WINDOWS 95

A PROGRAMMER'S CASE BOOK

STEVEN S. CHEN

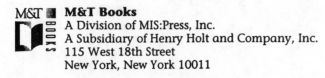

M&T Books
A Division of MIS:Press, Inc.
A Subsidiary of Henry Holt and Company, Inc.
115 West 18th Street
New York, New York 10011

This book is listed with the Library of Congress Cataloging-in-Publication Data.

ISBN 1-55851-411-2

97 96 95   4 3 2

Development Editor: Alla Efimova
Production Editor: Patricia Wallenburg
Copy Editor: Sara Black
Technical Editor: Ray Valdes

DEDICATION

To Jessica and her God!

ACKNOWLEDGEMENTS

The author would like to thank Brenda McLaughlin and Ray Valdes for making this book possible.

The author would also like to thank Patty Wallenburg and Alla Efimova for their excellent editing work.

The programming information in this book is based on information for developing applications for Windows 95 made public by Microsoft as of 9/8/94. Since this information was made public before the final release of the product, there may have been changes to some of the programming interfaces by the time the product is finally released. We encourage you to check the updated development information that should be part of your development system for resolving issues that might arise.

The end user information in this book is based on information on Windows 95 made public by Microsoft as of 9/8/94. Since this information was made public before the release of the product, we encourage you to visit your local bookstore at that time for updated books on Windows 95.

If you have a modem or access to the Internet, you can always get up-to-the-minute information on Windows 95 direct from Microsoft on WinNews:

On CompuServe: GO WINNEWS

On the Internet: ftp://ftp.microsoft.com/PerOpSys/Win_News/Chicago

http://www.microsoft.com

On AOL: keyword WINNEWS

On Prodigy: jumpword WINNEWS

On Genie: WINNEWS file area on Windows RTC

You can also subscribe to Microsoft's WinNews electronic Newsletter by sending Internet email to enews@microsoft.nwnet.com and putting the words SUBSCRIBE WINNEWS in the text of the email.

TABLE OF CONTENTS

CHAPTER THREE: CUSTOM CONTROLS 199

CHAPTER TEN: THE CLIPBOARD

INTRODUCTION

ABOUT THIS BOOK

In recent years, application programs for the Windows environment have entered the mainstream of the PC software industry. However, Windows has its own structure and graphic user interface that are rather unconventional when compared with the DOS environment. It takes a considerable amount of time and energy just to learn the basics of Windows programming.

Many Windows programming books available on the market today, including the reference books that accompany the software package *Windows 95 Software Development Kit by Microsoft*, only introduce the topic. They do not cover Windows programming with any depth. These books are undoubtedly useful for new players in the field, but there are still plenty of hurdles that programmers have to overcome before they can develop commercial-grade Windows software.

To overcome those hurdles in Windows programming, programmers can either spend a large chunk of time just to unscramble one problem (or develop one feature) themselves or find guidance in a reference book (like this one) to resolve it in a day or less. However, many of the books about Windows programming on the market today give only a few examples, which in most cases will not match the programmers' needs.

Windows 95: A Programmer's Case Book is not designed as the first book for the beginner. It is the kind of book that Windows programmers can use most effectively after they learn the simple basics of Windows programming from the literature that accompanies the Windows 95 SDK. This book is the product of many years of effort and experience and covers the field handily. Many examples in this book could very well be the foundation stones for new Windows programs. Every example is simple and straightforward and addresses only one feature of the Windows program. Many areas that are not covered by Microsoft books are covered in this book. It can help programmers to establish their Windows programming capability in an efficient and painless way.

This book provides 76 practical example programs (cases) that cover the most important issues in Windows 95 programming with emphasis on the Windows graphic user interface. It is a workbook for the beginner and a reference book for the more advanced programmer. Every example is simple, straightforward, and clear. Many examples in this book can also be used as utility programs for Windows program development. Because the book is for the programmers who already know the basics of Windows programming, there is no need to include the basics in this book. The comments at the beginning of each case are concise and focused only on the special technique or feature presented in that case. Also, for your convenience, comments have been added into the source code so that you can understand the code easily.

The cases in this book are divided into 12 chapters.

Chapter 1: Regular Controls. Most Windows programs contain many different types of controls. A control is a predefined child window that can handle a certain type of input or output task. Most controls presented in this chapter were introduced in previous versions of Windows environment. The owner-draw controls such as the push button, list box, and combo box have been discussed extensively.

Chapter 2: Common Controls. This chapter presents examples of controls that are new in Windows 95 SDK. Some controls were used in pre-Windows 95 programs, but they were not available to programmers. Simple examples are provided here to jump start programmer's capability of using these controls. Controls discussed include the progress bar, track bar, tool bar, tool tips, status bar, up-down control, and tab control.

Chapter 3: Custom Controls. This chapter introduces some useful techniques for customizing the regular controls and creating your own application-specific controls. It not only provides some useful examples but also demonstrates that the kinds of controls you can have in your program are limited only by your own imagination. For example, this chapter shows you how to divide one owner-draw push button into many areas so that it can actually behave like many push buttons with special shapes. Many user interface controls such as the spin button, direction button, switch, dial slider, analog meter, digital counter, and progress meter are presented in this chapter.

Chapter 4: Menus. This chapter demonstrates ways to put bitmap menu items into Windows main, pull-down, system, and floating menus.

Chapter 5: Drawing Functions. Most basic Windows graphics drawing functions such as line and pattern drawing functions as well as region drawing functions are presented here. These examples are the fundamentals of a more complicated drawing program. The use of metafiles to draw patterns is also discussed.

Chapter 6: Mouse, Cursor, and Graphics Drawing. This chapter provides three practical examples for drawing applications using the techniques described in previous chapters. The first example shows you how to change a cursor in a program. The second example is like a commercial program for drawing lines, rectangles and ellipses. The third example is a program for drawing color lines with a specified line width.

Chapter 7: Common Dialog Boxes. The common dialog box is a dialog box that can be displayed by calling a single function. Many common dialog boxes were introduced for Windows 3.1 SDK. Those common dialog boxes are also available in Windows 95 SDK. Common dialog boxes discussed in this chapter include the choose-color, choose-font, open-and-save file, print, and setup dialog boxes.

Chapter 8: Text and Fonts. This chapter shows you how to create fonts and draw text in windows. You can use the create font example program as a utility program to design and preview the fonts for your application. Two examples show you how to retrieve the font metrics information. Caret-related functions are also discussed.

Chapter 9: Bitmaps. This chapter tells you how to create bitmaps and display them on the screen. One example demonstrates the effect of raster operation code when a bitmap is painted on another bitmap.

Chapter 10: The Clipboard. This chapter shows you how to copy text and bitmaps into the Clipboard. It also shows you the way to retrieve the text or bitmap from the Clipboard and paste it in your Windows applications. Examples for handling the screen bitmap are also given.

Chapter 11: The Timer. This chapter shows you how to create and use the internal timer in a Windows program. Both single and multiple timers are discussed.

Chapter 12: Miscellaneous. Useful examples that do not fit into the previous 11 chapters are placed in this chapter. It shows you how to create the main window as a dialog box and how to start other Windows programs within a Windows program. It also provides a program for changing the Windows system color.

All source code files and compiled run-time programs are included in the companion compact disc. A typical case has the following files:

GLOBALS.H Header file containing global variables and function prototypes.

WINMAIN.C Standard WinMain function.

INIT.C Functions for registering main window class and creating main window among others.

CASEx.C Procedures for main window.

ABOUT.C Procedures for dialog box.

CASEx.RC Resource file.

ABOUT.DLG Resource file for dialog box.

CASEx.ICO Icon file.

CASEx.MAK Make file for compiling the program (no hard copy, stored in companion CD).

CASEx.EXE Compiled run-time program (stored on companion CD).

To compile or run the example programs in this book, you must have the following software installed in your system:

▲ Microsoft Windows 95

▲ The Windows 95 Software Development Kit (SDK)

▲ Microsoft Visual C++ 2.0

The make file (with **.mak** file extension) for each example has been included in the companion compact disc. To compile the program, simply type the following command at the DOS prompt:

```
nmake /f AppName.mak
```

where AppName.mak is the make file for the program named "AppName".

CHAPTER ONE

REGULAR CONTROLS

CASE 1-1: CUSTOM BITMAP PUSH BUTTONS IN MAIN WINDOW

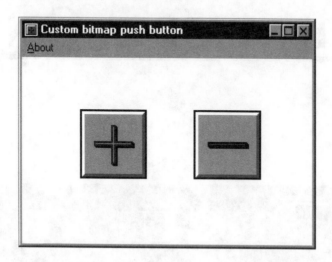

<u>FIGURE 1-1</u>

Most Windows programs contains many different types of controls. A *control* is a predefined child window that can handle a certain type of input or output task. The *push button* is a kind of control that is frequently used in most Windows programs. A *regular push button* has a standard look and can only display text on it. However, the push button can also be defined as an *owner-draw button*. The look of the owner-draw button can be determined by a bitmap or a drawing subroutine. To write a good commercial Windows program, a programmer must be able to design his/her own custom Windows controls, especially a push button.

This example shows you how to create a custom bitmap push button in the main window. In the file **mainbtn.c**, notice that two owner-draw buttons were created using the `CreateWindow()` function. The window class was specified as "button" and the button style was defined as BS_OWNER-DRAW. Once the button is defined as an owner-draw button, you must include a WM_DRAWITEM message case in the `WndProc()`, which is the procedure function for the main window. When WndProc() receives a WM_DRAWITEM message, the bitmap button is drawn using information stored in the LPDRAWITEMSTRUCT structure such as hDC, Control ID, or itemState. The DrawButtonUp() and DrawButtonDown() functions load the right bitmap according to the control ID and the item state then passes the bitmap handle to the PaintBitmap() function to draw the bitmaps in the predefined control area. These draw functions are extremely useful when you need to paint a large number of bitmap buttons in a single application.

Each button needs two bitmaps to show the item state. In this case, the BTNUP.BMP bitmap shows an up button and the BTNDOWN.BMP bitmap shows a pushed-down button. The procedures in case WM_DRAWITEM first checks the itemState in LPDRAWITEMSTRUCT structure. If itemState is ODS_SELECTED, the program calls the DrawButtonDown() function to load the "down" bitmap for the control item with the control ID defined as CtlID in the same structure and to pass the handle to the PaintBitmap() function to paint the bitmap. If the itemState is not ODS_SELECTED, the program calls the DrawButtonUp() function to load the "up" bitmap for that control and the PaintBitmap() function is then called to draw the loaded bitmap.

The reason to create two separate functions to load the bitmap is that, if you have a large number of custom controls in your application, it is more convenient to have a separate function to load the right bitmap in accordance with control ID. Because the drawing procedures are identical for all bitmap controls, it is convenient to use a separate function PaintBitmap() to do the job.

GLOBALS.H

```
// GLOBALS.H - header file for global variables
//              and function prototypes

// Product identifier string definitions
#define APPNAME       MainBtn
#define ICONFILE      MainBtn.ico
#define SZAPPNAME     "MainBtn"
#define SZDESCRIPTION "Custom bitmap push button"
```

```
#define SZVERSION       "Version 1.0"
#define SZCOMPANYNAME "\251 M&&T Books, 1994"
#define SZABOUT         "About"

// Global function prototypes
BOOL InitApplication(HINSTANCE);
BOOL InitInstance(HINSTANCE, int);
void PaintBitmap(HDC, HBITMAP);
void DrawButtonUp(HWND, HDC, int);
void DrawButtonDown(HWND, HDC, int);

// Callback functions called by Windows
LRESULT CALLBACK WndProc(HWND, UINT, WPARAM, LPARAM);
LRESULT CALLBACK About(HWND, UINT, WPARAM, LPARAM);

// Menu item ID
#define IDM_ABOUT       100

// Control ID
#define IDC_PUSHBUTTON  101
#define IDC_PUSHBUTTON2 102

// Global variable declarations.
extern HINSTANCE hInst;    // The current instance handle
extern char szAppName[];   // The name of this application
extern char szTitle[];     // The title bar text
```

WINMAIN.C

```
// WINMAIN.C
#include <windows.h>
#include "globals.h"

int APIENTRY WinMain(HINSTANCE hInstance,
                     HINSTANCE hPrevInstance,
                     LPSTR lpCmdLine,
                     int nCmdShow)
{
    MSG msg;

    // register the main window class
    if (!hPrevInstance)
        {
        if (!InitApplication(hInstance))
            {
            return FALSE;
```

```
        }
    }

// create the main window
if (!InitInstance(hInstance, nCmdShow))
   {
   return FALSE;
   }

// process window message
while (GetMessage(&msg, NULL, 0, 0))
   {
       TranslateMessage(&msg);
       DispatchMessage(&msg);
   }
return msg.wParam;
}
```

INIT.C

```
// INIT.C
#include <windows.h>
#include "globals.h"

HINSTANCE hInst;
char szAppName[] = SZAPPNAME;
char szTitle[] = SZDESCRIPTION;

// register the main window class
BOOL InitApplication(HINSTANCE hInstance)
{
    WNDCLASS  wc;

    wc.style         = CS_HREDRAW | CS_VREDRAW;
    wc.lpfnWndProc   = (WNDPROC)WndProc;
    wc.cbClsExtra    = 0;
    wc.cbWndExtra    = 0;
    wc.hInstance     = hInstance;
    wc.hIcon         = LoadIcon(hInstance, szAppName);
    wc.hCursor       = LoadCursor(NULL, IDC_ARROW);
    wc.hbrBackground = (HBRUSH)(COLOR_WINDOW + 1);
    wc.lpszMenuName  = szAppName;
    wc.lpszClassName = szAppName;

    return(RegisterClass(&wc));
}
```

```
// create and show main window
BOOL InitInstance(HINSTANCE hInstance, int nCmdShow)
{
    HWND    hWnd;
    hInst = hInstance;
    hWnd = CreateWindow(szAppName, szTitle,
                        WS_OVERLAPPEDWINDOW,
                        160, 120, 320, 240,
                        NULL, NULL, hInstance, NULL);

    // return FALSE if fail to create the main window
    if (!hWnd)
        {
        return FALSE;
        }

    ShowWindow(hWnd, nCmdShow);
    UpdateWindow(hWnd);

    return TRUE;
}
```

MAINBTN.C

```
// MAINBTN.C
#include <windows.h>
#include <windowsx.h>
#include "globals.h"

HWND hPushButton;
HWND hPushButton2;
HBITMAP hBitmap;

LRESULT CALLBACK WndProc(HWND hWnd,
                         UINT uMessage,
                         WPARAM wParam,
                         LPARAM lParam)
{
    LPDRAWITEMSTRUCT lpdis;

    switch (uMessage)
    {
        case WM_CREATE:
            // create two owner-draw push buttons
            hPushButton = CreateWindow("button", "",
```

```
                              BS_OWNERDRAW | WS_CHILD |
                              WS_VISIBLE,
                              63, 54, 72, 72,
                              hWnd, IDC_PUSHBUTTON,
                              hInst, NULL);

        hPushButton2 = CreateWindow("button", "",
                              BS_OWNERDRAW | WS_CHILD |
                              WS_VISIBLE,
                              185, 54, 72, 72,
                              hWnd, IDC_PUSHBUTTON2,
                              hInst, NULL);
        break;

case WM_DRAWITEM:

        lpdis = (LPDRAWITEMSTRUCT) lParam;

         // check itemState parameter in
         // LPDRAWITEMSTRUCT structure
        if(lpdis->itemState & ODS_SELECTED)
            // draw a down button bitmap if selected
            DrawButtonDown(hInst,
                        lpdis->hDC, lpdis->CtlID);
        else
            // draw an up button bitmap if not selected
            DrawButtonUp(hInst,
                        lpdis->hDC, lpdis->CtlID);
        break;

case WM_COMMAND:

        switch (GET_WM_COMMAND_ID(wParam,lParam))
        {
            case IDC_PUSHBUTTON:
            case IDC_PUSHBUTTON2:
                MessageBox(NULL,
                        "This is a custom push button!",
                        "Info",
                        MB_OK |
                        MB_ICONINFORMATION |
                        MB_SYSTEMMODAL);
                break;

            case IDM_ABOUT:
                // create an about dialog box
                DialogBox(hInst, "ABOUTDLG",
```

```
                                    hWnd, (DLGPROC)About);
                    break;

                default:
                    return DefWindowProc(hWnd, uMessage,
                                        wParam, lParam);
                }
                break;

        case WM_DESTROY:
            PostQuitMessage(0);
            break;

        default:
            return DefWindowProc(hWnd, uMessage,
                                wParam, lParam);
        }
        return 0;
}

// function for painting the button bitmap
void PaintBitmap (hDC, hBitmap)
HDC hDC;
HBITMAP hBitmap;
{
    BITMAP bmp;
    HDC hMemoryDC;
    hMemoryDC = CreateCompatibleDC(hDC);
    GetObject(hBitmap, sizeof(BITMAP), (LPSTR) &bmp) ;
    SelectObject(hMemoryDC, hBitmap) ;
    BitBlt(hDC, 0, 0, bmp.bmWidth, bmp.bmHeight,
                hMemoryDC, 0, 0, SRCCOPY);
    DeleteDC(hMemoryDC) ;
    DeleteObject(hBitmap) ;
}

// load a down button bitmap for drawing according to
// the CtlID parameter in LPDRAWITEMSTRUCT structure
// and pass the bitmap handle to PaintBitmap() function
void DrawButtonUp (hInstance, hDC, ButtonID)
HANDLE hInstance;
HDC hDC;
int ButtonID;
{
switch(ButtonID){

case IDC_PUSHBUTTON:
    hBitmap = LoadBitmap (hInstance, "BitmapButtonUp");
```

```
        break;

case IDC_PUSHBUTTON2:
        hBitmap = LoadBitmap (hInstance, "BitmapButtonUp2");
        break;
        }
        PaintBitmap(hDC, hBitmap);
}

// load an up button bitmap for drawing according to
// the CtlID parameter in LPDRAWITEMSTRUCT structure
// and pass the bitmap handle to PaintBitmap() function
void DrawButtonDown (hInstance, hDC, ButtonID)
HANDLE hInstance;
HDC hDC;
int ButtonID;
{
switch(ButtonID){
case IDC_PUSHBUTTON:
        hBitmap = LoadBitmap (hInstance, "BitmapButtonDown");
        break;

case IDC_PUSHBUTTON2:
        hBitmap = LoadBitmap (hInstance, "BitmapButtonDown2");
        break;
        }
        PaintBitmap(hDC, hBitmap);
}
```

ABOUT.C

```
// ABOUT.C
#include <windows.h>
#include <windowsx.h>
#include "globals.h"

// procedures for ABOUT dialog box
LRESULT CALLBACK About(HWND hDlg,
                       UINT uMessage,
                       WPARAM wParam,
                       LPARAM lParam)
{
    switch (uMessage)
      {
        case WM_COMMAND:
            switch (GET_WM_COMMAND_ID(wParam,lParam))
                {
```

```
                case IDOK:
                case IDCANCEL:
                    {
                    EndDialog(hDlg, TRUE);
                    return(TRUE);
                    }
                    break;
            }
        }
    return FALSE;
}
```

MAINBTN.RC

```
#include "windows.h"
#include "globals.h"
#include <winver.h>

BitmapButtonUp      BITMAP btnup.bmp
BitmapButtonDown    BITMAP btndown.bmp
BitmapButtonUp2     BITMAP btnup2.bmp
BitmapButtonDown2   BITMAP btndown2.bmp

APPNAME ICON ICONFILE

RCINCLUDE ABOUT.DLG

APPNAME MENU
BEGIN
  MENUITEM "&About",      IDM_ABOUT
END
```

ABOUT.DLG

```
ABOUTDLG DIALOG DISCARDABLE  22, 17, 167, 73
STYLE DS_MODALFRAME | WS_CAPTION | WS_SYSMENU
CAPTION SZABOUT
BEGIN
    DEFPUSHBUTTON   "OK", IDOK, 132, 2, 32, 14, WS_GROUP
    ICON            SZAPPNAME,      -1, 3, 2, 18, 20
    LTEXT           SZAPPNAME,      -1, 30, 12, 50, 8
    LTEXT           SZDESCRIPTION, -1, 30, 22, 150, 8
    LTEXT           SZVERSION,      -1, 30, 32, 150, 8
    LTEXT           SZCOMPANYNAME, -1, 30, 42, 150, 8
END
```

MAINBTN.ICO

BTNUP.BMP

BTNDOWN.BMP

BTNUP2.BMP

BTNDOWN2.BMP

CASE 1-2: CUSTOM BITMAP PUSH BUTTONS IN A DIALOG BOX

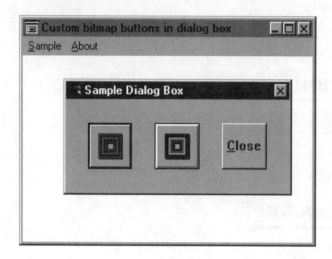

FIGURE 1-2

In this case two custom bitmap push buttons are placed in the same dialog box. Since they are child windows of a dialog box, their size, location, class, and style are defined in a dialog box resource file **SAMPLE.DLG**. There is a major difference in terms of button size between this case and Case 1-1. In Case 1-1, the button size was defined in pixels, whereas in this case, they are defined in dialog box base units. The size of the button is 24x24 in dialog base units, but the bitmap used 48x48 pixels to paint the button.

The dialog box base units in vertical and horizontal directions depend on the type of display. The X and Y dialog box base units can be obtained using the GetDialogBaseUnits() function. The dialog box base units for three different types of display devices are displayed in Table 1-1.

This table is useful for determining the size of a bitmap in terms of pixels for an owner-draw dialog box control, the size of which is defined in terms of dialog box base units.

TABLE 1-1

DISPLAY TYPE	VGA	SVGA	EGA
Resolution (pixels)	640x480	1024x768	640x350
X dialog box base unit	8	10	8
Y dialog box base unit	16	20	12
X pixel conversion factor	x2	x2.5	x2
Y pixel conversion factor	x2	x2.5	x1.5

For example, in this case, you can find that the size of the owner-draw button is defined as 24x24 in the resource file. To get the size of the bitmap in term of pixels that can fit into that control space on a VGA display, simply multiply the number in dialog box base units by the pixel conversion factor listed in Table 1-1. In this case, both factors are 2, so the bitmap size shall be 48 pixels x 48 pixels. However, it is not realistic to assume that all users of this application are using only VGA display. It is necessary to adjust the bitmap size when a display device other than the VGA monitor is detected before you show the dialog box. This can be done by writing a subroutine to check the dialog box base units before the application program paints the bitmap. If the dialog box base units correspond to a different type of display device, the bitmap can be resized using the StretchBlt() function. However, the new bitmap may not be as good as the original one especially for a small bitmap with fine details. The alternative way to handle this problem is to provide different bitmaps for different display devices.

In this case, a black frame is drawn around the button with the focus. The drawing procedures in this case are identical to those in Case 1-1. Since the itemState in the LPDRAWITEMSTRUCT structure provides the focus information, it is easy for the program to decide whether to draw a black rectangle around the button. In this case, the procedures for **WM_DRAWITEM** first draw the button according to its state (up or down). Then the itemState is checked again to see if it is ODS_FOCUS. If it is, the program draws a black rectangle around the item to show its focus state.

Because the button style has been defined as WS_TABSTOP, the button focus can be moved from button to button by pressing the **Tab** key. However, the IsDialogMessage() function must be called before the window passes the message to the WndProc. This occurs because the IsDialogMessage() function checks for keyboard messages and converts them into selection commands for the corresponding dialog box. Without it, the **Tab** key input will have no effect on the button focus. See Case 1-1 for more discussions about drawing custom bitmap buttons.

GLOBALS.H

```
// GLOBALS.H - header file for global variables
//             and function prototypes

// Product identifier string definitions.
#define APPNAME         DlgBtn
#define ICONFILE        DlgBtn.ico
#define SZAPPNAME       "DlgBtn"
#define SZDESCRIPTION   "Custom bitmap buttons in dialog box"
#define SZVERSION       "Version 1.0"
#define SZCOMPANYNAME   "\251 M&&T Books, 1994"
#define SZABOUT         "About"

// Global function prototypes.
BOOL InitApplication(HINSTANCE);
BOOL InitInstance(HINSTANCE, int);
void PaintBitmap(HDC, HBITMAP);
void DrawButtonUp(HWND, HDC, int);
void DrawButtonDown(HWND, HDC, int);

// Callback functions called by Windows.
LRESULT CALLBACK WndProc(HWND, UINT, WPARAM, LPARAM);
LRESULT CALLBACK About(HWND, UINT, WPARAM, LPARAM);
LRESULT CALLBACK SampleDlgProc(HWND, UINT, WPARAM, LPARAM);

// Menu item ID
#define IDM_ABOUT       101
#define IDM_SAMPLE      102

// Dialog box ID
#define IDD_SAMPLEDLG   103

// Dialog box control ID
#define IDC_PUSHBUTTON1 201
#define IDC_PUSHBUTTON2 202
#define IDC_CLOSE       203
```

```
// Global variable declarations.
extern HINSTANCE hInst;      // The current instance handle
extern char szAppName[];     // The name of this application
extern char szTitle[];       // The title bar text
extern HWND hWnd, hSample;
extern WORD Xfactor, Yfactor;
extern DLGPROC lpProcSample;
```

WINMAIN.C

```
// WINMAIN.C
#include <windows.h>
#include "globals.h"
HWND hSample;

int APIENTRY WinMain(HINSTANCE hInstance,
                     HINSTANCE hPrevInstance,
                     LPSTR lpCmdLine,
                     int nCmdShow)
{
    MSG msg;

    // register the main window class
    if (!hPrevInstance)
        {
        if (!InitApplication(hInstance))
            {
            return FALSE;
            }
        }

    // create the main window
    if (!InitInstance(hInstance, nCmdShow))
        {
        return FALSE;
        }

    // process window message
    // if sample dialog box is active,
    // process the dialog box keyboard message using
    // IsDialogMessage() function.
    while (GetMessage(&msg, NULL, 0, 0))
        { if(hSample == NULL ||
            !IsDialogMessage(hSample, &msg))
            {
            TranslateMessage(&msg);
```

```
                DispatchMessage(&msg);
                }
            }
        return msg.wParam;
    }
```

INIT.C

```c
// INIT.C
#include <windows.h>
#include "globals.h"

HINSTANCE hInst;
char szAppName[] = SZAPPNAME;
char szTitle[] = SZDESCRIPTION;

// register the main window class
BOOL InitApplication(HINSTANCE hInstance)
{
    WNDCLASS  wc;

    wc.style          = CS_HREDRAW | CS_VREDRAW;
    wc.lpfnWndProc    = (WNDPROC)WndProc;
    wc.cbClsExtra     = 0;
    wc.cbWndExtra     = 0;
    wc.hInstance      = hInstance;
    wc.hIcon          = LoadIcon(hInstance, szAppName);
    wc.hCursor        = LoadCursor(NULL, IDC_ARROW);
    wc.hbrBackground  = (HBRUSH)(COLOR_WINDOW + 1);
    wc.lpszMenuName   = szAppName;
    wc.lpszClassName  = szAppName;

    return(RegisterClass(&wc));
}

// create the main window
BOOL InitInstance(HINSTANCE hInstance, int nCmdShow)
{
    HWND     hWnd;
    hInst = hInstance;
    hWnd = CreateWindow(szAppName, szTitle,
                        WS_OVERLAPPEDWINDOW,
                        160, 120, 320, 240,
                        NULL, NULL, hInstance, NULL);

    if (!hWnd)
        {
        return FALSE;
```

```
        }

    ShowWindow(hWnd, nCmdShow);
    UpdateWindow(hWnd);

    return TRUE;
}
```

DLGBTN.C

```
// DLGBTN.C
#include <windows.h>
#include <windowsx.h>
#include "globals.h"
HWND hSample = 0;
DLGPROC lpProcSample;

LRESULT CALLBACK WndProc(HWND hWnd,
                         UINT uMessage,
                         WPARAM wParam,
                         LPARAM lParam)
{
    switch (uMessage)
    {
        case WM_COMMAND:

            switch (GET_WM_COMMAND_ID(wParam,lParam))
            {
                case IDM_SAMPLE:
                    // create a sample dialog box
                    lpProcSample = MakeProcInstance(
                        (FARPROC)SampleDlgProc, hInst);
                    hSample = CreateDialog(hInst,
                        MAKEINTRESOURCE(IDD_SAMPLEDLG),
                        hWnd, lpProcSample);
                    break;

                case IDM_ABOUT:
                    // create an about dialog box
                    DialogBox(hInst, "ABOUTDLG",
                            hWnd, (DLGPROC)About);
                    break;

                default:
                    return DefWindowProc(hWnd, uMessage,
                                        wParam, lParam);
            }
            break;
```

```
        case WM_DESTROY:
            PostQuitMessage(0);
            break;

        default:
            return DefWindowProc(hWnd, uMessage,
                                    wParam, lParam);
    }
    return 0;
}
```

SAMPLE.C

```
// SAMPLE.C
#include <windows.h>
#include <windowsx.h>
#include "globals.h"
HBITMAP hBitmap;

// procedures for sample dialog box
LRESULT CALLBACK SampleDlgProc(HWND hSample,
                               UINT uMessage,
                               WPARAM wParam,
                               LPARAM lParam)
{
    LPDRAWITEMSTRUCT lpdis;
    HPEN hPen;
    HBRUSH hBrush;

    switch (uMessage)
    {
        case WM_DRAWITEM:

            lpdis = (LPDRAWITEMSTRUCT) lParam;
             // check itemState parameter in

             // LPDRAWITEMSTRUCT structure
            if(lpdis-> itemState & ODS_SELECTED)
                // draw a down button bitmap if selected
              { DrawButtonDown(hInst,
                            lpdis->hDC, lpdis->CtlID);
                 goto drawfocus; }
            else
                // draw an up button bitmap if not selected
              DrawButtonUp(hInst,
                        lpdis->hDC, lpdis->CtlID);
```

```
                // draw a black rectangle around the button if focused
drawfocus:               if(lpdis-> itemState & ODS_FOCUS)
                           { hPen = SelectObject(lpdis->hDC,
                                CreatePen(PS_INSIDEFRAME,
                                          2, RGB(0, 0, 0)));
                             hBrush = SelectObject(lpdis->hDC,
                                   GetStockObject(NULL_BRUSH));
                             Rectangle(lpdis->hDC,
                                      lpdis->rcItem.left,
                                      lpdis->rcItem.top,
                                      lpdis->rcItem.right,
                                      lpdis->rcItem.bottom);
                             DeleteObject(SelectObject(
                                       lpdis->hDC, hPen));
                             DeleteObject(SelectObject(
                                       lpdis->hDC,hBrush));
                             break; }
                   break;

           case WM_COMMAND:
                   switch (GET_WM_COMMAND_ID(wParam,lParam))
                   {
                       case IDC_PUSHBUTTON1:
                       case IDC_PUSHBUTTON2:
                           MessageBeep(0);
                           break;

                       case IDCANCEL:
                       case IDC_CLOSE:
                           DestroyWindow(hSample);
                           hSample = NULL;
                           break;

                       default:
                           return DefWindowProc(hSample, uMessage,
                                               wParam, lParam);
                   }
                   break;

           default:
               return DefWindowProc(hSample, uMessage,
                                   wParam, lParam);
       }
    return 0;
}

// function for painting the button bitmap
void PaintBitmap (hDC, hBitmap)
```

```
HDC hDC;
HBITMAP hBitmap;
{
     BITMAP bmp;
     HDC hMemoryDC;
     hMemoryDC = CreateCompatibleDC(hDC);
     GetObject(hBitmap, sizeof(BITMAP), (LPSTR) &bmp);
     SelectObject(hMemoryDC, hBitmap);
     BitBlt(hDC, 0, 0, bmp.bmWidth, bmp.bmHeight,
                       hMemoryDC, 0, 0, SRCCOPY);
     DeleteDC(hMemoryDC);
     DeleteObject(hBitmap);
}

// load a down button bitmap for drawing according to the
// CtlID parameter in LPDRAWITEMSTRUCT structure and pass
// the bitmap handle to PaintBitmap() function.
void DrawButtonUp (hInstance, hDC, ButtonID)
HANDLE hInstance;
HDC hDC;
int ButtonID;
{
switch(ButtonID){
    case IDC_PUSHBUTTON1:
        hBitmap = LoadBitmap (hInstance,
                               "BitmapButton1Up");
        break;

    case IDC_PUSHBUTTON2:
        hBitmap = LoadBitmap (hInstance,
                               "BitmapButton2Up");
        break;
     }
     PaintBitmap(hDC, hBitmap);
}

// load an up button bitmap for drawing according to the
// CtlID parameter in LPDRAWITEMSTRUCT structure and pass
// the bitmap handle to PaintBitmap() function.
void DrawButtonDown (hInstance, hDC, ButtonID)
HANDLE hInstance;
HDC hDC;
int ButtonID;
{
switch(ButtonID){
    case IDC_PUSHBUTTON1:
        hBitmap = LoadBitmap (hInstance,
                               "BitmapButton1Down");
```

```
        break;

    case IDC_PUSHBUTTON2:
        hBitmap = LoadBitmap (hInstance,
                            "BitmapButton2Down");
        break;
    }
    PaintBitmap(hDC, hBitmap);
}
```

ABOUT.C

```
// ABOUT.C
#include <windows.h>
#include <windowsx.h>
#include "globals.h"

// procedures for ABOUT dialog box
LRESULT CALLBACK About(HWND hDlg,
                        UINT uMessage,
                        WPARAM wParam,
                        LPARAM lParam)
{
    switch (uMessage)
      {
        case WM_COMMAND:
            switch (GET_WM_COMMAND_ID(wParam,lParam))
              {
                case IDOK:
                case IDCANCEL:
                    {
                    EndDialog(hDlg, TRUE);
                    return(TRUE);
                    }
                    break;
              }
      }
    return FALSE;
}
```

DLGBTN.RC

```
#include "windows.h"
#include "globals.h"
#include <winver.h>

BitmapButton1Up    BITMAP btn1up.bmp
BitmapButton1Down  BITMAP btn1down.bmp
```

```
BitmapButton2Up    BITMAP btn2up.bmp
BitmapButton2Down BITMAP btn2down.bmp

APPNAME ICON ICONFILE

RCINCLUDE ABOUT.DLG
RCINCLUDE SAMPLE.DLG

APPNAME MENU
BEGIN
    MENUITEM "&Sample", IDM_SAMPLE
    MENUITEM "&About",  IDM_ABOUT
END
```

SAMPLE.DLG

```
DLGINCLUDE RCDATA DISCARDABLE
BEGIN
    "GLOBALS.H\0"
END

IDD_SAMPLEDLG DIALOG 20, 12, 120, 48
STYLE WS_BORDER | WS_POPUP | WS_VISIBLE | WS_CAPTION | WS_SYSMENU
CAPTION "Sample Dialog Box"
BEGIN
    CONTROL         "&R", IDC_PUSHBUTTON1, "Button",
                    BS_OWNERDRAW | WS_TABSTOP,
                    12, 12, 24, 24
    CONTROL         "&B", IDC_PUSHBUTTON2, "Button",
                    BS_OWNERDRAW | WS_TABSTOP,
                    48, 12, 24, 24
    PUSHBUTTON      "&Close", IDC_CLOSE, 84, 12, 24, 24
END
```

ABOUT.DLG

```
ABOUTDLG DIALOG DISCARDABLE  22, 17, 167, 73
STYLE DS_MODALFRAME | WS_CAPTION | WS_SYSMENU
CAPTION SZABOUT
BEGIN
    DEFPUSHBUTTON   "OK", IDOK, 132, 2, 32, 14, WS_GROUP
    ICON            SZAPPNAME,      -1, 3, 2, 18, 20
    LTEXT           SZAPPNAME,      -1, 30, 12,  50, 8
    LTEXT           SZDESCRIPTION, -1, 30, 22, 150, 8
    LTEXT           SZVERSION,      -1, 30, 32, 150, 8
    LTEXT           SZCOMPANYNAME, -1, 30, 42, 150, 8
END
```

DLGBTN.ICO

BTN1UP.BMP

BTN1DOWN.BMP

BTN2UP.BMP

BTN2DOWN.BMP

CASE 1-3: CUSTOM BITMAP PUSH BUTTONS ON A TOOL BAR

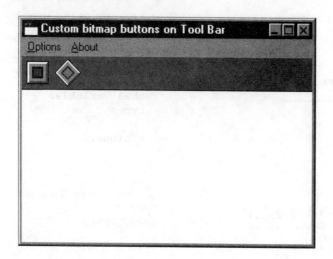

FIGURE 1-3

Y ou can use the tool bar common control functions as described in Chapter 2 to create a standard tool bar for your application. *Common controls* are a set of new controls introduced for Windows 95. Common controls include the tool bar, status bar, up-down control, and tab control. Please see Chapter 2 for examples of common controls. However, the common control function can only create a tool bar with standard look rectangular buttons on it. If you prefer to have more control over the look and function of the tool bar in your application, this case shows a simple example of creating a tool bar of your own style. In this case, two custom bitmap push buttons are placed in the gray area under the regular text menu bar. If you are already familiar with the ways to handle the custom bitmap buttons mentioned in the previous cases, this case is trivial.

Simply draw a gray rectangle under the text menu bar and also draw a thin black rectangle at the bottom of the gray rectangle as a boundary.

Then draw two custom bitmap buttons on the gray rectangle area. Because these controls are opened as windows, you can use the ShowWindow() function to hide them. If you are not familiar with the drawing of custom bitmap buttons, see the examples in Cases 1-1 and 1-2.

GLOBALS.H

```
// GLOBALS.H - header file for global variables
//              and function prototypes

// Product identifier string definitions.
#define APPNAME       ToolBar
#define ICONFILE      ToolBar.ico
#define SZAPPNAME     "ToolBar"
#define SZDESCRIPTION "Custom bitmap buttons on Tool Bar"
#define SZVERSION     "Version 1.0"
#define SZCOMPANYNAME "\251 M&&T Books, 1994"
#define SZABOUT       "About"

// Global function prototypes.
BOOL InitApplication(HINSTANCE);
BOOL InitInstance(HINSTANCE, int);
void PaintBitmap(HDC, HBITMAP);
void DrawButtonUp(HWND, HDC, int);
void DrawButtonDown(HWND, HDC, int);

// Callback functions called by Windows.
LRESULT CALLBACK WndProc(HWND, UINT, WPARAM, LPARAM);
LRESULT CALLBACK About(HWND, UINT, WPARAM, LPARAM);

// Menu item ID
#define IDM_ABOUT       101
#define IDM_SHOWTOOLBAR 102
#define IDM_HIDETOOLBAR 103

// Control ID
#define IDC_PUSHBUTTON1 104
#define IDC_PUSHBUTTON2 105

// Global variable declarations.
extern HINSTANCE hInst;      // The current instance handle
extern char szAppName[];     // The name of this application
extern char szTitle[];       // The title bar text
```

WINMAIN.C

```
// WINMAIN.C
#include <windows.h>
#include "globals.h"

int APIENTRY WinMain(HINSTANCE hInstance,
                     HINSTANCE hPrevInstance,
                     LPSTR lpCmdLine,
                     int nCmdShow)
{
    MSG msg;

    // register the main window class
    if (!hPrevInstance)
        {
        if (!InitApplication(hInstance))
            {
            return FALSE;
            }
        }

    // create the main window
    if (!InitInstance(hInstance, nCmdShow))
        {
        return FALSE;
        }

    // process window message
    while (GetMessage(&msg, NULL, 0, 0))
        {
            TranslateMessage(&msg);
            DispatchMessage(&msg);
        }
    return msg.wParam;
}
```

INIT.C

```
// INIT.C
#include <windows.h>
#include "globals.h"

HINSTANCE hInst;
char szAppName[] = SZAPPNAME;
char szTitle[] = SZDESCRIPTION;
```

```
// register the main window class
BOOL InitApplication(HINSTANCE hInstance)
{
    WNDCLASS  wc;

    wc.style          = CS_HREDRAW | CS_VREDRAW;
    wc.lpfnWndProc    = (WNDPROC)WndProc;
    wc.cbClsExtra     = 0;
    wc.cbWndExtra     = 0;
    wc.hInstance      = hInstance;
    wc.hIcon          = LoadIcon(hInstance, szAppName);
    wc.hCursor        = LoadCursor(NULL, IDC_ARROW);
    wc.hbrBackground  = (HBRUSH)(COLOR_WINDOW + 1);
    wc.lpszMenuName   = szAppName;
    wc.lpszClassName  = szAppName;

    return(RegisterClass(&wc));
}

// create the main window
BOOL InitInstance(HINSTANCE hInstance, int nCmdShow)
{
    HWND    hWnd;
    hInst = hInstance;
    hWnd = CreateWindow(szAppName, szTitle,
                        WS_OVERLAPPEDWINDOW,
                        160, 120, 320, 240,
                        NULL, NULL, hInstance, NULL);

    // return FALSE if create window failed
    if (!hWnd)
        {
        return FALSE;
        }

    ShowWindow(hWnd, nCmdShow);
    UpdateWindow(hWnd);

    return TRUE;
}
```

TOOLBAR.C

```
// TOOLBAR.C
#include <windows.h>
#include <windowsx.h>
#include "globals.h"
```

```
HWND hPushButton1, hPushButton2, hGrayRect, hBlackLine;
HBITMAP hBitmap;

LRESULT CALLBACK WndProc(HWND hWnd,
                         UINT uMessage,
                         WPARAM wParam,
                         LPARAM lParam)
{
    LPDRAWITEMSTRUCT lpdis;

    switch (uMessage)
    {
        case WM_CREATE:

                // create a gray rectangle as
                // the background of toolbar
                hGrayRect = CreateWindow("static", "",
                    SS_GRAYRECT | WS_CHILD | WS_VISIBLE,
                    0, 0, 640, 34, hWnd, NULL, hInst, NULL);

                // create a black rectangle as the bottom
                // boundary of the tool bar
                hBlackLine = CreateWindow("static", "",
                    SS_BLACKRECT | WS_CHILD | WS_VISIBLE,
                    0, 34, 640, 1, hWnd, NULL, hInst, NULL);

                // create two owner-draw push buttons
                hPushButton1 = CreateWindow("button", "",
                    BS_OWNERDRAW | WS_CHILD | WS_VISIBLE,
                    5, 5, 24, 24,
                    hWnd, IDC_PUSHBUTTON1, hInst, NULL);

                hPushButton2 = CreateWindow("button", "",
                    BS_OWNERDRAW | WS_CHILD | WS_VISIBLE,
                    36, 3, 28, 28,
                    hWnd, IDC_PUSHBUTTON2, hInst, NULL);
                break;

        case WM_DRAWITEM:

                lpdis = (LPDRAWITEMSTRUCT) lParam;

                // check the itemState parameter in
                // LPDRAWITEMSTRUCT structure lpdis
                if(lpdis->itemState & ODS_SELECTED)
                    // draw a down button bitmap if selected
                    DrawButtonDown(hInst,
                                lpdis->hDC, lpdis->CtlID);
```

```
        else
              // draw an up button bitmap if not selected
            DrawButtonUp(hInst,
                         lpdis->hDC, lpdis->CtlID);
        break;

case WM_COMMAND:

        switch (GET_WM_COMMAND_ID(wParam,lParam))
        {
         case IDM_ABOUT:

                // create an about dialog box
                DialogBox(hInst, "ABOUTDLG",
                          hWnd, (DLGPROC)About);
                break;

         case IDM_SHOWTOOLBAR:

                // show tool bar
                ShowWindow(hGrayRect, SW_SHOW);
                ShowWindow(hBlackLine, SW_SHOW);
                ShowWindow(hPushButton1, SW_SHOW);
                ShowWindow(hPushButton2, SW_SHOW);
                break;

         case IDM_HIDETOOLBAR:

                // hide tool bar
                ShowWindow(hGrayRect, SW_HIDE);
                ShowWindow(hBlackLine, SW_HIDE);
                ShowWindow(hPushButton1, SW_HIDE);
                ShowWindow(hPushButton2, SW_HIDE);
                break;

         case IDC_PUSHBUTTON1:
         case IDC_PUSHBUTTON2:

                MessageBox(NULL,
                        "This is a custom push button!",
                        "Info",
                        MB_OK | MB_ICONINFORMATION |
                        MB_SYSTEMMODAL);
                break;

        default:
                return DefWindowProc(hWnd, uMessage,
                                     wParam, lParam);
```

```
                }
                break;

        case WM_DESTROY:
                PostQuitMessage(0);
                break;

        default:
            return DefWindowProc(hWnd, uMessage,
                                    wParam, lParam);
    }
    return 0;
}

// function for painting the button bitmap
void PaintBitmap (hDC, hBitmap)
HDC hDC;
HBITMAP hBitmap;
{
    BITMAP bmp;
    HDC hMemoryDC;
    hMemoryDC = CreateCompatibleDC(hDC);
    GetObject(hBitmap, sizeof(BITMAP), (LPSTR) &bmp);
    SelectObject(hMemoryDC, hBitmap);
    BitBlt(hDC, 0, 0, bmp.bmWidth, bmp.bmHeight,
                    hMemoryDC, 0, 0, SRCCOPY);
    DeleteDC(hMemoryDC);
    DeleteObject(hBitmap);
}

// load a down button bitmap for drawing according to the
// CtlID paramter in LPDRAWITEMSTRUCT structure lpdis
// and pass the bitmap handle to PaintBitmap() funtion.
void DrawButtonUp (hInstance, hDC, ButtonID)
HWND hInstance;
HDC hDC;
int ButtonID;

{
switch(ButtonID){

case IDC_PUSHBUTTON1:
    hBitmap = LoadBitmap (hInstance, "BitmapButton1Up");
    break;

case IDC_PUSHBUTTON2:
    hBitmap = LoadBitmap (hInstance, "BitmapButton2Up");
    break;
    }
```

30

```
        PaintBitmap(hDC, hBitmap);
}

// load an up button bitmap for drawing according to the
// CtlID paramter in LPDRAWITEMSTRUCT structure lpdis
// and pass the bitmap handle to PaintBitmap() funtion.
void DrawButtonDown (hInstance, hDC, ButtonID)
HWND hInstance;
HDC hDC;
int ButtonID;

{
switch(ButtonID){

case IDC_PUSHBUTTON1:
    hBitmap = LoadBitmap (hInstance, "BitmapButton1Down");
    break;

case IDC_PUSHBUTTON2:
    hBitmap = LoadBitmap (hInstance, "BitmapButton2Down");
    break;
    }

    PaintBitmap(hDC, hBitmap);
}
```

ABOUT.C

```
// ABOUT.C
#include <windows.h>
#include <windowsx.h>
#include "globals.h"

// procedures for ABOUT dialog box
LRESULT CALLBACK About(HWND hDlg,
                       UINT uMessage,
                       WPARAM wParam,
                       LPARAM lParam)
{
    switch (uMessage)
      {
        case WM_COMMAND:
            switch (GET_WM_COMMAND_ID(wParam,lParam))
            {
                case IDOK:
                case IDCANCEL:
                    {
```

```
                        EndDialog(hDlg, TRUE);
                        return(TRUE);
                        }
                        break;
                }
        }
    return FALSE;
}
```

TOOLBAR.RC

```
#include "windows.h"
#include "globals.h"
#include <winver.h>

BitmapButton1Up    BITMAP btn1up.bmp
BitmapButton1Down  BITMAP btn1down.bmp
BitmapButton2Up    BITMAP btn2up.bmp
BitmapButton2Down  BITMAP btn2down.bmp

APPNAME ICON ICONFILE

RCINCLUDE ABOUT.DLG

APPNAME MENU
BEGIN
    POPUP         "&Options"
    BEGIN
        MENUITEM "&Show Tool Bar", IDM_SHOWTOOLBAR
        MENUITEM "&Hide Tool Bar", IDM_HIDETOOLBAR
    END
    MENUITEM "&About", IDM_ABOUT
END
```

ABOUT.DLG

```
ABOUTDLG DIALOG DISCARDABLE  22, 17, 167, 73
STYLE DS_MODALFRAME | WS_CAPTION | WS_SYSMENU
CAPTION SZABOUT
BEGIN
    DEFPUSHBUTTON    "OK", IDOK, 132, 2, 32, 14, WS_GROUP
    ICON             SZAPPNAME,      -1, 3, 2, 18, 20
    LTEXT            SZAPPNAME,      -1, 30, 12,  50, 8
    LTEXT            SZDESCRIPTION, -1, 30, 22, 150, 8
    LTEXT            SZVERSION,      -1, 30, 32, 150, 8
    LTEXT            SZCOMPANYNAME, -1, 30, 42, 150, 8
END
```

TOOLBAR.ICO

BTN1UP.BMP

BTN1DOWN.BMP

BTN2UP.BMP

BTN2DOWN.BMP

CASE 1-4: LIST BOX WITH HORIZONTAL SCROLL BAR

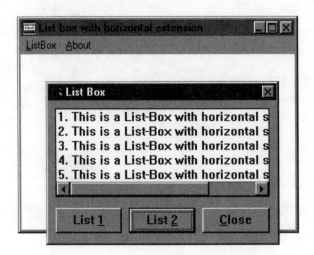

FIGURE 1-4

A *list box* usually displays a vertical scroll bar automatically when the number of items exceeds the number of rows in the box. However, this is not true when the length of the item exceeds the width of the list box even when the list box style was defined as WS_HSCROLL. To create a list box with horizontal scroll bar, you need to define the list box horizontal extent before you put any item into it. This is done by using the function:

```
SendDlgItemMessage(hLbox, IDC_LISTBOX,
          LB_SETHORIZONTALEXTENT 320, 0L);
```

You can check the length of items to be listed to determine how much extension is needed. Once you set the horizontal extension, a horizontal scroll bar will show up automatically when the length of the item exceeds the width of the list box. In this example, click List 1 button to see the vertical scroll bar and click List 2 button to see horizontal scroll bar. See Cases 1-5 and 1-6 for related examples.

GLOBALS.H

```
// GLOBALS.H - header file for global variables
//             and function prototypes

// Product identifier string definitions.
#define APPNAME       LboxH
#define ICONFILE      LboxH.ico
#define SZAPPNAME     "LboxH"
#define SZDESCRIPTION "List box with horizontal extension"
#define SZVERSION     "Version 1.0"
#define SZCOMPANYNAME "\251 M&&T Books, 1994"
#define SZABOUT       "About"

// Global function prototypes.
BOOL InitApplication(HINSTANCE);
BOOL InitInstance(HINSTANCE, int);

// Callback functions called by Windows.
LRESULT CALLBACK WndProc(HWND, UINT, WPARAM, LPARAM);
LRESULT CALLBACK About(HWND, UINT, WPARAM, LPARAM);
LRESULT CALLBACK LboxDlgProc(HWND, UINT, WPARAM, LPARAM);

// Menu item ID
#define IDM_ABOUT   101
#define IDM_LBOX    102

// Dialog box ID
#define IDD_LISTBOX 200

// Dialog box control ID
#define IDC_LISTBOX 103
#define IDC_LIST1   104
#define IDC_LIST2   105
#define IDC_CLOSE   106

// Global variable declarations.
extern HINSTANCE hInst;      // The current instance handle
extern char szAppName[];     // The name of this application
extern char szTitle[];       // The title bar text
extern HWND hWnd, hLbox;
extern DLGPROC lpProcLbox;
```

WINMAIN.C

```
// WINMAIN.C
#include <windows.h>
```

```
#include "globals.h"

HWND hLbox;

int APIENTRY WinMain(HINSTANCE hInstance,
                     HINSTANCE hPrevInstance,
                     LPSTR lpCmdLine,
                     int nCmdShow)
{
    MSG msg;

    // register the main window class
    if (!hPrevInstance)
        {
        if (!InitApplication(hInstance))
            {
            return FALSE;
            }
        }

    // create the main window
    if (!InitInstance(hInstance, nCmdShow))
        {
        return FALSE;
        }

    // process the message, if the message is the keyboard
    // input from list dialog box, use IsDialogMessage()
    // function to process the message.
    while (GetMessage(&msg, NULL, 0, 0))
        { if(hLbox == NULL || !IsDialogMessage(hLbox, &msg))
            {
             TranslateMessage(&msg);
             DispatchMessage(&msg);
            }
        }
    return msg.wParam;
}
```

INIT.C

```
// INIT.C
#include <windows.h>
#include "globals.h"

HINSTANCE hInst;
char szAppName[] = SZAPPNAME;
```

```
char szTitle[] = SZDESCRIPTION;

// register the main window class
BOOL InitApplication(HINSTANCE hInstance)
{
    WNDCLASS  wc;

    wc.style          = CS_HREDRAW | CS_VREDRAW;
    wc.lpfnWndProc    = (WNDPROC)WndProc;
    wc.cbClsExtra     = 0;
    wc.cbWndExtra     = 0;
    wc.hInstance      = hInstance;
    wc.hIcon          = LoadIcon(hInstance, szAppName);
    wc.hCursor        = LoadCursor(NULL, IDC_ARROW);
    wc.hbrBackground  = (HBRUSH)(COLOR_WINDOW + 1);
    wc.lpszMenuName   = szAppName;
    wc.lpszClassName  = szAppName;

    return(RegisterClass(&wc));
}

// create main window
BOOL InitInstance(HINSTANCE hInstance, int nCmdShow)
{
    HWND      hWnd;
    hInst = hInstance;
    hWnd = CreateWindow(szAppName, szTitle,
                        WS_OVERLAPPEDWINDOW,
                        160, 120, 320, 240,
                        NULL, NULL, hInstance, NULL);

    // return FALSE if create window failed
    if (!hWnd)
        {
        return FALSE;
        }

    ShowWindow(hWnd, nCmdShow);
    UpdateWindow(hWnd);

    return TRUE;
}
```

LBOXH.C

```
// LBOXH.C
#include <windows.h>
```

```
#include <windowsx.h>
#include "globals.h"

HWND hLbox;
DLGPROC lpProcLbox;

LRESULT CALLBACK WndProc(HWND hWnd,
                         UINT uMessage,
                         WPARAM wParam,
                         LPARAM lParam)
{
    switch (uMessage)
    {
        case WM_COMMAND:

            switch (GET_WM_COMMAND_ID(wParam,lParam))
            {
                case IDM_LBOX:

                    // create a dialog box to show
                    // the list box
                    lpProcLbox = MakeProcInstance(
                            (FARPROC)LboxDlgProc, hInst);
                    hLbox = CreateDialog(hInst,
                            MAKEINTRESOURCE(IDD_LISTBOX),
                                    hWnd, lpProcLbox);
                    break;

                case IDM_ABOUT:

                    // create an about dialog box
                    DialogBox(hInst, "ABOUTDLG",
                            hWnd, (DLGPROC)About);
                    break;

                default:
                    return DefWindowProc(hWnd, uMessage,
                                        wParam, lParam);
            }
            break;

        case WM_DESTROY:
            FreeProcInstance(lpProcLbox);
            PostQuitMessage(0);
            break;

        default:
            return DefWindowProc(hWnd, uMessage,
                                wParam, lParam);
```

```
        }
        return 0;
}
```

LIST.C

```
// LIST.C
#include <windows.h>
#include <windowsx.h>
#include <stdlib.h>
#include "globals.h"

HWND hLbox;

// procedure function for dialog box hLbox
LRESULT CALLBACK LboxDlgProc(HWND hLbox,
                        UINT uMessage,
                        WPARAM wParam,
                        LPARAM lParam)
{
    char buffer[55];
    char number[3];
    int i;

    switch (uMessage)
    {
        case WM_COMMAND:

            switch (GET_WM_COMMAND_ID(wParam,lParam))
            {
                case IDC_LIST1:

                    // reset the content of the list box
                    SendDlgItemMessage(hLbox, IDC_LISTBOX,
                            LB_RESETCONTENT, 0, 0L);

                    // set list box horizontal extent
                    SendDlgItemMessage(hLbox, IDC_LISTBOX,
                        LB_SETHORIZONTALEXTENT, 200, 0L);

                    // add list box contents
                    for(i=1; i<10; i++){
                        _itoa(i, number, 10);
                        strcpy(buffer, number);
                        strcat(buffer, ". ");
                        strcat(buffer,
                                "This is a List-Box!");
                        SendDlgItemMessage(hLbox,
```

39

```
                            IDC_LISTBOX,
                            LB_ADDSTRING,
                            0,
                            (LONG)(LPSTR)buffer);
            }
        break;

    case IDC_LIST2:

            // reset list box content
            SendDlgItemMessage(hLbox, IDC_LISTBOX,
                        LB_RESETCONTENT, 0, 0L);

            // set list box horizontal extent
            SendDlgItemMessage(hLbox, IDC_LISTBOX,
                LB_SETHORIZONTALEXTENT, 320, 0L);

            // add list box contents
            for(i=1; i<6; i++){
                _itoa(i, number, 10);
                strcpy(buffer, number);
                strcat(buffer, ". ");
                strcat(buffer,
                        "This is a List-Box ");
                strcat(buffer,
                    "with horizontal scroll bar!");
                SendDlgItemMessage(hLbox,
                        IDC_LISTBOX,
                        LB_ADDSTRING,
                        0,
                        (LONG)(LPSTR)buffer);
            }
        break;

    case IDCANCEL:
    case IDC_CLOSE:
        DestroyWindow(hLbox);
        hLbox = 0;
        break;

    default:
        return DefWindowProc(hLbox, uMessage,
                            wParam, lParam);
    }
    break;

default:
    return DefWindowProc(hLbox, uMessage,
```

```
                                    wParam, lParam);
    }
    return 0;
}
```

ABOUT.C

```
// ABOUT.C
#include <windows.h>
#include <windowsx.h>
#include "globals.h"

// procedures for ABOUT dialog box
LRESULT CALLBACK About(HWND hDlg,
                       UINT uMessage,
                       WPARAM wParam,
                       LPARAM lParam)
{
    switch (uMessage)
      {
        case WM_COMMAND:
              switch (GET_WM_COMMAND_ID(wParam,lParam))
              {
                  case IDOK:
                  case IDCANCEL:
                      {
                      EndDialog(hDlg, TRUE);
                      return(TRUE);
                      }
                      break;
              }
        }
    return FALSE;
}
```

LBOXH.RC

```
#include "windows.h"
#include "globals.h"
#include <winver.h>

APPNAME ICON ICONFILE

RCINCLUDE ABOUT.DLG
RCINCLUDE LIST.DLG
```

```
APPNAME MENU
BEGIN
    MENUITEM "&ListBox", IDM_LBOX
    MENUITEM "&About",   IDM_ABOUT
END
```

LIST.DLG

```
DLGINCLUDE RCDATA DISCARDABLE
BEGIN
    "GLOBALS.H\0"
END


IDD_LISTBOX DIALOG 15, 15, 130, 78
STYLE WS_POPUP | WS_VISIBLE | WS_CAPTION | WS_SYSMENU | WS_BORDER
CAPTION "List Box"
BEGIN
    LISTBOX         IDC_LISTBOX, 4, 4, 122, 49,
                    LBS_SORT | WS_VSCROLL |
                    WS_HSCROLL | WS_TABSTOP
    PUSHBUTTON      "List &1", IDC_LIST1, 4, 59, 38, 14
    PUSHBUTTON      "List &2", IDC_LIST2, 46, 59, 38, 14
    PUSHBUTTON      "&Close", IDC_CLOSE, 88, 59, 38, 14
END
```

ABOUT.DLG

```
ABOUTDLG DIALOG DISCARDABLE  22, 17, 167, 73
STYLE DS_MODALFRAME | WS_CAPTION | WS_SYSMENU
CAPTION SZABOUT
BEGIN
    DEFPUSHBUTTON   "OK", IDOK, 132, 2, 32, 14, WS_GROUP
    ICON            SZAPPNAME,      -1, 3, 2, 18, 20
    LTEXT           SZAPPNAME,      -1, 30, 12,  50, 8
    LTEXT           SZDESCRIPTION, -1, 30, 22, 150, 8
    LTEXT           SZVERSION,      -1, 30, 32, 150, 8
    LTEXT           SZCOMPANYNAME, -1, 30, 42, 150, 8
END
```

LBOXH.ICO

CASE 1-5: LIST BOX WITH COLOR ITEMS

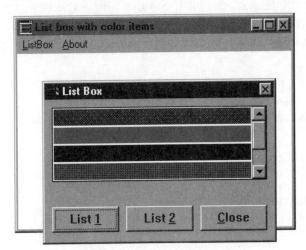

FIGURE 1-5

This example shows how to add single color items into a list box. In order for a program to paint color items with identical height in the list box, the list box style must be defined as LBS_OWNERDRAWFIXED in the dialog resource file **lbcolor.rc**. The following function call adds items to the list box:

```
SendDlgItemMessage(hLbox, IDC_LISTBOX,
          LB_ADDSTRING, 0, RGB(255, 0, 0));
```

Note that the last parameter in the function is the RGB color values for that item and that they are passed to the LPDRAWITEMSTRUCT structure as itemData. These data are then used in the WM_DRAWITEM procedure to define the color of the brush for painting the list box item. There is a rectangle associated with each item in an owner-draw list box. The rectangle data of the list box item is stored in the LPDRAWITEMSTRUCT structure as rcItem. When the WM_DRAWITEM message is received by LboxDlgProc(), the item rectangle gets filled with the color defined by itemData. The item height is defined as 20 pixels in the

LPMEASUREITEMSTRUCT structure when the window procedure handles the message WM_MEASUREITEM. Besides filling the item rectangle with one color as shown in this case, you can also paint a bitmap inside the item rectangle. See Case 1-6 for another example.

GLOBALS.H

```
// GLOBALS.H - header file for global variables
//              and function prototypes

// Product identifier string definitions.
#define APPNAME        LBColor
#define ICONFILE       LBColor.ico
#define SZAPPNAME      "LBColor"
#define SZDESCRIPTION  "List box with color items"
#define SZVERSION      "Version 1.0"
#define SZCOMPANYNAME  "\251 M&&T Books, 1994"
#define SZABOUT        "About"

// Global function prototypes.
BOOL InitApplication(HINSTANCE);
BOOL InitInstance(HINSTANCE, int);

// Callback functions called by Windows.
LRESULT CALLBACK WndProc(HWND, UINT, WPARAM, LPARAM);
LRESULT CALLBACK About(HWND, UINT, WPARAM, LPARAM);
LRESULT CALLBACK LboxDlgProc(HWND, UINT, WPARAM, LPARAM);

// Menu item ID
#define IDM_ABOUT   101
#define IDM_LBOX    102

// Dialog box ID
#define IDD_LISTBOX 200

// Dialog box control ID
#define IDC_LISTBOX 103
#define IDC_LIST1   104
#define IDC_LIST2   105
#define IDC_CLOSE   106

// Global variable declarations.
extern HINSTANCE hInst;     // The current instance handle
extern char szAppName[];    // The name of this application
extern char szTitle[];      // The title bar text
```

```
extern HWND hWnd, hLbox;
extern DLGPROC lpProcLbox;
```

WINMAIN.C

```c
// WINMAIN.C
#include <windows.h>
#include "globals.h"

HWND hLbox;

int APIENTRY WinMain(HINSTANCE hInstance,
                     HINSTANCE hPrevInstance,
                     LPSTR lpCmdLine,
                     int nCmdShow)
{
    MSG msg;

    // register the main window class
    if (!hPrevInstance)
        {
        if (!InitApplication(hInstance))
           {
           return FALSE;
           }
        }

    // create the main window
    if (!InitInstance(hInstance, nCmdShow))
       {
       return FALSE;
       }

    // process the message, if the message is the keyboard
    // input from list dialog box, use IsDialogMessage()
    // function to process the message.
    while (GetMessage(&msg, NULL, 0, 0))
        { if(hLbox == NULL || !IsDialogMessage(hLbox, &msg))
          {
          TranslateMessage(&msg);
          DispatchMessage(&msg);
          }
        }
    return msg.wParam;
}
```

INIT.C

```
// INIT.C
#include <windows.h>
#include "globals.h"

HINSTANCE hInst;
char szAppName[] = SZAPPNAME;
char szTitle[] = SZDESCRIPTION;

// register the main window class
BOOL InitApplication(HINSTANCE hInstance)
{
    WNDCLASS  wc;

    wc.style          = CS_HREDRAW | CS_VREDRAW;
    wc.lpfnWndProc    = (WNDPROC)WndProc;
    wc.cbClsExtra     = 0;
    wc.cbWndExtra     = 0;
    wc.hInstance      = hInstance;
    wc.hIcon          = LoadIcon(hInstance, szAppName);
    wc.hCursor        = LoadCursor(NULL, IDC_ARROW);
    wc.hbrBackground  = (HBRUSH)(COLOR_WINDOW + 1);
    wc.lpszMenuName   = szAppName;
    wc.lpszClassName  = szAppName;

    return(RegisterClass(&wc));
}


// create main window
BOOL InitInstance(HINSTANCE hInstance, int nCmdShow)
{
    HWND    hWnd;
    hInst = hInstance;
    hWnd = CreateWindow(szAppName, szTitle,
                    WS_OVERLAPPEDWINDOW,
                    160, 120, 320, 240,
                    NULL, NULL, hInstance, NULL);

    // return FALSE if create window failed
    if (!hWnd)
        {
        return FALSE;
        }

    ShowWindow(hWnd, nCmdShow);
    UpdateWindow(hWnd);
```

```
        return TRUE;
}
```

LBCOLOR.C

```
// LBCOLOR.C
#include <windows.h>
#include <windowsx.h>
#include "globals.h"

HWND hLbox;
DLGPROC lpProcLbox;

LRESULT CALLBACK WndProc(HWND hWnd,
                         UINT uMessage,
                         WPARAM wParam,
                         LPARAM lParam)
{
    switch (uMessage)
    {
        case WM_COMMAND:

            switch (GET_WM_COMMAND_ID(wParam,lParam))
            {
                case IDM_LBOX:

                    // create a dialog box with list box
                    lpProcLbox = MakeProcInstance(
                            (FARPROC)LboxDlgProc, hInst);
                    hLbox = CreateDialog(hInst,
                            MAKEINTRESOURCE(IDD_LISTBOX),
                                    hWnd, lpProcLbox);
                    break;

                case IDM_ABOUT:

                    // create an about dialog box
                    DialogBox(hInst, "ABOUTDLG",
                            hWnd, (DLGPROC)About);
                    break;

                default:
                    return DefWindowProc(hWnd, uMessage,
                                    wParam, lParam);
            }
```

```
            break;

        case WM_DESTROY:
            FreeProcInstance(lpProcLbox);
            PostQuitMessage(0);
            break;

        default:
            return DefWindowProc(hWnd, uMessage,
                                    wParam, lParam);
    }
    return 0;
}
```

LIST.C

```
// LIST.C
#include <windows.h>
#include <windowsx.h>
#include <stdlib.h>
#include "globals.h"

LRESULT CALLBACK LboxDlgProc(HWND hLbox,
                    UINT uMessage,
                    WPARAM wParam,
                    LPARAM lParam)
{
    LPDRAWITEMSTRUCT lpdis;
    LPMEASUREITEMSTRUCT lpmis;
    RECT rect;
    HBRUSH hBrush;

    switch (uMessage)
    {
        case WM_DRAWITEM:

            lpdis = (LPDRAWITEMSTRUCT)lParam;
            switch(lpdis->itemAction){
                case ODA_DRAWENTIRE:
                    // Fill the item rectangle with color
                    // specified by itemData parameter in
                    // LPDRAWITEMSTRUCT structure lpdis
                    CopyRect((LPRECT)&rect,
                            (LPRECT)&lpdis->rcItem);
                    InflateRect((LPRECT)&rect, -1, -1);
                    hBrush = CreateSolidBrush(
```

```
                           lpdis->itemData);
                FillRect(lpdis->hDC,
                         (LPRECT)&rect, hBrush);
                DeleteObject(hBrush);
                break;

        case ODA_SELECT:

                // frame the item rectangle if selected
                CopyRect((LPRECT)&rect,
                         (LPRECT)&lpdis->rcItem);
                InflateRect((LPRECT)&rect, 0, 0);
                if (lpdis->itemState & ODS_SELECTED)
                   hBrush = CreateSolidBrush(
                                   RGB(0, 0, 0));
                else
                   hBrush = CreateSolidBrush(
                          GetSysColor(COLOR_WINDOW));
                   FrameRect(lpdis->hDC,
                             (LPRECT)&rect, hBrush);
                   DeleteObject(hBrush);
                break;

        case ODA_FOCUS:

                // frame the item rectangle if focused
                CopyRect((LPRECT)&rect,
                         (LPRECT)&lpdis->rcItem);
                InflateRect((LPRECT)&rect, -1, -1);
                if(lpdis->itemState & ODS_FOCUS)
                   hBrush = CreateSolidBrush(
                            RGB(128, 128, 128));
                else
                   hBrush = CreateSolidBrush(
                          GetSysColor(COLOR_WINDOW));
                   FrameRect(lpdis->hDC,
                             (LPRECT)&rect, hBrush);
                   DeleteObject(hBrush);
                break;
        }
        return(TRUE);
        break;

    case WM_MEASUREITEM:

        // specify the height of list box items
        lpmis = (LPMEASUREITEMSTRUCT)lParam;
```

49

```
            if(lpmis->itemID == -1){
              lpmis->itemHeight = 20;
              return(TRUE);
              }
            lpmis->itemHeight = 20;
            break;

    case WM_COMMAND:

            switch (GET_WM_COMMAND_ID(wParam,lParam))
            {
                case IDC_LIST1:

                        // reset list box content
                        SendDlgItemMessage(hLbox, IDC_LISTBOX,
                                           LB_RESETCONTENT,
                                           0, 0L);
                        // set list box horizontal extent
                        SendDlgItemMessage(hLbox, IDC_LISTBOX,
                            LB_SETHORIZONTALEXTENT, 200, 0L);

                        // add list box color items
                        SendDlgItemMessage(hLbox, IDC_LISTBOX,
                                           LB_ADDSTRING, 0,
                                           RGB(255, 0, 0));
                        SendDlgItemMessage(hLbox, IDC_LISTBOX,
                                           LB_ADDSTRING, 0,
                                           RGB(0, 255, 0));
                        SendDlgItemMessage(hLbox, IDC_LISTBOX,
                                           LB_ADDSTRING, 0,
                                           RGB(0, 0, 255));
                        SendDlgItemMessage(hLbox, IDC_LISTBOX,
                                           LB_ADDSTRING, 0,
                                           RGB(255, 255, 0));
                        SendDlgItemMessage(hLbox, IDC_LISTBOX,
                                           LB_ADDSTRING, 0,
                                           RGB(255, 0, 255));
                        SendDlgItemMessage(hLbox, IDC_LISTBOX,
                                           LB_ADDSTRING, 0,
                                           RGB(0, 255, 255));
                        break;

                case IDC_LIST2:

                        // reset list box content
                        SendDlgItemMessage(hLbox, IDC_LISTBOX,
                                           LB_RESETCONTENT,
```

```
                                      0, 0L);
               // set list box horizontal extent such
               // that the horizontal scroll bar will
               // appear.
               SendDlgItemMessage(hLbox, IDC_LISTBOX,
                          LB_SETHORIZONTALEXTENT,
                          320, 0L);

               // add color items into list box
               SendDlgItemMessage(hLbox, IDC_LISTBOX,
                          LB_ADDSTRING, 0,
                          RGB(255, 0, 0));
               SendDlgItemMessage(hLbox, IDC_LISTBOX,
                          LB_ADDSTRING, 0,
                          RGB(0, 255, 0));
               SendDlgItemMessage(hLbox, IDC_LISTBOX,
                          LB_ADDSTRING, 0,
                          RGB(0, 0, 255));
               SendDlgItemMessage(hLbox, IDC_LISTBOX,
                          LB_ADDSTRING, 0,
                          RGB(255, 255, 0));
               SendDlgItemMessage(hLbox, IDC_LISTBOX,
                          LB_ADDSTRING, 0,
                          RGB(255, 0, 255));
               SendDlgItemMessage(hLbox, IDC_LISTBOX,
                          LB_ADDSTRING, 0,
                          RGB(0, 255, 255));
               break;

          case IDCANCEL:
          case IDC_CLOSE:
               DestroyWindow(hLbox);
               hLbox = 0;
               break;

          default:
               return DefWindowProc(hLbox, uMessage,
                                    wParam, lParam);
          }
          break;

     default:
          return DefWindowProc(hLbox, uMessage,
                               wParam, lParam);
     }
     return 0;
}
```

ABOUT.C

```
// ABOUT.C
#include <windows.h>
#include <windowsx.h>
#include "globals.h"

// procedures for ABOUT dialog box
LRESULT CALLBACK About(HWND hDlg,
                       UINT uMessage,
                       WPARAM wParam,
                       LPARAM lParam)
{
    switch (uMessage)
      {
        case WM_COMMAND:
            switch (GET_WM_COMMAND_ID(wParam,lParam))
            {
                case IDOK:
                case IDCANCEL:
                    {
                    EndDialog(hDlg, TRUE);
                    return(TRUE);
                    }
                    break;
            }
        }
    return FALSE;
}
```

LBCOLOR.RC

```
#include "windows.h"
#include "globals.h"
#include <winver.h>

APPNAME ICON ICONFILE

RCINCLUDE ABOUT.DLG
RCINCLUDE LIST.DLG

APPNAME MENU
BEGIN
    MENUITEM "&ListBox", IDM_LBOX
    MENUITEM "&About",   IDM_ABOUT
END
```

LIST.DLG

```
DLGINCLUDE RCDATA DISCARDABLE
BEGIN
    "GLOBALS.H\0"
END


IDD_LISTBOX DIALOG 15, 15, 130, 78
STYLE WS_POPUP | WS_VISIBLE | WS_CAPTION | WS_SYSMENU | WS_BORDER
CAPTION "List Box"
BEGIN
    LISTBOX         IDC_LISTBOX, 4, 4, 122, 49,
                    LBS_OWNERDRAWFIXED |
                    WS_VSCROLL | WS_HSCROLL | WS_TABSTOP
    PUSHBUTTON      "List &1", IDC_LIST1, 4, 59, 38, 14
    PUSHBUTTON      "List &2", IDC_LIST2, 46, 59, 38, 14
    PUSHBUTTON      "&Close", IDC_CLOSE, 88, 59, 38, 14
END
```

ABOUT.DLG

```
ABOUTDLG DIALOG DISCARDABLE  22, 17, 167, 73
STYLE DS_MODALFRAME | WS_CAPTION | WS_SYSMENU
CAPTION SZABOUT
BEGIN
    DEFPUSHBUTTON   "OK", IDOK, 132, 2, 32, 14, WS_GROUP
    ICON            SZAPPNAME,      -1, 3, 2, 18, 20
    LTEXT           SZAPPNAME,      -1, 30, 12,  50, 8
    LTEXT           SZDESCRIPTION, -1, 30, 22, 150, 8
    LTEXT           SZVERSION,      -1, 30, 32, 150, 8
    LTEXT           SZCOMPANYNAME, -1, 30, 42, 150, 8
END
```

LBCOLOR.ICO

CASE 1-6: LIST BOX WITH BITMAP ITEMS

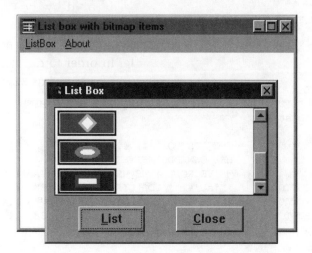

FIGURE 1-6

This case is similar to Case 1-5. However, instead of filling each list box item rectangle with color defined by itemData in LPDRAWITEMSTRUCT structure, a bitmap defined by itemData is loaded and painted in the listbox item rectangle. In order for the program to paint bitmap items with identical height in the list box, the list box style must be defined as LBS_OWNERDRAWFIXED in the dialog resource file **lbcolor.rc**. The following function call adds items to the list box:

```
SendDlgItemMessage(hLbox, IDC_LISTBOX,
    LB_ADDSTRING, 0,(LONG)(LPSTR)"ListItem1");
```

Note that the last parameter in the function is the bitmap name (defined in resource file **LBBITMAP.RC**) for that item and is passed to LPDRAWITEMSTRUCT structure as itemData. This data is then used in the WM_DRAWITEM procedure as the name of the bitmap to be painted for this item. The rectangle data of the list box item is stored in the LPDRAWITEMSTRUCT structure as rcItem. The PaintRectBitmap() function is the one that paints bitmaps in item rectangles. When

LboxDlgProc() receives the WM_DRAWITEM message, the coordinates of upper-left corner of item rectangle defined by rcItem in the LPDRAWITEMSTRUCT structure are passed to this function. A bitmap defined by itemData is then drawn with its upper-left corner positioned at the upper-left corner of the item rectangle. In order to accommodate the whole bitmap in the list box, the item height is defined as 32 pixels in the LPMEASUREITEMSTRUCT structure when the window procedure handles the message WM_MEASUREITEM.

GLOBALS.H

```
// GLOBALS.H - header file for global variables
//              and function prototypes

// Product identifier string definitions.
#define APPNAME        LBBitmap
#define ICONFILE       LBBitmap.ico
#define SZAPPNAME      "LBBitmap"
#define SZDESCRIPTION  "List box with bitmap items"
#define SZVERSION      "Version 1.0"
#define SZCOMPANYNAME  "\251 M&&T Books, 1994"
#define SZABOUT        "About"

// Global function prototypes.
BOOL InitApplication(HINSTANCE);
BOOL InitInstance(HINSTANCE, int);
void PaintRectBitmap(HDC, HBITMAP, WORD, WORD);

// Callback functions called by Windows.
LRESULT CALLBACK WndProc(HWND, UINT, WPARAM, LPARAM);
LRESULT CALLBACK About(HWND, UINT, WPARAM, LPARAM);
LRESULT CALLBACK LboxDlgProc(HWND, UINT, WPARAM, LPARAM);

// Menu item ID
#define IDM_ABOUT   101
#define IDM_LBOX    102

// Dialog box ID
#define IDD_LISTBOX 200

// Dialog box control ID
#define IDC_LISTBOX 103
#define IDC_LIST1   104
```

```
#define IDC_LIST2   105
#define IDC_CLOSE   106

// Global variable declarations.
extern HINSTANCE hInst;       // The current instance handle
extern char szAppName[];      // The name of this application
extern char szTitle[];        // The title bar text
extern HWND hWnd, hLbox;
extern DLGPROC lpProcLbox;
```

WINMAIN.C

```
// WINMAIN.C
#include <windows.h>
#include "globals.h"

HWND hLbox;

int APIENTRY WinMain(HINSTANCE hInstance,
                     HINSTANCE hPrevInstance,
                     LPSTR lpCmdLine,
                     int nCmdShow)
{
    MSG msg;

    // register the main window class
    if (!hPrevInstance)
        {
        if (!InitApplication(hInstance))
            {
            return FALSE;
            }
        }

    // create the main window
    if (!InitInstance(hInstance, nCmdShow))
        {
        return FALSE;
        }

    // process the message, if the message is the keyboard
    // input from list dialog box, use IsDialogMessage()
    // function to process the message.
    while (GetMessage(&msg, NULL, 0, 0))
        { if(hLbox == NULL || !IsDialogMessage(hLbox, &msg))
          {
```

```
            TranslateMessage(&msg);
            DispatchMessage(&msg);
          }
        }
    return msg.wParam;
}
```

INIT.C

```
// INIT.C
#include <windows.h>
#include "globals.h"

HINSTANCE hInst;
char szAppName[] = SZAPPNAME;
char szTitle[] = SZDESCRIPTION;

// register the main window class
BOOL InitApplication(HINSTANCE hInstance)
{
    WNDCLASS  wc;

    wc.style          = CS_HREDRAW | CS_VREDRAW;
    wc.lpfnWndProc    = (WNDPROC)WndProc;
    wc.cbClsExtra     = 0;
    wc.cbWndExtra     = 0;
    wc.hInstance      = hInstance;
    wc.hIcon          = LoadIcon(hInstance, szAppName);
    wc.hCursor        = LoadCursor(NULL, IDC_ARROW);
    wc.hbrBackground  = (HBRUSH)(COLOR_WINDOW + 1);
    wc.lpszMenuName   = szAppName;
    wc.lpszClassName  = szAppName;

    return(RegisterClass(&wc));
}

// create main window
BOOL InitInstance(HINSTANCE hInstance, int nCmdShow)
{
    HWND    hWnd;
    hInst = hInstance;
    hWnd = CreateWindow(szAppName, szTitle,
                        WS_OVERLAPPEDWINDOW,
                        160, 120, 320, 240,
                        NULL, NULL, hInstance, NULL);
```

```
        // return FALSE if create window failed
        if (!hWnd)
            {
            return FALSE;
            }

        ShowWindow(hWnd, nCmdShow);
        UpdateWindow(hWnd);

        return TRUE;
    }
```

LBBITMAP.C

```
// LBBITMAP.C
#include <windows.h>
#include <windowsx.h>
#include "globals.h"

HWND hLbox;
DLGPROC lpProcLbox;

LRESULT CALLBACK WndProc(HWND hWnd,
                         UINT uMessage,
                         WPARAM wParam,
                         LPARAM lParam)
{
    switch (uMessage)
    {
        case WM_COMMAND:
            switch (GET_WM_COMMAND_ID(wParam,lParam))
            {
                case IDM_LBOX:
                    // create a dialog box with list box
                    lpProcLbox = MakeProcInstance(
                            (FARPROC)LboxDlgProc, hInst);
                    hLbox = CreateDialog(hInst,
                            MAKEINTRESOURCE(IDD_LISTBOX),
                                    hWnd, lpProcLbox);
                    break;

                case IDM_ABOUT:
                    // create an about dialog
                    DialogBox(hInst, "ABOUTDLG",
                            hWnd, (DLGPROC)About);
                    break;
```

```
                    default:
                        return DefWindowProc(hWnd, uMessage,
                                                wParam, lParam);
                }
                break;

        case WM_DESTROY:
                FreeProcInstance(lpProcLbox);
                PostQuitMessage(0);
                break;

        default:
                return DefWindowProc(hWnd, uMessage,
                                        wParam, lParam);
        }
        return 0;
}
```

LIST.C

```
// LIST.C
#include <windows.h>
#include <windowsx.h>
#include <stdlib.h>
#include "globals.h"
HBITMAP hBitmap;

// procedures for dialog box hLbox
LRESULT CALLBACK LboxDlgProc(HWND hLbox,
                            UINT uMessage,
                            WPARAM wParam,
                            LPARAM lParam)
{
    LPDRAWITEMSTRUCT lpdis;
    LPMEASUREITEMSTRUCT lpmis;
    RECT rect;
    HBRUSH hBrush;

    switch (uMessage)
    {
        case WM_DRAWITEM:

                lpdis = (LPDRAWITEMSTRUCT)lParam;
                switch(lpdis->itemAction){
                    case ODA_DRAWENTIRE:
```

```
        // paint the item rectangle with the
        // bitmap specified by itemData
        // parameter in LPDRAWITEMSTRUCT lpdis
        CopyRect((LPRECT)&rect,
                (LPRECT)&lpdis->rcItem);
        InflateRect((LPRECT)&rect, -1, -1);
        hBitmap = LoadBitmap(hInst,
                (LPSTR)lpdis->itemData);
        PaintRectBitmap(lpdis->hDC, hBitmap,
                rect.left, rect.top);
        break;

case ODA_SELECT:

        // frame the item rectangle if selected
        CopyRect((LPRECT)&rect,
                (LPRECT)&lpdis->rcItem);
        InflateRect((LPRECT)&rect, 0, 0);
        if(lpdis->itemState & ODS_SELECTED)
           hBrush = CreateSolidBrush(
                        RGB(0, 0, 0));
        else
        hBrush = CreateSolidBrush(
                GetSysColor(COLOR_WINDOW));
        FrameRect(lpdis->hDC,
                (LPRECT)&rect, hBrush);
        DeleteObject(hBrush);
        break;

case ODA_FOCUS:

        // frame the item rectangle if focused
        CopyRect((LPRECT)&rect,
                (LPRECT)&lpdis->rcItem);
        InflateRect((LPRECT)&rect, -1, -1);
        if(lpdis->itemState & ODS_FOCUS)
           hBrush = CreateSolidBrush(
                        RGB(128, 128, 128));
        else
        hBrush = CreateSolidBrush(
                GetSysColor(COLOR_WINDOW));
        FrameRect(lpdis->hDC,
                (LPRECT)&rect, hBrush);
        DeleteObject(hBrush);
        DrawFocusRect(lpdis->hDC,
                (LPRECT)&lpdis->rcItem);
        break;
```

```
         }
      return(TRUE);
      break;

case WM_MEASUREITEM:

      // specify the height of list box items
      lpmis = (LPMEASUREITEMSTRUCT)lParam;
      if(lpmis->itemID == -1){
        lpmis->itemHeight = 32;
        return(TRUE);
        }
      lpmis->itemHeight = 32;
      break;

case WM_COMMAND:

      switch (GET_WM_COMMAND_ID(wParam,lParam))
      {
          case IDC_LIST1:

                 // reset list box contents
                 SendDlgItemMessage(hLbox, IDC_LISTBOX,
                             LB_RESETCONTENT, 0, 0L);

                 // add bitmap items to list box
                 SendDlgItemMessage(hLbox, IDC_LISTBOX,
                             LB_ADDSTRING, 0,
                         (LONG)(LPSTR)"ListItem1");
                 SendDlgItemMessage(hLbox, IDC_LISTBOX,
                             LB_ADDSTRING, 0,
                         (LONG)(LPSTR)"ListItem2");
                 SendDlgItemMessage(hLbox, IDC_LISTBOX,
                             LB_ADDSTRING, 0,
                         (LONG)(LPSTR)"ListItem3");
                 SendDlgItemMessage(hLbox, IDC_LISTBOX,
                             LB_ADDSTRING, 0,
                         (LONG)(LPSTR)"ListItem4");
                 SendDlgItemMessage(hLbox, IDC_LISTBOX,
                             LB_ADDSTRING, 0,
                         (LONG)(LPSTR)"ListItem5");
                 SendDlgItemMessage(hLbox, IDC_LISTBOX,
                             LB_ADDSTRING, 0,
                         (LONG)(LPSTR)"ListItem6");
                 break;

          case IDCANCEL:
```

```
                    case IDC_CLOSE:
                            DestroyWindow(hLbox);
                            hLbox = 0;
                            break;

                    default:
                            return DefWindowProc(hLbox, uMessage,
                                                    wParam, lParam);
                     }
                    break;

            default:
                    return DefWindowProc(hLbox, uMessage,
                                            wParam, lParam);
            }
        return 0;
}
```

```
// function for painting the bitmap in
// list box item rectangles
void PaintRectBitmap (hDC, hBitmap, rectX, rectY)
HDC hDC;
HBITMAP hBitmap;
WORD rectX, rectY;
{
    BITMAP bmp;
    HDC hMemoryDC;
    hMemoryDC = CreateCompatibleDC(hDC);
    GetObject(hBitmap, sizeof(BITMAP), (LPSTR) &bmp);
    SelectObject(hMemoryDC, hBitmap);
    BitBlt(hDC, rectX, rectY, bmp.bmWidth, bmp.bmHeight,
                    hMemoryDC, 0, 0, SRCCOPY);
    DeleteDC(hMemoryDC);
    DeleteObject(hBitmap);
}
```

ABOUT.C

```
// ABOUT.C
#include <windows.h>
#include <windowsx.h>
#include "globals.h"

// procedures for ABOUT dialog box
LRESULT CALLBACK About(HWND hDlg,
                        UINT uMessage,
```

```
                          WPARAM wParam,
                          LPARAM lParam)
{
    switch (uMessage)
      {
        case WM_COMMAND:
              switch (GET_WM_COMMAND_ID(wParam,lParam))
              {
                  case IDOK:
                  case IDCANCEL:
                      {
                      EndDialog(hDlg, TRUE);
                      return(TRUE);
                      }
                      break;
              }
      }
    return FALSE;
}
```

LBBITMAP.RC

```
#include "windows.h"
#include "globals.h"
#include <winver.h>

ListItem1 BITMAP item1.bmp
ListItem2 BITMAP item2.bmp
ListItem3 BITMAP item3.bmp
ListItem4 BITMAP item4.bmp
ListItem5 BITMAP item5.bmp
ListItem6 BITMAP item6.bmp

APPNAME ICON ICONFILE

RCINCLUDE ABOUT.DLG
RCINCLUDE LIST.DLG

APPNAME MENU
BEGIN
    MENUITEM "&ListBox", IDM_LBOX
    MENUITEM "&About",   IDM_ABOUT
END
```

LIST.DLG

```
DLGINCLUDE RCDATA DISCARDABLE
BEGIN
    "GLOBALS.H\0"
END


IDD_LISTBOX DIALOG 15, 15, 130, 78
STYLE WS_POPUP | WS_VISIBLE | WS_CAPTION | WS_SYSMENU | WS_BORDER
CAPTION "List Box"
BEGIN
    LISTBOX         IDC_LISTBOX, 4, 4, 122, 49,
                    LBS_OWNERDRAWFIXED |
                    WS_VSCROLL | WS_TABSTOP
    PUSHBUTTON      "&List", IDC_LIST1, 18, 59, 38, 14
    PUSHBUTTON      "&Close", IDC_CLOSE, 74, 59, 38, 14
END
```

ABOUT.DLG

```
ABOUTDLG DIALOG DISCARDABLE  22, 17, 167, 73
STYLE DS_MODALFRAME | WS_CAPTION | WS_SYSMENU
CAPTION SZABOUT
BEGIN
    DEFPUSHBUTTON   "OK", IDOK, 132, 2, 32, 14, WS_GROUP
    ICON            SZAPPNAME,      -1, 3, 2, 18, 20
    LTEXT           SZAPPNAME,      -1, 30, 12,  50, 8
    LTEXT           SZDESCRIPTION, -1, 30, 22, 150, 8
    LTEXT           SZVERSION,      -1, 30, 32, 150, 8
    LTEXT           SZCOMPANYNAME, -1, 30, 42, 150, 8
END
```

LBBITMAP.ICO

ITEM1.BMP

ITEM2.BMP

ITEM3.BMP

ITEM4.BMP

ITEM5.BMP

ITEM6.BMP

CASE 1-7: COMBO BOX WITH TEXT ITEMS

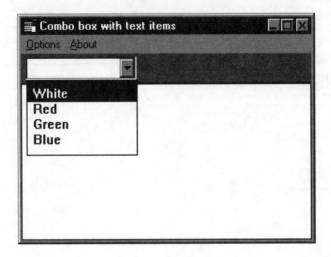

FIGURE 1-7

A *combo box* is a control that consists of a static or edit control box and a list box. The list box can be hidden until the user clicks the down-arrow button on the right-hand side of the static or edit control. When the list box is displayed, the user can choose one item in the list by clicking that item. The item chosen by the user is then displayed in the static or edit control box. The list box is usually closed after the selection.

This example shows how to handle a combo box with a drop-down list box. First, the combo box style is defined as CBS_DROPDOWNLIST. It adds four "text" items to the drop-down list box when the window processes the case CBN_DROPDOWN message. When any one of those four items is selected, the window automatically closes the drop down list box and displays that item in the combo box. See Cases 1-8 and 1-9 for more examples.

GLOBALS.H

```
// GLOBALS.H - header file for global variables
//             and function prototypes

// Product identifier string definitions.
#define APPNAME        ComboTx
#define ICONFILE       ComboTx.ico
#define SZAPPNAME      "ComboTx"
#define SZDESCRIPTION  "Combo box with text items"
#define SZVERSION      "Version 1.0"
#define SZCOMPANYNAME  "\251 M&&T Books, 1994"
#define SZABOUT        "About"

// Global function prototypes.
BOOL InitApplication(HINSTANCE);
BOOL InitInstance(HINSTANCE, int);

// Callback functions called by Windows.
LRESULT CALLBACK WndProc(HWND, UINT, WPARAM, LPARAM);
LRESULT CALLBACK About(HWND, UINT, WPARAM, LPARAM);

// Menu item ID
#define IDM_ABOUT       101
#define IDM_SHOWCOMBO   102
#define IDM_HIDECOMBO   103

// Control ID
#define IDC_COMBOBOX    104
#define IDC_COMBOEDIT   105

// Global variable declarations.
extern HINSTANCE hInst;      // The current instance handle
extern char szAppName[];     // The name of this application
extern char szTitle[];       // The title bar text
```

WINMAIN.C

```
// WINMAIN.C
#include <windows.h>
#include "globals.h"

int APIENTRY WinMain(HINSTANCE hInstance,
                     HINSTANCE hPrevInstance,
                     LPSTR lpCmdLine,
```

```
                        int nCmdShow)
{
    MSG msg;

    // register the main window class
    if (!hPrevInstance)
        {
        if (!InitApplication(hInstance))
            {
            return FALSE;
            }
        }

    // create and show main window
    if (!InitInstance(hInstance, nCmdShow))
        {
        return FALSE;
        }

    // process window message
    while (GetMessage(&msg, NULL, 0, 0))
        {
            TranslateMessage(&msg);
            DispatchMessage(&msg);
        }
    return msg.wParam;
}
```

INIT.C

```
// INIT.C
#include <windows.h>
#include "globals.h"

HINSTANCE hInst;
char szAppName[] = SZAPPNAME;
char szTitle[] = SZDESCRIPTION;

// register the main window class
BOOL InitApplication(HINSTANCE hInstance)
{
    WNDCLASS  wc;

    wc.style          = CS_HREDRAW | CS_VREDRAW;
    wc.lpfnWndProc    = (WNDPROC)WndProc;
    wc.cbClsExtra     = 0;
```

```
    wc.cbWndExtra      = 0;
    wc.hInstance       = hInstance;
    wc.hIcon           = LoadIcon(hInstance, szAppName);
    wc.hCursor         = LoadCursor(NULL, IDC_ARROW);
    wc.hbrBackground   = (HBRUSH)(COLOR_WINDOW + 1);
    wc.lpszMenuName    = szAppName;
    wc.lpszClassName   = szAppName;

    return(RegisterClass(&wc));
}

// create and show the main window
BOOL InitInstance(HINSTANCE hInstance, int nCmdShow)
{
    HWND    hWnd;
    hInst = hInstance;
    hWnd = CreateWindow(szAppName, szTitle,
                        WS_OVERLAPPEDWINDOW,
                        160, 120, 320, 240,
                        NULL, NULL, hInstance, NULL);

    if (!hWnd) return FALSE;

    ShowWindow(hWnd, nCmdShow);
    UpdateWindow(hWnd);

    return TRUE;
}
```

COMBOTX.C

```
// COMBOTX.C
#include <windows.h>
#include <windowsx.h>
#include "globals.h"

HWND hCombo, hGrayRect, hBlackLine;
HBRUSH hBrush, hBrushW, hBrushR, hBrushG, hBrushB;

LRESULT CALLBACK WndProc(HWND hWnd,
                         UINT uMessage,
                         WPARAM wParam,
                         LPARAM lParam)
{
    char buffer[6];
    WORD Index;
```

```
HDC hDC;
RECT rect;

switch (uMessage)
{
    case WM_CREATE:
            // create brushes for painting
            hBrushW = CreateSolidBrush(RGB(255, 255, 255));
            hBrushR = CreateSolidBrush(RGB(255,   0,   0));
            hBrushG = CreateSolidBrush(RGB(  0, 255,   0));
            hBrushB = CreateSolidBrush(RGB(  0,   0, 255));

            // create a gray rectangle below the menu area
            hGrayRect = CreateWindow("static", "",
                        SS_GRAYRECT |
                        WS_CHILD | WS_VISIBLE,
                        0, 0, 640, 30,
                        hWnd, NULL, hInst, NULL);

            // add a bottom black boundary to the gray area
            hBlackLine = CreateWindow("static", "",
                        SS_BLACKRECT |
                        WS_CHILD | WS_VISIBLE,
                        0, 30, 640, 1,
                        hWnd, NULL, hInst, NULL);

            // create a combo box
            hCombo = CreateWindow("combobox", "",
                        CBS_DROPDOWNLIST | WS_VSCROLL |
                        WS_GROUP | WS_CHILD |
                        WS_VISIBLE | WS_TABSTOP,
                        5, 3, 120, 90,
                        hWnd, IDC_COMBOBOX, hInst, NULL);
            break;

    case WM_COMMAND:
            switch (GET_WM_COMMAND_ID(wParam,lParam))
            {
                case IDM_SHOWCOMBO:
                        // show combo box and
                        // the gray rectangle
                        ShowWindow(hGrayRect, SW_SHOW);
                        ShowWindow(hBlackLine, SW_SHOW);
                        ShowWindow(hCombo, SW_SHOW);
                        break;

                case IDM_HIDECOMBO:
```

```
                // hide combo box and
                // the gray rectangle
                ShowWindow(hGrayRect, SW_HIDE);
                ShowWindow(hBlackLine, SW_HIDE);
                ShowWindow(hCombo, SW_HIDE);
                break;

        case IDC_COMBOBOX:
            switch(GET_WM_COMMAND_CMD(
                        wParam, lParam)){
              case CBN_DROPDOWN:
                    // reset the combo box content
                    SendMessage(hCombo,
                            CB_RESETCONTENT, 0, 0L);

                    // add text items to
                    // the combo box
                    strcpy(buffer, "White");
                    SendMessage(hCombo,
                            CB_ADDSTRING, 0,
                            (LONG)(LPSTR)buffer);
                    strcpy(buffer, "Red");
                    SendMessage(hCombo,
                            CB_ADDSTRING, 0,
                            (LONG)(LPSTR)buffer);
                    strcpy(buffer, "Green");
                    SendMessage(hCombo,
                            CB_ADDSTRING, 0,
                            (LONG)(LPSTR)buffer);
                    strcpy(buffer, "Blue");
                    SendMessage(hCombo,
                            CB_ADDSTRING, 0,
                            (LONG)(LPSTR)buffer);
                    break;

              case CBN_SELCHANGE:

                    // if item selection changed,
                    // choose the color brush
                    // specified by the item and
                    // paint the window client area
                    Index = (WORD)SendMessage(
                            hCombo,
                            CB_GETCURSEL, 0, 0L);
                    switch(Index){
                      case 0: hBrush = hBrushW;
                            break;
```

```
                          case 1: hBrush = hBrushR;
                                  break;
                          case 2: hBrush = hBrushG;
                                  break;
                          case 3: hBrush = hBrushB;
                                  break;
                          }
                    hDC = GetDC(hWnd);
                    GetClientRect(hWnd, &rect);
                    SelectObject(hDC, hBrush);
                    Rectangle(hDC,
                         rect.left, rect.top + 31,
                         rect.right, rect.bottom);
                    ReleaseDC(hWnd, hDC);
                    DeleteObject(hBrush);
                 break;
                 }
              break;

          case IDM_ABOUT:
                 // create an about box
                 DialogBox(hInst, "ABOUTDLG",
                          hWnd, (DLGPROC)About);
                 break;

          default:
              return DefWindowProc(hWnd, uMessage,
                                   wParam, lParam);
          }
          break;

      case WM_DESTROY:
          PostQuitMessage(0);
          break;

      default:
          return DefWindowProc(hWnd, uMessage,
                               wParam, lParam);
      }
   return 0;
}
```

ABOUT.C

```
// ABOUT.C
#include <windows.h>
```

```
#include <windowsx.h>
#include "globals.h"

// procedures for ABOUT dialog box
LRESULT CALLBACK About(HWND hDlg,
                       UINT uMessage,
                       WPARAM wParam,
                       LPARAM lParam)
{
    switch (uMessage)
      {
        case WM_COMMAND:
            switch (GET_WM_COMMAND_ID(wParam,lParam))
              {
                case IDOK:
                case IDCANCEL:
                    {
                    EndDialog(hDlg, TRUE);
                    return(TRUE);
                    }
                    break;
              }
      }
    return FALSE;
}
```

COMBOTX.RC

```
#include "windows.h"
#include "globals.h"
#include <winver.h>

APPNAME ICON ICONFILE

RCINCLUDE ABOUT.DLG

APPNAME MENU
BEGIN
    POPUP        "&Options"
    BEGIN
        MENUITEM "&Show COMBO Menu Bar", IDM_SHOWCOMBO
        MENUITEM "&Hide COMBO Menu Bar", IDM_HIDECOMBO
    END
    MENUITEM "&About", IDM_ABOUT
END
```

ABOUT.DLG

```
ABOUTDLG DIALOG DISCARDABLE  22, 17, 167, 73
STYLE DS_MODALFRAME | WS_CAPTION | WS_SYSMENU
CAPTION SZABOUT
BEGIN
    DEFPUSHBUTTON    "OK", IDOK, 132, 2, 32, 14, WS_GROUP
    ICON             SZAPPNAME,       -1, 3, 2, 18, 20
    LTEXT            SZAPPNAME,       -1, 30, 12,  50, 8
    LTEXT            SZDESCRIPTION, -1, 30, 22, 150, 8
    LTEXT            SZVERSION,       -1, 30, 32, 150, 8
    LTEXT            SZCOMPANYNAME, -1, 30, 42, 150, 8
END
```

COMBOTX.ICO

CASE 1-8: COMBO BOX WITH COLOR ITEMS

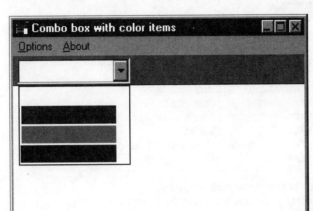

FIGURE 1-8

This case is similar to Case 1-7. The difference is that, in this case, color items instead of text items are added to the combo box drop-down list box. The procedures to paint single-color items in the drop-down list box are similar to those described in Case 1-5. To list the nontext item in the drop-down list box, the combo box must have the style of CBS_OWNERDRAWFIXED (if all items have the same height) or CBS_OWNERDRAWVARIABLE (if not all items have the same height). Please see Case 1-5 for more information. Like Case 1-7, when an item is selected, the window automatically closes the drop-down list box and paints the color item in the static box.

GLOBALS.H

```
// GLOBALS.H - header file for global variables
//              and function prototypes

// Product identifier string definitions.
#define APPNAME        ComboCol
#define ICONFILE       ComboCol.ico
#define SZAPPNAME      "ComboCol"
#define SZDESCRIPTION  "Combo box with color items"
#define SZVERSION      "Version 1.0"
#define SZCOMPANYNAME  "\251 M&&T Books, 1994"
#define SZABOUT        "About"

// Global function prototypes.
BOOL InitApplication(HINSTANCE);
BOOL InitInstance(HINSTANCE, int);

// Callback functions called by Windows.
LRESULT CALLBACK WndProc(HWND, UINT, WPARAM, LPARAM);
LRESULT CALLBACK About(HWND, UINT, WPARAM, LPARAM);

// Menu item ID
#define IDM_ABOUT       101
#define IDM_SHOWCOMBO   102
#define IDM_HIDECOMBO   103

// Control ID
#define IDC_COMBOBOX    104
#define IDC_COMBOEDIT   105

// Global variable declarations.
extern HINSTANCE hInst;     // The current instance handle
extern char szAppName[];    // The name of this application
extern char szTitle[];      // The title bar text
```

WINMAIN.C

```
// WINMAIN.C
#include <windows.h>
#include "globals.h"

int APIENTRY WinMain(HINSTANCE hInstance,
                     HINSTANCE hPrevInstance,
                     LPSTR lpCmdLine,
```

```
                        int nCmdShow)
{
    MSG msg;

    // register the main window class
    if (!hPrevInstance)
        {
        if (!InitApplication(hInstance))
            {
            return FALSE;
            }
        }

    // create and show main window
    if (!InitInstance(hInstance, nCmdShow))
        {
        return FALSE;
        }

    // process window message
    while (GetMessage(&msg, NULL, 0, 0))
        {
            TranslateMessage(&msg);
            DispatchMessage(&msg);
        }
    return msg.wParam;
}
```

INIT.C

```
// INIT.C
#include <windows.h>
#include "globals.h"

HINSTANCE hInst;
char szAppName[] = SZAPPNAME;
char szTitle[] = SZDESCRIPTION;

// register the main window class
BOOL InitApplication(HINSTANCE hInstance)
{
    WNDCLASS  wc;

    wc.style         = CS_HREDRAW | CS_VREDRAW;
    wc.lpfnWndProc   = (WNDPROC)WndProc;
    wc.cbClsExtra    = 0;
```

```
    wc.cbWndExtra    = 0;
    wc.hInstance     = hInstance;
    wc.hIcon         = LoadIcon(hInstance, szAppName);
    wc.hCursor       = LoadCursor(NULL, IDC_ARROW);
    wc.hbrBackground = (HBRUSH)(COLOR_WINDOW + 1);
    wc.lpszMenuName  = szAppName;
    wc.lpszClassName = szAppName;

    return(RegisterClass(&wc));
}

// create and show the main window
BOOL InitInstance(HINSTANCE hInstance, int nCmdShow)
{
    HWND    hWnd;
    hInst = hInstance;
    hWnd = CreateWindow(szAppName, szTitle,
                        WS_OVERLAPPEDWINDOW,
                        160, 120, 320, 240,
                        NULL, NULL, hInstance, NULL);

    if (!hWnd)
        {
        return FALSE;
        }

    ShowWindow(hWnd, nCmdShow);
    UpdateWindow(hWnd);

    return TRUE;
}
```

COMBOCOL.C

```
// COMBOCOL.C
#include <windows.h>
#include <windowsx.h>
#include "globals.h"

HWND hCombo, hGrayRect, hBlackLine;
HBRUSH hBrush, hBrushW, hBrushR, hBrushG, hBrushB;

LRESULT CALLBACK WndProc(HWND hWnd,
                    UINT uMessage,
                    WPARAM wParam,
                    LPARAM lParam)
```

```
{
    WORD Index;
    HDC hDC;
    LPDRAWITEMSTRUCT    lpdis;
    LPMEASUREITEMSTRUCT lpmis;
    RECT rect, rect1;
    HBRUSH hBrush;

    switch (uMessage)
    {
        case WM_CREATE:

                // create brushes for painting
                hBrushW = CreateSolidBrush(RGB(255, 255, 255));
                hBrushR = CreateSolidBrush(RGB(255,   0,   0));
                hBrushG = CreateSolidBrush(RGB(  0, 255,   0));
                hBrushB = CreateSolidBrush(RGB(  0,   0, 255));

                // create a gray rectangle below the menu area
                hGrayRect = CreateWindow("static", "",
                    SS_GRAYRECT | WS_CHILD | WS_VISIBLE,
                    0, 0, 640, 30, hWnd, NULL, hInst, NULL);

                // add a bottom black boundary to the gray area
                hBlackLine = CreateWindow("static", "",
                    SS_BLACKRECT | WS_CHILD | WS_VISIBLE,
                    0, 30, 640, 1, hWnd, NULL, hInst, NULL);

                // create an owner-draw combo box
                hCombo = CreateWindow("combobox", "",
                    CBS_DROPDOWNLIST | CBS_OWNERDRAWFIXED |
                    CBS_SIMPLE | WS_VSCROLL | WS_GROUP |
                    WS_CHILD | WS_VISIBLE | WS_TABSTOP,
                    5, 3, 120, 110,
                    hWnd, IDC_COMBOBOX, hInst, NULL);
                break;

        case WM_COMMAND:

                switch (GET_WM_COMMAND_ID(wParam,lParam))
                {
                    case IDM_ABOUT:

                            // create an about box
                            DialogBox(hInst, "ABOUTDLG",
                                    hWnd, (DLGPROC)About);
                            break;
```

```
case IDM_SHOWCOMBO:

    // show combo box and
    // the gray rectangle
    ShowWindow(hGrayRect, SW_SHOW);
    ShowWindow(hBlackLine, SW_SHOW);
    ShowWindow(hCombo, SW_SHOW);
    break;

case IDM_HIDECOMBO:

    // hide combo box and
    // the gray rectangle
    ShowWindow(hGrayRect, SW_HIDE);
    ShowWindow(hBlackLine, SW_HIDE);
    ShowWindow(hCombo, SW_HIDE);
    break;

case IDC_COMBOBOX:

    switch(GET_WM_COMMAND_CMD(
              wParam, lParam)){
    case CBN_DROPDOWN:

        // reset the combo box
        SendMessage(hCombo,
              CB_RESETCONTENT,
              0, 0L);

        // add color items to
        // the combo box
        SendMessage(hCombo,
              CB_ADDSTRING,
            0, RGB(255,255,255));
        SendMessage(hCombo,
              CB_ADDSTRING,
            0, RGB(255, 0, 0));
        SendMessage(hCombo,
              CB_ADDSTRING,
            0, RGB(0, 255, 0));
        SendMessage(hCombo,
              CB_ADDSTRING,
            0, RGB(0, 0, 255));
        break;

    case CBN_SELCHANGE:
```

```
                       // if item selection changed,
                       // choose the color brush
                       // specified by the item and
                       // paint the client area
                       Index = (WORD)SendMessage(
                                 hCombo,
                                 CB_GETCURSEL,
                                 0, 0L);
                       switch(Index){
                         case 0: hBrush = hBrushW;
                                 break;
                         case 1: hBrush = hBrushR;
                                 break;
                         case 2: hBrush = hBrushG;
                                 break;
                         case 3: hBrush = hBrushB;
                                 break;
                       }

                       hDC = GetDC(hWnd);
                       GetClientRect(hWnd, &rect1);
                       SelectObject(hDC, hBrush);
                       Rectangle(hDC,
                           rect1.left, rect1.top+31,
                           rect1.right, rect1.bottom);
                       ReleaseDC(hWnd, hDC);
                       DeleteObject(hBrush);
                   }
                 break;
        default:
            return DefWindowProc(hWnd, uMessage,
                              wParam, lParam);
      }
      break;

case WM_DRAWITEM:
      lpdis = (LPDRAWITEMSTRUCT)lParam;
      switch(lpdis->itemAction){

        case ODA_DRAWENTIRE:

                 // fill the item rectangle with color
                 CopyRect((LPRECT)&rect,
                         (LPRECT)&lpdis->rcItem);
                 InflateRect((LPRECT)&rect, -1, -1);
                 hBrush = CreateSolidBrush(
```

81

```
                                lpdis->itemData);
                FillRect(lpdis->hDC,
                                (LPRECT)&rect, hBrush);
                DeleteObject(hBrush);
                break;

        case ODA_SELECT:

                // frame the item rectangle if selected
                CopyRect((LPRECT)&rect,
                                (LPRECT)&lpdis->rcItem);
                InflateRect((LPRECT)&rect, 0, 0);
                if(lpdis->itemState & ODS_SELECTED)
                    hBrush = CreateSolidBrush(
                                        RGB(0, 0, 0));
                else
                    hBrush = CreateSolidBrush(
                                GetSysColor(COLOR_WINDOW));
                FrameRect(lpdis->hDC,
                                (LPRECT)&rect, hBrush);
                DeleteObject(hBrush);
                break;

        case ODA_FOCUS:

                // frame the item rectangle if focused
                CopyRect((LPRECT)&rect,
                                (LPRECT)&lpdis->rcItem);
                InflateRect((LPRECT)&rect, -1, -1);
                if(lpdis->itemState & ODS_FOCUS)
                    hBrush = CreateSolidBrush(
                                        RGB(128, 128, 128));
                else
                    hBrush = CreateSolidBrush(
                                GetSysColor(COLOR_WINDOW));
                FrameRect(lpdis->hDC,
                                (LPRECT)&rect, hBrush);
                DeleteObject(hBrush);
                break;
        }
        return(TRUE);
        break;

    case WM_MEASUREITEM:

        // specify the height of combo box item
        lpmis = (LPMEASUREITEMSTRUCT)lParam;
```

```
                    if(lpmis->itemID == -1){
                      lpmis->itemHeight = 20;
                      return(TRUE);
                      }
                    lpmis->itemHeight = 20;
                    break;

            case WM_DESTROY:
                    PostQuitMessage(0);
                    break;

            default:
                    return DefWindowProc(hWnd, uMessage,
                                         wParam, lParam);
        }
        return 0;
    }
```

ABOUT.C

```
// ABOUT.C
#include <windows.h>
#include <windowsx.h>
#include "globals.h"

// procedures for ABOUT dialog box
LRESULT CALLBACK About(HWND hDlg,
                       UINT uMessage,
                       WPARAM wParam,
                       LPARAM lParam)
{
    switch (uMessage)
      {
        case WM_COMMAND:
                switch (GET_WM_COMMAND_ID(wParam,lParam))
                {
                    case IDOK:
                    case IDCANCEL:
                        {
                        EndDialog(hDlg, TRUE);
                        return(TRUE);
                        }
                        break;
                }
        }
    return FALSE;
}
```

OL.RC

```
    e "windows.h"
    de "globals.h"
    ude <winver.h>

  NAME ICON ICONFILE

  CINCLUDE ABOUT.DLG

APPNAME MENU
BEGIN
    POPUP           "&Options"
    BEGIN
        MENUITEM "&Show COMBO Menu Bar", IDM_SHOWCOMBO
        MENUITEM "&Hide COMBO Menu Bar", IDM_HIDECOMBO
    END
    MENUITEM "&About", IDM_ABOUT
END
```

ABOUT.DLG

```
ABOUTDLG DIALOG DISCARDABLE  22, 17, 167, 73
STYLE DS_MODALFRAME | WS_CAPTION | WS_SYSMENU
CAPTION SZABOUT
BEGIN
    DEFPUSHBUTTON   "OK", IDOK, 132, 2, 32, 14, WS_GROUP
    ICON            SZAPPNAME,      -1, 3, 2, 18, 20
    LTEXT           SZAPPNAME,      -1, 30, 12,  50, 8
    LTEXT           SZDESCRIPTION, -1, 30, 22, 150, 8
    LTEXT           SZVERSION,      -1, 30, 32, 150, 8
    LTEXT           SZCOMPANYNAME, -1, 30, 42, 150, 8
END
```

COMBOCOL.ICO

CASE 1-9: COMBO BOX WITH BITMAP ITEMS

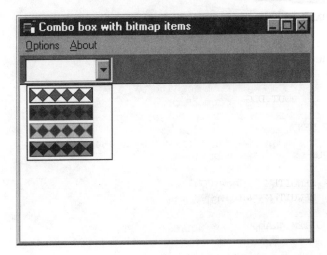

FIGURE 1-9

This case is similar to the previous cases. The difference is that, unlike Case 1-7, in which the items in the drop-down list are text items, or Case 1-8, in which the items in the drop-down list are color items, the items in the drop-down list are bitmaps. In order to draw these bitmaps, the combo box must have the style of CBS_OWNERDRAWFIXED. Please see Case 1-6 for the procedures that draw bitmaps in a list box.

```
  ... - header file for global variables
           and function prototypes

   ...t identifier string definitions.
      APPNAME        ComboBmp
   ...  ICONFILE      ComboBmp.ico
   ...e SZAPPNAME     "ComboBmp"
   ...ne SZDESCRIPTION "Combo box with bitmap items"
   ...ine SZVERSION   "Version 1.0"
  ...efine SZCOMPANYNAME "\251 M&&T Books, 1994"
  ...define SZABOUT    "About"


// Global function prototypes.
BOOL InitApplication(HINSTANCE);
BOOL InitInstance(HINSTANCE, int);
void PaintRectBitmap(HDC, HBITMAP, WORD, WORD);

// Callback functions called by Windows.
LRESULT CALLBACK WndProc(HWND, UINT, WPARAM, LPARAM);
LRESULT CALLBACK About(HWND, UINT, WPARAM, LPARAM);

// Menu item ID
#define IDM_ABOUT       101
#define IDM_SHOWCOMBO   102
#define IDM_HIDECOMBO   103


// Control ID
#define IDC_COMBOBOX    104


// Global variable declarations.
extern HINSTANCE hInst;      // The current instance handle
extern char szAppName[];     // The name of this application
extern char szTitle[];       // The title bar text
```

WINMAIN.C

```
// WINMAIN.C
#include <windows.h>
#include "globals.h"

int APIENTRY WinMain(HINSTANCE hInstance,
                     HINSTANCE hPrevInstance,
                     LPSTR lpCmdLine,
```

```
                        int nCmdShow)
{
    MSG msg;

    // register the main window class
    if (!hPrevInstance)
        {
        if (!InitApplication(hInstance))
            {
            return FALSE;
            }
        }

    // create and show main window
    if (!InitInstance(hInstance, nCmdShow))
        {
        return FALSE;
        }

    // process window message
    while (GetMessage(&msg, NULL, 0, 0))
        {
            TranslateMessage(&msg);
            DispatchMessage(&msg);
        }
    return msg.wParam;
}
```

INIT.C

```
// INIT.C
#include <windows.h>
#include "globals.h"

HINSTANCE hInst;
char szAppName[] = SZAPPNAME;
char szTitle[] = SZDESCRIPTION;

// register the main window class
BOOL InitApplication(HINSTANCE hInstance)
{
    WNDCLASS  wc;

    wc.style          = CS_HREDRAW | CS_VREDRAW;
    wc.lpfnWndProc    = (WNDPROC)WndProc;
    wc.cbClsExtra     = 0;
```

```
         a      = 0;
         e      = hInstance;
                = LoadIcon(hInstance, szAppName);
         r      = LoadCursor(NULL, IDC_ARROW);
      ckground  = (HBRUSH)(COLOR_WINDOW + 1);
      MenuName  = szAppName;
    szClassName = szAppName;

    urn(RegisterClass(&wc));


// reate and show the main window
L InitInstance(HINSTANCE hInstance, int nCmdShow)
{
    HWND    hWnd;
    hInst = hInstance;
    hWnd = CreateWindow(szAppName, szTitle,
                        WS_OVERLAPPEDWINDOW,
                        160, 120, 320, 240,
                        NULL, NULL, hInstance, NULL);

    if (!hWnd)
        {
        return FALSE;
        }

    ShowWindow(hWnd, nCmdShow);
    UpdateWindow(hWnd);

    return TRUE;
}
```

COMBOBMP.C

```
// COMBOBMP.C
#include <windows.h>
#include <windowsx.h>
#include "globals.h"

HWND hCombo, hGrayRect, hBlackLine;
HBRUSH hBrush, hBrushW, hBrushR, hBrushG, hBrushB;
HBITMAP hBitmap;

LRESULT CALLBACK WndProc(HWND hWnd,
                         UINT uMessage,
                         WPARAM wParam,
```

```
    wc.cbWndExtra    = 0;
    wc.hInstance     = hInstance;
    wc.hIcon         = LoadIcon(hInstance, szAppName);
    wc.hCursor       = LoadCursor(NULL, IDC_ARROW);
    wc.hbrBackground = (HBRUSH)(COLOR_WINDOW + 1);
    wc.lpszMenuName  = szAppName;
    wc.lpszClassName = szAppName;

    return(RegisterClass(&wc));
}

// create and show the main window
BOOL InitInstance(HINSTANCE hInstance, int nCmdShow)
{
    HWND    hWnd;
    hInst = hInstance;
    hWnd = CreateWindow(szAppName, szTitle,
                WS_OVERLAPPEDWINDOW,
                160, 120, 320, 240,
                NULL, NULL, hInstance, NULL);

    if (!hWnd)
        {
        return FALSE;
        }

    ShowWindow(hWnd, nCmdShow);
    UpdateWindow(hWnd);

    return TRUE;
}
```

COMBOBMP.C

```
// COMBOBMP.C
#include <windows.h>
#include <windowsx.h>
#include "globals.h"

HWND hCombo, hGrayRect, hBlackLine;
HBRUSH hBrush, hBrushW, hBrushR, hBrushG, hBrushB;
HBITMAP hBitmap;

LRESULT CALLBACK WndProc(HWND hWnd,
                            UINT uMessage,
                            WPARAM wParam,
```

```
                   int nCmdShow)
{
    MSG msg;

    // register the main window class
    if (!hPrevInstance)
        {
        if (!InitApplication(hInstance))
            {
            return FALSE;
            }
        }

    // create and show main window
    if (!InitInstance(hInstance, nCmdShow))
        {
        return FALSE;
        }

    // process window message
    while (GetMessage(&msg, NULL, 0, 0))
        {
            TranslateMessage(&msg);
            DispatchMessage(&msg);
        }
    return msg.wParam;
}
```

INIT.C

```
// INIT.C
#include <windows.h>
#include "globals.h"

HINSTANCE hInst;
char szAppName[] = SZAPPNAME;
char szTitle[] = SZDESCRIPTION;

// register the main window class
BOOL InitApplication(HINSTANCE hInstance)
{
    WNDCLASS  wc;

    wc.style        = CS_HREDRAW | CS_VREDRAW;
    wc.lpfnWndProc  = (WNDPROC)WndProc;
    wc.cbClsExtra   = 0;
```

```
                    LPARAM lParam)
{
    WORD Index;
    HDC hDC;
    LPDRAWITEMSTRUCT    lpdis;
    LPMEASUREITEMSTRUCT lpmis;
    RECT rect, rect1;
    HBRUSH hBrush;

    switch (uMessage)
    {
        case WM_CREATE:

                // create brushes for painting
                hBrushW = CreateSolidBrush(RGB(255, 255, 255));
                hBrushR = CreateSolidBrush(RGB(255,   0,   0));
                hBrushG = CreateSolidBrush(RGB(  0, 255,   0));
                hBrushB = CreateSolidBrush(RGB(  0,   0, 255));

                // create a gray rectangle below the menu area
                hGrayRect = CreateWindow("static", "",
                    SS_GRAYRECT | WS_CHILD | WS_VISIBLE,
                    0, 0, 640, 30, hWnd, NULL, hInst, NULL);
                // add a bottom black boundary to the gray area
                hBlackLine = CreateWindow("static", "",
                    SS_BLACKRECT | WS_CHILD | WS_VISIBLE,
                    0, 30, 640, 1, hWnd, NULL, hInst, NULL);

                // create an owner-draw combo box
                hCombo = CreateWindow("combobox", "",
                    CBS_DROPDOWNLIST | CBS_OWNERDRAWFIXED |
                    CBS_SIMPLE | WS_VSCROLL | WS_GROUP |
                    WS_CHILD | WS_VISIBLE | WS_TABSTOP,
                    5, 3, 94, 110,
                    hWnd, IDC_COMBOBOX, hInst, NULL);
                break;

        case WM_COMMAND:
                switch (GET_WM_COMMAND_ID(wParam,lParam))
                {
                    case IDM_SHOWCOMBO:
                            // show combo box and gray area
                            ShowWindow(hGrayRect, SW_SHOW);
                            ShowWindow(hBlackLine, SW_SHOW);
                            ShowWindow(hCombo, SW_SHOW);
                            break;
```

89

```
case IDM_HIDECOMBO:
        // hide combo box and gray area
        ShowWindow(hGrayRect, SW_HIDE);
        ShowWindow(hBlackLine, SW_HIDE);
        ShowWindow(hCombo, SW_HIDE);
        break;

case IDC_COMBOBOX:
        switch(GET_WM_COMMAND_CMD(
                        wParam, lParam))
        {
          case CBN_DROPDOWN:
                // reset combo box contents
                SendMessage(hCombo,
                        CB_RESETCONTENT,
                        0, 0L);

                // add bitmap items to
                // owner-draw combo box
                SendMessage(hCombo,
                        CB_ADDSTRING, 0,
                     (LONG)(LPSTR)"ListItem1");
                SendMessage(hCombo,
                        CB_ADDSTRING, 0,
                     (LONG)(LPSTR)"ListItem2");
                SendMessage(hCombo,
                        CB_ADDSTRING, 0,
                     (LONG)(LPSTR)"ListItem3");
                SendMessage(hCombo,
                        CB_ADDSTRING, 0,
                     (LONG)(LPSTR)"ListItem4");
                break;

          case CBN_SELCHANGE:
                // if item selection changed,
                // choose the color brush
                // associated with the item
                // and paint the client area
                Index = (WORD)SendMessage(
                        hCombo,
                        CB_GETCURSEL,
                        0, 0L);
                switch(Index){
                  case 0: hBrush = hBrushW;
                        break;
                  case 1: hBrush = hBrushR;
                        break;
```

```
                    case 2: hBrush = hBrushG;
                            break;
                    case 3: hBrush = hBrushB;
                            break;
                    }
                hDC = GetDC(hWnd);
                GetClientRect(hWnd, &rect1);
                SelectObject(hDC, hBrush);
                Rectangle(hDC,
                    rect1.left, rect1.top+31,
                    rect1.right, rect1.bottom);
                ReleaseDC(hWnd, hDC);
                DeleteObject(hBrush);
            break;
            }
        break;

    case IDM_ABOUT:
            // create an about dialog
        DialogBox(hInst, "ABOUTDLG",
                hWnd, (DLGPROC)About);
        break;

    default:
        return DefWindowProc(hWnd, uMessage,
                            wParam, lParam);
    }
    break;

case WM_DRAWITEM:
    lpdis = (LPDRAWITEMSTRUCT)lParam;
    switch(lpdis->itemAction){

    case ODA_DRAWENTIRE:
            // paint the item rectangle with bitmap
        CopyRect((LPRECT)&rect,
                (LPRECT)&lpdis->rcItem);
        InflateRect((LPRECT)&rect, -1, -1);
        hBitmap = LoadBitmap(hInst,
                    (LPSTR)lpdis->itemData);
        PaintRectBitmap(lpdis->hDC,
                hBitmap, rect.left, rect.top);
        break;

    case ODA_SELECT:
            // frame the item rectangle if selected
        CopyRect((LPRECT)&rect,
```

```
                              (LPRECT)&lpdis->rcItem);
              InflateRect((LPRECT)&rect, 0, 0);
              if(lpdis->itemState & ODS_SELECTED)
                 hBrush = CreateSolidBrush(
                                   RGB(0, 0, 0));
              else
                 hBrush = CreateSolidBrush(
                         GetSysColor(COLOR_WINDOW));
              FrameRect(lpdis->hDC,
                         (LPRECT)&rect, hBrush);
              DeleteObject(hBrush);
              break;

          case ODA_FOCUS:
              // frame the item rectangle if focused
              CopyRect((LPRECT)&rect,
                       (LPRECT)&lpdis->rcItem);
              InflateRect((LPRECT)&rect, -1, -1);
              if(lpdis->itemState & ODS_FOCUS)
                 hBrush = CreateSolidBrush(
                         RGB(128, 128, 128));
              else
                 hBrush = CreateSolidBrush(
                         GetSysColor(COLOR_WINDOW));
              FrameRect(lpdis->hDC,
                            (LPRECT)&rect, hBrush);
              DeleteObject(hBrush);
              DrawFocusRect(lpdis->hDC,
                         (LPRECT)&lpdis->rcItem);
              break;
          }
      return(TRUE);
      break;

   case WM_MEASUREITEM:
       // specify the height of combo box item
       lpmis = (LPMEASUREITEMSTRUCT)lParam;
       if(lpmis->itemID == -1){
         lpmis->itemHeight = 20;
         return(TRUE);
         }
       lpmis->itemHeight = 20;
       break;

   case WM_DESTROY:
       PostQuitMessage(0);
       break;
```

```
            default:
                return DefWindowProc(hWnd, uMessage,
                                     wParam, lParam);
        }
    return 0;
}


// function for painting the bitmap in
// combo box item rectangle
void PaintRectBitmap (hDC, hBitmap, rectX, rectY)
HDC hDC;
HBITMAP hBitmap;
WORD rectX, rectY;
{
    BITMAP bmp;
    HDC hMemoryDC;
    hMemoryDC = CreateCompatibleDC(hDC);
    GetObject(hBitmap, sizeof(BITMAP), (LPSTR) &bmp);
    SelectObject(hMemoryDC, hBitmap);
    BitBlt(hDC, rectX, rectY, bmp.bmWidth, bmp.bmHeight,
                hMemoryDC, 0, 0, SRCCOPY);
    DeleteDC(hMemoryDC);
    DeleteObject(hBitmap);
}
```

ABOUT.C

```
// ABOUT.C
#include <windows.h>
#include <windowsx.h>
#include "globals.h"


// procedures for ABOUT dialog box
LRESULT CALLBACK About(HWND hDlg,
                       UINT uMessage,
                       WPARAM wParam,
                       LPARAM lParam)
{
    switch (uMessage)
      {
        case WM_COMMAND:
            switch (GET_WM_COMMAND_ID(wParam,lParam))
              {
                case IDOK:
                case IDCANCEL:
```

```
                              {
                              EndDialog(hDlg, TRUE);
                              return(TRUE);
                              }
                              break;
                    }
          }
     return FALSE;
}
```

COMBOBMP.RC

```
#include "windows.h"
#include "globals.h"
#include <winver.h>


ListItem1 BITMAP item1.bmp
ListItem2 BITMAP item2.bmp
ListItem3 BITMAP item3.bmp
ListItem4 BITMAP item4.bmp


APPNAME ICON ICONFILE

RCINCLUDE ABOUT.DLG

APPNAME MENU
BEGIN
     POPUP          "&Options"
     BEGIN
          MENUITEM "&Show COMBO Menu Bar", IDM_SHOWCOMBO
          MENUITEM "&Hide COMBO Menu Bar", IDM_HIDECOMBO
     END
     MENUITEM "&About", IDM_ABOUT
END
```

ABOUT.DLG

```
ABOUTDLG DIALOG DISCARDABLE  22, 17, 167, 73
STYLE DS_MODALFRAME | WS_CAPTION | WS_SYSMENU
CAPTION SZABOUT
BEGIN
     DEFPUSHBUTTON   "OK", IDOK, 132, 2, 32, 14, WS_GROUP
     ICON            SZAPPNAME,     -1, 3, 2, 18, 20
     LTEXT           SZAPPNAME,     -1, 30, 12,  50, 8
```

```
        LTEXT           SZDESCRIPTION, -1, 30, 22, 150, 8
        LTEXT           SZVERSION,     -1, 30, 32, 150, 8
        LTEXT           SZCOMPANYNAME, -1, 30, 42, 150, 8
    END
```

COMBOBMP.ICO

ITEM1.BMP

ITEM2.BMP

ITEM3.BMP

ITEM4.BMP

CASE 1-10: COLOR SELECTION TABLE

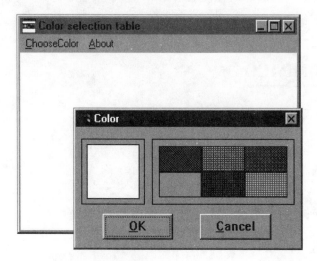

FIGURE 1-10

The Windows 95 SDK provides a general-purpose common dialog box for color selection and editing (see Case 7-1). However, this choose-color common dialog box may not be suitable for your application. For example, if the application is a drawing program where only a limited number of custom color selections are needed for the application, it is convenient for the user to have a custom color selection table constantly available on the screen.

This case allows you to make a color selection table specifically for your own application. Each color in the table is an owner-draw button. The show-color box on the left side of the selection table is also an owner-draw button. When the user clicks a specific color in the table, the program paints the show-color box with the same color. There is no bitmap involved in this case. The program simply uses the Window's GDI calls to paint a color rectangle in each color box. There are also other ways to create a color table. For another example, see Case 1-5. Also, to review how to draw owner-draw controls, see Cases 1-1 and 1-2.

GLOBALS.H

```
// GLOBALS.H - header file for global variables
//             and function prototypes

// Product identifier string definitions.
#define APPNAME        ColorTab
#define ICONFILE       ColorTab.ico
#define SZAPPNAME      "ColorTab"
#define SZDESCRIPTION  "Color selection table"
#define SZVERSION      "Version 1.0"
#define SZCOMPANYNAME  "\251 M&&T Books, 1994"
#define SZABOUT        "About"

// Global function prototypes.
BOOL InitApplication(HINSTANCE);
BOOL InitInstance(HINSTANCE, int);

// Callback functions called by Windows.
LRESULT CALLBACK WndProc(HWND, UINT, WPARAM, LPARAM);
LRESULT CALLBACK About(HWND, UINT, WPARAM, LPARAM);
LRESULT CALLBACK ColorDlgProc(HWND, UINT, WPARAM, LPARAM);

// Menu item ID
#define IDM_ABOUT    101
#define IDM_COLOR    102

// Dialog box ID
#define IDD_COLORDLGBOX 200

// Dialog box control ID
#define IDC_RED          103
#define IDC_GREEN        104
#define IDC_BLUE         105
#define IDC_MAGENTA      106
#define IDC_YELLOW       107
#define IDC_CYAN         108
#define IDC_SHOWCOLOR    109
#define IDC_CLOSE        110

// Global variable declarations.
extern HINSTANCE hInst;        // The current instance handle
extern char szAppName[];       // The name of this application
extern char szTitle[];         // The title bar text
extern HWND hWnd, hColor;
extern DLGPROC lpProcColor;
```

WINMAIN.C

```c
// WINMAIN.C
#include <windows.h>
#include "globals.h"

int APIENTRY WinMain(HINSTANCE hInstance,
                     HINSTANCE hPrevInstance,
                     LPSTR lpCmdLine,
                     int nCmdShow)
{
    MSG msg;

    // register main window class
    if (!hPrevInstance)
        {
        if (!InitApplication(hInstance))
            {
            return FALSE;
            }
        }

    // create and show main window
    if (!InitInstance(hInstance, nCmdShow))
        {
        return FALSE;
        }

    // process window message
    // if the message is the keyboard input
    // for the dialog box,
    // use IsDialogMessage function to process it
    while (GetMessage(&msg, NULL, 0, 0))
        { if( hColor == NULL ||
              !IsDialogMessage(hColor, &msg))
            {
            TranslateMessage(&msg);
            DispatchMessage(&msg);
            }
        }
    return msg.wParam;
}
```

INIT.C

```
// INIT.C
#include <windows.h>
#include "globals.h"

HINSTANCE hInst;
char szAppName[] = SZAPPNAME;
char szTitle[] = SZDESCRIPTION;

// register main window class
BOOL InitApplication(HINSTANCE hInstance)
{
    WNDCLASS  wc;

    wc.style         = CS_HREDRAW | CS_VREDRAW;
    wc.lpfnWndProc   = (WNDPROC)WndProc;
    wc.cbClsExtra    = 0;
    wc.cbWndExtra    = 0;
    wc.hInstance     = hInstance;
    wc.hIcon         = LoadIcon(hInstance, szAppName);
    wc.hCursor       = LoadCursor(NULL, IDC_ARROW);
    wc.hbrBackground = (HBRUSH)(COLOR_WINDOW + 1);
    wc.lpszMenuName  = szAppName;
    wc.lpszClassName = szAppName;

    return(RegisterClass(&wc));
}


// create and show main window
BOOL InitInstance(HINSTANCE hInstance, int nCmdShow)
{
    HWND    hWnd;
    hInst = hInstance;
    hWnd = CreateWindow(szAppName, szTitle,
                        WS_OVERLAPPEDWINDOW,
                        160, 120, 320, 240,
                        NULL, NULL, hInstance, NULL);

    if (!hWnd)
       {
       return FALSE;
       }

    ShowWindow(hWnd, nCmdShow);
    UpdateWindow(hWnd);
```

```
        return TRUE;
    }
```

COLORTAB.C

```c
// COLORTAB.C
#include <windows.h>
#include <windowsx.h>
#include "globals.h"

HWND hColor;
DLGPROC lpProcColor;

LRESULT CALLBACK WndProc(HWND hWnd,
                         UINT uMessage,
                         WPARAM wParam,
                         LPARAM lParam)
{
    switch (uMessage)
    {
        case WM_COMMAND:
            switch (GET_WM_COMMAND_ID(wParam,lParam))
            {
                case IDM_COLOR:
                    // create a dialog box with a
                    // color selection table in it
                    lpProcColor = MakeProcInstance(
                            (FARPROC)ColorDlgProc, hInst);
                    hColor = CreateDialog(hInst,
                        MAKEINTRESOURCE(IDD_COLORDLGBOX),
                                    hWnd, lpProcColor);
                    break;

                case IDM_ABOUT:
                    // create an about dialog box
                    DialogBox(hInst, "ABOUTDLG",
                            hWnd, (DLGPROC)About);
                    break;

                default:
                    return DefWindowProc(hWnd, uMessage,
                                    wParam, lParam);
            }
            break;

        case WM_DESTROY:
```

```
        FreeProcInstance(lpProcColor);
        PostQuitMessage(0);
        break;

    default:
        return DefWindowProc(hWnd, uMessage, wParam, lParam);
    }
    return 0;
}
```

COLOR.C

```
// COLOR.C
#include <windows.h>
#include <windowsx.h>
#include "globals.h"

HBITMAP hBitmap;
int Color_Choice = 0;

// procedures for dialog box hColor
LRESULT CALLBACK ColorDlgProc(HWND hColor,
                    UINT uMessage,
                    WPARAM wParam,
                    LPARAM lParam)
{
    LPDRAWITEMSTRUCT lpdis;
    HPEN hPen;
    HBRUSH hBrush;

    switch (uMessage)
    {
        case WM_DRAWITEM:
            lpdis = (LPDRAWITEMSTRUCT) lParam;
            switch(lpdis->CtlID){
                case IDC_RED:
                        // create the brush for
                        // painting the owner-draw button
                        // according to the button control ID
                        hBrush = SelectObject(lpdis->hDC,
                                CreateSolidBrush(
                                        RGB(255, 0, 0)));
                        goto drawit;

                case IDC_GREEN:
                        hBrush = SelectObject(lpdis->hDC,
```

```
                              CreateSolidBrush(
                                      RGB(0, 255, 0)));
                      goto drawit;

        case IDC_BLUE:
              hBrush = SelectObject(lpdis->hDC,
                      CreateSolidBrush(
                              RGB(0, 0, 255)));
                      goto drawit;

        case IDC_MAGENTA:
              hBrush = SelectObject(lpdis->hDC,
                      CreateSolidBrush(
                              RGB(255, 0, 255)));
                      goto drawit;

        case IDC_YELLOW:
              hBrush = SelectObject(lpdis->hDC,
                      CreateSolidBrush(
                              RGB(255, 255, 0)));
                      goto drawit;

        case IDC_CYAN:
              hBrush = SelectObject(lpdis->hDC,
                      CreateSolidBrush(
                              RGB(0, 255, 255)));
                      goto drawit;

        case IDC_SHOWCOLOR:
              // create the brush for painting
              // according to the Color_Choice number
              if(Color_Choice == 0)
                    { hBrush = SelectObject(
                              lpdis->hDC,
                              CreateSolidBrush(
                              RGB(255, 255, 255)));
                      goto drawit; }

              if(Color_Choice == 1)
                    { hBrush = SelectObject(
                              lpdis->hDC,
                              CreateSolidBrush(
                              RGB(255, 0, 0)));
                      goto drawit; }

              if(Color_Choice == 2)
                    { hBrush = SelectObject(
```

```
                              lpdis->hDC,
                              CreateSolidBrush(
                              RGB(0, 255, 0)));
                    goto drawit; }

          if(Color_Choice == 3)
               { hBrush = SelectObject(
                              lpdis->hDC,
                              CreateSolidBrush(
                              RGB(0, 0, 255)));
                    goto drawit; }

          if(Color_Choice == 4)
               { hBrush = SelectObject(
                              lpdis->hDC,
                              CreateSolidBrush(
                              RGB(255, 0, 255)));
                    goto drawit; }

          if(Color_Choice == 5)
               { hBrush = SelectObject(
                              lpdis->hDC,
                              CreateSolidBrush(
                              RGB(255, 255, 0)));
                    goto drawit; }

          if(Color_Choice == 6)
               { hBrush = SelectObject(
                              lpdis->hDC,
                              CreateSolidBrush(
                              RGB(0, 255, 255)));
                    goto drawit; }
          break;

// routine to draw color rectangles for
// color selection buttons
drawit:          { hPen = SelectObject(lpdis->hDC,
                    CreatePen(PS_INSIDEFRAME, 1,
                         RGB(0, 0, 0)));
               Rectangle(lpdis->hDC,
                    lpdis->rcItem.left,
                    lpdis->rcItem.top,
                    lpdis->rcItem.right,
                    lpdis->rcItem.bottom);
               DeleteObject(SelectObject(
                    lpdis->hDC, hPen));
               DeleteObject(SelectObject(
```

103

```
                              lpdis->hDC, hBrush));
                break; }
          break;

        default: return FALSE;
        }
        break;


    case WM_COMMAND:
        switch (GET_WM_COMMAND_ID(wParam,lParam))
        {
            // set the Color_Choice number
            // when the user click the button
          case IDC_RED:
                Color_Choice = 1;
                goto ShowColor;

          case IDC_GREEN:
                Color_Choice = 2;
                goto ShowColor;

          case IDC_BLUE:
                Color_Choice = 3;
                goto ShowColor;

          case IDC_MAGENTA:
                Color_Choice = 4;
                goto ShowColor;

          case IDC_YELLOW:
                Color_Choice = 5;
                goto ShowColor;

          case IDC_CYAN:
                Color_Choice = 6;
                goto ShowColor;

// toggle the state of owner-draw button (IDC_SHOWCOLOR) so
// the button can be redrawn to show the user selected color
ShowColor:
                SendDlgItemMessage(hColor, IDC_SHOWCOLOR,
                            BM_SETSTATE, NULL, NULL);
                SendDlgItemMessage(hColor, IDC_SHOWCOLOR,
                            BM_SETSTATE, TRUE, NULL);
                break;
```

```
            case IDOK:
            case IDCANCEL:
            case IDC_CLOSE:
                DestroyWindow(hColor);
                hColor = 0;
                break;

            default:
                return DefWindowProc(hColor, uMessage,
                                          wParam, lParam);
        }
        break;

    default:
        return DefWindowProc(hColor, uMessage,
                                  wParam, lParam);
    }
    return 0;
}
```

ABOUT.C

```
// ABOUT.C
#include <windows.h>
#include <windowsx.h>
#include "globals.h"

// procedures for ABOUT dialog box
LRESULT CALLBACK About(HWND hDlg,
                       UINT uMessage,
                       WPARAM wParam,
                       LPARAM lParam)
{
    switch (uMessage)
      {
        case WM_COMMAND:
            switch (GET_WM_COMMAND_ID(wParam,lParam))
              {
                case IDOK:
                case IDCANCEL:
                    {
                    EndDialog(hDlg, TRUE);
                    return(TRUE);
                    }
                    break;
              }
```

```
        }
    return FALSE;
}
```

COLORTAB.RC

```
#include "windows.h"
#include "globals.h"
#include <winver.h>

APPNAME ICON ICONFILE

RCINCLUDE ABOUT.DLG
RCINCLUDE COLOR.DLG

APPNAME MENU
BEGIN
    MENUITEM "&ChooseColor",  IDM_COLOR
    MENUITEM "&About",        IDM_ABOUT
END
```

COLOR.DLG

```
DLGINCLUDE RCDATA DISCARDABLE
BEGIN
    "GLOBALS.H\0"
END

IDD_COLORDLGBOX DIALOG 30, 30, 126, 65
STYLE DS_MODALFRAME | WS_POPUP | WS_VISIBLE |
      WS_CAPTION | WS_BORDER | WS_SYSMENU
CAPTION "Color"
BEGIN
    CONTROL     "&R", IDC_RED, "Button", BS_OWNERDRAW,
                47, 10, 24, 14
    CONTROL     "&G", IDC_GREEN, "Button", BS_OWNERDRAW,
                71, 10, 24, 14
    CONTROL     "&B", IDC_BLUE, "Button", BS_OWNERDRAW,
                95, 10, 24, 14
    CONTROL     "&M", IDC_MAGENTA, "Button", BS_OWNERDRAW,
                47, 24, 24, 14
    CONTROL     "&Y", IDC_YELLOW, "Button", BS_OWNERDRAW,
                71, 24, 24, 14
    CONTROL     "&C", IDC_CYAN, "Button", BS_OWNERDRAW,
```

```
                    95, 24, 24, 14
    CONTROL     "", -1, "Static", SS_BLACKFRAME,
                43, 6, 80, 36
    CONTROL     "", -1, "Static", SS_BLACKFRAME,
                3, 6, 36, 36
    CONTROL     "", IDC_SHOWCOLOR, "Button", BS_OWNERDRAW,
                6, 9, 30, 30
    PUSHBUTTON  "&OK", IDOK, 15, 47, 40, 14
    PUSHBUTTON  "&Cancel", IDCANCEL, 70, 47, 40, 14
END
```

ABOUT.DLG

```
ABOUTDLG DIALOG DISCARDABLE  22, 17, 167, 73
STYLE DS_MODALFRAME | WS_CAPTION | WS_SYSMENU
CAPTION SZABOUT
BEGIN
    DEFPUSHBUTTON   "OK", IDOK, 132, 2, 32, 14, WS_GROUP
    ICON            SZAPPNAME,      -1, 3, 2, 18, 20
    LTEXT           SZAPPNAME,      -1, 30, 12,  50, 8
    LTEXT           SZDESCRIPTION, -1, 30, 22, 150, 8
    LTEXT           SZVERSION,     -1, 30, 32, 150, 8
    LTEXT           SZCOMPANYNAME, -1, 30, 42, 150, 8
END
```

COLORTAB.ICO

CASE 1-11: COLOR EDITOR

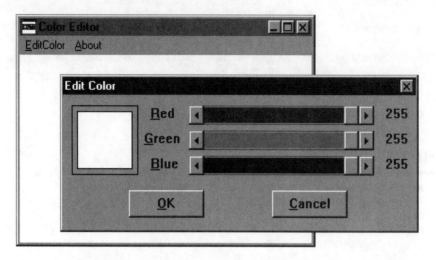

FIGURE 1-11

This case illustrates a different approach for specifying colors, compared to the approach outlined in Case 1-10, which allowed users to pick one color out of a palette of six colors. The approach in this new case allows users to select the color they want by easily specifying RGB values. The user can simply move the "thumb" of the color scroll bars to get the desired RGB values. The actions on scroll bars are passed to dialog box procedure function `EditColorDlgProc()` by sending the `WM_HSCROLL` message. The color that corresponds to the current RGB value is painted in the show-color box on the left side of the scroll bars when the user changes the RGB values. As shown in Case 1-10, the show-color box is an owner-draw button. The colors of the scroll bars are defined in the message case `WM_CTLCOLORSCROLLBAR` of the dialog procedure function `EditColorDlgProc()`.

GLOBALS.H

```
// GLOBALS.H - header file for global variables
//              and function prototypes

// Product identifier string definitions.
#define APPNAME        ColorEdt
#define ICONFILE       ColorEdt.ico
#define SZAPPNAME      "ColorEdt"
#define SZDESCRIPTION "Color Editor"
#define SZVERSION      "Version 1.0"
#define SZCOMPANYNAME "\251 M&&T Books, 1994"
#define SZABOUT        "About"

// Global function prototypes.
BOOL InitApplication(HINSTANCE);
BOOL InitInstance(HINSTANCE, int);

// Callback functions called by Windows.
LRESULT CALLBACK WndProc(HWND, UINT, WPARAM, LPARAM);
LRESULT CALLBACK About(HWND, UINT, WPARAM, LPARAM);
LRESULT CALLBACK EditColorDlgProc(HWND, UINT, WPARAM, LPARAM);

// Menu item ID
#define IDM_ABOUT    101
#define IDM_COLOR    102

// Dialog box ID
#define IDD_EDITCOLORDLG 200

// Dialog box control ID
#define IDC_REDSB        103
#define IDC_GREENSB      104
#define IDC_BLUESB       105
#define IDC_RN           106
#define IDC_GN           107
#define IDC_BN           108
#define IDC_SHOWCOLOR    109
#define IDC_CLOSE        110

// Global variable declarations.
extern HINSTANCE hInst;     // The current instance handle
extern char szAppName[];    // The name of this application
extern char szTitle[];      // The title bar text
extern HWND hWnd, hEditColor;
extern DLGPROC lpProcEditColor;
```

WINMAIN.C

```
// WINMAIN.C
#include <windows.h>
#include "globals.h"

extern HWND hEditColor;

int APIENTRY WinMain(HINSTANCE hInstance,
                     HINSTANCE hPrevInstance,
                     LPSTR lpCmdLine,
                     int nCmdShow)
{
    MSG msg;

    // register main window class
    if (!hPrevInstance)
        {
        if (!InitApplication(hInstance))
            {
            return FALSE;
            }
        }

    // create and show main window
    if (!InitInstance(hInstance, nCmdShow))
        {
        return FALSE;
        }

    // process window message
    // if the message is the keyboard input
    // from the dialog box
    // use IsDialogMessage function to process it
    while (GetMessage(&msg, NULL, 0, 0))
        { if( hEditColor == NULL ||
              !IsDialogMessage(hEditColor, &msg))
          {
          TranslateMessage(&msg);
          DispatchMessage(&msg);
          }
        }
    return msg.wParam;
}
```

INIT.C

```
// INIT.C
#include <windows.h>
#include "globals.h"

HINSTANCE hInst;
char szAppName[] = SZAPPNAME;
char szTitle[] = SZDESCRIPTION;

// register main window class
BOOL InitApplication(HINSTANCE hInstance)
{
    WNDCLASS  wc;

    wc.style         = CS_HREDRAW | CS_VREDRAW;
    wc.lpfnWndProc   = (WNDPROC)WndProc;
    wc.cbClsExtra    = 0;
    wc.cbWndExtra    = 0;
    wc.hInstance     = hInstance;
    wc.hIcon         = LoadIcon(hInstance, szAppName);
    wc.hCursor       = LoadCursor(NULL, IDC_ARROW);
    wc.hbrBackground = (HBRUSH)(COLOR_WINDOW + 1);
    wc.lpszMenuName  = szAppName;
    wc.lpszClassName = szAppName;

    return(RegisterClass(&wc));
}

// create and show main window
BOOL InitInstance(HINSTANCE hInstance, int nCmdShow)
{
    HWND    hWnd;
    hInst = hInstance;
    hWnd = CreateWindow(szAppName, szTitle,
                        WS_OVERLAPPEDWINDOW,
                        160, 120, 320, 240,
                        NULL, NULL, hInstance, NULL);

    if (!hWnd)
        {
        return FALSE;
        }

    ShowWindow(hWnd, nCmdShow);
    UpdateWindow(hWnd);
```

111

```
    return TRUE;
}
```

COLOREDT.C

```
// COLORTAB.C
#include <windows.h>
#include <windowsx.h>
#include "globals.h"

HWND hEditColor;
DLGPROC lpProcEditColor;

LRESULT CALLBACK WndProc(HWND hWnd,
                         UINT uMessage,
                         WPARAM wParam,
                         LPARAM lParam)
{
    switch (uMessage)
    {
        case WM_COMMAND:
            switch (GET_WM_COMMAND_ID(wParam,lParam))
            {
                case IDM_COLOR:
                    // create a dialog box with
                    // a color editor in it
                    lpProcEditColor = MakeProcInstance(
                        (FARPROC)EditColorDlgProc, hInst);
                    hEditColor = CreateDialog(hInst,
                        MAKEINTRESOURCE(IDD_EDITCOLORDLG),
                                    hWnd, lpProcEditColor);
                    break;

                case IDM_ABOUT:
                    // create an about dialog box
                    DialogBox(hInst, "ABOUTDLG",
                                hWnd, (DLGPROC)About);
                    break;

                default:
                    return DefWindowProc(hWnd, uMessage,
                                        wParam, lParam);
            }
            break;

        case WM_DESTROY:
```

```
                FreeProcInstance(lpProcEditColor);
                PostQuitMessage(0);
                break;

        default:
            return DefWindowProc(hWnd, uMessage,
                                     wParam, lParam);
    }
    return 0;
}
```

COLOR.C

```
// COLOR.C
#include <windows.h>
#include <windowsx.h>
#include <stdlib.h>
#include "globals.h"

HWND hEditColor;
HBRUSH hBrushR, hBrushG, hBrushB;
int RGBV[3];

// procedures for dialog box hEditColor
LRESULT CALLBACK EditColorDlgProc(HWND hEditColor,
                        UINT uMessage,
                        WPARAM wParam,
                        LPARAM lParam)
{
    HWND          hScrollBar;
    int           ScrollBarID, RGBindex;
    HBRUSH        hBrush;
    LPDRAWITEMSTRUCT lpdis;
    HPEN hPen;

    switch (uMessage)
    {
        case WM_INITDIALOG:

                // create brushes for painting
                // three R-G-B scroll bars
                hBrushR = CreateSolidBrush(RGB(255, 0, 0));
                hBrushG = CreateSolidBrush(RGB(0, 255, 0));
                hBrushB = CreateSolidBrush(RGB(0, 0, 255));

                // set initial RGB values
```

113

```
                RGBV[0]=255;
                RGBV[1]=255;
                RGBV[2]=255;

                // set RGB scroll bar range and position
                for(ScrollBarID = IDC_REDSB;
                   ScrollBarID < IDC_BLUESB+1; ScrollBarID++)
                  { hScrollBar = GetDlgItem(
                                    hEditColor, ScrollBarID);
                    SetScrollRange(hScrollBar, SB_CTL,
                                 0, 255, FALSE);
                    SetScrollPos(hScrollBar, SB_CTL,
                              RGBV[ScrollBarID-103],  FALSE);
                    SetDlgItemInt(hEditColor, ScrollBarID+3,
                              RGBV[ScrollBarID-103], FALSE);
                  } ;
                break;

        case WM_CTLCOLORSCROLLBAR:

                // specify the color of scroll bars
                hScrollBar = (HWND)lParam;
                ScrollBarID = GetWindowLong(
                                    hScrollBar, GWL_ID);
                switch(ScrollBarID)
                {
                  case IDC_REDSB:
                        return((DWORD)hBrushR);
                        break;

                  case IDC_GREENSB:
                        return((DWORD)hBrushG);
                        break;

                  case IDC_BLUESB:
                        return((DWORD)hBrushB);
                        break;

                  default:
                  return DefWindowProc (hEditColor, uMessage,
                                    wParam, lParam);
                }
                break;

        case WM_DRAWITEM:
                lpdis = (LPDRAWITEMSTRUCT) lParam;
                switch(lpdis->CtlID){
```

```
      case IDC_SHOWCOLOR:
            // paint the button rectangle according to
            // the RGB value specified by color editor
            hBrush = SelectObject(lpdis->hDC,
                              CreateSolidBrush(
                  RGB(RGBV[0], RGBV[1], RGBV[2])));
            hPen = SelectObject(lpdis->hDC,
                          CreatePen(PS_INSIDEFRAME, 1,
                          RGB(0, 0, 0)));
            Rectangle(lpdis->hDC,
                        lpdis->rcItem.left,
                        lpdis->rcItem.top,
                        lpdis->rcItem.right,
                        lpdis->rcItem.bottom);
            DeleteObject(SelectObject(
                        lpdis->hDC, hPen));
            DeleteObject(SelectObject(
                        lpdis->hDC, hBrush));
            break;

      default: return FALSE;
      }
      break;

case WM_HSCROLL:

      // process the color scroll bar message
      hScrollBar = (HWND)lParam;
      ScrollBarID = GetWindowLong(
                        hScrollBar, GWL_ID);
      RGBindex = ScrollBarID - 103;

      switch(LOWORD(wParam))
        {
        case SB_TOP:
            RGBV[RGBindex] = 0;
            break;

        case SB_BOTTOM:
            RGBV[RGBindex] = 255;
            break;

        case SB_PAGELEFT:
            RGBV[RGBindex] =
                        max(0, RGBV[RGBindex] - 16);
            break;
```

```
        case SB_LINELEFT:
            RGBV[RGBindex] =
                    max(0, RGBV[RGBindex] - 1);
            break;

        case SB_PAGERIGHT:
            RGBV[RGBindex] =
                    min(255, RGBV[RGBindex] + 16);
            break;

        case SB_LINERIGHT:
            RGBV[RGBindex] =
                    min(255, RGBV[RGBindex] + 1);
            break;

        case SB_THUMBPOSITION:
        case SB_THUMBTRACK:
            RGBV[RGBindex] = HIWORD(wParam);
            break;

        default :
            return FALSE ;
        }

    // set the scroll bar position
    SetScrollPos(hScrollBar, SB_CTL,
                RGBV[RGBindex], TRUE);
    // display the new RGB value
    SetDlgItemInt(hEditColor, ScrollBarID+3,
                    RGBV[RGBindex], FALSE);

    // toggle the state of owner-draw button
    // so the new color can be painted
    SendDlgItemMessage(hEditColor, IDC_SHOWCOLOR,
                BM_SETSTATE, (WPARAM)FALSE, 0);
    SendDlgItemMessage(hEditColor, IDC_SHOWCOLOR,
                BM_SETSTATE, (WPARAM)TRUE, 0);

    return FALSE ;
    break;

case WM_COMMAND:
    switch (GET_WM_COMMAND_ID(wParam,lParam))
    {
        case IDOK:
        case IDCANCEL:
        case IDC_CLOSE:
```

```
                            DeleteObject(hBrushR);
                            DeleteObject(hBrushG);
                            DeleteObject(hBrushB);
                            DestroyWindow(hEditColor);
                            hEditColor = 0;
                            break;

                        default:
                            return FALSE;
                    }
                    break;

            default:
                return DefWindowProc(hEditColor, uMessage, wParam,
        lParam);
            }
        return 0;
    }
```

ABOUT.C

```
// ABOUT.C
#include <windows.h>
#include <windowsx.h>
#include "globals.h"

// procedures for ABOUT dialog box
LRESULT CALLBACK About(HWND hDlg,
                        UINT uMessage,
                        WPARAM wParam,
                        LPARAM lParam)
{
    switch (uMessage)
        {
        case WM_COMMAND:
            switch (GET_WM_COMMAND_ID(wParam,lParam))
                {
                case IDOK:
                case IDCANCEL:
                    {
                    EndDialog(hDlg, TRUE);
                    return(TRUE);
                    }
                    break;
                }
            }
```

```
        return FALSE;
    }
```

COLOREDT.RC

```
#include "windows.h"
#include "globals.h"
#include <winver.h>

APPNAME ICON ICONFILE

RCINCLUDE ABOUT.DLG
RCINCLUDE COLOR.DLG

APPNAME MENU
BEGIN
    MENUITEM "&EditColor", IDM_COLOR
    MENUITEM "&About",     IDM_ABOUT
END
```

COLOR.DLG

```
DLGINCLUDE RCDATA DISCARDABLE
BEGIN
    "GLOBALS.H\0"
END

IDD_EDITCOLORDLG DIALOG 20, 10, 188, 69
STYLE DS_SYSMODAL | DS_MODALFRAME | WS_POPUP |
      WS_VISIBLE | WS_CAPTION
CAPTION "Edit Color"
BEGIN
    CONTROL     "", -1, "Static", SS_BLACKFRAME,
                5, 5, 36, 36
    CONTROL     "", IDC_SHOWCOLOR, "Button", BS_OWNERDRAW,
                8, 8, 30, 30
    CTEXT       "&Red", -1, 42, 5, 24, 10, NOT WS_GROUP
    SCROLLBAR   IDC_REDSB, 68, 5, 98, 10, WS_TABSTOP
    CTEXT       "", IDC_RN, 169, 5, 18, 10, NOT WS_GROUP
    CTEXT       "&Green", -1, 42, 18, 24, 10, NOT WS_GROUP
    SCROLLBAR   IDC_GREENSB, 68, 18, 98, 10, WS_TABSTOP
    CTEXT       "", IDC_GN, 169, 18, 18, 10, NOT WS_GROUP
    CTEXT       "&Blue", -1, 43, 31, 24, 10, NOT WS_GROUP
    SCROLLBAR   IDC_BLUESB, 68, 31, 98, 10, WS_TABSTOP
```

```
    CTEXT        "", IDC_BN, 169, 31, 18, 10, NOT WS_GROUP
    PUSHBUTTON   "&OK", IDOK, 36, 49, 40, 14
    PUSHBUTTON   "&Cancel", IDC_CLOSE, 112, 49, 40, 14
END
```

ABOUT.DLG

```
ABOUTDLG DIALOG DISCARDABLE  22, 17, 167, 73
STYLE DS_MODALFRAME | WS_CAPTION | WS_SYSMENU
CAPTION SZABOUT
BEGIN
    DEFPUSHBUTTON   "OK", IDOK, 132, 2, 32, 14, WS_GROUP
    ICON            SZAPPNAME,      -1, 3, 2, 18, 20
    LTEXT           SZAPPNAME,      -1, 30, 12,  50, 8
    LTEXT           SZDESCRIPTION, -1, 30, 22, 150, 8
    LTEXT           SZVERSION,      -1, 30, 32, 150, 8
    LTEXT           SZCOMPANYNAME, -1, 30, 42, 150, 8
END
```

COLOREDT.ICO

CHAPTER TWO

COMMON CONTROLS

CASE 2-1: PROGRESS BAR

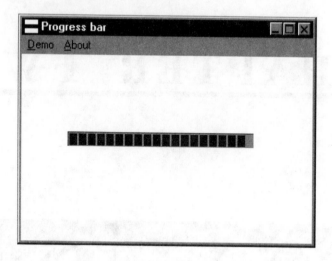

FIGURE 2-1

T he *common controls* are a set of controls supported by the common control library, which is a dynamic link library (DLL) included with the Windows 95 operating system. Similar to other window controls, a common control is a predefined child window used to handle input or output tasks.

This case is an example of using the progress bar common control to indicate the progress of a lengthy operation in an application. The CreateProgressBar() function creates a progress bar using CreateWindowEx() function with the PROGRESS_CLASS window class specified. The range and step of the progress bar are then set by sending the PBM_SETRANGE and PBM_SETSTEP messages to this child window control. The progress of an operation is indicated by a segmented blue bar. The progress bar position is updated during the operation by sending the PBM_STEPIT message to the progress bar. This common control does not draw tick marks to indicate the percentage of the progress. The programmer must write a subroutine to draw tick marks above or below the progress bar. See Chapter 5 for examples of drawing functions. A progress bar can display text to indicate the progress of an operation if the style PBS_SHOWPERCENT or PBS_SHOWPOS has been specified. When the user clicks on the demo menu item, the program increments the progress bar position from 0 to 100%.

GLOBALS.H

```
// GLOBALS.H - header file for global variables
//             and function prototypes

// Product identifier string definitions.
#define APPNAME        ProgBar
#define ICONFILE       ProgBar.ico
#define SZAPPNAME      "ProgBar"
#define SZDESCRIPTION  "Progress bar"
#define SZVERSION      "Version 1.0"
#define SZCOMPANYNAME  "\251 M&&T Books, 1994"
#define SZABOUT        "About"

// Global function prototypes.
BOOL InitApplication(HINSTANCE);
BOOL InitInstance(HINSTANCE, int);
HWND WINAPI CreateProgressBar(HWND, UINT, UINT, UINT,
                     UINT, UINT, UINT, UINT);

// Callback functions called by Windows.
LRESULT CALLBACK WndProc(HWND, UINT, WPARAM, LPARAM);
LRESULT CALLBACK About(HWND, UINT, WPARAM, LPARAM);

// Menu item ID
#define IDM_ABOUT      1000
#define IDM_DEMO       1001

// Global variable declarations.
extern HINSTANCE hInst;      // The current instance handle
extern char szAppName[];     // The name of this application
extern char szTitle[];       // The title bar text
```

WINMAIN.C

```
// WINMAIN.C
#include <windows.h>
#include "globals.h"
```

```c
int APIENTRY WinMain(HINSTANCE hInstance,
                     HINSTANCE hPrevInstance,
                     LPSTR lpCmdLine,
                     int nCmdShow)
{
    MSG msg;

    // register main window class
    if (!hPrevInstance)
        {
        if (!InitApplication(hInstance))
            {
            return FALSE;
            }
        }

    // create and show main window
    if (!InitInstance(hInstance, nCmdShow))
        {
        return FALSE;
        }

    // process window message
    while (GetMessage(&msg, NULL, 0, 0))
        {
            TranslateMessage(&msg);
            DispatchMessage(&msg);
        }
    return msg.wParam;
}
```

INIT.C

```c
// INIT.C
#include <windows.h>
#include "globals.h"

HINSTANCE hInst;
char szAppName[] = SZAPPNAME;
char szTitle[] = SZDESCRIPTION;

// register main window class
BOOL InitApplication(HINSTANCE hInstance)
{
    WNDCLASS  wc;
```

```
    wc.style          = CS_HREDRAW | CS_VREDRAW;
    wc.lpfnWndProc    = (WNDPROC)WndProc;
    wc.cbClsExtra     = 0;
    wc.cbWndExtra     = 0;
    wc.hInstance      = hInstance;
    wc.hIcon          = LoadIcon(hInstance, szAppName);
    wc.hCursor        = LoadCursor(NULL, IDC_ARROW);
    wc.hbrBackground  = (HBRUSH)(COLOR_WINDOW + 1);
    wc.lpszMenuName   = szAppName;
    wc.lpszClassName  = szAppName;

    return(RegisterClass(&wc));
}

// create and show main window
BOOL InitInstance(HINSTANCE hInstance, int nCmdShow)
{
    HWND    hWnd;
    hInst = hInstance;
    hWnd = CreateWindow(szAppName, szTitle,
                        WS_OVERLAPPEDWINDOW,
                        160, 120, 320, 240,
                        NULL, NULL, hInstance, NULL);

    if (!hWnd)
        {
        return FALSE;
        }

    ShowWindow(hWnd, nCmdShow);
    UpdateWindow(hWnd);

    return TRUE;
}
```

PROGBAR.C

```
// PROGBAR.C
#include <windows.h>
#include <windowsx.h>
#include <commctrl.h>     // required for common controls
#include "globals.h"

HWND hProgBar;
```

```
LRESULT CALLBACK WndProc(HWND hWnd,
                         UINT uMessage,
                         WPARAM wParam,
                         LPARAM lParam)
{
    int i;

    switch (uMessage)
    {
        case WM_CREATE:
            // create a progress bar
            hProgBar = CreateProgressBar(hWnd, 0, 100, 1,
                                         50, 80, 200, 16);
            break;

        case WM_COMMAND:
            switch (GET_WM_COMMAND_ID(wParam,lParam))
            {
                case IDM_DEMO:
                    // start a demo,
                    // set progress bar position
                    // from 0 to 100%
                    SendMessage(hProgBar,
                                PBM_SETPOS, (WPARAM)0, 0);
                    for(i=0; i<100; i++)
                      {
                        SendMessage(hProgBar,
                                    PBM_STEPIT, 0, 0);
                      }
                    break;

                case IDM_ABOUT:
                    // create an about dialog
                    DialogBox(hInst, "ABOUTDLG",
                              hWnd, (DLGPROC)About);
                    break;

                default:
                    return DefWindowProc(hWnd, uMessage,
                                         wParam, lParam);
            }
            break;

        case WM_DESTROY:
            PostQuitMessage(0);
            break;
```

```
        default:
            return DefWindowProc(hWnd, uMessage,
                                    wParam, lParam);
    }
    return 0;
}

// function for creating the progress bar
HWND WINAPI CreateProgressBar(
    HWND hWnd,      // handle of parent window
    UINT iMin,      // minimum value in progress bar range
    UINT iMax,      // maximum value in progress bar range
    UINT iStep,     // step increment for the progress bar
    UINT iPosX,     // x coord. of left end of progress bar
    UINT iPosY,     // y coord. of top of progress bar
    UINT iWidth,    // width (length) of progress bar
    UINT iHeight)   // height of progress bar
{
    HWND hProgBar;  // handle for progress bar

    InitCommonControls();  // load the common controls DLL

    hProgBar = CreateWindowEx(
                0,                    // no extended style
                PROGRESS_CLASS,       // class name for
                                      // progress bar
                (LPSTR)NULL,          // no caption (title)
                WS_CHILD |            // window style
                WS_VISIBLE |
                PBS_SHOWPERCENT,      // text indicates
                                      // percentage
                iPosX, iPosY,         // position
                iWidth, iHeight,      // width and height
                hWnd,                 // parent window
                (HMENU)NULL,          // no menu
                hInst,                // instance
                NULL                  // no WM_CREATE parameter
                );

    // set progress bar range
    SendMessage(hProgBar, PBM_SETRANGE, 0,
                    MAKELPARAM(iMin, iMax));

    // set progress bar increment step
    SendMessage(hProgBar, PBM_SETSTEP, (WPARAM)iStep, 0);

    SetFocus(hProgBar);
```

```
        return hProgBar;
}
```

ABOUT.C

```
// ABOUT.C
#include <windows.h>
#include <windowsx.h>
#include "globals.h"

// procedures for ABOUT dialog box
LRESULT CALLBACK About(HWND hDlg,
                       UINT uMessage,
                       WPARAM wParam,
                       LPARAM lParam)
{
    switch (uMessage)
      {
        case WM_COMMAND:
            switch (GET_WM_COMMAND_ID(wParam,lParam))
            {
                case IDOK:
                case IDCANCEL:
                    {
                    EndDialog(hDlg, TRUE);
                    return(TRUE);
                    }
                    break;
            }
      }
    return FALSE;
}
```

PROGBAR.RC

```
#include "windows.h"
#include "globals.h"
#include <winver.h>

APPNAME ICON ICONFILE

RCINCLUDE ABOUT.DLG

APPNAME MENU
```

```
BEGIN
  MENUITEM "&Demo",   IDM_DEMO
  MENUITEM "&About",  IDM_ABOUT
END
```

ABOUT.DLG

```
ABOUTDLG DIALOG DISCARDABLE  22, 17, 167, 73
STYLE DS_MODALFRAME | WS_CAPTION | WS_SYSMENU
CAPTION SZABOUT
BEGIN
    DEFPUSHBUTTON   "OK", IDOK, 132, 2, 32, 14, WS_GROUP
    ICON            SZAPPNAME,      -1, 3, 2, 18, 20
    LTEXT           SZAPPNAME,      -1, 30, 12,  50, 8
    LTEXT           SZDESCRIPTION, -1, 30, 22, 150, 8
    LTEXT           SZVERSION,      -1, 30, 32, 150, 8
    LTEXT           SZCOMPANYNAME, -1, 30, 42, 150, 8
END
```

PROGBAR.ICO

CASE 2-2: TRACK BARS

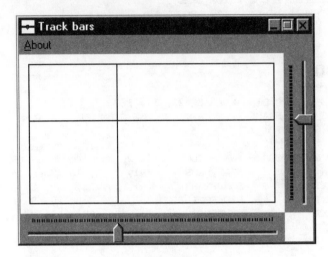

FIGURE 2-2

The *track bar common control* works similarly to the scroll bar. It can have either vertical or horizontal orientation depending on which style was specified—TBS_HORZ or TBS_VERT. However, unlike the scroll bar, both vertical and horizontal track bars notify their parent window of user actions by sending the parent a WM_HSCROLL message. In this case, our CreateTrackBar() function creates a vertical and a horizontal trackbar using windows CreateWindowEx() function with the TRACKBAR_CLASS window class specified. The track bar common control adds tick marks automatically.

In this application the horizontal line in the rectangle follows the motion of the "thumb" of the vertical trackbar. The vertical line in the rectangle follows the motion of the "thumb" of the horizontal track bar. You can also design you own track bar (slider). See Case 3-6 for an example of a slider.

GLOBALS.H

```
// GLOBALS.H - header file for global variables
//             and function prototypes

// Product identifier string definitions.
#define APPNAME        TrackBar
#define ICONFILE       TrackBar.ico
#define SZAPPNAME      "TrackBar"
#define SZDESCRIPTION  "Track bars"
#define SZVERSION      "Version 1.0"
#define SZCOMPANYNAME  "\251 M&&T Books, 1994"
#define SZABOUT        "About"

// Global function prototypes.
BOOL InitApplication(HINSTANCE);
BOOL InitInstance(HINSTANCE, int);
HWND WINAPI CreateTrackBar(HWND, UINT, UINT, UINT,
                UINT, UINT, UINT, DWORD, DWORD);

// Callback functions called by Windows.
LRESULT CALLBACK WndProc(HWND, UINT, WPARAM, LPARAM);
LRESULT CALLBACK About(HWND, UINT, WPARAM, LPARAM);

// Menu item ID
#define IDM_ABOUT   1000

// Global variable declarations.
extern HINSTANCE hInst;     // The current instance handle
extern char szAppName[];    // The name of this application
extern char szTitle[];      // The title bar text
```

WINMAIN.C

```
// WINMAIN.C
#include <windows.h>
#include "globals.h"

int APIENTRY WinMain(HINSTANCE hInstance,
                     HINSTANCE hPrevInstance,
                     LPSTR lpCmdLine,
                     int nCmdShow)
{
    MSG msg;

    // register main window class
```

```
    if (!hPrevInstance)
        {
        if (!InitApplication(hInstance))
            {
            return FALSE;
            }
        }

    // create and show main window
    if (!InitInstance(hInstance, nCmdShow))
        {
        return FALSE;
        }

    // process message
    while (GetMessage(&msg, NULL, 0, 0))
        {
            TranslateMessage(&msg);
            DispatchMessage(&msg);
        }
    return msg.wParam;
}
```

INIT.C

```
// INIT.C
#include <windows.h>
#include "globals.h"

HINSTANCE hInst;
char szAppName[] = SZAPPNAME;
char szTitle[] = SZDESCRIPTION;

// register main window class
BOOL InitApplication(HINSTANCE hInstance)
{
    WNDCLASS  wc;

    wc.style          = CS_HREDRAW | CS_VREDRAW;
    wc.lpfnWndProc    = (WNDPROC)WndProc;
    wc.cbClsExtra     = 0;
    wc.cbWndExtra     = 0;
    wc.hInstance      = hInstance;
    wc.hIcon          = LoadIcon(hInstance, szAppName);
    wc.hCursor        = LoadCursor(NULL, IDC_ARROW);
    wc.hbrBackground  = (HBRUSH)(COLOR_WINDOW + 1);
    wc.lpszMenuName   = szAppName;
```

```
    wc.lpszClassName = szAppName;

    return(RegisterClass(&wc));
}

// create and show main window
BOOL InitInstance(HINSTANCE hInstance, int nCmdShow)
{
    HWND    hWnd;
    hInst = hInstance;
    hWnd = CreateWindow(szAppName, szTitle,
                        WS_CAPTION | WS_BORDER |
                        WS_VISIBLE |
                        WS_SYSMENU | WS_MINIMIZEBOX,
                        160, 120, 320, 240,
                        NULL, NULL, hInstance, NULL);

    if (!hWnd)
        {
        return FALSE;
        }

    ShowWindow(hWnd, nCmdShow);
    UpdateWindow(hWnd);

    return TRUE;
}
```

TRACKBAR.C

```
// TRACKBAR.C
#include <windows.h>
#include <windowsx.h>
#include <commctrl.h>      // required for common controls
#include "globals.h"

HWND hWnd, hTrackBarH, hTrackBarV;

LRESULT CALLBACK WndProc(HWND hWnd,
                         UINT uMessage,
                         WPARAM wParam,
                         LPARAM lParam)
{
    static RECT rc, rc1;
    HDC hDC;
    PAINTSTRUCT ps;
    UINT xPos, yPos;
```

```
static UINT V_Pos = 50, H_Pos = 50;

switch (uMessage)
{
    case WM_CREATE:

            // get main window client rectangle
            GetClientRect(hWnd, &rc);

            // define a rectangle rc1 as drawing area
            rc1.left = rc.left + 10;
            rc1.right = rc.right - 40;
            rc1.top = rc.top + 10;
            rc1.bottom = rc.bottom - 40;

            // create a horizontal track bar
            hTrackBarH = CreateTrackBar(hWnd, 0, 100,
                            rc.left, rc.bottom - 30,
                            rc.right - rc.left - 30, 30,
                            TBS_HORZ, TBS_TOP);

            // create a vertical track bar
            hTrackBarV = CreateTrackBar(hWnd, 0, 100,
                            rc.right - 30, rc.top,
                            30, rc.bottom - rc.top - 30,
                            TBS_VERT, TBS_LEFT);
            break;


    case WM_HSCROLL:

            // process message for horizontal track bar
            if((HWND)lParam == hTrackBarH)
              {
              switch(LOWORD(wParam))
                {
                case TB_TOP:
                    H_Pos = 0;
                    break;

                case TB_BOTTOM:
                    H_Pos = 100;
                    break;

                case TB_PAGEUP:
                    H_Pos = max(0, H_Pos - 10);
                    break;

                case TB_LINEUP:
```

```
            H_Pos = max(0, H_Pos - 1);
            break;

    case TB_PAGEDOWN:
            H_Pos = min(100, H_Pos + 10);
            break;

    case TB_LINEDOWN:
            H_Pos = min(100, H_Pos + 1);
            break;

    case TB_THUMBPOSITION:
    case TB_THUMBTRACK:
            H_Pos = HIWORD(wParam);
            break;

    default :
            return FALSE ;
    }
  }

 // process message for vertical track bar
if((HWND)lParam == hTrackBarV)
  {
  switch(LOWORD(wParam))
    {
    case TB_TOP:
            V_Pos = 0;
            break;

    case TB_BOTTOM:
            V_Pos = 100;
            break;

    case TB_PAGEUP:
            V_Pos = max(0, V_Pos - 10);
            break;

    case TB_LINEUP:
            V_Pos = max(0, V_Pos - 1);
            break;

    case TB_PAGEDOWN:
            V_Pos = min(100, V_Pos + 10);
            break;

    case TB_LINEDOWN:
            V_Pos = min(100, V_Pos + 1);
```

```
              break;

          case TB_THUMBPOSITION:
          case TB_THUMBTRACK:
              V_Pos = HIWORD(wParam);
              break;

          default :
              return FALSE ;
          }
      }
      // repaint the area defined by rc1 rectangle
      InvalidateRect(hWnd, &rc1, TRUE);
      break;

  case WM_PAINT:

      hDC = BeginPaint(hWnd, &ps);
      SelectObject(hDC, GetStockObject(BLACK_PEN));
      SelectObject(hDC, GetStockObject(WHITE_BRUSH));

      GetClientRect(hWnd, &rc);
      // draw a rectangle
      Rectangle(hDC, rc.left + 10, rc.top + 10,
                     rc.right - 40, rc.bottom - 40);

      // draw a vertical line at the thumb position
      // of horizontal track bar
      xPos = rc.left + 10 +
             (rc.right - rc.left - 50) * H_Pos / 100;
      MoveToEx(hDC, xPos, rc.top + 10, NULL);
      LineTo(hDC, xPos, rc.bottom - 40);

      // draw a horizontal line at the thumb position
      // of vertical track bar
      yPos = rc.top + 10 +
             (rc.bottom - rc.top - 50) * V_Pos / 100;
      MoveToEx(hDC, rc.left + 10, yPos, NULL);
      LineTo(hDC, rc.right - 40, yPos);

      EndPaint(hWnd, &ps);
      break;

  case WM_COMMAND:

      switch (GET_WM_COMMAND_ID(wParam,lParam))
      {
          case IDM_ABOUT:
              // create an about dialog box
```

```
                        DialogBox(hInst, "ABOUTDLG",
                                hWnd, (DLGPROC)About);
                    break;

                default:
                    return DefWindowProc(hWnd, uMessage,
                                        wParam, lParam);
            }
            break;

        case WM_DESTROY:
            PostQuitMessage(0);
            break;

        default:
            return DefWindowProc(hWnd, uMessage,
                                wParam, lParam);
    }
    return 0;
}

// function for creating the track bar
HWND WINAPI CreateTrackBar(
    HWND  hWnd,      // handle of parent window
    UINT  iMin,      // minimum value in track bar range
    UINT  iMax,      // maximum value in track bar range
    UINT  iPosX,     // x coord. of left end of track bar
    UINT  iPosY,     // y coord. of top of track bar
    UINT  iWidth,    // width of track bar
    UINT  iHeight,   // height of track bar
    DWORD TBS_DIR,   // track bar orientation:
                     // TBS_HORZ or TBS_VERT
    DWORD TBS_TICK)  // tick mark location:
                     // TBS_TOP, TBS_BOTTOM,
                     // TBS_LEFT, TBS_RIGHT or TBS_BOTH
{
    HWND hTrackBar; // handle for track bar

    InitCommonControls(); // load the common controls DLL

    hTrackBar = CreateWindowEx(
                0,                 // no extended style
                TRACKBAR_CLASS,    // class name for
                                   // track bar
                (LPSTR)NULL,       // no caption (title)
                WS_CHILD |         // window style
                WS_VISIBLE |
                TBS_DIR |          // horizontal or
                                   // vertical style
```

137

```
                    TBS_AUTOTICKS |   // add tick marks
                                      // automatically
                    TBS_TICK,         // location of tick marks
                    iPosX, iPosY,     // position
                    iWidth, iHeight,  // width and height
                    hWnd,             // parent window
                    (HMENU)NULL,      // no menu
                    hInst,            // instance
                    NULL              // no WM_CREATE parameter
                    );

    // set track bar range
    SendMessage(hTrackBar, TBM_SETRANGE,
            (WPARAM)TRUE, MAKELPARAM(iMin, iMax));

    // set track bar page size
    SendMessage(hTrackBar, TBM_SETPAGESIZE, 0, (LPARAM)10);

    // set track bar to center position
    SendMessage(hTrackBar, TBM_SETPOS,
            (WPARAM)TRUE, (LPARAM)((iMax-iMin)/2));

    SetFocus(hTrackBar);
    return hTrackBar;
}
```

ABOUT.C

```
// ABOUT.C
#include <windows.h>
#include <windowsx.h>
#include "globals.h"

// procedures for ABOUT dialog box
LRESULT CALLBACK About(HWND hDlg,
                    UINT uMessage,
                    WPARAM wParam,
                    LPARAM lParam)
{
    switch (uMessage)
    {
        case WM_COMMAND:
            switch (GET_WM_COMMAND_ID(wParam,lParam))
            {
                case IDOK:
                case IDCANCEL:
                    {
```

```
                                EndDialog(hDlg, TRUE);
                                return(TRUE);
                                }
                                break;
                        }
                }
        return FALSE;
}
```

TRACKBAR.RC

```
#include "windows.h"
#include "globals.h"
#include <winver.h>

APPNAME ICON ICONFILE

RCINCLUDE ABOUT.DLG

APPNAME MENU
BEGIN
   MENUITEM "&About",   IDM_ABOUT
END
```

ABOUT.DLG

```
ABOUTDLG DIALOG DISCARDABLE  22, 17, 167, 73
STYLE DS_MODALFRAME | WS_CAPTION | WS_SYSMENU
CAPTION SZABOUT
BEGIN
        DEFPUSHBUTTON  "OK", IDOK, 132, 2, 32, 14, WS_GROUP
        ICON           SZAPPNAME,      -1, 3, 2, 18, 20
        LTEXT          SZAPPNAME,      -1, 30, 12,  50, 8
        LTEXT          SZDESCRIPTION, -1, 30, 22, 150, 8
        LTEXT          SZVERSION,     -1, 30, 32, 150, 8
        LTEXT          SZCOMPANYNAME, -1, 30, 42, 150, 8
END
```

TRACKBAR.ICO

CASE 2-3: TOOL BAR WITH TOOL TIPS (I)

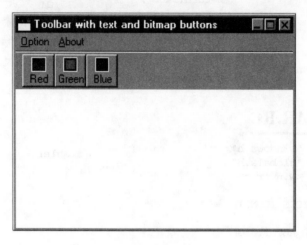

FIGURE 2-3

There are two ways to create a *tool bar common control* in an application—using the `CreateToolbarEx()` function or the `CreateWindowEx()` function with the `TOOLBARCLASSNAME` window class specified. If you want to display only the images (bitmaps without text next to it) on toolbar button faces, it can be done easily by using the `CreateToolbarEx()` function. The `CreateWindowEx()` function gives you more flexibility than the `CreateToolbarEx()` function. In this case our `CreateToolBar()` function uses the Windows `CreateWindowEx()` function to create a tool bar with tool tips.

Tool tip is a common control that provides instant help to any predefined controls in Windows 95. In this case, you specify the `TBSTYLE_TOOLTIPS` style when you create the tool bar. This means that the program will automatically create a tool tip control to provide instant help for buttons on the tool bar. When the cursor stays more than one second (adjustable) on top of any tool bar button, a small rectangle with tip text will appear next to the button to provide instant help. The texts for tool tip control are predefined in a string table in the resource file **TOOLBAR.RC**. The tool tip control gets the tip text by sending a `TTN_NEEDTEXT` notification message to its parent window.

Both image and text can be added to the tool bar button face. Three images appear for the three tool bar buttons are stored in the **TOOLBAR.BMP** bitmap file. The texts to be shown on tool bar buttons are predefined in a string table in the resource file **TOOLBAR.RC**. Please see Case 2-4 for an example of using the `CreateToolbarEx()` function to create a tool bar.

GLOBALS.H

```
// GLOBALS.H - header file for global variables
//                and function prototypes

// Product identifier string definitions.
#define APPNAME        ToolBar
#define ICONFILE       ToolBar.ico
#define SZAPPNAME      "ToolBar"
#define SZDESCRIPTION  "Toolbar with text and bitmap buttons"
#define SZVERSION      "Version 1.0"
#define SZCOMPANYNAME  "\251 M&&T Books, 1994"
#define SZABOUT        "About"

// Global function prototypes.
BOOL InitApplication(HINSTANCE);
BOOL InitInstance(HINSTANCE, int);
HWND CreateToolBar(HWND);

// Callback functions called by Windows.
LRESULT CALLBACK WndProc(HWND, UINT, WPARAM, LPARAM);
LRESULT CALLBACK About(HWND, UINT, WPARAM, LPARAM);

// Menu item ID
#define IDM_ABOUT    1000
#define IDM_SHOWTB   1001
#define IDM_HIDETB   1002

#define IDM_RED      1010
#define IDM_GREEN    1011
#define IDM_BLUE     1012

// String table ID
#define IDS_RED      1100
#define IDS_GREEN    1101
#define IDS_BLUE     1102
```

```
#define IDS_TIPS_RED    1200
#define IDS_TIPS_GREEN 1201
#define IDS_TIPS_BLUE  1202

// Bitmap ID
#define IDB_TOOLBAR 1300

// Child window ID
#define ID_TBar     1400

// Global variable declarations.
extern HINSTANCE hInst;      // The current instance handle
extern char szAppName[];     // The name of this application
extern char szTitle[];       // The title bar text
```

WINMAIN.C

```
// WINMAIN.C
#include <windows.h>
#include "globals.h"

int APIENTRY WinMain(HINSTANCE hInstance,
                     HINSTANCE hPrevInstance,
                     LPSTR lpCmdLine,
                     int nCmdShow)
{
    MSG msg;

    // register main window class
    if (!hPrevInstance)
        {
        if (!InitApplication(hInstance))
            {
            return FALSE;
            }
        }

    // create and show main window
    if (!InitInstance(hInstance, nCmdShow))
        {
        return FALSE;
        }

    // process window message
    while (GetMessage(&msg, NULL, 0, 0))
        {
```

```
            TranslateMessage(&msg);
            DispatchMessage(&msg);
        }
    return msg.wParam;
}
```

INIT.C

```
// INIT.C
#include <windows.h>
#include "globals.h"

HINSTANCE hInst;
char szAppName[] = SZAPPNAME;
char szTitle[] = SZDESCRIPTION;

// register main window class
BOOL InitApplication(HINSTANCE hInstance)
{
    WNDCLASS  wc;

    wc.style           = CS_HREDRAW | CS_VREDRAW;
    wc.lpfnWndProc     = (WNDPROC)WndProc;
    wc.cbClsExtra      = 0;
    wc.cbWndExtra      = 0;
    wc.hInstance       = hInstance;
    wc.hIcon           = LoadIcon(hInstance, szAppName);
    wc.hCursor         = LoadCursor(NULL, IDC_ARROW);
    wc.hbrBackground   = (HBRUSH)(COLOR_WINDOW + 1);
    wc.lpszMenuName    = szAppName;
    wc.lpszClassName   = szAppName;

    return(RegisterClass(&wc));
}

// create and show main window
BOOL InitInstance(HINSTANCE hInstance, int nCmdShow)
{
    HWND     hWnd;
    hInst = hInstance;
    hWnd = CreateWindow(szAppName, szTitle,
                        WS_OVERLAPPEDWINDOW,
                        160, 120, 320, 240,
                        NULL, NULL, hInstance, NULL);

    if (!hWnd)
```

143

```
        {
        return FALSE;
        }

    ShowWindow(hWnd, nCmdShow);
    UpdateWindow(hWnd);

    return TRUE;
}
```

TOOLBAR.C

```
// TOOLBAR.C
#include <windows.h>
#include <windowsx.h>
#include <commctrl.h>      // required for common controls
#include "globals.h"

HWND hToolBar;

LRESULT CALLBACK WndProc(HWND hWnd,
                         UINT uMessage,
                         WPARAM wParam,
                         LPARAM lParam)
{
    UINT ButtonID;

    switch (uMessage)
    {
        case WM_CREATE:

                // create a tool bar
            hToolBar = CreateToolBar(hWnd);
            break;

        case WM_COMMAND:
            switch (GET_WM_COMMAND_ID(wParam,lParam))
            {
                case IDM_RED:
                case IDM_GREEN:
                case IDM_BLUE:
                    MessageBeep(0);

                case IDM_SHOWTB:
                        // show tool bar
                    ShowWindow(hToolBar, SW_SHOW);
```

```
            break;

        case IDM_HIDETB:
            // hide tool bar
            ShowWindow(hToolBar, SW_HIDE);
            break;

        case IDM_ABOUT:
            // create an about dialog box
            DialogBox(hInst, "ABOUTDLG",
                    hWnd, (DLGPROC)About);
            break;

        default:
            return DefWindowProc(hWnd, uMessage,
                                wParam, lParam);
    }
    break;

case WM_NOTIFY:
    switch(((LPNMHDR)lParam) -> code)
    {
        // process tool tips control message
        case TTN_NEEDTEXT:
            {
            LPTOOLTIPTEXT lpttt;

            lpttt = (LPTOOLTIPTEXT)lParam;
            lpttt -> hinst = hInst;

            ButtonID = lpttt -> hdr.idFrom;
            switch(ButtonID)
            {
                case IDM_RED:
                    lpttt->lpszText =
                     MAKEINTRESOURCE(IDS_TIPS_RED);
                    break;

                case IDM_GREEN:
                    lpttt->lpszText =
                    MAKEINTRESOURCE(IDS_TIPS_GREEN);
                    break;

                case IDM_BLUE:
                    lpttt->lpszText =
                    MAKEINTRESOURCE(IDS_TIPS_BLUE);
                    break;
```

```
                    }
                break;
                }
            default: break;
        }
        break;

    case WM_DESTROY:
        PostQuitMessage(0);
        break;

    default:
        return DefWindowProc(hWnd, uMessage,
                             wParam, lParam);
    }
    return 0;
}


// function for creating a tool bar
HWND CreateToolBar(HWND hWnd)
{
    HWND hToolBar; // handle for tool bar
    TBADDBITMAP32 tbab;
    TBBUTTON tbb[3];
    char szBuffer[16];
    int iRed, iGreen, iBlue;
    int STR_LEN = 6;

    InitCommonControls(); // load the common controls DLL


    // create a toolbar with tooltip control
    hToolBar = CreateWindowEx(
            0,                    // no extended style
            TOOLBARCLASSNAME,     // class name for
                                  // tool bar
            (LPSTR)NULL,          // no caption (title)
            WS_CHILD |            // child window
            TBSTYLE_TOOLTIPS |    // create tooltip control
            CCS_ADJUSTABLE |      // enable customization
            CCS_NORESIZE,         // do not use default
                                  // width and height
            0, 0,                 // ignored
            640, 42,              // custom width
                                  // and height
            hWnd,                 // parent window
            (HMENU)ID_TBar,       // child window
```

```
                              // identifier
        hInst,                // instance
        NULL                  // no WM_CREATE parameter
        );


// Sned the message required for backward compatibility
SendMessage(hToolBar, TB_BUTTONSTRUCTSIZE,
        (WPARAM) sizeof(TBBUTTON), 0);


// Set button size
SendMessage(hToolBar, TB_SETBUTTONSIZE, 0,
            (LPARAM) MAKELONG(60, 40));


// Set button bitmap size
SendMessage(hToolBar, TB_SETBITMAPSIZE, 0,
            (LPARAM) MAKELONG(16, 16));


// Add the bitmap containing button images
// to the toolbar
tbab.hInst = NULL;
tbab.nID = (int) LoadBitmap(hInst,
            MAKEINTRESOURCE(IDB_TOOLBAR));
SendMessage(hToolBar, TB_ADDBITMAP32,
                (WPARAM)3, (LPARAM)&tbab);


// Add the button strings to the toolbar
LoadString(hInst, IDS_RED, (LPSTR)&szBuffer, STR_LEN);
iRed = SendMessage(hToolBar, TB_ADDSTRING, 0,
                        (LPARAM)(LPSTR)szBuffer);


LoadString(hInst, IDS_GREEN,
                (LPSTR)&szBuffer, STR_LEN);
iGreen = SendMessage(hToolBar, TB_ADDSTRING, 0,
                        (LPARAM)(LPSTR)szBuffer);


LoadString(hInst, IDS_BLUE, (LPSTR)&szBuffer, STR_LEN);
iBlue = SendMessage(hToolBar, TB_ADDSTRING, 0,
                        (LPARAM)(LPSTR)szBuffer);


// define the button parameters in TBBUTTON array
tbb[0].iBitmap   = 0;    // use 1st image in toolbar.bmp
tbb[0].idCommand = IDM_RED;
tbb[0].fsState   = TBSTATE_ENABLED;
tbb[0].fsStyle   = TBSTYLE_BUTTON;
tbb[0].dwData    = 0;
tbb[0].iString   = iRed;
```

```
    tbb[1].iBitmap    = 1;    // use 2nd image in toolbar.bmp
    tbb[1].idCommand  = IDM_GREEN;
    tbb[1].fsState    = TBSTATE_ENABLED;
    tbb[1].fsStyle    = TBSTYLE_BUTTON;
    tbb[1].dwData     = 0;
    tbb[1].iString    = iGreen;

    tbb[2].iBitmap    = 2;    // use 3rd image in toolbar.bmp
    tbb[2].idCommand  = IDM_BLUE;
    tbb[2].fsState    = TBSTATE_ENABLED;
    tbb[2].fsStyle    = TBSTYLE_BUTTON;
    tbb[2].dwData     = 0;
    tbb[2].iString    = iBlue;

    // add buttons to the toolbar
    SendMessage(hToolBar, TB_ADDBUTTONS, (WPARAM)3,
                          (LPARAM)(LPTBBUTTON)&tbb);

    ShowWindow(hToolBar, SW_SHOW);
    return hToolBar;
}
```

ABOUT.C

```
// ABOUT.C
#include <windows.h>
#include <windowsx.h>
#include "globals.h"

// procedures for ABOUT dialog box
LRESULT CALLBACK About(HWND hDlg,
                       UINT uMessage,
                       WPARAM wParam,
                       LPARAM lParam)
{
    switch (uMessage)
      {
        case WM_COMMAND:
            switch (GET_WM_COMMAND_ID(wParam,lParam))
              {
                case IDOK:
                case IDCANCEL:
                    {
                    EndDialog(hDlg, TRUE);
                    return(TRUE);
                    }
```

```
                    break;
              }
         }
     return FALSE;
}
```

TOOLBAR.RC

```
#include "windows.h"
#include "globals.h"
#include <winver.h>

IDB_TOOLBAR BITMAP toolbar.bmp

APPNAME ICON ICONFILE

RCINCLUDE ABOUT.DLG

APPNAME MENU
BEGIN
  POPUP    "&Option"
  BEGIN
    MENUITEM "&Show Toolbar",  IDM_SHOWTB
    MENUITEM "&Hide Toolbar",  IDM_HIDETB
  END
  MENUITEM "&About",  IDM_ABOUT
END

STRINGTABLE
BEGIN
    IDS_RED,      "Red"
    IDS_GREEN,    "Green"
    IDS_BLUE,     "Blue"
    IDS_TIPS_RED,    "choose red color"
    IDS_TIPS_GREEN, "choose green color"
    IDS_TIPS_BLUE,  "choose blue color"
END
```

ABOUT.DLG

```
ABOUTDLG DIALOG DISCARDABLE  22, 17, 167, 73
STYLE DS_MODALFRAME | WS_CAPTION | WS_SYSMENU
CAPTION SZABOUT
BEGIN
```

```
        DEFPUSHBUTTON   "OK", IDOK, 132, 2, 32, 14, WS_GROUP
        ICON            SZAPPNAME,      -1, 3, 2, 18, 20
        LTEXT           SZAPPNAME,      -1, 30, 12,  50, 8
        LTEXT           SZDESCRIPTION, -1, 30, 22, 150, 8
        LTEXT           SZVERSION,      -1, 30, 32, 150, 8
        LTEXT           SZCOMPANYNAME, -1, 30, 42, 150, 8
    END
```

TOOLBAR.ICO

TOOLBAR.BMP

CASE 2-4: TOOL BAR WITH TOOL TIPS (II)

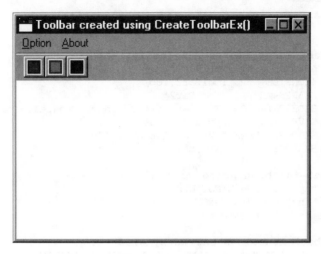

FIGURE 2-4

There are two ways to create a tool bar common control in an application—using the CreateToolbarEx() function or the CreateWindowEx() function and the TOOLBARCLASSNAME window class. In this case, our CreateToolBar() function uses the Windows 95 CreateToolbarEx() function to create a tool bar with tool tips. For more information on tool tips, see the Case 2-3. When the cursor stays more than one second on top of any tool bar button, a small rectangle with a tip will appear next to the button to provide instant help. The three images that appear on three tool bar buttons are stored in **TOOLBAR2.BMP** bitmap file. Please see Case 2-3 for an example of using the CreateWindowEx() function to create a tool bar.

GLOBALS.H

```
// GLOBALS.H - header file for global variables
//            and function prototypes

// Product identifier string definitions.
#define APPNAME        ToolBar2
#define ICONFILE       ToolBar2.ico
#define SZAPPNAME      "ToolBar2"
#define SZDESCRIPTION "Toolbar created using CreateToolbarEx()"
#define SZVERSION      "Version 1.0"
#define SZCOMPANYNAME "\251 M&&T Books, 1994"
#define SZABOUT        "About"

// Global function prototypes.
BOOL InitApplication(HINSTANCE);
BOOL InitInstance(HINSTANCE, int);
BOOL CreateToolBar(HWND);

// Callback functions called by Windows.
LRESULT CALLBACK WndProc(HWND, UINT, WPARAM, LPARAM);
LRESULT CALLBACK About(HWND, UINT, WPARAM, LPARAM);

// Menu item ID
#define IDM_TOOLBAR 1000
#define IDM_ABOUT    1001
#define IDM_SHOWTB   1002
#define IDM_HIDETB   1003

#define IDM_RED      1010
#define IDM_GREEN    1011
#define IDM_BLUE     1012

// String table ID
#define IDS_RED      1100
#define IDS_GREEN    1101
#define IDS_BLUE     1102

#define IDS_TIPS_RED    1200
#define IDS_TIPS_GREEN  1201
#define IDS_TIPS_BLUE   1202

// Bitmap ID
#define IDB_TOOLBAR 1300

// Global variable declarations.
extern HINSTANCE hInst;      // The current instance handle
extern char szAppName[];     // The name of this application
extern char szTitle[];       // The title bar text
```

WINMAIN.C

```c
// WINMAIN.C
#include <windows.h>
#include "globals.h"

int APIENTRY WinMain(HINSTANCE hInstance,
                     HINSTANCE hPrevInstance,
                     LPSTR lpCmdLine,
                     int nCmdShow)
{
    MSG msg;

    // register main window class
    if (!hPrevInstance)
        {
        if (!InitApplication(hInstance))
            {
            return FALSE;
            }
        }

    // create and show main window
    if (!InitInstance(hInstance, nCmdShow))
        {
        return FALSE;
        }

    // process window message
    while (GetMessage(&msg, NULL, 0, 0))
        {
            TranslateMessage(&msg);
            DispatchMessage(&msg);
        }
    return msg.wParam;
}
```

INIT.C

```c
// INIT.C
#include <windows.h>
#include "globals.h"

HINSTANCE hInst;
char szAppName[] = SZAPPNAME;
char szTitle[] = SZDESCRIPTION;
```

```
// register main window class
BOOL InitApplication(HINSTANCE hInstance)
{
    WNDCLASS  wc;

    wc.style         = CS_HREDRAW | CS_VREDRAW;
    wc.lpfnWndProc   = (WNDPROC)WndProc;
    wc.cbClsExtra    = 0;
    wc.cbWndExtra    = 0;
    wc.hInstance     = hInstance;
    wc.hIcon         = LoadIcon(hInstance, szAppName);
    wc.hCursor       = LoadCursor(NULL, IDC_ARROW);
    wc.hbrBackground = (HBRUSH)(COLOR_WINDOW + 1);
    wc.lpszMenuName  = szAppName;
    wc.lpszClassName = szAppName;

    return(RegisterClass(&wc));
}

// create and show main window
BOOL InitInstance(HINSTANCE hInstance, int nCmdShow)
{
    HWND    hWnd;
    hInst = hInstance;
    hWnd = CreateWindow(szAppName, szTitle,
                    WS_OVERLAPPEDWINDOW,
                    160, 120, 320, 240,
                    NULL, NULL, hInstance, NULL);

    if (!hWnd)
        {
        return FALSE;
        }

    ShowWindow(hWnd, nCmdShow);
    UpdateWindow(hWnd);

    return TRUE;
}
```

TOOLBAR2.C

```
// TOOLBAR2.C
#include <windows.h>
#include <windowsx.h>
#include <commctrl.h>      // required for common controls
#include "globals.h"
```

```
#define NUM_IMAGES      3  // number of images on tool bar
#define IMAGE_WIDTH     16  // image width in pixel
#define IMAGE_HEIGHT    16  // image height in pixel
#define BUTTON_WIDTH     0  // button width in pixel
                            // (use default)
#define BUTTON_HEIGHT    0  // button height in pixel
                            // (use default)

HWND hToolBar;

TBBUTTON tbb[] =
{
    {0, IDM_RED,    TBSTATE_ENABLED,   TBSTYLE_BUTTON, 0, 0},
    {1, IDM_GREEN,  TBSTATE_ENABLED,   TBSTYLE_BUTTON, 0, 0},
    {2, IDM_BLUE,   TBSTATE_ENABLED,   TBSTYLE_BUTTON, 0, 0},
};

LRESULT CALLBACK WndProc(HWND hWnd,
                         UINT uMessage,
                         WPARAM wParam,
                         LPARAM lParam)
{
    UINT ButtonID;

    switch (uMessage)
    {
        case WM_CREATE:
            // load common controls DLL
            InitCommonControls();

            // create a tool bar
            if(CreateToolBar(hWnd))
                return 0;
            else
                return -1;
            break;

        case WM_COMMAND:
            switch (GET_WM_COMMAND_ID(wParam,lParam))
            {
                case IDM_RED:
                case IDM_GREEN:
                case IDM_BLUE:
                    MessageBeep(0);

                case IDM_SHOWTB:
                    // show tool bar
```

```
                    ShowWindow(hToolBar, SW_SHOW);
                    break;

            case IDM_HIDETB:
                    // hide tool bar
                    ShowWindow(hToolBar, SW_HIDE);
                    break;

            case IDM_ABOUT:
                    // create an about dialog box
                    DialogBox(hInst, "ABOUTDLG",
                              hWnd, (DLGPROC)About);
                    break;

            default:
                return DefWindowProc(hWnd, uMessage,
                                     wParam, lParam);
        }
        break;

    case WM_NOTIFY:
        switch(((LPNMHDR)lParam) -> code)
        {
            // process tool tip control message
            case TTN_NEEDTEXT:
                {
                LPTOOLTIPTEXT lpttt;

                lpttt = (LPTOOLTIPTEXT)lParam;
                lpttt -> hinst = hInst;

                ButtonID = lpttt -> hdr.idFrom;
                switch(ButtonID)
                {
                    case IDM_RED:
                        lpttt->lpszText =
                          MAKEINTRESOURCE(IDS_TIPS_RED);
                        break;

                    case IDM_GREEN:
                        lpttt->lpszText =
                        MAKEINTRESOURCE(IDS_TIPS_GREEN);
                        break;

                    case IDM_BLUE:
                        lpttt->lpszText =
                        MAKEINTRESOURCE(IDS_TIPS_BLUE);
                        break;
```

```
                    }
                    break;
                    }
                default: break;
            }
            break;

        case WM_DESTROY:
            PostQuitMessage(0);
            break;

        default:
            return DefWindowProc(hWnd, uMessage,
                                    wParam, lParam);
    }
    return 0;
}


// function for creating a tool bar
BOOL CreateToolBar(HWND hWnd)
{
    hToolBar = CreateToolbarEx(
                    hWnd,
                    WS_CHILD | WS_VISIBLE |
                    TBSTYLE_TOOLTIPS,
                    IDM_TOOLBAR,
                    NUM_IMAGES,
                    hInst,
                    IDB_TOOLBAR,    // toolbar images
                                    // bitmap file
                    tbb,
                    sizeof(tbb)/sizeof(TBBUTTON),
                    BUTTON_WIDTH,
                    BUTTON_HEIGHT,
                    IMAGE_WIDTH,
                    IMAGE_HEIGHT,
                    sizeof(TBBUTTON));

    return (hToolBar != NULL);
}
```

ABOUT.C

```
// ABOUT.C
#include <windows.h>
#include <windowsx.h>
```

```
#include "globals.h"

// procedures for ABOUT dialog box
LRESULT CALLBACK About(HWND hDlg,
                       UINT uMessage,
                       WPARAM wParam,
                       LPARAM lParam)
{
    switch (uMessage)
     {
       case WM_COMMAND:
            switch (GET_WM_COMMAND_ID(wParam,lParam))
            {
                case IDOK:
                case IDCANCEL:
                     {
                     EndDialog(hDlg, TRUE);
                     return(TRUE);
                     }
                     break;
            }
     }
    return FALSE;
}
```

TOOLBAR2.RC

```
#include "windows.h"
#include "globals.h"
#include <winver.h>

IDB_TOOLBAR BITMAP toolbar2.bmp

APPNAME ICON ICONFILE

RCINCLUDE ABOUT.DLG

APPNAME MENU
BEGIN
  POPUP     "&Option"
  BEGIN
    MENUITEM "&Show Toolbar",  IDM_SHOWTB
    MENUITEM "&Hide Toolbar",  IDM_HIDETB
  END
  MENUITEM "&About",  IDM_ABOUT
END
```

```
STRINGTABLE
BEGIN
    IDS_RED,         "Red"
    IDS_GREEN,       "Green"
    IDS_BLUE,        "Blue"
    IDS_TIPS_RED,      "choose red color"
    IDS_TIPS_GREEN,  "choose green color"
    IDS_TIPS_BLUE,   "choose blue color"
END
```

ABOUT.DLG

```
ABOUTDLG DIALOG DISCARDABLE  22, 17, 167, 73
STYLE DS_MODALFRAME | WS_CAPTION | WS_SYSMENU
CAPTION SZABOUT
BEGIN
    DEFPUSHBUTTON    "OK", IDOK, 132, 2, 32, 14, WS_GROUP
    ICON             SZAPPNAME,      -1, 3, 2, 18, 20
    LTEXT            SZAPPNAME,      -1, 30, 12,  50, 8
    LTEXT            SZDESCRIPTION, -1, 30, 22, 150, 8
    LTEXT            SZVERSION,      -1, 30, 32, 150, 8
    LTEXT            SZCOMPANYNAME, -1, 30, 42, 150, 8
END
```

TOOLBAR2.ICO

TOOLBAR2.BMP

CASE 2-5: REGULAR STATUS BAR

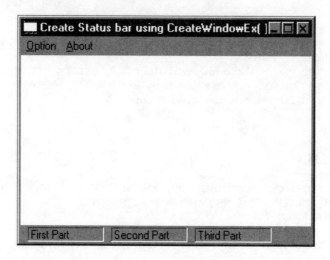

FIGURE 2-5

The *status bar common control* is a horizontal window at the top or bottom of a parent window. It can be divided into many parts to provide many different types of status information to the user. The status bar can be created using the CreateWindowEx() function with the STATUSCLASSNAME window class specified.

In this case the program creates a regular status bar (display text only) first and then sends an SB_SETPARTS message to the status bar to set the number and the coordinates of parts in the status window. In this case, each part of the status bar is more or less like a static control. You can set the text in each part by sending an SB_SETTEXT message to the status bar. In general, you can display any kind of information in a status bar. Please see Case 2-6 for an example of an owner-draw status bar.

GLOBALS.H

```
// GLOBALS.H - header file for global variables
//              and function prototypes

// Product identifier string definitions.
#define APPNAME        StatuBar
#define ICONFILE       StatuBar.ico
#define SZAPPNAME      "StatuBar"
#define SZDESCRIPTION  "Create Status bar using CreateWindowEx( )"
#define SZVERSION      "Version 1.0"
#define SZCOMPANYNAME  "\251 M&&T Books, 1994"
#define SZABOUT        "About"

// Global function prototypes.
BOOL InitApplication(HINSTANCE);
BOOL InitInstance(HINSTANCE, int);
HWND CreateAStatusBar(HWND);

// Callback functions called by Windows.
LRESULT CALLBACK WndProc(HWND, UINT, WPARAM, LPARAM);
LRESULT CALLBACK About(HWND, UINT, WPARAM, LPARAM);

// Menu item ID
#define IDM_ABOUT    1000
#define IDM_SHOWSB   1001
#define IDM_HIDESB   1002

// Child window ID
#define ID_SBar      1100

// Global variable declarations.
extern HINSTANCE hInst;      // The current instance handle
extern char szAppName[];     // The name of this application
extern char szTitle[];       // The title bar text
```

WINMAIN.C

```
// WINMAIN.C
#include <windows.h>
#include "globals.h"

int APIENTRY WinMain(HINSTANCE hInstance,
                     HINSTANCE hPrevInstance,
                     LPSTR lpCmdLine,
```

```
                    int nCmdShow)
{
    MSG msg;

    // register main window class
    if (!hPrevInstance)
        {
        if (!InitApplication(hInstance))
            {
            return FALSE;
            }
        }

    // create and show main window
    if (!InitInstance(hInstance, nCmdShow))
        {
        return FALSE;
        }

    // process window message
    while (GetMessage(&msg, NULL, 0, 0))
        {
            TranslateMessage(&msg);
            DispatchMessage(&msg);
        }
    return msg.wParam;
}
```

INIT.C

```
// INIT.C
#include <windows.h>
#include "globals.h"

HINSTANCE hInst;
char szAppName[] = SZAPPNAME;
char szTitle[] = SZDESCRIPTION;

// register main window class
BOOL InitApplication(HINSTANCE hInstance)
{
    WNDCLASS  wc;

    wc.style         = CS_HREDRAW | CS_VREDRAW;
    wc.lpfnWndProc   = (WNDPROC)WndProc;
    wc.cbClsExtra    = 0;
```

```
    wc.cbWndExtra    = 0;
    wc.hInstance     = hInstance;
    wc.hIcon         = LoadIcon(hInstance, szAppName);
    wc.hCursor       = LoadCursor(NULL, IDC_ARROW);
    wc.hbrBackground = (HBRUSH)(COLOR_WINDOW + 1);
    wc.lpszMenuName  = szAppName;
    wc.lpszClassName = szAppName;

    return(RegisterClass(&wc));
}

// create and show main window
BOOL InitInstance(HINSTANCE hInstance, int nCmdShow)
{
    HWND    hWnd;
    hInst = hInstance;
    hWnd = CreateWindow(szAppName, szTitle,
                        WS_OVERLAPPEDWINDOW,
                        160, 120, 320, 240,
                        NULL, NULL, hInstance, NULL);

    if (!hWnd)
        {
        return FALSE;
        }

    ShowWindow(hWnd, nCmdShow);
    UpdateWindow(hWnd);

    return TRUE;
}
```

STATUBAR.C

```
// STATUBAR.C
#include <windows.h>
#include <windowsx.h>
#include <commctrl.h>     // required for common controls
#include "globals.h"

HWND hStatusBar;

LRESULT CALLBACK WndProc(HWND hWnd,
                         UINT uMessage,
                         WPARAM wParam,
                         LPARAM lParam)
```

163

```
{
    switch (uMessage)
    {
    case WM_CREATE:
            // create a standard status bar
            // set text for each part in status bar
            hStatusBar = CreateAStatusBar(hWnd);

            // set text for each part in status bar
            SendMessage(hStatusBar, SB_SETTEXT,
                        (WPARAM) 0 | 0,
                        (LPARAM)(LPSTR)"First Part");
            SendMessage(hStatusBar, SB_SETTEXT,
                        (WPARAM) 1 | 0,
                        (LPARAM)(LPSTR)"Second Part");
            SendMessage(hStatusBar, SB_SETTEXT,
                        (WPARAM) 2 | 0,
                        (LPARAM)(LPSTR)"Third Part");
            break;

    case WM_COMMAND:
            switch (GET_WM_COMMAND_ID(wParam,lParam))
            {
            case IDM_SHOWSB:
                    // show status bar
                    ShowWindow(hStatusBar, SW_SHOW);
                    break;

            case IDM_HIDESB:
                    // hide status bar
                    ShowWindow(hStatusBar, SW_HIDE);
                    break;

            case IDM_ABOUT:
                    // create an about dialog box
                    DialogBox(hInst, "ABOUTDLG",
                            hWnd, (DLGPROC)About);
                    break;

            default:
                    return DefWindowProc(hWnd, uMessage,
                                        wParam, lParam);
            }
            break;

    case WM_DESTROY:
            PostQuitMessage(0);
```

164

```
            break;

        default:
            return DefWindowProc(hWnd, uMessage,
                                 wParam, lParam);
    }
    return 0;
}

// function for creating a status bar
HWND CreateAStatusBar(HWND hWnd)
{
    HWND hStatusBar; // handle for the status bar
    int aWidths[] = {90, 180, 270};  // width of each part
                                     // in status bar

    InitCommonControls(); // load the common controls DLL


    // create a status bar
    hStatusBar = CreateWindowEx(
            0,                  // no extended style
            STATUSCLASSNAME,    // class name for
                                // status bar
            (LPSTR)NULL,        // no caption (title)
            WS_CHILD |          // child window
            SBS_SIZEGRIP,       // include a sizing grip
            0, 0,               // ignored
            0, 0,               // ignored
            hWnd,               // parent window
            (HMENU)ID_SBar,     // child window
                                // identifier
            hInst,              // instance
            NULL                // no WM_CREATE parameter
            );

    // Set the number and coordinate of
    // parts in status window
    SendMessage(hStatusBar, SB_SETPARTS,
            (WPARAM) 3, (LPARAM)(LPINT)aWidths);

    ShowWindow(hStatusBar, SW_SHOW);
    return hStatusBar;
}
```

ABOUT.C

```
// ABOUT.C
#include <windows.h>
#include <windowsx.h>
#include "globals.h"

// procedures for ABOUT dialog box
LRESULT CALLBACK About(HWND hDlg,
                       UINT uMessage,
                       WPARAM wParam,
                       LPARAM lParam)
{
    switch (uMessage)
      {
        case WM_COMMAND:
            switch (GET_WM_COMMAND_ID(wParam,lParam))
              {
                case IDOK:
                case IDCANCEL:
                    {
                    EndDialog(hDlg, TRUE);
                    return(TRUE);
                    }
                    break;
              }
      }
    return FALSE;
}
```

STATUBAR.RC

```
#include "windows.h"
#include "globals.h"
#include <winver.h>

APPNAME ICON ICONFILE

RCINCLUDE ABOUT.DLG

APPNAME MENU
BEGIN
  POPUP     "&Option"
  BEGIN
    MENUITEM "&Show Status Bar",   IDM_SHOWSB
```

```
    MENUITEM "&Hide Status Bar",  IDM_HIDESB
  END
  MENUITEM "&About",  IDM_ABOUT
END
```

ABOUT.DLG

```
ABOUTDLG DIALOG DISCARDABLE  22, 17, 167, 73
STYLE DS_MODALFRAME | WS_CAPTION | WS_SYSMENU
CAPTION SZABOUT
BEGIN
    DEFPUSHBUTTON   "OK", IDOK, 132, 2, 32, 14, WS_GROUP
    ICON            SZAPPNAME,      -1, 3, 2, 18, 20
    LTEXT           SZAPPNAME,      -1, 30, 12,  50, 8
    LTEXT           SZDESCRIPTION, -1, 30, 22, 150, 8
    LTEXT           SZVERSION,      -1, 30, 32, 150, 8
    LTEXT           SZCOMPANYNAME, -1, 30, 42, 150, 8
END
```

STATUBAR.ICO

CASE 2-6: OWNER-DRAW STATUS BAR

FIGURE 2-6

The status bar common control is a horizontal window at the top or bottom of a parent window. It can be divided into many parts to provide many different types of status information to the user. The status bar can be created using the CreateWindowEx() function with the STATUSCLASSNAME window class specified.

In this case the program creates a three-part owner-draw bottom status bar using the procedures described in Case 2-5. A bitmap is painted into the rectangle that confines the first part of the status bar. A hatch brush is used to fill the rectangle for a second part of the bar. The third part displays a text string using a customized font. Unlike other owner-draw controls described in Chapter 1, an owner-draw status bar was not specified as "owner-draw" when created. The owner-draw style SBT_OWNERDRAW is specified when a SB_SETTEXT message is sent to a status bar for drawing a specific part of the status bar.

In this example, to draw a bitmap in first part of the status bar, the following message is sent to the status bar:

```
SendMessage(hStatusBar, SB_SETTEXT,
    WPARAM) 0 | SBT_OWNERDRAW, (LPARAM)(LPSTR)"PART1BMP");
```

The last parameter in the SendMessage() function is the bitmap name defined in the resource file **ODSB.RC**. When a status bar receives this message, this bitmap name is stored in the LPDRAWITEMSTRUCT structure as itemData, and a WM_DRAWITEM message is sent to its parent window to paint this part of the window. The second and third part of the status bar are drawn following similar procedures.

GLOBALS.H

```
// GLOBALS.H - header file for global variables
//              and function prototypes

// Product identifier string definitions.
#define APPNAME        ODSB
#define ICONFILE       ODSB.ico
#define SZAPPNAME      "ODSB"
#define SZDESCRIPTION  "Owner-Drawn status bar"
#define SZVERSION      "Version 1.0"
#define SZCOMPANYNAME  "\251 M&&T Books, 1994"
#define SZABOUT        "About"

// Global function prototypes.
BOOL InitApplication(HINSTANCE);
BOOL InitInstance(HINSTANCE, int);
HWND CreateAStatusBar(HWND);
void PaintRectBitmap(HDC, HBITMAP, LONG, LONG);

// Callback functions called by Windows.
LRESULT CALLBACK WndProc(HWND, UINT, WPARAM, LPARAM);
LRESULT CALLBACK About(HWND, UINT, WPARAM, LPARAM);

// Menu item ID
#define IDM_ABOUT    1000
#define IDM_SHOWSB   1001
#define IDM_HIDESB   1002

// Child window ID
#define ID_SBar      1100

// Global variable declarations.
```

```
extern HINSTANCE hInst;      // The current instance handle
extern char szAppName[];     // The name of this application
extern char szTitle[];       // The title bar text
```

WINMAIN.C

```
// WINMAIN.C
#include <windows.h>
#include "globals.h"

int APIENTRY WinMain(HINSTANCE hInstance,
                     HINSTANCE hPrevInstance,
                     LPSTR lpCmdLine,
                     int nCmdShow)
{
    MSG msg;

    // register main window class
    if (!hPrevInstance)
        {
        if (!InitApplication(hInstance))
            {
            return FALSE;
            }
        }

    // create and show main window
    if (!InitInstance(hInstance, nCmdShow))
        {
        return FALSE;
        }

    // process window message
    while (GetMessage(&msg, NULL, 0, 0))
        {
            TranslateMessage(&msg);
            DispatchMessage(&msg);
        }
    return msg.wParam;
}
```

INIT.C

```
// INIT.C
#include <windows.h>
```

```
#include "globals.h"

HINSTANCE hInst;
char szAppName[] = SZAPPNAME;
char szTitle[] = SZDESCRIPTION;

// register main window class
BOOL InitApplication(HINSTANCE hInstance)
{
    WNDCLASS   wc;

    wc.style         = CS_HREDRAW | CS_VREDRAW;
    wc.lpfnWndProc   = (WNDPROC)WndProc;
    wc.cbClsExtra    = 0;
    wc.cbWndExtra    = 0;
    wc.hInstance     = hInstance;
    wc.hIcon         = LoadIcon(hInstance, szAppName);
    wc.hCursor       = LoadCursor(NULL, IDC_ARROW);
    wc.hbrBackground = (HBRUSH)(COLOR_WINDOW + 1);
    wc.lpszMenuName  = szAppName;
    wc.lpszClassName = szAppName;

    return(RegisterClass(&wc));
}

// create and show main window
BOOL InitInstance(HINSTANCE hInstance, int nCmdShow)
{
    HWND    hWnd;
    hInst = hInstance;
    hWnd = CreateWindow(szAppName, szTitle,
                        WS_OVERLAPPEDWINDOW,
                        160, 120, 320, 240,
                        NULL, NULL, hInstance, NULL);

    if (!hWnd)
        {
        return FALSE;
        }

    ShowWindow(hWnd, nCmdShow);
    UpdateWindow(hWnd);

    return TRUE;
}
```

ODSB.C

```
// ODSB.C
#include <windows.h>
#include <windowsx.h>
#include <commctrl.h>      // required for common controls
#include "globals.h"

HWND hStatusBar;
HBITMAP hBitmap;

LRESULT CALLBACK WndProc(HWND hWnd,
                         UINT uMessage,
                         WPARAM wParam,
                         LPARAM lParam)
{
    LPDRAWITEMSTRUCT lpdis;
    RECT rect;
    HFONT hFont;
    HBRUSH hBrush;

    switch (uMessage)
    {
        case WM_CREATE:
            // create an owner-draw status bar
            hStatusBar = CreateAStatusBar(hWnd);

            // add contents to each part of the status bar
            SendMessage(hStatusBar, SB_SETTEXT,
                        (WPARAM) 0 | SBT_OWNERDRAW,
                        (LPARAM)(LPSTR)"PART1BMP");
            SendMessage(hStatusBar, SB_SETTEXT,
                        (WPARAM) 1 | SBT_OWNERDRAW,
                        (LPARAM)(LPSTR)NULL);
            SendMessage(hStatusBar, SB_SETTEXT,
                        (WPARAM) 2 | SBT_OWNERDRAW,
                        (LPARAM)(LPSTR)"Third Part");
            break;

        case WM_DRAWITEM:
            lpdis = (LPDRAWITEMSTRUCT)lParam;
            if(lpdis->CtlID == ID_SBar)
            {
                switch(lpdis->itemID)
                {
                    case 0:
                        // draw bitmap part1.bmp in
```

```
                    // part1 of status bar
                CopyRect((LPRECT)&rect,
                        (LPRECT)&lpdis->rcItem);
                hBitmap = LoadBitmap(hInst,
                        (LPSTR)lpdis->itemData);
                PaintRectBitmap(lpdis->hDC, hBitmap,
                                rect.left, rect.top);

                break;

            case 1:
                    // draw a rectangle in part 2
                    // of status bar
                CopyRect((LPRECT)&rect,
                        (LPRECT)&lpdis->rcItem);
                hBrush = CreateHatchBrush(
                        HS_DIAGCROSS, RGB(0, 0, 0));
                SelectObject(lpdis->hDC, hBrush);
                Rectangle(lpdis->hDC,
                        rect.left, rect.top,
                        rect.right, rect.bottom);
                DeleteObject(hBrush);
                break;

            case 2:
                    // draw text in part 3 of status bar
                hFont = CreateFont(14, 7, 0, 0, 400,
                        FALSE, FALSE, FALSE,
                        ANSI_CHARSET,
                        OUT_DEFAULT_PRECIS,
                        CLIP_DEFAULT_PRECIS,
                        PROOF_QUALITY,
                        DEFAULT_PITCH | FF_ROMAN,
                        (LPCTSTR)NULL);
                SelectObject(lpdis->hDC, hFont);
                SetBkMode(lpdis->hDC, TRANSPARENT);
                DrawText(lpdis->hDC, lpdis->itemData,
                        strlen(lpdis->itemData),
                        (LPRECT)&lpdis->rcItem,
                        DT_CENTER);
                DeleteObject(hFont);
                break;
            }
        }
        return(TRUE);
        break;

    case WM_COMMAND:
```

```
            switch (GET_WM_COMMAND_ID(wParam,lParam))
            {
            case IDM_SHOWSB:
                    // show status bar
                    ShowWindow(hStatusBar, SW_SHOW);
                    break;

            case IDM_HIDESB:
                     // hide status bar
                    ShowWindow(hStatusBar, SW_HIDE);
                    break;

            case IDM_ABOUT:
                     // create an about dialog box
                    DialogBox(hInst, "ABOUTDLG",
                              hWnd, (DLGPROC)About);
                    break;

              default:
                  return DefWindowProc(hWnd, uMessage,
                                          wParam, lParam);
            }
            break;

        case WM_DESTROY:
            PostQuitMessage(0);
            break;

        default:
            return DefWindowProc(hWnd, uMessage,
                                    wParam, lParam);
    }
    return 0;
}

// function for creating a status bar
HWND CreateAStatusBar(HWND hWnd)
{
    HWND hStatusBar; // handle for the status bar
    int aWidths[] = {90, 180, 270};

    InitCommonControls(); // load the common controls DLL

    // create a status bar
    hStatusBar = CreateWindowEx(
            0,                  // no extended style
            STATUSCLASSNAME,    // class name for
```

```
                                // status bar
            (LPSTR)NULL,         // no caption (title)
            WS_CHILD |           // child window
            SBS_SIZEGRIP,        // include a sizing grip
            0, 0,                // ignored
            0, 0,                // ignored
            hWnd,                // parent window
            (HMENU)ID_SBar,      // child window
                                 // identifier
            hInst,               // instance
            NULL                 // no WM_CREATE parameter
            );

    // Sets the number and coordinate of
    // parts in status window
    SendMessage(hStatusBar, SB_SETPARTS,
                (WPARAM) 3, (LPARAM)(LPINT)aWidths);

    ShowWindow(hStatusBar, SW_SHOW);
    return hStatusBar;
}


// function for painting the bitmap in part 1 of status bar
void PaintRectBitmap (hDC, hBitmap, rectX, rectY)
HDC hDC;
HBITMAP hBitmap;
LONG rectX, rectY;
{
    BITMAP bmp;
    HDC hMemoryDC;
    hMemoryDC = CreateCompatibleDC(hDC);
    GetObject(hBitmap, sizeof(BITMAP), (LPSTR) &bmp);
    SelectObject(hMemoryDC, hBitmap);
    BitBlt(hDC, rectX, rectY, bmp.bmWidth, bmp.bmHeight,
                hMemoryDC, 0, 0, SRCCOPY);
    DeleteDC(hMemoryDC);
    DeleteObject(hBitmap);
}
```

ABOUT.C

```
// ABOUT.C
#include <windows.h>
#include <windowsx.h>
#include "globals.h"
```

175

```
// procedures for ABOUT dialog box
LRESULT CALLBACK About(HWND hDlg,
                       UINT uMessage,
                       WPARAM wParam,
                       LPARAM lParam)
{
    switch (uMessage)
      {
        case WM_COMMAND:
             switch (GET_WM_COMMAND_ID(wParam,lParam))
             {
                 case IDOK:
                 case IDCANCEL:
                     {
                     EndDialog(hDlg, TRUE);
                     return(TRUE);
                     }
                     break;
             }
      }
    return FALSE;
}
```

ODSB.RC

```
#include "windows.h"
#include "globals.h"
#include <winver.h>

PART1BMP BITMAP part1.bmp

APPNAME ICON ICONFILE

RCINCLUDE ABOUT.DLG

APPNAME MENU
BEGIN
  POPUP     "&Option"
  BEGIN
    MENUITEM "&Show Status Bar",   IDM_SHOWSB
    MENUITEM "&Hide Status Bar",   IDM_HIDESB
  END
  MENUITEM "&About",   IDM_ABOUT
END
```

ABOUT.DLG

```
ABOUTDLG DIALOG DISCARDABLE  22, 17, 167, 73
STYLE DS_MODALFRAME | WS_CAPTION | WS_SYSMENU
CAPTION SZABOUT
BEGIN
    DEFPUSHBUTTON    "OK", IDOK, 132, 2, 32, 14, WS_GROUP
    ICON             SZAPPNAME,      -1, 3, 2, 18, 20
    LTEXT            SZAPPNAME,      -1, 30, 12,  50, 8
    LTEXT            SZDESCRIPTION, -1, 30, 22, 150, 8
    LTEXT            SZVERSION,      -1, 30, 32, 150, 8
    LTEXT            SZCOMPANYNAME, -1, 30, 42, 150, 8
END
```

ODSB.ICO

PART1.BMP

CASE 2-7: UP-DOWN CONTROL (SPIN BUTTONS)

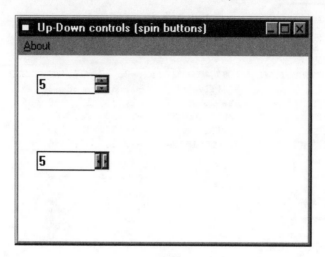

FIGURE 2-7

The *up-down common control* is like a pair of spin buttons that are used to increase/decrease a number in an edit box next to it. You can use the Windows 95 CreateUpDownControl() function to create an up-down control. However, before you do that, you shall create an edit control so that the handle of the edit box can be passed to the CreateUpDownControl() function as its "buddy" edit box.

Two up-down controls are created in this example, one vertical and one horizontal. The up-down control align to the right of its "buddy" edit boxes when the style flag is defined as UDS_ALIGNRIGHT. The default control orientation is vertical, and you can make it horizontal by specifying the style flag as UDS_HORZ. Both up-down controls send a WM_VSCROLL message to their parent window when their positions change.

GLOBALS.H

```
// GLOBALS.H - header file for global variables
//             and function prototypes

// Product identifier string definitions.
#define APPNAME         UpDown
#define ICONFILE        UpDown.ico
#define SZAPPNAME       "UpDown"
#define SZDESCRIPTION   "Up-Down controls (spin buttons)"
#define SZVERSION       "Version 1.0"
#define SZCOMPANYNAME   "\251 M&&T Books, 1994"
#define SZABOUT         "About"

// Global function prototypes.
BOOL InitApplication(HINSTANCE);
BOOL InitInstance(HINSTANCE, int);

// Callback functions called by Windows.
LRESULT CALLBACK WndProc(HWND, UINT, WPARAM, LPARAM);
LRESULT CALLBACK About(HWND, UINT, WPARAM, LPARAM);

// Menu item ID
#define IDM_ABOUT    1000

// Control ID
#define IDC_UPDOWN1 1010
#define IDC_UPDOWN2 1011
#define IDC_EDIT1    1012
#define IDC_EDIT2    1013

// Global variable declarations.
extern HINSTANCE hInst;      // The current instance handle
extern char szAppName[];     // The name of this application
extern char szTitle[];       // The title bar text
```

WINMAIN.C

```
// WINMAIN.C
#include <windows.h>
#include "globals.h"

int APIENTRY WinMain(HINSTANCE hInstance,
                     HINSTANCE hPrevInstance,
                     LPSTR lpCmdLine,
```

```
                          int nCmdShow)
{
    MSG msg;

    // register main window class
    if (!hPrevInstance)
       {
       if (!InitApplication(hInstance))
          {
          return FALSE;
          }
       }

    // create and show main window
    if (!InitInstance(hInstance, nCmdShow))
       {
       return FALSE;
       }

    // process window message
    while (GetMessage(&msg, NULL, 0, 0))
       {
          TranslateMessage(&msg);
          DispatchMessage(&msg);
       }
    return msg.wParam;
}
```

INIT.C

```
// INIT.C
#include <windows.h>
#include "globals.h"

HINSTANCE hInst;
char szAppName[] = SZAPPNAME;
char szTitle[] = SZDESCRIPTION;

// register main window class
BOOL InitApplication(HINSTANCE hInstance)
{
    WNDCLASS  wc;

    wc.style        = CS_HREDRAW | CS_VREDRAW;
    wc.lpfnWndProc  = (WNDPROC)WndProc;
    wc.cbClsExtra   = 0;
```

```
    wc.cbWndExtra    = 0;
    wc.hInstance     = hInstance;
    wc.hIcon         = LoadIcon(hInstance, szAppName);
    wc.hCursor       = LoadCursor(NULL, IDC_ARROW);
    wc.hbrBackground = (HBRUSH)(COLOR_WINDOW + 1);
    wc.lpszMenuName  = szAppName;
    wc.lpszClassName = szAppName;

    return(RegisterClass(&wc));
}

// create and show main window
BOOL InitInstance(HINSTANCE hInstance, int nCmdShow)
{
    HWND     hWnd;
    hInst = hInstance;
    hWnd = CreateWindow(szAppName, szTitle,
                    WS_OVERLAPPEDWINDOW,
                    160, 120, 320, 240,
                    NULL, NULL, hInstance, NULL);

    if (!hWnd)
        {
        return FALSE;
        }

    ShowWindow(hWnd, nCmdShow);
    UpdateWindow(hWnd);

    return TRUE;
}
```

UPDOWN.C

```
// UPDOWN.C
#include <windows.h>
#include <windowsx.h>
#include <commctrl.h>      // required for common controls
#include "globals.h"

HWND hUpDown1, hUpDown2, hEdit1, hEdit2;

LRESULT CALLBACK WndProc(HWND hWnd,
                    UINT uMessage,
                    WPARAM wParam,
                    LPARAM lParam)
{
```

```
switch (uMessage)
{
    case WM_CREATE:
        // load the common controls DLL
        InitCommonControls();

        // create a buddy edit window
        // for up-down control 1
        hEdit1 = CreateWindow("EDIT", NULL,
                            WS_BORDER | WS_CHILD |
                            WS_VISIBLE,
                            20, 20, 80, 20,
                            hWnd, (HMENU)IDC_EDIT1,
                            hInst, NULL);

        // create an up-down control for
        // hEdit1 edit box
        hUpDown1= CreateUpDownControl(
            WS_CHILD |          // window style
            WS_VISIBLE |
            UDS_ALIGNRIGHT |    // align to the right of
                                // buddy window
            UDS_SETBUDDYINT,    // sets the text of
                                // buddy window
            0, 0,               // left and top coordinate
                                // (ignored)
            0, 0,               // width and height
                                // (ignored)
            hWnd,               // parent window
            IDC_UPDOWN1,        // control ID
            hInst,              // instance
            hEdit1,             // handle of buddy window
            10, 1,              // upper and lower limit
            5                   // position of the control
            );

        // create a buddy edit window for
        // up-down control 2
        hEdit2 = CreateWindow("EDIT", NULL,
                            WS_BORDER | WS_CHILD |
                            WS_VISIBLE,
                            20, 100, 80, 20,
                            hWnd, (HMENU)IDC_EDIT2,
                            hInst, NULL);

        // create a horizontal up-down control for
        // hEdit2 edit box
```

```
        hUpDown2= CreateUpDownControl(
            WS_CHILD |          // window style
            WS_VISIBLE |
            UDS_SETBUDDYINT |   // sets the text of
                                // buddy window
            UDS_ALIGNRIGHT |    // align to the right of
                                // buddy window
            UDS_HORZ,           // horizontal style
            0, 0,               // left and top coordinate
                                // (ignored)
            0, 0,               // width and height
                                // (ignored)
            hWnd,               // parent window
            IDC_UPDOWN2,        // control ID
            hInst,              // instance
            hEdit2,             // handle of buddy window
            10, 1,              // upper and lower limit
            5                   // position of the control
            );

        break;

    case WM_COMMAND:
        switch (GET_WM_COMMAND_ID(wParam,lParam))
        {
            case IDM_ABOUT:
                // create an about dialog box
                DialogBox(hInst, "ABOUTDLG",
                        hWnd, (DLGPROC)About);
                break;

            default:
                return DefWindowProc(hWnd, uMessage,
                                    wParam, lParam);
        }
        break;

    case WM_DESTROY:
        PostQuitMessage(0);
        break;

    default:
        return DefWindowProc(hWnd, uMessage,
                            wParam, lParam);
    }
    return 0;
}
```

ABOUT.C

```
// ABOUT.C
#include <windows.h>
#include <windowsx.h>
#include "globals.h"

// procedures for ABOUT dialog box
LRESULT CALLBACK About(HWND hDlg,
                       UINT uMessage,
                       WPARAM wParam,
                       LPARAM lParam)
{
    switch (uMessage)
      {
      case WM_COMMAND:
            switch (GET_WM_COMMAND_ID(wParam,lParam))
            {
                case IDOK:
                case IDCANCEL:
                    {
                    EndDialog(hDlg, TRUE);
                    return(TRUE);
                    }
                    break;
            }
      }
    return FALSE;
}
```

UPDOWN.RC

```
#include "windows.h"
#include "globals.h"
#include <winver.h>

APPNAME ICON ICONFILE

RCINCLUDE ABOUT.DLG

APPNAME MENU
BEGIN
  MENUITEM "&About",   IDM_ABOUT
END
```

ABOUT.DLG

```
ABOUTDLG DIALOG DISCARDABLE  22, 17, 167, 73
STYLE DS_MODALFRAME | WS_CAPTION | WS_SYSMENU
CAPTION SZABOUT
BEGIN
    DEFPUSHBUTTON    "OK", IDOK, 132, 2, 32, 14, WS_GROUP
    ICON             SZAPPNAME,      -1, 3, 2, 18, 20
    LTEXT            SZAPPNAME,      -1, 30, 12,  50, 8
    LTEXT            SZDESCRIPTION, -1, 30, 22, 150, 8
    LTEXT            SZVERSION,     -1, 30, 32, 150, 8
    LTEXT            SZCOMPANYNAME, -1, 30, 42, 150, 8
END
```

UPDOWN.ICO

CASE 2-8: TAB CONTROL (WITH IMAGE LIST)

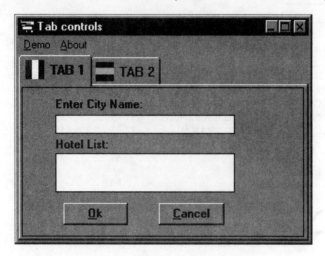

FIGURE 2-8

A tab control is like dividers in an organizer or notebook. You can create a tab control by using the `CreateWindowEx()` function and specifying the `WC_TABCONTROL` window class. If you wish to have the tabs show an image, you need to create an image list first using the Windows 95 `ImageList_Create()` function. Add images (bitmaps) to be used for the tab control into the image list. Once you create the tab control, you can add the tabs (with associated images) to it.

In this case, each tab has a dialog box associated with it. As a built-in feature, the text on the tab automatically becomes bold when it is selected (by clicking the tab). A `WM_NOTIFY` message is also sent to the control's parent window to notify it of this selection change. You can then use the Windows `ShowWindow()` function to display the associated dialog box for that tab and to hide all other dialog boxes.

GLOBALS.H

```
// GLOBALS.H - header file for global variables
//              and function prototypes

// Product identifier string definitions.
#define APPNAME        TabCtrl
#define ICONFILE       TabCtrl.ico
#define SZAPPNAME      "TabCtrl"
#define SZDESCRIPTION  "Tab controls"
#define SZVERSION      "Version 1.0"
#define SZCOMPANYNAME  "\251 M&&T Books, 1994"
#define SZABOUT        "About"

// Global function prototypes.
BOOL InitApplication(HINSTANCE);
BOOL InitInstance(HINSTANCE, int);
HWND CreateATabControl(HWND);
HIMAGELIST CreateAnImageList();

// Callback functions called by Windows.
LRESULT CALLBACK WndProc(HWND, UINT, WPARAM, LPARAM);
LRESULT CALLBACK TabDlgProc0(HWND, UINT, WPARAM, LPARAM);
LRESULT CALLBACK TabDlgProc1(HWND, UINT, WPARAM, LPARAM);
LRESULT CALLBACK About(HWND, UINT, WPARAM, LPARAM);

// Menu item ID
#define IDM_DEMO    1000
#define IDM_ABOUT   1001

// Dialog box ID
#define IDD_TAB1DLG 1050
#define IDD_TAB2DLG 1051

// Dialog box control ID
#define IDC_TAB1_EDIT 1100
#define IDC_TAB1_LIST 1101
#define IDC_TAB2_EDIT 1102
#define IDC_TAB2_LIST 1103

// String table ID
#define IDS_TIPS_TAB1 1200
#define IDS_TIPS_TAB2 1203

// Child window ID
#define ID_TC       1400
```

```c
// Global variable declarations.
extern HINSTANCE hInst;        // The current instance handle
extern char szAppName[];       // The name of this application
extern char szTitle[];         // The title bar text
extern HWND hWnd, hTabCtrl, hTabDlg0, hTabDlg1;
```

WINMAIN.C

```c
// WINMAIN.C
#include <windows.h>
#include <commctrl.h>
#include "globals.h"

int APIENTRY WinMain(HINSTANCE hInstance,
                     HINSTANCE hPrevInstance,
                     LPSTR lpCmdLine,
                     int nCmdShow)
{
    MSG msg;

    // register main window class
    if (!hPrevInstance)
        {
        if (!InitApplication(hInstance))
            {
            return FALSE;
            }
        }

    // create and show main window
    if (!InitInstance(hInstance, nCmdShow))
        {
        return FALSE;
        }

    // process window message
    while (GetMessage(&msg, NULL, 0, 0))
        {
            TranslateMessage(&msg);
            DispatchMessage(&msg);
        }
    return msg.wParam;
}
```

INIT.C

```c
// INIT.C
#include <windows.h>
#include <commctrl.h>
#include "globals.h"

HINSTANCE hInst;
char szAppName[] = SZAPPNAME;
char szTitle[] = SZDESCRIPTION;

// register main window class
BOOL InitApplication(HINSTANCE hInstance)
{
    WNDCLASS  wc;

    wc.style         = CS_HREDRAW | CS_VREDRAW;
    wc.lpfnWndProc   = (WNDPROC)WndProc;
    wc.cbClsExtra    = 0;
    wc.cbWndExtra    = 0;
    wc.hInstance     = hInstance;
    wc.hIcon         = LoadIcon(hInstance, szAppName);
    wc.hCursor       = LoadCursor(NULL, IDC_ARROW);
    wc.hbrBackground = (HBRUSH)(COLOR_WINDOW + 1);
    wc.lpszMenuName  = szAppName;
    wc.lpszClassName = szAppName;

    return(RegisterClass(&wc));
}

// create and show main window
BOOL InitInstance(HINSTANCE hInstance, int nCmdShow)
{
    HWND    hWnd;
    hInst = hInstance;
    hWnd = CreateWindow(szAppName, szTitle,
                        WS_OVERLAPPEDWINDOW,
                        160, 120, 320, 240,
                        NULL, NULL, hInstance, NULL);

    if (!hWnd)
        {
        return FALSE;
        }

    ShowWindow(hWnd, nCmdShow);
    UpdateWindow(hWnd);
```

```
    return TRUE;
}
```

TABCTRL.C

```
// TABCTRL.C
#include <windows.h>
#include <windowsx.h>
#include <commctrl.h>      // required for common controls
#include "globals.h"

HWND hTabCtrl, hTabDlg0, hTabDlg1;
HIMAGELIST hIML;
int i, iTab, iImage0, iImage1;
NMHDR FAR *pnmhdr;
DLGPROC lpProcTabDlg0;
DLGPROC lpProcTabDlg1;

LRESULT CALLBACK WndProc(HWND hWnd,
                         UINT uMessage,
                         WPARAM wParam,
                         LPARAM lParam)
{
    UINT ControlID;

    switch (uMessage)
    {
        case WM_CREATE:

            // load the common controls DLL
            InitCommonControls();

            // create an image list for tab control
            hIML = CreateAnImageList();
            break;

        case WM_COMMAND:
            switch(GET_WM_COMMAND_ID(wParam, lParam))
            {
                case IDM_DEMO:
                    // create a Tab control
                    hTabCtrl = CreateATabControl(hWnd);
                    break;
```

```
            case IDM_ABOUT:
                 // create an about dialog box
                 DialogBox(hInst, "ABOUTDLG",
                          hWnd, (DLGPROC)About);
                 break;

         default:
              return DefWindowProc(hWnd, uMessage,
                                   wParam, lParam);
      }
      break;

   case WM_NOTIFY:
      pnmhdr = (NMHDR FAR *)lParam;
      switch(pnmhdr->code)
      {
          // process tab control message
          case TCN_SELCHANGE:
               iTab = TabCtrl_GetCurSel(
                       (HWND)pnmhdr->hwndFrom);
               switch(iTab)
               {
                 case 0:
                    ShowWindow(hTabDlg1, SW_HIDE);
                    ShowWindow(hTabDlg0, SW_SHOW);
                    break;

                 case 1:
                    ShowWindow(hTabDlg0, SW_HIDE);
                    ShowWindow(hTabDlg1, SW_SHOW);
                    break;
               }
               break;

          // process tool tip control message
          case TTN_NEEDTEXT:
               {
               LPTOOLTIPTEXT lpttt;

               lpttt = (LPTOOLTIPTEXT)lParam;
               lpttt -> hinst = hInst;
               lpttt->lpszText =
                       MAKEINTRESOURCE(IDS_TIPS_TAB1);
               }
               break;

          default: break;
```

```
                      }
                      break;

              case WM_DESTROY:
                      FreeProcInstance(lpProcTabDlg0);
                      FreeProcInstance(lpProcTabDlg1);
                      PostQuitMessage(0);
                      break;

              default:
                      return DefWindowProc(hWnd, uMessage,
                                             wParam, lParam);
      }
      return 0;
}

// function for creating an image list
HIMAGELIST CreateAnImageList()
{
HIMAGELIST hIML;
HBITMAP hBitmap;

      // create an image list
      hIML = ImageList_Create(20, 20, FALSE, 2, 0);

      // add two bitmaps to the image list
      hBitmap = LoadBitmap(hInst, "TAB1BMP");
      iImage0 = ImageList_Add(hIML, hBitmap, (HBITMAP)NULL);

      hBitmap = LoadBitmap(hInst, "TAB2BMP");
      iImage1 = ImageList_Add(hIML, hBitmap, (HBITMAP)NULL);

      return hIML;
}

// function for creating a Tab control
HWND CreateATabControl(HWND hWnd)
{
      HWND hTabCtrl; // handle for tool bar
      RECT rc;
      TC_ITEM tcItem[2];

      GetClientRect(hWnd, &rc);

      // create a tab control with tooltips
      hTabCtrl = CreateWindowEx(
              0,                      // no extended style
```

```
            WC_TABCONTROL,       // class name for
                                 // tab control
             (LPSTR)NULL,        // no caption (title)
            WS_CHILD |           // child window
            WS_CLIPSIBLINGS |    //
            WS_VISIBLE |         // initial visiblea
            TCS_TOOLTIPS,        // create tooltip
                                 // control
            rc.left, rc.top,     // position
            rc.right, rc.bottom, // width and height
            hWnd,                // parent window
             (HMENU)ID_TC,       // child window
                                 // identifier
            hInst,               // instance
            NULL                 // no WM_CREATE
                                 //    parameter
         );

// Add tabs
tcItem[0].mask = TCIF_TEXT | TCIF_IMAGE;
tcItem[0].pszText = "TAB 1";
tcItem[0].iImage = iImage0;
SendMessage(hTabCtrl, TCM_INSERTITEM, (WPARAM)(int)0,
            (LPARAM)(const TC_ITEM FAR*)&tcItem[0]);

tcItem[1].mask = TCIF_TEXT | TCIF_IMAGE;
tcItem[1].pszText = "TAB 2";
tcItem[1].iImage = iImage1;
SendMessage(hTabCtrl, TCM_INSERTITEM, (WPARAM)(int)1,
            (LPARAM)(const TC_ITEM FAR*)&tcItem[1]);

// Set image list
SendMessage(hTabCtrl, TCM_SETIMAGELIST, (WPARAM)0,
                    (LPARAM)(HIMAGELIST)hIML);

// create dialog box for each tab
lpProcTabDlg0 = MakeProcInstance(TabDlgProc0, hInst);
hTabDlg0 = CreateDialog(hInst,
                    MAKEINTRESOURCE(IDD_TAB1DLG),
                    hWnd, lpProcTabDlg0);

lpProcTabDlg1 = MakeProcInstance(TabDlgProc1, hInst);
hTabDlg1 = CreateDialog(hInst,
                    MAKEINTRESOURCE(IDD_TAB2DLG),
                    hWnd, lpProcTabDlg1);

ShowWindow(hTabDlg0, SW_SHOW);
```

```
        ShowWindow(hTabDlg1, SW_HIDE);

        return hTabCtrl;
    }
```

TABDLG.C

```c
// TABDLG.C
#include <windows.h>
#include <windowsx.h>
#include <commctrl.h>
#include "globals.h"

HWND hTabCtrl;

// procedures for dialog box associate with first tab
LRESULT CALLBACK TabDlgProc0(HWND hDlg,
                             UINT uMessage,
                             WPARAM wParam,
                             LPARAM lParam)
{
    switch (uMessage)
      {
        case WM_COMMAND:
            switch (GET_WM_COMMAND_ID(wParam,lParam))
            {
                case IDOK:
                    MessageBeep(0);
                    break;

                case IDCANCEL:
                    {
                    DestroyWindow(hDlg);
                    DestroyWindow(hTabCtrl);
                    return(TRUE);
                    }
                    break;
            }
        }
    return FALSE;
}

// procedures for dialog box associate with second tab
LRESULT CALLBACK TabDlgProc1(HWND hDlg,
                             UINT uMessage,
                             WPARAM wParam,
```

```
                              LPARAM lParam)
{
    switch (uMessage)
      {
        case WM_COMMAND:
              switch (GET_WM_COMMAND_ID(wParam,lParam))
              {
                  case IDOK:
                      MessageBeep(0);
                      break;

                  case IDCANCEL:
                      {
                      DestroyWindow(hDlg);
                      DestroyWindow(hTabCtrl);
                      return(TRUE);
                      }
                      break;

              }
      }
    return FALSE;
}
```

ABOUT.C

```
// ABOUT.C
#include <windows.h>
#include <windowsx.h>
#include "globals.h"

// procedures for ABOUT dialog box
LRESULT CALLBACK About(HWND hDlg,
                       UINT uMessage,
                       WPARAM wParam,
                       LPARAM lParam)
{
    switch (uMessage)
      {
        case WM_COMMAND:
              switch (GET_WM_COMMAND_ID(wParam,lParam))
              {
                  case IDOK:
                  case IDCANCEL:
                      {
                      EndDialog(hDlg, TRUE);
                      return(TRUE);
```

```
                    }
                break;
            }
        }
    return FALSE;
}
```

TABCTRL.RC

```
#include "windows.h"
#include "globals.h"
#include <winver.h>

TAB1BMP BITMAP tab1.bmp
TAB2BMP BITMAP tab2.bmp

APPNAME ICON ICONFILE

RCINCLUDE ABOUT.DLG
RCINCLUDE TAB1.DLG
RCINCLUDE TAB2.DLG

APPNAME MENU
BEGIN
  MENUITEM "&Demo",   IDM_DEMO
  MENUITEM "&About", IDM_ABOUT
END

STRINGTABLE
BEGIN
    IDS_TIPS_TAB1, "Demo only, do nothing"
    IDS_TIPS_TAB2, "Demo only, do nothing"
END
```

TAB1.DLG

```
IDD_TAB1DLG DIALOG 4, 21, 172, 95
STYLE WS_CHILD | WS_VISIBLE | WS_BORDER
FONT 8, "MS Sans Serif"
BEGIN
    LTEXT       "Enter City Name:", -1, 20, 6, 59, 10
    EDITTEXT    IDC_TAB1_EDIT, 20, 17, 110, 12,
                ES_AUTOHSCROLL
    LTEXT       "Hotel List:", -1, 20, 32, 37, 8
```

```
        LISTBOX      IDC_TAB1_LIST, 20, 42, 110, 32,
                     LBS_SORT | WS_VSCROLL | WS_TABSTOP
        PUSHBUTTON   "&Ok", IDOK, 25, 74, 40, 14
        PUSHBUTTON   "&Cancel", IDCANCEL, 84, 74, 40, 14
    END
```

TAB2.DLG

```
    IDD_TAB2DLG DIALOG 4, 21, 172, 95
    STYLE WS_CHILD | WS_VISIBLE | WS_BORDER
    FONT 8, "MS Sans Serif"
    BEGIN
        LTEXT        "Enter District Name:", -1, 20, 6, 80, 10
        EDITTEXT     IDC_TAB2_EDIT, 20, 17, 110, 12,
                     ES_AUTOHSCROLL
        LTEXT        "Restaurant List:", -1, 20, 32, 80, 8
        LISTBOX      IDC_TAB2_LIST, 20, 42, 110, 32,
                     LBS_SORT | WS_VSCROLL | WS_TABSTOP
        PUSHBUTTON   "&Ok", IDOK, 25, 74, 40, 14
        PUSHBUTTON   "&Cancel", IDCANCEL, 84, 74, 40, 14
    END
```

ABOUT.DLG

```
    ABOUTDLG DIALOG DISCARDABLE  22, 17, 167, 73
    STYLE DS_MODALFRAME | WS_CAPTION | WS_SYSMENU
    CAPTION SZABOUT
    BEGIN
        DEFPUSHBUTTON   OK", IDOK, 132, 2, 32, 14, WS_GROUP
        ICON            SZAPPNAME,      -1, 3, 2, 18, 20
        LTEXT           SZAPPNAME,      -1, 30, 12, 50, 8
        LTEXT           SZDESCRIPTION, -1, 30, 22, 150, 8
        LTEXT           SZVERSION,      -1, 30, 32, 150, 8
        LTEXT           SZCOMPANYNAME, -1, 30, 42, 150, 8
    END
```

TABCTRL.ICO

TAB1.BMP

TAB2.BMP

CHAPTER THREE

CUSTOM CONTROLS

CASE 3-1: RECTANGULAR SPIN BUTTONS

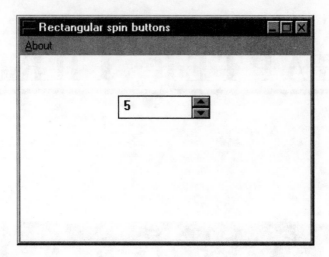

FIGURE 3-1

You can use the common control function in Windows 95 to create a standard spin button as shown in Case 2-7. However, you can also create your own spin buttons and have more control over the appearance and functions of the spin buttons. This case and the following one show you how to do this.

This case is an example of *rectangular spin buttons*. The two spin buttons next to the spin number edit box are implemented as two owner-draw push buttons. Please see Cases 1-1 and 1-2 for details about owner-draw push buttons. In this case, the spin number will increase/decrease by one when the spin-up/spin-down button is pushed. Please see Case 3-2 for an alternative (simpler) way to design spin buttons.

GLOBALS.H

```
// GLOBALS.H - header file for global variables
//            and function prototypes

// Product identifier string definitions.
#define APPNAME       SpinBtn
#define ICONFILE      SpinBtn.ico
#define SZAPPNAME     "SpinBtn"
#define SZDESCRIPTION "Rectangular spin buttons"
#define SZVERSION     "Version 1.0"
#define SZCOMPANYNAME "\251 M&&T Books, 1994"
#define SZABOUT       "About"

// Global function prototypes.
BOOL InitApplication(HINSTANCE);
BOOL InitInstance(HINSTANCE, int);
void PaintBitmap(HDC, HBITMAP);
void DrawButtonUp(HWND, HDC, int);
void DrawButtonDown(HWND, HDC, int);

// Callback functions called by Windows.
LRESULT CALLBACK WndProc(HWND, UINT, WPARAM, LPARAM);
LRESULT CALLBACK About(HWND, UINT, WPARAM, LPARAM);

// Menu item ID
#define IDM_ABOUT     100

// Control ID
#define IDC_SPINUP    101
#define IDC_SPINDOWN 102
#define IDC_EDIT      103

// Global variable declarations.
extern HINSTANCE hInst;     // The current instance handle
extern char szAppName[];    // The name of this application
extern char szTitle[];      // The title bar text
```

WINMAIN.C

```
// WINMAIN.C
#include <windows.h>
#include "globals.h"

int APIENTRY WinMain(HINSTANCE hInstance,
```

```
                    HINSTANCE hPrevInstance,
                    LPSTR lpCmdLine,
                    int nCmdShow)
{
    MSG msg;

    // register main window class
    if (!hPrevInstance)
        {
        if (!InitApplication(hInstance))
            {
            return FALSE;
            }
        }

    // create and show main window
    if (!InitInstance(hInstance, nCmdShow))
        {
        return FALSE;
        }

    // process window message
    while (GetMessage(&msg, NULL, 0, 0))
        {
            TranslateMessage(&msg);
            DispatchMessage(&msg);
        }
    return msg.wParam;
}
```

INIT.C

```
// INIT.C
#include <windows.h>
#include "globals.h"

HINSTANCE hInst;
char szAppName[] = SZAPPNAME;
char szTitle[] = SZDESCRIPTION;

// register main window class
BOOL InitApplication(HINSTANCE hInstance)
{
    WNDCLASS  wc;

    wc.style        = CS_HREDRAW | CS_VREDRAW;
```

```
    wc.lpfnWndProc   = (WNDPROC)WndProc;
    wc.cbClsExtra    = 0;
    wc.cbWndExtra    = 0;
    wc.hInstance     = hInstance;
    wc.hIcon         = LoadIcon(hInstance, szAppName);
    wc.hCursor       = LoadCursor(NULL, IDC_ARROW);
    wc.hbrBackground = (HBRUSH)(COLOR_WINDOW + 1);
    wc.lpszMenuName  = szAppName;
    wc.lpszClassName = szAppName;

    return(RegisterClass(&wc));
}

// create and show main window
BOOL InitInstance(HINSTANCE hInstance, int nCmdShow)
{
    HWND    hWnd;
    hInst = hInstance;
    hWnd = CreateWindow(szAppName, szTitle,
                        WS_OVERLAPPEDWINDOW,
                        160, 120, 320, 240,
                        NULL, NULL, hInstance, NULL);

    if (!hWnd)
        {
        return FALSE;
        }

    ShowWindow(hWnd, nCmdShow);
    UpdateWindow(hWnd);

    return TRUE;
}
```

SPINBTN.C

```
// SPINBTN.C
#include <windows.h>
#include <windowsx.h>
#include "globals.h"

HWND hSpinUpBtn, hSpinDownBtn, hEditBox;
HBITMAP hBitmap;
static int SpinNumber = 5;
static char EditText[3];
```

```
LRESULT CALLBACK WndProc(HWND hWnd,
                         UINT uMessage,
                         WPARAM wParam,
                         LPARAM lParam)
{
    LPDRAWITEMSTRUCT lpdis;
    int ButtonID;

    switch (uMessage)
    {
        case WM_CREATE:
            // create an edit box to display
            // the spin number
            hEditBox = CreateWindow("EDIT", "",
                        WS_BORDER | WS_CHILD | WS_VISIBLE,
                        106, 42, 80, 24,
                        hWnd, IDC_EDIT, hInst, NULL);

            // create an owner-draw spin-up push button
            // next to the spin number edit box
            hSpinUpBtn = CreateWindow("BUTTON", "",
                        BS_OWNERDRAW | WS_CHILD |
                        WS_VISIBLE,
                        185, 42, 20, 12,
                        hWnd, IDC_SPINUP, hInst, NULL);

            // create an ownerdraw spin-down push button
            // next to the spin number edit box
            hSpinDownBtn = CreateWindow("BUTTON", "",
                        BS_OWNERDRAW | WS_CHILD |
                        WS_VISIBLE,
                        185, 54, 20, 12,
                        hWnd, IDC_SPINDOWN, hInst, NULL);

            // display current spin number in the edit box
            sprintf(EditText, "%2d", SpinNumber);
            SetWindowText(hEditBox, EditText);
            break;

        case WM_DRAWITEM:
            // draw the owner-draw spin buttons
            lpdis = (LPDRAWITEMSTRUCT) lParam;
            if(lpdis->itemState & ODS_SELECTED)
                // draw a "down" button when selected
                DrawButtonDown(hInst,
                            lpdis->hDC, lpdis->CtlID);
            else
```

```
                    // draw an "up" button when not selected
            DrawButtonUp(hInst,
                        lpdis->hDC, lpdis->CtlID);
        break;

    case WM_COMMAND:
        switch (GET_WM_COMMAND_ID(wParam,lParam))
        {
            case IDM_ABOUT:
                    // create an about dialog box
                DialogBox(hInst, "ABOUTDLG",
                        hWnd, (DLGPROC)About);
                break;

            case IDC_SPINUP:
                    // beep when the spin number has
                    // reached the upper limit
                if(SpinNumber == 10) {
                        MessageBeep(0);
                        break; }

                    // increase the spin number by one when
                    // spin-up button was pushed
                SpinNumber += 1;

                    // display the new spin number
                sprintf(EditText, "%2d", SpinNumber);
                SetWindowText(hEditBox, EditText);
                break;

            case IDC_SPINDOWN:
                    // beep when the spin number has
                    // reached the lower limit
                if(SpinNumber ==  0) {
                        MessageBeep(0);
                        break; }

                    // decrease the spin number by one when
                    // spin-down button was pushed
                SpinNumber -= 1;

                    // display the new spin number
                sprintf(EditText, "%2d", SpinNumber);
                SetWindowText(hEditBox, EditText);
                break;

            default:
```

```
                       return DefWindowProc(hWnd, uMessage,
                                             wParam, lParam);
            }
            break;

        case WM_DESTROY:
            PostQuitMessage(0);
            break;

        default:
            return DefWindowProc(hWnd, uMessage,
                                 wParam, lParam);
    }
    return 0;
}


// function for painting the bitmap on ownerdraw buttons
void PaintBitmap (hDC, hBitmap)
HDC hDC;
HBITMAP hBitmap;
{
    BITMAP bmp;
    HDC hMemoryDC;
    hMemoryDC = CreateCompatibleDC(hDC);
    GetObject(hBitmap, sizeof(BITMAP), (LPSTR) &bmp) ;
    SelectObject(hMemoryDC, hBitmap) ;
    BitBlt(hDC, 0, 0, bmp.bmWidth, bmp.bmHeight,
                hMemoryDC, 0, 0, SRCCOPY);
    DeleteDC(hMemoryDC) ;
    DeleteObject(hBitmap) ;
}


// function for loading the bitmap for painting the
// non-selected ownerdraw buttons
void DrawButtonUp (hInstance, hDC, ButtonID)
HANDLE hInstance;
HDC hDC;
int ButtonID;
{
switch(ButtonID){
    case IDC_SPINUP:
        hBitmap = LoadBitmap (hInstance, "UpSpinUp");
        break;

    case IDC_SPINDOWN:
        hBitmap = LoadBitmap (hInstance, "DownSpinUp");
        break;
```

206

```
        }
    PaintBitmap(hDC, hBitmap);
}


// function for loading the bitmap for painting the
// selected ownerdraw buttons
void DrawButtonDown (hInstance, hDC, ButtonID)
HANDLE hInstance;
HDC hDC;
int ButtonID;
{
switch(ButtonID){
    case IDC_SPINUP:
        hBitmap = LoadBitmap (hInstance, "UpSpinDown");
        break;

    case IDC_SPINDOWN:
        hBitmap = LoadBitmap (hInstance, "DownSpinDown");
        break;
    }
    PaintBitmap(hDC, hBitmap);
}
```

ABOUT.C

```
// ABOUT.C
#include <windows.h>
#include <windowsx.h>
#include "globals.h"


// procedures for ABOUT dialog box
LRESULT CALLBACK About(HWND hDlg,
                       UINT uMessage,
                       WPARAM wParam,
                       LPARAM lParam)

{
    switch (uMessage)
      {
        case WM_COMMAND:
            switch (GET_WM_COMMAND_ID(wParam,lParam))
            {
                case IDOK:
                case IDCANCEL:
                    {
                    EndDialog(hDlg, TRUE);
                    return(TRUE);
```

```
                        }
                        break;
                }
        }
    return FALSE;
}
```

SPINBTN.RC

```
#include "windows.h"
#include "globals.h"
#include <winver.h>

UpSpinUp      BITMAP btn1up.bmp
UpSpinDown    BITMAP btn1down.bmp
DownSpinUp    BITMAP btn2up.bmp
DownSpinDown  BITMAP btn2down.bmp

APPNAME ICON ICONFILE

RCINCLUDE ABOUT.DLG

APPNAME MENU
BEGIN
    MENUITEM "&About", IDM_ABOUT
END
```

ABOUT.DLG

```
ABOUTDLG DIALOG DISCARDABLE  22, 17, 167, 73
STYLE DS_MODALFRAME | WS_CAPTION | WS_SYSMENU
CAPTION SZABOUT
BEGIN
    DEFPUSHBUTTON   "OK", IDOK, 132, 2, 32, 14, WS_GROUP
    ICON            SZAPPNAME,      -1, 3, 2, 18, 20
    LTEXT           SZAPPNAME,      -1, 30, 12,  50, 8
    LTEXT           SZDESCRIPTION, -1, 30, 22, 150, 8
    LTEXT           SZVERSION,      -1, 30, 32, 150, 8
    LTEXT           SZCOMPANYNAME, -1, 30, 42, 150, 8
END
```

SPINBTN.ICO

BTN1UP.BMP

BTN1DOWN.BMP

BTN2UP.BMP

BTN2DOWN.BMP

CASE 3-2: TRIANGULAR SPIN BUTTONS

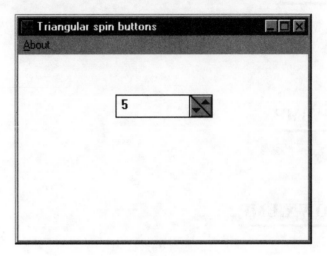

FIGURE 3-2

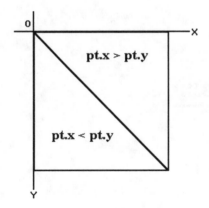

FIGURE 3-2A

T his example presents *triangular spin buttons* and is so doing, demonstrates an alternative way to design the spin buttons. See Case 3-1 for another method. In this case, you need only one owner-draw button to change the spin number displayed in the edit box. When the spin button is pushed, the program saves the current cursor position as (pt.x, pt.y). This cursor position is then converted from screen coordinates into spin button client coordinates (spin button local coordinates) using the Windows function ScreenToClient().

As shown in Figure 3-2a, if the cursor position is inside the upper-right triangle (*i.e.,* pt.x > pt.y) of the spin button, the bSpinUp flag is set to 1. If the cursor position is inside the lower-left triangle (*i.e.,* pt.x < pt.y) of the spin button, the bSpinUp flag is set to 0. The program then draws a pushed spin button according to the bSpinUp flag. If the bSpinUp flag is 1, the upper-right triangle of the spin button is drawn pushed down. If the bSpinUp flag is 0, the lower-left triangle of the spin button is drawn pushed down. The spin number is then changed according to the value of bSpinUp flag.

Please see Case 3-3 for a more sophisticated example. Please see Cases 1-1 and 1-2 for details about owner-draw push buttons.

GLOBALS.H

```
// GLOBALS.H - header file for global variables
//             and function prototypes

// Product identifier string definitions.
#define APPNAME        SpinBtn2
#define ICONFILE       SpinBtn2.ico
#define SZAPPNAME      "SpinBtn2"
#define SZDESCRIPTION  "Triangular spin buttons"
#define SZVERSION      "Version 1.0"
#define SZCOMPANYNAME  "\251 M&&T Books, 1994"
#define SZABOUT        "About"

// Global function prototypes.
BOOL InitApplication(HINSTANCE);
BOOL InitInstance(HINSTANCE, int);
void PaintBitmap(HDC, HBITMAP);
void DrawButtonUp(HWND, HDC, int);
void DrawButtonDown(HWND, HDC, int);

// Callback functions called by Windows.
LRESULT CALLBACK WndProc(HWND, UINT, WPARAM, LPARAM);
```

```
LRESULT CALLBACK About(HWND, UINT, WPARAM, LPARAM);

// Menu item ID
#define IDM_ABOUT    100

// Control ID
#define IDC_SPIN     101
#define IDC_EDIT     102

// Global variable declarations.
extern HINSTANCE hInst;        // The current instance handle
extern char szAppName[];       // The name of this application
extern char szTitle[];         // The title bar text
```

WINMAIN.C

```
// WINMAIN.C
#include <windows.h>
#include "globals.h"

int APIENTRY WinMain(HINSTANCE hInstance,
                     HINSTANCE hPrevInstance,
                     LPSTR lpCmdLine,
                     int nCmdShow)
{
    MSG msg;

    // register main window class
    if (!hPrevInstance)
        {
        if (!InitApplication(hInstance))
            {
            return FALSE;
            }
        }

    // create and show main window
    if (!InitInstance(hInstance, nCmdShow))
        {
        return FALSE;
        }

    // process window message
    while (GetMessage(&msg, NULL, 0, 0))
        {
            TranslateMessage(&msg);
```

```
            DispatchMessage(&msg);
        }
    return msg.wParam;
}
```

INIT.C

```
// INIT.C
#include <windows.h>
#include "globals.h"

HINSTANCE hInst;
char szAppName[] = SZAPPNAME;
char szTitle[] = SZDESCRIPTION;

// register main window class
BOOL InitApplication(HINSTANCE hInstance)
{
    WNDCLASS  wc;

    wc.style         = CS_HREDRAW | CS_VREDRAW;
    wc.lpfnWndProc   = (WNDPROC)WndProc;
    wc.cbClsExtra    = 0;
    wc.cbWndExtra    = 0;
    wc.hInstance     = hInstance;
    wc.hIcon         = LoadIcon(hInstance, szAppName);
    wc.hCursor       = LoadCursor(NULL, IDC_ARROW);
    wc.hbrBackground = (HBRUSH)(COLOR_WINDOW + 1);
    wc.lpszMenuName  = szAppName;
    wc.lpszClassName = szAppName;

    return(RegisterClass(&wc));
}

// create and show main window
BOOL InitInstance(HINSTANCE hInstance, int nCmdShow)
{
    HWND    hWnd;
    hInst = hInstance;
    hWnd = CreateWindow(szAppName, szTitle,
                    WS_OVERLAPPEDWINDOW,
                    160, 120, 320, 240,
                    NULL, NULL, hInstance, NULL);

    if (!hWnd)
        {
```

```
        return FALSE;
        }

    ShowWindow(hWnd, nCmdShow);
    UpdateWindow(hWnd);

    return TRUE;
}
```

SPINBTN2.C

```
// SPINBTN2.C
#include <windows.h>
#include <windowsx.h>
#include <stdio.h>
#include "globals.h"

HWND hSpinBtn, hEditBox;
HBITMAP hBitmap;
UINT SpinNumber = 5;
char EditText[3];
static BOOL bSpinUp;

LRESULT CALLBACK WndProc(HWND hWnd,
                         UINT uMessage,
                         WPARAM wParam,
                         LPARAM lParam)
{
    LPDRAWITEMSTRUCT lpdis;
    POINT pt;

    switch (uMessage)
    {
        case WM_CREATE:
            // create a spin number edit box
            hEditBox = CreateWindow("EDIT", "",
                    WS_BORDER | WS_CHILD | WS_VISIBLE,
                    106, 42, 80, 24,
                    hWnd, IDC_EDIT, hInst, NULL);

            // create an owner-draw spin button
            hSpinBtn = CreateWindow("BUTTON", "",
                    BS_OWNERDRAW | WS_CHILD |
                    WS_VISIBLE,
                    185, 42, 25, 24,
                    hWnd, IDC_SPIN, hInst, NULL);
```

```
                // display the current spin number in
                // edit box
                sprintf(EditText, "%2d", SpinNumber);
                SetWindowText(hEditBox, EditText);
                break;

    case WM_DRAWITEM:
                // save the cursor position as
                // (pt.x, pt.y) when the spin button
                // was pushed
                GetCursorPos(&pt);

                // convert the cursor position from screen
                // coordinate into client coordinate
                ScreenToClient(hSpinBtn, &pt);

                // if the cursor position is in the
                // upper right triangle
                // set the bSpinUp flag to 1
                if(pt.x > pt.y) bSpinUp = TRUE;

                // if the cursor position is in the
                // lower left triangle
                // set the bSpinUp flag to 0
                if(pt.x < pt.y) bSpinUp = FALSE;

                lpdis = (LPDRAWITEMSTRUCT) lParam;
                if(lpdis->itemState & ODS_SELECTED)
                    // if bSpinUp flag is TRUE -
                    // draw an upper-right down spin button
                    // if bSpinUp flag is FALSE -
                    // draw a lower-left down spin button
                    DrawButtonDown(hInst,
                            lpdis->hDC, lpdis->CtlID);
                else
                    // draw an up push button if not selected
                    DrawButtonUp(hInst,
                            lpdis->hDC, lpdis->CtlID);
                break;

    case WM_COMMAND:
                switch (GET_WM_COMMAND_ID(wParam,lParam))
                {
                    case IDM_ABOUT:
                        // create an about dialog box
                        DialogBox(hInst, "ABOUTDLG",
```

```
                               hWnd, (DLGPROC)About);
                break;

            case IDC_SPIN:

                if(bSpinUp){
                        // beep if spin number already
                        // reach the upper limit
                        if(SpinNumber == 10) {
                                MessageBeep(0); break; }
                        // increase the spin number
                        // by one
                        SpinNumber += 1; }

                if(!bSpinUp){
                        // beep if spin number already
                        // reach the lower limit
                        if(SpinNumber == 0) {
                                MessageBeep(0); break; }
                        // decrease the spin number
                        // by one
                        SpinNumber -= 1; }

                    // display the new spin number
                    sprintf(EditText, "%2d", SpinNumber);
                    SetWindowText(hEditBox, EditText);
                    break;

                default:
                    return DefWindowProc(hWnd, uMessage,
                                         wParam, lParam);
            }
            break;

        case WM_DESTROY:
            PostQuitMessage(0);
            break;

        default:
            return DefWindowProc(hWnd, uMessage,
                                 wParam, lParam);
    }
    return 0;
}

// function for painting the bitmap on
// owner-draw push buttons
```

```
void PaintBitmap (hDC, hBitmap)
HDC hDC;
HBITMAP hBitmap;
{
    BITMAP bmp;
    HDC hMemoryDC;
    hMemoryDC = CreateCompatibleDC(hDC);
    GetObject(hBitmap, sizeof(BITMAP), (LPSTR) &bmp) ;
    SelectObject(hMemoryDC, hBitmap) ;
    BitBlt(hDC, 0, 0, bmp.bmWidth, bmp.bmHeight,
                hMemoryDC, 0, 0, SRCCOPY);
    DeleteDC(hMemoryDC) ;
    DeleteObject(hBitmap) ;
}


// function for loading the bitmap for spin button
// when not selected
void DrawButtonUp (hInstance, hDC, ButtonID)
HANDLE hInstance;
HDC hDC;
int ButtonID;
{
switch(ButtonID){
case IDC_SPIN:
    hBitmap = LoadBitmap (hInstance, "UpUp");
    break;
    }
    PaintBitmap(hDC, hBitmap);
}


// function for loading the bitmap for spin button
// when selected
void DrawButtonDown (hInstance, hDC, ButtonID)
HANDLE hInstance;
HDC hDC;
int ButtonID;
{
switch(ButtonID){
case IDC_SPIN:
    if(bSpinUp)
            hBitmap = LoadBitmap (hInstance, "DownUp");
    else
            hBitmap = LoadBitmap (hInstance, "UpDown");
    break;
    }
    PaintBitmap(hDC, hBitmap);
}
```

217

ABOUT.C

```
// ABOUT.C
#include <windows.h>
#include <windowsx.h>
#include "globals.h"

// procedures for ABOUT dialog box
LRESULT CALLBACK About(HWND hDlg,
                       UINT uMessage,
                       WPARAM wParam,
                       LPARAM lParam)
{
    switch (uMessage)
      {
        case WM_COMMAND:
            switch (GET_WM_COMMAND_ID(wParam,lParam))
            {
                case IDOK:
                case IDCANCEL:
                    {
                    EndDialog(hDlg, TRUE);
                    return(TRUE);
                    }
                    break;
            }
      }
    return FALSE;
}
```

SPINBTN2.RC

```
#include "windows.h"
#include "globals.h"
#include <winver.h>

UpUp      BITMAP upup.bmp
UpDown    BITMAP updown.bmp
DownUp    BITMAP downup.bmp

APPNAME ICON ICONFILE

RCINCLUDE ABOUT.DLG

APPNAME MENU
BEGIN
  MENUITEM "&About",      IDM_ABOUT
END
```

ABOUT.DLG

```
ABOUTDLG DIALOG DISCARDABLE  22, 17, 167, 73
STYLE DS_MODALFRAME | WS_CAPTION | WS_SYSMENU
CAPTION SZABOUT
BEGIN
    DEFPUSHBUTTON    "OK", IDOK, 132, 2, 32, 14, WS_GROUP
    ICON             SZAPPNAME,      -1, 3, 2, 18, 20
    LTEXT            SZAPPNAME,      -1, 30, 12,  50, 8
    LTEXT            SZDESCRIPTION,  -1, 30, 22, 150, 8
    LTEXT            SZVERSION,      -1, 30, 32, 150, 8
    LTEXT            SZCOMPANYNAME,  -1, 30, 42, 150, 8
END
```

SPINBTN2.ICO

UPUP.BMP

UPDOWN.BMP

DOWNUP.BMP

CASE 3-3: DIRECTION BUTTONS

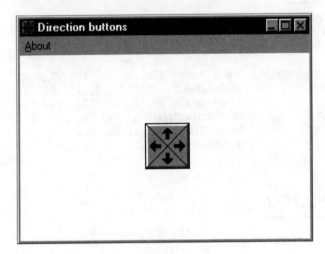

FIGURE 3-3

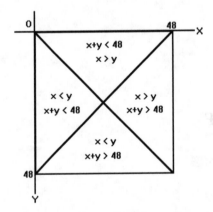

FIGURE 3-3A

This example demonstrates a technique similar to that discussed in Case 3-2 to design a *direction button*. As with Case 3-2, you need only one owner-draw direction button to change directions.

Although both this case and Case 3-2 rely on only one button, the button is subdivided into four triangular areas in this case (instead of two, as in the previous case). When the direction button is pushed, the program saves the current cursor position as (pt.x, pt.y). This cursor position is then converted from screen coordinates into direction button client coordinates (direction button local coordinates) using the Windows function ScreenToClient().

As shown in Figure 3-3a, if the cursor position is inside the right triangle (*i.e.*, pt.x > pt.y and pt.x + pt.y > 48) of the direction button, the iDir flag is set to 1. If the cursor position is inside the left triangle (*i.e.*, pt.x < pt.y and pt.x + pt.y < 48) of the direction button, the iDir flag is set to 2. If the cursor position is inside the lower triangle (*i.e.*, pt.x < pt.y and pt.x + pt.y > 48) of the direction button, the iDir flag is set to 3. If the cursor position is inside the upper triangle (*i.e.*, pt.x > pt.y and pt.x + pt.y < 48) of the direction button, the iDir flag is set to 4. The program then draws a pushed direction button according to the iDir flag. If the value of the iDir flag is 1, the right triangle of the direction button is drawn pushed down. Similarly, if the iDir flag is 2, 3, or 4 the left, lower, or upper triangle, respectively, of the direction button is drawn pushed down. Other actions can also be taken according to the value of iDir. Please see Cases 1-1 and 1-2 for details about owner-draw push buttons.

GLOBALS.H

```
// GLOBALS.H - header file for global variables
//              and function prototypes

// Product identifier string definitions.
#define APPNAME         DirBtn
#define ICONFILE        DirBtn.ico
#define SZAPPNAME       "DirBtn"
#define SZDESCRIPTION   "Direction buttons"
#define SZVERSION       "Version 1.0"
#define SZCOMPANYNAME   "\251 M&&T Books, 1994"
#define SZABOUT         "About"

// Global function prototypes.
BOOL InitApplication(HINSTANCE);
```

```
BOOL InitInstance(HINSTANCE, int);
void PaintBitmap(HDC, HBITMAP);
void DrawButtonUp(HWND, HDC, int);
void DrawButtonDown(HWND, HDC, int);

// Callback functions called by Windows.
LRESULT CALLBACK WndProc(HWND, UINT, WPARAM, LPARAM);
LRESULT CALLBACK About(HWND, UINT, WPARAM, LPARAM);

// Menu item ID
#define IDM_ABOUT    100

// Control ID
#define IDC_DIRBTN   101

// Global variable declarations.
extern HINSTANCE hInst;      // The current instance handle
extern char szAppName[];     // The name of this application
extern char szTitle[];       // The title bar text
```

WINMAIN.C

```
// WINMAIN.C
#include <windows.h>
#include "globals.h"

int APIENTRY WinMain(HINSTANCE hInstance,
                     HINSTANCE hPrevInstance,
                     LPSTR lpCmdLine,
                     int nCmdShow)
{
    MSG msg;

    // register main window class
    if (!hPrevInstance)
        {
        if (!InitApplication(hInstance))
            {
            return FALSE;
            }
        }

    // create and show main window
    if (!InitInstance(hInstance, nCmdShow))
        {
        return FALSE;
```

```
        }

        // process window message
    while (GetMessage(&msg, NULL, 0, 0))
        {
            TranslateMessage(&msg);
            DispatchMessage(&msg);
        }
    return msg.wParam;
}
```

INIT.C

```
// INIT.C
#include <windows.h>
#include "globals.h"

HINSTANCE hInst;
char szAppName[] = SZAPPNAME;
char szTitle[] = SZDESCRIPTION;

// register main window class
BOOL InitApplication(HINSTANCE hInstance)
{
    WNDCLASS  wc;

    wc.style          = CS_HREDRAW | CS_VREDRAW;
    wc.lpfnWndProc    = (WNDPROC)WndProc;
    wc.cbClsExtra     = 0;
    wc.cbWndExtra     = 0;
    wc.hInstance      = hInstance;
    wc.hIcon          = LoadIcon(hInstance, szAppName);
    wc.hCursor        = LoadCursor(NULL, IDC_ARROW);
    wc.hbrBackground  = (HBRUSH)(COLOR_WINDOW + 1);
    wc.lpszMenuName   = szAppName;
    wc.lpszClassName  = szAppName;

    return(RegisterClass(&wc));
}

// create and show main window
BOOL InitInstance(HINSTANCE hInstance, int nCmdShow)
{
    HWND    hWnd;
    hInst = hInstance;
    hWnd = CreateWindow(szAppName, szTitle,
```

223

```
                              WS_OVERLAPPEDWINDOW,
                              160, 120, 320, 240,
                              NULL, NULL, hInstance, NULL);

        if (!hWnd)
            {
            return FALSE;
            }

        ShowWindow(hWnd, nCmdShow);
        UpdateWindow(hWnd);

        return TRUE;
    }
```

DIRBTN.C

```
// DIRBTN.C
#include <windows.h>
#include <windowsx.h>
#include "globals.h"

HWND hDirBtn;
HBITMAP hBitmap;
static UINT iDir;

LRESULT CALLBACK WndProc(HWND hWnd,
                         UINT uMessage,
                         WPARAM wParam,
                         LPARAM lParam)
{
    LPDRAWITEMSTRUCT lpdis;
    POINT pt;

    switch (uMessage)
    {
        case WM_CREATE:
                // create a direction button
                hDirBtn = CreateWindow("BUTTON", "",
                        BS_OWNERDRAW | WS_CHILD |
                        WS_VISIBLE,
                        136, 72, 48, 48,
                        hWnd, IDC_DIRBTN, hInst, NULL);
                break;

        case WM_DRAWITEM:
```

```
// when direction button was pushed,
// save the current cursor position
// as (pt.x, pt.y)
GetCursorPos(&pt);

// convert the cursor position from screen
// coordinate into client coordinate
ScreenToClient(hDirBtn, &pt);

// if the cursor position is inside the right
// triangle, set iDir flag equal to 1
if((pt.x > pt.y) && (pt.x + pt.y > 48))
    iDir = 1;

// if the cursor position is inside the left
// triangle, set iDir flag equal to 2
if((pt.x < pt.y) && (pt.x + pt.y < 48))
    iDir = 2;

// if the cursor position is inside the lower
// triangle set iDir flag equal to 3
if((pt.x < pt.y) && (pt.x + pt.y > 48))
    iDir = 3;

// if the cursor position is inside the upper
// triangle set iDir flag equal to 4
if((pt.x > pt.y) && (pt.x + pt.y < 48))
    iDir = 4;

// draw direction button
lpdis = (LPDRAWITEMSTRUCT) lParam;
if(lpdis->itemState & ODS_SELECTED)
    // draw a down button according to iDir flag
    DrawButtonDown(hInst,
                   lpdis->hDC, lpdis->CtlID);
else
    // draw an up button if not selected
    DrawButtonUp(hInst,
                 lpdis->hDC, lpdis->CtlID);
break;

case WM_COMMAND:
    switch (GET_WM_COMMAND_ID(wParam,lParam))
    {
        case IDM_ABOUT:
            // create an about dialog box
            DialogBox(hInst, "ABOUTDLG",
```

```
                                    hWnd, (DLGPROC)About);
                    break;

            case IDC_DIRBTN:
                switch(iDir){
                    case 1:
                        // things to do when right
                        // triangle was pushed
                      break;
                    case 2:
                        // things to do when left
                        // triangle was pushed
                      break;
                    case 3:
                        // things to do when lower
                        // triangle was pushed
                      break;
                    case 4:
                        // things to do when upper
                        // triangle was pushed
                      break;

                    default: break;
                        }
                    break;

            default:
                return DefWindowProc(hWnd, uMessage,
                                        wParam, lParam);
            }
            break;

        case WM_DESTROY:
            PostQuitMessage(0);
            break;

        default:
            return DefWindowProc(hWnd, uMessage,
                                    wParam, lParam);
        }
    return 0;
}

// function for painting the bitmap on owner-draw button
void PaintBitmap (hDC, hBitmap)
HDC hDC;
HBITMAP hBitmap;
```

```
{
    BITMAP bmp;
    HDC hMemoryDC;
    hMemoryDC = CreateCompatibleDC(hDC);
    GetObject(hBitmap, sizeof(BITMAP), (LPSTR) &bmp) ;
    SelectObject(hMemoryDC, hBitmap) ;
    BitBlt(hDC, 0, 0, bmp.bmWidth, bmp.bmHeight,
                hMemoryDC, 0, 0, SRCCOPY);
    DeleteDC(hMemoryDC) ;
    DeleteObject(hBitmap) ;
}

// load the bitmap for an up direction button
void DrawButtonUp (hInstance, hDC, ButtonID)
HANDLE hInstance;
HDC hDC;
int ButtonID;
{
switch(ButtonID){
case IDC_DIRBTN:
    hBitmap = LoadBitmap (hInstance, "AllUp");
    break;
    }
    PaintBitmap(hDC, hBitmap);
}

// load the bitmap for a selected direction according to
// iDir flag
void DrawButtonDown (hInstance, hDC, ButtonID)
HANDLE hInstance;
HDC hDC;
int ButtonID;
{
switch(ButtonID){
case IDC_DIRBTN:
    switch(iDir){
                // load right triangle down bitmap
        case 1: hBitmap = LoadBitmap (hInstance, "EDown");
                break;

                // load left triangle down bitmap
        case 2: hBitmap = LoadBitmap (hInstance, "WDown");
                break;

                // load lower triangle down bitmap
        case 3: hBitmap = LoadBitmap (hInstance, "SDown");
                break;
```

```
                        // load upper triangle down bitmap
        case 4: hBitmap = LoadBitmap (hInstance, "NDown");
                break;
      }
    break;
    }
    PaintBitmap(hDC, hBitmap);
}
```

ABOUT.C

```
// ABOUT.C
#include <windows.h>
#include <windowsx.h>
#include "globals.h"

// procedures for ABOUT dialog box
LRESULT CALLBACK About(HWND hDlg,
                       UINT uMessage,
                       WPARAM wParam,
                       LPARAM lParam)
{
    switch (uMessage)
      {
        case WM_COMMAND:
            switch (GET_WM_COMMAND_ID(wParam,lParam))
            {
                case IDOK:
                case IDCANCEL:
                    {
                    EndDialog(hDlg, TRUE);
                    return(TRUE);
                    }
                    break;
            }
      }
    return FALSE;
}
```

DIRBTN.RC

```
#include "windows.h"
#include "globals.h"
#include <winver.h>
```

```
AllUp     BITMAP allup.bmp
EDown     BITMAP edown.bmp
WDown     BITMAP wdown.bmp
NDown     BITMAP ndown.bmp
SDown     BITMAP sdown.bmp


APPNAME ICON ICONFILE

RCINCLUDE ABOUT.DLG

APPNAME MENU
BEGIN
  MENUITEM "&About",      IDM_ABOUT
END
```

ABOUT.DLG

```
ABOUTDLG DIALOG DISCARDABLE  22, 17, 167, 73
STYLE DS_MODALFRAME | WS_CAPTION | WS_SYSMENU
CAPTION SZABOUT
BEGIN
    DEFPUSHBUTTON   "OK", IDOK, 132, 2, 32, 14, WS_GROUP
    ICON            SZAPPNAME,      -1, 3, 2, 18, 20
    LTEXT           SZAPPNAME,      -1, 30, 12,  50, 8
    LTEXT           SZDESCRIPTION, -1, 30, 22, 150, 8
    LTEXT           SZVERSION,      -1, 30, 32, 150, 8
    LTEXT           SZCOMPANYNAME, -1, 30, 42, 150, 8
END
```

DIRBTN.ICO

ALLUP.BMP

EDOWN.ICO

WDOWN.BMP

NDOWN.BMP

SDOWN.BMP

CASE 3-4: SWITCH

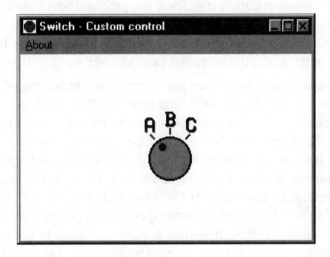

FIGURE 3-4

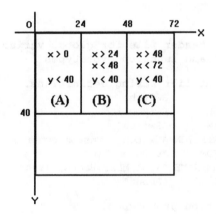

FIGURE 3-4A

This example also uses the button subdivision technique discussed in Cases 3-2 and 3-3 to design a *custom switch*. As in the previous cases, you need only one owner-draw switch button to change switch positons. In this case the target area is subdivided into four rectangles. When the switch button is pushed, the program saves the current cursor position as (pt.x, pt.y). This cursor position is then converted from screen coordinates into switch button client coordinates (switch button local coordinates) using the Windows function ScreenToClient().

As shown in Figure 3-4a, if the cursor position is inside the left rectangle (*i.e.*, pt.y < 40 and 0 < pt.x < 24) of the switch button, the iSwitch flag is set to 1. If the cursor position is inside the center rectangle (*i.e.*, pt.y < 40 and 24 < pt.x < 48) of the switch button, the iSwitch flag is set to 2. If the cursor position is inside the right rectangle (*i.e.*, pt.y < 40 and 48 < pt.x < 72) of the switch button, the iSwitch flag is set to 3. The program then draws a switch according to the value of the iSwitch flag. If the value of the iSwitch flag is 1, the switch is drawn pointing to position A. Similarly, if the iSwitch flag is 2 or 3, the switch is drawn pointing to position B or C. Other actions can also be taken according to the value of the iSwitch.

Please see Cases 1-1 and 1-2 for details about owner-draw push buttons.

GLOBALS.H

```
// GLOBALS.H - header file for global variables
//              and function prototypes

// Product identifier string definitions.
#define APPNAME        Switch
#define ICONFILE       Switch.ico
#define SZAPPNAME      "Switch"
#define SZDESCRIPTION  "Switch - Custom control"
#define SZVERSION      "Version 1.0"
#define SZCOMPANYNAME  "\251 M&&T Books, 1994"
#define SZABOUT        "About"

// Global function prototypes.
BOOL InitApplication(HINSTANCE);
BOOL InitInstance(HINSTANCE, int);
void PaintBitmap(HDC, HBITMAP);
void DrawSwitch(HWND, HDC, int);

// Callback functions called by Windows.
LRESULT CALLBACK WndProc(HWND, UINT, WPARAM, LPARAM);
LRESULT CALLBACK About(HWND, UINT, WPARAM, LPARAM);
```

```
// Menu item ID
#define IDM_ABOUT    100

// Control ID
#define IDC_SWITCH    101

// Global variable declarations.
extern HINSTANCE hInst;       // The current instance handle
extern char szAppName[];      // The name of this application
extern char szTitle[];        // The title bar text
```

WINMAIN.C

```
// WINMAIN.C
#include <windows.h>
#include "globals.h"

int APIENTRY WinMain(HINSTANCE hInstance,
                     HINSTANCE hPrevInstance,
                     LPSTR lpCmdLine,
                     int nCmdShow)
{
    MSG msg;

    // register main window class
    if (!hPrevInstance)
        {
        if (!InitApplication(hInstance))
            {
            return FALSE;
            }
        }

    // create and show main window
    if (!InitInstance(hInstance, nCmdShow))
        {
        return FALSE;
        }

    // process window message
    while (GetMessage(&msg, NULL, 0, 0))
        {
            TranslateMessage(&msg);
            DispatchMessage(&msg);
        }
    return msg.wParam;
}
```

INIT.C

```c
// INIT.C
#include <windows.h>
#include "globals.h"

HINSTANCE hInst;
char szAppName[] = SZAPPNAME;
char szTitle[] = SZDESCRIPTION;

// register main window class
BOOL InitApplication(HINSTANCE hInstance)
{
    WNDCLASS  wc;

    wc.style         = CS_HREDRAW | CS_VREDRAW;
    wc.lpfnWndProc   = (WNDPROC)WndProc;
    wc.cbClsExtra    = 0;
    wc.cbWndExtra    = 0;
    wc.hInstance     = hInstance;
    wc.hIcon         = LoadIcon(hInstance, szAppName);
    wc.hCursor       = LoadCursor(NULL, IDC_ARROW);
    wc.hbrBackground = (HBRUSH)(COLOR_WINDOW + 1);
    wc.lpszMenuName  = szAppName;
    wc.lpszClassName = szAppName;

    return(RegisterClass(&wc));
}

// create and show main window
BOOL InitInstance(HINSTANCE hInstance, int nCmdShow)
{
    HWND    hWnd;
    hInst = hInstance;
    hWnd = CreateWindow(szAppName, szTitle,
                        WS_OVERLAPPEDWINDOW,
                        160, 120, 320, 240,
                        NULL, NULL, hInstance, NULL);

    if (!hWnd)
        {
        return FALSE;
        }

    ShowWindow(hWnd, nCmdShow);
    UpdateWindow(hWnd);

    return TRUE;
}
```

SWITCH.C

```
// SWITCH.C
#include <windows.h>
#include <windowsx.h>
#include "globals.h"

HWND hSwitch;
HBITMAP hBitmap;
static UINT iSwitch = 1;

LRESULT CALLBACK WndProc(HWND hWnd,
                         UINT uMessage,
                         WPARAM wParam,
                         LPARAM lParam)
{
    LPDRAWITEMSTRUCT lpdis;
    POINT pt;

    switch (uMessage)
    {
        case WM_CREATE:
            // create an owner-draw switch button
            hSwitch = CreateWindow("BUTTON", "",
                        BS_OWNERDRAW | WS_CHILD |
                        WS_VISIBLE,
                        124, 60, 72, 72,
                        hWnd, IDC_SWITCH, hInst, NULL);
            break;

        case WM_DRAWITEM:
            // save current cursor position as (pt.x, pt.y)
            // when switch button was pushed
            GetCursorPos(&pt);

            // convert the cursor position position from
            // screen coordinate into client coordinate
            ScreenToClient(hSwitch, &pt);

            // if cursor position is near switch position A
            // set iSwitch flag to 1
            if(pt.x > 0  && pt.x < 24 && pt.y < 40)
                iSwitch = 1;

            // if cursor position is near switch position A
            // set iSwitch flag to 2
            if(pt.x > 24 && pt.x < 48 && pt.y < 40)
                iSwitch = 2;
```

235

```
            // if cursor position is near switch position A
            // set iSwitch flag to 3
            if(pt.x > 48 && pt.x < 72 && pt.y < 40)
               iSwitch = 3;

            // draw the switch according to the
            // value of iSwitch
            lpdis = (LPDRAWITEMSTRUCT) lParam;
            DrawSwitch(hInst, lpdis->hDC, lpdis->CtlID);
            break;

    case WM_COMMAND:
            switch (GET_WM_COMMAND_ID(wParam,lParam))
            {
               case IDM_ABOUT:
                      // create an about dialog box
                      DialogBox(hInst, "ABOUTDLG",
                               hWnd, (DLGPROC)About);
                      break;

               case IDC_SWITCH:
                      switch(iSwitch){
                         case 1: // things to do when switch
                                 // position A was selected
                               break;
                         case 2: // things to do when switch
                                 // position B was selected
                               break;
                         case 3: // things to do when switch
                                 // position C was selected
                               break;
                         default: break;
                         }
                      break;

               default:
                      return DefWindowProc(hWnd, uMessage,
                                           wParam, lParam);
            }
            break;

    case WM_DESTROY:
            PostQuitMessage(0);
            break;

    default:
            return DefWindowProc(hWnd, uMessage,
                                 wParam, lParam);
    }
    return 0;
```

```
}

// function to paint the bitmap on an ownerdraw button
void PaintBitmap (hDC, hBitmap)
HDC hDC;
HBITMAP hBitmap;
{
    BITMAP bmp;
    HDC hMemoryDC;
    hMemoryDC = CreateCompatibleDC(hDC);
    GetObject(hBitmap, sizeof(BITMAP), (LPSTR) &bmp) ;
    SelectObject(hMemoryDC, hBitmap) ;
    BitBlt(hDC, 0, 0, bmp.bmWidth, bmp.bmHeight,
             hMemoryDC, 0, 0, SRCCOPY);
    DeleteDC(hMemoryDC) ;
    DeleteObject(hBitmap) ;
}

// load the switch bitmap according to iSwitch flag
void DrawSwitch (hInstance, hDC, ButtonID)
HANDLE hInstance;
HDC hDC;
int ButtonID;
{
switch(ButtonID){
case IDC_SWITCH:
    switch(iSwitch){
      case 1: hBitmap = LoadBitmap (hInstance, "SwitchA");
             break;

      case 2: hBitmap = LoadBitmap (hInstance, "SwitchB");
             break;

      case 3: hBitmap = LoadBitmap (hInstance, "SWitchC");
             break;
    }
    break;
    }
    PaintBitmap(hDC, hBitmap);
}
```

ABOUT.C

```
// ABOUT.C
#include <windows.h>
#include <windowsx.h>
#include "globals.h"
```

```
// procedures for ABOUT dialog box
LRESULT CALLBACK About(HWND hDlg,
                       UINT uMessage,
                       WPARAM wParam,
                       LPARAM lParam)
{
    switch (uMessage)
      {
        case WM_COMMAND:
            switch (GET_WM_COMMAND_ID(wParam,lParam))
            {
                case IDOK:
                case IDCANCEL:
                    {
                    EndDialog(hDlg, TRUE);
                    return(TRUE);
                    }
                    break;
            }
      }
    return FALSE;
}
```

SWITCH.RC

```
#include "windows.h"
#include "globals.h"
#include <winver.h>

SwitchA  BITMAP switcha.bmp
SwitchB  BITMAP switchb.bmp
SwitchC  BITMAP switchc.bmp

APPNAME ICON ICONFILE

RCINCLUDE ABOUT.DLG

APPNAME MENU
BEGIN
  MENUITEM "&About",      IDM_ABOUT
END
```

ABOUT.DLG

```
ABOUTDLG DIALOG DISCARDABLE  22, 17, 167, 73
```

```
STYLE DS_MODALFRAME | WS_CAPTION | WS_SYSMENU
CAPTION SZABOUT
BEGIN
    DEFPUSHBUTTON    "OK", IDOK, 132, 2, 32, 14, WS_GROUP
    ICON             SZAPPNAME,      -1, 3, 2, 18, 20
    LTEXT            SZAPPNAME,      -1, 30, 12,  50, 8
    LTEXT            SZDESCRIPTION,  -1, 30, 22, 150, 8
    LTEXT            SZVERSION,      -1, 30, 32, 150, 8
    LTEXT            SZCOMPANYNAME,  -1, 30, 42, 150, 8
END
```

SWITCH.ICO

SWITCHA.BMP

SWITCHB.BMP

SWITCHC.BMP

CASE 3-5: DIAL

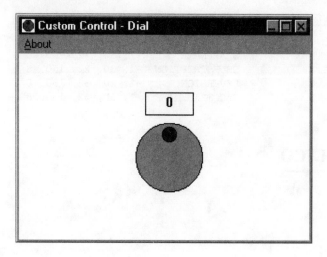

FIGURE 3-5

This case considers the situation in which a user needs to specify a range of values that have many increments, not just a few positions on a dial. In this case, one light gray circle with a dark gray dot marker on it represents a *dial*. When the user moves the cursor inside the dial area with left button down, the program tracks the cursor position and redraws the dot marker on the dial to match the cursor position. Also, the angle between the dot marker and the vertical line is calculated before the dial number is displayed in the edit box.

GLOBALS.H

```
// GLOBALS.H - header file for global variables
//              and function prototypes

// Product identifier string definitions.
#define APPNAME        Dial
#define ICONFILE       Dial.ico
#define SZAPPNAME      "Dial"
#define SZDESCRIPTION  "Custom Control - Dial"
#define SZVERSION      "Version 1.0"
#define SZCOMPANYNAME  "\251 M&&T Books, 1994"
#define SZABOUT        "About"

// Global function prototypes.
BOOL InitApplication(HINSTANCE);
BOOL InitInstance(HINSTANCE, int);

// Callback functions called by Windows.
LRESULT CALLBACK WndProc(HWND, UINT, WPARAM, LPARAM);
LRESULT CALLBACK About(HWND, UINT, WPARAM, LPARAM);

// Menu item ID
#define IDM_ABOUT   101

// Control ID
#define IDC_EDITBOX 102

// Global variable declarations.
extern HINSTANCE hInst;        // The current instance handle
extern char szAppName[];       // The name of this application
extern char szTitle[];         // The title bar text
```

WINMAIN.C

```
// WINMAIN.C
#include <windows.h>
#include "globals.h"

int APIENTRY WinMain(HINSTANCE hInstance,
                     HINSTANCE hPrevInstance,
                     LPSTR lpCmdLine,
                     int nCmdShow)
{
    MSG msg;
```

```
    // register main window class
    if (!hPrevInstance)
        {
        if (!InitApplication(hInstance))
            {
            return FALSE;
            }
        }

    // create and show main window
    if (!InitInstance(hInstance, nCmdShow))
        {
        return FALSE;
        }

    // process window message
    while (GetMessage(&msg, NULL, 0, 0))
        {
            TranslateMessage(&msg);
            DispatchMessage(&msg);
        }
    return msg.wParam;
}
```

INIT.C

```
// INIT.C
#include <windows.h>
#include "globals.h"

HINSTANCE hInst;
char szAppName[] = SZAPPNAME;
char szTitle[] = SZDESCRIPTION;

// register main window class
BOOL InitApplication(HINSTANCE hInstance)
{
    WNDCLASS  wc;

    wc.style        = CS_HREDRAW | CS_VREDRAW;
    wc.lpfnWndProc  = (WNDPROC)WndProc;
    wc.cbClsExtra   = 0;
    wc.cbWndExtra   = 0;
    wc.hInstance    = hInstance;
    wc.hIcon        = LoadIcon(hInstance, szAppName);
```

```
    wc.hCursor       = LoadCursor(NULL, IDC_ARROW);
    wc.hbrBackground = (HBRUSH)(COLOR_WINDOW + 1);
    wc.lpszMenuName  = szAppName;
    wc.lpszClassName = szAppName;

    return(RegisterClass(&wc));
}

// create and show main window
BOOL InitInstance(HINSTANCE hInstance, int nCmdShow)
{
    HWND    hWnd;
    hInst = hInstance;
    hWnd = CreateWindow(szAppName, szTitle,
                    WS_OVERLAPPEDWINDOW,
                    160, 120, 320, 240,
                    NULL, NULL, hInstance, NULL);

    if (!hWnd)
        {
        return FALSE;
        }

    ShowWindow(hWnd, nCmdShow);
    UpdateWindow(hWnd);

    return TRUE;
}
```

DIAL.C

```
// DIAL.C
#include <windows.h>
#include <windowsx.h>
#include <math.h>
#include "globals.h"

static HWND hEditBox;
HBITMAP hBitmap;
static UINT iDial = 0;
static BOOL bDial;

LRESULT CALLBACK WndProc(HWND hWnd,
                        UINT uMessage,
                        WPARAM wParam,
                        LPARAM lParam)
```

```
{
    PAINTSTRUCT ps;
    POINT pt;
    static RECT rc;
    int radius = 24;
    static int MarkerX = 36, MarkerY = 12;
    double Rpt = 24.;
    HDC hDC;
    int XX, YY;
    double Angle;
    static char EditText[6];

    switch (uMessage)
    {
        case WM_CREATE:
            // define an rectangle that confines the dial
            rc.left = 126;  rc.right = 198;
            rc.top = 72;    rc.bottom = 144;

            // create an edit box to display
            // the dial number
            hEditBox = CreateWindow("EDIT", "0",
                        WS_BORDER | WS_CHILD | WS_VISIBLE,
                        136, 40, 52, 24,
                        hWnd, IDC_EDITBOX, hInst, NULL);

            // display the initial dial number
            sprintf(EditText, "   %3d", iDial);
            SetWindowText(hEditBox, EditText);
            break;

        case WM_PAINT:
            hDC = BeginPaint(hWnd, &ps);

            // draw the circular light gray dial
            SelectObject(hDC, GetStockObject(BLACK_PEN));
            SelectObject(hDC,
                        GetStockObject(LTGRAY_BRUSH));
            Ellipse(hDC, rc.left, rc.top,
                        rc.right, rc.bottom);

            // draw the dark gray dot marker on the dial
            SelectObject(hDC,
                        GetStockObject(DKGRAY_BRUSH));
            Ellipse(hDC, rc.left + MarkerX - 8,
                        rc.top + MarkerY - 8,
                        rc.left + MarkerX + 8,
```

```
                    rc.top + MarkerY + 8);

        DeleteObject(SelectObject(
                    hDC, GetStockObject(BLACK_PEN)));
        DeleteObject(SelectObject(hDC,
                    GetStockObject(LTGRAY_BRUSH)));
        EndPaint(hWnd, &ps);
        break;

    case WM_LBUTTONDOWN:
        // save the current cursor position as
        // (pt.x, pt.y) when left mouse button is down
        GetCursorPos(&pt);

        // convert the cursor position from screen
        // coordinate into client area coordinate
        ScreenToClient(hWnd, &pt);

        // if the cursor position is inside the
        // rectangle that define the dial,
        // set the bDial flag to 1
        if(pt.x > rc.left && pt.x < rc.right
          && pt.y > rc.top && pt.y < rc.bottom){
          bDial = TRUE;
          }
        else bDial = FALSE;
        break;

    case WM_MOUSEMOVE:
        // if bDial flag is TRUE and the wParam
        // parameter of WM_MOUSEMOVE message is
        // MK_LBUTTON (i.e. left button is down),
        // redraw the dial with the dot
        // marker follow the cursor movement
        if(bDial && wParam == MK_LBUTTON)
        {
        GetCursorPos(&pt);
        ScreenToClient(hWnd, &pt);

        // calculate the relative position
        // (XX, YY) of cursor to the center of dial
        XX = pt.x - rc.left - 36;
        YY = pt.y - rc.top - 36;

        // calculate the distance (Rpt) between cursor
        // and the center of dial
        Rpt = sqrt(XX*XX + YY*YY);
```

```
        // calculate the position of dot marker
        // (MarkerX, MarkerY)
    MarkerX = XX * radius / Rpt + rc.left + 36;
    MarkerY = YY * radius / Rpt + rc.top + 36;

        // calculate the angle between the marker and
        // the vertical line
    Angle = asin((MarkerY - rc.top - 36.)/radius);

        // calculate the dial number from this angle
        // and times a constant such that one half turn
        // will increase the dial number by 100
    iDial = (Angle + 1.5707963268) * 31.8310155049;

        // display the new dial number
    sprintf(EditText, "   %3d", iDial);
    SetWindowText(hEditBox, EditText);

    hDC = GetDC(hWnd);

        // redraw the circular light gray dial
    SelectObject(hDC, GetStockObject(BLACK_PEN));
    SelectObject(hDC,
                GetStockObject(LTGRAY_BRUSH));
    Ellipse(hDC, rc.left, rc.top,
                rc.right, rc.bottom);

        // redraw the dark gray dot marker on the dial
    SelectObject(hDC,
                GetStockObject(DKGRAY_BRUSH));
    Ellipse(hDC, MarkerX - 8, MarkerY - 8,
                MarkerX + 8, MarkerY + 8);

    DeleteObject(SelectObject(
                hDC, GetStockObject(BLACK_PEN)));
    DeleteObject(SelectObject( hDC,
                GetStockObject(LTGRAY_BRUSH)));
    ReleaseDC(hWnd, hDC);
    }
    break;

case WM_COMMAND:
    switch (GET_WM_COMMAND_ID(wParam,lParam))
    {
        case IDM_ABOUT:
                // create an about dialog box
```

```
                    DialogBox(hInst, "ABOUTDLG",
                            hWnd, (DLGPROC)About);
                    break;

                case IDC_EDITBOX:
                    break;

                default:
                    return DefWindowProc(hWnd, uMessage,
                                        wParam, lParam);
            }
            break;

        case WM_DESTROY:
            PostQuitMessage(0);
            break;

        default:
            return DefWindowProc(hWnd, uMessage,
                                wParam, lParam);
    }
    return 0;
}
```

ABOUT.C

```
// ABOUT.C
#include <windows.h>
#include <windowsx.h>
#include "globals.h"

// procedures for ABOUT dialog box
LRESULT CALLBACK About(HWND hDlg,
                    UINT uMessage,
                    WPARAM wParam,
                    LPARAM lParam)
{
    switch (uMessage)
    {
        case WM_COMMAND:
            switch (GET_WM_COMMAND_ID(wParam,lParam))
            {
                case IDOK:
                case IDCANCEL:
                    {
                    EndDialog(hDlg, TRUE);
```

```
                                return(TRUE);
                            }
                            break;
                    }
            }
        return FALSE;
    }
```

DIAL.RC

```
#include "windows.h"
#include "globals.h"
#include <winver.h>

APPNAME ICON ICONFILE

RCINCLUDE ABOUT.DLG

APPNAME MENU
BEGIN
  MENUITEM "&About",      IDM_ABOUT
END
```

ABOUT.DLG

```
ABOUTDLG DIALOG DISCARDABLE  22, 17, 167, 73
STYLE DS_MODALFRAME | WS_CAPTION | WS_SYSMENU
CAPTION SZABOUT
BEGIN
    DEFPUSHBUTTON   "OK", IDOK, 132, 2, 32, 14, WS_GROUP
    ICON            SZAPPNAME,      -1, 3, 2, 18, 20
    LTEXT           SZAPPNAME,      -1, 30, 12,  50, 8
    LTEXT           SZDESCRIPTION, -1, 30, 22, 150, 8
    LTEXT           SZVERSION,     -1, 30, 32, 150, 8
    LTEXT           SZCOMPANYNAME, -1, 30, 42, 150, 8
END
```

DIAL.ICO

CASE 3-6: SLIDER

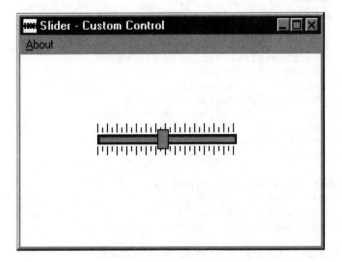

FIGURE 3-6

T his case presents a *horizontal slider* and is similar to Case 3-5 in that both provide an analog function for the user. The user can specify directly a range of values that can have many increments. In Case 3-5, the visual element is a round dial. In this case, the slider is a horizontal element consisting of a "thumb" that is moved along a track with rulerlike markings.

The slider is implemented using a bitmap that is drawn inside a predefined rectangle and a small gray rectangle (the thumb), which is then drawn on top of that. When the user moves the cursor inside the slider area with the left button down, the program tracks the cursor position and repaints the slider bitmap and the rectangular thumb to match the cursor postion.

GLOBALS.H

```
// GLOBALS.H - header file for global variables
//              and function prototypes

// Product identifier string definitions.
#define APPNAME       Slide
#define ICONFILE      Slide.ico
#define SZAPPNAME     "Slide"
#define SZDESCRIPTION "Slider - Custom Control"
#define SZVERSION     "Version 1.0"
#define SZCOMPANYNAME "\251 M&&T Books, 1994"
#define SZABOUT       "About"

// Global function prototypes.
BOOL InitApplication(HINSTANCE);
BOOL InitInstance(HINSTANCE, int);
void PaintRectBitmap(HDC, HBITMAP, WORD, WORD);

// Callback functions called by Windows.
LRESULT CALLBACK WndProc(HWND, UINT, WPARAM, LPARAM);
LRESULT CALLBACK About(HWND, UINT, WPARAM, LPARAM);

// Menu item ID
#define IDM_ABOUT 101

// Control ID
#define IDC_SLIDE 102

// Global variable declarations.
extern HINSTANCE hInst;      // The current instance handle
extern char szAppName[];     // The name of this application
extern char szTitle[];       // The title bar text
```

WINMAIN.C

```
// WINMAIN.C
#include <windows.h>
#include "globals.h"

int APIENTRY WinMain(HINSTANCE hInstance,
                     HINSTANCE hPrevInstance,
                     LPSTR lpCmdLine,
                     int nCmdShow)
{
```

```
    MSG msg;

    // register main window class
    if (!hPrevInstance)
        {
        if (!InitApplication(hInstance))
            {
            return FALSE;
            }
        }

    // create and show main window
    if (!InitInstance(hInstance, nCmdShow))
        {
        return FALSE;
        }

    // process window messages
    while (GetMessage(&msg, NULL, 0, 0))
        {
            TranslateMessage(&msg);
            DispatchMessage(&msg);
        }
    return msg.wParam;
}
```

INIT.C

```
// INIT.C
#include <windows.h>
#include "globals.h"

HINSTANCE hInst;
char szAppName[] = SZAPPNAME;
char szTitle[] = SZDESCRIPTION;

// register main window class
BOOL InitApplication(HINSTANCE hInstance)
{
    WNDCLASS  wc;

    wc.style          = CS_HREDRAW | CS_VREDRAW;
    wc.lpfnWndProc    = (WNDPROC)WndProc;
    wc.cbClsExtra     = 0;
    wc.cbWndExtra     = 0;
    wc.hInstance      = hInstance;
```

```
    wc.hIcon          = LoadIcon(hInstance, szAppName);
    wc.hCursor        = LoadCursor(NULL, IDC_ARROW);
    wc.hbrBackground  = (HBRUSH)(COLOR_WINDOW + 1);
    wc.lpszMenuName   = szAppName;
    wc.lpszClassName  = szAppName;

    return(RegisterClass(&wc));
}

// create and show main window
BOOL InitInstance(HINSTANCE hInstance, int nCmdShow)
{
    HWND    hWnd;
    hInst = hInstance;
    hWnd = CreateWindow(szAppName, szTitle,
                        WS_OVERLAPPEDWINDOW,
                        160, 120, 320, 240,
                        NULL, NULL, hInstance, NULL);

    if (!hWnd)
        {
        return FALSE;
        }

    ShowWindow(hWnd, nCmdShow);
    UpdateWindow(hWnd);

    return TRUE;
}
```

SLIDE.C

```
// SLIDE.C
#include <windows.h>
#include <windowsx.h>
#include <math.h>
#include "globals.h"

HBITMAP hBitmap;
static UINT iSlide = 0;
static BOOL bSlide;

LRESULT CALLBACK WndProc(HWND hWnd,
                         UINT uMessage,
                         WPARAM wParam,
                         LPARAM lParam)
```

```
{
    PAINTSTRUCT ps;
    static POINT pt;
    static RECT rc;
    HDC hDC;
    static int SlideY;

    switch (uMessage)
    {
        case WM_CREATE:

            // define the initial thumb position
            pt.x = 152;
            pt.y = 86;

            // define the slider vertical center position
            SlideY = 86;

            // define a rectangle that confine the slider
            rc.left = 80;
            rc.right = 224;
            rc.top = 70;
            rc.bottom = 102;
            break;

        case WM_PAINT:

            hDC = BeginPaint(hWnd, &ps);

            // load the slider bitmap and paint it inside
            // a rectangle rc
            hBitmap = LoadBitmap(hInst, "slider");
            PaintRectBitmap(hDC, hBitmap, rc.left, rc.top);

            // draw a small gray rectangle as the thumb
            // of the slider
            SelectObject(hDC, GetStockObject(BLACK_PEN));
            SelectObject(hDC,
                        GetStockObject(LTGRAY_BRUSH));
            Rectangle(hDC, pt.x - 6, SlideY - 10,
                        pt.x + 6, SlideY + 10);

            DeleteObject(SelectObject(
                        hDC, GetStockObject(BLACK_PEN)));
            DeleteObject(SelectObject(
                        hDC, GetStockObject(LTGRAY_BRUSH)));
            EndPaint(hWnd, &ps);
```

253

```
        break;

case WM_LBUTTONDOWN:

        // save the cursor position as (pt.x, pt.y)
        GetCursorPos(&pt);

        // convert the cursor position into
        // client area coordinate
        ScreenToClient(hWnd, &pt);

        // if the the cursor is inside the rectangle
        // that confine the slider,
        // set the bSlide flag to 1
        if(pt.x > rc.left && pt.x < rc.right
           && pt.y > rc.top && pt.y < rc.bottom){
           bSlide = TRUE;
           }
        else bSlide = FALSE;
        break;

case WM_MOUSEMOVE:

        // if bSlide flag is TRUE and the wParam
        // paramter of WM_MOUSEMOVE message is equal to
        // MK_LBUTTON (i.e. left button is down),
        // redraw the slider with the thumb position
        // equal to cursor position
        if(bSlide && wParam == MK_LBUTTON){
        GetCursorPos(&pt);
        ScreenToClient(hWnd, &pt);

        // check if the cursor position is within the
        // slide range
        if(pt.x > rc.left + 6 && pt.x < rc.right - 6
           && pt.y > rc.top && pt.y < rc.bottom)
        {
        hDC = GetDC(hWnd);

        // load the slider bitmap and paint it inside
        // the rectangle rc
        hBitmap = LoadBitmap(hInst, "slider");
        PaintRectBitmap(hDC, hBitmap, rc.left, rc.top);

        // draw a small gray rectangle as the
        // thumb of slider
        SelectObject(hDC, GetStockObject(BLACK_PEN));
```

```
            SelectObject(hDC,
                        GetStockObject(LTGRAY_BRUSH));
            Rectangle(hDC, pt.x - 6, SlideY - 10,
                        pt.x + 6, SlideY + 10);

            DeleteObject(SelectObject(
                        hDC, GetStockObject(BLACK_PEN)));
            DeleteObject(SelectObject(
                        hDC, GetStockObject(LTGRAY_BRUSH)));
            ReleaseDC(hWnd, hDC);
            }
            }
            break;

        case WM_COMMAND:
            switch (GET_WM_COMMAND_ID(wParam,lParam))
            {
                case IDM_ABOUT:
                        // create an about dialog
                        DialogBox(hInst, "ABOUTDLG",
                                hWnd, (DLGPROC)About);
                        break;

                default:
                    return DefWindowProc(hWnd, uMessage,
                                        wParam, lParam);
            }
            break;

        case WM_DESTROY:
            PostQuitMessage(0);
            break;

        default:
            return DefWindowProc(hWnd, uMessage,
                                wParam, lParam);
    }
    return 0;
}


// function to paint the slider bitmap
void PaintRectBitmap (hDC, hBitmap, rectX, rectY)
HDC hDC;
HBITMAP hBitmap;
WORD rectX, rectY;
{
    BITMAP bmp;
```

```
        HDC hMemoryDC;
        hMemoryDC = CreateCompatibleDC(hDC);
        GetObject(hBitmap, sizeof(BITMAP), (LPSTR) &bmp);
        SelectObject(hMemoryDC, hBitmap);
        BitBlt(hDC, rectX, rectY, bmp.bmWidth, bmp.bmHeight,
                        hMemoryDC, 0, 0, SRCCOPY);
        DeleteDC(hMemoryDC);
        DeleteObject(hBitmap);
}
```

ABOUT.C

```
// ABOUT.C
#include <windows.h>
#include <windowsx.h>
#include "globals.h"

// procedures for ABOUT dialog box
LRESULT CALLBACK About(HWND hDlg,
                        UINT uMessage,
                        WPARAM wParam,
                        LPARAM lParam)
{
    switch (uMessage)
      {
        case WM_COMMAND:
                switch (GET_WM_COMMAND_ID(wParam,lParam))
                {
                    case IDOK:
                    case IDCANCEL:
                        {
                        EndDialog(hDlg, TRUE);
                        return(TRUE);
                        }
                        break;
                }
      }
    return FALSE;
}
```

SLIDE.RC

```
#include "windows.h"
#include "globals.h"
```

```
#include <winver.h>

slider BITMAP slider.bmp

APPNAME ICON ICONFILE

RCINCLUDE ABOUT.DLG

APPNAME MENU
BEGIN
  MENUITEM "&About",      IDM_ABOUT
END
```

ABOUT.DLG

```
ABOUTDLG DIALOG DISCARDABLE  22, 17, 167, 73
STYLE DS_MODALFRAME | WS_CAPTION | WS_SYSMENU
CAPTION SZABOUT
BEGIN
    DEFPUSHBUTTON    "OK", IDOK, 132, 2, 32, 14, WS_GROUP
    ICON             SZAPPNAME,      -1, 3, 2, 18, 20
    LTEXT            SZAPPNAME,      -1, 30, 12,  50, 8
    LTEXT            SZDESCRIPTION, -1, 30, 22, 150, 8
    LTEXT            SZVERSION,     -1, 30, 32, 150, 8
    LTEXT            SZCOMPANYNAME, -1, 30, 42, 150, 8
END
```

SLIDE.ICO

SLIDER.BMP

CASE 3-7: ANALOG METER

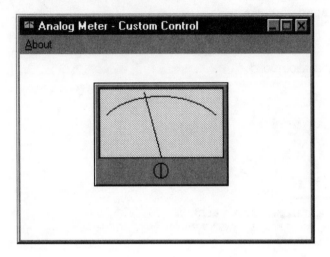

FIGURE 3-7

This case presents an analog meter, which is similar to the moving needle display you might find in a physical voltmeter. This user interface element, however, is not used to get input from the user (as is done in Cases 3-5 and 3-6). Rather, the purpose here is to display value in the analog style which provides many smooth increments.

To implement the meter, first paint a bitmap within a predefined rectangle. Then draw a black line on top of the bitmap to indicate the position of the needle. When it is necessary to change needle's position, the program erases the old needle and draws a new one.

GLOBALS.H

```
// GLOBALS.H - header file for global variables
//               and function prototypes

// Product identifier string definitions.
#define APPNAME        AMeter
#define ICONFILE       AMeter.ico
#define SZAPPNAME      "AMeter"
#define SZDESCRIPTION  "Analog Meter - Custom Control"
#define SZVERSION      "Version 1.0"
#define SZCOMPANYNAME  "\251 M&&T Books, 1994"
#define SZABOUT        "About"

// Global function prototypes.
BOOL InitApplication(HINSTANCE);
BOOL InitInstance(HINSTANCE, int);
void PaintMeterBitmap(HDC, HBITMAP, WORD, WORD);

// Callback functions called by Windows.
LRESULT CALLBACK WndProc(HWND, UINT, WPARAM, LPARAM);
LRESULT CALLBACK About(HWND, UINT, WPARAM, LPARAM);

// Menu item ID
#define IDM_ABOUT   1000

// Global variable declarations.
extern HINSTANCE hInst;       // The current instance handle
extern char szAppName[];      // The name of this application
extern char szTitle[];        // The title bar text
```

WINMAIN.C

```
// WINMAIN.C
#include <windows.h>
#include "globals.h"

int APIENTRY WinMain(HINSTANCE hInstance,
                     HINSTANCE hPrevInstance,
                     LPSTR lpCmdLine,
                     int nCmdShow)
{
    MSG msg;

    // register main window class
```

```
        if (!hPrevInstance)
          {
          if (!InitApplication(hInstance))
            {
            return FALSE;
            }
          }

        // create and show main window
        if (!InitInstance(hInstance, nCmdShow))
          {
          return FALSE;
          }

        // process window message
        while (GetMessage(&msg, NULL, 0, 0))
          {
            TranslateMessage(&msg);
            DispatchMessage(&msg);
          }
        return msg.wParam;
}
```

INIT.C

```
// INIT.C
#include <windows.h>
#include "globals.h"

HINSTANCE hInst;
char szAppName[] = SZAPPNAME;
char szTitle[] = SZDESCRIPTION;

// register main window class
BOOL InitApplication(HINSTANCE hInstance)
{
    WNDCLASS  wc;

    wc.style         = CS_HREDRAW | CS_VREDRAW;
    wc.lpfnWndProc   = (WNDPROC)WndProc;
    wc.cbClsExtra    = 0;
    wc.cbWndExtra    = 0;
    wc.hInstance     = hInstance;
    wc.hIcon         = LoadIcon(hInstance, szAppName);
    wc.hCursor       = LoadCursor(NULL, IDC_ARROW);
    wc.hbrBackground = (HBRUSH)(COLOR_WINDOW + 1);
```

260

```
    wc.lpszMenuName  = szAppName;
    wc.lpszClassName = szAppName;

    return(RegisterClass(&wc));
}

// create and show main window
BOOL InitInstance(HINSTANCE hInstance, int nCmdShow)
{
    HWND    hWnd;
    hInst = hInstance;
    hWnd = CreateWindow(szAppName, szTitle,
                        WS_OVERLAPPEDWINDOW,
                        160, 120, 320, 240,
                        NULL, NULL, hInstance, NULL);

    if (!hWnd)
        {
        return FALSE;
        }

    ShowWindow(hWnd, nCmdShow);
    UpdateWindow(hWnd);

    return TRUE;
}
```

AMETER.C

```
// AMETER.C
#include <windows.h>
#include <windowsx.h>
#include <math.h>
#include "globals.h"

LRESULT CALLBACK WndProc(HWND hWnd,
                         UINT uMessage,
                         WPARAM wParam,
                         LPARAM lParam)
{
    HBITMAP hBitmap;
    PAINTSTRUCT ps;
    static POINT pt;
    static RECT rc;
    HDC hDC;
    HRGN hRgnRect;
```

```
double Angle;
int i, j;

switch (uMessage)
{
    case WM_CREATE:
            // define a recatngle that confines
            // the analog meter
            rc.left = 80;    rc.right = 224;
            rc.top = 30;     rc.bottom = 138;

            // define a meter display region
            hRgnRect = CreateRectRgn(rc.left + 7,
                                     rc.top + 7,
                                     rc.left + 137,
                                     rc.top + 77);
            break;

    case WM_PAINT:
            hDC = BeginPaint(hWnd, &ps);

            // load the ameter bitmap and paint it inside
            // the rectangle rc
            hBitmap = LoadBitmap(hInst, "ametera");
            PaintMeterBitmap(hDC, hBitmap,
                                  rc.left, rc.top);
            SelectClipRgn(hDC, hRgnRect);

            // draw a needle that swing back and forth
            // four times
            for(j=0; j<4; j++){
            for(i=0; i<85; i++){
              Angle = 0.7 + 0.02*i;
              SetROP2(hDC, R2_MERGEPENNOT);
              SelectObject(hDC, GetStockObject(BLACK_PEN));
              MoveToEx(hDC, rc.left + 72,
                            rc.top + 90, NULL);
              LineTo(hDC, rc.left + 72 + 85*cos(Angle),
                          rc.top + 90 - 85*sin(Angle));

              SetROP2(hDC, R2_MASKPENNOT);
              SelectObject(hDC, GetStockObject(WHITE_PEN));
              MoveToEx(hDC, rc.left + 72,
                            rc.top + 90, NULL);
              LineTo(hDC, rc.left + 72 + 85*cos(Angle),
                          rc.top + 90 - 85*sin(Angle));
            }
```

```
      for(i=0; i<85; i++){
        Angle = 2.4 - 0.02*i;
        SetROP2(hDC, R2_MERGEPENNOT);
        SelectObject(hDC, GetStockObject(BLACK_PEN));
        MoveToEx(hDC, rc.left + 72,
                      rc.top + 90, NULL);
        LineTo(hDC, rc.left + 72 + 85*cos(Angle),
                    rc.top + 90 - 85*sin(Angle));

        SetROP2(hDC, R2_MASKPENNOT);
        SelectObject(hDC, GetStockObject(WHITE_PEN));
        MoveToEx(hDC, rc.left + 72,
                      rc.top + 90, NULL);
        LineTo(hDC, rc.left + 72 + 85*cos(Angle),
                    rc.top + 90 - 85*sin(Angle));
      }
      }

      DeleteObject(SelectObject(
                  hDC, GetStockObject(BLACK_PEN)));
      DeleteObject(SelectObject(
                  hDC, GetStockObject(WHITE_PEN)));

      EndPaint(hWnd, &ps);
      break;

case WM_COMMAND:
      switch (GET_WM_COMMAND_ID(wParam,lParam))
      {
         case IDM_ABOUT:
                // create an about dialog box
                DialogBox(hInst, "ABOUTDLG",
                        hWnd, (DLGPROC)About);
                break;

         default:
                return DefWindowProc(hWnd, uMessage,
                                      wParam, lParam);

      }
      break;

case WM_DESTROY:
      PostQuitMessage(0);
      break;

default:
      return DefWindowProc(hWnd, uMessage,
```

```
                                    wParam, lParam);
    }
    return 0;
}


// function for painting the analog meter bitmap
void PaintMeterBitmap (hDC, hBitmap, rectX, rectY)
HDC hDC;
HBITMAP hBitmap;
WORD rectX, rectY;
{
    BITMAP bmp;
    HDC hMemoryDC;
    hMemoryDC = CreateCompatibleDC(hDC);
    GetObject(hBitmap, sizeof(BITMAP), (LPSTR) &bmp);
    SelectObject(hMemoryDC, hBitmap);
    BitBlt(hDC, rectX, rectY, bmp.bmWidth, bmp.bmHeight,
                    hMemoryDC, 0, 0, SRCCOPY);
    DeleteDC(hMemoryDC);
    DeleteObject(hBitmap);
}
```

ABOUT.C

```
// ABOUT.C
#include <windows.h>
#include <windowsx.h>
#include "globals.h"


// procedures for ABOUT dialog box
LRESULT CALLBACK About(HWND hDlg,
                       UINT uMessage,
                       WPARAM wParam,
                       LPARAM lParam)
{
    switch (uMessage)
      {
        case WM_COMMAND:
            switch (GET_WM_COMMAND_ID(wParam,lParam))
              {
                case IDOK:
                case IDCANCEL:
                    {
                    EndDialog(hDlg, TRUE);
                    return(TRUE);
                    }
```

```
                        break;
            }
        }
    return FALSE;
}
```

AMETER.RC

```
#include "windows.h"
#include "globals.h"
#include <winver.h>

ametera BITMAP ametera.bmp

APPNAME ICON ICONFILE

RCINCLUDE ABOUT.DLG

APPNAME MENU
BEGIN
  MENUITEM "&About",      IDM_ABOUT
END
```

ABOUT.DLG

```
ABOUTDLG DIALOG DISCARDABLE  22, 17, 167, 73
STYLE DS_MODALFRAME | WS_CAPTION | WS_SYSMENU
CAPTION SZABOUT
BEGIN
    DEFPUSHBUTTON   "OK", IDOK, 132, 2, 32, 14, WS_GROUP
    ICON            SZAPPNAME,      -1, 3, 2, 18, 20
    LTEXT           SZAPPNAME,      -1, 30, 12,  50, 8
    LTEXT           SZDESCRIPTION, -1, 30, 22, 150, 8
    LTEXT           SZVERSION,      -1, 30, 32, 150, 8
    LTEXT           SZCOMPANYNAME, -1, 30, 42, 150, 8
END
```

AMETER.ICO

265

CASE 3-8: DIGITAL COUNTER

FIGURE 3-8

This case presents a *digital counter* that looks like a liquid crystal display (LCD). The digital counter is a way of presenting a set of specific values to the user, as opposed to the range of indefinite increments handled by the analog meter in Case 3-7.

This element displays a three-digit decimal number and is driven by a half-second internal timer. The timer is implemented using the Windows function `SetTimer()`, which will generate a `WM_TIMER` message to your window procedure every *N* milliseconds, where *N* is the integer specified in the third argument (in this case, 500).

When the `WM_TIMER` message is received, the internal data value is incremented, and three bitmaps are drawn, one for each digit position. The bitmaps are selected from a set of ten possible bitmaps, one for each decimal digit. As you can see, the bitmaps resemble the digits in an LCD such as a digital watch.

GLOBALS.H

```
// GLOBALS.H - header file for global variables
//             and function prototypes

// Product identifier string definitions.
#define APPNAME        Digital
#define ICONFILE       Digital.ico
#define SZAPPNAME      "Digital"
#define SZDESCRIPTION  "Digital Counter"
#define SZVERSION      "Version 1.0"
#define SZCOMPANYNAME  "\251 M&&T Books, 1994"
#define SZABOUT        "About"

// Global function prototypes.
BOOL InitApplication(HINSTANCE);
BOOL InitInstance(HINSTANCE, int);
void PaintBitmap(HDC, HBITMAP, int, int);
void DrawNumber(HINSTANCE, HDC, UINT, int, int);

// Callback functions called by Windows.
LRESULT CALLBACK WndProc(HWND, UINT, WPARAM, LPARAM);
LRESULT CALLBACK About(HWND, UINT, WPARAM, LPARAM);

// Menu item ID
#define IDM_ABOUT   1000

// Global variable declarations.
extern HINSTANCE hInst;     // The current instance handle
extern char szAppName[];    // The name of this application
extern char szTitle[];      // The title bar text
```

WINMAIN.C

```
// WINMAIN.C
#include <windows.h>
#include "globals.h"

int APIENTRY WinMain(HINSTANCE hInstance,
                     HINSTANCE hPrevInstance,
                     LPSTR lpCmdLine,
                     int nCmdShow)
{
    MSG msg;

    // register main window class
```

```
          if (!hPrevInstance)
             {
             if (!InitApplication(hInstance))
                {
                return FALSE;
                }
             }

          // create and show main window
          if (!InitInstance(hInstance, nCmdShow))
             {
             return FALSE;
             }

          // process window message
          while (GetMessage(&msg, NULL, 0, 0))
             {
                 TranslateMessage(&msg);
                 DispatchMessage(&msg);
             }
          return msg.wParam;
     }
```

INIT.C

```
// INIT.C
#include <windows.h>
#include "globals.h"

HINSTANCE hInst;
char szAppName[] = SZAPPNAME;
char szTitle[] = SZDESCRIPTION;

// register main window class
BOOL InitApplication(HINSTANCE hInstance)
{
    WNDCLASS  wc;

    wc.style         = CS_HREDRAW | CS_VREDRAW;
    wc.lpfnWndProc   = (WNDPROC)WndProc;
    wc.cbClsExtra    = 0;
    wc.cbWndExtra    = 0;
    wc.hInstance     = hInstance;
    wc.hIcon         = LoadIcon(hInstance, szAppName);
    wc.hCursor       = LoadCursor(NULL, IDC_ARROW);
    wc.hbrBackground = (HBRUSH)(COLOR_WINDOW + 1);
```

268

```
    wc.lpszMenuName  = szAppName;
    wc.lpszClassName = szAppName;

    return(RegisterClass(&wc));
}

// create and show main window
BOOL InitInstance(HINSTANCE hInstance, int nCmdShow)
{
    HWND     hWnd;
    hInst = hInstance;
    hWnd = CreateWindow(szAppName, szTitle,
                        WS_OVERLAPPEDWINDOW,
                        160, 120, 320, 240,
                        NULL, NULL, hInstance, NULL);

    if (!hWnd)
        {
        return FALSE;
        }

    ShowWindow(hWnd, nCmdShow);
    UpdateWindow(hWnd);

    return TRUE;
}
```

DIGITAL.C

```
// DIGITAL.C
#include <windows.h>
#include <windowsx.h>
#include "globals.h"

LRESULT CALLBACK WndProc(HWND hWnd,
                         UINT uMessage,
                         WPARAM wParam,
                         LPARAM lParam)
{
    HDC hDC;
    static UINT iDigit_1 = 0, iDigit_2 = 0, iDigit_3 = 0;
    POINT pt1 = { 150, 50 }; /* position of 1st digit */
    POINT pt2 = { 125, 50 }; /* position of 2nd digit */
    POINT pt3 = { 100, 50 }; /* position of 3rd digit */

    switch (uMessage)
```

269

```
    {
    case WM_CREATE:
            // create a half second timer
            SetTimer(hWnd, 1, 500, NULL);
            break;

    case WM_TIMER:
            // increase 1st digit by one for
            // every half second
            iDigit_1 += 1;

            // if 1st digit is equal to 10,
            // increase 2nd digit by one
            // and reset 1st digit to 0
            if(iDigit_1 == 10){
               iDigit_2 += 1;
               iDigit_1 = 0; }

            // if 2nd digit is equal to 10,
            // increase 3rd digit by one
            // and reset 2nd digit to 0
            if(iDigit_2 == 10){
               iDigit_3 += 1;
               iDigit_2 = 0; }

            hDC = GetDC(hWnd);

            // draw digit bitmaps
            DrawNumber(hInst, hDC, iDigit_1, pt1.x, pt1.y);
            DrawNumber(hInst, hDC, iDigit_2, pt2.x, pt2.y);
            DrawNumber(hInst, hDC, iDigit_3, pt3.x, pt3.y);
            ReleaseDC(hWnd, hDC);
            break;

    case WM_COMMAND:
            switch (GET_WM_COMMAND_ID(wParam,lParam))
            {
               case IDM_ABOUT:
                       // create an about dialog box
                       DialogBox(hInst, "ABOUTDLG",
                                 hWnd, (DLGPROC)About);
                       break;

               default:
                   return DefWindowProc(hWnd, uMessage,
                                        wParam, lParam);
            }
```

```
            break;

        case WM_DESTROY:
            KillTimer(hWnd, 1);
            PostQuitMessage(0);
            break;

        default:
            return DefWindowProc(hWnd, uMessage,
                                 wParam, lParam);
    }
    return 0;
}
```

```
// function to paint the digit bitmap
void PaintBitmap (hDC, hBitmap, RectX, RectY)
HDC hDC;
HBITMAP hBitmap;
int RectX, RectY;
{
    BITMAP bmp;
    HDC hMemoryDC;
    hMemoryDC = CreateCompatibleDC(hDC);
    GetObject(hBitmap, sizeof(BITMAP), (LPSTR) &bmp);
    SelectObject(hMemoryDC, hBitmap);
    BitBlt(hDC, RectX, RectY, bmp.bmWidth, bmp.bmHeight,
               hMemoryDC, 0, 0, SRCCOPY);
    DeleteDC(hMemoryDC);
    DeleteObject(hBitmap);
}
```

```
// function to load the digit bitmap
void DrawNumber(hInstance, hDC, iDigit, RectX, RectY)
HANDLE hInstance;
HDC hDC;
UINT iDigit;
int RectX, RectY;
{
HBITMAP hBitmap;
switch(iDigit){
        case 0:  hBitmap = LoadBitmap (hInstance, "Zero");
                 break;

        case 1:  hBitmap = LoadBitmap (hInstance, "One");
                 break;

        case 2:  hBitmap = LoadBitmap (hInstance, "Two");
```

```
                    break;

        case 3:  hBitmap = LoadBitmap (hInstance, "Three");
                 break;

        case 4:  hBitmap = LoadBitmap (hInstance, "Four");
                 break;

        case 5:  hBitmap = LoadBitmap (hInstance, "Five");
                 break;

        case 6:  hBitmap = LoadBitmap (hInstance, "Six");
                 break;

        case 7:  hBitmap = LoadBitmap (hInstance, "Seven");
                 break;

        case 8:  hBitmap = LoadBitmap (hInstance, "Eight");
                 break;

        case 9:  hBitmap = LoadBitmap (hInstance, "Nine");
                 break;
        }
     PaintBitmap(hDC, hBitmap, RectX, RectY);
}
```

ABOUT.C

```
// ABOUT.C
#include <windows.h>
#include <windowsx.h>
#include "globals.h"

// procedures for ABOUT dialog box
LRESULT CALLBACK About(HWND hDlg,
                       UINT uMessage,
                       WPARAM wParam,
                       LPARAM lParam)
{
    switch (uMessage)
      {
        case WM_COMMAND:
            switch (GET_WM_COMMAND_ID(wParam,lParam))
            {
                case IDOK:
                case IDCANCEL:
```

```
                              {
                              EndDialog(hDlg, TRUE);
                              return(TRUE);
                              }
                              break;
                    }
          }
     return FALSE;
}
```

DIGITAL.RC

```
#include "windows.h"
#include "globals.h"
#include <winver.h>

Zero   BITMAP zero.bmp
One    BITMAP one.bmp
Two    BITMAP two.bmp
Three  BITMAP three.bmp
Four   BITMAP four.bmp
Five   BITMAP five.bmp
Six    BITMAP six.bmp
Seven  BITMAP seven.bmp
Eight  BITMAP eight.bmp
Nine   BITMAP nine.bmp

APPNAME ICON ICONFILE

RCINCLUDE ABOUT.DLG

APPNAME MENU
BEGIN
  MENUITEM "&About",      IDM_ABOUT
END
```

ABOUT.DLG

```
ABOUTDLG DIALOG DISCARDABLE  22, 17, 167, 73
STYLE DS_MODALFRAME | WS_CAPTION | WS_SYSMENU
CAPTION SZABOUT
BEGIN
    DEFPUSHBUTTON   "OK", IDOK, 132, 2, 32, 14, WS_GROUP
    ICON            SZAPPNAME,     -1, 3, 2, 18, 20
```

```
        LTEXT        SZAPPNAME,        -1, 30, 12,  50, 8
        LTEXT        SZDESCRIPTION,    -1, 30, 22, 150, 8
        LTEXT        SZVERSION,        -1, 30, 32, 150, 8
        LTEXT        SZCOMPANYNAME,    -1, 30, 42, 150, 8
   END
```

DIGITAL.ICO

ONE.BMP

1

TWO.BMP

2

THREE.BMP

3

FOUR.BMP

4

FIVE.BMP

5

SIX.BMP

6

SEVEN.BMP

7

EIGHT.BMP

8

NINE.BMP

9

ZERO.BMP

0

CASE 3-9: PROGRESS METER

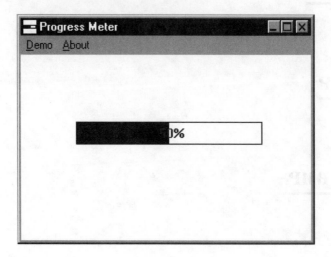

FIGURE 3-9

The *progress meter* is a user interface element frequently used to provide feedback to the user when an application carries out a lengthy operation such as a file download in a telecom program or a file copy in an install program. The progress meter consists of a white rectangle that is slowly filled from left to right as the operation moves from beginning to completion. In addition, a number is displayed in the center that provides a running total of the percent of completion.

To implement the progress bar, you need to draw a white rectangle with a black boundary followed by the blue rectangle that fills from left to right. The progress number centers on the white rectangle. Please see Case 2-1 for another example.

GLOBALS.H

```
// GLOBALS.H - header file for global variables
//              and function prototypes

// Product identifier string definitions.
#define APPNAME       Meter
#define ICONFILE      Meter.ico
#define SZAPPNAME     "Meter"
#define SZDESCRIPTION "Progress Meter"
#define SZVERSION     "Version 1.0"
#define SZCOMPANYNAME "\251 M&&T Books, 1994"
#define SZABOUT       "About"

// Global function prototypes.
BOOL InitApplication(HINSTANCE);
BOOL InitInstance(HINSTANCE, int);
void PaintRectBitmap(HDC, HBITMAP, WORD, WORD);

// Callback functions called by Windows.
LRESULT CALLBACK WndProc(HWND, UINT, WPARAM, LPARAM);
LRESULT CALLBACK About(HWND, UINT, WPARAM, LPARAM);

// Menu item ID
#define IDM_DEMO  100
#define IDM_ABOUT 101

// Global variable declarations.
extern HINSTANCE hInst;      // The current instance handle
extern char szAppName[];     // The name of this application
extern char szTitle[];       // The title bar text
```

WINMAIN.C

```
// WINMAIN.C
#include <windows.h>
#include "globals.h"

int APIENTRY WinMain(HINSTANCE hInstance,
                     HINSTANCE hPrevInstance,
                     LPSTR lpCmdLine,
                     int nCmdShow)
{
    MSG msg;

    // register main window class
```

```
        if (!hPrevInstance)
          {
          if (!InitApplication(hInstance))
            {
            return FALSE;
            }
          }

        // create and show main window
        if (!InitInstance(hInstance, nCmdShow))
          {
          return FALSE;
          }

        // process window message
        while (GetMessage(&msg, NULL, 0, 0))
          {
              TranslateMessage(&msg);
              DispatchMessage(&msg);
          }
        return msg.wParam;
}
```

INIT.C

```
// INIT.C
#include <windows.h>
#include "globals.h"

HINSTANCE hInst;
char szAppName[] = SZAPPNAME;
char szTitle[] = SZDESCRIPTION;

// register main window class
BOOL InitApplication(HINSTANCE hInstance)
{
    WNDCLASS  wc;

    wc.style          = CS_HREDRAW | CS_VREDRAW;
    wc.lpfnWndProc    = (WNDPROC)WndProc;
    wc.cbClsExtra     = 0;
    wc.cbWndExtra     = 0;
    wc.hInstance      = hInstance;
    wc.hIcon          = LoadIcon(hInstance, szAppName);
    wc.hCursor        = LoadCursor(NULL, IDC_ARROW);
    wc.hbrBackground  = (HBRUSH)(COLOR_WINDOW + 1);
```

```
    wc.lpszMenuName  = szAppName;
    wc.lpszClassName = szAppName;

    return(RegisterClass(&wc));
}


// create and show main window
BOOL InitInstance(HINSTANCE hInstance, int nCmdShow)
{
    HWND    hWnd;
    hInst = hInstance;
    hWnd = CreateWindow(szAppName, szTitle,
                        WS_OVERLAPPEDWINDOW,
                        160, 120, 320, 240,
                        NULL, NULL, hInstance, NULL);

    if (!hWnd)
        {
        return FALSE;
        }

    ShowWindow(hWnd, nCmdShow);
    UpdateWindow(hWnd);

    return TRUE;
}
```

METER.C

```
// METER.C
#include <windows.h>
#include <windowsx.h>
#include "globals.h"

HBITMAP hBitmap;
static UINT iMeter_percent = 50;

LRESULT CALLBACK WndProc(HWND hWnd,
                         UINT uMessage,
                         WPARAM wParam,
                         LPARAM lParam)
{
    PAINTSTRUCT ps;
    static RECT rc;
    HDC hDC;
    HBRUSH hBlueBrush;
```

```
char meter_text[4];
int i, j;

switch (uMessage)
{
    case WM_CREATE:
            // define a rectangle that confines the meter
            rc.left = 60;
            rc.right = 260;
            rc.top = 70;
            rc.bottom = 94;
            break;

    case WM_PAINT:
            hDC = BeginPaint(hWnd, &ps);

            // draw a background rectangle
            SelectObject(hDC, GetStockObject(WHITE_BRUSH));
            Rectangle(hDC, rc.left, rc.top,
                        rc.right, rc.bottom);

            // paint a blue rectangle that indicate the
            // progress of the job
            hBlueBrush = CreateSolidBrush(RGB(0, 0, 255));
            SelectObject(hDC, hBlueBrush);
            Rectangle(hDC, rc.left, rc.top,
                        rc.left + iMeter_percent * 2,
                        rc.bottom);

            // draw the percentage text on the meter
            sprintf(meter_text, "%3d%%", iMeter_percent);
            SetTextColor(hDC, RGB(255, 0, 0));
            SetBkMode(hDC, TRANSPARENT);
            SetTextAlign(hDC, TA_CENTER);
            TextOut(hDC, (rc.left + rc.right)/2,
                        rc.top + 4, meter_text, 4);

            DeleteObject(SelectObject(hDC, hBlueBrush));
            EndPaint(hWnd, &ps);
            break;

    case WM_COMMAND:
            switch (GET_WM_COMMAND_ID(wParam,lParam))
            {
                case IDM_DEMO:
                    for(i=0; i<101; i++){
                        for(j=0; j<10000; j++){};
```

```
                    iMeter_percent = i;
        hDC = GetDC(hWnd);

            // draw a background rectangle
            SelectObject(hDC, GetStockObject(WHITE_BRUSH));
            Rectangle(hDC, rc.left, rc.top,
                        rc.right, rc.bottom);

            // paint a blue rectangle that indicate the
            // progress of the job
            hBlueBrush = CreateSolidBrush(RGB(0, 0, 255));
            SelectObject(hDC, hBlueBrush);
            Rectangle(hDC, rc.left, rc.top,
                        rc.left + iMeter_percent * 2,
                        rc.bottom);

            // draw the percentage text on the meter
            sprintf(meter_text, "%3d%%", iMeter_percent);
            SetTextColor(hDC, RGB(255, 0, 0));
            SetBkMode(hDC, TRANSPARENT);
            SetTextAlign(hDC, TA_CENTER);
            TextOut(hDC, (rc.left + rc.right)/2,
                        rc.top + 4, meter_text, 4);

            DeleteObject(SelectObject(hDC,
                        GetStockObject(WHITE_BRUSH)));
            DeleteObject(SelectObject(hDC, hBlueBrush));
            ReleaseDC(hWnd, hDC);
                    }
                break;

            case IDM_ABOUT:
                    // create an about dialog box
                    DialogBox(hInst, "ABOUTDLG",
                            hWnd, (DLGPROC)About);
                    break;

            default:
                return DefWindowProc(hWnd, uMessage,
                                    wParam, lParam);
        }
        break;

case WM_DESTROY:
        PostQuitMessage(0);
        break;
```

```
        default:
            return DefWindowProc(hWnd, uMessage,
                                 wParam, lParam);
    }
    return 0;
}
```

ABOUT.C

```
// ABOUT.C
#include <windows.h>
#include <windowsx.h>
#include "globals.h"

// procedures for ABOUT dialog box
LRESULT CALLBACK About(HWND hDlg,
                       UINT uMessage,
                       WPARAM wParam,
                       LPARAM lParam)
{
    switch (uMessage)
      {
        case WM_COMMAND:
            switch (GET_WM_COMMAND_ID(wParam,lParam))
            {
                case IDOK:
                case IDCANCEL:
                    {
                    EndDialog(hDlg, TRUE);
                    return(TRUE);
                    }
                    break;
            }
      }
    return FALSE;
}
```

METER.RC

```
#include "windows.h"
#include "globals.h"
#include <winver.h>

APPNAME ICON ICONFILE
```

```
RCINCLUDE ABOUT.DLG

APPNAME MENU
BEGIN
    MENUITEM "&Demo",   IDM_DEMO
    MENUITEM "&About",  IDM_ABOUT
END
```

ABOUT.DLG

```
ABOUTDLG DIALOG DISCARDABLE  22, 17, 167, 73
STYLE DS_MODALFRAME | WS_CAPTION | WS_SYSMENU
CAPTION SZABOUT
BEGIN
    DEFPUSHBUTTON   "OK", IDOK, 132, 2, 32, 14, WS_GROUP
    ICON            SZAPPNAME,      -1, 3, 2, 18, 20
    LTEXT           SZAPPNAME,      -1, 30, 12,  50, 8
    LTEXT           SZDESCRIPTION, -1, 30, 22, 150, 8
    LTEXT           SZVERSION,     -1, 30, 32, 150, 8
    LTEXT           SZCOMPANYNAME, -1, 30, 42, 150, 8
END
```

METER.ICO

CHAPTER FOUR

MENUS

CASE 4-1: BITMAP MENU ITEMS

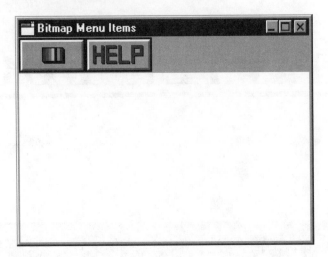

<u>FIGURE 4-1</u>

This case shows how to display bitmaps in a Windows menu. In this case, the two bitmaps shown in Figure 4-1 comprise the top-level menu choices. Subsequent cases will illustrate how to display bitmaps as part of the drop-down list of menu items.

Of the two items in the top-level menu here, the left one is a *regular item*—that is, it has an immediate action, as opposed to invoking a pop-up or secondary menu list. The menu item on the right (the "Help" bitmap) invokes a secondary drop-down menu, in this case, a command to show the About box. The list of items for the Help menu choice is defined in the resource file MENUBMP.RC.

The menu is created in the handler for the WM_CREATE message, which is received by the window procedure before the window is displayed on the screen. As you can see from the code listing, the first step is to load the bitmaps using the names specified in the resource file. This is accomplished via the Windows functin LoadBitmap(). Then an emply main menu is created with CreateMenu() and populated with a couple of calls to AppendMenu(). The secondary menu needs to be loaded via

`LoadMenu()` before being added to the top-level menu with `AppendMenu()`. Lastly, the `SetMenu()` function establishes the connection between this menu and our main application window. In this sequence of calls, the main difference between a text-only menu and one with a bitmap is in the parameters to the calls, passing `MF_BITMAP` to `AppendMenu()`. Of course, if you had a text-only menu, you would not need to load and append each item manually; all this could be done automatically in a resource file definition.

As with text menu items, Windows sends a `WM_COMMAND` message to your window procedure when a menu item is sleected. The code in the listing that handles the `WM_COMMAND` message is no different for the case of bitmap menu items.

Note that, unlike owner-draw push buttons in which you have to supply the code for painting the push-down state, here Windows automatically changes the bitmap colors when the menu item is selected.

GLOBALS.H

```
// GLOBALS.H - header file for global variables
//              and function prototypes

// Product identifier string definitions.
#define APPNAME        MenuBmp
#define ICONFILE       MenuBmp.ico
#define SZAPPNAME      "MenuBmp"
#define SZDESCRIPTION  "Bitmap Menu Items"
#define SZVERSION      "Version 1.0"
#define SZCOMPANYNAME  "\251 M&&T Books, 1994"
#define SZABOUT        "About"

// Global function prototypes.
BOOL InitApplication(HINSTANCE);
BOOL InitInstance(HINSTANCE, int);

// Callback functions called by Windows.
LRESULT CALLBACK WndProc(HWND, UINT, WPARAM, LPARAM);
LRESULT CALLBACK About(HWND, UINT, WPARAM, LPARAM);

// Menu item ID
#define IDM_PUSHBUTTON  1001
```

```
#define IDM_ABOUT        1002

// Global variable declarations.
extern HINSTANCE hInst;
extern char szAppName[];
extern char szTitle[];
```

WINMAIN.C

```
// WINMAIN.C
#include <windows.h>
#include "globals.h"

int APIENTRY WinMain(HINSTANCE hInstance,
                     HINSTANCE hPrevInstance,
                     LPSTR lpCmdLine,
                     int nCmdShow)
{
    MSG msg;
    HANDLE hAccelTable;

    // register main window class
    if (!hPrevInstance)
        {
        if (!InitApplication(hInstance))
            {
            return FALSE;
            }
        }

    // create and show main window
    if (!InitInstance(hInstance, nCmdShow))
        {
        return FALSE;
        }

    hAccelTable = LoadAccelerators(hInstance, szAppName);

    // process window messages
    while (GetMessage(&msg, NULL, 0, 0))
        {
        if (!TranslateAccelerator(msg.hwnd,
                                  hAccelTable, &msg))
            {
            TranslateMessage(&msg);
            DispatchMessage(&msg);
            }
        }
```

```
    return msg.wParam;
}
```

INIT.C

```
// INIT.C
#include <windows.h>
#include "globals.h"

HINSTANCE hInst;
char szAppName[] = SZAPPNAME;
char szTitle[] = SZDESCRIPTION;

// register main window class
BOOL InitApplication(HINSTANCE hInstance)
{
    WNDCLASS  wc;

    wc.style         = CS_HREDRAW | CS_VREDRAW;
    wc.lpfnWndProc   = (WNDPROC)WndProc;
    wc.cbClsExtra    = 0;
    wc.cbWndExtra    = 0;
    wc.hInstance     = hInstance;
    wc.hIcon         = LoadIcon(hInstance, szAppName);
    wc.hCursor       = LoadCursor(NULL, IDC_ARROW);
    wc.hbrBackground = (HBRUSH)(COLOR_WINDOW + 1);
    wc.lpszMenuName  = szAppName;
    wc.lpszClassName = szAppName;

    return(RegisterClass(&wc));
}

// create and show main window
BOOL InitInstance(HINSTANCE hInstance, int nCmdShow)
{
    HWND    hWnd;
    hInst = hInstance;
    hWnd = CreateWindow(szAppName, szTitle,
                        WS_OVERLAPPEDWINDOW,
                        160, 120, 320, 240,
                        NULL, NULL, hInstance, NULL);

    if (!hWnd)
        {
        return FALSE;
        }

    ShowWindow(hWnd, nCmdShow);
```

```
        UpdateWindow(hWnd);

        return TRUE;
    }
```

MENUBMP.C

```
// MENUBMP.C
#include <windows.h>
#include <windowsx.h>
#include "globals.h"

LRESULT CALLBACK WndProc(HWND hWnd,
                         UINT uMessage,
                         WPARAM wParam,
                         LPARAM lParam)

{
HMENU hMenu, hMenuHelp;
HBITMAP hBitmap, hBitmapH;

    switch (uMessage)
    {
        case WM_CREATE:
            // load menu item bitmaps
            hBitmap = LoadBitmap(hInst, "BitmapButton");
            hBitmapH = LoadBitmap(hInst, "BitmapHelp");

            // create an empty main menu
            hMenu = CreateMenu();

            // load submenu for main menu item HELP
            hMenuHelp = LoadMenu(hInst, "MenuHelp");

            // add first bitmap menu item to main menu
            AppendMenu(hMenu, MF_BITMAP,
                    (UINT)IDM_PUSHBUTTON,
                    (LPCTSTR)MAKELONG(hBitmap, 0));

            // add help bitmap menu item (with submenu)
            // to main menu
            AppendMenu(hMenu, MF_POPUP | MF_BITMAP,
                    hMenuHelp,
                    (LPCTSTR)MAKELONG(hBitmapH, 0));
            SetMenu(hWnd, hMenu);
            break;

        case WM_COMMAND:
```

```
          switch (GET_WM_COMMAND_ID(wParam,lParam))
          {
              case IDM_PUSHBUTTON:
                  MessageBox(NULL,
                      "This is a custom manu push button!",
                      "Info", MB_OK | MB_ICONINFORMATION |
                      MB_SYSTEMMODAL);
                  break;

              case IDM_ABOUT:
                  // create an about box
                  DialogBox(hInst, "ABOUTDLG",
                          hWnd, (DLGPROC)About);
                  break;

              default:
                  return DefWindowProc(hWnd, uMessage,
                                          wParam, lParam);
          }
          break;

      case WM_DESTROY:
          PostQuitMessage(0);
          break;

      default:
          return DefWindowProc(hWnd, uMessage,
                                  wParam, lParam);
      }
      return 0;
}
```

ABOUT.C

```
// ABOUT.C
#include <windows.h>
#include <windowsx.h>
#include "globals.h"

// procedures for ABOUT dialog box
LRESULT CALLBACK About(HWND hDlg,
                    UINT uMessage,
                    WPARAM wParam,
                    LPARAM lParam)
{
    switch (uMessage)
      {
        case WM_COMMAND:
```

```
                    switch (GET_WM_COMMAND_ID(wParam,lParam))
                    {
                        case IDOK:
                        case IDCANCEL:
                            {
                            EndDialog(hDlg, TRUE);
                            return(TRUE);
                            }
                            break;
                    }
            }
        return FALSE;
    }
```

MENUBMP.RC

```
#include "windows.h"
#include "globals.h"
#include <winver.h>

APPNAME ICON ICONFILE

RCINCLUDE ABOUT.DLG

BitmapButton   BITMAP mbtn.bmp
BitmapHelp     BITMAP mhelp.bmp

MenuHelp MENU
BEGIN
    MENUITEM "&About  F1", IDM_ABOUT
END

APPNAME ACCELERATORS
BEGIN
    VK_F1, IDM_ABOUT, VIRTKEY
END
```

ABOUT.DLG

```
ABOUTDLG DIALOG DISCARDABLE  22, 17, 167, 73
STYLE DS_MODALFRAME | WS_CAPTION | WS_SYSMENU
CAPTION SZABOUT
BEGIN
    DEFPUSHBUTTON   "OK", IDOK, 132, 2, 32, 14, WS_GROUP
    ICON            SZAPPNAME,     -1, 3, 2, 18, 20
    LTEXT           SZAPPNAME,     -1, 30, 12,  50, 8
    LTEXT           SZDESCRIPTION, -1, 30, 22, 150, 8
```

```
        LTEXT           SZVERSION,      -1, 30, 32, 150, 8
        LTEXT           SZCOMPANYNAME, -1, 30, 42, 150, 8
    END
```

MENUBMP.ICO

MBTN.BMP

MHELP.BMP

CASE 4-2: BITMAP ITEMS IN PULL-DOWN MENU

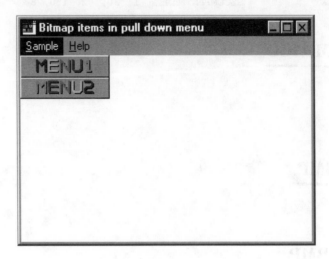

FIGURE 4-2

This case shows how to use bitmap items in a pull-down menu. Unlike Case 4-1, in which the top-level menu choices were bitmaps, here the top-level menu contains purely text items. However, each of the two top-level choices invokes a secondary pull-down menu that consists of bitmap items.

Unlike Case 4-1, the menu structure is entirely defined at run time, via Windows API calls, instead of being partially specified in a resource file. Here the resource file MENUBMPP.RC contains only the names of the bitmaps used by the Windows API calls.

As in Case 4-1, menu creation happens in the WM_CREATE handler using a sequence of Windows API calls. As you can see from the code listing, the first step is to load the various bitmaps using the names specifed in the resource file, via a call to LoadBitmap(). Then an empty main menu is created with CreateMenu() and populated with a couple of calls to AppendMenu(). To append a menu item that is a bitmap, you use MF_BITMAP as one of the parameters to AppendMenu(). Also, note that there is no call to LoadMenu() because the menu is specified entirely

294

at run time, instead of a static definition in the resource file. A call to `SetMenu()` establishes the connection between this menu and our main application window.

For all menu items, Windows sends a `WM_COMMAND` message to your WndProc when a menu item is selected. The code in the `WM_COMMAND` handler makes no distinction between text and bitmap menu items.

GLOBALS.H

```
// GLOBALS.H - header file for global variables
//             and function prototypes

// Product identifier string definitions.
#define APPNAME       MenuBmpp
#define ICONFILE      MenuBmpp.ico
#define SZAPPNAME     "MenuBmpp"
#define SZDESCRIPTION "Bitmap items in pull down menu"
#define SZVERSION     "Version 1.0"
#define SZCOMPANYNAME "\251 M&&T Books, 1994"
#define SZABOUT       "About"

// Global function prototypes.
BOOL InitApplication(HINSTANCE);
BOOL InitInstance(HINSTANCE, int);

// Callback functions.  These are called by Windows.
LRESULT CALLBACK WndProc(HWND, UINT, WPARAM, LPARAM);
LRESULT CALLBACK About(HWND, UINT, WPARAM, LPARAM);

// Menu item ID
#define IDM_ABOUT  1001
#define IDM_SAMPLE 1002
#define IDM_MENU1  1003
#define IDM_MENU2  1004

// Global variable declarations.
extern HINSTANCE hInst;      // The current instance handle
extern char szAppName[];     // The name of this application
extern char szTitle[];       // The title bar text
```

WINMAIN.C

```
// WINMAIN.C
#include <windows.h>
```

```c
#include "globals.h"

int APIENTRY WinMain(HINSTANCE hInstance,
                     HINSTANCE hPrevInstance,
                     LPSTR lpCmdLine,
                     int nCmdShow)
{
    MSG msg;

    // register main window class
    if (!hPrevInstance)
        {
        if (!InitApplication(hInstance))
            {
            return FALSE;
            }
        }

    // create and show main window
    if (!InitInstance(hInstance, nCmdShow))
        {
        return FALSE;
        }

    // process window messages
    while (GetMessage(&msg, NULL, 0, 0))
        {
            TranslateMessage(&msg);
            DispatchMessage(&msg);
        }
    return msg.wParam;
}
```

INIT.C

```c
// INIT.C
#include <windows.h>
#include "globals.h"

HINSTANCE hInst;
char szAppName[] = SZAPPNAME;
char szTitle[] = SZDESCRIPTION;

// register main window class
BOOL InitApplication(HINSTANCE hInstance)
{
```

```
    WNDCLASS  wc;

    wc.style          = CS_HREDRAW | CS_VREDRAW;
    wc.lpfnWndProc    = (WNDPROC)WndProc;
    wc.cbClsExtra     = 0;
    wc.cbWndExtra     = 0;
    wc.hInstance      = hInstance;
    wc.hIcon          = LoadIcon(hInstance, szAppName);
    wc.hCursor        = LoadCursor(NULL, IDC_ARROW);
    wc.hbrBackground  = (HBRUSH)(COLOR_WINDOW + 1);
    wc.lpszMenuName   = szAppName;
    wc.lpszClassName  = szAppName;

    return(RegisterClass(&wc));
}

// create and show main window
BOOL InitInstance(HINSTANCE hInstance, int nCmdShow)
{
    HWND     hWnd;
    hInst = hInstance;
    hWnd = CreateWindow(szAppName, szTitle,
                        WS_OVERLAPPEDWINDOW,
                        160, 120, 320, 240,
                        NULL, NULL, hInstance, NULL);

    if (!hWnd)
        {
        return FALSE;
        }

    ShowWindow(hWnd, nCmdShow);
    UpdateWindow(hWnd);

    return TRUE;
}
```

MENUBMPP.C

```
// MENUBMPP.C
#include <windows.h>
#include <windowsx.h>
#include "globals.h"

LRESULT CALLBACK WndProc(HWND hWnd,
                         UINT uMessage,
```

297

```
                        WPARAM wParam,
                        LPARAM lParam)
{
HMENU hMenu, hMenuSample, hMenuHelp;
HBITMAP hBitmap1, hBitmap2, hBitmapA;

    switch (uMessage)
    {
        case WM_CREATE:
            // load menu item bitmaps
            hBitmap1 = LoadBitmap(hInst,
                                "BitmapPopUpMenu1");
            hBitmap2 = LoadBitmap(hInst,
                                "BitmapPopUpMenu2");
            hBitmapA = LoadBitmap(hInst, "BitmapAbout");

            // create an empty main menu
            hMenu = CreateMenu();

            // create an empty submenu for
            // menu item "Sample"
            hMenuSample = CreateMenu();

            // add menu item "Sample" to main menu
            AppendMenu(hMenu, MF_STRING | MF_POPUP,
                    hMenuSample, "&Sample");

            // add menu items to "Sample" submenu
            AppendMenu(hMenuSample, MF_BITMAP,
                    (UINT)IDM_MENU1,
                    (LPCTSTR)MAKELONG(hBitmap1, 0));
            AppendMenu(hMenuSample, MF_SEPARATOR, 0, NULL);
            AppendMenu(hMenuSample, MF_BITMAP,
                    (UINT)IDM_MENU2,
                    (LPCTSTR)MAKELONG(hBitmap2, 0));

            // create an empty submenu for menu item "Help"
            hMenuHelp = CreateMenu();

            // add menu item "Help" to main menu
            AppendMenu(hMenu, MF_STRING | MF_POPUP,
                    hMenuHelp, "&Help");

            // add menu item to "Help" submenu
            AppendMenu(hMenuHelp, MF_BITMAP,
                    (UINT)IDM_ABOUT,
                    (LPCTSTR)MAKELONG(hBitmapA, 0));
```

```
                SetMenu(hWnd, hMenu);
                break;

        case WM_COMMAND:
                switch (GET_WM_COMMAND_ID(wParam,lParam))
                {
                    case IDM_ABOUT:
                            // create an about dialog box
                            DialogBox(hInst, "ABOUTDLG",
                                        hWnd, (DLGPROC)About);
                            break;

                    case IDM_MENU1:
                            // things to do
                            MessageBox(NULL,
                                "This is a custom popup menu item!",
                                "Info", MB_OK | MB_ICONINFORMATION |
                                MB_SYSTEMMODAL);
                            break;

                    case IDM_MENU2:
                            // things to do
                            MessageBox(NULL,
                                "This is a custom popup menu item!",
                                "Info", MB_OK | MB_ICONINFORMATION |
                                MB_SYSTEMMODAL);
                            break;

                    default:
                            return DefWindowProc(hWnd, uMessage,
                                                    wParam, lParam);
                }
                break;

        case WM_DESTROY:
                PostQuitMessage(0);
                break;

        default:
                return DefWindowProc(hWnd, uMessage,
                                        wParam, lParam);
    }
    return 0;
}
```

ABOUT.C

```
// ABOUT.C
#include <windows.h>
#include <windowsx.h>
#include "globals.h"

// procedures for ABOUT dialog box
LRESULT CALLBACK About(HWND hDlg,
                       UINT uMessage,
                       WPARAM wParam,
                       LPARAM lParam)
{
    switch (uMessage)
      {
        case WM_COMMAND:
            switch (GET_WM_COMMAND_ID(wParam,lParam))
              {
                case IDOK:
                case IDCANCEL:
                    {
                    EndDialog(hDlg, TRUE);
                    return(TRUE);
                    }
                    break;
              }
      }
    return FALSE;
}
```

MENUBMPP.RC

```
#include "windows.h"
#include "globals.h"
#include <winver.h>

APPNAME ICON ICONFILE

RCINCLUDE ABOUT.DLG

BitmapPopupMenu1 BITMAP menu1.bmp
BitmapPopupMenu2 BITMAP menu2.bmp
BitmapAbout      BITMAP mabout.bmp
```

ABOUT.DLG

```
ABOUTDLG DIALOG DISCARDABLE  22, 17, 167, 73
STYLE DS_MODALFRAME | WS_CAPTION | WS_SYSMENU
CAPTION SZABOUT
BEGIN
    DEFPUSHBUTTON    "OK", IDOK, 132, 2, 32, 14, WS_GROUP
    ICON             SZAPPNAME,      -1, 3, 2, 18, 20
    LTEXT            SZAPPNAME,      -1, 30, 12,  50, 8
    LTEXT            SZDESCRIPTION, -1, 30, 22, 150, 8
    LTEXT            SZVERSION,      -1, 30, 32, 150, 8
    LTEXT            SZCOMPANYNAME, -1, 30, 42, 150, 8
END
```

MENUBMPP.ICO

MENU1.BMP

MENU2.BMP

CASE 4-3: BITMAP ITEMS IN MAIN MENU AND PULL DOWN MENUS

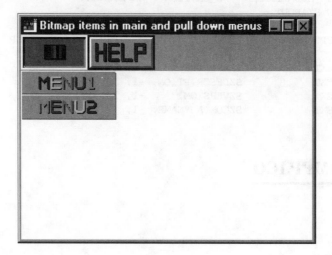

FIGURE 4-3

This case is a combination of Case 4-1 and 4-2, in that bitmap items are used for the top-level menu as well as the secondary pull-down menus.

As in the previous cases, the menus are created and populated entirely at run time via Windows API calls rather than statically via a resource file definition. The code here is a straightforward combination of the techniques used in the previous two cases. Please see the discussion there for more details on the implementation.

GLOBALS.H

```
// GLOBALS.H - header file for global variables
//              and function prototypes

// Product identifier string definitions.
#define APPNAME       MenuBmpa
#define ICONFILE      MenuBmpa.ico
#define SZAPPNAME     "MenuBmpa"
#define SZDESCRIPTION "Bitmap items in main and pull down menus"
#define SZVERSION     "Version 1.0"
#define SZCOMPANYNAME "\251 M&&T Books, 1994"
#define SZABOUT       "About"

// Global function prototypes.
BOOL InitApplication(HINSTANCE);
BOOL InitInstance(HINSTANCE, int);

// Callback functions.  These are called by Windows.
LRESULT CALLBACK WndProc(HWND, UINT, WPARAM, LPARAM);
LRESULT CALLBACK About(HWND, UINT, WPARAM, LPARAM);

// Menu item ID
#define IDM_ABOUT 101
#define IDM_MENU1 102
#define IDM_MENU2 103

// Global variable declarations.
extern HINSTANCE hInst;      // The current instance handle
extern char szAppName[];     // The name of this application
extern char szTitle[];       // The title bar text
```

WINMAIN.C

```
// WINMAIN.C
#include <windows.h>
#include "globals.h"

int APIENTRY WinMain(HINSTANCE hInstance,
                     HINSTANCE hPrevInstance,
                     LPSTR lpCmdLine,
                     int nCmdShow)
{
    MSG msg;

    // register main window class
```

```
            if (!hPrevInstance)
                {
                if (!InitApplication(hInstance))
                    {
                    return FALSE;
                    }
                }

            // create and show main window
            if (!InitInstance(hInstance, nCmdShow))
                {
                return FALSE;
                }

            // process window messages
            while (GetMessage(&msg, NULL, 0, 0))
                {
                    TranslateMessage(&msg);
                    DispatchMessage(&msg);
                }
            return msg.wParam;
}
```

INIT.C

```
// INIT.C
#include <windows.h>
#include "globals.h"

HINSTANCE hInst;
char szAppName[] = SZAPPNAME;
char szTitle[] = SZDESCRIPTION;

// register main window class
BOOL InitApplication(HINSTANCE hInstance)
{
    WNDCLASS  wc;

    wc.style         = CS_HREDRAW | CS_VREDRAW;
    wc.lpfnWndProc   = (WNDPROC)WndProc;
    wc.cbClsExtra    = 0;
    wc.cbWndExtra    = 0;
    wc.hInstance     = hInstance;
    wc.hIcon         = LoadIcon(hInstance, szAppName);
    wc.hCursor       = LoadCursor(NULL, IDC_ARROW);
    wc.hbrBackground = (HBRUSH)(COLOR_WINDOW + 1);
```

```
    wc.lpszMenuName  = szAppName;
    wc.lpszClassName = szAppName;

    return(RegisterClass(&wc));
}

// create and show main window
BOOL InitInstance(HINSTANCE hInstance, int nCmdShow)
{
    HWND     hWnd;
    hInst = hInstance;
    hWnd = CreateWindow(szAppName, szTitle,
                        WS_OVERLAPPEDWINDOW,
                        160, 120, 320, 240,
                        NULL, NULL, hInstance, NULL);

    if (!hWnd)
        {
        return FALSE;
        }

    ShowWindow(hWnd, nCmdShow);
    UpdateWindow(hWnd);

    return TRUE;
}
```

MENUBMPA.C

```
// MENUBMPA.C
#include <windows.h>
#include <windowsx.h>
#include "globals.h"

LRESULT CALLBACK WndProc(HWND hWnd,
                         UINT uMessage,
                         WPARAM wParam,
                         LPARAM lParam)
{
HMENU hMenu, hMenuSample, hMenuHelp;
HBITMAP hBitmapS, hBitmap1, hBitmap2, hBitmapH, hBitmapA;

    switch (uMessage)
    {
        case WM_CREATE:
            // load bitmaps for menu item
            hBitmapS = LoadBitmap(hInst, "BitmapSample");
```

```
                  hBitmap1 = LoadBitmap(hInst,
                                    "BitmapPopUpMenu1");
                  hBitmap2 = LoadBitmap(hInst,
                                    "BitmapPopUpMenu2");
                  hBitmapH = LoadBitmap(hInst, "BitmapHelp");
                  hBitmapA = LoadBitmap(hInst, "BitmapAbout");

                  // create an empty main menu
                  hMenu = CreateMenu();

                  // create an empty "Sample" submenu
                  hMenuSample = CreateMenu();

                  // add item "Sample" to main menu
                  AppendMenu(hMenu, MF_BITMAP | MF_POPUP,
                          hMenuSample,
                          (LPCTSTR)MAKELONG(hBitmapS, 0));

                  // add items to submenu "Sample"
                  AppendMenu(hMenuSample, MF_BITMAP,
                          (UINT)IDM_MENU1,
                          (LPCTSTR)MAKELONG(hBitmap1, 0));
                  AppendMenu(hMenuSample, MF_SEPARATOR, 0, NULL);
                  AppendMenu(hMenuSample, MF_BITMAP,
                          (UINT)IDM_MENU2,
                          (LPCTSTR)MAKELONG(hBitmap2, 0));

                  // create an empty "Help" submenu
                  hMenuHelp = CreateMenu();

                  // add item "Help" to main menu
                  AppendMenu(hMenu, MF_BITMAP | MF_POPUP,
                          hMenuHelp,
                          (LPCTSTR)MAKELONG(hBitmapH, 0));

                  // add items to "Help" submenu
                  AppendMenu(hMenuHelp, MF_BITMAP,
                          (UINT)IDM_ABOUT,
                          (LPCTSTR)MAKELONG(hBitmapA, 0));

              SetMenu(hWnd, hMenu);
              break;

      case WM_COMMAND:
          switch (GET_WM_COMMAND_ID(wParam,lParam))
          {
             case IDM_ABOUT:
                      // create an about dialog box
```

```
                        DialogBox(hInst, "ABOUTDLG",
                                    hWnd, (DLGPROC)About);
                    break;

                case IDM_MENU1:
                        // things to do
                        MessageBox(NULL,
                            "This is a custom popup menu item!",
                            "Info", MB_OK | MB_ICONINFORMATION |
                            MB_SYSTEMMODAL);
                        break;

                case IDM_MENU2:
                        // things to do
                        MessageBox(NULL,
                            "This is a custom popup menu item!",
                            "Info", MB_OK | MB_ICONINFORMATION |
                            MB_SYSTEMMODAL);
                        break;

                default:
                        return DefWindowProc(hWnd, uMessage,
                                            wParam, lParam);
            }
            break;

        case WM_DESTROY:
            PostQuitMessage(0);
            break;

        default:
            return DefWindowProc(hWnd, uMessage,
                                wParam, lParam);
    }
    return 0;
}
```

ABOUT.C

```
// ABOUT.C
#include <windows.h>
#include <windowsx.h>
#include "globals.h"

// procedures for ABOUT dialog box
LRESULT CALLBACK About(HWND hDlg,
```

```
                    UINT uMessage,
                    WPARAM wParam,
                    LPARAM lParam)
    {
        switch (uMessage)
          {
            case WM_COMMAND:
                    switch (GET_WM_COMMAND_ID(wParam,lParam))
                    {
                        case IDOK:
                        case IDCANCEL:
                            {
                            EndDialog(hDlg, TRUE);
                            return(TRUE);
                            }
                            break;
                    }
          }
        return FALSE;
    }
```

MENUBMPA.RC

```
#include "windows.h"
#include "globals.h"
#include <winver.h>

APPNAME ICON ICONFILE

RCINCLUDE ABOUT.DLG

BitmapSample       BITMAP mbtnup.bmp
BitmapPopupMenu1   BITMAP menu1.bmp
BitmapPopupMenu2   BITMAP menu2.bmp
BitmapHelp         BITMAP mhelp.bmp
BitmapAbout        BITMAP mabout.bmp
```

ABOUT.DLG

```
ABOUTDLG DIALOG DISCARDABLE  22, 17, 167, 73
STYLE DS_MODALFRAME | WS_CAPTION | WS_SYSMENU
CAPTION SZABOUT
BEGIN
    DEFPUSHBUTTON    "OK", IDOK, 132, 2, 32, 14, WS_GROUP
    ICON             SZAPPNAME,    -1, 3, 2, 18, 20
```

```
        LTEXT          SZAPPNAME,       -1, 30, 12,  50, 8
        LTEXT          SZDESCRIPTION,   -1, 30, 22, 150, 8
        LTEXT          SZVERSION,       -1, 30, 32, 150, 8
        LTEXT          SZCOMPANYNAME,   -1, 30, 42, 150, 8
    END
```

MENUBMPA.ICO

MBTNUP.BMP

MHELP.BMP

MENU1.BMP

MENU2.BMP

MABOUT.BMP

CASE 4-4: BITMAP ITEMS IN SYSTEM MENU

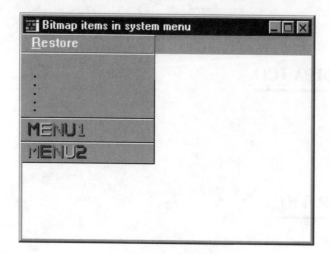

Bitmap items in system menu

Restore

MENU1

MENU2

FIGURE 4-4

This case shows you how to add custom bitmap menu items to the Windows system menu. As in the previous cases, menu creation is accomplished in the WM_CREATE handler in your window procedure. First, the bitmaps for the menu items must be loaded with LoadBitmap(). Then, you get a handle to the system menu by calling GetSystemMenu(). This handle is passed as a parameter to a series of AppendMenu() calls that add bitmap items to the system menu. As you can see from the code, a separator is first added by using the MF_SEPARATOR parameter in AppendMenu().

To process the menu commands when the user selects these menu choices, you need to add a handler for the WM_SYSCOMMAND message. Note that, as in the previous cases, regular menu processing gets done in the WM_COMMAND handler. The code is basically the same for either case: a switch statement that dispatches to the appropriate function depending on the WPARAM value that represents the resource ID for the menu item.

GLOBALS.H

```
// GLOBALS.H - header file for global variables
//              and function prototypes

// Product identifier string definitions.
#define APPNAME        MenuSys
#define ICONFILE       MenuSys.ico
#define SZAPPNAME      "MenuSys"
#define SZDESCRIPTION  "Bitmap items in system menu"
#define SZVERSION      "Version 1.0"
#define SZCOMPANYNAME  "\251 M&&T Books, 1994"
#define SZABOUT        "About"

// Global function prototypes.
BOOL InitApplication(HINSTANCE);
BOOL InitInstance(HINSTANCE, int);

// Callback functions.  These are called by Windows.
LRESULT CALLBACK WndProc(HWND, UINT, WPARAM, LPARAM);
LRESULT CALLBACK About(HWND, UINT, WPARAM, LPARAM);

// Menu item ID
#define IDM_ABOUT 101
#define IDM_MENU1 102
#define IDM_MENU2 103

// Global variable declarations.
extern HINSTANCE hInst;       // The current instance handle
extern char szAppName[];      // The name of this application
extern char szTitle[];        // The title bar text
```

WINMAIN.C

```
// WINMAIN.C
#include <windows.h>
#include "globals.h"

int APIENTRY WinMain(HINSTANCE hInstance,
                     HINSTANCE hPrevInstance,
                     LPSTR lpCmdLine,
                     int nCmdShow)
{
    MSG msg;

    // register main window class
```

```
      if (!hPrevInstance)
         {
         if (!InitApplication(hInstance))
            {
            return FALSE;
            }
         }

      // create and show main window
      if (!InitInstance(hInstance, nCmdShow))
         {
         return FALSE;
         }

      // process window message
      while (GetMessage(&msg, NULL, 0, 0))
         {
            TranslateMessage(&msg);
            DispatchMessage(&msg);
         }
      return msg.wParam;
}
```

INIT.C

```
// INIT.C
#include <windows.h>
#include "globals.h"

HINSTANCE hInst;
char szAppName[] = SZAPPNAME;
char szTitle[] = SZDESCRIPTION;

// register main window class
BOOL InitApplication(HINSTANCE hInstance)
{
    WNDCLASS  wc;

    wc.style          = CS_HREDRAW | CS_VREDRAW;
    wc.lpfnWndProc    = (WNDPROC)WndProc;
    wc.cbClsExtra     = 0;
    wc.cbWndExtra     = 0;
    wc.hInstance      = hInstance;
    wc.hIcon          = LoadIcon(hInstance, szAppName);
    wc.hCursor        = LoadCursor(NULL, IDC_ARROW);
    wc.hbrBackground  = (HBRUSH)(COLOR_WINDOW + 1);
```

```
    wc.lpszMenuName  = szAppName;
    wc.lpszClassName = szAppName;

    return(RegisterClass(&wc));
}

// create and show main window
BOOL InitInstance(HINSTANCE hInstance, int nCmdShow)
{
    HWND    hWnd;
    hInst = hInstance;
    hWnd = CreateWindow(szAppName, szTitle,
                        WS_OVERLAPPEDWINDOW,
                        160, 120, 320, 240,
                        NULL, NULL, hInstance, NULL);

    if (!hWnd)
        {
        return FALSE;
        }

    ShowWindow(hWnd, nCmdShow);
    UpdateWindow(hWnd);

    return TRUE;
}
```

MENUSYS.C

```
// MENUSYS.C
#include <windows.h>
#include <windowsx.h>
#include "globals.h"

LRESULT CALLBACK WndProc(HWND hWnd,
                         UINT uMessage,
                         WPARAM wParam,
                         LPARAM lParam)
{
HMENU hSysMenu;
HBITMAP hBitmap1, hBitmap2;

    switch (uMessage)
        {
        case WM_CREATE:
                // load bitmaps for system menu items
```

313

```
    hBitmap1 = LoadBitmap(hInst, "BitmapSysMenu1");
    hBitmap2 = LoadBitmap(hInst, "BitmapSysMenu2");

    // get system menu handle
    hSysMenu = GetSystemMenu(hWnd, 0);

    // add items to system menu
    AppendMenu(hSysMenu, MF_SEPARATOR, 0, NULL);
    AppendMenu(hSysMenu, MF_BITMAP,
            (UINT)IDM_MENU1,
            (LPCTSTR)MAKELONG(hBitmap1, 0));
    AppendMenu(hSysMenu, MF_SEPARATOR, 0, NULL);
    AppendMenu(hSysMenu, MF_BITMAP,
            (UINT)IDM_MENU2,
            (LPCTSTR)MAKELONG(hBitmap2, 0));
    break;

case WM_SYSCOMMAND:
    switch (wParam){
      case IDM_MENU1:
            // things to do
            MessageBox(NULL,
              "This is a custom system menu item!",
              "Info", MB_OK | MB_ICONINFORMATION |
              MB_SYSTEMMODAL);
            break;

      case IDM_MENU2:
            // things to do
            MessageBox(NULL,
              "This is a custom system menu item!",
              "Info", MB_OK | MB_ICONINFORMATION |
              MB_SYSTEMMODAL);
            break;

      default:
        return (DefWindowProc(hWnd, uMessage,
                              wParam, lParam));
    }
    break;

case WM_COMMAND:
    switch (GET_WM_COMMAND_ID(wParam,lParam))
    {
       case IDM_ABOUT:
            // create an about dialog box
            DialogBox(hInst, "ABOUTDLG",
```

```
                        hWnd, (DLGPROC)About);
                break;


            default:
                return DefWindowProc(hWnd, uMessage,
                                        wParam, lParam);
            }
            break;

        case WM_DESTROY:
            PostQuitMessage(0);
            break;

        default:
            return DefWindowProc(hWnd, uMessage,
                                    wParam, lParam);
        }
        return 0;
}
```

ABOUT.C

```
// ABOUT.C
#include <windows.h>
#include <windowsx.h>
#include "globals.h"

// procedures for ABOUT dialog box
LRESULT CALLBACK About(HWND hDlg,
                        UINT uMessage,
                        WPARAM wParam,
                        LPARAM lParam)
{
    switch (uMessage)
      {
        case WM_COMMAND:
            switch (GET_WM_COMMAND_ID(wParam,lParam))
              {
                case IDOK:
                case IDCANCEL:
                    {
                    EndDialog(hDlg, TRUE);
                    return(TRUE);
                    }
                    break;
```

```
            }
        }
    return FALSE;
}
```

MENUSYS.RC

```
#include "windows.h"
#include "globals.h"
#include <winver.h>

APPNAME ICON ICONFILE

RCINCLUDE ABOUT.DLG

BitmapSysMenu1 BITMAP menu1.bmp
BitmapSysMenu2 BITMAP menu2.bmp

APPNAME MENU
BEGIN
    POPUP "&Help"
    BEGIN
     MENUITEM "&About", IDM_ABOUT
    END
END
```

ABOUT.DLG

```
ABOUTDLG DIALOG DISCARDABLE  22, 17, 167, 73
STYLE DS_MODALFRAME | WS_CAPTION | WS_SYSMENU
CAPTION SZABOUT
BEGIN
    DEFPUSHBUTTON   "OK", IDOK, 132, 2, 32, 14, WS_GROUP
    ICON            SZAPPNAME,      -1, 3, 2, 18, 20
    LTEXT           SZAPPNAME,      -1, 30, 12,  50, 8
    LTEXT           SZDESCRIPTION, -1, 30, 22, 150, 8
    LTEXT           SZVERSION,      -1, 30, 32, 150, 8
    LTEXT           SZCOMPANYNAME, -1, 30, 42, 150, 8
END
```

MENUSYS.ICO

MENU1.BMP

MENU2.BMP

CASE 4-5: CHECK ITEMS IN PULL DOWN MENU

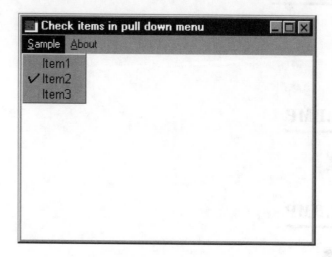

FIGURE 4-5

This case shows how to place check marks next to a particular menu item. This technique is commonly used in many applications. It is used when the program needs to convey to the user information about the current state—for example, which is the current point size in a menu list of various point sizes.

The code here is a straightforward use of the Windows API. The processing happens in the WM_COMMAND handler in the main WndProc. For any given menu item, say IDM_MENU1, you need to first get a handle to the menu via a call to GetMenu(). Using the handle returned by GetMenu(), call the Windows API function CheckMenuItem() with either MF_CHECKED or MF_UNCHECKED parameter. Of course, your code needs a static variable of some sort to remember the current state of this aspect of your application. In the code here, the boolean variable bCheck1 is used to remember the checked/unchecked state and is toggled accordingly.

GLOBALS.H

```
// GLOBALS.H - header file for global variables
//              and function prototypes

// Product identifier string definitions.
#define APPNAME        MenuChk
#define ICONFILE       MenuChk.ico
#define SZAPPNAME      "MenuChk"
#define SZDESCRIPTION  "Check items in pull down menu"
#define SZVERSION      "Version 1.0"
#define SZCOMPANYNAME  "\251 M&&T Books, 1994"
#define SZABOUT        "About"

// Global function prototypes.
BOOL InitApplication(HINSTANCE);
BOOL InitInstance(HINSTANCE, int);

// Callback functions.  These are called by Windows.
LRESULT CALLBACK WndProc(HWND, UINT, WPARAM, LPARAM);
LRESULT CALLBACK About(HWND, UINT, WPARAM, LPARAM);

// Menu item ID
#define IDM_ABOUT   101
#define IDM_SAMPLE  102
#define IDM_MENU1   103
#define IDM_MENU2   104
#define IDM_MENU3   105

// Global variable declarations.
extern HINSTANCE hInst;      // The current instance handle
extern char szAppName[];     // The name of this application
extern char szTitle[];       // The title bar text
```

WINMAIN.C

```
// WINMAIN.C
#include <windows.h>
#include "globals.h"

int APIENTRY WinMain(HINSTANCE hInstance,
                     HINSTANCE hPrevInstance,
                     LPSTR lpCmdLine,
                     int nCmdShow)
{
```

```
    MSG msg;

    // register main window class
    if (!hPrevInstance)
        {
        if (!InitApplication(hInstance))
            {
            return FALSE;
            }
        }

    // create and show main window
    if (!InitInstance(hInstance, nCmdShow))
        {
        return FALSE;
        }

    // process window messages
    while (GetMessage(&msg, NULL, 0, 0))
        {
        TranslateMessage(&msg);
        DispatchMessage(&msg);
        }
    return msg.wParam;
}
```

INIT.C

```
// INIT.C
#include <windows.h>
#include "globals.h"

HINSTANCE hInst;
char szAppName[] = SZAPPNAME;
char szTitle[] = SZDESCRIPTION;

// register main window class
BOOL InitApplication(HINSTANCE hInstance)
{
    WNDCLASS  wc;

    wc.style          = CS_HREDRAW | CS_VREDRAW;
    wc.lpfnWndProc    = (WNDPROC)WndProc;
    wc.cbClsExtra     = 0;
    wc.cbWndExtra     = 0;
    wc.hInstance      = hInstance;
```

```
    wc.hIcon          = LoadIcon(hInstance, szAppName);
    wc.hCursor        = LoadCursor(NULL, IDC_ARROW);
    wc.hbrBackground  = (HBRUSH)(COLOR_WINDOW + 1);
    wc.lpszMenuName   = szAppName;
    wc.lpszClassName  = szAppName;

    return(RegisterClass(&wc));
}

// create and show main window
BOOL InitInstance(HINSTANCE hInstance, int nCmdShow)
{
    HWND    hWnd;
    hInst = hInstance;
    hWnd = CreateWindow(szAppName, szTitle,
                        WS_OVERLAPPEDWINDOW,
                        160, 120, 320, 240,
                        NULL, NULL, hInstance, NULL);

    if (!hWnd)
       {
       return FALSE;
       }

    ShowWindow(hWnd, nCmdShow);
    UpdateWindow(hWnd);

    return TRUE;
}
```

MENUCHK.C

```
// MENUCHK.C
#include <windows.h>
#include <windowsx.h>
#include "globals.h"

HMENU hMenu;
BOOL  bCheck1=FALSE, bCheck2=FALSE, bCheck3=FALSE;

LRESULT CALLBACK WndProc(HWND hWnd,
                         UINT uMessage,
                         WPARAM wParam,
                         LPARAM lParam)
{
    switch (uMessage)
```

```
        {
    case WM_COMMAND:
        switch (GET_WM_COMMAND_ID(wParam,lParam))
        {
        case IDM_ABOUT:
                // create an about dialog box
                DialogBox(hInst, "ABOUTDLG",
                        hWnd, (DLGPROC)About);
                break;

        case IDM_MENU1:
                hMenu = GetMenu(hWnd);
                if(bCheck1)
                    CheckMenuItem(hMenu, IDM_MENU1,
                                MF_UNCHECKED);
                else
                    CheckMenuItem(hMenu, IDM_MENU1,
                                MF_CHECKED);
                bCheck1 = !bCheck1;
                break;

        case IDM_MENU2:
                hMenu = GetMenu(hWnd);
                if(bCheck2)
                    CheckMenuItem(hMenu, IDM_MENU2,
                                MF_UNCHECKED);
                else
                    CheckMenuItem(hMenu, IDM_MENU2,
                                MF_CHECKED);
                bCheck2 = !bCheck2;
                break;

        case IDM_MENU3:
                hMenu = GetMenu(hWnd);
                if(bCheck3)
                    CheckMenuItem(hMenu, IDM_MENU3,
                                MF_UNCHECKED);
                else
                    CheckMenuItem(hMenu, IDM_MENU3,
                                MF_CHECKED);
                bCheck3 = !bCheck3;
                break;

        default:
            return DefWindowProc(hWnd, uMessage,
                                wParam, lParam);
        }
```

```
            break;

        case WM_DESTROY:
            PostQuitMessage(0);
            break;

        default:
            return DefWindowProc(hWnd, uMessage,
                                     wParam, lParam);
    }
    return 0;
}
```

ABOUT.C

```
// ABOUT.C
#include <windows.h>
#include <windowsx.h>
#include "globals.h"

// procedures for ABOUT dialog box
LRESULT CALLBACK About(HWND hDlg,
                     UINT uMessage,
                     WPARAM wParam,
                     LPARAM lParam)
{
    switch (uMessage)
      {
        case WM_COMMAND:
            switch (GET_WM_COMMAND_ID(wParam,lParam))
            {
                case IDOK:
                case IDCANCEL:
                    {
                    EndDialog(hDlg, TRUE);
                    return(TRUE);
                    }
                    break;
            }
      }
    return FALSE;
}
```

MENUCHK.RC

```
#include "windows.h"
#include "globals.h"
#include <winver.h>

APPNAME ICON ICONFILE

RCINCLUDE ABOUT.DLG

APPNAME MENU
BEGIN
   POPUP "&Sample"
   BEGIN
     MENUITEM "Item&1", IDM_MENU1
     MENUITEM "Item&2", IDM_MENU2
     MENUITEM "Item&3", IDM_MENU3
   END
   MENUITEM "&About",    IDM_ABOUT
END
```

ABOUT.DLG

```
ABOUTDLG DIALOG DISCARDABLE  22, 17, 167, 73
STYLE DS_MODALFRAME | WS_CAPTION | WS_SYSMENU
CAPTION SZABOUT
BEGIN
    DEFPUSHBUTTON    "OK", IDOK, 132, 2, 32, 14, WS_GROUP
    ICON             SZAPPNAME,      -1, 3, 2, 18, 20
    LTEXT            SZAPPNAME,      -1, 30, 12,  50, 8
    LTEXT            SZDESCRIPTION, -1, 30, 22, 150, 8
    LTEXT            SZVERSION,      -1, 30, 32, 150, 8
    LTEXT            SZCOMPANYNAME, -1, 30, 42, 150, 8
END
```

MENUCHK.ICO

CASE 4-6: FLOATING POPUP MENU WITH TEXT ITEMS

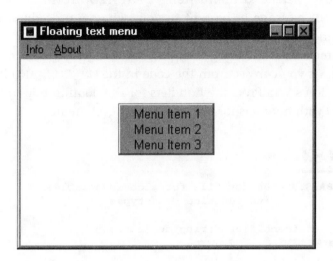

FIGURE 4-6

This case shows how to implement a floating pop-up menu via the CreatePopupMenu() and TrackPopupMenu() functions in the Windows API.

The main window in this application has a conventional text-only menu that is statically defined in the resource file FMTEXT.RC, as is done in many Windows applications.

The floating pop-up menu is created dynamically at run time, in response to a right-button mouse click. The floating menu is created so that its upper-left corner is at the current cursor position.

The code to create the menu is in the WM_RBUTTONDOWN handler in the main window procedure. As you can see from the code, first an empty pop-up menu is created via a call to CreatePopupMenu(). Then, this menu is populated just like any other menu, using calls to AppendMenu(). Next, the API function TrackPopupMenu() is called to display the menu in the window and to track the user's mouse movements. Lastly, once processing has completed, the menu is destroyed with `DestroyMenu()`.

If the user selects a menu item, `TrackPopupMenu()` causes a `WM_COMMAND` message to be sent to your window procedure. Handling menu commands for a floating pop-up menu is no different than for a pull-down menu. All handling is dispatched using the resource ID for the menu item. As you can see from the code in the `WM_COMMAND` handler in the application's WndProc, the handlers for the floating pop-up items are interspersed with handlers for the regular top-level menu.

GLOBALS.H

```
// GLOBALS.H - header file for global variables
//              and function prototypes

// Product identifier string definitions.
#define APPNAME        FmText
#define ICONFILE       FmText.ico
#define SZAPPNAME      "FmText"
#define SZDESCRIPTION "Floating text menu"
#define SZVERSION      "Version 1.0"
#define SZCOMPANYNAME "\251 M&&T Books, 1994"
#define SZABOUT        "About"

// Global function prototypes.
BOOL InitApplication(HINSTANCE);
BOOL InitInstance(HINSTANCE, int);

// Callback functions.  These are called by Windows.
LRESULT CALLBACK WndProc(HWND, UINT, WPARAM, LPARAM);
LRESULT CALLBACK About(HWND, UINT, WPARAM, LPARAM);

// Menu item ID
#define IDM_ABOUT 101
#define IDM_MENU1 102
#define IDM_MENU2 103
#define IDM_MENU3 104
#define IDM_INFO  105

// Global variable declarations.
extern HINSTANCE hInst;      // The current instance handle
extern char szAppName[];     // The name of this application
extern char szTitle[];       // The title bar text
```

WINMAIN.C

```
// WINMAIN.C
#include <windows.h>
#include "globals.h"

int APIENTRY WinMain(HINSTANCE hInstance,
                     HINSTANCE hPrevInstance,
                     LPSTR lpCmdLine,
                     int nCmdShow)
{
    MSG msg;

    // register main window class
    if (!hPrevInstance)
        {
        if (!InitApplication(hInstance))
            {
            return FALSE;
            }
        }

    // create and show main window
    if (!InitInstance(hInstance, nCmdShow))
        {
        return FALSE;
        }

    // process window messages
    while (GetMessage(&msg, NULL, 0, 0))
        {
            TranslateMessage(&msg);
            DispatchMessage(&msg);
        }
    return msg.wParam;
}
```

INIT.C

```
// INIT.C
#include <windows.h>
#include "globals.h"

HINSTANCE hInst;
char szAppName[] = SZAPPNAME;
char szTitle[] = SZDESCRIPTION;

// register main window class
```

```
BOOL InitApplication(HINSTANCE hInstance)
{
    WNDCLASS  wc;

    wc.style         = CS_HREDRAW | CS_VREDRAW;
    wc.lpfnWndProc   = (WNDPROC)WndProc;
    wc.cbClsExtra    = 0;
    wc.cbWndExtra    = 0;
    wc.hInstance     = hInstance;
    wc.hIcon         = LoadIcon(hInstance, szAppName);
    wc.hCursor       = LoadCursor(NULL, IDC_ARROW);
    wc.hbrBackground = (HBRUSH)(COLOR_WINDOW + 1);
    wc.lpszMenuName  = szAppName;
    wc.lpszClassName = szAppName;

    return(RegisterClass(&wc));
}

// create and show main window
BOOL InitInstance(HINSTANCE hInstance, int nCmdShow)
{
    HWND    hWnd;
    hInst = hInstance;
    hWnd = CreateWindow(szAppName, szTitle,
                        WS_OVERLAPPEDWINDOW,
                        160, 120, 320, 240,
                        NULL, NULL, hInstance, NULL);

    if (!hWnd)
        {
        return FALSE;
        }

    ShowWindow(hWnd, nCmdShow);
    UpdateWindow(hWnd);

    return TRUE;
}
```

FMTEXT.C

```
// FMTEXT.C
#include <windows.h>
#include <windowsx.h>
#include "globals.h"

LRESULT CALLBACK WndProc(HWND hWnd,
                         UINT uMessage,
```

```
                    WPARAM wParam,
                    LPARAM lParam)
{
    POINT CursorPos;
    HMENU hFloatingMenu;

    switch (uMessage)
    {
        case WM_RBUTTONDOWN:
            GetCursorPos(&CursorPos);

            // create an empty popup menu
            hFloatingMenu = CreatePopupMenu();

            // add items to the popup menu
            AppendMenu(hFloatingMenu, MF_ENABLED,
                       IDM_MENU1, "Menu Item &1");
            AppendMenu(hFloatingMenu, MF_ENABLED,
                       IDM_MENU2, "Menu Item &2");
            AppendMenu(hFloatingMenu, MF_ENABLED,
                       IDM_MENU3, "Menu Item &3");

            // display the popup menu at cursor position
            TrackPopupMenu(hFloatingMenu,
                       TPM_LEFTALIGN | TPM_RIGHTBUTTON,
                       CursorPos.x, CursorPos.y,
                       (int)NULL, hWnd, NULL);
            DestroyMenu(hFloatingMenu);
            break;

        case WM_COMMAND:
            switch (GET_WM_COMMAND_ID(wParam,lParam))
            {
                case IDM_ABOUT:
                    // create an about dialog box
                    DialogBox(hInst, "ABOUTDLG",
                              hWnd, (DLGPROC)About);
                    break;

                case IDM_INFO:
                    MessageBox(NULL,
                        "Press right mouse button
                        for popup menu!",
                        "Info", MB_OK |
                        MB_ICONINFORMATION |
                        MB_SYSTEMMODAL);
                    break;
```

```
                case IDM_MENU1:
                case IDM_MENU2:
                case IDM_MENU3:
                    MessageBox(NULL,
                        "This is a floating menu item!",
                        "Info", MB_OK | MB_ICONINFORMATION |
                        MB_SYSTEMMODAL);
                    break;

                default:
                    return DefWindowProc(hWnd, uMessage,
                                    wParam, lParam);
            }
            break;

        case WM_DESTROY:
            PostQuitMessage(0);
            break;

        default:
            return DefWindowProc(hWnd, uMessage,
                            wParam, lParam);
    }
    return 0;
}
```

ABOUT.C

```
// ABOUT.C
#include <windows.h>
#include <windowsx.h>
#include "globals.h"

// procedures for ABOUT dialog box
LRESULT CALLBACK About(HWND hDlg,
                    UINT uMessage,
                    WPARAM wParam,
                    LPARAM lParam)
{
    switch (uMessage)
      {
        case WM_COMMAND:
            switch (GET_WM_COMMAND_ID(wParam,lParam))
            {
                case IDOK:
                case IDCANCEL:
                    {
```

```
                    EndDialog(hDlg, TRUE);
                    return(TRUE);
                    }
                    break;
                }
        }
    return FALSE;
}
```

FMTEXT.RC

```
#include "windows.h"
#include "globals.h"
#include <winver.h>

APPNAME ICON ICONFILE

RCINCLUDE ABOUT.DLG

APPNAME MENU
BEGIN
    MENUITEM "&Info",   IDM_INFO
    MENUITEM "&About",  IDM_ABOUT
END
```

ABOUT.DLG

```
ABOUTDLG DIALOG DISCARDABLE  22, 17, 167, 73
STYLE DS_MODALFRAME | WS_CAPTION | WS_SYSMENU
CAPTION SZABOUT
BEGIN
    DEFPUSHBUTTON    "OK", IDOK, 132, 2, 32, 14, WS_GROUP
    ICON             SZAPPNAME,      -1, 3, 2, 18, 20
    LTEXT            SZAPPNAME,      -1, 30, 12, 50, 8
    LTEXT            SZDESCRIPTION, -1, 30, 22, 150, 8
    LTEXT            SZVERSION,      -1, 30, 32, 150, 8
    LTEXT            SZCOMPANYNAME, -1, 30, 42, 150, 8
END
```

FMTEXT.ICO

CASE 4-7: FLOATING POPUP MENU WITH BITMAP ITEMS

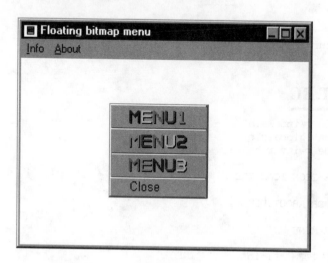

FIGURE 4-7

This case builds on Case 4-6, which showed how to create and use a floating pop-up menu of text items. In this case, the text items are now bitmap items.

As before, the CreatePopupMenu() and TrackPopupMenu() functions in the Windows API are used. The floating pop-up menu is created in response to a WM_RBUTTONDOWN message (when the user clicks on the right mouse button). The sequence of calls is basically the same as in Case 4-6, except for loading the bitmaps with LoadBitmap() and then specifying the MF_BITMAP parameter to AppendMenu(). For more details on specifying bitmap items in a menu, see Case 4-1.

GLOBALS.H

```
// GLOBALS.H - header file for global variables
//             and function prototypes

// Product identifier string definitions.
#define APPNAME         FmBmp
#define ICONFILE        FmBmp.ico
#define SZAPPNAME       "FmBmp"
#define SZDESCRIPTION   "Floating bitmap menu"
#define SZVERSION       "Version 1.0"
#define SZCOMPANYNAME   "\251 M&&T Books, 1994"
#define SZABOUT         "About"

// Global function prototypes.
BOOL InitApplication(HINSTANCE);
BOOL InitInstance(HINSTANCE, int);

// Callback functions.  These are called by Windows.
LRESULT CALLBACK WndProc(HWND, UINT, WPARAM, LPARAM);
LRESULT CALLBACK About(HWND, UINT, WPARAM, LPARAM);

// Menu item ID
#define IDM_ABOUT 101
#define IDM_MENU1 102
#define IDM_MENU2 103
#define IDM_MENU3 104
#define IDM_INFO  105
#define IDM_CLOSE 106

// Global variable declarations.
extern HINSTANCE hInst;     // The current instance handle
extern char szAppName[];    // The name of this application
extern char szTitle[];      // The title bar text
```

WINMAIN.C

```
// WINMAIN.C
#include <windows.h>
#include "globals.h"

int APIENTRY WinMain(HINSTANCE hInstance,
                     HINSTANCE hPrevInstance,
                     LPSTR lpCmdLine,
                     int nCmdShow)
{
```

```
        MSG msg;

        // register main window class
        if (!hPrevInstance)
            {
            if (!InitApplication(hInstance))
                {
                return FALSE;
                }
            }

        // create and show main window
        if (!InitInstance(hInstance, nCmdShow))
            {
            return FALSE;
            }

        // process window messages
        while (GetMessage(&msg, NULL, 0, 0))
            {
                TranslateMessage(&msg);
                DispatchMessage(&msg);
            }
        return msg.wParam;
    }
```

INIT.C

```
    // INIT.C
    #include <windows.h>
    #include "globals.h"

    HINSTANCE hInst;
    char szAppName[] = SZAPPNAME;
    char szTitle[] = SZDESCRIPTION;

    // register main window class
    BOOL InitApplication(HINSTANCE hInstance)
    {
        WNDCLASS  wc;

        wc.style        = CS_HREDRAW | CS_VREDRAW;
        wc.lpfnWndProc  = (WNDPROC)WndProc;
        wc.cbClsExtra   = 0;
        wc.cbWndExtra   = 0;
        wc.hInstance    = hInstance;
```

```
    wc.hIcon        = LoadIcon(hInstance, szAppName);
    wc.hCursor      = LoadCursor(NULL, IDC_ARROW);
    wc.hbrBackground = (HBRUSH)(COLOR_WINDOW + 1);
    wc.lpszMenuName  = szAppName;
    wc.lpszClassName = szAppName;

    return(RegisterClass(&wc));
}


// create and show main window
BOOL InitInstance(HINSTANCE hInstance, int nCmdShow)
{
    HWND    hWnd;
    hInst = hInstance;
    hWnd = CreateWindow(szAppName, szTitle,
                        WS_OVERLAPPEDWINDOW,
                        160, 120, 320, 240,
                        NULL, NULL, hInstance, NULL);

    if (!hWnd)
        {
        return FALSE;
        }

    ShowWindow(hWnd, nCmdShow);
    UpdateWindow(hWnd);

    return TRUE;
}
```

FMBMP.C

```
// FMB MP.C
#include <windows.h>
#include <windowsx.h>
#include "globals.h"

LRESULT CALLBACK WndProc(HWND hWnd,
                         UINT uMessage,
                         WPARAM wParam,
                         LPARAM lParam)
{
    POINT CursorPos;
    HMENU hFloatingMenu;
    HBITMAP hBitmap1, hBitmap2, hBitmap3;

    switch (uMessage)
```

335

```
{
    case WM_RBUTTONDOWN:
        GetCursorPos(&CursorPos);

        // load bitmaps for popup menu items
        hBitmap1 = LoadBitmap(hInst, "MENU1");
        hBitmap2 = LoadBitmap(hInst, "MENU2");
        hBitmap3 = LoadBitmap(hInst, "MENU3");

        // create an empty popup menu
        hFloatingMenu = CreatePopupMenu();

        // add items to popup menu
        AppendMenu(hFloatingMenu,
                MF_ENABLED | MF_BITMAP,
                (UINT)IDM_MENU1,
                (LPSTR)MAKELONG(hBitmap1, 0));
        AppendMenu(hFloatingMenu,
                MF_SEPARATOR, (UINT)NULL, NULL);
        AppendMenu(hFloatingMenu,
                MF_ENABLED | MF_BITMAP,
                (UINT)IDM_MENU2,
                (LPSTR)MAKELONG(hBitmap2, 0));
        AppendMenu(hFloatingMenu,
                MF_SEPARATOR, (UINT)NULL, NULL);
        AppendMenu(hFloatingMenu,
                MF_ENABLED | MF_BITMAP,
                (UINT)IDM_MENU3,
                (LPSTR)MAKELONG(hBitmap3, 0));
        AppendMenu(hFloatingMenu,
                MF_SEPARATOR, (UINT)NULL, NULL);
        AppendMenu(hFloatingMenu,
                MF_ENABLED | MF_STRING,
                (UINT)IDM_CLOSE, "&Close");

        // display popup menu at cursor position
        TrackPopupMenu(hFloatingMenu,
                TPM_LEFTALIGN | TPM_RIGHTBUTTON,
                CursorPos.x, CursorPos.y,
                (int)NULL, hWnd, NULL);
        DestroyMenu(hFloatingMenu);
        break;

    case WM_COMMAND:
        switch (GET_WM_COMMAND_ID(wParam,lParam))
        {
            case IDM_ABOUT:
                    // create an about dialog box
```

```
                    DialogBox(hInst, "ABOUTDLG",
                            hWnd, (DLGPROC)About);
                break;

        case IDM_INFO:
                MessageBox(NULL,
         "Press right mouse button for popup menu!",
                        "Info", MB_OK |
                        MB_ICONINFORMATION |
                        MB_SYSTEMMODAL);
                break;

        case IDM_MENU1:
        case IDM_MENU2:
        case IDM_MENU3:
                MessageBox(NULL,
                        "This is a floating menu item!",
                        "Info", MB_OK |
                        MB_ICONINFORMATION |
                        MB_SYSTEMMODAL);
                break;

        case IDM_CLOSE:
                break;

        default:
                return DefWindowProc(hWnd, uMessage,
                                        wParam, lParam);
        }
        break;

    case WM_DESTROY:
        PostQuitMessage(0);
        break;

    default:
        return DefWindowProc(hWnd, uMessage,
                                wParam, lParam);
    }
    return 0;
}
```

ABOUT.C

```
// ABOUT.C
#include <windows.h>
```

```c
#include <windowsx.h>
#include "globals.h"

// procedures for ABOUT dialog box
LRESULT CALLBACK About(HWND hDlg,
                       UINT uMessage,
                       WPARAM wParam,
                       LPARAM lParam)
{
    switch (uMessage)
      {
        case WM_COMMAND:
             switch (GET_WM_COMMAND_ID(wParam,lParam))
             {
                 case IDOK:
                 case IDCANCEL:
                     {
                     EndDialog(hDlg, TRUE);
                     return(TRUE);
                     }
                     break;
             }
      }
    return FALSE;
}
```

FMBMP.RC

```c
#include "windows.h"
#include "globals.h"
#include <winver.h>

APPNAME ICON ICONFILE

RCINCLUDE ABOUT.DLG

MENU1 BITMAP menu1.bmp
MENU2 BITMAP menu2.bmp
MENU3 BITMAP menu3.bmp

APPNAME MENU
BEGIN
    MENUITEM "&Info",   IDM_INFO
    MENUITEM "&About",  IDM_ABOUT
END
```

ABOUT.DLG

```
ABOUTDLG DIALOG DISCARDABLE  22, 17, 167, 73
STYLE DS_MODALFRAME | WS_CAPTION | WS_SYSMENU
CAPTION SZABOUT
BEGIN
    DEFPUSHBUTTON    "OK", IDOK, 132, 2, 32, 14, WS_GROUP
    ICON             SZAPPNAME,      -1, 3, 2, 18, 20
    LTEXT            SZAPPNAME,      -1, 30, 12,  50, 8
    LTEXT            SZDESCRIPTION, -1, 30, 22, 150, 8
    LTEXT            SZVERSION,      -1, 30, 32, 150, 8
    LTEXT            SZCOMPANYNAME, -1, 30, 42, 150, 8
END
```

FMBMP.ICO

MENU1.BMP

MENU1

MENU2.BMP

MENU2

MENU3.BMP

MENU3

Chapter Five

Drawing Functions

CASE 5-1: DRAW LINES

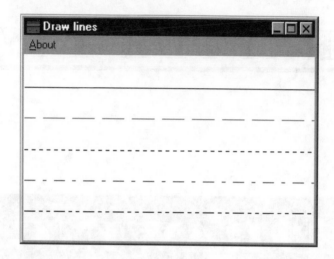

FIGURE 5-1

The graphics device interface (GDI) is one of the largest and most important subsystems in the Windows API. In a nutshell, GDI consists of functions to draw basic graphic shapes such as lines, rectangles, and ellipses, as well as additional functions that support graphics drawing, such as creating pens and brushes, and recording and playing back metafiles (stored sequences of graphics commands). The cases in this chapter illustrate the use of the Windows GDI for some simple graphic effects, such as drawing dashed lines, filled rectangles, and pie charts.

This particular case is a simple example that shows how to draw lines in a window. In general, most Windows programs draw graphics inside the *client area*, which is the main part of the window, the portion framed by the window border, and window title bar. The cases in this chapter are no exception.

The user can adjust the size of the window, so it is necessary to use the CS_HREDRAW and CS_VREDRAW parameters to the CreateWindow() API, so that the client area can be repainted when the window size changes. When the client area of the window needs repainting, Windows sends a WM_PAINT message to the window procedure WndProc(). Here the WM_PAINT handler follows the standard protocol by first calling BeginPaint() and then making the necessary graphics calls and calling EndPaint().

In this case, the graphics calls consist of first calling CreatePen() to set up for line drawing and then using GetClientRect() to get the current size of the client area. Drawing is accomplished by a series of MoveToEx() and LineTo() calls. Lastly, DeleteObject() is called for each pen that was created.

Perhaps the most complicated part of this case is the use of mapping modes. Here, the MM_ANISOTROPIC parameter is specified for the Windows SetMapMode() function. This means that window coordinates will be *stretched* (scaled as necessary) to fit into the viewport coordinates and that, unlike the MM_ISOTROPIC mode, this scaling will be done independently in both the horizontal and vertical dimension. The SetMapMode() call is followed by SetViewportExtEx() and SetWindowExtEx() to specify the size of the viewport and the size of the window that corresponds to the viewport. In this case the application window is specified to be 250 units wide by 120 deep; the viewport is specified to be whatever size is returned by GetClientRect(). After the correspondence between window and viewport has been established, Windows will automatically scale all GDI drawing calls according to the window/viewport ratio. In this example, all LineTo() calls use a width of 250. Because of the mapping mode in effect, the lines will always be drawn across the entire window width, regardless of how much the user adjusts the window size.

GLOBALS.H

```
// GLOBALS.H - header file for global variables
//              and function prototypes

// Product identifier string definitions
#define APPNAME     Line
#define ICONFILE    Line.ico
#define SZAPPNAME   "Line"
```

```
#define SZDESCRIPTION "Draw lines"
#define SZVERSION     "Version 1.0"
#define SZCOMPANYNAME "\251 M&&T Books, 1994"
#define SZABOUT       "About"

// Global function prototypes.
BOOL InitApplication(HINSTANCE);
BOOL InitInstance(HINSTANCE, int);

// Callback functions.  These are called by Windows.
LRESULT CALLBACK WndProc(HWND, UINT, WPARAM, LPARAM);
LRESULT CALLBACK About(HWND, UINT, WPARAM, LPARAM);

// Menu item ID
#define IDM_ABOUT    1000

// Global variable declarations.
extern HINSTANCE hInst;       // The current instance handle
extern char szAppName[];      // The name of this application
extern char szTitle[];        // The title bar text
```

WINMAIN.C

```
// WINMAIN.C
#include <windows.h>
#include "globals.h"

int APIENTRY WinMain(HINSTANCE hInstance,
                     HINSTANCE hPrevInstance,
                     LPSTR lpCmdLine,
                     int nCmdShow)
{
    MSG msg;

    // register main window class
    if (!hPrevInstance)
       {
       if (!InitApplication(hInstance))
          {
          return FALSE;
          }
       }

    // create and show main windows
    if (!InitInstance(hInstance, nCmdShow))
       {
```

```
        return FALSE;
        }

    // process window messages
    while (GetMessage(&msg, NULL, 0, 0))
        {
            TranslateMessage(&msg);
            DispatchMessage(&msg);
        }
    return msg.wParam;
}
```

INIT.C

```
// INIT.C
#include <windows.h>
#include "globals.h"

HINSTANCE hInst;
char szAppName[] = SZAPPNAME;
char szTitle[] = SZDESCRIPTION;

// register main window class
BOOL InitApplication(HINSTANCE hInstance)
{
    WNDCLASS  wc;

    wc.style          = CS_HREDRAW | CS_VREDRAW;
    wc.lpfnWndProc    = (WNDPROC)WndProc;
    wc.cbClsExtra     = 0;
    wc.cbWndExtra     = 0;
    wc.hInstance      = hInstance;
    wc.hIcon          = LoadIcon(hInstance, szAppName);
    wc.hCursor        = LoadCursor(NULL, IDC_ARROW);
    wc.hbrBackground  = (HBRUSH)(COLOR_WINDOW + 1);
    wc.lpszMenuName   = szAppName;
    wc.lpszClassName  = szAppName;

    return(RegisterClass(&wc));
}

// create and show main windows
BOOL InitInstance(HINSTANCE hInstance, int nCmdShow)
{
    HWND    hWnd;
    hInst = hInstance;
```

```
        hWnd = CreateWindow(szAppName, szTitle,
                        WS_OVERLAPPEDWINDOW,
                        160, 120, 320, 240,
                        NULL, NULL, hInstance, NULL);

    if (!hWnd)
        {
        return FALSE;
        }

    ShowWindow(hWnd, nCmdShow);
    UpdateWindow(hWnd);

    return TRUE;
}
```

LINE.C

```
// LINE.C
#include <windows.h>
#include <windowsx.h>
#include "globals.h"

LRESULT CALLBACK WndProc(HWND hWnd,
                        UINT uMessage,
                        WPARAM wParam,
                        LPARAM lParam)
{
    HDC hDC;
    HPEN hPenRed, hPenGreen, hPenBlue;
    HPEN hPenYellow, hPenBlack;
    PAINTSTRUCT ps;
    RECT rect;

    switch (uMessage)
        {
        case WM_PAINT:
            hDC = BeginPaint(hWnd, &ps);

            // create pens for drawing
            hPenRed = CreatePen(0, 1, RGB(255, 0, 0));
            hPenGreen = CreatePen(1, 1, RGB(0, 255, 0));
            hPenBlue = CreatePen(2, 1, RGB(0, 0, 255));
            hPenYellow = CreatePen(3, 1, RGB(128, 128, 0));
            hPenBlack = CreatePen(4, 1, RGB(0, 0, 0));
```

```
SetMapMode(hDC, MM_ANISOTROPIC);
GetClientRect(hWnd, &rect);
SetViewportExtEx(hDC, rect.right,
                 rect.bottom, NULL);
SetWindowExtEx(hDC, 250, 120, NULL);

// choose pen and draw lines
SelectObject(hDC, hPenRed);
MoveToEx(hDC, 1, 21, NULL);
LineTo(hDC, 250, 21);

SelectObject(hDC, hPenGreen);
MoveToEx(hDC, 1, 41, NULL);
LineTo(hDC, 250, 41);

SelectObject(hDC, hPenBlue);
MoveToEx(hDC, 1, 61, NULL);
LineTo(hDC, 250, 61);

SelectObject(hDC, hPenYellow);
MoveToEx(hDC, 1, 81, NULL);
LineTo(hDC, 250, 81);

SelectObject(hDC, hPenBlack);
MoveToEx(hDC, 1, 101, NULL);
LineTo(hDC, 250, 101);

EndPaint(hWnd, &ps);
DeleteObject(hPenRed);
DeleteObject(hPenGreen);
DeleteObject(hPenBlue);
DeleteObject(hPenYellow);
DeleteObject(hPenBlack);
break;

case WM_COMMAND:
    switch (GET_WM_COMMAND_ID(wParam,lParam))
    {
        case IDM_ABOUT:
            DialogBox(hInst, "ABOUTDLG",
                      hWnd, (DLGPROC)About);
            break;

        default:
            return DefWindowProc(hWnd, uMessage,
            wParam, lParam);
    }
```

```
                    break;

            case WM_DESTROY:
                PostQuitMessage(0);
                break;

            default:
                return DefWindowProc(hWnd, uMessage,
                                     wParam, lParam);
        }
        return 0;
}
```

ABOUT.C

```
// ABOUT.C
#include <windows.h>
#include <windowsx.h>
#include "globals.h"

// procedures for ABOUT dialog box
LRESULT CALLBACK About(HWND hDlg,
                       UINT uMessage,
                       WPARAM wParam,
                       LPARAM lParam)
{
    switch (uMessage)
      {
        case WM_COMMAND:
            switch (GET_WM_COMMAND_ID(wParam,lParam))
            {
                case IDOK:
                case IDCANCEL:
                    {
                    EndDialog(hDlg, TRUE);
                    return(TRUE);
                    }
                    break;
            }
      }
    return FALSE;
}
```

LINE.RC

```
#include "windows.h"
#include "globals.h"
#include <winver.h>

APPNAME ICON ICONFILE

RCINCLUDE ABOUT.DLG

APPNAME MENU
BEGIN
  MENUITEM "&About", IDM_ABOUT
END
```

ABOUT.DLG

```
ABOUTDLG DIALOG DISCARDABLE  22, 17, 167, 73
STYLE DS_MODALFRAME | WS_CAPTION | WS_SYSMENU
CAPTION SZABOUT
BEGIN
    DEFPUSHBUTTON    "OK", IDOK, 132, 2, 32, 14, WS_GROUP
    ICON             SZAPPNAME,      -1, 3, 2, 18, 20
    LTEXT            SZAPPNAME,      -1, 30, 12,  50, 8
    LTEXT            SZDESCRIPTION, -1, 30, 22, 150, 8
    LTEXT            SZVERSION,     -1, 30, 32, 150, 8
    LTEXT            SZCOMPANYNAME, -1, 30, 42, 150, 8
END
```

LINE.ICO

CASE 5-2: DRAW RECTANGLES USING SOLID AND HATCH BRUSHES

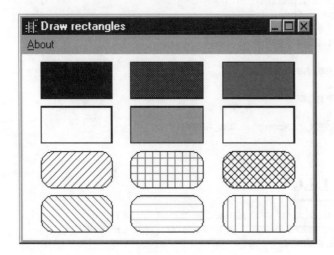

FIGURE 5-2

This case continues the task of exploring the Windows GDI that began in Case 5-1. Here, the code fills the client area of the window with a series of rectangles filled in various ways.

To paint a rectangle with a pattern in it, first specify the rectangle's width and depth using the SetRect() function. Then, you can either select a stock brush with GetStockObject() or create a hatch brush using the CreateHatchBrush() function.

As in Case 5-1, all drawing code is in the WM_PAINT handler of the window procedure. Windows will send a paint message to your application whenever the contents of a window needs repainting. By specifying the CS_HREDRAW and CS_VREDRAW parameters to the CreateWindow() function, the window procedure will receive a WM_PAINT message whenever the user resizes the window.

As also was done in Case 5-1, we use the MM_ANISOTROPIC mapping mode, combined with calls to SetViewportExtEx() and

`SetWindowExtEx()`, to set things up so that the graphics drawing calls will occupy the entire client area of the window regardless of how the user resizes it.

In this case, after the mapping mode has been set up, the code in the `WM_PAINT` handler draws rectangles, first using stock brushes such as `GetStockObject()` and `FillRect()`. Except for the `BLACK_BRUSH` rectangle, all rectangles are "framed" after being filled. The `FrameRect()` function outlines the border of the rectangle with the current pen.

After drawing rectangles with six stock brushes, the code draws six rounded rectangles using hatch brushes. The `CreateHatchBrush()` function accepts parameters such as `HS_DIAGONAL`, `HS_CROSS`, and `HS_HORIZONTAL` to create different styles of hatch brushes. This result is passed to the `SelectObject()` function. The `RoundRect()` primitive uses the currently selected brush.

GLOBALS.H

```
// GLOBALS.H - header file for global variables
//               and function prototypes

// Product identifier string definitions
#define APPNAME        Rect
#define ICONFILE       Rect.ico
#define SZAPPNAME      "Rect"
#define SZDESCRIPTION  "Draw rectangles"
#define SZVERSION      "Version 1.0"
#define SZCOMPANYNAME  "\251 M&&T Books, 1994"
#define SZABOUT        "About"

// Global function prototypes.
BOOL InitApplication(HINSTANCE);
BOOL InitInstance(HINSTANCE, int);

// Callback functions.  These are called by Windows.
LRESULT CALLBACK WndProc(HWND, UINT, WPARAM, LPARAM);
LRESULT CALLBACK About(HWND, UINT, WPARAM, LPARAM);

// Menu item ID
#define IDM_ABOUT   1000
```

```
// Global variable declarations.
extern HINSTANCE hInst;        // The current instance handle
extern char szAppName[];       // The name of this application
extern char szTitle[];         // The title bar text
```

WINMAIN.C

```
// WINMAIN.C
#include <windows.h>
#include "globals.h"

int APIENTRY WinMain(HINSTANCE hInstance,
                     HINSTANCE hPrevInstance,
                     LPSTR lpCmdLine,
                     int nCmdShow)
{
    MSG msg;

    // register main window class
    if (!hPrevInstance)
        {
        if (!InitApplication(hInstance))
            {
            return FALSE;
            }
        }

    // create and show main window
    if (!InitInstance(hInstance, nCmdShow))
        {
        return FALSE;
        }

    // process window messages
    while (GetMessage(&msg, NULL, 0, 0))
        {
            TranslateMessage(&msg);
            DispatchMessage(&msg);
        }
    return msg.wParam;
}
```

INIT.C

```
// INIT.C
#include <windows.h>
```

```
#include "globals.h"

HINSTANCE hInst;
char szAppName[] = SZAPPNAME;
char szTitle[] = SZDESCRIPTION;

// register main window class
BOOL InitApplication(HINSTANCE hInstance)
{
    WNDCLASS  wc;

    wc.style          = CS_HREDRAW | CS_VREDRAW;
    wc.lpfnWndProc    = (WNDPROC)WndProc;
    wc.cbClsExtra     = 0;
    wc.cbWndExtra     = 0;
    wc.hInstance      = hInstance;
    wc.hIcon          = LoadIcon(hInstance, szAppName);
    wc.hCursor        = LoadCursor(NULL, IDC_ARROW);
    wc.hbrBackground  = (HBRUSH)(COLOR_WINDOW + 1);
    wc.lpszMenuName   = szAppName;
    wc.lpszClassName  = szAppName;


    return(RegisterClass(&wc));
}

// create and show main window
BOOL InitInstance(HINSTANCE hInstance, int nCmdShow)
{
    HWND     hWnd;
    hInst = hInstance;
    hWnd = CreateWindow(szAppName, szTitle,
                        WS_OVERLAPPEDWINDOW,
                        160, 120, 320, 240,
                        NULL, NULL, hInstance, NULL);

    if (!hWnd)
       {
       return FALSE;
       }

    ShowWindow(hWnd, nCmdShow);
    UpdateWindow(hWnd);

    return TRUE;
}
```

RECT.C

```c
// RECT.C
#include <windows.h>
#include <windowsx.h>
#include "globals.h"

LRESULT CALLBACK WndProc(HWND hWnd,
                         UINT uMessage,
                         WPARAM wParam,
                         LPARAM lParam)
{
    HDC hDC;
    PAINTSTRUCT ps;
    RECT rect, rect1;
    HBRUSH hBrush, hBrushBlack;

    switch (uMessage)
    {
        case WM_PAINT:
            hDC = BeginPaint(hWnd, &ps);
            SetMapMode(hDC, MM_ANISOTROPIC);
            GetClientRect(hWnd, &rect);
            SetViewportExtEx(hDC, rect.right,
                             rect.bottom, NULL);
            SetWindowExtEx(hDC, 240, 150, NULL);

            // define a rectangle and paint it using
            // selected brush
            SetRect(&rect1, 15, 6, 75, 36);
              hBrushBlack = GetStockObject(BLACK_BRUSH);
              FillRect(hDC, &rect1, hBrushBlack);
            SetRect(&rect1, 90, 6, 150, 36);
              hBrush = GetStockObject(DKGRAY_BRUSH);
              FillRect(hDC, &rect1, hBrush);
              FrameRect(hDC, &rect1, hBrushBlack);
            SetRect(&rect1, 165, 6, 225, 36);
              hBrush = GetStockObject(GRAY_BRUSH);
              FillRect(hDC, &rect1, hBrush);
              FrameRect(hDC, &rect1, hBrushBlack);

            SetRect(&rect1, 15, 42, 75, 72);
              hBrush = GetStockObject(HOLLOW_BRUSH);
              FillRect(hDC, &rect1, hBrush);
              FrameRect(hDC, &rect1, hBrushBlack);
            SetRect(&rect1, 90, 42, 150, 72);
              hBrush = GetStockObject(LTGRAY_BRUSH);
```

```
      FillRect(hDC, &rect1, hBrush);
      FrameRect(hDC, &rect1, hBrushBlack);
    SetRect(&rect1, 165, 42, 225, 72);
      hBrush = GetStockObject(WHITE_BRUSH);
      FillRect(hDC, &rect1, hBrush);
      FrameRect(hDC, &rect1, hBrushBlack);

    // create a hatch brush and use it to paint
    // a round rectangle
    hBrush = SelectObject(hDC,
              CreateHatchBrush(HS_BDIAGONAL,
              RGB(255, 0, 0)));
      RoundRect(hDC, 15, 78, 75, 108, 20, 20);
    hBrush = SelectObject(hDC,
              CreateHatchBrush(HS_CROSS,
              RGB(0, 255, 0)));
      RoundRect(hDC, 90, 78, 150, 108, 20, 20);
    hBrush = SelectObject(hDC,
              CreateHatchBrush(HS_DIAGCROSS,
              RGB(0, 0, 255)));
      RoundRect(hDC, 165, 78, 225, 108, 20, 20);

    hBrush = SelectObject(hDC,
              CreateHatchBrush(HS_FDIAGONAL,
              RGB(255, 0, 255)));
      RoundRect(hDC, 15, 114, 75, 144, 20, 20);
    hBrush = SelectObject(hDC,
              CreateHatchBrush(HS_HORIZONTAL,
              RGB(255, 255, 0)));
      RoundRect(hDC, 90, 114, 150, 144, 20, 20);
    hBrush = SelectObject(hDC,
              CreateHatchBrush(HS_VERTICAL,
              RGB(0, 255, 255)));
      RoundRect(hDC, 165, 114, 225, 144, 20, 20);

    EndPaint(hWnd, &ps);
    DeleteObject(hBrush);
    DeleteObject(hBrushBlack);
    break;

case WM_COMMAND:
    switch (GET_WM_COMMAND_ID(wParam,lParam))
    {
      case IDM_ABOUT:
            // create an about dialog box
            DialogBox(hInst, "ABOUTDLG",
                hWnd, (DLGPROC)About);
```

```
                              break;

                      default:
                          return DefWindowProc(hWnd, uMessage,
                                                  wParam, lParam);
                  }
                  break;

              case WM_DESTROY:
                  PostQuitMessage(0);
                  break;

              default:
                  return DefWindowProc(hWnd, uMessage,
                                          wParam, lParam);
          }
          return 0;
      }
```

ABOUT.C

```
// ABOUT.C
#include <windows.h>
#include <windowsx.h>
#include "globals.h"

// procedures for ABOUT dialog box
LRESULT CALLBACK About(HWND hDlg,
                       UINT uMessage,
                       WPARAM wParam,
                       LPARAM lParam)
{
    switch (uMessage)
      {
        case WM_COMMAND:
            switch (GET_WM_COMMAND_ID(wParam,lParam))
            {
                case IDOK:
                case IDCANCEL:
                    {
                    EndDialog(hDlg, TRUE);
                    return(TRUE);
                    }
                    break;
            }
      }
```

```
        return FALSE;
    }
```

RECT.RC

```
#include "windows.h"
#include "globals.h"
#include <winver.h>

APPNAME ICON ICONFILE

RCINCLUDE ABOUT.DLG

APPNAME MENU
BEGIN
    MENUITEM "&About", IDM_ABOUT
END
```

ABOUT.DLG

```
ABOUTDLG DIALOG DISCARDABLE  22, 17, 167, 73
STYLE DS_MODALFRAME | WS_CAPTION | WS_SYSMENU
CAPTION SZABOUT
BEGIN
    DEFPUSHBUTTON   "OK", IDOK, 132, 2, 32, 14, WS_GROUP
    ICON            SZAPPNAME,      -1, 3, 2, 18, 20
    LTEXT           SZAPPNAME,      -1, 30, 12,  50, 8
    LTEXT           SZDESCRIPTION,  -1, 30, 22, 150, 8
    LTEXT           SZVERSION,      -1, 30, 32, 150, 8
    LTEXT           SZCOMPANYNAME,  -1, 30, 42, 150, 8
END
```

RECT.ICO

CASE 5-3: FILL AREAS USING BITMAP BRUSH

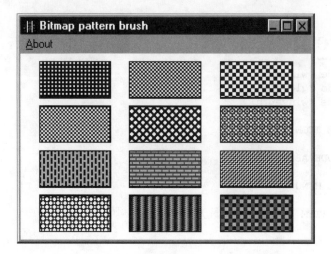

FIGURE 5-3

This case continues our exploration of the Windows GDI by illustrating using a bitmap brush to fill rectangles. As in the previous cases, drawing is done in the WM_PAINT handler of the window procedure. As before, the mapping mode is MM_ANISOTROPIC.

In this case, the rectangles are filled with a bitmap brush created with the CreatePatternBrush() function. This function requires a bitmap handle as a parameter, which is obtained by first calling LoadBitmap(). The bitmaps used for the pattern brushes are 8 x 8 pixels. The 12 bitmaps used are in files named BRUSH1.BMP, BRUSH2.BMP, and so on.

As in the previous case, the SetRect() function is used to specify the size of the rectangle, which is then filled with FillRect() and outlined with FrameRect().

GLOBALS.H

```
// GLOBALS.H - header file for global variables
//             and function prototypes

// Product identifier string definitions
#define APPNAME        BmpBrush
#define ICONFILE       BmpBrush.ico
#define SZAPPNAME      "BmpBrush"
#define SZDESCRIPTION  "Bitmap pattern brush"
#define SZVERSION      "Version 1.0"
#define SZCOMPANYNAME  "\251 M&&T Books, 1994"
#define SZABOUT        "About"

// Global function prototypes.
BOOL InitApplication(HINSTANCE);
BOOL InitInstance(HINSTANCE, int);

// Callback functions.  These are called by Windows.
LRESULT CALLBACK WndProc(HWND, UINT, WPARAM, LPARAM);
LRESULT CALLBACK About(HWND, UINT, WPARAM, LPARAM);

// Menu item ID
#define IDM_ABOUT    1000

// Global variable declarations.
extern HINSTANCE hInst;     // The current instance handle
extern char szAppName[];    // The name of this application
extern char szTitle[];      // The title bar text
```

WINMAIN.C

```
// WINMAIN.C
#include <windows.h>
#include "globals.h"

int APIENTRY WinMain(HINSTANCE hInstance,
                     HINSTANCE hPrevInstance,
                     LPSTR lpCmdLine,
                     int nCmdShow)
{
    MSG msg;

    // register main window class
    if (!hPrevInstance)
```

```
    {
    if (!InitApplication(hInstance))
        {
        return FALSE;
        }
    }

    // create and show main window
    if (!InitInstance(hInstance, nCmdShow))
        {
        return FALSE;
        }

    // process window messages
    while (GetMessage(&msg, NULL, 0, 0))
        {
            TranslateMessage(&msg);
            DispatchMessage(&msg);
        }
    return msg.wParam;
}
```

INIT.C

```
// INIT.C
#include <windows.h>
#include "globals.h"

HINSTANCE hInst;
char szAppName[] = SZAPPNAME;
char szTitle[] = SZDESCRIPTION;

// register main window class
BOOL InitApplication(HINSTANCE hInstance)
{
    WNDCLASS  wc;

    wc.style         = CS_HREDRAW | CS_VREDRAW;
    wc.lpfnWndProc   = (WNDPROC)WndProc;
    wc.cbClsExtra    = 0;
    wc.cbWndExtra    = 0;
    wc.hInstance     = hInstance;
    wc.hIcon         = LoadIcon(hInstance, szAppName);
    wc.hCursor       = LoadCursor(NULL, IDC_ARROW);
    wc.hbrBackground = (HBRUSH)(COLOR_WINDOW + 1);
    wc.lpszMenuName  = szAppName;
```

```
    wc.lpszClassName = szAppName;

    return(RegisterClass(&wc));
}

// create and show main window
BOOL InitInstance(HINSTANCE hInstance, int nCmdShow)
{
    HWND    hWnd;
    hInst = hInstance;
    hWnd = CreateWindow(szAppName, szTitle,
                        WS_OVERLAPPEDWINDOW,
                        160, 120, 320, 240,
                        NULL, NULL, hInstance, NULL);

    if (!hWnd)
        {
        return FALSE;
        }

    ShowWindow(hWnd, nCmdShow);
    UpdateWindow(hWnd);

    return TRUE;
}
```

BMPBRUSH.C

```
// BMPBRUSH.C
#include <windows.h>
#include <windowsx.h>
#include "globals.h"

LRESULT CALLBACK WndProc(HWND hWnd,
                         UINT uMessage,
                         WPARAM wParam,
                         LPARAM lParam)
{
    HDC hDC;
    PAINTSTRUCT ps;
    RECT rect, rect1;
    HBRUSH hBrush, hBrushBlack;
    HBITMAP hBitmap;

    switch (uMessage)
        {
```

```
case WM_PAINT:
     hDC = BeginPaint(hWnd, &ps);
     SetMapMode(hDC, MM_ANISOTROPIC);
     GetClientRect(hWnd, &rect);
     SetViewportExtEx(hDC, rect.right,
                           rect.bottom, NULL);
     SetWindowExtEx(hDC, 240, 150, NULL);
     hBrushBlack = GetStockObject(BLACK_BRUSH);

      // define a rectangle
      // create a bitmap brush to paint it
     SetRect(&rect1, 15, 6, 75, 36);
       hBitmap = LoadBitmap(hInst, "Brush1");
       hBrush = CreatePatternBrush(hBitmap);
       FillRect(hDC, &rect1, hBrush);
       FrameRect(hDC, &rect1, hBrushBlack);
     SetRect(&rect1, 90, 6, 150, 36);
       hBitmap = LoadBitmap(hInst, "Brush2");
       hBrush = CreatePatternBrush(hBitmap);
       FillRect(hDC, &rect1, hBrush);
       FrameRect(hDC, &rect1, hBrushBlack);
     SetRect(&rect1, 165, 6, 225, 36);
       hBitmap = LoadBitmap(hInst, "Brush3");
       hBrush = CreatePatternBrush(hBitmap);
       FillRect(hDC, &rect1, hBrush);
       FrameRect(hDC, &rect1, hBrushBlack);

     SetRect(&rect1, 15, 42, 75, 72);
       hBitmap = LoadBitmap(hInst, "Brush4");
       hBrush = CreatePatternBrush(hBitmap);
       FillRect(hDC, &rect1, hBrush);
       FrameRect(hDC, &rect1, hBrushBlack);
     SetRect(&rect1, 90, 42, 150, 72);
       hBitmap = LoadBitmap(hInst, "Brush5");
       hBrush = CreatePatternBrush(hBitmap);
       FillRect(hDC, &rect1, hBrush);
       FrameRect(hDC, &rect1, hBrushBlack);
     SetRect(&rect1, 165, 42, 225, 72);
       hBitmap = LoadBitmap(hInst, "Brush6");
       hBrush = CreatePatternBrush(hBitmap);
       FillRect(hDC, &rect1, hBrush);
       FrameRect(hDC, &rect1, hBrushBlack);

     SetRect(&rect1, 15, 78, 75, 108);
       hBitmap = LoadBitmap(hInst, "Brush7");
       hBrush = CreatePatternBrush(hBitmap);
       FillRect(hDC, &rect1, hBrush);
```

```
        FrameRect(hDC, &rect1, hBrushBlack);
    SetRect(&rect1, 90, 78, 150, 108);
        hBitmap = LoadBitmap(hInst, "Brush8");
        hBrush = CreatePatternBrush(hBitmap);
        FillRect(hDC, &rect1, hBrush);
        FrameRect(hDC, &rect1, hBrushBlack);
    SetRect(&rect1, 165, 78, 225, 108);
        hBitmap = LoadBitmap(hInst, "Brush9");
        hBrush = CreatePatternBrush(hBitmap);
        FillRect(hDC, &rect1, hBrush);
        FrameRect(hDC, &rect1, hBrushBlack);

    SetRect(&rect1, 15, 114, 75, 144);
        hBitmap = LoadBitmap(hInst, "Brush10");
        hBrush = CreatePatternBrush(hBitmap);
        FillRect(hDC, &rect1, hBrush);
        FrameRect(hDC, &rect1, hBrushBlack);
    SetRect(&rect1, 90, 114, 150, 144);
        hBitmap = LoadBitmap(hInst, "Brush11");
        hBrush = CreatePatternBrush(hBitmap);
        FillRect(hDC, &rect1, hBrush);
        FrameRect(hDC, &rect1, hBrushBlack);
    SetRect(&rect1, 165, 114, 225, 144);
        hBitmap = LoadBitmap(hInst, "Brush12");
        hBrush = CreatePatternBrush(hBitmap);
        FillRect(hDC, &rect1, hBrush);
        FrameRect(hDC, &rect1, hBrushBlack);

    EndPaint(hWnd, &ps);
    DeleteObject(hBitmap);
    DeleteObject(hBrush);
    DeleteObject(hBrushBlack);
    break;

case WM_COMMAND:
    switch (GET_WM_COMMAND_ID(wParam,lParam))
    {
      case IDM_ABOUT:
            // create an about dialog box
            DialogBox(hInst, "ABOUTDLG",
                    hWnd, (DLGPROC)About);
            break;

      default:
            return DefWindowProc(hWnd, uMessage,
                                wParam, lParam);
    }
```

```
                break;

            case WM_DESTROY:
                PostQuitMessage(0);
                break;

            default:
                return DefWindowProc(hWnd, uMessage,
                                     wParam, lParam);
        }
        return 0;
    }
```

ABOUT.C

```
// ABOUT.C
#include <windows.h>
#include <windowsx.h>
#include "globals.h"

// procedures for ABOUT dialog box
LRESULT CALLBACK About(HWND hDlg,
                       UINT uMessage,
                       WPARAM wParam,
                       LPARAM lParam)
{
    switch (uMessage)
      {
        case WM_COMMAND:
            switch (GET_WM_COMMAND_ID(wParam,lParam))
            {
                case IDOK:
                case IDCANCEL:
                    {
                    EndDialog(hDlg, TRUE);
                    return(TRUE);
                    }
                    break;
            }
      }
    return FALSE;
}
```

BMPBRUSH.RC

```
#include "windows.h"
#include "globals.h"
#include <winver.h>


Brush1  BITMAP brush1.bmp
Brush2  BITMAP brush2.bmp
Brush3  BITMAP brush3.bmp
Brush4  BITMAP brush4.bmp
Brush5  BITMAP brush5.bmp
Brush6  BITMAP brush6.bmp
Brush7  BITMAP brush7.bmp
Brush8  BITMAP brush8.bmp
Brush9  BITMAP brush9.bmp
Brush10 BITMAP brush10.bmp
Brush11 BITMAP brush11.bmp
Brush12 BITMAP brush12.bmp


APPNAME ICON ICONFILE

RCINCLUDE ABOUT.DLG

APPNAME MENU
BEGIN
    MENUITEM "&About", IDM_ABOUT
END
```

ABOUT.DLG

```
ABOUTDLG DIALOG DISCARDABLE  22, 17, 167, 73
STYLE DS_MODALFRAME | WS_CAPTION | WS_SYSMENU
CAPTION SZABOUT
BEGIN
    DEFPUSHBUTTON   "OK", IDOK, 132, 2, 32, 14, WS_GROUP
    ICON            SZAPPNAME,      -1, 3, 2, 18, 20
    LTEXT           SZAPPNAME,      -1, 30, 12,  50, 8
    LTEXT           SZDESCRIPTION,  -1, 30, 22, 150, 8
    LTEXT           SZVERSION,      -1, 30, 32, 150, 8
    LTEXT           SZCOMPANYNAME,  -1, 30, 42, 150, 8
END
```

BMPBRUSH.ICO

BRUSH1.BMP

BRUSH2.BMP

BRUSH3.BMP

BRUSH4.BMP

BRUSH5.BMP

BRUSH6.BMP

BRUSH7.BMP

BRUSH8.BMP

BRUSH9.BMP

BRUSH10.BMP

BRUSH11.BMP

BRUSH12.BMP

CASE 5-4: DRAW COLOR PIES

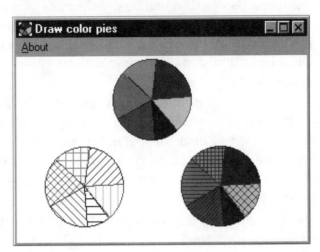

FIGURE 5-4

This case builds upon techniques introduced in the previous cases in this chapter to draw a more palatable shape: the proverbial pie used in many charts. Here the code draws three circular pies which are colored and shaded differently.

Unlike, say, rounded rectangles, the Windows GDI does not offer a primitive to draw an entire pie. However, it does have a primitive that draws a single filled slice of a pie, called Pie().

As in the previous cases, drawing is done in the WM_PAINT handler of the window procedure. Unlike the previous cases, the mapping mode is MM_ISOTROPIC, rather than MM_ANISOTROPIC, to preserve the circularity of the pie shapes.

The code in the WM_PAINT handler first creates a number of pens and brushes in different colors to use in drawing the different slices. This is done with calls to CreatePen() and CreateSolidBrush(). Then, for each of the three pies, each of the six slices is drawn by calling Pie(). The Pie() function are similar to those in the Arc() function. The first set of parameters specifies the bounding rectangle of the ellipse (or, in this

369

case, circle), which will enclose the arc of the slice by specifying the *X* and *Y* coordinates of the upper-left and bottom-right corners of the rectangle. The next set of parameters to `Pie()` specifies the *XY* coordinates of the starting and ending points of the arc. For each slice, these parameters are calculated using `sin()` and `cos()` in combination with the radius and center point of the total pie.

The entire process is driven by an array of floats called `ItemPercent[]`. This array contains the percentage of the total circle that each slice of the pie will hold. The pie in this example has six slices, so the array will have six elements. All calculations are done using floating point arithmetic. Because `sin()` and `cos()` are used, you must specify the #include file `math.h`.

For each pie, the code steps through a `for()` loop that gets the corresponding percentage value from `ItemPercent[]`. The percentage value is used to calculate a starting and ending angle, which is then transformed into the starting and ending coordinate points.

In the first pie, at the top center of the window, the slices are drawn with solid brushes created with the `CreateSolidBrush()` function. In the second pie, positioned at the bottom left of the window, the slices are filled with hatch brushes created using the `CreateHatchBrush()` function. Lastly, in the third pie at the bottom right of the window, the code uses brushes created with `CreatePatternBrush()`. For more information on using hatch brushes, see Case 5-2. For details on using bitmap brushes, see Case 5-3.

GLOBALS.H

```
// GLOBALS.H - header file for global variables
//              and function prototypes

// Product identifier string definitions
#define APPNAME        ColorPie
#define ICONFILE       ColorPie.ico
#define SZAPPNAME      "ColorPie"
#define SZDESCRIPTION  "Draw color pies"
#define SZVERSION      "Version 1.0"
#define SZCOMPANYNAME  "\251 M&&T Books, 1994"
```

```
#define SZABOUT          "About"

// Global function prototypes.
BOOL InitApplication(HINSTANCE);
BOOL InitInstance(HINSTANCE, int);

// Callback functions.  These are called by Windows.
LRESULT CALLBACK WndProc(HWND, UINT, WPARAM, LPARAM);
LRESULT CALLBACK About(HWND, UINT, WPARAM, LPARAM);

// Menu item ID
#define IDM_ABOUT    1000

// Global variable declarations.
extern HINSTANCE hInst;       // The current instance handle
extern char szAppName[];      // The name of this application
extern char szTitle[];        // The title bar text
```

WINMAIN.C

```
// WINMAIN.C
#include <windows.h>
#include "globals.h"

int APIENTRY WinMain(HINSTANCE hInstance,
                     HINSTANCE hPrevInstance,
                     LPSTR lpCmdLine,
                     int nCmdShow)
{
    MSG msg;

    // register main window class
    if (!hPrevInstance)
        {
        if (!InitApplication(hInstance))
            {
            return FALSE;
            }
        }

    // create and show main window
    if (!InitInstance(hInstance, nCmdShow))
        {
        return FALSE;
        }
```

```
    // process window messages
    while (GetMessage(&msg, NULL, 0, 0))
        {
            TranslateMessage(&msg);
            DispatchMessage(&msg);
        }
    return msg.wParam;
}
```

INIT.C

```
// INIT.C
#include <windows.h>
#include "globals.h"

HINSTANCE hInst;
char szAppName[] = SZAPPNAME;
char szTitle[] = SZDESCRIPTION;

// register main window class
BOOL InitApplication(HINSTANCE hInstance)
{
    WNDCLASS  wc;

    wc.style         = CS_HREDRAW | CS_VREDRAW;
    wc.lpfnWndProc   = (WNDPROC)WndProc;
    wc.cbClsExtra    = 0;
    wc.cbWndExtra    = 0;
    wc.hInstance     = hInstance;
    wc.hIcon         = LoadIcon(hInstance, szAppName);
    wc.hCursor       = LoadCursor(NULL, IDC_ARROW);
    wc.hbrBackground = (HBRUSH)(COLOR_WINDOW + 1);
    wc.lpszMenuName  = szAppName;
    wc.lpszClassName = szAppName;

    return(RegisterClass(&wc));
}

// create and show main window
BOOL InitInstance(HINSTANCE hInstance, int nCmdShow)
{
    HWND    hWnd;
    hInst = hInstance;
    hWnd = CreateWindow(szAppName, szTitle,
                        WS_OVERLAPPEDWINDOW,
                        160, 120, 320, 240,
                        NULL, NULL, hInstance, NULL);
```

```
        if (!hWnd)
           {
           return FALSE;
           }

        ShowWindow(hWnd, nCmdShow);
        UpdateWindow(hWnd);

        return TRUE;
    }
```

COLORPIE.C

```
// COLORPIE.C
#include <windows.h>
#include <windowsx.h>
#include "globals.h"
#include <math.h>
#define PI 3.1415926

LRESULT CALLBACK WndProc(HWND hWnd,
                         UINT uMessage,
                         WPARAM wParam,
                         LPARAM lParam)
{
    HDC hDC;
    PAINTSTRUCT ps;
    RECT rect;
    HPEN hPenI[6], hPen;
    HBRUSH hBrushI[6], hBrush;
    HBITMAP hBitmap;
    float Pie_radius, Pie_centerX, Pie_centerY;
    float Percent, ItemPercent[6];
    int i;
    double Angle1, Angle2;

    // specify the percentage of each slice of the pie
    ItemPercent[0] = 23;
    ItemPercent[1] = 15;
    ItemPercent[2] = 20;
    ItemPercent[3] = 18;
    ItemPercent[4] = 10;
    ItemPercent[5] = 15;

    switch (uMessage)
    {
```

```
case WM_PAINT:
    hDC = BeginPaint(hWnd, &ps);
    SetMapMode(hDC, MM_ISOTROPIC);
    GetClientRect(hWnd, &rect);
    SetViewportExtEx(hDC, rect.right,
                          rect.bottom, NULL);
    SetWindowExtEx(hDC, 320, 200, NULL);

    // create pens for painting
    hPenI[0] = CreatePen(0, 1, RGB(128, 0, 0));
    hPenI[1] = CreatePen(0, 1, RGB(0, 128, 128));
    hPenI[2] = CreatePen(0, 1, RGB(0, 128, 0));
    hPenI[3] = CreatePen(0, 1, RGB(128, 0, 128));
    hPenI[4] = CreatePen(0, 1, RGB(0, 0, 128));
    hPenI[5] = CreatePen(0, 1, RGB(128, 128, 0));

    // create solid brush for painting
    hBrushI[0] = CreateSolidBrush(RGB(255, 0, 0));
    hBrushI[1] = CreateSolidBrush(
                          RGB(0, 255, 255));
    hBrushI[2] = CreateSolidBrush(RGB(0, 255, 0));
    hBrushI[3] = CreateSolidBrush(
                          RGB(255, 0, 255));
    hBrushI[4] = CreateSolidBrush(RGB(0, 0, 255));
    hBrushI[5] = CreateSolidBrush(
                          RGB(255, 255, 0));

    // draw a pie using solid brushes
    Pie_radius = 70.;
    Pie_centerX = 240.;
    Pie_centerY = 75.;
    Percent = 0;
    for(i=0; i<6; i++){
        Angle1 = (Percent*2.*PI)/100.;
        Percent += ItemPercent[i];
        Angle2 = (Percent*2.*PI)/100.;
        hPen = SelectObject(hDC, hPenI[i]);
        hBrush = SelectObject(hDC, hBrushI[i]);
        Pie(hDC,
            Pie_centerX - Pie_radius,
            Pie_centerY - Pie_radius,
            Pie_centerX + Pie_radius,
            Pie_centerY + Pie_radius,
            (short)(Pie_centerX +
                    Pie_radius * cos(Angle1)),
            (short)(Pie_centerY -
                    Pie_radius * sin(Angle1)),
            (short)(Pie_centerX +
```

```
                        Pie_radius * cos(Angle2)),
          (short)(Pie_centerY -
                        Pie_radius * sin(Angle2)));
    }

// create hatch brushes for painting
hBrushI[0] = CreateHatchBrush(HS_BDIAGONAL,
                                RGB(255, 0, 0));

hBrushI[1] = CreateHatchBrush(HS_CROSS,
                                RGB(0, 255, 255));

hBrushI[2] = CreateHatchBrush(HS_DIAGCROSS,
                                RGB(0, 255, 0));

hBrushI[3] = CreateHatchBrush(HS_FDIAGONAL,
                                RGB(255, 0, 255));

hBrushI[4] = CreateHatchBrush(HS_HORIZONTAL,
                                RGB(0, 0, 255));

hBrushI[5] = CreateHatchBrush(HS_VERTICAL,
                                RGB(255, 255, 0));

// draw a pie using hatch brushes
Pie_radius = 70.;
Pie_centerX = 120.;
Pie_centerY = 225.;
Percent = 0;
for(i=0; i<6; i++){
    Angle1 = (Percent*2.*PI)/100.;
    Percent += ItemPercent[i];
    Angle2 = (Percent*2.*PI)/100.;
    hPen = SelectObject(hDC, hPenI[i]);
    hBrush = SelectObject(hDC, hBrushI[i]);
    Pie(hDC,
        Pie_centerX - Pie_radius,
        Pie_centerY - Pie_radius,
        Pie_centerX + Pie_radius,
        Pie_centerY + Pie_radius,
        (short)(Pie_centerX +
                Pie_radius * cos(Angle1)),
        (short)(Pie_centerY -
                Pie_radius * sin(Angle1)),
        (short)(Pie_centerX +
                Pie_radius * cos(Angle2)),
        (short)(Pie_centerY -
                Pie_radius * sin(Angle2)));
    }

// create bitmap brushes for painting
hBitmap = LoadBitmap(hInst, "Brush0");
hBrushI[0] = CreatePatternBrush(hBitmap);
```

375

```
hBitmap = LoadBitmap(hInst, "Brush1");
hBrushI[1] = CreatePatternBrush(hBitmap);
hBitmap = LoadBitmap(hInst, "Brush2");
hBrushI[2] = CreatePatternBrush(hBitmap);
hBitmap = LoadBitmap(hInst, "Brush3");
hBrushI[3] = CreatePatternBrush(hBitmap);
hBitmap = LoadBitmap(hInst, "Brush4");
hBrushI[4] = CreatePatternBrush(hBitmap);
hBitmap = LoadBitmap(hInst, "Brush5");
hBrushI[5] = CreatePatternBrush(hBitmap);

 // draw a pie using bitmap brushes
Pie_radius = 70.;
Pie_centerX = 360.;
Pie_centerY = 225.;
Percent = 0;
for(i=0; i<6; i++){
    Angle1 = (Percent*2.*PI)/100.;
    Percent += ItemPercent[i];
    Angle2 = (Percent*2.*PI)/100.;
    hPen = SelectObject(hDC, hPenI[i]);
    hBrush = SelectObject(hDC, hBrushI[i]);
    Pie(hDC,
        Pie_centerX - Pie_radius,
        Pie_centerY - Pie_radius,
        Pie_centerX + Pie_radius,
        Pie_centerY + Pie_radius,
        (short)(Pie_centerX +
                Pie_radius * cos(Angle1)),
        (short)(Pie_centerY -
                Pie_radius * sin(Angle1)),
        (short)(Pie_centerX +
                Pie_radius * cos(Angle2)),
        (short)(Pie_centerY -
                Pie_radius * sin(Angle2)));
    }

EndPaint(hWnd, &ps);
DeleteObject(SelectObject(hDC, hPen));
DeleteObject(SelectObject(hDC, hBrush));
break;

case WM_COMMAND:
    switch (GET_WM_COMMAND_ID(wParam,lParam))
    {
        case IDM_ABOUT:
            // create an about dialog box
```

```
                        DialogBox(hInst,  "ABOUTDLG",
                                    hWnd,  (DLGPROC)About);
                        break;

                default:
                    return DefWindowProc(hWnd, uMessage,
                                              wParam, lParam);
            }
            break;

        case WM_DESTROY:
            PostQuitMessage(0);
            break;

        default:
            return DefWindowProc(hWnd, uMessage,
                                      wParam, lParam);
    }
    return 0;
}
```

ABOUT.C

```
// ABOUT.C
#include <windows.h>
#include <windowsx.h>
#include "globals.h"

// procedures for ABOUT dialog box
LRESULT CALLBACK About(HWND hDlg,
                        UINT uMessage,
                        WPARAM wParam,
                        LPARAM lParam)
{
    switch (uMessage)
      {
        case WM_COMMAND:
            switch (GET_WM_COMMAND_ID(wParam,lParam))
              {
                case IDOK:
                case IDCANCEL:
                    {
                    EndDialog(hDlg, TRUE);
                    return(TRUE);
                    }
                    break;
```

```
            }
        }
    return FALSE;
}
```

COLORPIE.RC

```
#include "windows.h"
#include "globals.h"
#include <winver.h>

Brush0 BITMAP brush0.bmp
Brush1 BITMAP brush1.bmp
Brush2 BITMAP brush2.bmp
Brush3 BITMAP brush3.bmp
Brush4 BITMAP brush4.bmp
Brush5 BITMAP brush5.bmp

APPNAME ICON ICONFILE

RCINCLUDE ABOUT.DLG

APPNAME MENU
BEGIN
    MENUITEM "&About", IDM_ABOUT
END
```

ABOUT.DLG

```
ABOUTDLG DIALOG DISCARDABLE  22, 17, 167, 73
STYLE DS_MODALFRAME | WS_CAPTION | WS_SYSMENU
CAPTION SZABOUT
BEGIN
    DEFPUSHBUTTON   "OK", IDOK, 132, 2, 32, 14, WS_GROUP
    ICON            SZAPPNAME,      -1, 3, 2, 18, 20
    LTEXT           SZAPPNAME,      -1, 30, 12,  50, 8
    LTEXT           SZDESCRIPTION, -1, 30, 22, 150, 8
    LTEXT           SZVERSION,      -1, 30, 32, 150, 8
    LTEXT           SZCOMPANYNAME, -1, 30, 42, 150, 8
END
```

COLORPIE.ICO

BRUSH0.BMP

BRUSH1.BMP

BRUSH2.BMP

BRUSH3.BMP

BRUSH4.BMP

BRUSH5.BMP

CASE 5-5: DRAWING A 3D COLOR PIE

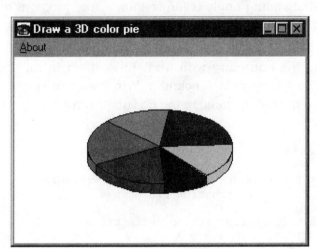

FIGURE 5-5

This case draws a single pie in 3D viewed from a side angle, instead of the flat 2D view used in Case 5-4. Unlike the previous cases, only a single instance of the pie is drawn.

As in Case 5-4, all calculations are done using floating point arithmetic. Because `sin()` and `cos()` are used, you must specify the #include file `math.h`. Like all previous cases in this chapter, the drawing code is found in the `WM_PAINT` handler. After a call to `BeginPaint()`, the code sets the map mode to `MM_ANISOTROPIC` and uses the `SetMapMode()`, `SetViewportExtEx()`, and `SetWindowExtEx()` as is done in Case 5-1. Then various brushes are created with `CreateSolidBrush()`, again as in previous cases.

Then, as in Case 5-4, the `Pie()` function in Windows is used to draw a single slice. This slice, however, is only in 2D. To get the 3D effect, it is necessary to check the starting and ending angles of each slice, in order to determine if drawing the side wall is needed. There are various possible cases for any given slice. If the starting angle and ending angle of the slice are both larger than π, the program draws a side wall, using the values for the starting and ending angle. However, if the starting angle is smaller than π and the ending angle is larger than π, the program draws a side wall starting at π to the ending angle.

To draw the side wall, the program calculates the coordinates of the points along the boundary wall and stores them in an array named point[]. The Polygon() function in Windows is used to draw the side wall, by using the points stored in the point[] array.

GLOBALS.H

```
// GLOBALS.H - header file for global variables
//                and function prototypes

// Product identifier string definitions
#define APPNAME        Pie3D
#define ICONFILE       Pie3D.ico
#define SZAPPNAME      "Pie3D"
#define SZDESCRIPTION  "Draw a 3D color pie"
#define SZVERSION      "Version 1.0"
#define SZCOMPANYNAME  "\251 M&&T Books, 1994"
#define SZABOUT        "About"

// Global function prototypes.
BOOL InitApplication(HINSTANCE);
BOOL InitInstance(HINSTANCE, int);

// Callback functions.  These are called by Windows.
LRESULT CALLBACK WndProc(HWND, UINT, WPARAM, LPARAM);
LRESULT CALLBACK About(HWND, UINT, WPARAM, LPARAM);

// Menu item ID
#define IDM_ABOUT   1000

// Global variable declarations.
extern HINSTANCE hInst;      // The current instance handle
extern char szAppName[];     // The name of this application
extern char szTitle[];       // The title bar text
```

WINMAIN.C

```
// WINMAIN.C
#include <windows.h>
```

```
#include "globals.h"

int APIENTRY WinMain(HINSTANCE hInstance,
                     HINSTANCE hPrevInstance,
                     LPSTR lpCmdLine,
                     int nCmdShow)
{
    MSG msg;

    // register main window class
    if (!hPrevInstance)
        {
        if (!InitApplication(hInstance))
            {
            return FALSE;
            }
        }

    // create and show main window
    if (!InitInstance(hInstance, nCmdShow))
        {
        return FALSE;
        }

    // process window messages
    while (GetMessage(&msg, NULL, 0, 0))
        {
            TranslateMessage(&msg);
            DispatchMessage(&msg);
        }
    return msg.wParam;
}
```

INIT.C

```
// INIT.C
#include <windows.h>
#include "globals.h"

HINSTANCE hInst;
char szAppName[] = SZAPPNAME;
char szTitle[] = SZDESCRIPTION;

// register main window class
BOOL InitApplication(HINSTANCE hInstance)
{
```

383

```
        WNDCLASS  wc;

        wc.style          = CS_HREDRAW | CS_VREDRAW;
        wc.lpfnWndProc    = (WNDPROC)WndProc;
        wc.cbClsExtra     = 0;
        wc.cbWndExtra     = 0;
        wc.hInstance      = hInstance;
        wc.hIcon          = LoadIcon(hInstance, szAppName);
        wc.hCursor        = LoadCursor(NULL, IDC_ARROW);
        wc.hbrBackground  = (HBRUSH)(COLOR_WINDOW + 1);
        wc.lpszMenuName   = szAppName;
        wc.lpszClassName  = szAppName;

        return(RegisterClass(&wc));
    }


// create and show main window
BOOL InitInstance(HINSTANCE hInstance, int nCmdShow)
{
    HWND    hWnd;
    hInst = hInstance;
    hWnd = CreateWindow(szAppName, szTitle,
                        WS_OVERLAPPEDWINDOW,
                        160, 120, 320, 240,
                        NULL, NULL, hInstance, NULL);

    if (!hWnd)
        {
        return FALSE;
        }

    ShowWindow(hWnd, nCmdShow);
    UpdateWindow(hWnd);

    return TRUE;
}
```

PIE3D.C

```
// PIE3D.C
#include <windows.h>
#include <windowsx.h>
#include "globals.h"
#include <math.h>
#define PI 3.1415926
```

```
LRESULT CALLBACK WndProc(HWND hWnd,
                         UINT uMessage,
                         WPARAM wParam,
                         LPARAM lParam)
{
    HDC hDC;
    PAINTSTRUCT ps;
    RECT rect;
    HPEN hPenBlack;
    HBRUSH hBrushI[6], hBrush;
    float Pie_radius, Pie_centerX, Pie_centerY;
    float Pie_thickness;
    float Percent, ItemPercent[6];
    int i,j,k;
    double Angle1, Angle2, Angle, dAngle;
    POINT point[42];

    // specify the percentage of each slice of the pie
    ItemPercent[0] = 23;
    ItemPercent[1] = 15;
    ItemPercent[2] = 20;
    ItemPercent[3] = 18;
    ItemPercent[4] = 10;
    ItemPercent[5] = 15;

    Pie_centerX = 120.;
    Pie_centerY = 145.;
    Pie_radius = 60.;
    Pie_thickness = 15;

    switch (uMessage)
    {
        case WM_PAINT:
            hDC = BeginPaint(hWnd, &ps);
            SetMapMode(hDC, MM_ANISOTROPIC);
            GetClientRect(hWnd, &rect);
            SetViewportExtEx(hDC, rect.right,
                             rect.bottom, NULL);
            SetWindowExtEx(hDC, 240, 300, NULL);

            // create solid brushes for painting
            hPenBlack = GetStockObject(BLACK_PEN);
            hBrushI[0] = CreateSolidBrush(RGB(255, 0, 0));
            hBrushI[1] = CreateSolidBrush(
                             RGB(0, 255, 255));
            hBrushI[2] = CreateSolidBrush(RGB(0, 255, 0));
            hBrushI[3] = CreateSolidBrush(
```

```
                                    RGB(255, 0, 255));
hBrushI[4] = CreateSolidBrush(RGB(0, 0, 255));
hBrushI[5] = CreateSolidBrush(
                                    RGB(255, 255, 0));

 // draw a 3D color pie
Percent = 0;
SelectObject(hDC, hPenBlack);
for(i=0; i<6; i++){
    Angle1 = (Percent*2.*PI)/100.;
    Percent += ItemPercent[i];
    Angle2 = (Percent*2.*PI)/100.;
    SelectObject(hDC, hBrushI[i]);
    Pie(hDC,
        Pie_centerX - Pie_radius,
        Pie_centerY - Pie_radius,
        Pie_centerX + Pie_radius,
        Pie_centerY + Pie_radius,
        (short)(Pie_centerX +
                Pie_radius * cos(Angle1)),
        (short)(Pie_centerY -
                Pie_radius * sin(Angle1)),
        (short)(Pie_centerX +
                Pie_radius * cos(Angle2)),
        (short)(Pie_centerY -
                Pie_radius * sin(Angle2)));

    if(Angle1 < PI && Angle2 > PI){
        j = ceil((Angle2 - PI)*20/PI);
        dAngle = (Angle2 - PI)/j;
        Angle = PI;
        for(k=0; k<j+1; k++){
            point[k].x = (short)(Pie_centerX
                    + Pie_radius * cos(Angle));
            point[k].y = (short)(Pie_centerY
                    - Pie_radius * sin(Angle));
            Angle += dAngle;
        }
        Angle = Angle2;
        for(k=j+1; k<2*(j+1); k++){
            point[k].x = (short)(Pie_centerX
                    + Pie_radius * cos(Angle));
            point[k].y = (short)(Pie_centerY
                    - Pie_radius * sin(Angle)
                    + Pie_thickness);
            Angle -= dAngle;
        }
```

```
                Polygon(hDC, point, 2*(j+1));
                }
           if(Angle1 > PI && Angle2 > PI){
                j = ceil((Angle2 - Angle1)*20/PI);
                dAngle = (Angle2 - Angle1)/j;
                Angle = Angle1;
                for(k=0; k<j+1; k++){
                    point[k].x = (short)(Pie_centerX
                            + Pie_radius * cos(Angle));
                    point[k].y = (short)(Pie_centerY
                            - Pie_radius * sin(Angle));
                    Angle += dAngle;
                }
                Angle = Angle2;
                for(k= j+1; k<2*(j+1); k++){
                    point[k].x = (short)(Pie_centerX
                            + Pie_radius * cos(Angle));
                    point[k].y = (short)(Pie_centerY
                            - Pie_radius * sin(Angle)
                            + Pie_thickness);
                    Angle -= dAngle;
                }
                Polygon(hDC, point, 2*(j+1));
                }
            }
        EndPaint(hWnd, &ps);
        break;

    case WM_COMMAND:
        switch (GET_WM_COMMAND_ID(wParam,lParam))
        {
            case IDM_ABOUT:
                // create an about dialog box
                DialogBox(hInst, "ABOUTDLG",
                        hWnd, (DLGPROC)About);
                break;

            default:
                return DefWindowProc(hWnd, uMessage,
                                    wParam, lParam);
        }
        break;

    case WM_DESTROY:
        PostQuitMessage(0);
        break;
```

```
            default:
                return DefWindowProc(hWnd, uMessage,
                                        wParam, lParam);
        }
        return 0;
}
```

ABOUT.C

```
// ABOUT.C
#include <windows.h>
#include <windowsx.h>
#include "globals.h"

// procedures for ABOUT dialog box
LRESULT CALLBACK About(HWND hDlg,
                        UINT uMessage,
                        WPARAM wParam,
                        LPARAM lParam)
{
    switch (uMessage)
      {
        case WM_COMMAND:
            switch (GET_WM_COMMAND_ID(wParam,lParam))
            {
                case IDOK:
                case IDCANCEL:
                    {
                    EndDialog(hDlg, TRUE);
                    return(TRUE);
                    }
                    break;
            }
      }
    return FALSE;
}
```

PIE3D.RC

```
#include "windows.h"
#include "globals.h"
#include <winver.h>

APPNAME ICON ICONFILE
```

```
RCINCLUDE ABOUT.DLG

APPNAME MENU
BEGIN
    MENUITEM "&About", IDM_ABOUT
END
```

ABOUT.DLG

```
ABOUTDLG DIALOG DISCARDABLE  22, 17, 167, 73
STYLE DS_MODALFRAME | WS_CAPTION | WS_SYSMENU
CAPTION SZABOUT
BEGIN
        DEFPUSHBUTTON    "OK", IDOK, 132, 2, 32, 14, WS_GROUP
        ICON             SZAPPNAME,      -1, 3, 2, 18, 20
        LTEXT            SZAPPNAME,      -1, 30, 12,  50, 8
        LTEXT            SZDESCRIPTION, -1, 30, 22, 150, 8
        LTEXT            SZVERSION,      -1, 30, 32, 150, 8
        LTEXT            SZCOMPANYNAME, -1, 30, 42, 150, 8
END
```

PIE3D.ICO

CASE 5-6: DRAWING MODE

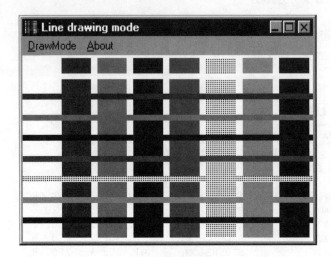

FIGURE 5-6

This case illustrates the use of *drawing modes* in Windows. Drawing mode is a concept that applies only to raster devices such as screen displays. It does not apply to vector or plotting devices. Drawing mode refers to the way in which bits are combined on a raster display when new bits are added. The SetROP2() function in Windows specifies the result of binary raster operation when bits are transferred to the screen. For example, if you use the R2_COPYPEN parameter, then the bits of the drawing pen overwrite the bits already present on the raster grid. If you specify the R2_NOT transfer mode, then the existing bits on the raster are inverted. There are 16 drawing modes to choose from, including the popular R2_XORPEN.

For black-and-white images, it is not difficult to figure out the result of the 16 possible boolean combinations of AND, NOT, OR, and XOR operations. However, in the case of color images, in which the operations are undertaken on color values, it is more difficult to visualize the outcome.

The program in this case illustrates the outcome color when a pen draws lines on a color background. In this case, eight vertical color stripes are painted in the window client area. Then, eight horizontal color lines are draw on the already colored area. The color of the result depends on the drawing mode used, which the user specifies by selecting menu items in the pull-down menu Draw Mode.

The `SetROP2()` function is one that is used in many other drawing examples in this book, see examples in the cases in Chapter 6.

GLOBALS.H

```
// GLOBALS.H - header file for global variables
//              and function prototypes

// Product identifier string definitions
#define APPNAME       LineMode
#define ICONFILE      LineMode.ico
#define SZAPPNAME     "LineMode"
#define SZDESCRIPTION "Line drawing mode"
#define SZVERSION     "Version 1.0"
#define SZCOMPANYNAME "\251 M&&T Books, 1994"
#define SZABOUT       "About"

// Global function prototypes.
BOOL InitApplication(HINSTANCE);
BOOL InitInstance(HINSTANCE, int);

// Callback functions.  These are called by Windows.
LRESULT CALLBACK WndProc(HWND, UINT, WPARAM, LPARAM);
LRESULT CALLBACK About(HWND, UINT, WPARAM, LPARAM);

// Menu item ID
#define IDM_ABOUT            100
#define IDM_R2_BLACK         101
#define IDM_R2_WHITE         102
#define IDM_R2_NOP           103
#define IDM_R2_NOT           104
#define IDM_R2_COPYPEN       105
#define IDM_R2_NOTCOPYPEN    106
#define IDM_R2_MERGEPENNOT   107
#define IDM_R2_MASKPENNOT    108
#define IDM_R2_MERGENOTPEN   109
#define IDM_R2_MASKNOTPEN    110
#define IDM_R2_MERGEPEN      111
#define IDM_R2_NOTMERGEPEN   112
#define IDM_R2_MASKPEN       113
```

```
#define IDM_R2_NOTMASKPEN    114
#define IDM_R2_XORPEN        115
#define IDM_R2_NOTXORPEN     116

// Global variable declarations.
extern HINSTANCE hInst;       // The current instance handle
extern char szAppName[];      // The name of this application
extern char szTitle[];        // The title bar text
```

WINMAIN.C

```
// WINMAIN.C
#include <windows.h>
#include "globals.h"

int APIENTRY WinMain(HINSTANCE hInstance,
                     HINSTANCE hPrevInstance,
                     LPSTR lpCmdLine,
                     int nCmdShow)
{
    MSG msg;

    // register main window class
    if (!hPrevInstance)
        {
        if (!InitApplication(hInstance))
            {
            return FALSE;
            }
        }

    // create and show main window
    if (!InitInstance(hInstance, nCmdShow))
        {
        return FALSE;
        }

    // process window messages
    while (GetMessage(&msg, NULL, 0, 0))
        {
            TranslateMessage(&msg);
            DispatchMessage(&msg);
        }
    return msg.wParam;
}
```

INIT.C

```
// INIT.C
#include <windows.h>
#include "globals.h"

HINSTANCE hInst;
char szAppName[] = SZAPPNAME;
char szTitle[] = SZDESCRIPTION;

// register main window class
BOOL InitApplication(HINSTANCE hInstance)
{
    WNDCLASS  wc;

    wc.style          = CS_HREDRAW | CS_VREDRAW;
    wc.lpfnWndProc    = (WNDPROC)WndProc;
    wc.cbClsExtra     = 0;
    wc.cbWndExtra     = 0;
    wc.hInstance      = hInstance;
    wc.hIcon          = LoadIcon(hInstance, szAppName);
    wc.hCursor        = LoadCursor(NULL, IDC_ARROW);
    wc.hbrBackground  = (HBRUSH)(COLOR_WINDOW + 1);
    wc.lpszMenuName   = szAppName;
    wc.lpszClassName  = szAppName;

    return(RegisterClass(&wc));
}

// create and show main window
BOOL InitInstance(HINSTANCE hInstance, int nCmdShow)
{
    HWND    hWnd;
    hInst = hInstance;
    hWnd = CreateWindow(szAppName, szTitle,
                        WS_OVERLAPPEDWINDOW,
                        160, 120, 320, 240,
                        NULL, NULL, hInstance, NULL);

    if (!hWnd)
        {
        return FALSE;
        }

    ShowWindow(hWnd, nCmdShow);
    UpdateWindow(hWnd);
```

```
        return TRUE;
}
```

LINEMODE.C

```
// LINEMODE.C
#include <windows.h>
#include <windowsx.h>
#include "globals.h"

LRESULT CALLBACK WndProc(HWND hWnd,
                         UINT uMessage,
                         WPARAM wParam,
                         LPARAM lParam)
{
    HDC hDC;
    HPEN hPenRed, hPenGreen, hPenBlue, hPenWhite, hPenBlack;
    HPEN hPenCyan, hPenYellow, hPenMagenta;
    HBRUSH hBrushRed, hBrushGreen, hBrushBlue;
    HBRUSH hBrushBlack, hBrushWhite;
    HBRUSH hBrushCyan, hBrushYellow, hBrushMagenta;
    PAINTSTRUCT ps;
    RECT rect;
    static short nDrawMode = R2_COPYPEN;

    switch (uMessage)
    {
        case WM_PAINT:
            hDC = BeginPaint(hWnd, &ps);

            // create pens for drawing
            hPenRed = CreatePen(0, 8, RGB(255, 0, 0));
            hPenGreen = CreatePen(0, 8, RGB(0, 255, 0));
            hPenBlue = CreatePen(0, 8, RGB(0, 0, 255));
            hPenCyan = CreatePen(0, 8, RGB(0, 255, 255));
            hPenMagenta = CreatePen(0, 8,
                                RGB(255, 0, 255));
            hPenYellow = CreatePen(0, 8, RGB(255, 255, 0));
            hPenWhite = CreatePen(0, 8,
                                RGB(255, 255, 255));
            hPenBlack = CreatePen(0, 8, RGB(0, 0, 0));

            // create solid brushes for painting
            hBrushRed = CreateSolidBrush(RGB(255, 0, 0));
            hBrushGreen = CreateSolidBrush(RGB(0, 255, 0));
            hBrushBlue = CreateSolidBrush(RGB(0, 0, 255));
```

```
hBrushCyan = CreateSolidBrush(
                         RGB(0, 255, 255));
hBrushMagenta = CreateSolidBrush(
                         RGB(255, 0, 255));
hBrushYellow = CreateSolidBrush(
                         RGB(255, 255, 0));
hBrushWhite = CreateSolidBrush(
                         RGB(255, 255, 255));
hBrushBlack = CreateSolidBrush(RGB(0, 0, 0));

SetMapMode(hDC, MM_ANISOTROPIC);
GetClientRect(hWnd, &rect);
SetViewportExtEx(hDC, rect.right,
                 rect.bottom, NULL);
SetWindowExtEx(hDC, 400, 180, NULL);

// draw eight vertical retangles
// using eight different color brushes
SelectObject(hDC, hPenWhite);
SelectObject(hDC, hBrushWhite);
Rectangle(hDC, 0, 0, 50, 180);

SelectObject(hDC, hBrushRed);
Rectangle(hDC, 50, 0, 100, 180);

SelectObject(hDC, hBrushGreen);
Rectangle(hDC, 100, 0, 150, 180);

SelectObject(hDC, hBrushBlue);
Rectangle(hDC, 150, 0, 200, 180);

SelectObject(hDC, hBrushMagenta);
Rectangle(hDC, 200, 0, 250, 180);

SelectObject(hDC, hBrushYellow);
Rectangle(hDC, 250, 0, 300, 180);

SelectObject(hDC, hBrushCyan);
Rectangle(hDC, 300, 0, 350, 180);

SelectObject(hDC, hBrushBlack);
Rectangle(hDC, 350, 0, 400, 180);

// draw eight horizontal lines
// using eight different color pens
SetROP2(hDC, nDrawMode);
```

```
SelectObject(hDC, hPenWhite);
MoveToEx(hDC, 1, 20, NULL);
LineTo(hDC, 400, 20);

SelectObject(hDC, hPenRed);
MoveToEx(hDC, 1, 40, NULL);
LineTo(hDC, 400, 40);

SelectObject(hDC, hPenGreen);
MoveToEx(hDC, 1, 60, NULL);
LineTo(hDC, 400, 60);

SelectObject(hDC, hPenBlue);
MoveToEx(hDC, 1, 80, NULL);
LineTo(hDC, 400, 80);

SelectObject(hDC, hPenMagenta);
MoveToEx(hDC, 1, 100, NULL);
LineTo(hDC, 400, 100);

SelectObject(hDC, hPenYellow);
MoveToEx(hDC, 1, 120, NULL);
LineTo(hDC, 400, 120);

SelectObject(hDC, hPenCyan);
MoveToEx(hDC, 1, 140, NULL);
LineTo(hDC, 400, 140);

SelectObject(hDC, hPenBlack);
MoveToEx(hDC, 1, 160, NULL);
LineTo(hDC, 400, 160);

EndPaint(hWnd, &ps);
DeleteObject(hPenRed);
DeleteObject(hPenGreen);
DeleteObject(hPenBlue);
DeleteObject(hPenWhite);
DeleteObject(hPenBlack);
DeleteObject(hPenCyan);
DeleteObject(hPenYellow);
DeleteObject(hPenMagenta);

DeleteObject(hBrushRed);
DeleteObject(hBrushGreen);
DeleteObject(hBrushBlue);
DeleteObject(hBrushWhite);
DeleteObject(hBrushBlack);
```

```
        DeleteObject(hBrushCyan);
        DeleteObject(hBrushYellow);
        DeleteObject(hBrushMagenta);
        break;

case WM_COMMAND:
        switch (GET_WM_COMMAND_ID(wParam,lParam))
        {
            case IDM_R2_BLACK:
                    nDrawMode = R2_BLACK;
                    break;

            case IDM_R2_WHITE:
                    nDrawMode = R2_WHITE;
                    break;

            case IDM_R2_NOP:
                    nDrawMode = R2_NOP;
                    break;

            case IDM_R2_NOT:
                    nDrawMode = R2_NOT;
                    break;

            case IDM_R2_COPYPEN:
                    nDrawMode = R2_COPYPEN;
                    break;

            case IDM_R2_NOTCOPYPEN:
                    nDrawMode = R2_NOTCOPYPEN;
                    break;

            case IDM_R2_MERGEPENNOT:
                    nDrawMode = R2_MERGEPENNOT;
                    break;

            case IDM_R2_MASKPENNOT:
                    nDrawMode = R2_MASKPENNOT;
                    break;

            case IDM_R2_MERGENOTPEN:
                    nDrawMode = R2_MERGENOTPEN;
                    break;

            case IDM_R2_MASKNOTPEN:
                    nDrawMode = R2_MASKNOTPEN;
                    break;
```

```
                    case IDM_R2_MERGEPEN:
                        nDrawMode = R2_MERGEPEN;
                        break;

                    case IDM_R2_NOTMERGEPEN:
                        nDrawMode = R2_NOTMERGEPEN;
                        break;

                    case IDM_R2_MASKPEN:
                        nDrawMode = R2_MASKPEN;
                        break;

                    case IDM_R2_NOTMASKPEN:
                        nDrawMode = R2_NOTMASKPEN;
                        break;

                    case IDM_R2_XORPEN:
                        nDrawMode = R2_XORPEN;
                        break;

                    case IDM_R2_NOTXORPEN:
                        nDrawMode = R2_NOTXORPEN;
                        break;

                    case IDM_ABOUT:
                        DialogBox(hInst, "ABOUTDLG",
                                    hWnd, (DLGPROC)About);
                        break;

                    default:
                        return DefWindowProc(hWnd, uMessage,
                                                wParam, lParam);
                }
                InvalidateRect(hWnd, NULL, FALSE);
                break;

        case WM_DESTROY:
                PostQuitMessage(0);
                break;

        default:
            return DefWindowProc(hWnd, uMessage,
                                    wParam, lParam);
    }
    return 0;
}
```

ABOUT.C

```
// ABOUT.C
#include <windows.h>
#include <windowsx.h>
#include "globals.h"

// procedures for ABOUT dialog box
LRESULT CALLBACK About(HWND hDlg,
                       UINT uMessage,
                       WPARAM wParam,
                       LPARAM lParam)

{
    switch (uMessage)
      {
        case WM_COMMAND:
            switch (GET_WM_COMMAND_ID(wParam,lParam))
              {
                case IDOK:
                case IDCANCEL:
                    {
                    EndDialog(hDlg, TRUE);
                    return(TRUE);
                    }
                    break;
              }
      }
    return FALSE;
}
```

LINEMODE.RC

```
#include "windows.h"
#include "globals.h"
#include <winver.h>

APPNAME ICON ICONFILE

RCINCLUDE ABOUT.DLG

APPNAME MENU
BEGIN
    POPUP         "&DrawMode"
    BEGIN
        MENUITEM "R2_BLACK",         IDM_R2_BLACK
```

```
        MENUITEM "R2_WHITE",         IDM_R2_WHITE
        MENUITEM "R2_NOP",           IDM_R2_NOP
        MENUITEM "R2_NOT",           IDM_R2_NOT
        MENUITEM "R2_COPYPEN",       IDM_R2_COPYPEN
        MENUITEM "R2_NOTCOPYPEN",    IDM_R2_NOTCOPYPEN
        MENUITEM "R2_MERGEPENNOT",   IDM_R2_MERGEPENNOT
        MENUITEM "R2_MASKPENNOT",    IDM_R2_MASKPENNOT
        MENUITEM "R2_MERGENOTPEN",   IDM_R2_MERGENOTPEN
        MENUITEM "R2_MASKNOTPEN",    IDM_R2_MASKNOTPEN
        MENUITEM "R2_MERGEPEN",      IDM_R2_MERGEPEN
        MENUITEM "R2_NOTMERGEPEN",   IDM_R2_NOTMERGEPEN
        MENUITEM "R2_MASKPEN",       IDM_R2_MASKPEN
        MENUITEM "R2_NOTMASKPEN",    IDM_R2_NOTMASKPEN
        MENUITEM "R2_XORPEN",        IDM_R2_XORPEN
        MENUITEM "R2_NOTXORPEN",     IDM_R2_NOTXORPEN
    END
    MENUITEM "&About", IDM_ABOUT
END
```

ABOUT.DLG

```
ABOUTDLG DIALOG DISCARDABLE  22, 17, 167, 73
STYLE DS_MODALFRAME | WS_CAPTION | WS_SYSMENU
CAPTION SZABOUT
BEGIN
    DEFPUSHBUTTON   "OK", IDOK, 132, 2, 32, 14, WS_GROUP
    ICON            SZAPPNAME,      -1, 3, 2, 18, 20
    LTEXT           SZAPPNAME,      -1, 30, 12,  50, 8
    LTEXT           SZDESCRIPTION, -1, 30, 22, 150, 8
    LTEXT           SZVERSION,     -1, 30, 32, 150, 8
    LTEXT           SZCOMPANYNAME, -1, 30, 42, 150, 8
END
```

LINEMODE.ICO

CASE 5-7: DRAW BARS IN COLOR

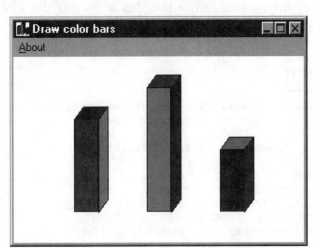

FIGURE 5-7

This case shows how to draw a series of color bars of the kind used in many business bar charts. The Windows API does not provide a primitive to draw a 3D-style bar in color, so the program here provides one. The function is called DrawBar(), and it takes ten parameters. The first parameter is the handle to the device context hDC, which is almost universally used by Windows GDI functions. As explained in your programming reference, a device context enables drawing to a window by packaging the state of the drawing process (current brush, current pen, current mapping mode, and so on).

The next two parameters specify the bottom-left coordinates of the bar. The following three parameters specify the height, width, and depth, respectively, of the bar. The next parameter is a handle to a pen to use in drawing the edges of the bar faces. The last three parameters are handles to brushes that are used in drawing the face, side, and top of the bar, respectively. The DrawBar() function first draws a rectangle as the bar front surface and then draws a polygon for the top using the Windows Polygon() function and finally draws another polygon for the side. The points for polygons are stored in the array point[] and are derived from the values for the bottom-left point plus or minus the height, depth, and/or width.

GLOBALS.H

```
// GLOBALS.H - header file for global variables
//              and function prototypes

// Product identifier string definitions
#define APPNAME       ColorBar
#define ICONFILE      ColorBar.ico
#define SZAPPNAME     "ColorBar"
#define SZDESCRIPTION "Draw color bars"
#define SZVERSION     "Version 1.0"
#define SZCOMPANYNAME "\251 M&&T Books, 1994"
#define SZABOUT       "About"

// Global function prototypes.
BOOL InitApplication(HINSTANCE);
BOOL InitInstance(HINSTANCE, int);
void DrawBar(HDC, int, int, int, int, int, HPEN, HBRUSH, HBRUSH,
             HBRUSH);

// Callback functions called by Windows.
LRESULT CALLBACK WndProc(HWND, UINT, WPARAM, LPARAM);
LRESULT CALLBACK About(HWND, UINT, WPARAM, LPARAM);

// Menu item ID
#define IDM_ABOUT   1000

// Global variable declarations.
extern HINSTANCE hInst;      // The current instance handle
extern char szAppName[];     // The name of this application
extern char szTitle[];       // The title bar text
```

WINMAIN.C

```
// WINMAIN.C
#include <windows.h>
#include "globals.h"

int APIENTRY WinMain(HINSTANCE hInstance,
                     HINSTANCE hPrevInstance,
```

```
                     LPSTR lpCmdLine,
                     int nCmdShow)
{
    MSG msg;

    // register main window class
    if (!hPrevInstance)
        {
        if (!InitApplication(hInstance))
            {
            return FALSE;
            }
        }

    // create and show main window
    if (!InitInstance(hInstance, nCmdShow))
        {
        return FALSE;
        }

    // process window mesages
    while (GetMessage(&msg, NULL, 0, 0))
        {
            TranslateMessage(&msg);
            DispatchMessage(&msg);
        }
    return msg.wParam;
}
```

INIT.C

```
// INIT.C
#include <windows.h>
#include "globals.h"

HINSTANCE hInst;
char szAppName[] = SZAPPNAME;
char szTitle[] = SZDESCRIPTION;

// register main window class
BOOL InitApplication(HINSTANCE hInstance)
{
    WNDCLASS  wc;

    wc.style        = CS_HREDRAW | CS_VREDRAW;
    wc.lpfnWndProc  = (WNDPROC)WndProc;
```

```
      wc.cbClsExtra     = 0;
      wc.cbWndExtra     = 0;
      wc.hInstance      = hInstance;
      wc.hIcon          = LoadIcon(hInstance, szAppName);
      wc.hCursor        = LoadCursor(NULL, IDC_ARROW);
      wc.hbrBackground  = (HBRUSH)(COLOR_WINDOW + 1);
      wc.lpszMenuName   = szAppName;
      wc.lpszClassName  = szAppName;

      return(RegisterClass(&wc));
}


// create and show main window
BOOL InitInstance(HINSTANCE hInstance, int nCmdShow)
{
      HWND    hWnd;
      hInst = hInstance;
      hWnd = CreateWindow(szAppName, szTitle,
                          WS_OVERLAPPEDWINDOW,
                          160, 120, 320, 240,
                          NULL, NULL, hInstance, NULL);

      if (!hWnd)
          {
          return FALSE;
          }

      ShowWindow(hWnd, nCmdShow);
      UpdateWindow(hWnd);

      return TRUE;
}
```

COLORBAR.C

```
// COLORBAR.C
#include <windows.h>
#include <windowsx.h>
#include "globals.h"

LRESULT CALLBACK WndProc(HWND hWnd,
                         UINT uMessage,
                         WPARAM wParam,
                         LPARAM lParam)
{
      HDC hDC;
```

```
HPEN hPenBlack;
HBRUSH hBrushRed, hBrushGreen, hBrushBlue;
PAINTSTRUCT ps;
RECT rect;

switch (uMessage)
{
    case WM_PAINT:
        hDC = BeginPaint(hWnd, &ps);

            // create pen and brushes for drawing
        hPenBlack = CreatePen(0, 1, RGB(0, 0, 0));
        hBrushRed = CreateSolidBrush(RGB(255, 0, 0));
        hBrushGreen = CreateSolidBrush(RGB(0, 255, 0));
        hBrushBlue = CreateSolidBrush(RGB(0, 0, 255));

        SetMapMode(hDC, MM_ANISOTROPIC);
        GetClientRect(hWnd, &rect);
        SetViewportExtEx(hDC, rect.right,
                        rect.bottom, NULL);
        SetWindowExtEx(hDC, 240, 120, NULL);
        SetPolyFillMode(hDC, WINDING);

            // draw three 3D color bars
        DrawBar(hDC, 50, 100, 60, 20, 8,
                hPenBlack, hBrushRed,
                hBrushGreen, hBrushBlue);
        DrawBar(hDC, 110, 100, 80, 20, 8,
                hPenBlack, hBrushGreen,
                hBrushBlue, hBrushRed);
        DrawBar(hDC, 170, 100, 40, 20, 8,
                hPenBlack, hBrushBlue,
                hBrushRed, hBrushGreen);

        EndPaint(hWnd, &ps);
        DeleteObject(hBrushRed);
        DeleteObject(hBrushGreen);
        DeleteObject(hBrushBlue);
        DeleteObject(hPenBlack);
        break;

    case WM_COMMAND:
        switch (GET_WM_COMMAND_ID(wParam,lParam))
        {
            case IDM_ABOUT:
                    // create an about dialog box
                DialogBox(hInst, "ABOUTDLG",
```

405

```
                                        hWnd, (DLGPROC)About);
                        break;

                default:
                        return DefWindowProc(hWnd, uMessage,
                                                wParam, lParam);
                }
                break;

        case WM_DESTROY:
                PostQuitMessage(0);
                break;

        default:
                return DefWindowProc(hWnd, uMessage,
                                        wParam, lParam);
        }
        return 0;
}


// function for drawing a 3D color bar
void DrawBar(hDC, X_left, Y_bottom,
                Bar_height, Bar_width, Bar_depth,
                hPen, hBrushFace, hBrushSide, hBrushTop)
HDC hDC;
int X_left, Y_bottom, Bar_height, Bar_width, Bar_depth;
HPEN hPen;
HBRUSH hBrushFace, hBrushSide, hBrushTop;
{
static POINT point[4];
        SelectObject(hDC, hPen);
        SelectObject(hDC, hBrushFace);
        Rectangle(hDC, X_left, Y_bottom - Bar_height,
                        X_left + Bar_width, Y_bottom);

        point[0].x = X_left;
        point[0].y = Y_bottom - Bar_height;
        point[1].x = X_left + Bar_depth;
        point[1].y = Y_bottom - Bar_height - Bar_depth;
        point[2].x = X_left + Bar_width + Bar_depth;
        point[2].y = Y_bottom - Bar_height - Bar_depth;
        point[3].x = X_left + Bar_width;
        point[3].y = Y_bottom - Bar_height;
        SelectObject(hDC, hBrushTop);
        Polygon(hDC, point, 4);

        point[0].x = X_left + Bar_width;
        point[0].y = Y_bottom - Bar_height;
```

```
                point[1].x = X_left + Bar_width + Bar_depth;
                point[1].y = Y_bottom - Bar_height - Bar_depth;
                point[2].x = X_left + Bar_width + Bar_depth;
                point[2].y = Y_bottom - Bar_depth;
                point[3].x = X_left + Bar_width;
                point[3].y = Y_bottom;
                SelectObject(hDC, hBrushSide);
                Polygon(hDC, point, 4);
        }
```

ABOUT.C

```
// ABOUT.C
#include <windows.h>
#include <windowsx.h>
#include "globals.h"

// procedures for ABOUT dialog box
LRESULT CALLBACK About(HWND hDlg,
                       UINT uMessage,
                       WPARAM wParam,
                       LPARAM lParam)
{
    switch (uMessage)
      {
        case WM_COMMAND:
              switch (GET_WM_COMMAND_ID(wParam,lParam))
              {
                  case IDOK:
                  case IDCANCEL:
                      {
                      EndDialog(hDlg, TRUE);
                      return(TRUE);
                      }
                      break;
              }
      }
    return FALSE;
}
```

COLORBAR.RC

```
#include "windows.h"
#include "globals.h"
#include <winver.h>
```

```
APPNAME ICON ICONFILE

RCINCLUDE ABOUT.DLG

APPNAME MENU
BEGIN
   MENUITEM "&About",      IDM_ABOUT
END
```

ABOUT.DLG

```
ABOUTDLG DIALOG DISCARDABLE  22, 17, 167, 73
STYLE DS_MODALFRAME | WS_CAPTION | WS_SYSMENU
CAPTION SZABOUT
BEGIN
    DEFPUSHBUTTON    "OK", IDOK, 132, 2, 32, 14, WS_GROUP
    ICON             SZAPPNAME,      -1, 3, 2, 18, 20
    LTEXT            SZAPPNAME,      -1, 30, 12, 50, 8
    LTEXT            SZDESCRIPTION, -1, 30, 22, 150, 8
    LTEXT            SZVERSION,     -1, 30, 32, 150, 8
    LTEXT            SZCOMPANYNAME, -1, 30, 42, 150, 8
END
```

COLORBAR.ICO

CASE 5-8: DRAW ELLIPSE IN VARIOUS MODE

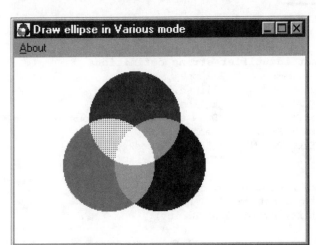

FIGURE 5-8

This program draws three ellipses in red, green, and blue using the
Ellipse() function in the Windows GDI. The tricky part in this
case is positioning the overlapped areas so that they look good. We
want the overlapped areas to show merged colors. For example, the center
area should be white because the color that results from merging red,
green, and blue is white. And when the red and green ellipses overlap, the
intersection of the two will have a merged color of yellow. To make these
colors appear properly, we first set the drawing mode to R2_COPYPEN
using the SetROP2() function. Then, we draw the red, blue, and green
ellipses. Next, we change the drawing mode to R2_MERGEPEN and draw
the red and green ellipses.

GLOBALS.H

```
// GLOBALS.H - header file for global variables
//              and function prototypes

// Product identifier string definitions
#define APPNAME       Ellipse
#define ICONFILE      Ellipse.ico
#define SZAPPNAME     "Ellipse"
#define SZDESCRIPTION "Draw ellipse in Various mode"
#define SZVERSION     "Version 1.0"
#define SZCOMPANYNAME "\251 M&&T Books, 1994"
#define SZABOUT       "About"

// Global function prototypes.
BOOL InitApplication(HINSTANCE);
BOOL InitInstance(HINSTANCE, int);

// Callback functions called by Windows.
LRESULT CALLBACK WndProc(HWND, UINT, WPARAM, LPARAM);
LRESULT CALLBACK About(HWND, UINT, WPARAM, LPARAM);

// Menu item ID
#define IDM_ABOUT   1000

// Global variable declarations.
extern HINSTANCE hInst;     // The current instance handle
extern char szAppName[];    // The name of this application
extern char szTitle[];      // The title bar text
```

WINMAIN.C

```
// WINMAIN.C
#include <windows.h>
#include "globals.h"

int APIENTRY WinMain(HINSTANCE hInstance,
                     HINSTANCE hPrevInstance,
                     LPSTR lpCmdLine,
                     int nCmdShow)
{
    MSG msg;

    // register main window class
    if (!hPrevInstance)
        {
        if (!InitApplication(hInstance))
```

```
              {
              return FALSE;
              }
          }

      // create and show main window
      if (!InitInstance(hInstance, nCmdShow))
          {
          return FALSE;
          }

      // process window messages
      while (GetMessage(&msg, NULL, 0, 0))
          {
              TranslateMessage(&msg);
              DispatchMessage(&msg);
          }
      return msg.wParam;
  }
```

INIT.C

```
// INIT.C
#include <windows.h>
#include "globals.h"

HINSTANCE hInst;
char szAppName[] = SZAPPNAME;
char szTitle[] = SZDESCRIPTION;

// register main window class
BOOL InitApplication(HINSTANCE hInstance)
{
    WNDCLASS  wc;

    wc.style         = CS_HREDRAW | CS_VREDRAW;
    wc.lpfnWndProc   = (WNDPROC)WndProc;
    wc.cbClsExtra    = 0;
    wc.cbWndExtra    = 0;
    wc.hInstance     = hInstance;
    wc.hIcon         = LoadIcon(hInstance, szAppName);
    wc.hCursor       = LoadCursor(NULL, IDC_ARROW);
    wc.hbrBackground = (HBRUSH)(COLOR_WINDOW + 1);
    wc.lpszMenuName  = szAppName;
    wc.lpszClassName = szAppName;

    return(RegisterClass(&wc));
```

411

```
}

// create and show main window
BOOL InitInstance(HINSTANCE hInstance, int nCmdShow)
{
    HWND    hWnd;
    hInst = hInstance;
    hWnd = CreateWindow(szAppName, szTitle,
                        WS_OVERLAPPEDWINDOW,
                        160, 120, 320, 240,
                        NULL, NULL, hInstance, NULL);

    if (!hWnd)
        {
        return FALSE;
        }

    ShowWindow(hWnd, nCmdShow);
    UpdateWindow(hWnd);

    return TRUE;
}
```

ELLIPSE.C

```
// ELLIPSE.C
#include <windows.h>
#include <windowsx.h>
#include "globals.h"

LRESULT CALLBACK WndProc(HWND hWnd,
                         UINT uMessage,
                         WPARAM wParam,
                         LPARAM lParam)
{
    HDC hDC;
    HPEN hPenRed, hPenGreen, hPenBlue;
    HBRUSH hBrushRed, hBrushGreen, hBrushBlue;
    PAINTSTRUCT ps;
    RECT rect;

    switch (uMessage)
    {
        case WM_PAINT:
            hDC = BeginPaint(hWnd, &ps);
```

```
    // create pens and brushes for drawing
    hPenRed = CreatePen(0, 1, RGB(255, 0, 0));
    hPenGreen = CreatePen(0, 1, RGB(0, 255, 0));
    hPenBlue = CreatePen(0, 1, RGB(0, 0, 255));
    hBrushRed = CreateSolidBrush(RGB(255, 0, 0));
    hBrushGreen = CreateSolidBrush(RGB(0, 255, 0));
    hBrushBlue = CreateSolidBrush(RGB(0, 0, 255));

    SetMapMode(hDC, MM_ISOTROPIC);
    GetClientRect(hWnd, &rect);
    SetViewportExtEx(hDC, rect.right,
                     rect.bottom, NULL);
    SetWindowExtEx(hDC, 120, 80, NULL);

// draw 3 overlapped ellipse
SetROP2(hDC, R2_COPYPEN);
    SelectObject(hDC, hPenRed);
    SelectObject(hDC, hBrushRed);
    Ellipse(hDC, 50, 10, 110, 70);
    SelectObject(hDC, hPenGreen);
    SelectObject(hDC, hBrushGreen);
    Ellipse(hDC, 33, 40, 93, 100);
    SelectObject(hDC, hPenBlue);
    SelectObject(hDC, hBrushBlue);
    Ellipse(hDC, 67, 40, 127, 100);

// redraw 1st and 2nd ellipses so the
// overlapped areas can have the merged color
SetROP2(hDC, R2_MERGEPEN);
    SelectObject(hDC, hPenRed);
    SelectObject(hDC, hBrushRed);
    Ellipse(hDC, 50, 10, 110, 70);
    SelectObject(hDC, hPenGreen);
    SelectObject(hDC, hBrushGreen);
    Ellipse(hDC, 33, 40, 93, 100);

    EndPaint(hWnd, &ps);

    DeleteObject(hPenRed);
    DeleteObject(hBrushRed);
    DeleteObject(hPenGreen);
    DeleteObject(hBrushGreen);
    DeleteObject(hPenBlue);
    DeleteObject(hBrushBlue);
    break;

case WM_COMMAND:
```

```
        switch (GET_WM_COMMAND_ID(wParam,lParam))
        {
            case IDM_ABOUT:
                    // create an about dialog box
                    DialogBox(hInst, "ABOUTDLG",
                            hWnd, (DLGPROC)About);
                    break;

            default:
                return DefWindowProc(hWnd, uMessage,
                                        wParam, lParam);
        }
        break;

    case WM_DESTROY:
        PostQuitMessage(0);
        break;

    default:
        return DefWindowProc(hWnd, uMessage,
                            wParam, lParam);
    }
    return 0;
}
```

ABOUT.C

```
// ABOUT.C
#include <windows.h>
#include <windowsx.h>
#include "globals.h"

// procedures for ABOUT dialog box
LRESULT CALLBACK About(HWND hDlg,
                    UINT uMessage,
                    WPARAM wParam,
                    LPARAM lParam)
{
    switch (uMessage)
    {
        case WM_COMMAND:
            switch (GET_WM_COMMAND_ID(wParam,lParam))
            {
                case IDOK:
                case IDCANCEL:
                    {
                    EndDialog(hDlg, TRUE);
```

```
                            return(TRUE);
                        }
                        break;
                }
            }
        return FALSE;
    }
```

ELLIPSE.RC

```
#include "windows.h"
#include "globals.h"
#include <winver.h>

APPNAME ICON ICONFILE

RCINCLUDE ABOUT.DLG

APPNAME MENU
BEGIN
  MENUITEM "&About",      IDM_ABOUT
END
```

ABOUT.DLG

```
ABOUTDLG DIALOG DISCARDABLE  22, 17, 167, 73
STYLE DS_MODALFRAME | WS_CAPTION | WS_SYSMENU
CAPTION SZABOUT
BEGIN
    DEFPUSHBUTTON    "OK", IDOK, 132, 2, 32, 14, WS_GROUP
    ICON             SZAPPNAME,      -1, 3, 2, 18, 20
    LTEXT            SZAPPNAME,      -1, 30, 12,  50, 8
    LTEXT            SZDESCRIPTION, -1, 30, 22, 150, 8
    LTEXT            SZVERSION,      -1, 30, 32, 150, 8
    LTEXT            SZCOMPANYNAME, -1, 30, 42, 150, 8
END
```

ELLIPSE.ICO

CASE 5-9: DRAW POLYGONS USING POLYPOLYGON() FUNCTION

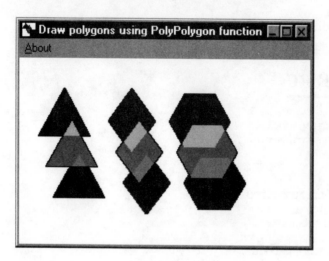

FIGURE 5-9

This example shows how to use the PolyPolygon() function in the Windows API to draw many polygons at once. Using this function can result in gains in efficiency and convenience when undertaking a complicated drawing task.

The first step is to put the coordinates of all the polygon edges into an array named points[]. You must place both the starting and ending points for each polygon in the point[] array, even though they are always identical. The numbers of points in each polygon are stored in the array PolyCount[].

The PolyPolygon() function simply reads the information in the points[] and PolyCount[] arrays and draws the set of polygons. As is typical of Windows GDI functions, drawing happens using the currently selected pen and brush.

In this example the code first draws the top row of three polygons using PolyPolygon(). Then a for-loop goes through the points[]

array and shifts the coordinates to define the next row of three polygons. This is done one more time for the bottom row of three polygons.

In order to show the overlapping areas in the proper merged color, the program sets the drawing mode to R2_MERGEPEN and then draws the top two rows of polygons again.

GLOBALS.H

```
// GLOBALS.H - header file for global variables
//             and function prototypes

// Product identifier string definitions
#define APPNAME      Polygon
#define ICONFILE     Polygon.ico
#define SZAPPNAME    "Polygon"
#define SZDESCRIPTION "Draw polygons using PolyPolygon function"
#define SZVERSION    "Version 1.0"
#define SZCOMPANYNAME "\251 M&&T Books, 1994"
#define SZABOUT      "About"

// Global function prototypes.
BOOL InitApplication(HINSTANCE);
BOOL InitInstance(HINSTANCE, int);

// Callback functions called by Windows.
LRESULT CALLBACK WndProc(HWND, UINT, WPARAM, LPARAM);
LRESULT CALLBACK About(HWND, UINT, WPARAM, LPARAM);

// Menu item ID
#define IDM_ABOUT   1000

// Global variable declarations.
extern HINSTANCE hInst;     // The current instance handle
extern char szAppName[];    // The name of this application
extern char szTitle[];      // The title bar text
```

WINMAIN.C

```
// WINMAIN.C
#include <windows.h>
#include "globals.h"

int APIENTRY WinMain(HINSTANCE hInstance,
```

```
                    HINSTANCE hPrevInstance,
                    LPSTR lpCmdLine,
                    int nCmdShow)
{
    MSG msg;

    // register main window class
    if (!hPrevInstance)
        {
        if (!InitApplication(hInstance))
            {
            return FALSE;
            }
        }

    // create and show main window
    if (!InitInstance(hInstance, nCmdShow))
        {
        return FALSE;
        }

    // process window messages
    while (GetMessage(&msg, NULL, 0, 0))
        {
            TranslateMessage(&msg);
            DispatchMessage(&msg);
        }
    return msg.wParam;
}
```

INIT.C

```
// INIT.C
#include <windows.h>
#include "globals.h"

HINSTANCE hInst;
char szAppName[] = SZAPPNAME;
char szTitle[] = SZDESCRIPTION;

// register main window class
BOOL InitApplication(HINSTANCE hInstance)
{
    WNDCLASS  wc;

    wc.style        = CS_HREDRAW | CS_VREDRAW;
```

```
        wc.lpfnWndProc   = (WNDPROC)WndProc;
        wc.cbClsExtra    = 0;
        wc.cbWndExtra    = 0;
        wc.hInstance     = hInstance;
        wc.hIcon         = LoadIcon(hInstance, szAppName);
        wc.hCursor       = LoadCursor(NULL, IDC_ARROW);
        wc.hbrBackground = (HBRUSH)(COLOR_WINDOW + 1);
        wc.lpszMenuName  = szAppName;
        wc.lpszClassName = szAppName;

        return(RegisterClass(&wc));
}

// create and show main window
BOOL InitInstance(HINSTANCE hInstance, int nCmdShow)
{
        HWND    hWnd;
        hInst = hInstance;
        hWnd = CreateWindow(szAppName, szTitle,
                            WS_OVERLAPPEDWINDOW,
                            160, 120, 320, 240,
                            NULL, NULL, hInstance, NULL);

        if (!hWnd)
            {
            return FALSE;
            }

        ShowWindow(hWnd, nCmdShow);
        UpdateWindow(hWnd);

        return TRUE;
}
```

POLYGON.C

```
// POLYGON.C
#include <windows.h>
#include <windowsx.h>
#include "globals.h"

LRESULT CALLBACK WndProc(HWND hWnd,
                         UINT uMessage,
                         WPARAM wParam,
                         LPARAM lParam)
{
```

```
HDC hDC;
HPEN hPenBlack;
HBRUSH hBrushRed, hBrushGreen, hBrushBlue;
PAINTSTRUCT ps;
RECT rect;
int i;
POINT points[] = { 30, 20, 13, 50, 47, 50, 30, 20,
                   75, 20, 60, 40, 75, 60, 90, 40,
                   75, 20, 100, 40, 110, 57, 130, 57,
                   140, 40, 130, 23, 110, 23, 100, 40 };
int PolyCounts[] = { 4, 5, 7 };

switch (uMessage)
{
    case WM_PAINT:
        hDC = BeginPaint(hWnd, &ps);

        // create pen and brushes for drawing
        hPenBlack = CreatePen(0, 1, RGB(0, 0, 0));
        hBrushRed = CreateSolidBrush(RGB(255, 0, 0));
        hBrushGreen = CreateSolidBrush(RGB(0, 255, 0));
        hBrushBlue = CreateSolidBrush(RGB(0, 0, 255));

        SetMapMode(hDC, MM_ISOTROPIC);
        GetClientRect(hWnd, &rect);
        SetViewportExtEx(hDC, rect.right,
                         rect.bottom, NULL);
        SetWindowExtEx(hDC, 120,   80, NULL);
        SetPolyFillMode(hDC, WINDING);

        // draw first set of polygons
        SetROP2(hDC, R2_COPYPEN);
        SelectObject(hDC, hPenBlack);
        SelectObject(hDC, hBrushRed);
        PolyPolygon(hDC, points, PolyCounts, 3);

        // shift the polygon definition points
        for(i=0; i<16; i++){
            points[i].x += 5; points[i].y += 20; }
        // draw 2nd set of polygons using new points
        SelectObject(hDC, hPenBlack);
        SelectObject(hDC, hBrushGreen);
        PolyPolygon(hDC, points, PolyCounts, 3);

        // shift the polygon definition points again
        for(i=0; i<16; i++){
            points[i].x += 5; points[i].y += 20; }
```

```
        // draw 3rd set of polygons using new points
        SelectObject(hDC, hPenBlack);
        SelectObject(hDC, hBrushBlue);
        PolyPolygon(hDC, points, PolyCounts, 3);

        // change raster operation mode redraw the
        // 1st and 2nd set of polygons so the
        // operlapped areas can show merged color
        SetROP2(hDC, R2_MERGEPEN);
        for(i=0; i<16; i++){
            points[i].x -= 10; points[i].y -= 40; }
        SelectObject(hDC, hPenBlack);
        SelectObject(hDC, hBrushRed);
        PolyPolygon(hDC, points, PolyCounts, 3);

        for(i=0; i<16; i++){
            points[i].x += 5; points[i].y += 20; }
        SelectObject(hDC, hPenBlack);
        SelectObject(hDC, hBrushGreen);
        PolyPolygon(hDC, points, PolyCounts, 3);

        EndPaint(hWnd, &ps);
        DeleteObject(hBrushRed);
        DeleteObject(hBrushGreen);
        DeleteObject(hBrushBlue);
        DeleteObject(hPenBlack);
        break;

case WM_COMMAND:
        switch (GET_WM_COMMAND_ID(wParam,lParam))
        {
            case IDM_ABOUT:
                    // create an about dialog box
                DialogBox(hInst, "ABOUTDLG",
                            hWnd, (DLGPROC)About);
                break;

            default:
                return DefWindowProc(hWnd, uMessage,
                                        wParam, lParam);
        }
        break;

case WM_DESTROY:
        PostQuitMessage(0);
        break;
```

```
        default:
            return DefWindowProc(hWnd, uMessage,
                                    wParam, lParam);
    }
    return 0;
}
```

ABOUT.C

```
// ABOUT.C
#include <windows.h>
#include <windowsx.h>
#include "globals.h"

// procedures for ABOUT dialog box
LRESULT CALLBACK About(HWND hDlg,
                        UINT uMessage,
                        WPARAM wParam,
                        LPARAM lParam)
{
    switch (uMessage)
      {
        case WM_COMMAND:
            switch (GET_WM_COMMAND_ID(wParam,lParam))
            {
                case IDOK:
                case IDCANCEL:
                    {
                    EndDialog(hDlg, TRUE);
                    return(TRUE);
                    }
                    break;
            }
      }
    return FALSE;
}
```

POLYGON.RC

```
#include "windows.h"
#include "globals.h"
#include <winver.h>

APPNAME ICON ICONFILE
```

```
RCINCLUDE ABOUT.DLG

APPNAME MENU
BEGIN
  MENUITEM "&About",      IDM_ABOUT
END
```

ABOUT.DLG

```
ABOUTDLG DIALOG DISCARDABLE  22, 17, 167, 73
STYLE DS_MODALFRAME | WS_CAPTION | WS_SYSMENU
CAPTION SZABOUT
BEGIN
    DEFPUSHBUTTON   "OK", IDOK, 132, 2, 32, 14, WS_GROUP
    ICON            SZAPPNAME,      -1, 3, 2, 18, 20
    LTEXT           SZAPPNAME,      -1, 30, 12,  50, 8
    LTEXT           SZDESCRIPTION,  -1, 30, 22, 150, 8
    LTEXT           SZVERSION,      -1, 30, 32, 150, 8
    LTEXT           SZCOMPANYNAME,  -1, 30, 42, 150, 8
END
```

POLYGON.ICO

CASE 5-10: REGION DRAWING FUNCTIONS

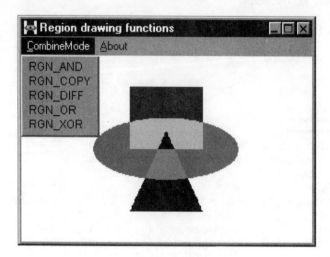

FIGURE 5-10

This case shows how to use the region functions in the GDI portion of the Windows API. The code first defines three different regions, using the functions CreateRectRgn(), CreateEllipticRgn(), and CreatePolygonRgn(), respectively. These regions are then combined into one single region using the CombineRgn() function with a specific combine mode. The user can choose one of five possible combine modes such as RGN_AND, RGN_COPY, and RGN_DIFF. These choices are listed in the pull-down menu entitled CombineMode.

424

GLOBALS.H

```
// GLOBALS.H - header file for global variables
//             and function prototypes

// Product identifier string definitions
#define APPNAME        Region
#define ICONFILE       Region.ico
#define SZAPPNAME      "Region"
#define SZDESCRIPTION  "Region drawing functions"
#define SZVERSION      "Version 1.0"
#define SZCOMPANYNAME  "\251 M&&T Books, 1994"
#define SZABOUT        "About"

// Global function prototypes.
BOOL InitApplication(HINSTANCE);
BOOL InitInstance(HINSTANCE, int);

// Callback functions called by Windows.
LRESULT CALLBACK WndProc(HWND, UINT, WPARAM, LPARAM);
LRESULT CALLBACK About(HWND, UINT, WPARAM, LPARAM);

// Menu item ID
#define IDM_ABOUT      100
#define IDM_RGN_AND    101
#define IDM_RGN_COPY   102
#define IDM_RGN_DIFF   103
#define IDM_RGN_OR     104
#define IDM_RGN_XOR    105

// Global variable declarations.
extern HINSTANCE hInst;      // The current instance handle
extern char szAppName[];     // The name of this application
extern char szTitle[];       // The title bar text
```

WINMAIN.C

```
// WINMAIN.C
#include <windows.h>
#include "globals.h"

int APIENTRY WinMain(HINSTANCE hInstance,
                     HINSTANCE hPrevInstance,
                     LPSTR lpCmdLine,
                     int nCmdShow)
{
```

```
        MSG msg;

        // register main window class
        if (!hPrevInstance)
            {
            if (!InitApplication(hInstance))
                {
                return FALSE;
                }
            }

        // create and show main window
        if (!InitInstance(hInstance, nCmdShow))
            {
            return FALSE;
            }

        // process window messages
        while (GetMessage(&msg, NULL, 0, 0))
            {
                TranslateMessage(&msg);
                DispatchMessage(&msg);
            }
        return msg.wParam;
    }
```

INIT.C

```
    // INIT.C
    #include <windows.h>
    #include "globals.h"

    HINSTANCE hInst;
    char szAppName[] = SZAPPNAME;
    char szTitle[] = SZDESCRIPTION;

    // register main window class
    BOOL InitApplication(HINSTANCE hInstance)
    {
        WNDCLASS  wc;

        wc.style        = CS_HREDRAW | CS_VREDRAW;
        wc.lpfnWndProc  = (WNDPROC)WndProc;
        wc.cbClsExtra   = 0;
        wc.cbWndExtra   = 0;
        wc.hInstance    = hInstance;
```

```
    wc.hIcon         = LoadIcon(hInstance, szAppName);
    wc.hCursor       = LoadCursor(NULL, IDC_ARROW);
    wc.hbrBackground = (HBRUSH)(COLOR_WINDOW + 1);
    wc.lpszMenuName  = szAppName;
    wc.lpszClassName = szAppName;

    return(RegisterClass(&wc));
}

// create and show main window
BOOL InitInstance(HINSTANCE hInstance, int nCmdShow)
{
    HWND    hWnd;
    hInst = hInstance;
    hWnd = CreateWindow(szAppName, szTitle,
                        WS_OVERLAPPEDWINDOW,
                        160, 120, 320, 240,
                        NULL, NULL, hInstance, NULL);

    if (!hWnd)
        {
        return FALSE;
        }

    ShowWindow(hWnd, nCmdShow);
    UpdateWindow(hWnd);

    return TRUE;
}
```

REGION.C

```
// REGION.C
#include <windows.h>
#include <windowsx.h>
#include "globals.h"

LRESULT CALLBACK WndProc(HWND hWnd,
                         UINT uMessage,
                         WPARAM wParam,
                         LPARAM lParam)
{
    HDC hDC;
    HBRUSH hBrushRed, hBrushGreen, hBrushBlue, hBrushBlack;
    PAINTSTRUCT ps;
    HRGN hRgnRect, hRgnElliptic, hRgnPolygon;
```

```
HRGN hRgnCombine, hRgnCombine1, hRgnCombine2;
RECT rect;
POINT point[3];
static short nCombineMode = RGN_AND;

switch (uMessage)
{
    case WM_PAINT:
        hDC = BeginPaint(hWnd, &ps);

        // create solid brushes for drawing
        hBrushRed = CreateSolidBrush(RGB(255, 0, 0));
        hBrushGreen = CreateSolidBrush(RGB(0, 255, 0));
        hBrushBlue = CreateSolidBrush(RGB(0, 0, 255));
        hBrushBlack = CreateSolidBrush(RGB(0, 0, 0));

        SetMapMode(hDC, MM_ANISOTROPIC);
        GetClientRect(hWnd, &rect);
        SetViewportExtEx(hDC, rect.right,
                         rect.bottom, NULL);
        SetWindowExtEx(hDC, 400, 300, NULL);

        // create a rectangular resion
        hRgnRect = CreateRectRgn(150, 50, 250, 150);
        // create an elliptic region
        hRgnElliptic = CreateEllipticRgn(
                           100, 100, 300, 200);

        // create a triangular region
        point[0].x = 150; point[0].y = 250;
        point[1].x = 200; point[1].y = 120;
        point[2].x = 250; point[2].y = 250;
        hRgnPolygon = CreatePolygonRgn(
                          point, 3, WINDING);

        // draw 3 regions
        SetROP2(hDC, R2_COPYPEN);
        FillRgn(hDC, hRgnRect, hBrushRed);
        FillRgn(hDC, hRgnElliptic, hBrushGreen);
        FillRgn(hDC, hRgnPolygon, hBrushBlue);
        SetROP2(hDC, R2_MERGEPEN);
        FillRgn(hDC, hRgnRect, hBrushRed);
        FillRgn(hDC, hRgnElliptic, hBrushGreen);

        // combine 3 regions with specified
        // Combine Mode
        hRgnCombine = CreateRectRgn(
```

```
                                 150, 100, 250, 200);
        hRgnCombine1 = CreateRectRgn(
                                 150, 100, 250, 200);
        hRgnCombine2 = CreateRectRgn(
                                 150, 100, 250, 200);
        CombineRgn(hRgnCombine1, hRgnRect,
                   hRgnElliptic, nCombineMode);
        CombineRgn(hRgnCombine2, hRgnPolygon,
                   hRgnElliptic, nCombineMode);
        CombineRgn(hRgnCombine, hRgnCombine1,
                   hRgnCombine2, nCombineMode);

         // fill combined region with black color
        SetROP2(hDC, R2_COPYPEN);
        FillRgn(hDC, hRgnCombine, hBrushBlack);

        EndPaint(hWnd, &ps);

        DeleteObject(hBrushRed);
        DeleteObject(hBrushGreen);
        DeleteObject(hBrushBlue);
        DeleteObject(hBrushBlack);

        DeleteObject(hRgnRect);
        DeleteObject(hRgnElliptic);
        DeleteObject(hRgnPolygon);
        DeleteObject(hRgnCombine1);
        DeleteObject(hRgnCombine2);
        break;

    case WM_COMMAND:
        switch (GET_WM_COMMAND_ID(wParam,lParam))
        {
            case IDM_RGN_AND:
                nCombineMode = RGN_AND;
                break;

            case IDM_RGN_COPY:
                nCombineMode = RGN_COPY;
                break;

            case IDM_RGN_DIFF:
                nCombineMode = RGN_DIFF;
                break;

            case IDM_RGN_OR:
                nCombineMode = RGN_OR;
```

```
                        break;

                case IDM_RGN_XOR:
                    nCombineMode = RGN_XOR;
                    break;

                case IDM_ABOUT:
                    // create an about dialog boc
                    DialogBox(hInst, "ABOUTDLG",
                            hWnd, (DLGPROC)About);
                    break;

                default:
                    return DefWindowProc(hWnd, uMessage,
                                    wParam, lParam);
            }
            // repaint the client area to reflect the change
            InvalidateRect(hWnd, NULL, FALSE);
            break;

        case WM_DESTROY:
            PostQuitMessage(0);
            break;

        default:
            return DefWindowProc(hWnd, uMessage,
                            wParam, lParam);
    }
    return 0;
}
```

ABOUT.C

```
// ABOUT.C
#include <windows.h>
#include <windowsx.h>
#include "globals.h"

// procedures for ABOUT dialog box
LRESULT CALLBACK About(HWND hDlg,
                    UINT uMessage,
                    WPARAM wParam,
                    LPARAM lParam)
{
    switch (uMessage)
        {
```

```
      case WM_COMMAND:
          switch (GET_WM_COMMAND_ID(wParam,lParam))
          {
              case IDOK:
              case IDCANCEL:
                  {
                  EndDialog(hDlg, TRUE);
                  return(TRUE);
                  }
                  break;

          }
      }
    return FALSE;
}
```

REGION.RC

```
#include "windows.h"
#include "globals.h"
#include <winver.h>

APPNAME ICON ICONFILE

RCINCLUDE ABOUT.DLG

APPNAME MENU
BEGIN
    POPUP          "&CombineMode"
    BEGIN
        MENUITEM "RGN_AND",      IDM_RGN_AND
        MENUITEM "RGN_COPY",     IDM_RGN_COPY
        MENUITEM "RGN_DIFF",     IDM_RGN_DIFF
        MENUITEM "RGN_OR",       IDM_RGN_OR
        MENUITEM "RGN_XOR",      IDM_RGN_XOR
    END
    MENUITEM "&About", IDM_ABOUT
END
```

ABOUT.DLG

```
ABOUTDLG DIALOG DISCARDABLE  22, 17, 167, 73
STYLE DS_MODALFRAME | WS_CAPTION | WS_SYSMENU
CAPTION SZABOUT
BEGIN
```

```
    DEFPUSHBUTTON    "OK", IDOK, 132, 2, 32, 14, WS_GROUP
    ICON             SZAPPNAME,      -1, 3, 2, 18, 20
    LTEXT            SZAPPNAME,      -1, 30, 12,  50, 8
    LTEXT            SZDESCRIPTION, -1, 30, 22, 150, 8
    LTEXT            SZVERSION,      -1, 30, 32, 150, 8
    LTEXT            SZCOMPANYNAME, -1, 30, 42, 150, 8
END
```

REGION.ICO

CASE 5-11: LineDDA Function

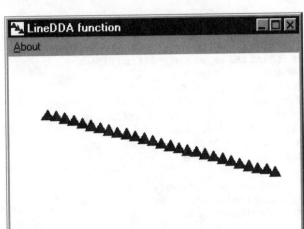

FIGURE 5-11

This case shows how to use the LineDDA() function in the GDI portion of the Windows API. The LineDDA() function tells the GDI subsystem to draw a line, but it also sets up a callback function in your code that is called as the line is drawn. The "DDA" refers to the line-drawing algorithm used, which steps through the line one horizontal pixel at a time, calculating the position of the corresponding vertical pixel or pixels. At each step in the line-drawing process, Windows makes a call to your callback routine, which is of type LINEDDAPROC.

In this case, we have defined a function called LineDDAFunc() that draws a small triangle each time it is called back. When LineDDAFunc() is called, it is passed the *XY* coordinates of the current point. The LineDDAFunc() varies the color of the triangles depending on the point coordinates.

433

GLOBALS.H

```
// GLOBALS.H - header file for global variables
//              and function prototypes

// Product identifier string definitions
#define APPNAME        LineDDA
#define ICONFILE       LineDDA.ico
#define SZAPPNAME      "LineDDA"
#define SZDESCRIPTION  "LineDDA function"
#define SZVERSION      "Version 1.0"
#define SZCOMPANYNAME  "\251 M&&T Books, 1994"
#define SZABOUT        "About"

// Global function prototypes.
BOOL InitApplication(HINSTANCE);
BOOL InitInstance(HINSTANCE, int);

// Callback functions called by Windows.
LRESULT CALLBACK WndProc(HWND, UINT, WPARAM, LPARAM);
LRESULT CALLBACK About(HWND, UINT, WPARAM, LPARAM);
VOID CALLBACK LineDDAFunc(int, int, LPARAM);

// Menu item ID
#define IDM_ABOUT   1000

// Global variable declarations.
extern HINSTANCE hInst;      // The current instance handle
extern char szAppName[];     // The name of this application
extern char szTitle[];       // The title bar text
```

WINMAIN.C

```
// WINMAIN.C
#include <windows.h>
#include "globals.h"

int APIENTRY WinMain(HINSTANCE hInstance,
                     HINSTANCE hPrevInstance,
                     LPSTR lpCmdLine,
                     int nCmdShow)
{
    MSG msg;

    // register main window class
    if (!hPrevInstance)
```

```
        {
        if (!InitApplication(hInstance))
            {
            return FALSE;
            }
        }

    // create and show main window
    if (!InitInstance(hInstance, nCmdShow))
        {
        return FALSE;
        }

    // process window messages
    while (GetMessage(&msg, NULL, 0, 0))
        {
            TranslateMessage(&msg);
            DispatchMessage(&msg);
        }
    return msg.wParam;
}
```

INIT.C

```
// INIT.C
#include <windows.h>
#include "globals.h"

HINSTANCE hInst;
char szAppName[] = SZAPPNAME;
char szTitle[] = SZDESCRIPTION;

// register main window class
BOOL InitApplication(HINSTANCE hInstance)
{
    WNDCLASS  wc;

    wc.style          = CS_HREDRAW | CS_VREDRAW;
    wc.lpfnWndProc    = (WNDPROC)WndProc;
    wc.cbClsExtra     = 0;
    wc.cbWndExtra     = 0;
    wc.hInstance      = hInstance;
    wc.hIcon          = LoadIcon(hInstance, szAppName);
    wc.hCursor        = LoadCursor(NULL, IDC_ARROW);
    wc.hbrBackground  = (HBRUSH)(COLOR_WINDOW + 1);
    wc.lpszMenuName   = szAppName;
```

```
        wc.lpszClassName = szAppName;

        return(RegisterClass(&wc));
}

// create and show main window
BOOL InitInstance(HINSTANCE hInstance, int nCmdShow)
{
    HWND    hWnd;
    hInst = hInstance;
    hWnd = CreateWindow(szAppName, szTitle,
                        WS_OVERLAPPEDWINDOW,
                        160, 120, 320, 240,
                        NULL, NULL, hInstance, NULL);

    if (!hWnd)
        {
        return FALSE;
        }

    ShowWindow(hWnd, nCmdShow);
    UpdateWindow(hWnd);

    return TRUE;
}
```

LINEDDA.C

```
// LINEDDA.C
#include <windows.h>
#include <windowsx.h>
#include "globals.h"

LRESULT CALLBACK WndProc(HWND hWnd,
                         UINT uMessage,
                         WPARAM wParam,
                         LPARAM lParam)
{
    HDC hDC;
    PAINTSTRUCT ps;
    RECT rect;

    switch (uMessage)
    {
        case WM_PAINT:
            hDC = BeginPaint(hWnd, &ps);
```

```
        SetMapMode(hDC, MM_ANISOTROPIC);
        GetClientRect(hWnd, &rect);
        SetViewportExtEx(hDC, rect.right,
                         rect.bottom, NULL);
        SetWindowExtEx(hDC, 200, 150, NULL);

         // draw color triangles along a line
        LineDDA(20, 50, 180, 100,
                (LINEDDAPROC)LineDDAFunc,
                (LPARAM)&hDC);
        EndPaint(hWnd, &ps);
        break;

    case WM_COMMAND:
        switch (GET_WM_COMMAND_ID(wParam,lParam))
        {
            case IDM_ABOUT:
                    // create an about dialog box
                DialogBox(hInst, "ABOUTDLG",
                          hWnd, (DLGPROC)About);
                break;

            default:
                return DefWindowProc(hWnd, uMessage,
                                     wParam, lParam);
        }
        break;

    case WM_DESTROY:
        PostQuitMessage(0);
        break;

    default:
        return DefWindowProc(hWnd, uMessage,
                             wParam, lParam);
    }
    return 0;
}

// function for drawing color triangles
VOID CALLBACK LineDDAFunc(X, Y, lpData)
int X, Y;
LPARAM lpData;
{
HPEN hPenBlack;
HBRUSH hBrush;
POINT point[3];
```

```
static short R_index=255, B_index=0;
static short i = 0;
if(i == 0){
    hPenBlack = GetStockObject(BLACK_PEN);
    SelectObject(*(HDC far *)lpData, hPenBlack);
    hBrush = CreateSolidBrush(RGB(R_index, 0, B_index));
    SelectObject(*(HDC far *)lpData, hBrush);
    point[0].x = X; point[0].y = Y;
    point[1].x = X+8; point[1].y = Y;
    point[2].x = X+4; point[2].y = Y-8;
    Polygon(*(HDC far *)lpData, point, 3);
    R_index -= 16; B_index += 16;
    }
i = (i + 1) % 6;
}
```

ABOUT.C

```
// ABOUT.C
#include <windows.h>
#include <windowsx.h>
#include "globals.h"

// procedures for ABOUT dialog box
LRESULT CALLBACK About(HWND hDlg,
                       UINT uMessage,
                       WPARAM wParam,
                       LPARAM lParam)
{
    switch (uMessage)
      {
        case WM_COMMAND:
            switch (GET_WM_COMMAND_ID(wParam,lParam))
            {
                case IDOK:
                case IDCANCEL:
                    {
                    EndDialog(hDlg, TRUE);
                    return(TRUE);
                    }
                    break;
            }
      }
    return FALSE;
}
```

LINEDDA.RC

```
#include "windows.h"
#include "globals.h"
#include <winver.h>

APPNAME ICON ICONFILE

RCINCLUDE ABOUT.DLG

APPNAME MENU
BEGIN
  MENUITEM "&About",        IDM_ABOUT
END
```

ABOUT.DLG

```
ABOUTDLG DIALOG DISCARDABLE  22, 17, 167, 73
STYLE DS_MODALFRAME | WS_CAPTION | WS_SYSMENU
CAPTION SZABOUT
BEGIN
    DEFPUSHBUTTON    "OK", IDOK, 132, 2, 32, 14, WS_GROUP
    ICON             SZAPPNAME,      -1, 3, 2, 18, 20
    LTEXT            SZAPPNAME,      -1, 30, 12,  50, 8
    LTEXT            SZDESCRIPTION, -1, 30, 22, 150, 8
    LTEXT            SZVERSION,      -1, 30, 32, 150, 8
    LTEXT            SZCOMPANYNAME, -1, 30, 42, 150, 8
END
```

LINEDDA.ICO

CASE 5-12: DRAW COMBINED REGION (REGION CLIPPING FUNCTIONS)

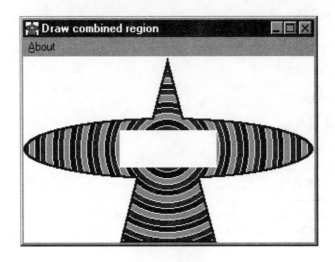

FIGURE 5-12

This case illustrates use of some of the region functions in the GDI subsystem of the Windows API. The setup portion of the program happens during the processing of the WM_SIZE message in the main window procedure. Windows sends the WM_SIZE message to your WndProc when the window is first created and whenever the user resizes the window. The code in this handler creates an elliptical region, and a triangle region using the functions CreateEllipticRgn() and CreatePolygonRgn(). These two regions are then combined into a third region using RGN_OR as the region combine mode.

The rest of the code is found in the WM_PAINT handler of the window procedure, which is called whenever the window client area needs to be repainted. To restrict all drawing operations to take effect only within the boundary of the combined region, the code uses the SelectClipRgn() function. To make things more interesting, the code uses the ExcludeClipRect() function to specify a rectangular area in the middle of the combined region that will be excluded from drawing operations.

Then, the code draws a series of concentric ellipses in different colors. As you can see, all painting is clipped within the combined region and outside the "exclude" rectangle. Lastly, a call to the `FrameRgn()` function adds a black boundary that outlines the combined region.

GLOBALS.H

```
// GLOBALS.H - header file for global variables
//              and function prototypes

// Product identifier string definitions.
#define APPNAME        CRegion
#define ICONFILE       CRegion.ico
#define SZAPPNAME      "CRegion"
#define SZDESCRIPTION "Draw combined region"
#define SZVERSION      "Version 1.0"
#define SZCOMPANYNAME "\251 M&&T Books, 1994"
#define SZABOUT        "About"

// Global function prototypes.
BOOL InitApplication(HINSTANCE);
BOOL InitInstance(HINSTANCE, int);

// Callback functions called by Windows.
LRESULT CALLBACK WndProc(HWND, UINT, WPARAM, LPARAM);
LRESULT CALLBACK About(HWND, UINT, WPARAM, LPARAM);

// Menu item ID
#define IDM_ABOUT   1000

// Global variable declarations.
extern HINSTANCE hInst;      // The current instance handle
extern char szAppName[];     // The name of this application
extern char szTitle[];       // The title bar text
```

WINMAIN.C

```
// WINMAIN.C
#include <windows.h>
#include "globals.h"

int APIENTRY WinMain(HINSTANCE hInstance,
                     HINSTANCE hPrevInstance,
```

```
                            LPSTR lpCmdLine,
                            int nCmdShow)
{
    MSG msg;

    // register main window class
    if (!hPrevInstance)
        {
        if (!InitApplication(hInstance))
            {
            return FALSE;
            }
        }

    // create and show main window
    if (!InitInstance(hInstance, nCmdShow))
        {
        return FALSE;
        }

    // process window messages
    while (GetMessage(&msg, NULL, 0, 0))
        {
        TranslateMessage(&msg);
        DispatchMessage(&msg);
        }
    return msg.wParam;
}
```

INIT.C

```
// INIT.C
#include <windows.h>
#include "globals.h"

HINSTANCE hInst;
char szAppName[] = SZAPPNAME;
char szTitle[] = SZDESCRIPTION;

// register main window class
BOOL InitApplication(HINSTANCE hInstance)
{
    WNDCLASS  wc;

    wc.style        = CS_HREDRAW | CS_VREDRAW;
    wc.lpfnWndProc  = (WNDPROC)WndProc;
```

```
    wc.cbClsExtra    = 0;
    wc.cbWndExtra    = 0;
    wc.hInstance     = hInstance;
    wc.hIcon         = LoadIcon(hInstance, szAppName);
    wc.hCursor       = LoadCursor(NULL, IDC_ARROW);
    wc.hbrBackground = (HBRUSH)(COLOR_WINDOW + 1);
    wc.lpszMenuName  = szAppName;
    wc.lpszClassName = szAppName;

    return(RegisterClass(&wc));
}

// create and show main window
BOOL InitInstance(HINSTANCE hInstance, int nCmdShow)
{
    HWND    hWnd;
    hInst = hInstance;
    hWnd = CreateWindow(szAppName, szTitle,
                        WS_OVERLAPPEDWINDOW,
                        160, 120, 320, 240,
                        NULL, NULL, hInstance, NULL);

    if (!hWnd)
        {
        return FALSE;
        }

    ShowWindow(hWnd, nCmdShow);
    UpdateWindow(hWnd);

    return TRUE;
}
```

CREGION.C

```
// CREGION.C
#include <windows.h>
#include <windowsx.h>
#include "globals.h"

LRESULT CALLBACK WndProc(HWND hWnd,
                         UINT uMessage,
                         WPARAM wParam,
                         LPARAM lParam)
{
    HDC hDC;
```

```
PAINTSTRUCT ps;
HBRUSH hBrushRed, hBrushGreen, hBrushBlue;
HRGN hRgnElliptic, hRgnPolygon;
static HRGN hRgnCombine;
POINT point[3];
static short Client_X, Client_Y;
double Radius;
int i;

switch (uMessage)
{
    case WM_SIZE:
            // get client area dimension
            Client_X = LOWORD(lParam);
            Client_Y = HIWORD(lParam);

            // create an elliptic region
            hRgnElliptic = CreateEllipticRgn(0, Client_Y/3,
                        Client_X, Client_Y*2/3);

            // create a triangular region
            point[0].x = Client_X/3;
            point[0].y = Client_Y;
            point[1].x = Client_X/2;
            point[1].y = 0;
            point[2].x = Client_X*2/3;
            point[2].y = Client_Y;
            hRgnPolygon = CreatePolygonRgn(
                            point, 3, WINDING);

            // create a dummy region
            hRgnCombine = CreateRectRgn(0, 0, 1, 1);

            // combine elliptic and triangular regions
            CombineRgn(hRgnCombine, hRgnPolygon,
                    hRgnElliptic, RGN_OR);
            DeleteObject(hRgnElliptic);
            DeleteObject(hRgnPolygon);
            break;

    case WM_PAINT:
            hDC = BeginPaint(hWnd, &ps);

            // define a clip region
            SelectClipRgn(hDC, hRgnCombine);
            point[0].x = Client_X/3;
            point[0].y = Client_Y*2/5;
```

```
point[1].x = Client_X*2/3;
point[1].y = Client_Y*3/5;
DPtoLP(hDC, point, 2);

  // exclude the clip region from
  // the combined region
ExcludeClipRect(hDC, point[0].x, point[0].y,
                point[1].x, point[1].y);

  // create pen and brushes for painting
  // the combined region
SelectObject(hDC, CreatePen(0, 1,
                  RGB(255, 255, 255)));
hBrushRed = CreateSolidBrush(RGB(255, 0, 0));
hBrushGreen = CreateSolidBrush(RGB(0, 255, 0));
hBrushBlue = CreateSolidBrush(RGB(0, 0, 255));

  // draw red, green and blue ellipses
  // in combined region
i = 0;
for(Radius = Client_X/2; Radius > 2;
    Radius -= Client_X/50.)
  {
    if(i == 0) SelectObject(hDC, hBrushRed);
    if(i == 1) SelectObject(hDC, hBrushGreen);
    if(i == 2) SelectObject(hDC, hBrushBlue);
    Ellipse(hDC, Client_X/2 - Radius,
                 Client_Y/2 + Radius,
                 Client_X/2 + Radius,
                 Client_Y/2 - Radius);
    i = (i+1) % 3;
  }

  // frame the combined region
FrameRgn(hDC, hRgnCombine,
        CreateSolidBrush(RGB(0, 0, 0)), 2, 2);
EndPaint(hWnd, &ps);

DeleteObject(hRgnCombine);
DeleteObject(hBrushRed);
DeleteObject(hBrushGreen);
DeleteObject(hBrushBlue);
break;

case WM_COMMAND:
    switch (GET_WM_COMMAND_ID(wParam,lParam))
    {
```

```
                        case IDM_ABOUT:
                                // create an about box
                                DialogBox(hInst, "ABOUTDLG",
                                            hWnd, (DLGPROC)About);
                                break;

                        default:
                                return DefWindowProc(hWnd, uMessage,
                                                        wParam, lParam);
                        }
                        break;

                case WM_DESTROY:
                        PostQuitMessage(0);
                        break;

                default:
                        return DefWindowProc(hWnd, uMessage,
                                                wParam, lParam);
                }
        return 0;
}
```

ABOUT.C

```
// ABOUT.C
#include <windows.h>
#include <windowsx.h>
#include "globals.h"

// procedures for ABOUT dialog box
LRESULT CALLBACK About(HWND hDlg,
                        UINT uMessage,
                        WPARAM wParam,
                        LPARAM lParam)
{
    switch (uMessage)
      {
        case WM_COMMAND:
                switch (GET_WM_COMMAND_ID(wParam,lParam))
                {
                    case IDOK:
                    case IDCANCEL:
                        {
                        EndDialog(hDlg, TRUE);
                        return(TRUE);
```

```
                            }
                        break;
                }
            }
        return FALSE;
    }
```

CREGION.RC

```
#include "windows.h"
#include "globals.h"
#include <winver.h>

APPNAME ICON ICONFILE

RCINCLUDE ABOUT.DLG

APPNAME MENU
BEGIN
  MENUITEM "&About",      IDM_ABOUT
END
```

ABOUT.DLG

```
ABOUTDLG DIALOG DISCARDABLE  22, 17, 167, 73
STYLE DS_MODALFRAME | WS_CAPTION | WS_SYSMENU
CAPTION SZABOUT
BEGIN
    DEFPUSHBUTTON   "OK", IDOK, 132, 2, 32, 14, WS_GROUP
    ICON            SZAPPNAME,      -1, 3, 2, 18, 20
    LTEXT           SZAPPNAME,      -1, 30, 12, 50, 8
    LTEXT           SZDESCRIPTION, -1, 30, 22, 150, 8
    LTEXT           SZVERSION,      -1, 30, 32, 150, 8
    LTEXT           SZCOMPANYNAME, -1, 30, 42, 150, 8
END
```

CREGION.ICO

CASE 5-13: METAFILES

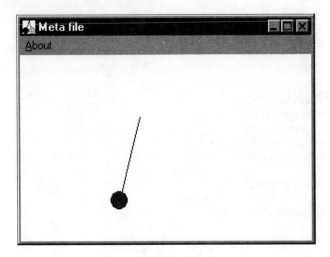

FIGURE 5-13

This case illustrates how to use the metafile facility in the Windows GDI subsystem. A *metafile* is a stored sequence of GDI calls. Metafiles can be played back to reproduce the sequence of GDI calls, in the order in which they were originally made. Metafiles can exist only in memory, or they can be stored on disk for future recall. Metafiles are useful for drawing complex graphical objects that need to be redrawn in different parts of your program.

In this example, two metafiles are created. The first one draws a simple figure, which consists of a line that angles to the left and a red ellipse at the bottom end of the line, as shown in Figure 5-13. The second metafile is almost identical to the first, except that the position is different: the line angles over to the right. If these two metafiles are played repeatedly in alternating sequence, we can see the red ball move back and forth from left to right, similar to the motion of a pendulum. We use a timer to define the time interval between movements.

GLOBALS.H

```
// GLOBALS.H - header file for global variables
//            and function prototypes

// Product identifier string definitions
#define APPNAME        Meta
#define ICONFILE       Meta.ico
#define SZAPPNAME      "Meta"
#define SZDESCRIPTION  "Meta file"
#define SZVERSION      "Version 1.0"
#define SZCOMPANYNAME  "\251 M&&T Books, 1994"
#define SZABOUT        "About"

// Global function prototypes.
BOOL InitApplication(HINSTANCE);
BOOL InitInstance(HINSTANCE, int);

// Callback functions called by Windows.
LRESULT CALLBACK WndProc(HWND, UINT, WPARAM, LPARAM);
LRESULT CALLBACK About(HWND, UINT, WPARAM, LPARAM);

// Menu item ID
#define IDM_ABOUT   1000

// Global variable declarations.
extern HINSTANCE hInst;      // The current instance handle
extern char szAppName[];     // The name of this application
extern char szTitle[];       // The title bar text
```

WINMAIN.C

```
// WINMAIN.C
#include <windows.h>
#include "globals.h"

int APIENTRY WinMain(HINSTANCE hInstance,
                     HINSTANCE hPrevInstance,
                     LPSTR lpCmdLine,
                     int nCmdShow)
{
    MSG msg;

    // register main window class
    if (!hPrevInstance)
        {
```

```
        if (!InitApplication(hInstance))
            {
            return FALSE;
            }
        }

    // create and show main window
    if (!InitInstance(hInstance, nCmdShow))
        {
        return FALSE;
        }

    // process window messages
    while (GetMessage(&msg, NULL, 0, 0))
        {
            TranslateMessage(&msg);
            DispatchMessage(&msg);
        }
    return msg.wParam;
}
```

INIT.C

```
// INIT.C
#include <windows.h>
#include "globals.h"

HINSTANCE hInst;
char szAppName[] = SZAPPNAME;
char szTitle[] = SZDESCRIPTION;

// register main window class
BOOL InitApplication(HINSTANCE hInstance)
{
    WNDCLASS  wc;

    wc.style          = CS_HREDRAW | CS_VREDRAW;
    wc.lpfnWndProc    = (WNDPROC)WndProc;
    wc.cbClsExtra     = 0;
    wc.cbWndExtra     = 0;
    wc.hInstance      = hInstance;
    wc.hIcon          = LoadIcon(hInstance, szAppName);
    wc.hCursor        = LoadCursor(NULL, IDC_ARROW);
    wc.hbrBackground  = (HBRUSH)(COLOR_WINDOW + 1);
    wc.lpszMenuName   = szAppName;
    wc.lpszClassName  = szAppName;
```

```
        return(RegisterClass(&wc));
}

// create and show main window
BOOL InitInstance(HINSTANCE hInstance, int nCmdShow)
{
    HWND    hWnd;
    hInst = hInstance;
    hWnd = CreateWindow(szAppName, szTitle,
                        WS_OVERLAPPEDWINDOW,
                        160, 120, 320, 240,
                        NULL, NULL, hInstance, NULL);

    if (!hWnd)
        {
        return FALSE;
        }

    ShowWindow(hWnd, nCmdShow);
    UpdateWindow(hWnd);

    return TRUE;
}
```

META.C

```
// META.C
#include <windows.h>
#include <windowsx.h>
#include "globals.h"

LRESULT CALLBACK WndProc(HWND hWnd,
                         UINT uMessage,
                         WPARAM wParam,
                         LPARAM lParam)
{
    HDC hDC, hMetaDC1, hMetaDC2;
    static HANDLE hMetaFile1, hMetaFile2;
    static BOOL bTiTa = TRUE;
    HBRUSH hBrushRed;
    PAINTSTRUCT ps;
    RECT rect;

    switch (uMessage)
        {
```

```
case WM_CREATE:
      SetTimer(hWnd, 1, 1000, NULL);

      hBrushRed = CreateSolidBrush(RGB(255, 0, 0));

      // create 1st meta file
      hMetaDC1 = CreateMetaFile(NULL);
      SelectObject(hMetaDC1, hBrushRed);
      MoveToEx(hMetaDC1, 200, 100, NULL);
      LineTo(hMetaDC1, 165, 235);
      Ellipse(hMetaDC1, 150, 220, 180, 250);
      hMetaFile1 = CloseMetaFile(hMetaDC1);

      // create 2nd meta file
      hMetaDC2 = CreateMetaFile(NULL);
      SelectObject(hMetaDC2, hBrushRed);
      MoveToEx(hMetaDC2, 200, 100, NULL);
      LineTo(hMetaDC2, 235, 235);
      Ellipse(hMetaDC2, 220, 220, 250, 250);
      hMetaFile2 = CloseMetaFile(hMetaDC2);
      break;

case WM_TIMER:
      bTiTa = !bTiTa;
      // repaint client area
      InvalidateRect(hWnd, NULL, FALSE);
      break;

case WM_PAINT:
      hDC = BeginPaint(hWnd, &ps);
      SetMapMode(hDC, MM_ISOTROPIC);
      GetClientRect(hWnd, &rect);
      SetViewportExtEx(hDC, rect.right,
                            rect.bottom, NULL);
      SetWindowExtEx(hDC, 300, 200, NULL);

      if(bTiTa == TRUE){
      SetROP2(hDC, R2_WHITE);
      PlayMetaFile(hDC, hMetaFile2);
      SetROP2(hDC, R2_COPYPEN);
      PlayMetaFile(hDC, hMetaFile1); };

      if(bTiTa == FALSE){
      SetROP2(hDC, R2_WHITE);
      PlayMetaFile(hDC, hMetaFile1);
      SetROP2(hDC, R2_COPYPEN);
      PlayMetaFile(hDC, hMetaFile2); };
```

```
            EndPaint(hWnd, &ps);
            DeleteObject(hBrushRed);
            break;

        case WM_COMMAND:
            switch (GET_WM_COMMAND_ID(wParam,lParam))
            {
                case IDM_ABOUT:
                        // create an about dialog box
                    DialogBox(hInst, "ABOUTDLG",
                                hWnd, (DLGPROC)About);
                    break;

                default:
                    return DefWindowProc(hWnd, uMessage,
                                        wParam, lParam);
            }
            break;

        case WM_DESTROY:
            KillTimer(hWnd, 1);
             // delete meta files
            DeleteMetaFile(hMetaFile1);
            DeleteMetaFile(hMetaFile2);
            PostQuitMessage(0);
            break;

        default:
            return DefWindowProc(hWnd, uMessage,
                                wParam, lParam);
    }
    return 0;
}
```

ABOUT.C

```
// ABOUT.C
#include <windows.h>
#include <windowsx.h>
#include "globals.h"

// procedures for ABOUT dialog box
LRESULT CALLBACK About(HWND hDlg,
                        UINT uMessage,
                        WPARAM wParam,
```

453

```
                        LPARAM lParam)
{
    switch (uMessage)
      {
        case WM_COMMAND:
              switch (GET_WM_COMMAND_ID(wParam,lParam))
              {
                  case IDOK:
                  case IDCANCEL:
                      {
                      EndDialog(hDlg, TRUE);
                      return(TRUE);
                      }
                      break;
              }
      }
    return FALSE;
}
```

META.RC

```
#include "windows.h"
#include "globals.h"
#include <winver.h>

APPNAME ICON ICONFILE

RCINCLUDE ABOUT.DLG

APPNAME MENU
BEGIN
  MENUITEM "&About",       IDM_ABOUT
END
```

ABOUT.DLG

```
ABOUTDLG DIALOG DISCARDABLE  22, 17, 167, 73
STYLE DS_MODALFRAME | WS_CAPTION | WS_SYSMENU
CAPTION SZABOUT
BEGIN
    DEFPUSHBUTTON   "OK", IDOK, 132, 2, 32, 14, WS_GROUP
    ICON            SZAPPNAME,      -1, 3, 2, 18, 20
    LTEXT           SZAPPNAME,      -1, 30, 12,  50, 8
    LTEXT           SZDESCRIPTION, -1, 30, 22, 150, 8
```

```
        LTEXT           SZVERSION,      -1, 30, 32, 150, 8
        LTEXT           SZCOMPANYNAME, -1, 30, 42, 150, 8
    END
```

META.ICO

CASE 5-14: SAVING METAFILES

This example shows how to create a Windows metafile and save it in an external file. This case builds upon concepts introduced in Case 5-13, which showed metafiles created and used solely in memory. The two metafiles used in this example are identical to those in Case 5-13; however, each metafile is saved into a file on disk. The file names used are "left.met" and "right.met". The next case shows how to retrieve these metafiles and play them back in a Windows program.

The difference between creating a metafile for in-memory use and one that is stored on disk is the parameter to the `CreateMetaFile()` function. If the parameter is `NULL`, the metafile is in memory; otherwise, the parameter is the file name to use for storing it on disk.

The program here is probably one of the shortest possible Windows programs, because, although it uses the Windows API, it does not have a window procedure or much of the other baggage present in Windows programs.

SAVEMETA.C

```
// SAVEMETA.C
#include <windows.h>

int APIENTRY WinMain(HINSTANCE hInstance,
                     HINSTANCE hPrevInstance,
                     LPSTR lpCmdLine,
                     int nCmdShow)
{
    HDC hMetaDC1, hMetaDC2;
    HANDLE hMetaFile1, hMetaFile2;
    HBRUSH hBrushRed;

    hBrushRed = CreateSolidBrush(RGB(255, 0, 0));

    // create a meta file with file name left.met
    hMetaDC1 = CreateMetaFile((LPSTR) "left.met");
    SelectObject(hMetaDC1, hBrushRed);
    MoveToEx(hMetaDC1, 200, 100, NULL);
    LineTo(hMetaDC1, 165, 235);
    Ellipse(hMetaDC1, 150, 220, 180, 250);
    hMetaFile1 = CloseMetaFile(hMetaDC1);
    DeleteMetaFile(hMetaFile1);

    // create a meta file with file name right.met
    hMetaDC2 = CreateMetaFile((LPSTR) "right.met");
    SelectObject(hMetaDC2, hBrushRed);
    MoveToEx(hMetaDC2, 200, 100, NULL);
    LineTo(hMetaDC2, 235, 235);
    Ellipse(hMetaDC2, 220, 220, 250, 250);
    hMetaFile2 = CloseMetaFile(hMetaDC2);
    DeleteMetaFile(hMetaFile2);

    DeleteObject(hBrushRed);
    return TRUE;
}
```

CASE 5-15: PLAYING BACK METAFILES STORED ON DISK

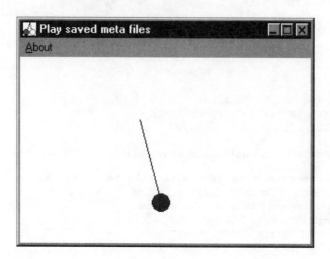

FIGURE 5-15

This program is similar to the one in Case 5-13. However, instead of creating its own metafile and playing them back, it relies on the two metafiles created by the program in Case 5-14. This is a simple process. In the WM_CREATE handler of the main window procedure, the code loads each metafile using a call to the GetMetaFile() function. This function requires only a file name as a parameter. As in Case 5-13, a timer is used to control when each of the two files is played back. In response to a WM_PAINT message, the code uses PlayMetaFile() to redraw the pendulum.

GLOBALS.H

```
// GLOBALS.H - header file for global variables
//            and function prototypes

// Product identifier string definitions
#define APPNAME       PlayMeta
#define ICONFILE      PlayMeta.ico
#define SZAPPNAME     "PlayMeta"
#define SZDESCRIPTION "Play saved meta files"
#define SZVERSION     "Version 1.0"
#define SZCOMPANYNAME "\251 M&&T Books, 1994"
#define SZABOUT       "About"

// Global function prototypes.
BOOL InitApplication(HINSTANCE);
BOOL InitInstance(HINSTANCE, int);

// Callback functions called by Windows.
LRESULT CALLBACK WndProc(HWND, UINT, WPARAM, LPARAM);
LRESULT CALLBACK About(HWND, UINT, WPARAM, LPARAM);

// Menu item ID
#define IDM_ABOUT   1000

// Global variable declarations.
extern HINSTANCE hInst;       // The current instance handle
extern char szAppName[];      // The name of this application
extern char szTitle[];        // The title bar text
```

WINMAIN.C

```
// WINMAIN.C
#include <windows.h>
#include "globals.h"

int APIENTRY WinMain(HINSTANCE hInstance,
                     HINSTANCE hPrevInstance,
                     LPSTR lpCmdLine,
                     int nCmdShow)
{
    MSG msg;

    // register main window class
    if (!hPrevInstance)
```

```
        {
        if (!InitApplication(hInstance))
            {
            return FALSE;
            }
        }

    // create and show main window
    if (!InitInstance(hInstance, nCmdShow))
        {
        return FALSE;
        }

    // process window messages
    while (GetMessage(&msg, NULL, 0, 0))
        {
            TranslateMessage(&msg);
            DispatchMessage(&msg);
        }
    return msg.wParam;
}
```

INIT.C

```
// INIT.C
#include <windows.h>
#include "globals.h"

HINSTANCE hInst;
char szAppName[] = SZAPPNAME;
char szTitle[] = SZDESCRIPTION;

// register main window class
BOOL InitApplication(HINSTANCE hInstance)
{
    WNDCLASS  wc;

    wc.style          = CS_HREDRAW | CS_VREDRAW;
    wc.lpfnWndProc    = (WNDPROC)WndProc;
    wc.cbClsExtra     = 0;
    wc.cbWndExtra     = 0;
    wc.hInstance      = hInstance;
    wc.hIcon          = LoadIcon(hInstance, szAppName);
    wc.hCursor        = LoadCursor(NULL, IDC_ARROW);
    wc.hbrBackground  = (HBRUSH)(COLOR_WINDOW + 1);
    wc.lpszMenuName   = szAppName;
```

```
    wc.lpszClassName = szAppName;

    return(RegisterClass(&wc));
}


// create and show main window
BOOL InitInstance(HINSTANCE hInstance, int nCmdShow)
{
    HWND    hWnd;
    hInst = hInstance;
    hWnd = CreateWindow(szAppName, szTitle,
                        WS_OVERLAPPEDWINDOW,
                        160, 120, 320, 240,
                        NULL, NULL, hInstance, NULL);

    if (!hWnd)
        {
        return FALSE;
        }

    ShowWindow(hWnd, nCmdShow);
    UpdateWindow(hWnd);

    return TRUE;
}
```

PLAYMETA.C

```
// PLAYMETA.C
#include <windows.h>
#include <windowsx.h>
#include "globals.h"

LRESULT CALLBACK WndProc(HWND hWnd,
                         UINT uMessage,
                         WPARAM wParam,
                         LPARAM lParam)
{
    HDC hDC;
    static HANDLE hMetaFile1, hMetaFile2;
    static BOOL bTiTa = TRUE;
    HBRUSH hBrushRed;
    PAINTSTRUCT ps;
    RECT rect;

    switch (uMessage)
```

```
{
    case WM_CREATE:
        SetTimer(hWnd, 1, 1000, NULL);
        hBrushRed = CreateSolidBrush(RGB(255, 0, 0));

        // load meta files
        hMetaFile1 = GetMetaFile((LPSTR) "left.met");
        hMetaFile2 = GetMetaFile((LPSTR) "right.met");
        break;

    case WM_TIMER:
        bTiTa = !bTiTa;
        // repaint client area
        InvalidateRect(hWnd, NULL, FALSE);
        break;

    case WM_PAINT:
        hDC = BeginPaint(hWnd, &ps);
        SetMapMode(hDC, MM_ISOTROPIC);
        GetClientRect(hWnd, &rect);
        SetViewportExtEx(hDC, rect.right,
                            rect.bottom, NULL);
        SetWindowExtEx(hDC, 300, 200, NULL);

        if(bTiTa == TRUE){
        SetROP2(hDC, R2_WHITE);
        PlayMetaFile(hDC, hMetaFile2);
        SetROP2(hDC, R2_COPYPEN);
        PlayMetaFile(hDC, hMetaFile1); };

        if(bTiTa == FALSE){
        SetROP2(hDC, R2_WHITE);
        PlayMetaFile(hDC, hMetaFile1);
        SetROP2(hDC, R2_COPYPEN);
        PlayMetaFile(hDC, hMetaFile2); };

        EndPaint(hWnd, &ps);
        break;

    case WM_COMMAND:
        switch (GET_WM_COMMAND_ID(wParam,lParam))
        {
            case IDM_ABOUT:
                // create an about dialog box
                DialogBox(hInst, "ABOUTDLG",
                        hWnd, (DLGPROC)About);
                break;
```

```
                    default:
                        return DefWindowProc(hWnd, uMessage,
                                                wParam, lParam);
                    }
                break;

            case WM_DESTROY:
                KillTimer(hWnd, 1);
                DeleteObject(hBrushRed);
                 // delete meta files
                DeleteMetaFile(hMetaFile1);
                DeleteMetaFile(hMetaFile2);
                PostQuitMessage(0);
                break;

            default:
                return DefWindowProc(hWnd, uMessage,
                                        wParam, lParam);
            }
        return 0;
    }
```

ABOUT.C

```
// ABOUT.C
#include <windows.h>
#include <windowsx.h>
#include "globals.h"

// procedures for ABOUT dialog box
LRESULT CALLBACK About(HWND hDlg,
                        UINT uMessage,
                        WPARAM wParam,
                        LPARAM lParam)

{
    switch (uMessage)
      {
        case WM_COMMAND:
            switch (GET_WM_COMMAND_ID(wParam,lParam))
              {
                case IDOK:
                case IDCANCEL:
                    {
                    EndDialog(hDlg, TRUE);
                    return(TRUE);
```

463

```
                    }
                break;
            }
        }
    return FALSE;
}
```

PLAYMETA.RC

```
#include "windows.h"
#include "globals.h"
#include <winver.h>

APPNAME ICON ICONFILE

RCINCLUDE ABOUT.DLG

APPNAME MENU
BEGIN
  MENUITEM "&About",      IDM_ABOUT
END
```

ABOUT.DLG

```
ABOUTDLG DIALOG DISCARDABLE  22, 17, 167, 73
STYLE DS_MODALFRAME | WS_CAPTION | WS_SYSMENU
CAPTION SZABOUT
BEGIN
    DEFPUSHBUTTON   "OK", IDOK, 132, 2, 32, 14, WS_GROUP
    ICON            SZAPPNAME,      -1, 3, 2, 18, 20
    LTEXT           SZAPPNAME,      -1, 30, 12,  50, 8
    LTEXT           SZDESCRIPTION, -1, 30, 22, 150, 8
    LTEXT           SZVERSION,      -1, 30, 32, 150, 8
    LTEXT           SZCOMPANYNAME, -1, 30, 42, 150, 8
END
```

PLAYMETA.ICO

CHAPTER SIX

MOUSE, CURSOR, AND GRAPHICS DRAWING

CASE 6-1: CURSOR FUNCTIONS

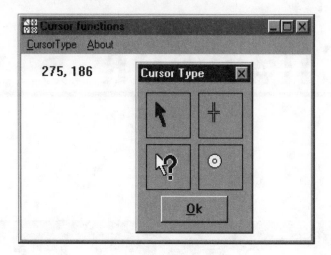

<u>FIGURE 6-1</u>

The cases in this chapter, unlike those in previous chapters, represent more substantial programs and are larger in size than previous cases. They combine concepts that have been discussed in earlier chapters with new techniques.

This case shows how to change the standard cursor or mouse pointer into one that is more application-specific. This user interface idea can be seen in many Windows programs when the user enters into some kind of "mode." For example, in a drawing program, the user can pick a tool, such as a Rectangle tool, from a tool palette. The user is then in rectangle drawing mode, and the cursor changes shape to reflect this change. Once the user is finished drawing rectangles, he or she can select the Paint Bucket tool. The cursor changes shape appropriately, and the user enters fill mode, which will fill already drawn shapes with a color or pattern. These examples should give you a good idea about how the cursor function works.

This program boils the task down to the essentials. It lets the user change the cursor by clicking on one of four cursor bitmap buttons in a cursor selection dialog box similar to the one shown in Figure 6.1. This is done by using the owner-drawn buttons discussed in Case 1-2. In response to a WM_COMMAND message in the dialog box procedure, the code loads the appropriate cursor using the LoadCursor() function. Cursor bitmaps are stored in files such as CURSO1.CUR and CURSOR2.CUR. The correspondence between the file names and the cursor name used by LoadCursor() is established in the resource file CCURSOR.RC. The LoadCursor() function returns to the loaded cursor a handle, which is placed in the global variable hNewCursor.

The cursor change actually occurs in the main window procedure, in response to a WM_SETCURSOR message. The code in this handler changes the cursor to the newly selected cursor using the SetCursor() function.

This program does one other thing: it displays information about the current position, in the form of a single line of text in the uppe-left corner of the main window's client area. The code obtains the current cursor position using the GetCursorPos() function and converts this position from screen coordinates to local window coordinates using the ScreenToClient() function.

GLOBALS.H

```
// GLOBALS.H - header file for global variables
//                 and function prototypes

// Product identifier string definitions
#define APPNAME        CCursor
#define ICONFILE       CCursor.ico
#define SZAPPNAME      "CCursor"
#define SZDESCRIPTION  "Cursor functions"
#define SZVERSION      "Version 1.0"
#define SZCOMPANYNAME  "\251 M&&T Books, 1994"
#define SZABOUT        "About"

// Global function prototypes.
BOOL InitApplication(HINSTANCE);
BOOL InitInstance(HINSTANCE, int);
void PaintBitmap(HDC, HBITMAP);
void DrawCursorBitmap(HWND, HDC, int);

// Callback functions called by Windows.
```

467

```
LRESULT CALLBACK WndProc(HWND, UINT, WPARAM, LPARAM);
LRESULT CALLBACK CursorType(HWND, UINT, WPARAM, LPARAM);
LRESULT CALLBACK About(HWND, UINT, WPARAM, LPARAM);

// Menu item ID
#define IDM_ABOUT        101
#define IDM_CURSOR_TYPE 102

// Dialog Control ID
#define IDC_BLACKFRAME  103
#define IDC_CURSOR1     104
#define IDC_CURSOR2     105
#define IDC_CURSOR3     106
#define IDC_CURSOR4     107
#define IDC_OK          108

// Global variable declarations.
extern HINSTANCE hInst;      // The current instance handle
extern char szAppName[];     // The name of this application
extern char szTitle[];       // The title bar text
```

WINMAIN.C

```
// WINMAIN.C
#include <windows.h>
#include "globals.h"

int APIENTRY WinMain(HINSTANCE hInstance,
                     HINSTANCE hPrevInstance,
                     LPSTR lpCmdLine,
                     int nCmdShow)
{
    MSG msg;

    // register main window class
    if (!hPrevInstance)
        {
        if (!InitApplication(hInstance))
            {
            return FALSE;
            }
        }

    // create and show main window
    if (!InitInstance(hInstance, nCmdShow))
        {
        return FALSE;
```

```
    }

    // process window messages
    while (GetMessage(&msg, NULL, 0, 0))
        {
            TranslateMessage(&msg);
            DispatchMessage(&msg);
        }
    return msg.wParam;
}
```

INIT.C

```
// INIT.C
#include <windows.h>
#include "globals.h"

HINSTANCE hInst;
char szAppName[] = SZAPPNAME;
char szTitle[] = SZDESCRIPTION;

// register main window class
BOOL InitApplication(HINSTANCE hInstance)
{
    WNDCLASS  wc;

    wc.style           = CS_HREDRAW | CS_VREDRAW;
    wc.lpfnWndProc     = (WNDPROC)WndProc;
    wc.cbClsExtra      = 0;
    wc.cbWndExtra      = 0;
    wc.hInstance       = hInstance;
    wc.hIcon           = LoadIcon(hInstance, szAppName);
    wc.hCursor         = LoadCursor(NULL, IDC_ARROW);
    wc.hbrBackground   = (HBRUSH)(COLOR_WINDOW + 1);
    wc.lpszMenuName    = szAppName;
    wc.lpszClassName   = szAppName;

    return(RegisterClass(&wc));
}

// create and show main window
BOOL InitInstance(HINSTANCE hInstance, int nCmdShow)
{
    HWND    hWnd;
    hInst = hInstance;
    hWnd = CreateWindow(szAppName, szTitle,
```

```
                        WS_OVERLAPPEDWINDOW,
                        160, 120, 320, 240,
                        NULL, NULL, hInstance, NULL);

    if (!hWnd)
        {
        return FALSE;
        }

    ShowWindow(hWnd, nCmdShow);
    UpdateWindow(hWnd);

    return TRUE;
    }
```

CCURSOR.C

```
// CCURSOR.C
#include <windows.h>
#include <windowsx.h>
#include "globals.h"

LRESULT CALLBACK WndProc(HWND hWnd,
                         UINT uMessage,
                         WPARAM wParam,
                         LPARAM lParam)
{
    POINT point;
    HDC hDC;
    char CursorPos[20];

    switch (uMessage)
    {
        case WM_CREATE:
            GetClientRect(hWnd, &rect);
            hNewCursor = LoadCursor(NULL, IDC_ARROW);
            SetCursor(hNewCursor);
            break;

        case WM_COMMAND:
            switch (GET_WM_COMMAND_ID(wParam,lParam))
            {
                case IDM_CURSOR_TYPE:
                    // create the choose cursor dialog box
                    hCTypeDlg = CreateDialog(hInst,
                            "CURSORTYPE",
                            hWnd,
```

```
                              (DLGPROC)CursorType);
             break;
        case IDM_ABOUT:
             // create an about dialog box
             DialogBox(hInst, "ABOUTDLG",
                       hWnd, (DLGPROC)About);
             break;

        default:
            return DefWindowProc(hWnd, uMessage,
                                 wParam, lParam);
    }
    break;

case WM_MOUSEMOVE:
    // update the cursor position when mouse moves
    // get cursor current position
    GetCursorPos(&point);

    // convert the cursor position from screen
    // coordinate to client coordinate of
    // main window
    ScreenToClient(hWnd, &point);

    // print the cursor position into
    // the string "CursorPos"
    sprintf(CursorPos, "    %3d, %3d   ",
                        point.x, point.y);
    hDC = GetDC(hWnd);
    // paint the string "CursorPos" near the upper
    // left corner of main window client area
    TextOut(hDC, 10, 10,
               CursorPos, strlen(CursorPos));
    ReleaseDC(hWnd, hDC);
    break;

case WM_SETCURSOR:
    // change cursor
    SetCursor(hNewCursor);
    break;

case WM_DESTROY:
    PostQuitMessage(0);
    break;

default:
    return DefWindowProc(hWnd, uMessage,
                         wParam, lParam);
```

```
                        DeleteObject(SelectObject(
                                   lpdis->hDC, hPen));
                        DeleteObject(SelectObject(
                                   lpdis->hDC, hBrush));
                   }
           break;

      case WM_COMMAND:
           switch(GET_WM_COMMAND_ID(wParam, lParam))
           {
                   // load new cursor when selected
               case IDC_CURSOR1:
                   hNewCursor = LoadCursor(hInst,
                                            "CURSOR1");
                   break;

               case IDC_CURSOR2:
                   hNewCursor = LoadCursor(hInst,
                                            "CURSOR2");
                   break;

               case IDC_CURSOR3:
                   hNewCursor = LoadCursor(hInst,
                                            "CURSOR3");
                   break;

               case IDC_CURSOR4:
                   hNewCursor = LoadCursor(hInst,
                                            "CURSOR4");
                   break;

               case IDC_OK:
               case IDCANCEL:
                   DestroyWindow(hCTypeDlg);
                   hCTypeDlg = 0;
                   break;

               default: return FALSE;
           }
           break;

      case WM_SETCURSOR:
               // change cursor
           SetCursor(hNewCursor);
           break;

   default: return FALSE;
   }
```

```
        }
        return 0;
}
```

CTYPE.C

```
// CTYPE.C
#include <windows.h>
#include <windowsx.h>
#include "globals.h"

HBITMAP  hBitmap;
HWND     hCTypeDlg;
HCURSOR  hNewCursor;
RECT     rect;

LRESULT CALLBACK CursorType(HWND hCTypeDlg,
                            UINT uMessage,
                            WPARAM wParam,
                            LPARAM lParam)
{
    LPDRAWITEMSTRUCT lpdis;
    HPEN hPen;
    HBRUSH hBrush;

    switch (uMessage) {
        case WM_DRAWITEM:
            lpdis = (LPDRAWITEMSTRUCT) lParam;

            // draw bitmap buttons
            DrawCursorBitmap(hInst,
                        lpdis->hDC, lpdis->CtlID);

            // draw a black rectangle around the
            // selected cursor bitmap button
            if(lpdis-> itemState & ODS_FOCUS)
            { hPen = SelectObject(lpdis->hDC,
                    CreatePen(PS_INSIDEFRAME, 2,
                            RGB(0, 0, 0)));
                hBrush = SelectObject(lpdis->hDC,
                        GetStockObject(NULL_BRUSH));
                Rectangle(lpdis->hDC,
                        lpdis->rcItem.left,
                        lpdis->rcItem.top,
                        lpdis->rcItem.right,
                        lpdis->rcItem.bottom);
```

```
        return TRUE;
}


// function for painting bitmap buttons in
// choose cursor dialog box
void PaintBitmap (hDC, hBitmap)
HDC hDC;
HBITMAP hBitmap;
{
    BITMAP bmp;
    HDC hMemoryDC ;
    hMemoryDC = CreateCompatibleDC(hDC);
    GetObject(hBitmap, sizeof(BITMAP), (LPSTR) &bmp);
    SelectObject(hMemoryDC, hBitmap) ;
    BitBlt(hDC, 0, 0, bmp.bmWidth, bmp.bmHeight,
            hMemoryDC, 0, 0, SRCCOPY);
    DeleteDC(hMemoryDC);
    DeleteObject(hBitmap);
}


// function for loading the bitmap of cursor
// selection button
void DrawCursorBitmap (hInstance, hDC, ButtonID)
HANDLE hInstance;
HDC hDC;
int ButtonID;
{
switch(ButtonID){
    case IDC_CURSOR1:
        hBitmap = LoadBitmap (hInstance, "Cursor1");
        break;

    case IDC_CURSOR2:
        hBitmap = LoadBitmap (hInstance, "Cursor2");
        break;

    case IDC_CURSOR3:
        hBitmap = LoadBitmap (hInstance, "Cursor3");
        break;

    case IDC_CURSOR4:
        hBitmap = LoadBitmap (hInstance, "Cursor4");
        break;
    }

    PaintBitmap(hDC, hBitmap);
}
```

474

ABOUT.C

```
// ABOUT.C
#include <windows.h>
#include <windowsx.h>
#include "globals.h"

// procedures for ABOUT dialog box
LRESULT CALLBACK About(HWND hDlg,
                       UINT uMessage,
                       WPARAM wParam,
                       LPARAM lParam)
{
    switch (uMessage)
      {
        case WM_COMMAND:
            switch (GET_WM_COMMAND_ID(wParam,lParam))
            {
                case IDOK:
                case IDCANCEL:
                    {
                    EndDialog(hDlg, TRUE);
                    return(TRUE);
                    }
                    break;
            }
      }
    return FALSE;
}
```

CCURSOR.RC

```
#include "windows.h"
#include "globals.h"
#include <winver.h>

Cursor1 BITMAP cursor1.bmp
Cursor2 BITMAP cursor2.bmp
Cursor3 BITMAP cursor3.bmp
Cursor4 BITMAP cursor4.bmp

CURSOR1 CURSOR cursor1.cur
CURSOR2 CURSOR cursor2.cur
CURSOR3 CURSOR cursor3.cur
CURSOR4 CURSOR cursor4.cur
```

```
APPNAME ICON ICONFILE

RCINCLUDE CTYPE.DLG
RCINCLUDE ABOUT.DLG

APPNAME MENU
BEGIN
    MENUITEM "&CursorType", IDM_CURSOR_TYPE
    MENUITEM "&About", IDM_ABOUT
END
```

CTYPE.DLG

```
CURSORTYPE DIALOG 30, 30, 60, 77
STYLE WS_POPUP | WS_VISIBLE | WS_CAPTION
CAPTION "Cursor Type"
BEGIN
    CONTROL     "", -1, "Static", SS_BLACKFRAME,
                4, 5, 24, 24
    CONTROL     "", IDC_CURSOR1, "Button", BS_OWNERDRAW,
                9, 10, 14, 14
    CONTROL     "", -1, "Static", SS_BLACKFRAME,
                32, 5, 24, 24
    CONTROL     "", IDC_CURSOR2, "Button", BS_OWNERDRAW,
                37, 10, 14, 14
    CONTROL     "", -1, "Static", SS_BLACKFRAME,
                4, 32, 24, 24
    CONTROL     "", IDC_CURSOR3, "Button", BS_OWNERDRAW,
                9, 37, 14, 14
    CONTROL     "", -1, "Static", SS_BLACKFRAME,
                32, 32, 24, 24
    CONTROL     "", IDC_CURSOR4, "Button", BS_OWNERDRAW,
                37, 37, 14, 14
    PUSHBUTTON  "&Ok", IDC_OK, 12, 59, 36, 14
END
```

ABOUT.DLG

```
ABOUTDLG DIALOG DISCARDABLE  22, 17, 167, 73
STYLE DS_MODALFRAME | WS_CAPTION | WS_SYSMENU
CAPTION SZABOUT
BEGIN
    DEFPUSHBUTTON   "OK", IDOK, 132, 2, 32, 14, WS_GROUP
```

```
    ICON        SZAPPNAME,      -1, 3, 2, 18, 20
    LTEXT       SZAPPNAME,      -1, 30, 12,  50, 8
    LTEXT       SZDESCRIPTION, -1, 30, 22, 150, 8
    LTEXT       SZVERSION,      -1, 30, 32, 150, 8
    LTEXT       SZCOMPANYNAME, -1, 30, 42, 150, 8
END
```

CCURSOR.ICO

CURSOR1.BMP

CURSOR2.BMP

CURSOR3.BMP

CURSOR4.BMP

CASE 6-2: DRAW BASIC PATTERNS

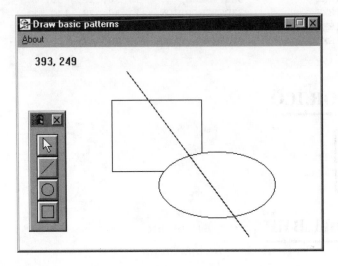

FIGURE 6-2

T his case builds upon techniques used in Case 6-2 to show how to create a simple drawing program. This program allows the users to draw one of three basic graphical shapes: a line, an ellipse, or a rectangle. They select these shapes from a tool palette that is implemented as a modeless dialog box with owner-drawn buttons. For more on owner-drawn push buttons, see Cases 1-2 and 6-1. The tool palette can be dragged anywhere on the screen so that the users can have an unobstructed view of their work. The users select one of several shapes from the tool palette, and the cursor changes to reflect the current state or mode.

As you look through the code, you will note many references to patterns, as in the *pattern* dialog box or the global variable Pattern_Choice. Note that these patterns are not bitmap-style patterns as found in the Windows GDI but merely my terminology for different graphical shapes such as ellipses, rectangles, and lines. The global variable Pattern_Choice refers to the currently selected shape. As in the Case 6-1, the cursor-changing code is in the WM_SETCURSOR handler of the main window procedure. Once the mouse is clicked, the bDrawMode flag is set to

TRUE, and the program is in drawing mode so that users can draw whichever is the currently selected shape. As users move the mouse around the window, Windows sends a WM_MOUSEMOVE message to the main window procedure. The handler for these messages updates the screen display to reflect the mouse movements, which involves getting the cursor position, erasing the previously drawn temporary shape, and drawing a new temporary shape at the current cursor position. When users click the mouse a second time, the previously drawn temporary shape is erased and a "permanent" version of that shape is drawn. The bOrder flag is used to track the state of the drawing process. This flag is initially zero and is then set to one when the first mouse click happens (remember that the bDrawMode flag becomes TRUE at that time). When the second mouse click is received, bDrawMode is set to FALSE, and bOrder is set back to 0. Also, the cursor is changed back to the system default arrow cursor.

Note that in a "real" drawing program, the code would maintain a data structure that remembers which shapes were drawn and where. This data structure, which might be a list or tree structure, is used during WM_PAINT messages to refresh the contents of the screen. Also, a commercial-grade program would allow users to save and retrieve this data structure from the disk, as well as to delete shapes by removing them from the data structure. In order to keep the examples simple and understandable, I have not implemented these more advanced features in this example.

GLOBALS.H

```
// GLOBALS.H - header file for global variables
//              and function prototypes

// Product identifier string definitions.
#define APPNAME        DrawPat
#define ICONFILE       DrawPat.ico
#define SZAPPNAME      "DrawPat"
#define SZDESCRIPTION  "Draw basic patterns"
#define SZVERSION      "Version 1.0"
#define SZCOMPANYNAME  "\251 M&&T Books, 1994"
#define SZABOUT        "About"

// Global function prototypes.
BOOL InitApplication(HINSTANCE);
```

```
BOOL InitInstance(HINSTANCE, int);
void PaintBitmap(HDC, HBITMAP);
void DrawPatternUpBitmap(HWND, HDC, int);
void DrawPatternDownBitmap(HWND, HDC, int);

// Callback functions called by Windows.
LRESULT CALLBACK WndProc(HWND, UINT, WPARAM, LPARAM);
LRESULT CALLBACK About(HWND, UINT, WPARAM, LPARAM);
LRESULT CALLBACK PatternTypeDlgProc(HWND, UINT, WPARAM, LPARAM);

// Menu item ID
#define IDM_ABOUT   1000

// Dialog box ID
#define IDD_PATTERNTYPE 900

// Dialog box control ID
#define IDC_PTN0    1001
#define IDC_PTN1    1002
#define IDC_PTN2    1003
#define IDC_PTN3    1004

// Global variable declarations.
extern HINSTANCE hInst;
extern char szAppName[];
extern char szTitle[];
extern HWND hWnd, hPatternDlg;
extern DLGPROC lpPatternType;
extern HBITMAP hBitmap;
extern HCURSOR hNewCursor;
extern RECT rect;
extern UINT Pattern_Choice;
extern BOOL bOrder;
extern BOOL bDrawMode;
extern POINT pt, pt1, pt2, ptx;
```

WINMAIN.C

```
// WINMAIN.C
#include <windows.h>
#include "globals.h"

int APIENTRY WinMain(HINSTANCE hInstance,
                     HINSTANCE hPrevInstance,
                     LPSTR lpCmdLine,
                     int nCmdShow)
{
```

```
        MSG msg;

        // register main window class
        if (!hPrevInstance)
            {
            if (!InitApplication(hInstance))
                {
                return FALSE;
                }
            }

        // create and show main window
        if (!InitInstance(hInstance, nCmdShow))
            {
            return FALSE;
            }

        // process window messages
        while (GetMessage(&msg, NULL, 0, 0))
            {
                TranslateMessage(&msg);
                DispatchMessage(&msg);
            }
        return msg.wParam;
}
```

INIT.C

```
// INIT.C
#include <windows.h>
#include "globals.h"

HINSTANCE hInst;
char szAppName[] = SZAPPNAME;
char szTitle[] = SZDESCRIPTION;

// register main window class
BOOL InitApplication(HINSTANCE hInstance)
{
    WNDCLASS  wc;

    wc.style        = (UINT)NULL;
    wc.lpfnWndProc  = (WNDPROC)WndProc;
    wc.cbClsExtra   = 0;
    wc.cbWndExtra   = 0;
    wc.hInstance    = hInstance;
    wc.hIcon        = LoadIcon(hInstance, szAppName);
```

481

```
    wc.hCursor         = LoadCursor(NULL, IDC_ARROW);
    wc.hbrBackground   = (HBRUSH)(COLOR_WINDOW + 1);
    wc.lpszMenuName    = szAppName;
    wc.lpszClassName   = szAppName;

    return(RegisterClass(&wc));
}

// create and show main window
BOOL InitInstance(HINSTANCE hInstance, int nCmdShow)
{
    HWND     hWnd;
    hInst = hInstance;
    hWnd = CreateWindow(szAppName, szTitle,
                WS_BORDER | WS_CAPTION | WS_MINIMIZEBOX |
                WS_SYSMENU | WS_VISIBLE,
                120, 90, 400, 300,
                NULL, NULL, hInstance, NULL);

    if (!hWnd)
        {
        return FALSE;
        }

    ShowWindow(hWnd, nCmdShow);
    UpdateWindow(hWnd);

    return TRUE;
}
```

DRAWPAT.C

```
// DRAWPAT.C
#include <windows.h>
#include <windowsx.h>
#include <stdio.h>
#include <stdlib.h>
#include "globals.h"

HWND hPatternDlg;
DLGPROC lpPatternType;
HCURSOR hNewCursor;
UINT Pattern_Choice;
BOOL bOrder;
BOOL bDrawMode;
RECT rect;
```

482

```
POINT pt, pt1, pt2, ptx;

LRESULT CALLBACK WndProc(HWND hWnd,
                        UINT uMessage,
                        WPARAM wParam,
                        LPARAM lParam)
{
    HDC hDC;
    char CursorPos[20];
    RECT rc1;
    HPEN hWhitePen = GetStockObject(WHITE_PEN);
    HPEN hBlackPen = GetStockObject(BLACK_PEN);

    switch (uMessage)
    {
        case WM_CREATE:
            Pattern_Choice = 0;
            bOrder = FALSE;
            bDrawMode = FALSE;
            GetClientRect(hWnd, &rect);
            hNewCursor = LoadCursor(NULL, IDC_ARROW);
            SetCursor(hNewCursor);

            // create the pattern selection dialog box
            lpPatternType = MakeProcInstance(
                    (FARPROC)PatternTypeDlgProc, hInst);
            hPatternDlg = CreateDialog(hInst,
                    MAKEINTRESOURCE(IDD_PATTERNTYPE),
                    hWnd, lpPatternType);
            break;

        case WM_COMMAND:
            switch (GET_WM_COMMAND_ID(wParam,lParam))
            {
                case IDM_ABOUT:
                    // create an about dialog box
                    DialogBox(hInst, "ABOUTDLG",
                            hWnd, (DLGPROC)About);
                    break;

                default:
                    return DefWindowProc(hWnd, uMessage,
                                    wParam, lParam);
            }
            break;

        case WM_MOUSEMOVE:
```

483

```
        // paint cursor position near upper left
        // corner of window client area when
        // mouse moves
GetCursorPos(&pt);
ScreenToClient(hWnd, &pt);
sprintf(CursorPos, "    %3d, %3d    ",
                        pt.x, pt.y);
hDC = GetDC(hWnd);
SetMapMode(hDC, MM_TEXT);
SetTextColor(hDC, RGB(0, 0, 0));
SetBkColor(hDC, RGB(255, 255, 255));
TextOut(hDC, 10, 10,
            CursorPos, strlen(CursorPos));
ReleaseDC(hWnd, hDC);


        // if the Draw-Mode is ON and the point Order
        // flag is 1 (i.e. the user is moving the mouse
        // to find the position of second point to
        // define the pattern), use the current cursor
        // position as the second point position to
        // draw a temperary pattern so user can preview
        // the the pattern to be drawn. This temperary
        // pattern is immediately erased when user move
        // the cursor to other position. A new
        // temperary pattern will be drawn according to
        // new cursor potition

if(bDrawMode && bOrder){
    hDC = GetDC(hWnd);
    if(Pattern_Choice ==1){
            // erase old temporary line
            SetROP2(hDC, R2_MASKPENNOT);
            SelectObject(hDC, hWhitePen);
            MoveToEx(hDC, pt1.x, pt1.y, NULL);
            LineTo(hDC, ptx.x, ptx.y);

            // draw new temporary line
            SetROP2(hDC, R2_MERGEPENNOT);
            SelectObject(hDC, hBlackPen);
            MoveToEx(hDC, pt1.x, pt1.y, NULL);
            LineTo(hDC, pt.x, pt.y); }

    if(Pattern_Choice ==2){
            // erase old temporary ellipse
            SelectObject(hDC, hWhitePen);
            SetROP2(hDC, R2_MASKPENNOT);
            rc1.left = min(pt1.x, ptx.x);
            rc1.right = max(pt1.x, ptx.x);
```

```
        rc1.top = min(pt1.y, ptx.y);
        rc1.bottom = max(pt1.y, ptx.y);
        Arc(hDC, rc1.left, rc1.top,
            rc1.right, rc1.bottom,
            (rc1.left + rc1.right)/2,
            rc1.bottom,
            (rc1.left + rc1.right)/2,
            rc1.bottom);

        // draw new temporary ellipse
        SelectObject(hDC, hBlackPen);
        SetROP2(hDC, R2_MERGEPENNOT);
        rc1.left = min(pt1.x, pt.x);
        rc1.right = max(pt1.x, pt.x);
        rc1.top = min(pt1.y, pt.y);
        rc1.bottom = max(pt1.y, pt.y);
        Arc(hDC, rc1.left, rc1.top,
            rc1.right, rc1.bottom,
            (rc1.left + rc1.right)/2,
            rc1.bottom,
            (rc1.left + rc1.right)/2,
            rc1.bottom);
    }

if(Pattern_Choice == 3){
        // erase old temporary rectangle
        SelectObject(hDC, hWhitePen);
        SetROP2(hDC, R2_MASKPENNOT);
        rc1.left = min(pt1.x, ptx.x);
        rc1.right = max(pt1.x, ptx.x);
        rc1.top = min(pt1.y, ptx.y);
        rc1.bottom = max(pt1.y, ptx.y);
        SetRect(&rc1, rc1.left, rc1.top,
            rc1.right, rc1.bottom);
        FrameRect(hDC, &rc1,
            GetStockObject(WHITE_BRUSH));

        // draw new temporary rectangle
        SelectObject(hDC, hBlackPen);
        SetROP2(hDC, R2_MERGEPENNOT);
        rc1.left = min(pt1.x, pt.x);
        rc1.right = max(pt1.x, pt.x);
        rc1.top = min(pt1.y, pt.y);
        rc1.bottom = max(pt1.y, pt.y);
        SetRect(&rc1, rc1.left, rc1.top,
        rc1.right, rc1.bottom);
        FrameRect(hDC, &rc1,
            GetStockObject(BLACK_BRUSH));
```

```
            }
          }
      // position of new temporary second point
      // became the position of old
      // temporary second point after
      // one erase-draw cycle is completed
      ptx.x = pt.x;
      ptx.y = pt.y;
      DeleteObject(SelectObject(hDC, hWhitePen));
      DeleteObject(SelectObject(hDC, hBlackPen));
      ReleaseDC(hWnd, hDC);
      break;

case WM_LBUTTONDOWN:
      // check if the Pattern_Choice is not system
      // cursor and the Draw Mode is "ON"
      if((Pattern_Choice != 0) &&
         (bDrawMode == TRUE))
         {
         if(bOrder == 0) {
            // get the position of first point that
            // defines the starting position of a
            // line or the corner of a rectangle
            GetCursorPos(&pt1);
            ScreenToClient(hWnd, &pt1);
            }
         if(bOrder != 0) {
            // get the position of second point that
            // defines the ending position of a line
            // or the corner of a rectangle
            GetCursorPos(&pt2);
            ScreenToClient(hWnd, &pt2);
            hDC = GetDC(hWnd);
            SetROP2(hDC, R2_COPYPEN);

            // draw patterns
            if(Pattern_Choice == 1){
               MoveToEx(hDC, pt1.x, pt1.y, NULL);
               LineTo(hDC, pt2.x, pt2.y);
               }
            if(Pattern_Choice == 2){
               Ellipse(hDC, pt1.x, pt1.y,
                       pt2.x, pt2.y);
               }
            if(Pattern_Choice == 3){
            rc1.left = min(pt1.x, pt2.x);
            rc1.right = max(pt1.x, pt2.x);
```

```
                rc1.top = min(pt1.y, pt2.y);
                rc1.bottom = max(pt1.y, pt2.y);
                Rectangle(hDC, rc1.left, rc1.top,
                                rc1.right, rc1.bottom);
                    }
                DeleteObject(SelectObject(
                                hDC, hWhitePen));
                DeleteObject(SelectObject(
                                hDC, hBlackPen));
                ReleaseDC(hWnd, hDC);
                  // turn off the Draw Mode when drawing is
                  // done
                bDrawMode = FALSE;
                  // change the cursor back to system
                  //cursor
                hNewCursor = LoadCursor(NULL, IDC_ARROW);
                  }
                // toggle the point Order flag
            bOrder = !bOrder;
            }


        break;

    case WM_SETCURSOR:
        SetCursor(hNewCursor);
        break;

    case WM_DESTROY:
        FreeProcInstance(lpPatternType);
        PostQuitMessage(0);
        break;

    default:
        return DefWindowProc(hWnd, uMessage, wParam, lParam);
    }
    return 0;
}
```

PATTYPE.C

```
// PATTYPE.C
#include <windows.h>
#include <windowsx.h>
#include "globals.h"

HBITMAP hBitmap;
```

```
HCURSOR hNewCursor;
UINT Pattern_Choice;
BOOL bDrawMode;

LRESULT CALLBACK PatternTypeDlgProc(HWND    hPatternDlg,
                                    UINT    uMessage,
                                    WPARAM wParam,
                                    LPARAM lParam )
{
LPDRAWITEMSTRUCT lpdis;

    switch (uMessage)
    {
        case WM_DRAWITEM:
            // draw bitmap buttons in pattern selection
            //dialog box
            lpdis = (LPDRAWITEMSTRUCT) lParam;
            if(lpdis-> itemState & ODS_SELECTED)
                DrawPatternDownBitmap(hInst,
                            lpdis->hDC, lpdis->CtlID);
            else
                DrawPatternUpBitmap(hInst,
                            lpdis->hDC, lpdis->CtlID);
            break;

        case WM_COMMAND:
            switch (GET_WM_COMMAND_ID(wParam,lParam))
            {
                case IDC_PTN0:  // system cursor button
                    // load the system default cursor
                    hNewCursor = LoadCursor(
                                    NULL, IDC_ARROW);
                    // set the Pattern_Choice flag
                    Pattern_Choice = 0;
                    // set the Draw Mode to FALSE such
                    // that no pattern will be drawn when
                    // user click the left mouse button
                    bDrawMode = FALSE;
                    break;

                case IDC_PTN1: // line pattern button
                    // load the cursor for line drawing
                    hNewCursor = LoadCursor(
                                    hInst, "PTN1");

                    // set the Pattern_Choice flag to
                    // line pattern
```

```
            Pattern_Choice = 1;

              // Turn on the Draw Mode so user can
              // draw a line by clicking the left
              // mouse button to determine the
              // starting and ending positions of
              // the line
            bDrawMode = TRUE;
            break;

    case IDC_PTN2: // ellipse pattern button
              // load the cursor for ellipse
              // drawing
            hNewCursor = LoadCursor(
                        hInst, "PTN2");

              // set the Pattern_Choice flag to
              // ellipse pattern
            Pattern_Choice = 2;

              // Turn on the Draw Mode so user can
              // draw a ellipse by clicking the
              // left mouse button to determine the
              // positions of two opposite corners
              // of the rectangle that confine the
              // ellipse
            bDrawMode = TRUE;
            break;

    case IDC_PTN3: // rectangle pattern button
              // load the cursor for rectangle
              // drawing
            hNewCursor = LoadCursor(
                            hInst, "PTN3");

              // set the Pattern_Choice flag to
              // rectangle pattern
            Pattern_Choice = 3;

              // Turn on the Draw Mode so user can
              // draw a rectangle by clicking the
              // left mouse button to determine the
              // positions of two opposite corners
              // of the rectangle
            bDrawMode = TRUE;
            break;
```

489

```
                        default: return FALSE;
                        }
                break;

            case WM_SETCURSOR:
                SetCursor(hNewCursor);
                break;

    default: return FALSE;
    }
    return TRUE;
}


// function for painting the pattern bitmap buttons
// in pattern selection dialog box
void PaintBitmap (hDC, hBitmap)
HDC hDC;
HBITMAP hBitmap;
{
    BITMAP bmp;
    HDC hMemoryDC;
    hMemoryDC = CreateCompatibleDC(hDC);
    GetObject(hBitmap, sizeof(BITMAP), (LPSTR) &bmp);
    SelectObject(hMemoryDC, hBitmap) ;
    BitBlt(hDC, 0, 0, bmp.bmWidth, bmp.bmHeight,
                      hMemoryDC, 0, 0, SRCCOPY);
    DeleteDC(hMemoryDC);
    DeleteObject(hBitmap);
}


// load the corresponding bitmap for the "UP" state
// of the clicked pattern selection button
void DrawPatternUpBitmap (hInstance, hDC, ButtonID)
HANDLE hInstance;
HDC hDC;
int ButtonID;
{
switch(ButtonID){
    case IDC_PTN0:
        hBitmap = LoadBitmap (hInstance, "ptn0up");
        break;

    case IDC_PTN1:
        hBitmap = LoadBitmap (hInstance, "ptn1up");
        break;

    case IDC_PTN2:
```

```
                hBitmap = LoadBitmap (hInstance, "ptn2up");
                break;

        case IDC_PTN3:
                hBitmap = LoadBitmap (hInstance, "ptn3up");
                break;

        }
        PaintBitmap(hDC, hBitmap);
}

// load the corresponding bitmap for the "DOWN" state
// of the clicked pattern selection button
void DrawPatternDownBitmap (hInstance, hDC, ButtonID)
HANDLE hInstance;
HDC hDC;
int ButtonID;
{
switch(ButtonID){
        case IDC_PTN0:
                hBitmap = LoadBitmap (hInstance, "ptn0down");
                break;

        case IDC_PTN1:
                hBitmap = LoadBitmap (hInstance, "ptn1down");
                break;

        case IDC_PTN2:
                hBitmap = LoadBitmap (hInstance, "ptn2down");
                break;

        case IDC_PTN3:
                hBitmap = LoadBitmap (hInstance, "ptn3down");
                break;

        }
        PaintBitmap(hDC, hBitmap);
}
```

ABOUT.C

```
// ABOUT.C
#include <windows.h>
#include <windowsx.h>
#include "globals.h"
```

```
// procedures for ABOUT dialog box
LRESULT CALLBACK About(HWND hDlg,
                       UINT uMessage,
                       WPARAM wParam,
                       LPARAM lParam)
{
    switch (uMessage)
      {
        case WM_COMMAND:
            switch (GET_WM_COMMAND_ID(wParam,lParam))
            {
                case IDOK:
                case IDCANCEL:
                    {
                    EndDialog(hDlg, TRUE);
                    return(TRUE);
                    }
                    break;
            }
      }
    return FALSE;
}
```

DRAWPAT.RC

```
#include "windows.h"
#include "globals.h"
#include <winver.h>

APPNAME ICON ICONFILE

RCINCLUDE ABOUT.DLG
RCINCLUDE PATTYPE.DLG

ptn0up BITMAP ptn0up.bmp
ptn1up BITMAP ptn1up.bmp
ptn2up BITMAP ptn2up.bmp
ptn3up BITMAP ptn3up.bmp

ptn0down BITMAP ptn0down.bmp
ptn1down BITMAP ptn1down.bmp
ptn2down BITMAP ptn2down.bmp
ptn3down BITMAP ptn3down.bmp

PTN1 CURSOR ptn1.cur
PTN2 CURSOR ptn2.cur
```

```
PTN3 CURSOR ptn3.cur

APPNAME MENU
BEGIN
    MENUITEM "&About", IDM_ABOUT
END
```

PATTYPE.DLG

```
IDD_PATTERNTYPE DIALOG 6, 40, 22, 64
STYLE WS_POPUP | WS_VISIBLE | WS_CAPTION | WS_SYSMENU
BEGIN
    CONTROL   "", IDC_PTN0, "Button", BS_OWNERDRAW,
              4, 4, 14, 14
    CONTROL   "", IDC_PTN1, "Button", BS_OWNERDRAW,
              4, 18, 14, 14
    CONTROL   "", IDC_PTN2, "Button", BS_OWNERDRAW,
              4, 32, 14, 14
    CONTROL   "", IDC_PTN3, "Button", BS_OWNERDRAW,
              4, 46, 14, 14
END
```

ABOUT.DLG

```
ABOUTDLG DIALOG DISCARDABLE  22, 17, 167, 73
STYLE DS_MODALFRAME | WS_CAPTION | WS_SYSMENU
CAPTION SZABOUT
BEGIN
    DEFPUSHBUTTON   "OK", IDOK, 132, 2, 32, 14, WS_GROUP
    ICON            SZAPPNAME,      -1, 3, 2, 18, 20
    LTEXT           SZAPPNAME,      -1, 30, 12,  50, 8
    LTEXT           SZDESCRIPTION, -1, 30, 22, 150, 8
    LTEXT           SZVERSION,      -1, 30, 32, 150, 8
    LTEXT           SZCOMPANYNAME, -1, 30, 42, 150, 8
END
```

DRAWPAT.ICO

PTN0UP.BMP

PTN0DOWN.BMP

PTN1UP.BMP

PTN1DOWN.BMP

PTN2UP.BMP

PTN2DOWN.BMP

PTN3UP.BMP

PTN3DOWN.BMP

PTN1.CUR

PTN2.CUR

PTN3.CUR

CASE 6-3: DRAW COLOR LINES

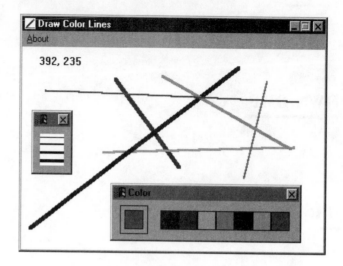

FIGURE 6-3

This case builds upon techniques used in Case 6-2 to show how to create another kind of simple drawing program. This program allows users to draw lines in various colors and thicknesses. As in Case 6-2, users select shapes from a tool palette that is implemented as a modeless dialog box with owner-drawn buttons. Unlike Case 6-2, these shapes are not ellipses or rectangles, but instead lines of various thickness. In addition to this line selection palette, there is an additional palette for color selection. The color selection palette is implemented in a similar way, as a modeless dialog box with owner-drawn buttons. For more on owner-drawn push buttons, see Cases 1-2 and 6-2.

Either palette can be dragged anywhere on the screen to minimize visual obstruction of the client area. As in Case 6-2, the cursor-changing code is in the WM_SETCURSOR handler of the main window procedure. Once the mouse is clicked, the bDrawMode flag is set to TRUE, and the program is in drawing mode so that users can draw whichever is the currently selected line. As the user moves the mouse around the window, Windows sends the WM_MOUSEMOVE message to the main window procedure. The handler for these messages updates the screen display to reflect the mouse movements, which involves getting the cursor position, erasing the previously drawn temporary line, and drawing a new temporary line at the current cursor position. When users click the mouse a second time, the previously drawn temporary line is erased and a "permanent" version of that line is drawn. The bOrder flag is used to track the state of the drawing process. This flag is initially 0 and is then set to 1 when the first mouse click happens (remember that the bDrawMode flag becomes TRUE at that time). When the second mouse click is received, bDrawMode is set to FALSE, and bOrder is set back to 0. Also, the cursor is changed back to the system default arrow cursor.

Note that in a "real" drawing program, the code would maintain a data structure that remembers which shapes were drawn and where. This data structure, which might be a list or tree structure, is used during WM_PAINT messages to refresh the contents of the screen. Also, a commercial-grade program would allow users to save and retrieve this data structure from the disk, as well as to delete shapes by removing them from the data structure. In order to keep the examples simple and understandable, I have not implemented these more advanced features in this example.

GLOBALS.H

```
// GLOBALS.H - header file for global variables
//              and function prototypes

// Product identifier string definions
#define APPNAME        DrawLine
#define ICONFILE       DrawLine.ico
#define SZAPPNAME      "DrawLine"
#define SZDESCRIPTION  "Draw Color Lines"
#define SZVERSION      "Version 1.0"
#define SZCOMPANYNAME  "\251 M&&T Books, 1994"
#define SZABOUT        "About"

// Global function prototypes.
BOOL InitApplication(HINSTANCE);
BOOL InitInstance(HINSTANCE, int);
void PaintBitmap(HDC, HBITMAP);
void DrawLineBitmap(HWND, HDC, int);
```

```
void DrawLineSBitmap(HWND, HDC, int);

// Callback functions called by Windows.
LRESULT CALLBACK WndProc(HWND, UINT, WPARAM, LPARAM);
LRESULT CALLBACK About(HWND, UINT, WPARAM, LPARAM);
LRESULT CALLBACK LineWidthDlgProc(HWND, UINT, WPARAM, LPARAM);
LRESULT CALLBACK LineColorDlgProc(HWND, UINT, WPARAM, LPARAM);

// Menu item ID
#define IDM_ABOUT   100

// Dialog box ID
#define IDD_LINEWIDTH 200
#define IDD_LINECOLOR 201

// Dialog box control ID
#define IDC_LINE1   101
#define IDC_LINE2   102
#define IDC_LINE3   103
#define IDC_LINE4   104

#define IDC_BLACK   105
#define IDC_RED     106
#define IDC_YELLOW 107
#define IDC_GREEN   108
#define IDC_BLUE    109
#define IDC_CYAN    110
#define IDC_MAGENTA 111
#define IDC_SHOWCOLOR 112

// Global variable declarations.
extern HINSTANCE hInst;
extern char szAppName[];
extern char szTitle[];
extern HWND hWnd, hColorDlg, hLineDlg;
extern DLGPROC lpProcColor, lpProcLine;
```

WINMAIN.C

```
// WINMAIN.C
#include <windows.h>
#include "globals.h"

HWND hLineDlg, hColorDlg;

int APIENTRY WinMain(HINSTANCE hInstance,
                     HINSTANCE hPrevInstance,
```

```
                         LPSTR lpCmdLine,
                         int nCmdShow)
{
    MSG msg;

    // register main window class
    if (!hPrevInstance)
        {
        if (!InitApplication(hInstance))
            {
            return FALSE;
            }
        }

    // create and show main window
    if (!InitInstance(hInstance, nCmdShow))
        {
        return FALSE;
        }

    // process window messages
    // if the message is the keyboard input for dialog box,
    // use IsDailogMessage() function to process it
    while (GetMessage(&msg, NULL, 0, 0))
        { if(!IsWindow(hColorDlg) ||
             !IsDialogMessage(hColorDlg, &msg))
        {
          TranslateMessage(&msg);
          DispatchMessage(&msg);
        }
        }
    return msg.wParam;
}
```

INIT.C

```
// INIT.C
#include <windows.h>
#include "globals.h"

HINSTANCE hInst;
char szAppName[] = SZAPPNAME;
char szTitle[] = SZDESCRIPTION;

// register main window class
BOOL InitApplication(HINSTANCE hInstance)
{
```

```
        WNDCLASS  wc;

        wc.style          = (UINT)NULL;
        wc.lpfnWndProc    = (WNDPROC)WndProc;
        wc.cbClsExtra     = 0;
        wc.cbWndExtra     = 0;
        wc.hInstance      = hInstance;
        wc.hIcon          = LoadIcon(hInstance, szAppName);
        wc.hCursor        = LoadCursor(NULL, IDC_ARROW);
        wc.hbrBackground  = (HBRUSH)(COLOR_WINDOW + 1);
        wc.lpszMenuName   = szAppName;
        wc.lpszClassName  = szAppName;

        return(RegisterClass(&wc));
}

// create and show main window
BOOL InitInstance(HINSTANCE hInstance, int nCmdShow)
{
    HWND    hWnd;
    hInst = hInstance;
    hWnd = CreateWindow(szAppName, szTitle,
                    WS_BORDER | WS_CAPTION | WS_MINIMIZEBOX |
                    WS_SYSMENU | WS_VISIBLE,
                    120, 90, 400, 300,
                    NULL, NULL, hInstance, NULL);

    if (!hWnd)
        {
        return FALSE;
        }

    ShowWindow(hWnd, nCmdShow);
    UpdateWindow(hWnd);

    return TRUE;
}
```

DRAWLINE.C

```
// DRAWLINE.C
#include <windows.h>
#include <windowsx.h>
#include <stdio.h>
#include <stdlib.h>
#include "globals.h"
```

```
HWND hLineDlg, hColorDlg;
DLGPROC lpProcLine, lpProcColor;
HCURSOR hNewCursor;
BOOL bOrder, bDrawMode;
POINT pt, pt1, pt2, ptx;
LOGPEN lp;

LRESULT CALLBACK WndProc(HWND hWnd,
                         UINT uMessage,
                         WPARAM wParam,
                         LPARAM lParam)
{
    HDC hDC;
    char CursorPos[20];
    HPEN hPen;
    HPEN hWhitePen = GetStockObject(WHITE_PEN);
    HPEN hBlackPen = GetStockObject(BLACK_PEN);

    switch (uMessage)
    {
        case WM_CREATE:
            bOrder = FALSE;
            bDrawMode = FALSE;
             // set pen style for drawing to PS_SOLID
            lp.lopnStyle = PS_SOLID;
            hNewCursor = LoadCursor(NULL, IDC_ARROW);
            SetCursor(hNewCursor);

             // create line width selection dialog box
            lpProcLine = MakeProcInstance(
                            LineWidthDlgProc, hInst);
            hLineDlg = CreateDialog(hInst,
                        MAKEINTRESOURCE(IDD_LINEWIDTH),
                            hWnd, lpProcLine);

             // create color selection table dialog box
            lpProcColor = MakeProcInstance(
                            LineColorDlgProc, hInst);
            hColorDlg = CreateDialog(hInst,
                        MAKEINTRESOURCE(IDD_LINECOLOR),
                            hWnd, lpProcColor);
            break;

        case WM_COMMAND:
            switch (GET_WM_COMMAND_ID(wParam,lParam))
            {
                case IDM_ABOUT:
                     // create an about dialog box
```

```
                    DialogBox(hInst, "ABOUTDLG",
                              hWnd, (DLGPROC)About);
                    break;

              default:
                  return DefWindowProc(hWnd, uMessage,
                                       wParam, lParam);
          }
          break;

      case WM_MOUSEMOVE:
          // get the current cursor position and
          // display it near the upper left corner
          // of window client area
          GetCursorPos(&pt);
          ScreenToClient(hWnd, &pt);
          sprintf(CursorPos, "   %3d, %3d   ",
                             pt.x, pt.y);
          hDC = GetDC(hWnd);
          TextOut(hDC, 10, 10,
                       CursorPos, strlen(CursorPos));
          ReleaseDC(hWnd, hDC);

          // if the bDrawMode is TRUE and the point Order
          // flag is 1 (i.e. the user is moving the mouse
          // to find the position of second point to
          // define a line), use the current cursor
          // position as the second point position to
          // draw a temperary line so user can preview
          // the the line to be drawn. This temperary
          // line is immediately erased when user move
          // the cursor to other position. A new
          // temperary line will be drawn according to
          // new cursor potition

          if(bDrawMode && bOrder){
              hDC = GetDC(hWnd);

              // erase old temporary line
              SetROP2(hDC, R2_MASKPENNOT);
              SelectObject(hDC, hWhitePen);
              MoveToEx(hDC, pt1.x, pt1.y, NULL);
              LineTo(hDC, ptx.x, ptx.y);

              // draw new temporary line
              SetROP2(hDC, R2_MERGEPENNOT);
              SelectObject(hDC, hBlackPen);
              MoveToEx(hDC, pt1.x, pt1.y, NULL);
```

```
        LineTo(hDC, pt.x, pt.y);
        }

    // position of new temporary second point
    // became the position of old
    // temporary second point after
    // one erase-draw cycle is completed
    ptx.x = pt.x;
    ptx.y = pt.y;
    DeleteObject(SelectObject(hDC, hWhitePen));
    DeleteObject(SelectObject(hDC, hBlackPen));
    ReleaseDC(hWnd, hDC);
    break;

case WM_LBUTTONDOWN:
        // check if bDrawMode flag is TRUE
    if(bDrawMode){
        if(bOrder == 0)
                // get the position of first point that
                // defines the starting position of a
                // line
            { GetCursorPos(&pt1);
              ScreenToClient(hWnd, &pt1);
              }
        if(bOrder != 0)
                // get the position of second point that
                // defines the ending position of a line
            { GetCursorPos(&pt2);
              hDC = GetDC(hWnd);
              hPen = CreatePenIndirect(&lp);
              SelectObject(hDC, hPen);
              ScreenToClient(hWnd, &pt2);

                // draw line
              SetROP2(hDC, R2_COPYPEN);
                  MoveToEx(hDC, pt1.x, pt1.y, NULL);
                  LineTo(hDC, pt2.x, pt2.y);
              DeleteObject(SelectObject(hDC, hPen));
              ReleaseDC(hWnd, hDC);

                // turn off the Draw Mode when drawing
                // is done
              bDrawMode = FALSE;

                // change the cursor back to system
                // cursor
              hNewCursor = LoadCursor(NULL, IDC_ARROW);
              }
```

```
                    // toggle the point Order flag
               bOrder = !bOrder;
               }

          break;

     case WM_SETCURSOR:
          SetCursor(hNewCursor);
          break;

     case WM_DESTROY:
          FreeProcInstance(lpProcColor);
          FreeProcInstance(lpProcLine);
          PostQuitMessage(0);
          break;

     default:
          return DefWindowProc(hWnd, uMessage,
                                    wParam, lParam);
     }
     return 0;
}
```

LINE.C

```
// LINE.C
#include <windows.h>
#include <windowsx.h>
#include "globals.h"

HBITMAP hBitmap;
HCURSOR hNewCursor;
LOGPEN lp;
BOOL bDrawMode;

LRESULT CALLBACK LineWidthDlgProc(HWND    hLineDlg,
                                  UINT    uMessage,
                                  WPARAM wParam,
                                  LPARAM lParam )
{
     LPDRAWITEMSTRUCT lpdis;

     switch (uMessage)
     {
          case WM_DRAWITEM:
               // draw line width selection buttons
```

```
    lpdis = (LPDRAWITEMSTRUCT) lParam;
    if(lpdis-> itemState & ODS_FOCUS)
        DrawLineSBitmap(hInst,
                lpdis->hDC, lpdis->CtlID);
    else
        DrawLineBitmap(hInst,
                    lpdis->hDC, lpdis->CtlID);
    break;

case WM_COMMAND:
    switch (GET_WM_COMMAND_ID(wParam,lParam))
    {
        case IDC_LINE1:
                // load line drawing cursor
                hNewCursor = LoadCursor(hInst, "line");
                // set line width equal to 1
                lp.lopnWidth.x = 1;
                // turn on the bDrawMode flag
                bDrawMode = TRUE;
                break;

        case IDC_LINE2:
                // load line drawing cursor
                hNewCursor = LoadCursor(hInst, "line");
                // set line width equal to 2
                lp.lopnWidth.x = 2;
                // turn on the bDrawMode flag
                bDrawMode = TRUE;
                break;

        case IDC_LINE3:
                // load line drawing cursor
                hNewCursor = LoadCursor(hInst, "line");
                // set line width equal to 3
                lp.lopnWidth.x = 3;
                // turn on the bDrawMode flag
                bDrawMode = TRUE;
                break;

        case IDC_LINE4:
                // load line drawing cursor
                hNewCursor = LoadCursor(hInst, "line");
                // set line width equal to 4
                lp.lopnWidth.x = 4;
                // turn on the bDrawMode flag
                bDrawMode = TRUE;
                break;
```

```
                        default: return FALSE;
                        }
                break;

            case WM_SETCURSOR:
                    SetCursor(hNewCursor);
                    break;

        default: return FALSE;
        }
        return TRUE;
}


// function for painting the bitmaps in line width
// selection dialog box
void PaintBitmap (hDC, hBitmap)
HDC hDC;
HBITMAP hBitmap;
{
        BITMAP bmp;
        HDC hMemoryDC;
        hMemoryDC = CreateCompatibleDC(hDC);
        GetObject(hBitmap, sizeof(BITMAP), (LPSTR) &bmp);
        SelectObject(hMemoryDC, hBitmap) ;
        BitBlt(hDC, 0, 0, bmp.bmWidth, bmp.bmHeight,
                        hMemoryDC, 0, 0, SRCCOPY);
        DeleteDC(hMemoryDC);
        DeleteObject(hBitmap);
}


// function for loading the line-width bitmap
void DrawLineBitmap (hInstance, hDC, ButtonID)
HANDLE hInstance;
HDC hDC;
int ButtonID;
{
switch(ButtonID){
    case IDC_LINE1:
            hBitmap = LoadBitmap (hInstance, "line1");
            break;

    case IDC_LINE2:
            hBitmap = LoadBitmap (hInstance, "line2");
            break;

    case IDC_LINE3:
```

```
            hBitmap = LoadBitmap (hInstance, "line3");
            break;

      case IDC_LINE4:
            hBitmap = LoadBitmap (hInstance, "line4");
            break;
        }
      PaintBitmap(hDC, hBitmap);
}


// function for loading the selected line-width bitmap
void DrawLineSBitmap (hInstance, hDC, ButtonID)
HANDLE hInstance;
HDC hDC;
int ButtonID;
{
switch(ButtonID){
      case IDC_LINE1:
            hBitmap = LoadBitmap (hInstance, "line1s");
            break;

      case IDC_LINE2:
            hBitmap = LoadBitmap (hInstance, "line2s");
            break;

      case IDC_LINE3:
            hBitmap = LoadBitmap (hInstance, "line3s");
            break;

      case IDC_LINE4:
            hBitmap = LoadBitmap (hInstance, "line4s");
            break;
        }
      PaintBitmap(hDC, hBitmap);
}
```

COLOR.C

```
// COLOR.C
#include <windows.h>
#include <windowsx.h>
#include "globals.h"

HWND hColorDlg;
BOOL bDrawMode;
int Line_Color = 0;
```

```
LOGPEN lp;

LRESULT CALLBACK LineColorDlgProc(HWND    hColorDlg,
                                  UINT    uMessage,
                                  WPARAM wParam,
                                  LPARAM lParam )
{
    LPDRAWITEMSTRUCT lpdis;
    HPEN hPen;
    HBRUSH hBrush;

    switch (uMessage)
    {
        case WM_DRAWITEM:
                // draw color selection table
                lpdis = (LPDRAWITEMSTRUCT) lParam;
                switch(lpdis->CtlID){

                    case IDC_BLACK:
                        hBrush = SelectObject(lpdis->hDC,
                            CreateSolidBrush(RGB(0, 0, 0)));
                                goto drawit;

                    case IDC_RED:
                        hBrush = SelectObject(lpdis->hDC,
                            CreateSolidBrush(RGB(255, 0, 0)));
                                goto drawit;

                    case IDC_GREEN:
                        hBrush = SelectObject(lpdis->hDC,
                            CreateSolidBrush(RGB(0, 255, 0)));
                                goto drawit;

                    case IDC_BLUE:
                        hBrush = SelectObject(lpdis->hDC,
                            CreateSolidBrush(RGB(0, 0, 255)));
                                goto drawit;

                    case IDC_MAGENTA:
                        hBrush = SelectObject(lpdis->hDC,
                            CreateSolidBrush(RGB(255, 0, 255)));
                                goto drawit;

                    case IDC_YELLOW:
                        hBrush = SelectObject(lpdis->hDC,
                            CreateSolidBrush(RGB(255, 255, 0)));
                                goto drawit;

                    case IDC_CYAN:
```

```
         hBrush = SelectObject(lpdis->hDC,
            CreateSolidBrush(RGB(0, 255, 255)));
                  goto drawit;

   case IDC_SHOWCOLOR:
       if(Line_Color == 0)
         { hBrush = SelectObject(lpdis->hDC,
             CreateSolidBrush(RGB(0, 0, 0)));
           goto drawit;
         }

       if(Line_Color == 1)
         { hBrush = SelectObject(lpdis->hDC,
             CreateSolidBrush(RGB(255, 0, 0)));
           goto drawit;
         }

       if(Line_Color == 2)
         { hBrush = SelectObject(lpdis->hDC,
           CreateSolidBrush(RGB(255, 255, 0)));
           goto drawit;
         }

       if(Line_Color == 3)
         { hBrush = SelectObject(lpdis->hDC,
             CreateSolidBrush(RGB(0, 255, 0)));
           goto drawit;
         }

       if(Line_Color == 4)
         { hBrush = SelectObject(lpdis->hDC,
             CreateSolidBrush(RGB(0, 0, 255)));
           goto drawit;
         }

       if(Line_Color == 5)
         { hBrush = SelectObject(lpdis->hDC,
           CreateSolidBrush(RGB(0, 255, 255)));
            goto drawit;
         }

       if(Line_Color == 6)
         { hBrush = SelectObject(lpdis->hDC,
           CreateSolidBrush(RGB(255, 0, 255)));
            goto drawit;
         }

drawit:           // draw the buttons in color
```

```
                         // selection table
                  { hPen = SelectObject(lpdis->hDC,
                       CreatePen(PS_SOLID, 1, RGB(0, 0, 0)));
                     Rectangle(lpdis->hDC,
                         lpdis->rcItem.left,
                         lpdis->rcItem.top,
                         lpdis->rcItem.right,
                         lpdis->rcItem.bottom);
                     DeleteObject(SelectObject(
                                   lpdis->hDC, hPen));
                     DeleteObject(SelectObject(
                                   lpdis->hDC, hBrush));
                     break; }
              break;
              default: return FALSE;
              }
              break;

      case WM_COMMAND:
              switch (GET_WM_COMMAND_ID(wParam,lParam))
              {
                  case IDC_BLACK:
                          // set Line_Color flag to 0
                        Line_Color = 0;
                          // set line color to black
                        lp.lopnColor = RGB(0, 0, 0);
                          // turn off the bDrawMode flag
                        bDrawMode = FALSE;
                        goto ShowColor;

                  case IDC_RED:
                          // set Line_Color flag to 1
                        Line_Color = 1;
                          // set line color to red
                        lp.lopnColor = RGB(255, 0, 0);
                        bDrawMode = FALSE;
                        goto ShowColor;

                  case IDC_YELLOW:
                          // set Line_Color flag to 2
                        Line_Color = 2;
                          // set line color to yellow
                        lp.lopnColor = RGB(255, 255, 0);
                        bDrawMode = FALSE;
                        goto ShowColor;

                  case IDC_GREEN:
                          // set Line_Color flag to 3
```

```
                              Line_Color = 3;
                                  // set line color to green
                              lp.lopnColor = RGB(0, 255, 0);
                              bDrawMode = FALSE;
                              goto ShowColor;

                      case IDC_BLUE:
                                  // set Line_Color flag to 4
                              Line_Color = 4;
                                  // set line color to blue
                              lp.lopnColor = RGB(0, 0, 255);
                              bDrawMode = FALSE;
                              goto ShowColor;

                      case IDC_CYAN:
                                  // set Line_Color flag to 5
                              Line_Color = 5;
                                  // set line color to cyan
                              lp.lopnColor = RGB(0, 255, 255);
                              bDrawMode = FALSE;
                              goto ShowColor;

                      case IDC_MAGENTA:
                                  // set Line_Color flag to 6
                              Line_Color = 6;
                                  // set line color to magenta
                              lp.lopnColor = RGB(255, 0, 255);
                              bDrawMode = FALSE;
                              goto ShowColor;

ShowColor:
                                  // toggle the state of ShowColor button
                                  // so the button can be repainted to
                                  // show the selected color
                              SendDlgItemMessage(hColorDlg,
                                      IDC_SHOWCOLOR, BM_SETSTATE,
                                      (WPARAM)FALSE, (LPARAM)NULL);
                              SendDlgItemMessage(hColorDlg,
                                      IDC_SHOWCOLOR, BM_SETSTATE,
                                      (WPARAM)TRUE, (LPARAM)NULL);
                              break;
                          }
                      break;

          default: return FALSE;
          }
          return TRUE;
}
```

ABOUT.C

```c
// ABOUT.C
#include <windows.h>
#include <windowsx.h>
#include "globals.h"

// procedures for ABOUT dialog box
LRESULT CALLBACK About(HWND hDlg,
                       UINT uMessage,
                       WPARAM wParam,
                       LPARAM lParam)
{
    switch (uMessage)
      {
        case WM_COMMAND:
            switch (GET_WM_COMMAND_ID(wParam,lParam))
            {
                case IDOK:
                case IDCANCEL:
                    {
                    EndDialog(hDlg, TRUE);
                    return(TRUE);
                    }
                    break;
            }
      }
    return FALSE;
}
```

DRAWLINE.RC

```c
#include "windows.h"
#include "globals.h"
#include <winver.h>

line1  BITMAP line1.bmp
line2  BITMAP line2.bmp
line3  BITMAP line3.bmp
line4  BITMAP line4.bmp
line1s BITMAP line1s.bmp
line2s BITMAP line2s.bmp
line3s BITMAP line3s.bmp
line4s BITMAP line4s.bmp

line CURSOR line.cur
```

```
APPNAME ICON ICONFILE

RCINCLUDE ABOUT.DLG
RCINCLUDE COLOR.DLG
RCINCLUDE LINE.DLG

APPNAME MENU
BEGIN
  MENUITEM "&About", IDM_ABOUT
END
```

LINE.DLG

```
IDD_LINEWIDTH DIALOG 6, 40, 24, 28
STYLE WS_POPUP | WS_VISIBLE | WS_CAPTION | WS_SYSMENU
BEGIN
    CONTROL    "", IDC_LINE1, "Button", BS_OWNERDRAW |
               WS_TABSTOP, 4, 4, 16, 4
    CONTROL    "", IDC_LINE2, "Button", BS_OWNERDRAW |
               WS_TABSTOP, 4, 8, 16, 5
    CONTROL    "", IDC_LINE3, "Button", BS_OWNERDRAW |
               WS_TABSTOP, 4, 13, 16, 5
    CONTROL    "", IDC_LINE4, "Button", BS_OWNERDRAW |
               WS_TABSTOP, 4, 18, 16, 6
END
```

COLOR.DLG

```
DLGINCLUDE RCDATA DISCARDABLE
BEGIN
    "GLOBALS.H\0"
END

IDD_LINECOLOR DIALOG 60, 90, 121, 24
STYLE WS_POPUP | WS_VISIBLE | WS_CAPTION | WS_SYSMENU
CAPTION "Color"
BEGIN
    CONTROL    "", -1, "Static", SS_BLACKFRAME, 5, 3, 18, 18
    CONTROL    "", IDC_SHOWCOLOR, "Button", BS_OWNERDRAW |
               WS_TABSTOP, 8, 6, 12, 12
    CONTROL    "", IDC_BLACK, "Button", BS_OWNERDRAW |
               WS_TABSTOP, 31, 6, 12, 12
    CONTROL    "", IDC_RED, "Button", BS_OWNERDRAW |
               WS_TABSTOP, 43, 6, 12, 12
```

513

```
    CONTROL    "", IDC_YELLOW, "Button", BS_OWNERDRAW |
               WS_TABSTOP, 55, 6, 12, 12
    CONTROL    "", IDC_GREEN, "Button", BS_OWNERDRAW |
               WS_TABSTOP, 67, 6, 12, 12
    CONTROL    "", IDC_BLUE, "Button", BS_OWNERDRAW |
               WS_TABSTOP, 79, 6, 12, 12
    CONTROL    "", IDC_CYAN, "Button", BS_OWNERDRAW |
               WS_TABSTOP, 91, 6, 12, 12
    CONTROL    "", IDC_MAGENTA, "Button", BS_OWNERDRAW |
               WS_TABSTOP, 103, 6, 12, 12
END
```

ABOUT.DLG

```
ABOUTDLG DIALOG DISCARDABLE  22, 17, 167, 73
STYLE DS_MODALFRAME | WS_CAPTION | WS_SYSMENU
CAPTION SZABOUT
BEGIN
    DEFPUSHBUTTON    "OK", IDOK, 132, 2, 32, 14, WS_GROUP
    ICON             SZAPPNAME,      -1, 3, 2, 18, 20
    LTEXT            SZAPPNAME,      -1, 30, 12,  50, 8
    LTEXT            SZDESCRIPTION, -1, 30, 22, 150, 8
    LTEXT            SZVERSION,     -1, 30, 32, 150, 8
    LTEXT            SZCOMPANYNAME, -1, 30, 42, 150, 8
END
```

DRAWLINE.ICO

LINE.CUR

LINE1.BMP

LINE1S.BMP

LINE2.BMP

LINE2S.BMP

LINE3.BMP

LINE3S.BMP

LINE4.BMP

LINE4S.BMP

CHAPTER SEVEN

COMMON DIALOG BOXES

CASE 7-1: CHOOSE COLOR COMMON DIALOG BOX

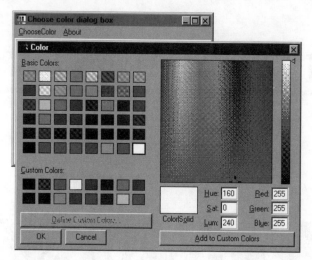

FIGURE 7-1

This chapter shows how to use various common dialog boxes provided by the Windows environment. *Common dialog boxes* are standard dialog boxes implemented in the Windows API that carry out commonly needed tasks—work that just about every application needs to do. Examples of these tasks are choosing a color, choosing a font, and selecting a printer.

This case shows the choose color common dialog box, which is a general-purpose color selection dialog box. It lets users choose a color from 48 basic colors or 16 custom colors. Users can also edit a custom color by specifying the RGB values (or the analogous HSL color metric) or by clicking the mouse in a color space.

Using this dialog box is very straightforward. A menu item is defined with the menu ID IDM_CHOOSE_COLOR. When this menu choice is made, the corresponding code in the WM_COMMAND handler is executed. The first step is to set up the CHOOSECOLOR data structure, which serves as input to the ChooseColor() function provided by the Windows API. As you can see from the code, parameters stored in this data structure include the handle of the application window, a pointer to an array of custom colors, and an element in which to store the result, cc.rgbResult. Once the CHOOSECOLOR data structure is set up, the code calls ChooseColor() to show the dialog box. When it returns, the code paints the client area with the color defined by the parameter cc.rgbResult.

GLOBALS.H

```
// GLOBALS.H - header file for global variables
//              and function prototypes

// Product identifier string definitions
#define APPNAME        CColor
#define ICONFILE       CColor.ico
#define SZAPPNAME      "CColor"
#define SZDESCRIPTION "Choose color dialog box"
#define SZVERSION      "Version 1.0"
#define SZCOMPANYNAME "\251 M&&T Books, 1994"
#define SZABOUT        "About"

// Global function prototypes.
BOOL InitApplication(HINSTANCE);
BOOL InitInstance(HINSTANCE, int);

// Callback functions called by Windows.
LRESULT CALLBACK WndProc(HWND, UINT, WPARAM, LPARAM);
LRESULT CALLBACK About(HWND, UINT, WPARAM, LPARAM);

// Menu item ID
#define IDM_ABOUT         101
#define IDM_CHOOSE_COLOR 102

// Global variable declarations.
extern HINSTANCE hInst;     // The current instance handle
extern char szAppName[];    // The name of this application
extern char szTitle[];      // The title bar text
```

WINMAIN.C

```
// WINMAIN.C
#include <windows.h>
#include "globals.h"

int APIENTRY WinMain(HINSTANCE hInstance,
```

```
                    HINSTANCE hPrevInstance,
                    LPSTR lpCmdLine,
                    int nCmdShow)
{
    MSG msg;

    // register main window class
    if (!hPrevInstance)
        {
        if (!InitApplication(hInstance))
            {
            return FALSE;
            }
        }

    // create and show main window
    if (!InitInstance(hInstance, nCmdShow))
        {
        return FALSE;
        }

    // process window messages
    while (GetMessage(&msg, NULL, 0, 0))
        {
            TranslateMessage(&msg);
            DispatchMessage(&msg);
        }
    return msg.wParam;
}
```

INIT.C

```
// INIT.C
#include <windows.h>
#include "globals.h"

HINSTANCE hInst;
char szAppName[] = SZAPPNAME;
char szTitle[] = SZDESCRIPTION;

// register main window class
BOOL InitApplication(HINSTANCE hInstance)
{
    WNDCLASS  wc;

    wc.style         = CS_HREDRAW | CS_VREDRAW;
    wc.lpfnWndProc   = (WNDPROC)WndProc;
```

```
    wc.cbClsExtra    = 0;
    wc.cbWndExtra    = 0;
    wc.hInstance     = hInstance;
    wc.hIcon         = LoadIcon(hInstance, szAppName);
    wc.hCursor       = LoadCursor(NULL, IDC_ARROW);
    wc.hbrBackground = (HBRUSH)(COLOR_WINDOW + 1);
    wc.lpszMenuName  = szAppName;
    wc.lpszClassName = szAppName;

    return(RegisterClass(&wc));
}

// create and show main window
BOOL InitInstance(HINSTANCE hInstance, int nCmdShow)
{
    HWND    hWnd;
    hInst = hInstance;
    hWnd = CreateWindow(szAppName, szTitle,
                        WS_OVERLAPPEDWINDOW,
                        160, 120, 320, 240,
                        NULL, NULL, hInstance, NULL);

    if (!hWnd)
        {
        return FALSE;
        }

    ShowWindow(hWnd, nCmdShow);
    UpdateWindow(hWnd);

    return TRUE;
}
```

CCOLOR.C

```
// CCOLOR.C
#include <windows.h>
#include <windowsx.h>
#include <commdlg.h>
#include "globals.h"

LRESULT CALLBACK WndProc(HWND hWnd,
                         UINT uMessage,
                         WPARAM wParam,
                         LPARAM lParam)
{
    PAINTSTRUCT ps;
    HDC hDC;
```

521

```
RECT rect;
HPEN hPen;
HBRUSH hBrush;
CHOOSECOLOR cc;
COLORREF ResultColor;
// define custom colors in choose color dialog box
COLORREF CustomColor[16] = {
                RGB(0, 0, 0),        RGB(63, 63, 63),
                RGB(127, 127, 127),  RGB(255, 255, 255),
                RGB(255, 0, 0),      RGB(127, 0, 0),
                RGB(0, 255, 0),      RGB(0, 127, 0),
                RGB(0, 0, 255),      RGB(0, 0, 127),
                RGB(0, 255, 255),    RGB(0, 127, 127),
                RGB(255, 0, 255),    RGB(127, 0, 127),
                RGB(255, 255, 0),    RGB(127, 127, 0)    } ;

switch (uMessage)
{
    case WM_COMMAND:
        switch (GET_WM_COMMAND_ID(wParam,lParam))
        {
            case IDM_ABOUT:
                // create an about dialog box
                DialogBox(hInst, "ABOUTDLG",
                        hWnd, (DLGPROC)About);
                break;

            case IDM_CHOOSE_COLOR:
                // set parameters in CHOOSECOLOR
                // structure cc
                ResultColor = RGB(255, 255, 255);
                memset(&cc, 0, sizeof(CHOOSECOLOR));
                cc.lStructSize = sizeof(CHOOSECOLOR);
                cc.hwndOwner = hWnd;
                cc.hInstance = NULL;
                cc.rgbResult = ResultColor;
                cc.lpCustColors = CustomColor;
                cc.Flags = CC_RGBINIT;
                cc.lCustData = 0L;
                cc.lpfnHook = NULL;
                cc.lpTemplateName = (LPSTR)NULL;

                // open choose color common dialog box
                ChooseColor(&cc);

                // paint the client area with color
                // defined by the parameter rgbResult
                // in CHOOSECOLOR structure cc
                hDC = GetDC(hWnd);
                GetClientRect(hWnd, &rect);
                hPen = GetStockObject(WHITE_PEN);
                hBrush = CreateSolidBrush(
```

```
                                        cc.rgbResult);
                SelectObject(hDC, hPen);
                SelectObject(hDC, hBrush);
                Rectangle(hDC, rect.left, rect.top,
                        rect.right, rect.bottom);
                EndPaint(hWnd, &ps);

                DeleteObject(hPen);
                DeleteObject(hBrush);
                DeleteDC(hDC);
                break;

            default:
                return DefWindowProc(hWnd, uMessage,
                                wParam, lParam);
            }
            break;

        case WM_DESTROY:
            PostQuitMessage(0);
            break;

        default:
            return DefWindowProc(hWnd, uMessage,
                            wParam, lParam);
        }
    return 0;
}
```

ABOUT.C

```
// ABOUT.C
#include <windows.h>
#include <windowsx.h>
#include "globals.h"

// procedures for ABOUT dialog box
LRESULT CALLBACK About(HWND hDlg,
                    UINT uMessage,
                    WPARAM wParam,
                    LPARAM lParam)
{
    switch (uMessage)
        {
        case WM_COMMAND:
            switch (GET_WM_COMMAND_ID(wParam,lParam))
                {
                case IDOK:
                case IDCANCEL:
                    {
                    EndDialog(hDlg, TRUE);
```

```
                            return(TRUE);
                        }
                        break;
                }
            }
        return FALSE;
    }
```

CCOLOR.RC

```
#include "windows.h"
#include "globals.h"
#include <winver.h>

APPNAME ICON ICONFILE

RCINCLUDE ABOUT.DLG

APPNAME MENU
BEGIN
    MENUITEM "&ChooseColor", IDM_CHOOSE_COLOR
    MENUITEM "&About",       IDM_ABOUT
END
```

ABOUT.DLG

```
ABOUTDLG DIALOG DISCARDABLE  22, 17, 167, 73
STYLE DS_MODALFRAME | WS_CAPTION | WS_SYSMENU
CAPTION SZABOUT
BEGIN
    DEFPUSHBUTTON    "OK", IDOK, 132, 2, 32, 14, WS_GROUP
    ICON             SZAPPNAME,      -1, 3, 2, 18, 20
    LTEXT            SZAPPNAME,      -1, 30, 12, 50, 8
    LTEXT            SZDESCRIPTION, -1, 30, 22, 150, 8
    LTEXT            SZVERSION,      -1, 30, 32, 150, 8
    LTEXT            SZCOMPANYNAME, -1, 30, 42, 150, 8
END
```

CCOLOR.ICO

CASE 7-2: CHOOSE FONT COMMON DIALOG BOX

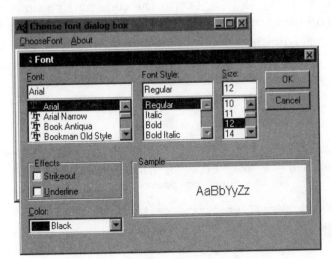

FIGURE 7-2

C hoosing a font is another task that many applications need to provide. To save you the trouble of creating this dialog box and to ensure consistency of user interface among different Windows applications, the Windows environment provides a common dialog box for font selection.

This dialog box lets users select: a font from a list of font names (such as Bookman Old Style), a font style from a list of styles (such as Italic or Bold), and a font size from a list of sizes (such as 10 point or 12 point). In addition, users can select effects such as strikeout or underline, as well as specify a color. The dialog box also provides a short preview of the font you've chosen by showing a small text string in the currently selected size and style.

As with most other common dialog boxes, using this dialog box is straightforward. In Case 7-1, the code had to set up the CHOOSECOLOR data structure before calling the ChooseColor() function. In this case, our code needs to setup the CHOOSEFONT data structure, before calling the ChooseFont() function. As before, we invoke this dialog box via a menu selection. The menu choice generates a WM_COMMAND message with the parameter IDM_CHOOSE_FONT. The code puts parameters such as minimum and maximum font sizes in this data structure. When the ChooseFont() function is called, the dialog box shown in Figureure 7-2 is displayed. After users have made a selection and closed the dialog box, the code shows a text string (in this case, an alphabet) in the client area of the main application window.

GLOBALS.H

```
// GLOBALS.H - header file for global variables
//              and function prototypes

// Product identifier string definitions
#define APPNAME         CFont
#define ICONFILE        CFont.ico
#define SZAPPNAME       "CFont"
#define SZDESCRIPTION   "Choose font dialog box"
#define SZVERSION       "Version 1.0"
#define SZCOMPANYNAME   "\251 M&&T Books, 1994"
#define SZABOUT         "About"

// Global function prototypes.
BOOL InitApplication(HINSTANCE);
BOOL InitInstance(HINSTANCE, int);

// Callback functions called by Windows.
LRESULT CALLBACK WndProc(HWND, UINT, WPARAM, LPARAM);
LRESULT CALLBACK About(HWND, UINT, WPARAM, LPARAM);

// Menu item ID
#define IDM_ABOUT       1000
#define IDM_CHOOSE_FONT 1001

// Global variable declarations.
extern HINSTANCE hInst;      // The current instance handle
extern char szAppName[];     // The name of this application
extern char szTitle[];       // The title bar text
```

WINMAIN.C

```
// WINMAIN.C
#include <windows.h>
#include "globals.h"
```

```
int APIENTRY WinMain(HINSTANCE hInstance,
                     HINSTANCE hPrevInstance,
                     LPSTR lpCmdLine,
                     int nCmdShow)
{
    MSG msg;

    // register main window class
    if (!hPrevInstance)
        {
        if (!InitApplication(hInstance))
            {
            return FALSE;
            }
        }

    // create and show main window
    if (!InitInstance(hInstance, nCmdShow))
        {
        return FALSE;
        }

    // process window messages
    while (GetMessage(&msg, NULL, 0, 0))
        {
            TranslateMessage(&msg);
            DispatchMessage(&msg);
        }
    return msg.wParam;
}
```

INIT.C

```
// INIT.C
#include <windows.h>
#include "globals.h"

HINSTANCE hInst;
char szAppName[] = SZAPPNAME;
char szTitle[] = SZDESCRIPTION;

// register main window class
BOOL InitApplication(HINSTANCE hInstance)
{
    WNDCLASS  wc;
```

```
    wc.style         = CS_HREDRAW | CS_VREDRAW;
    wc.lpfnWndProc   = (WNDPROC)WndProc;
    wc.cbClsExtra    = 0;
    wc.cbWndExtra    = 0;
    wc.hInstance     = hInstance;
    wc.hIcon         = LoadIcon(hInstance, szAppName);
    wc.hCursor       = LoadCursor(NULL, IDC_ARROW);
    wc.hbrBackground = (HBRUSH)(COLOR_WINDOW + 1);
    wc.lpszMenuName  = szAppName;
    wc.lpszClassName = szAppName;

    return(RegisterClass(&wc));
}

// create and show main window
BOOL InitInstance(HINSTANCE hInstance, int nCmdShow)
{
    HWND     hWnd;
    hInst = hInstance;
    hWnd = CreateWindow(szAppName, szTitle,
                    WS_OVERLAPPEDWINDOW,
                    160, 120, 320, 240,
                    NULL, NULL, hInstance, NULL);

    if (!hWnd)
        {
        return FALSE;
        }

    ShowWindow(hWnd, nCmdShow);
    UpdateWindow(hWnd);

    return TRUE;
}
```

CFONT.C

```
// CFONT.C
#include <windows.h>
#include <windowsx.h>
#include <commdlg.h>
#include "globals.h"

LRESULT CALLBACK WndProc(HWND hWnd,
                    UINT uMessage,
                    WPARAM wParam,
                    LPARAM lParam)
```

```
{
    LOGFONT lf;
    CHOOSEFONT cf;
    HFONT hFont, hFontOld;
    HDC hDC;
    LPSTR lpText = "ABCDEFGHIJKLMNOPQRSTUVWXYZ";
    LPSTR lpTexts = "abcdefghijklmnopqrstuvwxyz";

    switch (uMessage)
    {
        case WM_COMMAND:
            switch (GET_WM_COMMAND_ID(wParam,lParam))
            {
                case IDM_ABOUT:
                    // create an about dialog box
                    DialogBox(hInst, "ABOUTDLG",
                            hWnd, (DLGPROC)About);
                    break;

                case IDM_CHOOSE_FONT:
                    // set parameters in CHOOSEFONT
                    // structure cf
                    memset(&cf, 0, sizeof(CHOOSEFONT));
                    cf.lStructSize = sizeof(CHOOSEFONT);
                    cf.hwndOwner = hWnd;
                    cf.hDC = hDC;
                    cf.lpLogFont = &lf;
                    cf.iPointSize = 12;
                    cf.Flags = CF_SCREENFONTS | CF_EFFECTS |
                            CF_LIMITSIZE;
                    cf.rgbColors = RGB(0, 0, 0);
                    cf.lCustData = 0L;
                    cf.lpfnHook = NULL;
                    cf.lpTemplateName = (LPSTR)NULL;
                    cf.hInstance = NULL;
                    cf.lpszStyle = (LPSTR)NULL;
                    cf.nFontType = SCREEN_FONTTYPE;
                    cf.nSizeMin = 6;
                    cf.nSizeMax = 48;

                    // open choose font common dialog box
                    ChooseFont(&cf);

                    // display sample text in client area
                    // use the font chosen by user
                    hDC = GetDC(hWnd);
                    hFont = CreateFontIndirect(
                                    cf.lpLogFont);
```

529

```
                        hFontOld = SelectObject(hDC, hFont);
                        SetTextColor(hDC, cf.rgbColors);
                        TextOut(hDC, 5, 5,
                                lpText, strlen(lpText));
                        TextOut(hDC, 5, 100,
                                lpTexts, strlen(lpTexts));
                        SelectObject(hDC, hFontOld);
                        DeleteObject(hFont);
                        break;

                default:
                        return DefWindowProc(hWnd, uMessage,
                                                wParam, lParam);
                }
                break;

        case WM_DESTROY:
                PostQuitMessage(0);
                break;

        default:
                return DefWindowProc(hWnd, uMessage,
                                        wParam, lParam);
        }
        return 0;
}
```

ABOUT.C

```
// ABOUT.C
#include <windows.h>
#include <windowsx.h>
#include "globals.h"

// procedures for ABOUT dialog box
LRESULT CALLBACK About(HWND hDlg,
                       UINT uMessage,
                       WPARAM wParam,
                       LPARAM lParam)
{
    switch (uMessage)
      {
      case WM_COMMAND:
            switch (GET_WM_COMMAND_ID(wParam,lParam))
            {
                case IDOK:
                case IDCANCEL:
                    {
```

```
                        EndDialog(hDlg, TRUE);
                        return(TRUE);
                        }
                        break;
                }
        }
    return FALSE;
}
```

CFONT.RC

```
#include "windows.h"
#include "globals.h"
#include <winver.h>

APPNAME ICON ICONFILE

RCINCLUDE ABOUT.DLG

APPNAME MENU
BEGIN
    MENUITEM "&ChooseFont", IDM_CHOOSE_FONT
    MENUITEM "&About",      IDM_ABOUT
END
```

ABOUT.DLG

```
ABOUTDLG DIALOG DISCARDABLE  22, 17, 167, 73
STYLE DS_MODALFRAME | WS_CAPTION | WS_SYSMENU
CAPTION SZABOUT
BEGIN
    DEFPUSHBUTTON    "OK", IDOK, 132, 2, 32, 14, WS_GROUP
    ICON             SZAPPNAME,      -1, 3, 2, 18, 20
    LTEXT            SZAPPNAME,      -1, 30, 12,  50, 8
    LTEXT            SZDESCRIPTION, -1, 30, 22, 150, 8
    LTEXT            SZVERSION,      -1, 30, 32, 150, 8
    LTEXT            SZCOMPANYNAME, -1, 30, 42, 150, 8
END
```

CFONT.ICO

CASE 7-3: OPEN AND SAVEAS
COMMON DIALOG BOXES

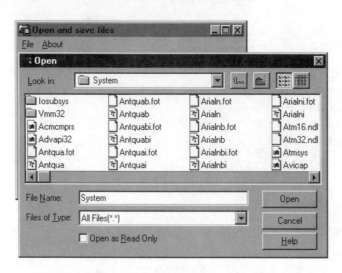

FIGURE 7-3A

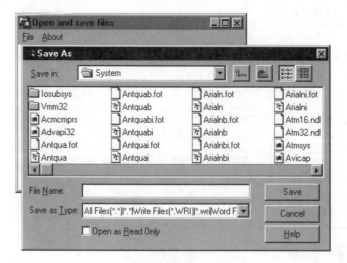

FIGURE 7-3B

Opening a disk file and later saving work onto another disk file are perhaps the two most common tasks that an application must carry out. These tasks are carried out by the Open and SaveAs common dialog boxes provided by the Windows API.

One benefit of using a common dialog box is that, if and when the underlying operating environment changes, it is likely that your application code won't need to change in order to support new features. This is case with these file-related dialog boxes. In Windows95, the design and layout of these dialog boxes have been spiffed up and made easier to use. However, your code from Windows 3.1 does not need to change. It is just as straightforward as it was before.

As in Cases 7-1 and 7-2, the common dialog box is activated by a menu choice, in this case IDM_OPEN_FILE. As before, the WM_COMMAND handler in the window procedure sets up a data structure and calls the API function to invoke the common dialog box. However, before doing this, a call to GetSystemDirectory() is needed to retrieve the name of the Windows system directory. Note that a related function GetWindowsDirectory() returns the name of the directory where Windows is (for example, C:\WINDOWS). The next step is to load the file name filter string. A filter string is of the form *.* or *.DOC and acts as a way of selecting all files of a certain type. For example, Microsoft Word files typically end with a .DOC suffix. The filter string can be a constant defined in your source code; in this case, we define it as a string resource in the resource file OPENSAVE.RC. After loading it from the resource file with LoadString(), some "massaging" of the string is needed, to separate each filter specification with a NULL byte and to terminate the string with a double NULL. After this, the code sets up the OPENFILENAME structure with values such as the filter string, the directory name, and so on. Then, the GetOpenFileName() function invokes the dialog box. When the dialog box returns, the file is opened with CreateFile(). The code for the IDM_SAVE_FILE menu choice is very similar, but instead of GetOpenFileName(), the call is to GetSaveFileName().

The "Open" and "SaveAs" common dialog boxes are used to open files and save material into files. Both are associated with an OPENFILENAME structure. Before you open the common dialog box, the program gets the current system directory and loads the file name filter string. This information is stored in an OPENFILENAME structure ofn. The user selected file name was stored as the member lpstrFile in structure ofn. The program can then open this user selected file for further work.

GLOBALS.H

```
// GLOBALS.H - header file for global variables
//              and function prototypes

// Product identifier string definitions
#define APPNAME         OpenSave
#define ICONFILE        OpenSave.ico
#define SZAPPNAME       "OpenSave"
#define SZDESCRIPTION   "Open and save files"
#define SZVERSION       "Version 1.0"
#define SZCOMPANYNAME   "\251 M&&T Books, 1994"
#define SZABOUT         "About"

// Global function prototypes.
BOOL InitApplication(HINSTANCE);
BOOL InitInstance(HINSTANCE, int);

// Callback functions called by Windows.
LRESULT CALLBACK WndProc(HWND, UINT, WPARAM, LPARAM);
LRESULT CALLBACK About(HWND, UINT, WPARAM, LPARAM);

// Menu item ID
#define IDM_ABOUT       101
#define IDM_OPEN_FILE   102
#define IDM_SAVE_FILE   103

// String ID
#define IDS_FILTERSTRING 104

// Global variable declarations.
extern HINSTANCE hInst;     // The current instance handle
extern char szAppName[];    // The name of this application
extern char szTitle[];      // The title bar text
```

WINMAIN.C

```
// WINMAIN.C
#include <windows.h>
```

```
#include "globals.h"

int APIENTRY WinMain(HINSTANCE hInstance,
                     HINSTANCE hPrevInstance,
                     LPSTR lpCmdLine,
                     int nCmdShow)
{
    MSG msg;

    // register main window class
    if (!hPrevInstance)
        {
        if (!InitApplication(hInstance))
            {
            return FALSE;
            }
        }

    // create and show main window
    if (!InitInstance(hInstance, nCmdShow))
        {
        return FALSE;
        }

    // process window messages
    while (GetMessage(&msg, NULL, 0, 0))
        {
        TranslateMessage(&msg);
        DispatchMessage(&msg);
        }
    return msg.wParam;
}
```

INIT.C

```
// INIT.C
#include <windows.h>
#include "globals.h"

HINSTANCE hInst;
char szAppName[] = SZAPPNAME;
char szTitle[] = SZDESCRIPTION;

// register main window class
BOOL InitApplication(HINSTANCE hInstance)
{
```

```
        WNDCLASS  wc;

        wc.style         = CS_HREDRAW | CS_VREDRAW;
        wc.lpfnWndProc   = (WNDPROC)WndProc;
        wc.cbClsExtra    = 0;
        wc.cbWndExtra    = 0;
        wc.hInstance     = hInstance;
        wc.hIcon         = LoadIcon(hInstance, szAppName);
        wc.hCursor       = LoadCursor(NULL, IDC_ARROW);
        wc.hbrBackground = (HBRUSH)(COLOR_WINDOW + 1);
        wc.lpszMenuName  = szAppName;
        wc.lpszClassName = szAppName;

        return(RegisterClass(&wc));
    }


// create and show main window
BOOL InitInstance(HINSTANCE hInstance, int nCmdShow)
{
    HWND    hWnd;
    hInst = hInstance;
    hWnd = CreateWindow(szAppName, szTitle,
                        WS_OVERLAPPEDWINDOW,
                        160, 120, 320, 240,
                        NULL, NULL, hInstance, NULL);

    if (!hWnd)
        {
        return FALSE;
        }

    ShowWindow(hWnd, nCmdShow);
    UpdateWindow(hWnd);

    return TRUE;
}
```

OPENSAVE.C

```
// OPENSAVE.C
#include <windows.h>
#include <windowsx.h>
#include <commdlg.h>    // must be included for common dialog box
#include "globals.h"

LRESULT CALLBACK WndProc(HWND hWnd,
```

```
                        UINT uMessage,
                        WPARAM wParam,
                        LPARAM lParam)
{
    static OPENFILENAME ofn;
    char szDirName[256];        // system directory name
    char szFile[256];           // file name
    char szFileTitle[256];      // file title
    char chReplace;             // szFilter string separator
    char szFilter[256];         // file name filter
    HFILE hf;                   // file handle
    UINT i, cbString;

    switch (uMessage)
    {
        case WM_COMMAND:
            switch (GET_WM_COMMAND_ID(wParam,lParam))
            {
                case IDM_ABOUT:
                        // create an about dialog box
                        DialogBox(hInst, "ABOUTDLG",
                                    hWnd, (DLGPROC)About);
                        break;

                case IDM_OPEN_FILE:

                        // get the system directory name
                        GetSystemDirectory(szDirName,
                                        sizeof(szDirName));

                        // add a null terminating character
                        // to szFile
                        szFile[0] = '\0';

                        // load the file name filter string
                        cbString = LoadString(hInst,
                                        IDS_FILTERSTRING,
                                        szFilter,
                                        sizeof(szFilter));

                        // add a null terminating character
                        //to szFilter
                        chReplace = szFilter[cbString - 1];
                        for(i = 0; szFilter[i] != '\0'; i++)
                            {
                            if(szFilter[i] == chReplace)
                                szFilter[i] = '\0';
                            }
```

537

```
                    // set parameters in OPENFILENAME
                    // structure ofn
          memset(&ofn, 0, sizeof(OPENFILENAME));
          ofn.lStructSize = sizeof(OPENFILENAME);
          ofn.hwndOwner = hWnd;
          ofn.hInstance = NULL;
          ofn.lpstrFilter = szFilter;
          ofn.lpstrCustomFilter = (LPSTR)NULL;
          ofn.nFilterIndex = 1;
          ofn.lpstrFile = szFile;
          ofn.nMaxFile = sizeof(szFile);
          ofn.lpstrFileTitle = szFileTitle;
          ofn.nMaxFileTitle =
                      sizeof(szFileTitle);
          ofn.lpstrInitialDir = szDirName;
          ofn.lpstrTitle = (LPSTR)NULL;
          ofn.Flags = OFN_SHOWHELP |
                      OFN_PATHMUSTEXIST |
                      OFN_FILEMUSTEXIST;
          ofn.nFileOffset = NULL;
          ofn.nFileExtension = NULL;
          ofn.lpstrDefExt = (LPSTR)NULL;
          ofn.lCustData = 0L;
          ofn.lpfnHook = (FARPROC)NULL;
          ofn.lpTemplateName = (LPSTR)NULL;

                    // open an open file common dialog box
          GetOpenFileName(&ofn);

                    // open the file
          hf = CreateFile(ofn.lpstrFile,
                      GENERIC_READ,
                      0,
                      (LPSECURITY_ATTRIBUTES)NULL,
                      OPEN_EXISTING,
                      FILE_ATTRIBUTE_NORMAL,
                      (HANDLE)NULL);

              //
              // things to do after the file is open
              //

              // close the file
          CloseHandle(hf);
          break;

      case IDM_SAVE_FILE:
```

```
// get the system directory name
GetSystemDirectory(szDirName,
                   sizeof(szDirName));

// add a null terminating character
// to szFile
szFile[0] = '\0';

// load the file name filter string
cbString = LoadString(hInst,
           IDS_FILTERSTRING,
           szFilter, sizeof(szFilter));

// add a null terminating character
// to szFilter
for(i = 0; szFilter[i] != '\0'; i++)
  {
    if(szFilter[i] == chReplace)
       szFilter[i] = '\0';
  }

// set parameters in OPENFILENAME
// structure ofn
memset(&ofn, 0, sizeof(OPENFILENAME));
ofn.lStructSize = sizeof(OPENFILENAME);
ofn.hwndOwner = hWnd;
ofn.hInstance = NULL;
ofn.lpstrFilter = szFilter;
ofn.lpstrCustomFilter = (LPSTR)NULL;
ofn.nFilterIndex = 1;
ofn.lpstrFile = szFile;
ofn.nMaxFile = sizeof(szFile);
ofn.lpstrFileTitle = szFileTitle;
ofn.nMaxFileTitle =
              sizeof(szFileTitle);
ofn.lpstrInitialDir = szDirName;
ofn.lpstrTitle = (LPSTR)NULL;
ofn.Flags = OFN_SHOWHELP |
            OFN_OVERWRITEPROMPT;
ofn.nFileOffset = NULL;
ofn.nFileExtension = NULL;
ofn.lpstrDefExt = (LPSTR)NULL;
ofn.lCustData = 0L;
ofn.lpfnHook = (FARPROC)NULL;
ofn.lpTemplateName = (LPSTR)NULL;

// open a SaveAs common dialog box
```

539

```
                    GetSaveFileName(&ofn);

                    // open the file
                    hf = CreateFile(ofn.lpstrFile,
                            GENERIC_WRITE,
                            0,
                            (LPSECURITY_ATTRIBUTES)NULL,
                            CREATE_ALWAYS,
                            FILE_ATTRIBUTE_NORMAL,
                            (HANDLE)NULL);

                //
                // things to do,
                // example: write text into a file
                //

                // close the file
                    CloseHandle(hf);
                    break;

            default:
                    return DefWindowProc(hWnd, uMessage,
                                        wParam, lParam);
            }
            break;

        case WM_DESTROY:
            PostQuitMessage(0);
            break;

        default:
            return DefWindowProc(hWnd, uMessage,
                                wParam, lParam);
    }
    return 0;
}
```

ABOUT.C

```
// ABOUT.C
#include <windows.h>
#include <windowsx.h>
#include "globals.h"

// procedures for ABOUT dialog box
LRESULT CALLBACK About(HWND hDlg,
```

```
                        UINT uMessage,
                        WPARAM wParam,
                        LPARAM lParam)
{
    switch (uMessage)
      {
        case WM_COMMAND:
            switch (GET_WM_COMMAND_ID(wParam,lParam))
            {
                case IDOK:
                case IDCANCEL:
                    {
                    EndDialog(hDlg, TRUE);
                    return(TRUE);
                    }
                    break;
            }
      }
    return FALSE;
}
```

OPENSAVE.RC

```
#include "windows.h"
#include "globals.h"
#include <winver.h>

APPNAME ICON ICONFILE

RCINCLUDE ABOUT.DLG

APPNAME MENU
BEGIN
    POPUP     "&File"
    BEGIN
        MENUITEM "&Open",     IDM_OPEN_FILE
        MENUITEM "&Save As", IDM_SAVE_FILE
    END
    MENUITEM "&About", IDM_ABOUT
END

STRINGTABLE
BEGIN
  IDS_FILTERSTRING "All Files(*.*)|*.*|Write Files(*.WRI)|
                    *.wri|Word Files(*.DOC)|*.doc|"
END
```

ABOUT.DLG

```
ABOUTDLG DIALOG DISCARDABLE  22, 17, 167, 73
STYLE DS_MODALFRAME | WS_CAPTION | WS_SYSMENU
CAPTION SZABOUT
BEGIN
    DEFPUSHBUTTON    "OK", IDOK, 132, 2, 32, 14, WS_GROUP
    ICON             SZAPPNAME,      -1, 3, 2, 18, 20
    LTEXT            SZAPPNAME,      -1, 30, 12,  50, 8
    LTEXT            SZDESCRIPTION, -1, 30, 22, 150, 8
    LTEXT            SZVERSION,      -1, 30, 32, 150, 8
    LTEXT            SZCOMPANYNAME, -1, 30, 42, 150, 8
END
```

OPENSAVE.ICO

CASE 7-4: PRINT AND PRINT SETUP COMMON DIALOG BOX

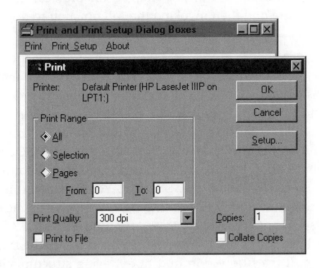

FIGURE 7-4A

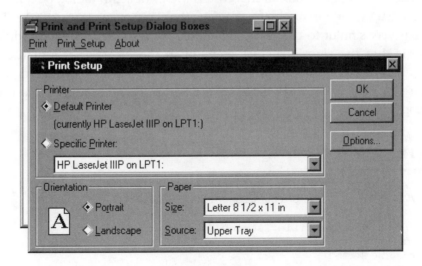

FIGURE 7-4B

T he print and print setup dialog boxes are used in any Windows application that needs to print something on the printer. As with Cases 7-1 through 7-3 in this chapter, the protocol involves setting up a data structure and then invoking the API function to display the dialog box.

As before, the code is in the WM_COMMAND handler for the appropriate menu choice, in this case: IDM_PRINT. The data structure that holds the parameters is of type PRINTDLG. It contains parameters such as the page number to start from and number of copies. In our case, these values are mostly set to NULL. The PrintDlg() function shows the common dialog box and returns nonzero if there is something to print. Our code then prints a simple page to the printer, using the device context handle returned by the print dialog box, pd.hDC. You will note the use of the Escape() commands used in printing from Windows applications, with parameters such as STARTDOC, NEWFRAME, and ENDDOC. After printing is done, the device context must be released via a call to the DeleteDC() function. Also, if the hDevMode and hDevNames structure elements are not NULL, they should be freed with calls to GlobalFree().

The second dialog box in this case is the print setup dialog box, and it is invoked by the menu choice that has the ID IDM_PRINT_SETUP. The code is very similar to the print dialog box just discussed. The main difference is that the Flags structure element in the PRINTDLG structure is PD_PRINTSETUP, instead of PD_RETURNDC. The print setup dialog box is also invoked if the user clicks on the **Setup...** pushbutton in the print dialog box.

GLOBALS.H

```
// GLOBALS.H - header file for global variables
//             and function prototypes

// Product identifier string definitions
#define APPNAME      Print
#define ICONFILE     Print.ico
#define SZAPPNAME    "Print"
#define SZDESCRIPTION "Print and Print Setup Dialog Boxes"
#define SZVERSION    "Version 1.0"
```

```
#define SZCOMPANYNAME "\251 M&&T Books, 1994"
#define SZABOUT       "About"

// Global function prototypes.
BOOL InitApplication(HINSTANCE);
BOOL InitInstance(HINSTANCE, int);

// Callback functions called by Windows.
LRESULT CALLBACK WndProc(HWND, UINT, WPARAM, LPARAM);
LRESULT CALLBACK About(HWND, UINT, WPARAM, LPARAM);

// Menu item ID
#define IDM_ABOUT        101
#define IDM_PRINT        102
#define IDM_PRINT_SETUP 103


// Global variable declarations.
extern HINSTANCE hInst;        // The current instance handle
extern char szAppName[];       // The name of this application
extern char szTitle[];         // The title bar text
```

WINMAIN.C

```
// WINMAIN.C
#include <windows.h>
#include "globals.h"

int APIENTRY WinMain(HINSTANCE hInstance,
                     HINSTANCE hPrevInstance,
                     LPSTR lpCmdLine,
                     int nCmdShow)
{
    MSG msg;

    // register main window class
    if (!hPrevInstance)
        {
        if (!InitApplication(hInstance))
            {
            return FALSE;
            }
        }

    // create and show main window
    if (!InitInstance(hInstance, nCmdShow))
```

```
        {
        return FALSE;
        }

    // process window messages
    while (GetMessage(&msg, NULL, 0, 0))
        {
        TranslateMessage(&msg);
        DispatchMessage(&msg);
        }
    return msg.wParam;
    }
```

INIT.C

```
// INIT.C
#include <windows.h>
#include "globals.h"

HINSTANCE hInst;
char szAppName[] = SZAPPNAME;
char szTitle[] = SZDESCRIPTION;

// register main window class
BOOL InitApplication(HINSTANCE hInstance)
{
    WNDCLASS  wc;

    wc.style         = CS_HREDRAW | CS_VREDRAW;
    wc.lpfnWndProc   = (WNDPROC)WndProc;
    wc.cbClsExtra    = 0;
    wc.cbWndExtra    = 0;
    wc.hInstance     = hInstance;
    wc.hIcon         = LoadIcon(hInstance, szAppName);
    wc.hCursor       = LoadCursor(NULL, IDC_ARROW);
    wc.hbrBackground = (HBRUSH)(COLOR_WINDOW + 1);
    wc.lpszMenuName  = szAppName;
    wc.lpszClassName = szAppName;

    return(RegisterClass(&wc));
}

// create and show main window
BOOL InitInstance(HINSTANCE hInstance, int nCmdShow)
{
    HWND    hWnd;
```

```
    hInst = hInstance;
    hWnd = CreateWindow(szAppName, szTitle,
                        WS_OVERLAPPEDWINDOW,
                        160, 120, 320, 240,
                        NULL, NULL, hInstance, NULL);

    if (!hWnd)
        {
        return FALSE;
        }

    ShowWindow(hWnd, nCmdShow);
    UpdateWindow(hWnd);

    return TRUE;
}
```

PRINT.C

```
// PRINT.C
#include <windows.h>
#include <windowsx.h>
#include <commdlg.h>
#include "globals.h"

LRESULT CALLBACK WndProc(HWND hWnd,
                         UINT uMessage,
                         WPARAM wParam,
                         LPARAM lParam)
{
    PRINTDLG pd;
    switch (uMessage)
    {
        case WM_COMMAND:
            switch (GET_WM_COMMAND_ID(wParam,lParam))
            {
                case IDM_ABOUT:
                    // create an about dialog box
                    DialogBox(hInst, "ABOUTDLG",
                            hWnd, (DLGPROC)About);
                    break;

                case IDM_PRINT:
                    // set parameters in PRINTDLG
                    // structure pd
                    memset(&pd, 0, sizeof(PRINTDLG));
```

```
                          pd.lStructSize = sizeof(PRINTDLG);
                          pd.hwndOwner = hWnd;
                          pd.hDevMode = NULL;
                          pd.hDevNames = NULL;
                          pd.hDC = NULL;
                          pd.Flags = PD_RETURNDC;
                          pd.nFromPage = (WORD)NULL;
                          pd.nToPage = (WORD)NULL;
                          pd.nMinPage = (WORD)NULL;
                          pd.nMaxPage = (WORD)NULL;
                          pd.nCopies = (WORD)NULL;
                          pd.hInstance = NULL;
                          pd.lCustData = 0L;
                          pd.lpfnPrintHook = NULL;
                          pd.lpfnSetupHook = NULL;
                          pd.lpPrintTemplateName = (LPSTR)NULL;
                          pd.lpSetupTemplateName = (LPSTR)NULL;
                          pd.hPrintTemplate = NULL;
                          pd.hSetupTemplate = NULL;

                            // open print common dialog box
                            // and print sample text
                          if(PrintDlg(&pd) != 0) {
                          Escape(pd.hDC, STARTDOC, 8,
                                          "Test-Doc", NULL);
                          TextOut(pd.hDC, 50, 50,
                                    "Common Dialog Test Page",23);
                          Rectangle(pd.hDC, 50, 90, 625, 105);
                          Escape(pd.hDC, NEWFRAME, 0, NULL, NULL);
                          Escape(pd.hDC, ENDDOC, 0, NULL, NULL);
                          DeleteDC(pd.hDC);
                          if(pd.hDevMode != NULL)
                                          GlobalFree(pd.hDevMode);
                          if(pd.hDevNames != NULL)
                                          GlobalFree(pd.hDevNames);
                          }
                          break;

                      case IDM_PRINT_SETUP:
                            // set parameters in PRINTDLG
                            // structure pd
                          memset(&pd, 0, sizeof(PRINTDLG));
                          pd.lStructSize = sizeof(PRINTDLG);
                          pd.hwndOwner = hWnd;
                          pd.hDevMode = NULL;
                          pd.hDevNames = NULL;
                          pd.hDC = NULL;
```

```
                pd.Flags = PD_PRINTSETUP;
                pd.nFromPage = (WORD)NULL;
                pd.nToPage = (WORD)NULL;
                pd.nMinPage = (WORD)NULL;
                pd.nMaxPage = (WORD)NULL;
                pd.nCopies = (WORD)NULL;
                pd.hInstance = NULL;
                pd.lCustData = 0L;
                pd.lpfnPrintHook = NULL;
                pd.lpfnSetupHook = NULL;
                pd.lpPrintTemplateName = (LPSTR)NULL;
                pd.lpSetupTemplateName = (LPSTR)NULL;
                pd.hPrintTemplate = NULL;
                pd.hSetupTemplate = NULL;

                // open print setup common dialog box
                PrintDlg(&pd);
                break;

            default:
                return DefWindowProc(hWnd, uMessage,
                                     wParam, lParam);
            }
            break;

        case WM_DESTROY:
            PostQuitMessage(0);
            break;

        default:
            return DefWindowProc(hWnd, uMessage,
                                 wParam, lParam);
    }
    return 0;
}
```

ABOUT.C

```
// ABOUT.C
#include <windows.h>
#include <windowsx.h>
#include "globals.h"

// procedures for ABOUT dialog box
LRESULT CALLBACK About(HWND hDlg,
                       UINT uMessage,
```

```
                    WPARAM wParam,
                    LPARAM lParam)
{
    switch (uMessage)
      {
        case WM_COMMAND:
            switch (GET_WM_COMMAND_ID(wParam,lParam))
            {
                case IDOK:
                case IDCANCEL:
                    {
                    EndDialog(hDlg, TRUE);
                    return(TRUE);
                    }
                    break;
            }
      }
    return FALSE;
}
```

PRINT.RC

```
#include "windows.h"
#include "globals.h"
#include <winver.h>

APPNAME ICON ICONFILE

RCINCLUDE ABOUT.DLG

APPNAME MENU
BEGIN
    MENUITEM "&Print",        IDM_PRINT
    MENUITEM "Print_&Setup",  IDM_PRINT_SETUP
    MENUITEM "&About",        IDM_ABOUT
END
```

ABOUT.DLG

```
ABOUTDLG DIALOG DISCARDABLE  22, 17, 167, 73
STYLE DS_MODALFRAME | WS_CAPTION | WS_SYSMENU
CAPTION SZABOUT
BEGIN
    DEFPUSHBUTTON   "OK", IDOK, 132, 2, 32, 14, WS_GROUP
    ICON            SZAPPNAME,    -1, 3, 2, 18, 20
```

550

```
    LTEXT         SZAPPNAME,      -1, 30, 12,  50, 8
    LTEXT         SZDESCRIPTION,  -1, 30, 22, 150, 8
    LTEXT         SZVERSION,      -1, 30, 32, 150, 8
    LTEXT         SZCOMPANYNAME,  -1, 30, 42, 150, 8
END
```

PRINT.ICO

CHAPTER EIGHT

TEXT AND FONTS

CASE 8-1: DRAWING SAMPLE FORMATTED TEXT

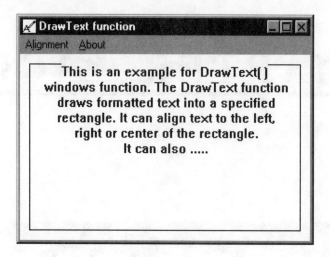

FIGURE 8-1

S ome of the cases in previous chapters have involved displaying short text strings in the client area using the TextOut() function of the Windows GDI. Mostly this use has gone unremarked. The cases in this chapter show how to use a variety of text and font services provided by the Windows environment.

This case presents the DrawText() function, which is in some ways more powerful than the TextOut() function in that it will display multiple lines of text formatted to fit into a specified rectangle. The lines of text can be aligned to the left, right, or center of the rectangle. In this example, the code draws the outline of the rectangle that encloses the text, in order to clarify how the DrawText() function works.

You can change the text alignment via the choices in the Alignment menu. The WM_COMMAND handler for these menu items (IDM_LEFT, IDM_RIGHT, and IDM_CENTER) places the corresponding alignment parameter into the global variable fuFormat, and then calls the InvalidateRect() function to cause the window to be repainted.

Text drawing occurs in the `WM_PAINT` handler in the main window procedure. Each time the window is redrawn, the size of the client area is calculated with a call to `GetClientRect()`. This rectangle is then inset by 10 pixels using the utility function `InflateRect()`. Then the call to `DrawText()` is made using the inset rectangle and the current alignment parameter.

GLOBALS.H

```
// GLOBALS.H - header file for global variables
//              and function prototypes

// Product identifier string definitions
#define APPNAME        DText
#define ICONFILE       DText.ico
#define SZAPPNAME      "DText"
#define SZDESCRIPTION "DrawText function"
#define SZVERSION      "Version 1.0"
#define SZCOMPANYNAME "\251 M&&T Books, 1994"
#define SZABOUT        "About"

// Global function prototypes.
BOOL InitApplication(HINSTANCE);
BOOL InitInstance(HINSTANCE, int);

// Callback functions called by Windows.
LRESULT CALLBACK WndProc(HWND, UINT, WPARAM, LPARAM);
LRESULT CALLBACK About(HWND, UINT, WPARAM, LPARAM);

// Menu item ID
#define IDM_ABOUT    101
#define IDM_LEFT     102
#define IDM_RIGHT    103
#define IDM_CENTER   104

// Global variable declarations.
extern HINSTANCE hInst;       // The current instance handle
extern char szAppName[];      // The name of this application
extern char szTitle[];        // The title bar text
```

WINMAIN.C

```
// WINMAIN.C
#include <windows.h>
#include "globals.h"
```

```c
int APIENTRY WinMain(HINSTANCE hInstance,
                     HINSTANCE hPrevInstance,
                     LPSTR lpCmdLine,
                     int nCmdShow)
{
    MSG msg;

    // register main window class
    if (!hPrevInstance)
        {
        if (!InitApplication(hInstance))
            {
            return FALSE;
            }
        }

    // create and show main window
    if (!InitInstance(hInstance, nCmdShow))
        {
        return FALSE;
        }

    // process window messages
    while (GetMessage(&msg, NULL, 0, 0))
        {
            TranslateMessage(&msg);
            DispatchMessage(&msg);
        }
    return msg.wParam;
}
```

INIT.C

```c
// INIT.C
#include <windows.h>
#include "globals.h"

HINSTANCE hInst;
char szAppName[] = SZAPPNAME;
char szTitle[] = SZDESCRIPTION;

// register main window class
BOOL InitApplication(HINSTANCE hInstance)
{
    WNDCLASS  wc;

    wc.style          = CS_HREDRAW | CS_VREDRAW;
    wc.lpfnWndProc    = (WNDPROC)WndProc;
```

```
    wc.cbClsExtra    = 0;
    wc.cbWndExtra    = 0;
    wc.hInstance     = hInstance;
    wc.hIcon         = LoadIcon(hInstance, szAppName);
    wc.hCursor       = LoadCursor(NULL, IDC_ARROW);
    wc.hbrBackground = (HBRUSH)(COLOR_WINDOW + 1);
    wc.lpszMenuName  = szAppName;
    wc.lpszClassName = szAppName;

    return(RegisterClass(&wc));
}

// create and show main window
BOOL InitInstance(HINSTANCE hInstance, int nCmdShow)
{
    HWND    hWnd;
    hInst = hInstance;
    hWnd = CreateWindow(szAppName, szTitle,
                        WS_OVERLAPPEDWINDOW,
                        160, 120, 320, 240,
                        NULL, NULL, hInstance, NULL);

    if (!hWnd)
        {
        return FALSE;
        }

    ShowWindow(hWnd, nCmdShow);
    UpdateWindow(hWnd);

    return TRUE;
}
```

DTEXT.C

```
// DRAWTEXT.C
#include <windows.h>
#include <windowsx.h>
#include "globals.h"

LRESULT CALLBACK WndProc(HWND hWnd,
                         UINT uMessage,
                         WPARAM wParam,
                         LPARAM lParam)
{
    PAINTSTRUCT ps;
    HDC hDC;
    RECT rect;
    static UINT fuFormat = DT_LEFT;
```

```
// define sample text
LPCSTR lpcstr = "This is an example for DrawText( )\n
          windows function. The DrawText function\n
          draws formatted text into a specified\n
          rectangle. It can align text to the left,\n
          right or center of the rectangle.\n
          It can also .....";

switch (uMessage)
{
    case WM_COMMAND:
        switch (GET_WM_COMMAND_ID(wParam,lParam))
        {
            case IDM_ABOUT:
                // create an about dialog box
                DialogBox(hInst, "ABOUTDLG",
                          hWnd, (DLGPROC)About);
                break;

            // set text alignment
            case IDM_LEFT:
                fuFormat = DT_LEFT;
                InvalidateRect(hWnd, NULL, TRUE);
                break;

            case IDM_RIGHT:
                fuFormat = DT_RIGHT;
                InvalidateRect(hWnd, NULL, TRUE);
                break;

            case IDM_CENTER:
                fuFormat = DT_CENTER;
                InvalidateRect(hWnd, NULL, TRUE);
                break;

            default:
                return DefWindowProc(hWnd, uMessage,
                                     wParam, lParam);
        }
        break;

    case WM_PAINT:
        hDC = BeginPaint(hWnd, &ps);
        GetClientRect(hWnd, &rect);

        // shrink the client rectange by 10 pixels
        InflateRect(&rect, -10, -10);

        // draw the new rectangle
```

```
                    Rectangle(hDC, rect.left, rect.top,
                              rect.right, rect.bottom);
                    SetMapMode(hDC, MM_TEXT);

                    // Draw the text in new rectangle
                    // according to the alignment
                    // flag -> fuFormat
                    DrawText(hDC, lpcstr,  strlen(lpcstr),
                              &rect, fuFormat);
                    EndPaint(hWnd, &ps);
                    break;

            case WM_DESTROY:
                    PostQuitMessage(0);
                    break;

            default:
                    return DefWindowProc(hWnd, uMessage,
                                        wParam, lParam);
        }
        return 0;
}
```

ABOUT.C

```
// ABOUT.C
#include <windows.h>
#include <windowsx.h>
#include "globals.h"

// procedures for ABOUT dialog box
LRESULT CALLBACK About(HWND hDlg,
                       UINT uMessage,
                       WPARAM wParam,
                       LPARAM lParam)
{
    switch (uMessage)
      {
        case WM_COMMAND:
                switch (GET_WM_COMMAND_ID(wParam,lParam))
                {
                    case IDOK:
                    case IDCANCEL:
                        {
                        EndDialog(hDlg, TRUE);
                        return(TRUE);
                        }
                        break;
```

```
                }
            }
        return FALSE;
    }
```

DTEXT.RC

```
#include "windows.h"
#include "globals.h"
#include <winver.h>

APPNAME ICON ICONFILE

RCINCLUDE ABOUT.DLG

APPNAME MENU
BEGIN
    POPUP           "A&lignment"
    BEGIN
        MENUITEM "&Left",    IDM_LEFT
        MENUITEM "&Right",   IDM_RIGHT
        MENUITEM "&Center",  IDM_CENTER
    END
    MENUITEM "&About",       IDM_ABOUT
END
```

ABOUT.DLG

```
ABOUTDLG DIALOG DISCARDABLE  22, 17, 167, 73
STYLE DS_MODALFRAME | WS_CAPTION | WS_SYSMENU
CAPTION SZABOUT
BEGIN
    DEFPUSHBUTTON   "OK", IDOK, 132, 2, 32, 14, WS_GROUP
    ICON            SZAPPNAME,       -1, 3, 2, 18, 20
    LTEXT           SZAPPNAME,       -1, 30, 12, 50, 8
    LTEXT           SZDESCRIPTION,   -1, 30, 22, 150, 8
    LTEXT           SZVERSION,       -1, 30, 32, 150, 8
    LTEXT           SZCOMPANYNAME,   -1, 30, 42, 150, 8
END
```

DTEXT.ICO

CASE 8-2: TEXT OUT( ) FUNCTION

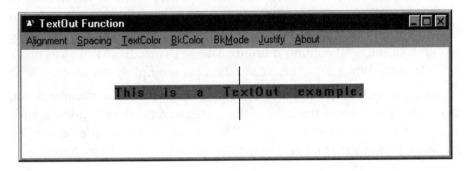

FIGURE 8-2

The TextOut() function is in some ways simpler than the DrawText() function described in Case 8-1. However, you can also use TextOut() in conjunction with other text API functions to achieve a finer degree of control over text output than you can get with DrawText(). However, TextOut() places more of the burden on the individual programmer.

This case shows some of the basic functionality of TextOut() when used with related functions such as SetTextAlign(), SetTextColor(), SetTextCharacterExtra(), SetBkColor(), SetBkMode(), and SetTextJustification().

For purposes of clarifying what's going on, the code draws a vertical line in the center of the client area to serve as an alignment marker. The SetTextAlign() function sets the alignment flags. The user can use the Alignment menu to change these flags. The code uses the SetTextCharacterExtra() function to change the intercharacter spacing. The user can select different values via the Spacing menu. Likewise, users can use the TextColor menu to change the color of the text. This results in a call to the SetTextColor() function.

Continuing with this approach, the BkColor menu lets users change the text background color. This results in a call to the SetBkColor() function. Further, a BkMode menu that changes the background mode to either opaque or transparent which is accomplished via the SetBkMode() function. Lastly, the Justify menu controls *justification* of text (justification is the process of taking the extra space at the end of a line and distributing it among the intermediate spaces so that the line of text ends at the right column margin). The SetTextJustification() function is the Windows API function used to accomplish this effect.

As in Case 8-1, the handler in WM_COMMAND for the various menu choices merely changes the state of the corresponding global variable, such as fuAlign and nExtraSpace. Then a call to InvalidateRect() invokes a paint message. The text gets drawn in the WM_PAINT handler.

GLOBALS.H

```
// GLOBALS.H - header file for global variables
//             and function prototypes

// Product identifier string definitions
#define APPNAME        TOut
#define ICONFILE       TOut.ico
#define SZAPPNAME      "TOut"
#define SZDESCRIPTION  "TextOut Function"
#define SZVERSION      "Version 1.0"
#define SZCOMPANYNAME  "\251 M&&T Books, 1994"
#define SZABOUT        "About"

// Global function prototypes.
BOOL InitApplication(HINSTANCE);
BOOL InitInstance(HINSTANCE, int);

// Callback functions called by Windows.
LRESULT CALLBACK WndProc(HWND, UINT, WPARAM, LPARAM);
LRESULT CALLBACK About(HWND, UINT, WPARAM, LPARAM);

// Menu item ID
#define IDM_ABOUT      101

#define IDM_LEFT       102
#define IDM_RIGHT      103
#define IDM_CENTER     104

#define IDM_SMALL      105
#define IDM_MEDIUM     106
#define IDM_LARGE      107
```

```
#define IDM_WHITE     108
#define IDM_BLACK     109
#define IDM_RED       110
#define IDM_GREEN     111
#define IDM_BLUE      112

#define IDM_BK_WHITE 113
#define IDM_BK_BLACK 114
#define IDM_BK_RED   115
#define IDM_BK_GREEN 116
#define IDM_BK_BLUE  117

#define IDM_OPAQUE       118
#define IDM_TRANSPARENT 119

#define IDM_JUSTIFY_YES 120
#define IDM_JUSTIFY_NO  121

// Global variable declarations.
extern HINSTANCE hInst;      // The current instance handle
extern char szAppName[];     // The name of this application
extern char szTitle[];       // The title bar text
```

WINMAIN.C

```
// WINMAIN.C
#include <windows.h>
#include "globals.h"

int APIENTRY WinMain(HINSTANCE hInstance,
                     HINSTANCE hPrevInstance,
                     LPSTR lpCmdLine,
                     int nCmdShow)
{
    MSG msg;

    // register main window class
    if (!hPrevInstance)
        {
        if (!InitApplication(hInstance))
            {
            return FALSE;
            }
        }
```

```
    // create and show main window
    if (!InitInstance(hInstance, nCmdShow))
        {
        return FALSE;
        }

    // process window messages
    while (GetMessage(&msg, NULL, 0, 0))
        {
            TranslateMessage(&msg);
            DispatchMessage(&msg);
        }
    return msg.wParam;
}
```

INIT.C

```
// INIT.C
#include <windows.h>
#include "globals.h"

HINSTANCE hInst;
char szAppName[] = SZAPPNAME;
char szTitle[] = SZDESCRIPTION;

// register main window class
BOOL InitApplication(HINSTANCE hInstance)
{
    WNDCLASS  wc;

    wc.style         = CS_HREDRAW | CS_VREDRAW;
    wc.lpfnWndProc   = (WNDPROC)WndProc;
    wc.cbClsExtra    = 0;
    wc.cbWndExtra    = 0;
    wc.hInstance     = hInstance;
    wc.hIcon         = LoadIcon(hInstance, szAppName);
    wc.hCursor       = LoadCursor(NULL, IDC_ARROW);
    wc.hbrBackground = (HBRUSH)(COLOR_WINDOW + 1);
    wc.lpszMenuName  = szAppName;
    wc.lpszClassName = szAppName;

    return(RegisterClass(&wc));
}

// create and show main window
BOOL InitInstance(HINSTANCE hInstance, int nCmdShow)
{
```

```
HWND    hWnd;
hInst = hInstance;
hWnd = CreateWindow(szAppName, szTitle,
                    WS_OVERLAPPEDWINDOW,
                    70, 120, 500, 240,
                    NULL, NULL, hInstance, NULL);

if (!hWnd)
   {
   return FALSE;
   }

ShowWindow(hWnd, nCmdShow);
UpdateWindow(hWnd);

return TRUE;
}
```

TOUT.C

```
// TOUT.C
#include <windows.h>
#include <windowsx.h>
#include "globals.h"

LRESULT CALLBACK WndProc(HWND hWnd,
                         UINT uMessage,
                         WPARAM wParam,
                         LPARAM lParam)
{
    PAINTSTRUCT ps;
    HDC hDC;
    static UINT fuAlign = TA_LEFT;
    static int nExtraSpace = 0;
    static COLORREF clrref = RGB(0, 0, 0);
    static COLORREF bk_clrref = RGB(255, 255, 255);
    static int fnBkMode = OPAQUE;
    static BOOL bJustify = FALSE;
    LPCSTR lpcstr = "This is a TextOut example.";

    switch (uMessage)
    {
        case WM_COMMAND:
            switch (GET_WM_COMMAND_ID(wParam,lParam))
            {
                case IDM_ABOUT:
                    // create an about dialog box
                    DialogBox(hInst, "ABOUTDLG",
```

```
                         hWnd, (DLGPROC)About);
         break;

    // set text alignment
    case IDM_LEFT:
         fuAlign = TA_LEFT;
         InvalidateRect(hWnd, NULL, TRUE);
         break;

    case IDM_RIGHT:
         fuAlign = TA_RIGHT;
         InvalidateRect(hWnd, NULL, TRUE);
         break;

    case IDM_CENTER:
         fuAlign = TA_CENTER;
         InvalidateRect(hWnd, NULL, TRUE);
         break;

    // set space between characters
    case IDM_SMALL:
         nExtraSpace = 0;
         InvalidateRect(hWnd, NULL, TRUE);
         break;

    case IDM_MEDIUM:
         nExtraSpace = 1;
         InvalidateRect(hWnd, NULL, TRUE);
         break;

    case IDM_LARGE:
         nExtraSpace = 2;
         InvalidateRect(hWnd, NULL, TRUE);
       break;

    // set text color
    case IDM_WHITE:
         clrref = RGB(255, 255, 255);
         InvalidateRect(hWnd, NULL, TRUE);
         break;

    case IDM_BLACK:
         clrref = RGB(0, 0, 0);
         InvalidateRect(hWnd, NULL, TRUE);
         break;

    case IDM_RED:
         clrref = RGB(255, 0, 0);
```

```
                InvalidateRect(hWnd, NULL, TRUE);
                break;

        case IDM_GREEN:
                clrref = RGB(0, 255, 0);
                InvalidateRect(hWnd, NULL, TRUE);
                break;

        case IDM_BLUE:
                clrref = RGB(0, 0, 255);
                InvalidateRect(hWnd, NULL, TRUE);
                break;

        // set text background color
        case IDM_BK_WHITE:
                bk_clrref = RGB(255, 255, 255);
                InvalidateRect(hWnd, NULL, TRUE);
                break;

        case IDM_BK_BLACK:
                bk_clrref = RGB(0, 0, 0);
                InvalidateRect(hWnd, NULL, TRUE);
                break;

        case IDM_BK_RED:
                bk_clrref = RGB(255, 0, 0);
                InvalidateRect(hWnd, NULL, TRUE);
                break;

        case IDM_BK_GREEN:
                bk_clrref = RGB(0, 255, 0);
                InvalidateRect(hWnd, NULL, TRUE);
                break;

        case IDM_BK_BLUE:
                bk_clrref = RGB(0, 0, 255);
                InvalidateRect(hWnd, NULL, TRUE);
                break;

        // set background mode
        case IDM_OPAQUE:
                fnBkMode = OPAQUE;
                InvalidateRect(hWnd, NULL, TRUE);
                break;

        case IDM_TRANSPARENT:
                fnBkMode = TRANSPARENT;
                InvalidateRect(hWnd, NULL, TRUE);
```

```
                    break;

                // set justification
            case IDM_JUSTIFY_YES:
                bJustify = TRUE;
                InvalidateRect(hWnd, NULL, TRUE);
                break;

            case IDM_JUSTIFY_NO:
                bJustify = FALSE;
                InvalidateRect(hWnd, NULL, TRUE);
                break;

            default:
                return DefWindowProc(hWnd, uMessage,
                                     wParam, lParam);
        }
        break;

    case WM_PAINT:
        hDC = BeginPaint(hWnd, &ps);
        SetMapMode(hDC, MM_TEXT);

        // draw a line as alignment mark
        MoveToEx(hDC, 250, 20, NULL);
        LineTo(hDC, 250, 80);

        SetTextAlign(hDC, fuAlign);
        SetTextCharacterExtra(hDC, nExtraSpace);
        SetTextColor(hDC, clrref);
        SetBkColor(hDC, bk_clrref);
        SetBkMode(hDC, fnBkMode);
        if(bJustify) SetTextJustification(hDC, 60, 4);
        if(!bJustify) SetTextJustification(hDC, 0, 4);
        TextOut(hDC, 250, 40, lpcstr, strlen(lpcstr));
        EndPaint(hWnd, &ps);
        break;

    case WM_DESTROY:
        PostQuitMessage(0);
        break;

    default:
        return DefWindowProc(hWnd, uMessage,
                             wParam, lParam);
    }
    return 0;
}
```

ABOUT.C

```
// ABOUT.C
#include <windows.h>
#include <windowsx.h>
#include "globals.h"

// procedures for ABOUT dialog box
LRESULT CALLBACK About(HWND hDlg,
                       UINT uMessage,
                       WPARAM wParam,
                       LPARAM lParam)
{
    switch (uMessage)
      {
        case WM_COMMAND:
            switch (GET_WM_COMMAND_ID(wParam,lParam))
            {
                case IDOK:
                case IDCANCEL:
                    {
                    EndDialog(hDlg, TRUE);
                    return(TRUE);
                    }
                    break;
            }
      }
    return FALSE;
}
```

TOUT.RC

```
#include "windows.h"
#include "globals.h"
#include <winver.h>

APPNAME ICON ICONFILE

RCINCLUDE ABOUT.DLG

APPNAME MENU
BEGIN
    POPUP        "A&lignment"
      BEGIN
        MENUITEM "&Left",    IDM_LEFT
        MENUITEM "&Right",   IDM_RIGHT
```

```
            MENUITEM "&Center",   IDM_CENTER
        END
    POPUP       "&Spacing"
      BEGIN
        MENUITEM "&Small",    IDM_SMALL
        MENUITEM "&Medium",   IDM_MEDIUM
        MENUITEM "&Large",    IDM_LARGE
      END
    POPUP       "&TextColor"
      BEGIN
        MENUITEM "&White"     IDM_WHITE
        MENUITEM "B&lack"     IDM_BLACK
        MENUITEM "&Red",      IDM_RED
        MENUITEM "&Green",    IDM_GREEN
        MENUITEM "&Blue",     IDM_BLUE
      END
    POPUP       "&BkColor"
      BEGIN
        MENUITEM "&White"     IDM_BK_WHITE
        MENUITEM "B&lack"     IDM_BK_BLACK
        MENUITEM "&Red",      IDM_BK_RED
        MENUITEM "&Green",    IDM_BK_GREEN
        MENUITEM "&Blue",     IDM_BK_BLUE
      END
    POPUP       "Bk&Mode"
      BEGIN
        MENUITEM "&Opaque"        IDM_OPAQUE
        MENUITEM "&Transparent" IDM_TRANSPARENT
      END
    POPUP       "&Justify"
      BEGIN
        MENUITEM "&Yes"       IDM_JUSTIFY_YES
        MENUITEM "&No"        IDM_JUSTIFY_NO
      END
    MENUITEM "&About", IDM_ABOUT
END
```

ABOUT.DLG

```
ABOUTDLG DIALOG DISCARDABLE  22, 17, 167, 73
STYLE DS_MODALFRAME | WS_CAPTION | WS_SYSMENU
CAPTION SZABOUT
BEGIN
    DEFPUSHBUTTON   "OK", IDOK, 132, 2, 32, 14, WS_GROUP
    ICON            SZAPPNAME,      -1, 3, 2, 18, 20
    LTEXT           SZAPPNAME,      -1, 30, 12,  50, 8
```

```
        LTEXT           SZDESCRIPTION,  -1, 30, 22, 150, 8
        LTEXT           SZVERSION,      -1, 30, 32, 150, 8
        LTEXT           SZCOMPANYNAME,  -1, 30, 42, 150, 8
    END
```

TOUT.ICO

CASE 8-3: CREATE FONT

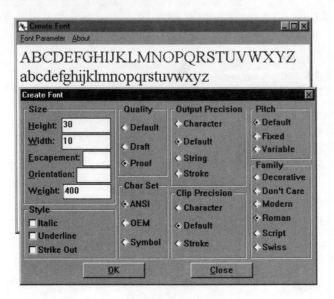

FIGURE 8-3

Sometimes an application must use a specific font that is chosen according to very specific parameters such as height, weight and width. This program lets users create and preview a font. First, the users specify various parameters via the dialog box shown in Figure 8-3. When the OK button is clicked, these font parameters are passed to the `CreateFont()` function, which creates what is known in Windows as a *logical font*. Then the font mapper mechanism in Windows maps this logical font to the *physical font* that most closely matches the parameters (physical fonts are fonts that have actually been installed into the Windows environment). The handle returned by `CreateFont()` is passed to the `SelectObject()` function to associate this font with the current device context. Then the code uses the `TextOut()` function to draw the 26 characters of the alphabet (both upper- and lower-case) in the main window client area.

GLOBALS.H

```
// GLOBALS.H - header file for global variables
//              and function prototypes

// Product identifier string definitions
#define APPNAME         CrFont
#define ICONFILE        CrFont.ico
#define SZAPPNAME       "CrFont"
#define SZDESCRIPTION   "Create Font"
#define SZVERSION       "Version 1.0"
#define SZCOMPANYNAME   "\251 M&&T Books, 1994"
#define SZABOUT         "About"

// Global function prototypes.
BOOL InitApplication(HINSTANCE);
BOOL InitInstance(HINSTANCE, int);

// Callback functions called by Windows.
LRESULT CALLBACK WndProc(HWND, UINT, WPARAM, LPARAM);
LRESULT CALLBACK About(HWND, UINT, WPARAM, LPARAM);
LRESULT CALLBACK FontDlgProc(HWND, UINT, WPARAM, LPARAM);

// Menu item ID
#define IDM_ABOUT               99
#define IDM_FONT_PARAMETER      100

// Dialog box ID
#define IDD_CREATEFONT          200

// Dialog box control ID
#define IDC_FONT_HEIGHT         101
#define IDC_FONT_WIDTH          102
#define IDC_FONT_ESCAPEMENT     103
#define IDC_FONT_ORIENTATION    104
#define IDC_FONT_WEIGHT         105

#define IDC_STYLE_ITALIC        106
#define IDC_STYLE_UNDERLINE     107
#define IDC_STYLE_STRIKEOUT     108

#define IDC_QUALITY_DEFAULT     109
#define IDC_QUALITY_DRAFT       110
#define IDC_QUALITY_PROOF       111

#define IDC_PITCH_DEFAULT       112
#define IDC_PITCH_FIXED         113
#define IDC_PITCH_VARIABLE      114
```

```
#define IDC_CHARSET_ANSI       115
#define IDC_CHARSET_OEM        116
#define IDC_CHARSET_SYMBOL     117

#define IDC_OP_CHARACTER       118
#define IDC_OP_DEFAULT         119
#define IDC_OP_STRING          120
#define IDC_OP_STROKE          121

#define IDC_CP_CHARACTER       122
#define IDC_CP_DEFAULT         123
#define IDC_CP_STROKE          124

#define IDC_FAMILY_DECORATIVE  125
#define IDC_FAMILY_DONTCARE    126
#define IDC_FAMILY_MODERN      127
#define IDC_FAMILY_ROMAN       128
#define IDC_FAMILY_SCRIPT      129
#define IDC_FAMILY_SWISS       130

#define IDC_CLOSE              132

// Global variable declarations.
extern HINSTANCE hInst;        // The current instance handle
extern char szAppName[];       // The name of this application
extern char szTitle[];         // The title bar text
extern HWND hWnd, hFontDlg;
extern DLGPROC lpProcFont;

extern int nHeight, nWidth, nWeight;
extern int nEscapement, nOrientation;
extern BYTE cItalic, cUnderline, cStrikeOut;
extern BYTE cCharSet, cOutputPrecision;
extern BYTE cClipPrecision, cQuality;
extern BYTE cPitchAndFamily;
extern RECT rect;
```

WINMAIN.C

```
// WINMAIN.C
#include <windows.h>
#include "globals.h"

extern HWND hFontDlg;
```

```
int APIENTRY WinMain(HINSTANCE hInstance,
                     HINSTANCE hPrevInstance,
                     LPSTR lpCmdLine,
                     int nCmdShow)
{
    MSG msg;

    // register main window class
    if (!hPrevInstance)
        {
        if (!InitApplication(hInstance))
            {
            return FALSE;
            }
        }

    // create and show main window
    if (!InitInstance(hInstance, nCmdShow))
        {
        return FALSE;
        }

    // process window messages
    while (GetMessage(&msg, NULL, 0, 0))
        {
            TranslateMessage(&msg);
            DispatchMessage(&msg);
        }
    return msg.wParam;
}
```

INIT.C

```
// INIT.C
#include <windows.h>
#include "globals.h"

HINSTANCE hInst;
char szAppName[] = SZAPPNAME;
char szTitle[] = SZDESCRIPTION;

// register main window class
BOOL InitApplication(HINSTANCE hInstance)
{
    WNDCLASS  wc;

    wc.style          = CS_HREDRAW | CS_VREDRAW;
```

```
    wc.lpfnWndProc   = (WNDPROC)WndProc;
    wc.cbClsExtra    = 0;
    wc.cbWndExtra    = 0;
    wc.hInstance     = hInstance;
    wc.hIcon         = LoadIcon(hInstance, szAppName);
    wc.hCursor       = LoadCursor(NULL, IDC_ARROW);
    wc.hbrBackground = (HBRUSH)(COLOR_WINDOW + 1);
    wc.lpszMenuName  = szAppName;
    wc.lpszClassName = szAppName;

    return(RegisterClass(&wc));
}

// create and show main window
BOOL InitInstance(HINSTANCE hInstance, int nCmdShow)
{
    HWND    hWnd;
    hInst = hInstance;
    hWnd = CreateWindow(szAppName, szTitle,
                        WS_OVERLAPPEDWINDOW,
                        CW_USEDEFAULT, CW_USEDEFAULT,
                        CW_USEDEFAULT, CW_USEDEFAULT,
                        NULL, NULL, hInstance, NULL);

    if (!hWnd)
       {
       return FALSE;
       }

    ShowWindow(hWnd, nCmdShow);
    UpdateWindow(hWnd);

    return TRUE;
}
```

CRFONT.C

```
// CRFONT.C
#include <windows.h>
#include <windowsx.h>
#include "globals.h"

int nHeight, nWidth, nWeight;
int nEscapement, nOrientation;
BYTE cItalic, cUnderline, cStrikeOut;
BYTE cCharSet, cOutputPrecision;
BYTE cClipPrecision, cQuality;
```

```
BYTE cPitchAndFamily;
RECT rect;

HWND hFontDlg;
DLGPROC lpProcFont;

LRESULT CALLBACK WndProc(HWND hWnd,
                         UINT uMessage,
                         WPARAM wParam,
                         LPARAM lParam)
{
    PAINTSTRUCT ps;
    HFONT hFont;
    HDC hDC;
    BOOL lpTranslated;
    // define sample text
    LPSTR lpText = "ABCDEFGHIJKLMNOPQRSTUVWXYZ";
    LPSTR lpTexts = "abcdefghijklmnopqrstuvwxyz";

    switch (uMessage)
    {
        case WM_CREATE:
            // set initial parameter values for
            // CreateFont function
            nHeight = 30; nWidth = 10; nWeight = 400;
            cCharSet = ANSI_CHARSET;
            cOutputPrecision = OUT_DEFAULT_PRECIS;
            cClipPrecision = CLIP_DEFAULT_PRECIS;
            cQuality = DEFAULT_QUALITY;
            break;

        case WM_PAINT:
            hDC = BeginPaint(hWnd, &ps);
            SetMapMode(hDC, MM_TEXT);
            SetTextColor(hDC, RGB(0, 0, 0));
            SetBkColor(hDC, RGB(255, 255, 255));
            GetClientRect(hWnd, &rect);
            if(hFontDlg){
              // set font parameters
             nHeight = GetDlgItemInt(hFontDlg,
                                IDC_FONT_HEIGHT,
                                &lpTranslated, FALSE);
             if(nHeight < 1) nHeight = 30;
             nWidth = GetDlgItemInt(hFontDlg,
                                IDC_FONT_WIDTH,
                                &lpTranslated, FALSE);
             nEscapement = GetDlgItemInt(hFontDlg,
                                IDC_FONT_ESCAPEMENT,
```

```
                                    &lpTranslated, TRUE);
        nOrientation = GetDlgItemInt(hFontDlg,
                           IDC_FONT_ORIENTATION,
                           &lpTranslated, TRUE);
        nWeight = GetDlgItemInt(hFontDlg,
                           IDC_FONT_WEIGHT,
                           &lpTranslated, FALSE);
        cItalic = (BYTE)(IsDlgButtonChecked(hFontDlg,
                           IDC_STYLE_ITALIC) ? 1 : 0);
        cUnderline = (BYTE)(IsDlgButtonChecked(
                           hFontDlg,
                           IDC_STYLE_UNDERLINE) ? 1 : 0);
        cStrikeOut = (BYTE)(IsDlgButtonChecked(
                           hFontDlg,
                           IDC_STYLE_STRIKEOUT) ? 1 : 0);
    }

    // create font
    hFont = CreateFont(nHeight, nWidth,nEscapement,
                       nOrientation,
                       nWeight, cItalic, cUnderline,
                       cStrikeOut,
                       cCharSet, cOutputPrecision,
                       cClipPrecision,
                       cQuality, cPitchAndFamily,
                       NULL);
    SelectObject(hDC, hFont);

    // display sample text in client area
    TextOut(hDC, 5, 5, lpText, strlen(lpText));
    TextOut(hDC, 5, 5+nHeight,
                       lpTexts, strlen(lpTexts));
    EndPaint(hWnd, &ps);
    break;

case WM_COMMAND:
    switch (GET_WM_COMMAND_ID(wParam,lParam))
    {
        case IDM_FONT_PARAMETER:
            // create a set-font-parameter
            // dialog box
            lpProcFont = MakeProcInstance(
                    (FARPROC)FontDlgProc, hInst);
            hFontDlg = CreateDialog(hInst,
                MAKEINTRESOURCE(IDD_CREATEFONT),
                            hWnd, lpProcFont);
            break;
```

```
                case IDM_ABOUT:
                        // create an about dialog box
                        DialogBox(hInst, "ABOUTDLG",
                                    hWnd, (DLGPROC)About);
                        break;

                default:
                        return DefWindowProc(hWnd, uMessage,
                                               wParam, lParam);

            }
            break;

        case WM_DESTROY:
            FreeProcInstance(lpProcFont);
            PostQuitMessage(0);
            break;

        default:
            return DefWindowProc(hWnd, uMessage,
                                   wParam, lParam);

    }
    return 0;
}
```

FONT.C

```
// FONT.C
#include <windows.h>
#include <windowsx.h>
#include "globals.h"

HWND hWnd, hFontDlg;
int nHeight, nWidth, nWeight;
int nEscapement, nOrientation;
BYTE cItalic, cUnderline, cStrikeOut;
BYTE cCharSet, cOutputPrecision;
BYTE cClipPrecision, cQuality;
BYTE cPitchAndFamily;

LRESULT CALLBACK FontDlgProc(HWND hFontDlg,
                                UINT uMessage,
                                WPARAM wParam,
                                LPARAM lParam)
{
    switch (uMessage)
    {
        case WM_INITDIALOG:
```

```
              // set default values
          SetDlgItemText(hFontDlg,
                      IDC_FONT_HEIGHT, "30");
          SetDlgItemText(hFontDlg, IDC_FONT_WIDTH, "10");
          SetDlgItemText(hFontDlg,
                      IDC_FONT_WEIGHT, "400");
          CheckRadioButton(hFontDlg, IDC_QUALITY_DEFAULT,
                      IDC_QUALITY_PROOF,
                      IDC_QUALITY_DEFAULT);
          CheckRadioButton(hFontDlg, IDC_CHARSET_ANSI,
                      IDC_CHARSET_SYMBOL,
                      IDC_CHARSET_ANSI);
          CheckRadioButton(hFontDlg, IDC_OP_CHARACTER,
                      IDC_OP_STROKE, IDC_OP_DEFAULT);
          CheckRadioButton(hFontDlg, IDC_CP_CHARACTER,
                      IDC_CP_STROKE, IDC_CP_DEFAULT);
          CheckRadioButton(hFontDlg, IDC_PITCH_DEFAULT,
                      IDC_PITCH_VARIABLE,
                      IDC_PITCH_DEFAULT);
          CheckRadioButton(hFontDlg,
                      IDC_FAMILY_DECORATIVE,
                      IDC_FAMILY_SWISS,
                      IDC_FAMILY_SWISS);
      break;

  case WM_COMMAND:
      switch (GET_WM_COMMAND_ID(wParam,lParam))
      {
         case IDC_STYLE_ITALIC:
         case IDC_STYLE_UNDERLINE:
         case IDC_STYLE_STRIKEOUT:
              CheckDlgButton(hFontDlg, wParam,
                  IsDlgButtonChecked(hFontDlg,
                          wParam) ? 0 : 1);
              break;

         case IDC_QUALITY_DEFAULT:
              CheckRadioButton(hFontDlg,
                      IDC_QUALITY_DEFAULT,
                      IDC_QUALITY_PROOF,
                      IDC_QUALITY_DEFAULT);
              cQuality = (BYTE)DEFAULT_QUALITY;
              break;

         case IDC_QUALITY_DRAFT:
              CheckRadioButton(hFontDlg,
                       IDC_QUALITY_DEFAULT,
                       IDC_QUALITY_PROOF,
```

```
                         IDC_QUALITY_DRAFT);
          cQuality = (BYTE)DRAFT_QUALITY;
          break;

case IDC_QUALITY_PROOF:
     CheckRadioButton(hFontDlg,
                    IDC_QUALITY_DEFAULT,
                    IDC_QUALITY_PROOF,
                    IDC_QUALITY_PROOF);
          cQuality = (BYTE)PROOF_QUALITY;
          break;

case IDC_CHARSET_ANSI:
     CheckRadioButton(hFontDlg,
                    IDC_CHARSET_ANSI,
                    IDC_CHARSET_SYMBOL,
                    IDC_CHARSET_ANSI);
          cCharSet = (BYTE)ANSI_CHARSET;
          break;

case IDC_CHARSET_OEM:
     CheckRadioButton(hFontDlg,
                    IDC_CHARSET_ANSI,
                    IDC_CHARSET_SYMBOL,
                    IDC_CHARSET_OEM);
          cCharSet = (BYTE)OEM_CHARSET;
          break;

case IDC_CHARSET_SYMBOL:
     CheckRadioButton(hFontDlg,
                    IDC_CHARSET_ANSI,
                    IDC_CHARSET_SYMBOL,
                    IDC_CHARSET_SYMBOL);
          cCharSet = (BYTE)SYMBOL_CHARSET;
          break;

case IDC_OP_CHARACTER:
     CheckRadioButton(hFontDlg,
          IDC_OP_CHARACTER,
          IDC_OP_STROKE, IDC_OP_CHARACTER);
          cOutputPrecision =
                    (BYTE)OUT_CHARACTER_PRECIS;
          break;

case IDC_OP_DEFAULT:
     CheckRadioButton(hFontDlg,
          IDC_OP_CHARACTER,
          IDC_OP_STROKE, IDC_OP_DEFAULT);
```

581

```
            cOutputPrecision =
                (BYTE)OUT_DEFAULT_PRECIS;
            break;

        case IDC_OP_STRING:
            CheckRadioButton(hFontDlg,
                IDC_OP_CHARACTER,
                IDC_OP_STROKE, IDC_OP_STRING);
            cOutputPrecision =
                (BYTE)OUT_STRING_PRECIS;
            break;

        case IDC_OP_STROKE:
            CheckRadioButton(hFontDlg,
                IDC_OP_CHARACTER,
                IDC_OP_STROKE, IDC_OP_STROKE);
            cOutputPrecision =
                (BYTE)OUT_STROKE_PRECIS;
            break;

        case IDC_CP_CHARACTER:
            CheckRadioButton(hFontDlg,
                IDC_CP_CHARACTER,
                IDC_CP_STROKE, IDC_CP_CHARACTER);
            cClipPrecision =
                (BYTE)CLIP_CHARACTER_PRECIS;
            break;

        case IDC_CP_DEFAULT:
            CheckRadioButton(hFontDlg,
                IDC_CP_CHARACTER,
                IDC_CP_STROKE, IDC_CP_DEFAULT);
            cClipPrecision =
                (BYTE)CLIP_DEFAULT_PRECIS;
            break;

        case IDC_CP_STROKE:
            CheckRadioButton(hFontDlg,
                IDC_CP_CHARACTER,
                IDC_CP_STROKE, IDC_CP_STROKE);
            cClipPrecision =
                (BYTE)CLIP_STROKE_PRECIS;
            break;

        case IDC_PITCH_DEFAULT:
            CheckRadioButton(hFontDlg,
                IDC_PITCH_DEFAULT,
                IDC_PITCH_VARIABLE,
```

```
                    IDC_PITCH_DEFAULT);
        cPitchAndFamily &= 0xF0;
        cPitchAndFamily |= (BYTE)DEFAULT_PITCH;
        break;

case IDC_PITCH_FIXED:
        CheckRadioButton(hFontDlg,
                IDC_PITCH_DEFAULT,
                IDC_PITCH_VARIABLE,
                IDC_PITCH_FIXED);
        cPitchAndFamily &= 0xF0;
        cPitchAndFamily |= (BYTE)FIXED_PITCH;
        break;

case IDC_PITCH_VARIABLE:
        CheckRadioButton(hFontDlg,
                IDC_PITCH_DEFAULT,
                IDC_PITCH_VARIABLE,
                IDC_PITCH_VARIABLE);
        cPitchAndFamily &= 0xF0;
        cPitchAndFamily |=
                (BYTE)VARIABLE_PITCH;
        break;

case IDC_FAMILY_DECORATIVE:
        CheckRadioButton(hFontDlg,
                IDC_FAMILY_DECORATIVE,
                IDC_FAMILY_SWISS,
                IDC_FAMILY_DECORATIVE);
        cPitchAndFamily &= 0x0F;
        cPitchAndFamily |=
                (BYTE)(FF_DECORATIVE);
        break;

case IDC_FAMILY_DONTCARE:
        CheckRadioButton(hFontDlg,
                IDC_FAMILY_DECORATIVE,
                IDC_FAMILY_SWISS,
                IDC_FAMILY_DONTCARE);
        cPitchAndFamily &= 0x0F;
        cPitchAndFamily |= (BYTE)(FF_DONTCARE);
        break;

case IDC_FAMILY_MODERN:
        CheckRadioButton(hFontDlg,
                IDC_FAMILY_DECORATIVE,
                IDC_FAMILY_SWISS,
                IDC_FAMILY_MODERN);
```

```
            cPitchAndFamily &= 0x0F;
            cPitchAndFamily |= (BYTE)(FF_MODERN);
            break;

    case IDC_FAMILY_ROMAN:
            CheckRadioButton(hFontDlg,
                IDC_FAMILY_DECORATIVE,
                IDC_FAMILY_SWISS,
                IDC_FAMILY_ROMAN);
            cPitchAndFamily &= 0x0F;
            cPitchAndFamily |= (BYTE)(FF_ROMAN);
            break;

    case IDC_FAMILY_SCRIPT:
            CheckRadioButton(hFontDlg,
                IDC_FAMILY_DECORATIVE,
                IDC_FAMILY_SWISS,
                IDC_FAMILY_SCRIPT);
            cPitchAndFamily &= 0x0F;
            cPitchAndFamily |= (BYTE)(FF_SCRIPT);
            break;

    case IDC_FAMILY_SWISS:
            CheckRadioButton(hFontDlg,
                IDC_FAMILY_DECORATIVE,
                IDC_FAMILY_SWISS,
                IDC_FAMILY_SWISS);
            cPitchAndFamily &= 0x0F;
            cPitchAndFamily |= (BYTE)(FF_SWISS);
            break;

    case IDOK:
            InvalidateRect(hWnd, &rect, TRUE);
            break;

    case IDCANCEL:
    case IDC_CLOSE:
            DestroyWindow(hFontDlg);
            hFontDlg = 0;
            break;

    default:
     return FALSE;
  }
  break;

default:
    return FALSE;
```

```
    }
    return 0;
}
```

ABOUT.C

```
// ABOUT.C
#include <windows.h>
#include <windowsx.h>
#include "globals.h"

// procedures for ABOUT dialog box
LRESULT CALLBACK About(HWND hDlg,
                       UINT uMessage,
                       WPARAM wParam,
                       LPARAM lParam)
{
    switch (uMessage)
      {
        case WM_COMMAND:
            switch (GET_WM_COMMAND_ID(wParam,lParam))
              {
                case IDOK:
                case IDCANCEL:
                    {
                    EndDialog(hDlg, TRUE);
                    return(TRUE);
                    }
                    break;
              }
      }
    return FALSE;
}
```

CRFONT.RC

```
#include "windows.h"
#include "globals.h"
#include <winver.h>

APPNAME ICON ICONFILE

RCINCLUDE ABOUT.DLG
RCINCLUDE FONT.DLG
```

```
APPNAME MENU
BEGIN
    MENUITEM "&Font Parameter", IDM_FONT_PARAMETER
    MENUITEM "&About", IDM_ABOUT
END
```

FONT.DLG

```
DLGINCLUDE RCDATA DISCARDABLE
BEGIN
    "GLOBALS.H\0"
END


IDD_CREATEFONT DIALOG 27, 19, 237, 143
STYLE WS_POPUP | WS_VISIBLE | WS_CAPTION
CAPTION "Create Font"
BEGIN
    GROUPBOX      "Size", -1, 2, 2, 75, 79, WS_TABSTOP
    LTEXT         "&Height:", -1, 6, 15, 24, 10
    EDITTEXT      IDC_FONT_HEIGHT, 33, 13, 40, 12
    LTEXT         "&Width:", -1, 6, 27, 24, 10
    EDITTEXT      IDC_FONT_WIDTH, 33, 26, 40, 12
    LTEXT         "&Escapement:", -1, 6, 40, 43, 10
    EDITTEXT      IDC_FONT_ESCAPEMENT, 50, 39, 23, 12,
                  ES_AUTOHSCROLL
    LTEXT         "&Orientation:", -1, 6, 53, 38, 10
    EDITTEXT      IDC_FONT_ORIENTATION, 45, 52, 28, 12,
                  ES_AUTOHSCROLL
    LTEXT         "W&eight:", -1, 6, 66, 29, 10
    EDITTEXT      IDC_FONT_WEIGHT, 34, 65, 39, 12
    GROUPBOX      "Style", -1, 2, 81, 75, 43, WS_TABSTOP
    CHECKBOX      "Italic", IDC_STYLE_ITALIC, 6, 91, 68, 10
    CHECKBOX      "Underline", IDC_STYLE_UNDERLINE,
                  6, 101, 68, 10
    CHECKBOX      "Strike Out", IDC_STYLE_STRIKEOUT,
                  6, 112, 68, 10
    GROUPBOX      "Quality", -1, 79, 2, 40, 57, WS_TABSTOP
    CONTROL       "Default", IDC_QUALITY_DEFAULT, "Button",
                  BS_RADIOBUTTON | WS_GROUP | WS_TABSTOP,
                  81, 16, 36, 10
    CONTROL       "Draft", IDC_QUALITY_DRAFT, "Button",
                  BS_RADIOBUTTON |
                  WS_GROUP | WS_TABSTOP, 81, 31, 36, 10
    CONTROL       "Proof", IDC_QUALITY_PROOF, "Button",
                  BS_RADIOBUTTON |
                  WS_TABSTOP, 81, 44, 36, 10
```

```
GROUPBOX      "Char Set", -1, 79, 62, 40, 62, WS_TABSTOP
CONTROL       "ANSI", IDC_CHARSET_ANSI, "Button",
              BS_RADIOBUTTON |
              WS_TABSTOP, 81, 76, 36, 10
CONTROL       "OEM", IDC_CHARSET_OEM, "Button",
              BS_RADIOBUTTON |
              WS_TABSTOP, 81, 91, 36, 10
CONTROL       "Symbol", IDC_CHARSET_SYMBOL, "Button",
              BS_RADIOBUTTON | WS_TABSTOP, 81, 106, 36, 10
GROUPBOX      "Output Precision", -1, 121, 2, 61, 65,
              WS_TABSTOP
CONTROL       "Character", IDC_OP_CHARACTER, "Button",
              BS_RADIOBUTTON | WS_TABSTOP, 124, 13, 55, 10
CONTROL       "Default", IDC_OP_DEFAULT, "Button",
              BS_RADIOBUTTON |
              WS_TABSTOP, 124, 27, 55, 10
CONTROL       "String", IDC_OP_STRING, "Button",
              BS_RADIOBUTTON |
              WS_TABSTOP, 124, 40, 54, 10
CONTROL       "Stroke", IDC_OP_STROKE, "Button",
              BS_RADIOBUTTON |
              WS_TABSTOP, 124, 52, 55, 10
GROUPBOX      "Clip Precision", -1, 121, 68, 61, 56,
              WS_TABSTOP
CONTROL       "Character", IDC_CP_CHARACTER, "Button",
              BS_RADIOBUTTON | WS_TABSTOP, 124, 79, 55, 10
CONTROL       "Default", IDC_CP_DEFAULT, "Button",
              BS_RADIOBUTTON |
              WS_TABSTOP, 124, 93, 55, 10
CONTROL       "Stroke", IDC_CP_STROKE, "Button",
              BS_RADIOBUTTON |
              WS_TABSTOP, 124, 107, 55, 10
GROUPBOX      "Pitch", -1, 185, 2, 49, 44, WS_TABSTOP
CONTROL       "Default", IDC_PITCH_DEFAULT, "Button",
              BS_RADIOBUTTON | WS_TABSTOP, 187, 12, 38, 10
CONTROL       "Fixed", IDC_PITCH_FIXED, "Button",
              BS_RADIOBUTTON |
              WS_TABSTOP, 187, 23, 38, 10
CONTROL       "Variable", IDC_PITCH_VARIABLE, "Button",
              BS_RADIOBUTTON | WS_TABSTOP, 187, 33, 38, 10
GROUPBOX      "Family", -1, 185, 46, 49, 78, WS_TABSTOP
CONTROL       "Decorative", IDC_FAMILY_DECORATIVE,
              "Button", BS_RADIOBUTTON | WS_TABSTOP,
              187, 55, 45, 10
CONTROL       "Don't Care", IDC_FAMILY_DONTCARE, "Button",
              BS_RADIOBUTTON | WS_TABSTOP, 187, 66, 46, 10
CONTROL       "Modern", IDC_FAMILY_MODERN, "Button",
```

587

```
                    BS_RADIOBUTTON | WS_TABSTOP, 187, 76, 38, 10
        CONTROL     "Roman", IDC_FAMILY_ROMAN, "Button",
                    BS_RADIOBUTTON |
                    WS_TABSTOP, 187, 87, 38, 10
        CONTROL     "Script", IDC_FAMILY_SCRIPT, "Button",
                    BS_RADIOBUTTON | WS_TABSTOP, 187, 99, 38, 10
        CONTROL     "Swiss", IDC_FAMILY_SWISS, "Button",
                    BS_RADIOBUTTON |
                    WS_TABSTOP, 187, 110, 38, 10
        PUSHBUTTON  "&OK", IDOK, 50, 127, 50, 12
        PUSHBUTTON  "&Close", IDC_CLOSE, 137, 127, 50, 12
    END
```

ABOUT.DLG

```
    ABOUTDLG DIALOG DISCARDABLE  22, 17, 167, 73
    STYLE DS_MODALFRAME | WS_CAPTION | WS_SYSMENU
    CAPTION SZABOUT
    BEGIN
        DEFPUSHBUTTON    "OK", IDOK, 132, 2, 32, 14, WS_GROUP
        ICON             SZAPPNAME,      -1, 3, 2, 18, 20
        LTEXT            SZAPPNAME,      -1, 30, 12,  50, 8
        LTEXT            SZDESCRIPTION, -1, 30, 22, 150, 8
        LTEXT            SZVERSION,      -1, 30, 32, 150, 8
        LTEXT            SZCOMPANYNAME, -1, 30, 42, 150, 8
    END
```

FONT.ICO

CASE 8-4: GET TEXT METRICS

Get Text Metrics			
Choose-Font About			
Height	16	Italic	No
Ascent	13	Underlined	No
Descent	3	Struck Out	No
Int Leading	3	First Char	32
Ext leading	0	Last Char	255
Ave Char Width	7	Default Char	128
Max Char Width	14	Break Char	32
Weight	700		
		Pitch	Fixed Pitch
Overhang	0	Family	Swiss
Digitized Aspect X	96	Char Set	ANSI
Digitized Aspect Y	96		

FIGURE 8-4

F onts, as you have perhaps gathered by now, are much more than simple letters of the alphabet. Every font has associated with it a number properties and attributes, known as *font metrics*. These metrics include font height, font weight, font ascent, font descent, and maximum character width. All font properties are stored in a TEXTMETRIC structure.

This case uses the GetTextMetrics() function to retrieve these properties for a non-TrueType font. The font metrics information is then displayed in the main window client area, using a long series of TextOut() calls.

The user can choose any font available in the system by using the choose font dialog box. This common dialog box was presented in Case 7-2. The dialog box is activated using the Choose Font menu item. The following case shows how to obtain the text metrics for a TrueType font.

GLOBALS.H

```
// GLOBALS.H - header file for global variables
//               and function prototypes

// Product identifier string definitions
#define APPNAME       TMetrics
#define ICONFILE      TMetrics.ico
#define SZAPPNAME     "TMetrics"
#define SZDESCRIPTION "Get Text Metrics"
#define SZVERSION     "Version 1.0"
#define SZCOMPANYNAME "\251 M&&T Books, 1994"
#define SZABOUT       "About"

// Global function prototypes.
BOOL InitApplication(HINSTANCE);
BOOL InitInstance(HINSTANCE, int);

// Callback functions called by Windows.
LRESULT CALLBACK WndProc(HWND, UINT, WPARAM, LPARAM);
LRESULT CALLBACK About(HWND, UINT, WPARAM, LPARAM);

// Menu item ID
#define IDM_ABOUT       101
#define IDM_CHOOSE_FONT 102

// Global variable declarations.
extern HINSTANCE hInst;       // The current instance handle
extern char szAppName[];      // The name of this application
extern char szTitle[];        // The title bar text
```

WINMAIN.C

```
// WINMAIN.C
#include <windows.h>
#include "globals.h"

int APIENTRY WinMain(HINSTANCE hInstance,
                     HINSTANCE hPrevInstance,
                     LPSTR lpCmdLine,
                     int nCmdShow)
{
    MSG msg;

    // register main window class
    if (!hPrevInstance)
```

```
        {
        if (!InitApplication(hInstance))
            {
            return FALSE;
            }
        }

    // create and show main window
    if (!InitInstance(hInstance, nCmdShow))
        {
        return FALSE;
        }

    // process window messages
    while (GetMessage(&msg, NULL, 0, 0))
        {
            TranslateMessage(&msg);
            DispatchMessage(&msg);
        }
    return msg.wParam;
}
```

INIT.C

```
// INIT.C
#include <windows.h>
#include "globals.h"

HINSTANCE hInst;
char szAppName[] = SZAPPNAME;
char szTitle[] = SZDESCRIPTION;

// register main window class
BOOL InitApplication(HINSTANCE hInstance)
{
    WNDCLASS  wc;

    wc.style          = CS_HREDRAW | CS_VREDRAW;
    wc.lpfnWndProc    = (WNDPROC)WndProc;
    wc.cbClsExtra     = 0;
    wc.cbWndExtra     = 0;
    wc.hInstance      = hInstance;
    wc.hIcon          = LoadIcon(hInstance, szAppName);
    wc.hCursor        = LoadCursor(NULL, IDC_ARROW);
    wc.hbrBackground  = (HBRUSH)(COLOR_WINDOW + 1);
    wc.lpszMenuName   = szAppName;
```

591

```
    wc.lpszClassName = szAppName;

    return(RegisterClass(&wc));
}

// create and show main window
BOOL InitInstance(HINSTANCE hInstance, int nCmdShow)
{
    HWND    hWnd;
    hInst = hInstance;
    hWnd = CreateWindow(szAppName, szTitle,
                        WS_OVERLAPPEDWINDOW,
                        80, 60, 440, 300,
                        NULL, NULL, hInstance, NULL);

    if (!hWnd)
        {
        return FALSE;
        }

    ShowWindow(hWnd, nCmdShow);
    UpdateWindow(hWnd);

    return TRUE;
}
```

TMETRICS.C

```
// TMETRICS.C
#include <windows.h>
#include <windowsx.h>
#include <commdlg.h>
#include <stdlib.h>
#include <string.h>
#include "globals.h"

LRESULT CALLBACK WndProc(HWND hWnd,
                         UINT uMessage,
                         WPARAM wParam,
                         LPARAM lParam)
{
    LOGFONT lf;
    CHOOSEFONT cf;
    HFONT hFont, hSysFont;
    HDC hDC;
    static TEXTMETRIC tm;
```

```
PAINTSTRUCT ps;
char xx[8], yy[12];

switch (uMessage)
{
    case WM_COMMAND:
        switch (GET_WM_COMMAND_ID(wParam,lParam))
        {
        case IDM_ABOUT:
                // create an about dialog box
                DialogBox(hInst, "ABOUTDLG",
                        hWnd, (DLGPROC)About);
                break;

        case IDM_CHOOSE_FONT:
                hDC = GetDC(hWnd);

                // set parameters in CHOOSEFONT
                // structure cf
                memset(&cf, 0, sizeof(CHOOSEFONT));
                cf.lStructSize = sizeof(CHOOSEFONT);
                cf.hwndOwner = hWnd;
                cf.hDC = hDC;
                cf.lpLogFont = &lf;
                cf.Flags = CF_SCREENFONTS | CF_EFFECTS;
                cf.rgbColors = RGB(0, 0, 0);
                cf.nFontType = SCREEN_FONTTYPE;

                // open choose font common dialog box
                ChooseFont(&cf);

                // create font
                hFont = CreateFontIndirect(
                                    cf.lpLogFont);
                SelectObject(hDC, hFont);

                // get text metrics of selected font
                GetTextMetrics(hDC, &tm);
                DeleteObject(SelectObject(hDC, hFont));

                // repaint client area
                InvalidateRect(hWnd, NULL, TRUE);
                break;

        default:
                return DefWindowProc(hWnd, uMessage,
                                wParam, lParam);
```

```
        }
        break;

case WM_PAINT:
        hDC = BeginPaint(hWnd, &ps);
        SetMapMode(hDC, MM_TEXT);
        hSysFont = GetStockObject(SYSTEM_FONT);
        SelectObject(hDC, hSysFont);

        // display font text metrics
        TextOut(hDC, 5, 5, "Height",  6);
        _itoa(tm.tmHeight, xx, 10);
        TextOut(hDC, 140, 5, xx, strlen(xx));
        TextOut(hDC, 5, 25, "Ascent",  6);
        _itoa(tm.tmAscent, xx, 10);
        TextOut(hDC, 140, 25, xx, strlen(xx));
        TextOut(hDC, 5, 45, "Descent",  7);
        _itoa(tm.tmDescent, xx, 10);
        TextOut(hDC, 140, 45, xx, strlen(xx));
        TextOut(hDC, 5, 65, "Int Leading", 11);
        _itoa(tm.tmInternalLeading, xx, 10);
        TextOut(hDC, 140, 65, xx, strlen(xx));

        TextOut(hDC, 5, 85, "Ext leading", 11);
        _itoa(tm.tmExternalLeading, xx, 10);
        TextOut(hDC, 140, 85, xx, strlen(xx));
        TextOut(hDC, 5, 105, "Ave Char Width", 14);
        _itoa(tm.tmAveCharWidth, xx, 10);
        TextOut(hDC, 140, 105, xx, strlen(xx));
        TextOut(hDC, 5, 125, "Max Char Width", 14);
        _itoa(tm.tmMaxCharWidth, xx, 10);
        TextOut(hDC, 140, 125, xx, strlen(xx));
        TextOut(hDC, 5, 145, "Weight",  6);
        _itoa(tm.tmWeight, xx, 10);
        TextOut(hDC, 140, 145, xx, strlen(xx));

        TextOut(hDC, 5, 175, "Overhang",  8);
        _itoa(tm.tmOverhang, xx, 10);
        TextOut(hDC, 140, 175, xx, strlen(xx));
        TextOut(hDC, 5, 195, "Digitized Aspect X", 18);
        _itoa(tm.tmDigitizedAspectX, xx, 10);
        TextOut(hDC, 140, 195, xx, strlen(xx));
        TextOut(hDC, 5, 215, "Digitized Aspect Y", 18);
        _itoa(tm.tmDigitizedAspectY, xx, 10);
        TextOut(hDC, 140, 215, xx, strlen(xx));

        TextOut(hDC, 200, 5, "Italic",  6);
```

```
  { if(tm.tmItalic == 0x00) strcpy(xx, "No");
    else strcpy(xx, "Yes"); }
TextOut(hDC, 335, 5, xx, strlen(xx));
TextOut(hDC, 200, 25, "Underlined", 10);
  { if(tm.tmUnderlined == 0x00)
                         strcpy(xx, "No");
    else strcpy(xx, "Yes"); }
TextOut(hDC, 335, 25, xx, strlen(xx));
TextOut(hDC, 200, 45, "Struck Out", 10);
  { if(tm.tmStruckOut != 0) strcpy(xx, "Yes");
    else strcpy(xx, "No"); }
TextOut(hDC, 335, 45, xx, strlen(xx));
TextOut(hDC, 200, 75, "First Char", 10);
_itoa(tm.tmFirstChar, xx, 10);
TextOut(hDC, 335, 75, xx, strlen(xx));

TextOut(hDC, 200, 95, "Last Char", 9);
_itoa(tm.tmLastChar, xx, 10);
TextOut(hDC, 335, 95, xx, strlen(xx));
TextOut(hDC, 200, 115, "Default Char", 12);
_itoa(tm.tmDefaultChar, xx, 10);
TextOut(hDC, 335, 115, xx, strlen(xx));
TextOut(hDC, 200, 135, "Break Char", 10);
_itoa(tm.tmBreakChar, xx, 10);
TextOut(hDC, 335, 135, xx, strlen(xx));

TextOut(hDC, 200, 165, "Pitch", 5);
  { if((tm.tmPitchAndFamily & 0x0F) ==
                         TMPF_FIXED_PITCH)
        strcpy(yy, "Fixed Pitch");
else if((tm.tmPitchAndFamily & 0x0F) ==
                         TMPF_VECTOR)
        strcpy(yy, "Vector");
else if((tm.tmPitchAndFamily & 0x0F) ==
                         TMPF_TRUETYPE)
        strcpy(yy, "True Type");
else if((tm.tmPitchAndFamily & 0x0F) ==
                         TMPF_DEVICE)
        strcpy(yy, "Device");
    else strcpy(yy, "Don't know!"); }
TextOut(hDC, 335, 165, yy, strlen(yy));

TextOut(hDC, 200, 185, "Family", 6);
  { if((tm.tmPitchAndFamily & 0xF0) ==
                         FF_DONTCARE)
        strcpy(yy, "Don't Care");
else if((tm.tmPitchAndFamily & 0xF0) ==
```

```
                                           FF_ROMAN)
               strcpy(yy, "Roman");
         else if((tm.tmPitchAndFamily & 0xF0) ==
                                           FF_SWISS)
               strcpy(yy, "Swiss");
         else if((tm.tmPitchAndFamily & 0xF0) ==
                                           FF_MODERN)
               strcpy(yy, "Modern");
         else if((tm.tmPitchAndFamily & 0xF0) ==
                                           FF_SCRIPT)
               strcpy(yy, "Script");
         else if((tm.tmPitchAndFamily & 0xF0) ==
                                           FF_DECORATIVE)
               strcpy(yy, "Decorative");
           else strcpy(yy, "Don't know!"); }
      TextOut(hDC, 335, 185, yy, strlen(yy));

      TextOut(hDC, 200, 205, "Char Set",  8);
         { if(tm.tmCharSet == 0x00)
                               strcpy(yy, "ANSI");
         else if (tm.tmCharSet == 0x01)
                               strcpy(yy, "DEFAULT");
         else if(tm.tmCharSet == 0x02)
                               strcpy(yy, "SYMBOL");
         else if(tm.tmCharSet == 0x80)
                               strcpy(yy, "SHIFTJIS");
         else if(tm.tmCharSet == 0xFF)
                               strcpy(yy, "OEM");
            else strcpy(yy, "Don't know!"); }
      TextOut(hDC, 335, 205, yy, strlen(yy));

      DeleteObject(SelectObject(hDC, hSysFont));
      EndPaint(hWnd, &ps);
      break;

   case WM_DESTROY:
      PostQuitMessage(0);
      break;

   default:
      return DefWindowProc(hWnd, uMessage,
                           wParam, lParam);
   }
   return 0;
}
```

ABOUT.C

```
// ABOUT.C
#include <windows.h>
#include <windowsx.h>
#include "globals.h"

// procedures for ABOUT dialog box
LRESULT CALLBACK About(HWND hDlg,
                       UINT uMessage,
                       WPARAM wParam,
                       LPARAM lParam)
{
    switch (uMessage)
      {
        case WM_COMMAND:
              switch (GET_WM_COMMAND_ID(wParam,lParam))
                {
                    case IDOK:
                    case IDCANCEL:
                        {
                        EndDialog(hDlg, TRUE);
                        return(TRUE);
                        }
                        break;
                }
      }
    return FALSE;
}
```

TMETRICS.RC

```
#include "windows.h"
#include "globals.h"
#include <winver.h>

APPNAME ICON ICONFILE

RCINCLUDE ABOUT.DLG

APPNAME MENU
BEGIN
    MENUITEM "Choose-Font", IDM_CHOOSE_FONT
    MENUITEM "&About",      IDM_ABOUT
END
```

ABOUT.DLG

```
ABOUTDLG DIALOG DISCARDABLE  22, 17, 167, 73
STYLE DS_MODALFRAME | WS_CAPTION | WS_SYSMENU
CAPTION SZABOUT
BEGIN
        DEFPUSHBUTTON    "OK", IDOK, 132, 2, 32, 14, WS_GROUP
        ICON             SZAPPNAME,      -1, 3, 2, 18, 20
        LTEXT            SZAPPNAME,      -1, 30, 12,  50, 8
        LTEXT            SZDESCRIPTION, -1, 30, 22, 150, 8
        LTEXT            SZVERSION,      -1, 30, 32, 150, 8
        LTEXT            SZCOMPANYNAME, -1, 30, 42, 150, 8
END
```

TMETRICS.ICO

CASE 8-5: GET OUTLINE TEXT METRICS OF TRUETYPE FONTS

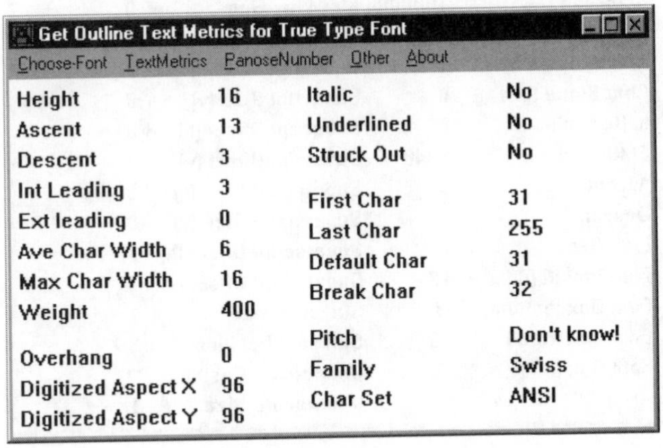

Get Outline Text Metrics for True Type Font

Choose-Font   TextMetrics   PanoseNumber   Other   About

Height	16	Italic	No
Ascent	13	Underlined	No
Descent	3	Struck Out	No
Int Leading	3	First Char	31
Ext leading	0	Last Char	255
Ave Char Width	6	Default Char	31
Max Char Width	16	Break Char	32
Weight	400		
		Pitch	Don't know!
Overhang	0	Family	Swiss
Digitized Aspect X	96	Char Set	ANSI
Digitized Aspect Y	96		

FIGURE 8-5A

Get Outline Text Metrics for True Type Font

Choose-Font   TextMetrics   PanoseNumber   Other   About

Family Type	2
Serif Style	11
Weight	6
Proportion	4
Contrast	2
Stroke Variation	2
Arm Style	2
Letter form	2
Mid line	2
XHeight	4

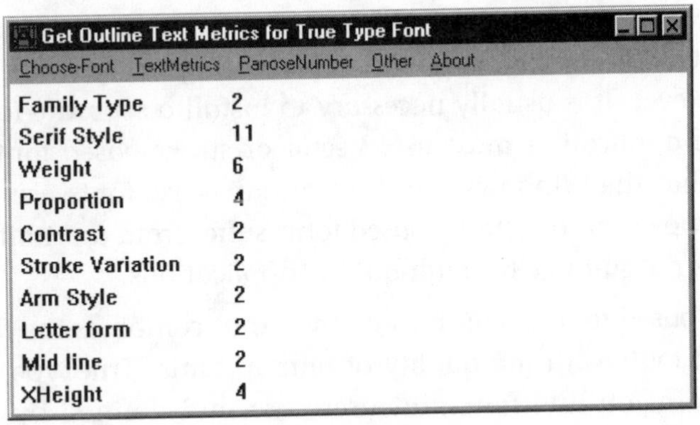

FIGURE 8-5B

599

Get Outline Text Metrics for True Type Font			
Choose-Font	TextMetrics	PanoseNumber	Other	About

Size	278	Mac Ascent	12
Filler	0	Mac Descent	-3
Selection	1000000	Mac Line Gap	0
Type	0	Minimum PPEM	11
Char Slope Rise	1	Subscript Size (h)	9
Char Slope Run	0	Subscript Size (v)	8
Italic Angle	0	Subscript Offset (h)	0
EMSquare	2048	Subscript Offset (v)	2
Ascent	9	Superscript Size (h)	9
Descent	-3	Superscript Size (v)	8
Line Gap	2	Superscript Offset (h)	0
Font Box (top)	12	Superscript Offset (v)	6
Font Box (bottom)	-3	Strikeout Size	1
Font Box (right)	13	Strikeout Position	3
Font Box (left)	-3	Underscore Position	-1
		Underscore Size	1

FIGURE 8-5c

As you perhaps know, there are different ways to represent text characters on a computer. One way, if your computer has a bitmap display, is with raster fonts, in which each character of a given size is represented by an array of bits or pixels. Another approach is to use simple lines or strokes to represent a character. These two approaches were used in early versions of Windows. *Raster fonts* (also known as bitmap fonts) can do a good job of representing complex typographical shapes. However, it is usually necessary to install a separate font for each size that an application must use. Vector or stroke-based fonts are more flexible in that the Windows can draw variable-size fonts using the same set of data. However, the stroke-based fonts suffer from a primitive-looking result that is not suitable for high-quality applications.

Outline-based fonts are a third method that combines the flexibility of stroke-based fonts with the quality of bitmap fonts. TrueType fonts are a certain kind of outline font that uses a format defined by Apple and Microsoft and used by many other vendors. (Another popular outline font format is Adobe Type 1 fonts from Adobe Systems.)

In version 3.1 of Windows, Microsoft added support for TrueType fonts to the Windows API. The GetOutlineTextMetrics() function is used to obtain the text metrics for a given TrueType font. These data are returned in an OUTLINETEXTMETRIC structure. The program here displays this information in the client area, again using a long sequence of TextOut() calls.

Users can choose any font from those available in the system by means of the Choose Font dialog box (this common dialog box was presented in Case 7-2). The Choose Font dialog box is invoked via the Choose Font menu item. When users click on the TextMetrics menu item, the information returned in the TEXTMETRIC structure is displayed in the main window client area, as shown in Figure 8-5a. The users click on the PanoseNumber menu item, the information returned in the PANOSE structure is displayed in the main window client area. Lastly, when the users click on the Other menu item, other information returned in the OUTLINETEXTMETRIC structure is displayed, as shown in Figure 8-5c. Please see Case 8-4 for details on getting the text metrics information for a non-TrueType font.

GLOBALS.H

```
// GLOBALS.H - header file for global variables
//             and function prototypes

// Product identifier string definitions
#define APPNAME        OTM
#define ICONFILE       OTM.ico
#define SZAPPNAME      "OTM"
#define SZDESCRIPTION "Get Outline Text Metrics for True Type
    Font"
#define SZVERSION      "Version 1.0"
#define SZCOMPANYNAME "\251 M&&T Books, 1994"
#define SZABOUT        "About"

// Global function prototypes.
BOOL InitApplication(HINSTANCE);
BOOL InitInstance(HINSTANCE, int);

// Callback functions called by Windows.
LRESULT CALLBACK WndProc(HWND, UINT, WPARAM, LPARAM);
```

```
LRESULT CALLBACK About(HWND, UINT, WPARAM, LPARAM);

// Menu item ID
#define IDM_ABOUT        101
#define IDM_CHOOSE_FONT 102
#define IDM_TEXTMETRICS 103
#define IDM_PANOSE       104
#define IDM_OTHER        105

// Global variable declarations.
extern HINSTANCE hInst;     // The current instance handle
extern char szAppName[];    // The name of this application
extern char szTitle[];      // The title bar text
```

WINMAIN.C

```
// WINMAIN.C
#include <windows.h>
#include "globals.h"

int APIENTRY WinMain(HINSTANCE hInstance,
                     HINSTANCE hPrevInstance,
                     LPSTR lpCmdLine,
                     int nCmdShow)
{
    MSG msg;

    // register main window class
    if (!hPrevInstance)
        {
        if (!InitApplication(hInstance))
            {
            return FALSE;
            }
        }

    // create and show main window
    if (!InitInstance(hInstance, nCmdShow))
        {
        return FALSE;
        }

    // process window messages
    while (GetMessage(&msg, NULL, 0, 0))
        {
            TranslateMessage(&msg);
            DispatchMessage(&msg);
```

```
        }
    return msg.wParam;
}
```

INIT.C

```c
// INIT.C
#include <windows.h>
#include "globals.h"

HINSTANCE hInst;
char szAppName[] = SZAPPNAME;
char szTitle[] = SZDESCRIPTION;

// register main window class
BOOL InitApplication(HINSTANCE hInstance)
{
    WNDCLASS  wc;

    wc.style          = CS_HREDRAW | CS_VREDRAW;
    wc.lpfnWndProc    = (WNDPROC)WndProc;
    wc.cbClsExtra     = 0;
    wc.cbWndExtra     = 0;
    wc.hInstance      = hInstance;
    wc.hIcon          = LoadIcon(hInstance, szAppName);
    wc.hCursor        = LoadCursor(NULL, IDC_ARROW);
    wc.hbrBackground  = (HBRUSH)(COLOR_WINDOW + 1);
    wc.lpszMenuName   = szAppName;
    wc.lpszClassName  = szAppName;

    return(RegisterClass(&wc));
}

// create and show main window
BOOL InitInstance(HINSTANCE hInstance, int nCmdShow)
{
    HWND    hWnd;
    hInst = hInstance;
    hWnd = CreateWindow(szAppName, szTitle,
                        WS_OVERLAPPEDWINDOW,
                        80, 60, 440, 380,
                        NULL, NULL, hInstance, NULL);

    if (!hWnd)
        {
        return FALSE;
```

```
        }

    ShowWindow(hWnd, nCmdShow);
    UpdateWindow(hWnd);

    return TRUE;
}
```

OTM.C

```c
// OTM.C
#include <windows.h>
#include <windowsx.h>
#include <stdlib.h>
#include <string.h>
#include <commdlg.h>
#include "globals.h"

LRESULT CALLBACK WndProc(HWND hWnd,
                         UINT uMessage,
                         WPARAM wParam,
                         LPARAM lParam)
{
    LOGFONT lf;
    CHOOSEFONT cf;
    HFONT hFont, hSysFont;
    HDC hDC;
    static OUTLINETEXTMETRIC otm;
    PAINTSTRUCT ps;
    static int iOtm = 0;
    UINT cbData;
    char xx[8], yy[12];

    switch (uMessage)
    {
        case WM_COMMAND:
            switch (GET_WM_COMMAND_ID(wParam,lParam))
            {
                case IDM_CHOOSE_FONT:
                    hDC = GetDC(hWnd);

                    // set parameters in CHOOSEFONT
                    // structure cf
                    memset(&cf, 0, sizeof(CHOOSEFONT));
                    cf.lStructSize = sizeof(CHOOSEFONT);
                    cf.hwndOwner = hWnd;
```

```
cf.hDC = hDC;
cf.lpLogFont = &lf;
cf.Flags = CF_SCREENFONTS | CF_EFFECTS;
cf.rgbColors = RGB(0, 0, 0);
cf.nFontType = SCREEN_FONTTYPE;

    // open the choose font common
    // dialog box
ChooseFont(&cf);

    // create and select the font
hFont = CreateFontIndirect(
                 cf.lpLogFont);
SelectObject(hDC, hFont);

    // get the size of outline text metrics
cbData = GetOutlineTextMetrics(
                 hDC,(UINT)NULL, NULL);

    // get outline text metrics
GetOutlineTextMetrics(hDC,
                      cbData, &otm);
DeleteObject(SelectObject(hDC, hFont));
ReleaseDC(hWnd, hDC);
iOtm = 0;

    // repaint client area
InvalidateRect(hWnd, NULL, TRUE);
break;

case IDM_TEXTMETRICS:
    iOtm = 1;
        // repaint client area
    InvalidateRect(hWnd, NULL, TRUE);
    break;

case IDM_PANOSE:
    iOtm = 2;
        // repaint client area
    InvalidateRect(hWnd, NULL, TRUE);
    break;

case IDM_OTHER:
    iOtm = 3;
        // repaint client area
    InvalidateRect(hWnd, NULL, TRUE);
    break;
```

605

```
                    case IDM_ABOUT:
                        // create an about dialog box
                        DialogBox(hInst, "ABOUTDLG",
                                    hWnd, (DLGPROC)About);
                        break;

                default:
                    return DefWindowProc(hWnd, uMessage,
                                            wParam, lParam);
            }
            break;

        case WM_PAINT:
            hDC = BeginPaint(hWnd, &ps);
            SetMapMode(hDC, MM_TEXT);
            hSysFont = GetStockObject(SYSTEM_FONT);
            SelectObject(hDC, hSysFont);

            // display text metrics parameters in client area
            if(iOtm == 1){
                TextOut(hDC, 5, 5, "Height", 6);
                _itoa(otm.otmTextMetrics.tmHeight, xx, 10);
                TextOut(hDC, 140, 5, xx, strlen(xx));
                TextOut(hDC, 5, 25, "Ascent", 6);
                _itoa(otm.otmTextMetrics.tmAscent, xx, 10);
                TextOut(hDC, 140, 25, xx, strlen(xx));
                TextOut(hDC, 5, 45, "Descent", 7);
                _itoa(otm.otmTextMetrics.tmDescent, xx, 10);
                TextOut(hDC, 140, 45, xx, strlen(xx));
                TextOut(hDC, 5, 65, "Int Leading", 11);
                _itoa(otm.otmTextMetrics.tmInternalLeading,
                                            xx, 10);
                TextOut(hDC, 140, 65, xx, strlen(xx));

                TextOut(hDC, 5, 85, "Ext leading", 11);
                _itoa(otm.otmTextMetrics.tmExternalLeading,
                                            xx, 10);
                TextOut(hDC, 140, 85, xx, strlen(xx));
                TextOut(hDC, 5, 105, "Ave Char Width", 14);
                _itoa(otm.otmTextMetrics.tmAveCharWidth,
                                            xx, 10);
                TextOut(hDC, 140, 105, xx, strlen(xx));
                TextOut(hDC, 5, 125, "Max Char Width", 14);
                _itoa(otm.otmTextMetrics.tmMaxCharWidth,
                                            xx, 10);
                TextOut(hDC, 140, 125, xx, strlen(xx));
                TextOut(hDC, 5, 145, "Weight", 6);
```

```
_itoa(otm.otmTextMetrics.tmWeight, xx, 10);
TextOut(hDC, 140, 145, xx, strlen(xx));

TextOut(hDC, 5, 175, "Overhang", 8);
_itoa(otm.otmTextMetrics.tmOverhang, xx, 10);
TextOut(hDC, 140, 175, xx, strlen(xx));
TextOut(hDC, 5, 195, "Digitized Aspect X", 18);
_itoa(otm.otmTextMetrics.tmDigitizedAspectX,
                              xx, 10);
TextOut(hDC, 140, 195, xx, strlen(xx));
TextOut(hDC, 5, 215, "Digitized Aspect Y", 18);
_itoa(otm.otmTextMetrics.tmDigitizedAspectY,
                              xx, 10);
TextOut(hDC, 140, 215, xx, strlen(xx));

TextOut(hDC, 200, 5, "Italic", 6);
  { if(otm.otmTextMetrics.tmItalic == 0x00)
      strcpy(xx, "No");
    else strcpy(xx, "Yes"); }
TextOut(hDC, 335, 5, xx, strlen(xx));
TextOut(hDC, 200, 25, "Underlined", 10);
  { if(otm.otmTextMetrics.tmUnderlined == 0x00)
      strcpy(xx, "No");
    else strcpy(xx, "Yes"); }
TextOut(hDC, 335, 25, xx, strlen(xx));
TextOut(hDC, 200, 45, "Struck Out", 10);
  { if(otm.otmTextMetrics.tmStruckOut == 0x00)
      strcpy(xx, "No");
    else strcpy(xx, "Yes"); }

TextOut(hDC, 335, 45, xx, strlen(xx));
TextOut(hDC, 200, 75, "First Char", 10);
_itoa(otm.otmTextMetrics.tmFirstChar, xx, 10);
TextOut(hDC, 335, 75, xx, strlen(xx));

TextOut(hDC, 200, 95, "Last Char", 9);
_itoa(otm.otmTextMetrics.tmLastChar, xx, 10);
TextOut(hDC, 335, 95, xx, strlen(xx));
TextOut(hDC, 200, 115, "Default Char", 12);
_itoa(otm.otmTextMetrics.tmDefaultChar,
                              xx, 10);
TextOut(hDC, 335, 115, xx, strlen(xx));
TextOut(hDC, 200, 135, "Break Char", 10);
_itoa(otm.otmTextMetrics.tmBreakChar, xx, 10);
TextOut(hDC, 335, 135, xx, strlen(xx));

TextOut(hDC, 200, 165, "Pitch", 5);
```

607

```
     { if((otm.otmTextMetrics.tmPitchAndFamily &
         0x0F) == TMPF_FIXED_PITCH)
         strcpy(yy, "Fixed Pitch");
   else if((otm.otmTextMetrics.tmPitchAndFamily &
         0x0F) == TMPF_VECTOR)
         strcpy(yy, "Vector");
   else if((otm.otmTextMetrics.tmPitchAndFamily &
         0x0F) == TMPF_TRUETYPE)
         strcpy(yy, "True Type");
   else if((otm.otmTextMetrics.tmPitchAndFamily &
         0x0F) == TMPF_DEVICE)
         strcpy(yy, "Device");
     else strcpy(yy, "Don't know!"); }
 TextOut(hDC, 335, 165, yy, strlen(yy));

 TextOut(hDC, 200, 185, "Family",  6);
    { if((otm.otmTextMetrics.tmPitchAndFamily &
         0xF0) == FF_DONTCARE)
         strcpy(yy, "Don't Care");
   else if((otm.otmTextMetrics.tmPitchAndFamily &
         0xF0) == FF_ROMAN)
         strcpy(yy, "Roman");
   else if((otm.otmTextMetrics.tmPitchAndFamily &
         0xF0) == FF_SWISS)
         strcpy(yy, "Swiss");
   else if((otm.otmTextMetrics.tmPitchAndFamily &
         0xF0) == FF_MODERN)
         strcpy(yy, "Modern");
   else if((otm.otmTextMetrics.tmPitchAndFamily &
         0xF0) == FF_SCRIPT)
         strcpy(yy, "Script");
   else if((otm.otmTextMetrics.tmPitchAndFamily &
         0xF0) == FF_DECORATIVE)
         strcpy(yy, "Decorative");
     else strcpy(yy, "Don't know!"); }
 TextOut(hDC, 335, 185, yy, strlen(yy));

 TextOut(hDC, 200, 205, "Char Set",  8);
    { if(otm.otmTextMetrics.tmCharSet == 0x00)
        strcpy(yy, "ANSI");
   else if (otm.otmTextMetrics.tmCharSet == 0x01)
        strcpy(yy, "DEFAULT");
   else if(otm.otmTextMetrics.tmCharSet == 0x02)
        strcpy(yy, "SYMBOL");
   else if(otm.otmTextMetrics.tmCharSet == 0x80)
        strcpy(yy, "SHIFTJIS");
   else if(otm.otmTextMetrics.tmCharSet == 0xFF)
```

```
        strcpy(yy, "OEM");
      else strcpy(yy, "Don't know!"); }
  TextOut(hDC, 335, 205, yy, strlen(yy));
  }


// display parameters in PANOSE structure
if(iOtm == 2){
  TextOut(hDC, 5, 5, "Family Type", 11);
  _itoa(otm.otmPanoseNumber.bFamilyType, xx, 10);
  TextOut(hDC, 140, 5, xx, strlen(xx));
  TextOut(hDC, 5, 25, "Serif Style", 11);
  _itoa(otm.otmPanoseNumber.bSerifStyle, xx, 10);
  TextOut(hDC, 140, 25, xx, strlen(xx));
  TextOut(hDC, 5, 45, "Weight",  6);
  _itoa(otm.otmPanoseNumber.bWeight, xx, 10);
  TextOut(hDC, 140, 45, xx, strlen(xx));
  TextOut(hDC, 5, 65, "Proportion", 10);
  _itoa(otm.otmPanoseNumber.bProportion, xx, 10);
  TextOut(hDC, 140, 65, xx, strlen(xx));

  TextOut(hDC, 5, 85, "Contrast",  8);
  _itoa(otm.otmPanoseNumber.bContrast, xx, 10);
  TextOut(hDC, 140, 85, xx, strlen(xx));
  TextOut(hDC, 5, 105, "Stroke Variation", 16);
  _itoa(otm.otmPanoseNumber.bStrokeVariation,
          xx, 10);
  TextOut(hDC, 140, 105, xx, strlen(xx));
  TextOut(hDC, 5, 125, "Arm Style",  9);
  _itoa(otm.otmPanoseNumber.bArmStyle, xx, 10);
  TextOut(hDC, 140, 125, xx, strlen(xx));
  TextOut(hDC, 5, 145, "Letter form", 11);
  _itoa(otm.otmPanoseNumber.bLetterform, xx, 10);
  TextOut(hDC, 140, 145, xx, strlen(xx));

  TextOut(hDC, 5, 165, "Mid line",  8);
  _itoa(otm.otmPanoseNumber.bMidline, xx, 10);
  TextOut(hDC, 140, 165, xx, strlen(xx));
  TextOut(hDC, 5, 185, "XHeight",  7);
  _itoa(otm.otmPanoseNumber.bXHeight, xx, 10);
  TextOut(hDC, 140, 185, xx, strlen(xx));
  }


// display other parameter in outline text
// metrics structure
if(iOtm == 3){
  TextOut(hDC, 5, 5, "Size",  4);
  _itoa(otm.otmSize, xx, 10);
```

```
TextOut(hDC, 140, 5, xx, strlen(xx));
TextOut(hDC, 5, 25, "Filler", 6);
_itoa(otm.otmFiller, xx, 10);
TextOut(hDC, 140, 25, xx, strlen(xx));
TextOut(hDC, 5, 45, "Selection", 9);
_itoa(otm.otmfsSelection, xx, 2);
TextOut(hDC, 140, 45, xx, strlen(xx));
TextOut(hDC, 5, 65, "Type", 4);
_itoa(otm.otmfsType, xx, 2);
TextOut(hDC, 140, 65, xx, strlen(xx));

TextOut(hDC, 5, 85, "Char Slope Rise", 15);
_itoa(otm.otmsCharSlopeRise, xx, 10);
TextOut(hDC, 140, 85, xx, strlen(xx));
TextOut(hDC, 5, 105, "Char Slope Run", 14);
_itoa(otm.otmsCharSlopeRun, xx, 10);
TextOut(hDC, 140, 105, xx, strlen(xx));
TextOut(hDC, 5, 125, "Italic Angle", 12);
_itoa(otm.otmItalicAngle, xx, 10);
TextOut(hDC, 140, 125, xx, strlen(xx));
TextOut(hDC, 5, 145, "EMSquare", 8);
_itoa(otm.otmEMSquare, xx, 10);
TextOut(hDC, 140, 145, xx, strlen(xx));

TextOut(hDC, 5, 165, "Ascent", 6);
_itoa(otm.otmAscent, xx, 10);
TextOut(hDC, 140, 165, xx, strlen(xx));
TextOut(hDC, 5, 185, "Descent", 7);
_itoa(otm.otmDescent, xx, 10);
TextOut(hDC, 140, 185, xx, strlen(xx));
TextOut(hDC, 5, 205, "Line Gap", 8);
_itoa(otm.otmLineGap, xx, 10);
TextOut(hDC, 140, 205, xx, strlen(xx));

TextOut(hDC, 5, 225, "Font Box (top)", 14);
_itoa(otm.otmrcFontBox.top, xx, 10);
TextOut(hDC, 140, 225, xx, strlen(xx));
TextOut(hDC, 5, 245, "Font Box (bottom)", 17);
_itoa(otm.otmrcFontBox.bottom, xx, 10);
TextOut(hDC, 140, 245, xx, strlen(xx));
TextOut(hDC, 5, 265, "Font Box (right)", 16);
_itoa(otm.otmrcFontBox.right, xx, 10);
TextOut(hDC, 140, 265, xx, strlen(xx));
TextOut(hDC, 5, 285, "Font Box (left)", 15);
_itoa(otm.otmrcFontBox.left, xx, 10);
TextOut(hDC, 140, 285, xx, strlen(xx));
```

```
TextOut(hDC, 200, 5, "Mac Ascent", 10);
_itoa(otm.otmMacAscent, xx, 10);
TextOut(hDC, 350, 5, xx, strlen(xx));
TextOut(hDC, 200, 25, "Mac Descent", 11);
_itoa(otm.otmMacDescent, xx, 10);
TextOut(hDC, 350, 25, xx, strlen(xx));
TextOut(hDC, 200, 45, "Mac Line Gap", 12);
_itoa(otm.otmMacLineGap, xx, 10);
TextOut(hDC, 350, 45, xx, strlen(xx));

TextOut(hDC, 200, 65, "Minimum PPEM", 12);
_itoa(otm.otmusMinimumPPEM, xx, 10);
TextOut(hDC, 350, 65, xx, strlen(xx));

TextOut(hDC, 200, 85,
        "Subscript Size (h)", 18);
_itoa(otm.otmptSubscriptSize.x, xx, 10);
TextOut(hDC, 350, 85, xx, strlen(xx));
TextOut(hDC, 200, 105,
        "Subscript Size (v)", 18);
_itoa(otm.otmptSubscriptSize.y, xx, 10);
TextOut(hDC, 350, 105, xx, strlen(xx));
TextOut(hDC, 200, 125,
        "Subscript Offset (h)", 20);
_itoa(otm.otmptSubscriptOffset.x, xx, 10);
TextOut(hDC, 350, 125, xx, strlen(xx));
TextOut(hDC, 200, 145,
        "Subscript Offset (v)", 20);
_itoa(otm.otmptSubscriptOffset.y, xx, 10);
TextOut(hDC, 350, 145, xx, strlen(xx));

TextOut(hDC, 200, 165,
        "Superscript Size (h)", 20);
_itoa(otm.otmptSuperscriptSize.x, xx, 10);
TextOut(hDC, 350, 165, xx, strlen(xx));
TextOut(hDC, 200, 185,
        "Superscript Size (v)", 20);
_itoa(otm.otmptSuperscriptSize.y, xx, 10);
TextOut(hDC, 350, 185, xx, strlen(xx));
TextOut(hDC, 200, 205,
        "Superscript Offset (h)", 22);
_itoa(otm.otmptSuperscriptOffset.x, xx, 10);
TextOut(hDC, 350, 205, xx, strlen(xx));
TextOut(hDC, 200, 225,
        "Superscript Offset (v)", 22);
_itoa(otm.otmptSuperscriptOffset.y, xx, 10);
TextOut(hDC, 350, 225, xx, strlen(xx));
```

```
                        TextOut(hDC, 200, 245, "Strikeout Size", 14);
                        _itoa(otm.otmsStrikeoutSize, xx, 10);
                        TextOut(hDC, 350, 245, xx, strlen(xx));
                        TextOut(hDC, 200, 265,
                                "Strikeout Position", 18);
                        _itoa(otm.otmsStrikeoutPosition, xx, 10);
                        TextOut(hDC, 350, 265, xx, strlen(xx));
                        TextOut(hDC, 200, 285,
                                "Underscore Position", 19);
                        _itoa(otm.otmsUnderscorePosition, xx, 10);
                        TextOut(hDC, 350, 285, xx, strlen(xx));
                        TextOut(hDC, 200, 305,
                                "Underscore Size", 15);
                        _itoa(otm.otmsUnderscoreSize, xx, 10);
                        TextOut(hDC, 350, 305, xx, strlen(xx));

                        TextOut(hDC, 200, 325, "Family Name", 11);
                        TextOut(hDC, 350, 325, otm.otmpFamilyName,
                                        strlen(otm.otmpFamilyName));
                        TextOut(hDC, 200, 345, "Face Name", 9);
                        TextOut(hDC, 350, 345, otm.otmpFaceName,
                                        strlen(otm.otmpFaceName));
                        TextOut(hDC, 200, 365, "Style Name", 10);
                        TextOut(hDC, 350, 365, otm.otmpStyleName,
                                        strlen(otm.otmpStyleName));
                        TextOut(hDC,   5, 385, "Full Name", 9);
                        TextOut(hDC, 140, 385, otm.otmpFullName,
                                        strlen(otm.otmpFullName));

            }

                        DeleteObject(SelectObject(hDC, hSysFont));;
                        EndPaint(hWnd, &ps);
                        break;

                case WM_DESTROY:
                        PostQuitMessage(0);
                        break;

                default:
                        return DefWindowProc(hWnd, uMessage,
                                        wParam, lParam);
        }
        return 0;
}
```

ABOUT.C

```
// ABOUT.C
#include <windows.h>
#include <windowsx.h>
#include "globals.h"

// procedures for ABOUT dialog box
LRESULT CALLBACK About(HWND hDlg,
                       UINT uMessage,
                       WPARAM wParam,
                       LPARAM lParam)
{
    switch (uMessage)
      {
        case WM_COMMAND:
            switch (GET_WM_COMMAND_ID(wParam,lParam))
              {
                case IDOK:
                case IDCANCEL:
                    {
                    EndDialog(hDlg, TRUE);
                    return(TRUE);
                    }
                    break;
              }
      }
    return FALSE;
}
```

OTM.RC

```
#include "windows.h"
#include "globals.h"
#include <winver.h>

APPNAME ICON ICONFILE

RCINCLUDE ABOUT.DLG

APPNAME MENU
BEGIN
    MENUITEM "&Choose-Font",   IDM_CHOOSE_FONT
    MENUITEM "&TextMetrics",   IDM_TEXTMETRICS
    MENUITEM "&PanoseNumber"   IDM_PANOSE
```

613

```
    MENUITEM "&Other",          IDM_OTHER
    MENUITEM "&About",          IDM_ABOUT
END
```

ABOUT.DLG

```
ABOUTDLG DIALOG DISCARDABLE  22, 17, 167, 73
STYLE DS_MODALFRAME | WS_CAPTION | WS_SYSMENU
CAPTION SZABOUT
BEGIN
    DEFPUSHBUTTON  "OK", IDOK, 132, 2, 32, 14, WS_GROUP
    ICON           SZAPPNAME,      -1, 3, 2, 18, 20
    LTEXT          SZAPPNAME,      -1, 30, 12,  50, 8
    LTEXT          SZDESCRIPTION, -1, 30, 22, 150, 8
    LTEXT          SZVERSION,      -1, 30, 32, 150, 8
    LTEXT          SZCOMPANYNAME, -1, 30, 42, 150, 8
END
```

OTM.ICO

CASE 8-6: CHANGE CARET STYLE

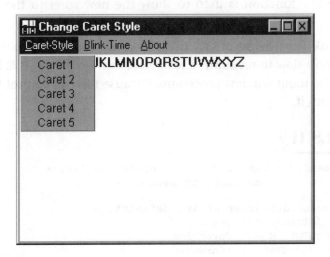

FIGURE 8-6

The final case in this chapter shows how to create and change the caret in an edit box. The *caret* is the visual marker that shows where text characters will appear when users type at the keyboard. It is different from the mouse pointer, because the mouse pointer tracks the position of the mouse on the screen wherever it happens to be. By convention, the caret is usually set only when users click on the mouse button (which is sometimes confusing to new users).

When the main window is created, the WM_CREATE handler of the main window procedure creates an edit control that is a child of the main window. This edit control is then told to display a sample text string (in this case, an alphabet) via the SetWindowText().

Three custom carets have been defined, and these are stored in the files CARET1.BMP, CARET2.BMP and so on. Using the Caret-Style menu, users can select among these different carets. The code in the WM_COMMAND handler that processes these menu choices first uses DestroyCaret() to remove the current caret. Then the code loads the custom caret bitmaps via the LoadBitmap() function, and then uses the CreateCaret()

615

function to create a caret from the loaded bitmap. Finally, the ShowCaret() function is used to show the new caret in the edit child window.

The Blink-Time menu allows users to set or change the blink time of the caret, from slow to medium to fast. Note that no WM_PAINT handler is needed in the main window procedure, because the edit control takes care of painting itself.

GLOBALS.H

```
// GLOBALS.H - header file for global variables
//             and function prototypes

// Product identifier string definitions
#define APPNAME        Caret
#define ICONFILE       Caret.ico
#define SZAPPNAME      "Caret"
#define SZDESCRIPTION  "Change Caret Style"
#define SZVERSION      "Version 1.0"
#define SZCOMPANYNAME  "\251 M&&T Books, 1994"
#define SZABOUT        "About"

// Global function prototypes.
BOOL InitApplication(HINSTANCE);
BOOL InitInstance(HINSTANCE, int);

// Callback functions called by Windows.
LRESULT CALLBACK WndProc(HWND, UINT, WPARAM, LPARAM);
LRESULT CALLBACK About(HWND, UINT, WPARAM, LPARAM);

// Menu item ID
#define IDM_ABOUT             100
#define IDM_CARET1            101
#define IDM_CARET2            102
#define IDM_CARET3            103
#define IDM_CARET4            104
#define IDM_CARET5            105
#define IDM_BLINKTIME_SLOW    106
#define IDM_BLINKTIME_MEDIUM  107
#define IDM_BLINKTIME_FAST    108

// Global variable declarations.
extern HINSTANCE hInst;      // The current instance handle
extern char szAppName[];     // The name of this application
extern char szTitle[];       // The title bar text
```

WINMAIN.C

```
// WINMAIN.C
#include <windows.h>
#include "globals.h"

int APIENTRY WinMain(HINSTANCE hInstance,
                     HINSTANCE hPrevInstance,
                     LPSTR lpCmdLine,
                     int nCmdShow)
{
    MSG msg;

    // register main window class
    if (!hPrevInstance)
        {
        if (!InitApplication(hInstance))
            {
            return FALSE;
            }
        }

    // create and show main window
    if (!InitInstance(hInstance, nCmdShow))
        {
        return FALSE;
        }

    // process window messages
    while (GetMessage(&msg, NULL, 0, 0))
        {
            TranslateMessage(&msg);
            DispatchMessage(&msg);
        }
    return msg.wParam;
}
```

INIT.C

```
// INIT.C
#include <windows.h>
#include "globals.h"

HINSTANCE hInst;
char szAppName[] = SZAPPNAME;
char szTitle[] = SZDESCRIPTION;
```

```
// register main window class
BOOL InitApplication(HINSTANCE hInstance)
{
    WNDCLASS  wc;

    wc.style         = CS_HREDRAW | CS_VREDRAW;
    wc.lpfnWndProc   = (WNDPROC)WndProc;
    wc.cbClsExtra    = 0;
    wc.cbWndExtra    = 0;
    wc.hInstance     = hInstance;
    wc.hIcon         = LoadIcon(hInstance, szAppName);
    wc.hCursor       = LoadCursor(NULL, IDC_ARROW);
    wc.hbrBackground = (HBRUSH)(COLOR_WINDOW + 1);
    wc.lpszMenuName  = szAppName;
    wc.lpszClassName = szAppName;

    return(RegisterClass(&wc));
}


// create and show main window
BOOL InitInstance(HINSTANCE hInstance, int nCmdShow)
{
    HWND    hWnd;
    hInst = hInstance;
    hWnd = CreateWindow(szAppName, szTitle,
                        WS_OVERLAPPEDWINDOW,
                        160, 120, 320, 240,
                        NULL, NULL, hInstance, NULL);

    if (!hWnd)
        {
        return FALSE;
        }

    ShowWindow(hWnd, nCmdShow);
    UpdateWindow(hWnd);

    return TRUE;
}
```

CARET.C

```
// CARET.C
#include <windows.h>
#include <windowsx.h>
#include "globals.h"
```

```
HBITMAP hBitmap;
HWND hEdit;

LRESULT CALLBACK WndProc(HWND hWnd,
                         UINT uMessage,
                         WPARAM wParam,
                         LPARAM lParam)
{
    char *buffer = "ABCDEFGHIJKLMNOPQRSTUVWXYZ";

    switch (uMessage)
    {
        case WM_CREATE:
            // create an edit child window in
            // main window client area
            hEdit = CreateWindow("edit", "",
                    ES_LEFT | ES_MULTILINE |
                    WS_VISIBLE | WS_CHILD,
                    0, 0, 320, 240,
                    hWnd, NULL, hInst, NULL);

            // display text stored in buffer in edit window
            SetWindowText(hEdit, buffer);
            break;

        case WM_COMMAND:
            switch (GET_WM_COMMAND_ID(wParam,lParam))
            {
                case IDM_CARET1:
                    // remove current caret
                    DestroyCaret();

                    // load the selected caret bitmap
                    hBitmap = LoadBitmap(
                            hInst, "BitmapCaret1");

                    // create a new caret
                    CreateCaret(hEdit, hBitmap,
                            (int)NULL, (int)NULL);

                    // show new caret
                    ShowCaret(hEdit);
                    break;

                case IDM_CARET2:
                    DestroyCaret();
                    hBitmap = LoadBitmap(
                            hInst, "BitmapCaret2");
```

619

```
            CreateCaret(hEdit, hBitmap,
                        (int)NULL, (int)NULL);
            ShowCaret(hEdit);
            break;

    case IDM_CARET3:
            DestroyCaret();
            hBitmap = LoadBitmap(
                        hInst, "BitmapCaret3");
            CreateCaret(hEdit, hBitmap,
                        (int)NULL, (int)NULL);
            ShowCaret(hEdit);
            break;

    case IDM_CARET4:
            DestroyCaret();
            // create a solid caret
            CreateCaret(hEdit, NULL, 8, 20);
            ShowCaret(hEdit);
            break;

    case IDM_CARET5:
            DestroyCaret();
            // create a gray caret
            CreateCaret(hEdit, 1, 8, 20);
            ShowCaret(hEdit);
            break;

    // set caret blink time
    case IDM_BLINKTIME_SLOW:
            SetCaretBlinkTime(1000);
            break;

    case IDM_BLINKTIME_MEDIUM:
            SetCaretBlinkTime(500);
            break;

    case IDM_BLINKTIME_FAST:
            SetCaretBlinkTime(200);
            break;

    case IDM_ABOUT:
            // create an about dialog box
            DialogBox(hInst, "ABOUTDLG",
                    hWnd, (DLGPROC)About);
            break;

    default:
```

620

```
                     return DefWindowProc(hWnd, uMessage,
                                          wParam, lParam);

            }
            break;

        case WM_DESTROY:
            DestroyCaret();
            PostQuitMessage(0);
            break;

        default:
            return DefWindowProc(hWnd, uMessage,
                                 wParam, lParam);

    }
    return 0;
}
```

ABOUT.C

```
// ABOUT.C
#include <windows.h>
#include <windowsx.h>
#include "globals.h"

// procedures for ABOUT dialog box
LRESULT CALLBACK About(HWND hDlg,
                       UINT uMessage,
                       WPARAM wParam,
                       LPARAM lParam)

{
    switch (uMessage)
      {
        case WM_COMMAND:
            switch (GET_WM_COMMAND_ID(wParam,lParam))
            {
                case IDOK:
                case IDCANCEL:
                    {
                    EndDialog(hDlg, TRUE);
                    return(TRUE);
                    }
                    break;

            }
      }
    return FALSE;
}
```

CARET.RC

```
#include "windows.h"
#include "globals.h"
#include <winver.h>

BitmapCaret1 BITMAP caret1.bmp
BitmapCaret2 BITMAP caret2.bmp
BitmapCaret3 BITMAP caret3.bmp

APPNAME ICON ICONFILE

RCINCLUDE ABOUT.DLG

APPNAME MENU
BEGIN
    POPUP "&Caret-Style"
    BEGIN
      MENUITEM "Caret &1",  IDM_CARET1
      MENUITEM "Caret &2",  IDM_CARET2
      MENUITEM "Caret &3",  IDM_CARET3
      MENUITEM "Caret &4",  IDM_CARET4
      MENUITEM "Caret &5",  IDM_CARET5
    END
    POPUP "&Blink-Time"
    BEGIN
      MENUITEM "&Slow",   IDM_BLINKTIME_SLOW
      MENUITEM "&Medium", IDM_BLINKTIME_MEDIUM
      MENUITEM "&Fast",   IDM_BLINKTIME_FAST
    END
    MENUITEM "&About", IDM_ABOUT
END
```

ABOUT.DLG

```
ABOUTDLG DIALOG DISCARDABLE  22, 17, 167, 73
STYLE DS_MODALFRAME | WS_CAPTION | WS_SYSMENU
CAPTION SZABOUT
BEGIN
    DEFPUSHBUTTON   "OK", IDOK, 132, 2, 32, 14, WS_GROUP
    ICON            SZAPPNAME,      -1, 3, 2, 18, 20
    LTEXT           SZAPPNAME,      -1, 30, 12,  50, 8
    LTEXT           SZDESCRIPTION, -1, 30, 22, 150, 8
    LTEXT           SZVERSION,      -1, 30, 32, 150, 8
    LTEXT           SZCOMPANYNAME, -1, 30, 42, 150, 8
END
```

CARET.ICO

CHAPTER NINE

BITMAPS

CASE 9-1: CREATE BITMAP() FUNCTION

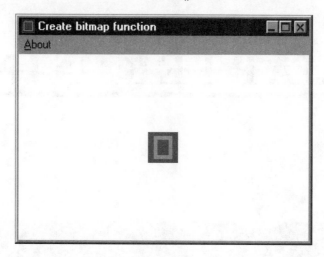

FIGURE 9-1

The cases in this chapter deal with bitmaps. The first case shows the hard way to create a bitmap: using the CreateBitmap() function.

The bitmap in this case consists of a 32 x 32 pixel design that is stored in a BYTE array named Sample[]. This bitmap is a monochrome bitmap in which each pixel can be either zero or one. The on/off status of the bits in the bitmap is expressed in the source code as an array of hexadecimal values. For example, the fifth row of the Sample[] array consists of the values 0x03, 0xff, 0xff, 0xc0. This set of values corresponds to the following sequence of bits: 00000011111111111111111111000000 (i.e., first six bits off, then twenty bits on, then six more bits off). The SetTextColor() function is used to specify the color of the ON bits, and the SetBkColor() function is used to specify the color of the OFF bits.

The important code is in the WM_PAINT handler of the main window procedure. After setting the text and background colors, the code creates a device context (DC) in memory using the CreateCompatibleDC() function. Then CreateBitmap() is used to create the bitmap, which is then selected into the memory DC. This bitmap is transferred to the screen display from the memory DC using the `BitBlt()` function. Finally, cleanup is done using `DeleteDC()` and `DeleteObject()`.

GLOBALS.H

```
// GLOBALS.H - header file for global variables
//              and function prototypes

// Product identifier string definitions
#define APPNAME      CrBmp
#define ICONFILE     CrBmp.ico
#define SZAPPNAME    "CrBmp"
#define SZDESCRIPTION "Create bitmap function"
#define SZVERSION    "Version 1.0"
#define SZCOMPANYNAME "\251 M&&T Books, 1994"
#define SZABOUT      "About"

// Global function prototypes.
BOOL InitApplication(HINSTANCE);
BOOL InitInstance(HINSTANCE, int);

// Callback functions called by Windows.
LRESULT CALLBACK WndProc(HWND, UINT, WPARAM, LPARAM);
LRESULT CALLBACK About(HWND, UINT, WPARAM, LPARAM);

// Menu item ID
#define IDM_ABOUT    1000

// Global variable declarations.
extern HINSTANCE hInst;      // The current instance handle
extern char szAppName[];     // The name of this application
extern char szTitle[];       // The title bar text
```

WINMAIN.C

```
// WINMAIN.C
#include <windows.h>
#include "globals.h"

int APIENTRY WinMain(HINSTANCE hInstance,
                     HINSTANCE hPrevInstance,
                     LPSTR lpCmdLine,
                     int nCmdShow)
```

```
{
    MSG msg;

    // register main window class
    if (!hPrevInstance)
        {
        if (!InitApplication(hInstance))
            {
            return FALSE;
            }
        }

    // create and show main window
    if (!InitInstance(hInstance, nCmdShow))
        {
        return FALSE;
        }

    // process window messages
    while (GetMessage(&msg, NULL, 0, 0))
        {
            TranslateMessage(&msg);
            DispatchMessage(&msg);
        }
    return msg.wParam;
}
```

INIT.C

```
// INIT.C
#include <windows.h>
#include "globals.h"

HINSTANCE hInst;
char szAppName[] = SZAPPNAME;
char szTitle[] = SZDESCRIPTION;

// register main window class
BOOL InitApplication(HINSTANCE hInstance)
{
    WNDCLASS  wc;

    wc.style          = CS_HREDRAW | CS_VREDRAW;
    wc.lpfnWndProc    = (WNDPROC)WndProc;
    wc.cbClsExtra     = 0;
    wc.cbWndExtra     = 0;
    wc.hInstance      = hInstance;
```

```
    wc.hIcon          = LoadIcon(hInstance, szAppName);
    wc.hCursor        = LoadCursor(NULL, IDC_ARROW);
    wc.hbrBackground  = (HBRUSH)(COLOR_WINDOW + 1);
    wc.lpszMenuName   = szAppName;
    wc.lpszClassName  = szAppName;

    return(RegisterClass(&wc));
}

// create and show main window
BOOL InitInstance(HINSTANCE hInstance, int nCmdShow)
{
    HWND    hWnd;
    hInst = hInstance;
    hWnd = CreateWindow(szAppName, szTitle,
                        WS_OVERLAPPEDWINDOW,
                        160, 120, 320, 240,
                        NULL, NULL, hInstance, NULL);

    if (!hWnd)
        {
        return FALSE;
        }

    ShowWindow(hWnd, nCmdShow);
    UpdateWindow(hWnd);

    return TRUE;
}
```

CRBMP.C

```
// CRBMP.C
#include <windows.h>
#include <windowsx.h>
#include "globals.h"

LRESULT CALLBACK WndProc(HWND hWnd,
                         UINT uMessage,
                         WPARAM wParam,
                         LPARAM lParam)
{
    PAINTSTRUCT ps;
    HBITMAP hBitmap;
    BITMAP bmp;
    HDC hDC, hMemoryDC;
    static int Client_X, Client_Y;
```

```
// define bits in the bitmap
static BYTE Sample[] = {
                    0x00, 0x00, 0x00, 0x00,
                    0x00, 0x00, 0x00, 0x00,
                    0x00, 0x00, 0x00, 0x00,
                    0x00, 0x00, 0x00, 0x00,
                    0x03, 0xff, 0xff, 0xc0,
                    0x03, 0xff, 0xff, 0xc0,
                    0x03, 0xff, 0xff, 0xc0,
                    0x03, 0xff, 0xff, 0xc0,
                    0x03, 0xc0, 0x03, 0xc0,
                    0x03, 0xc0, 0x03, 0xc0,
                    0x03, 0xc0, 0x03, 0xc0,
                    0x03, 0xc0, 0x03, 0xc0,
                    0x03, 0xc0, 0x03, 0xc0,
                    0x03, 0xc0, 0x03, 0xc0,
                    0x03, 0xc0, 0x03, 0xc0,
                    0x03, 0xc0, 0x03, 0xc0,
                    0x03, 0xc0, 0x03, 0xc0,
                    0x03, 0xc0, 0x03, 0xc0,
                    0x03, 0xc0, 0x03, 0xc0,
                    0x03, 0xc0, 0x03, 0xc0,
                    0x03, 0xc0, 0x03, 0xc0,
                    0x03, 0xc0, 0x03, 0xc0,
                    0x03, 0xc0, 0x03, 0xc0,
                    0x03, 0xc0, 0x03, 0xc0,
                    0x03, 0xff, 0xff, 0xc0,
                    0x03, 0xff, 0xff, 0xc0,
                    0x03, 0xff, 0xff, 0xc0,
                    0x03, 0xff, 0xff, 0xc0,
                    0x00, 0x00, 0x00, 0x00,
                    0x00, 0x00, 0x00, 0x00,
                    0x00, 0x00, 0x00, 0x00,
                    0x00, 0x00, 0x00, 0x00 };

switch (uMessage)
{
    case WM_SIZE:
        Client_X = LOWORD(lParam);
        Client_Y = HIWORD(lParam);
        break;

    case WM_PAINT:
        hDC = BeginPaint(hWnd, &ps);

        // set bit 1 color
        SetTextColor(hDC, RGB(255, 0, 0));
```

```
                // set bit 0 color
            SetBkColor(hDC, RGB(0, 255, 0));
            hMemoryDC = CreateCompatibleDC(hDC);

                // create the bitmap
            hBitmap = CreateBitmap(32, 32, 1, 1,
                                    (LPSTR)Sample);
            GetObject(hBitmap, sizeof(BITMAP),
                                (LPSTR) &bmp);

                // select the created bitmap for hMemoryDC
            SelectObject(hMemoryDC, hBitmap);

                // copy the bitmap from hMemoryDC to hDC
            BitBlt(hDC, Client_X/2 - bmp.bmWidth/2,
                Client_Y/2 - bmp.bmHeight/2,
                bmp.bmWidth, bmp.bmHeight,
                hMemoryDC, 0, 0, SRCCOPY);

            ReleaseDC(hWnd, hDC);
            EndPaint(hWnd, &ps);

            DeleteDC(hMemoryDC);
            DeleteObject(hBitmap);
            break;

    case WM_COMMAND:
            switch (GET_WM_COMMAND_ID(wParam,lParam))
            {
                case IDM_ABOUT:
                        // create an about dialog box
                    DialogBox(hInst, "ABOUTDLG",
                                hWnd, (DLGPROC)About);
                    break;

                default:
                    return DefWindowProc(hWnd, uMessage,
                                            wParam, lParam);
            }
            break;

    case WM_DESTROY:
            PostQuitMessage(0);
            break;

    default:
```

```
                return DefWindowProc(hWnd, uMessage,
                                        wParam, lParam);
        }
        return 0;
}
```

ABOUT.C

```
// ABOUT.C
#include <windows.h>
#include <windowsx.h>
#include "globals.h"

// procedures for ABOUT dialog box
LRESULT CALLBACK About(HWND hDlg,
                        UINT uMessage,
                        WPARAM wParam,
                        LPARAM lParam)
{
    switch (uMessage)
      {
        case WM_COMMAND:
            switch (GET_WM_COMMAND_ID(wParam,lParam))
            {
                case IDOK:
                case IDCANCEL:
                    {
                    EndDialog(hDlg, TRUE);
                    return(TRUE);
                    }
                    break;
            }
      }
    return FALSE;
}
```

CRBMP.RC

```
#include "windows.h"
#include "globals.h"
#include <winver.h>

APPNAME ICON ICONFILE
```

632

```
RCINCLUDE ABOUT.DLG

APPNAME MENU
BEGIN
  MENUITEM "&About",      IDM_ABOUT
END
```

ABOUT.DLG

```
ABOUTDLG DIALOG DISCARDABLE  22, 17, 167, 73
STYLE DS_MODALFRAME | WS_CAPTION | WS_SYSMENU
CAPTION SZABOUT
BEGIN
    DEFPUSHBUTTON    "OK", IDOK, 132, 2, 32, 14, WS_GROUP
    ICON             SZAPPNAME,      -1, 3, 2, 18, 20
    LTEXT            SZAPPNAME,      -1, 30, 12,  50, 8
    LTEXT            SZDESCRIPTION, -1, 30, 22, 150, 8
    LTEXT            SZVERSION,     -1, 30, 32, 150, 8
    LTEXT            SZCOMPANYNAME, -1, 30, 42, 150, 8
END
```

CRBMP.ICO

CASE 9-2: THE CREATEBITMAPINDIRECT( ) FUNCTION

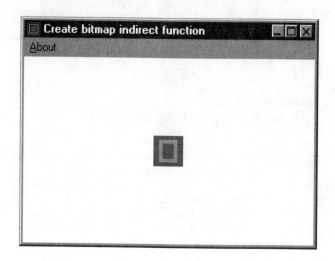

FIGURE 9-2

This case shows another hard way to create a bitmap, using the CreateBitmapIndirect() function. This case is almost identical to Case 9-1, except for the use of CreateBitmapIndirect() in place of CreateBitmap(). Basically, parameters that would normally be passed directly to the CreateBitmap() function are placed into a data structure of type BITMAP. A pointer to this structure is passed to the CreateBitmapIndirect() function. In all other respects, the code in this case is identical to Case 9-1, so please consult the description there for more information.

GLOBALS.H

```
// GLOBALS.H - header file for global variables
//            and function prototypes

// Product identifier string definitions
#define APPNAME         CrBmpI
#define ICONFILE        CrBmpI.ico
#define SZAPPNAME       "CrBmpI"
#define SZDESCRIPTION   "Create bitmap indirect function"
#define SZVERSION       "Version 1.0"
#define SZCOMPANYNAME   "\251 M&&T Books, 1994"
#define SZABOUT         "About"

// Global function prototypes.
BOOL InitApplication(HINSTANCE);
BOOL InitInstance(HINSTANCE, int);

// Callback functions called by Windows.
LRESULT CALLBACK WndProc(HWND, UINT, WPARAM, LPARAM);
LRESULT CALLBACK About(HWND, UINT, WPARAM, LPARAM);

// Menu item ID
#define IDM_ABOUT    1000

// Global variable declarations.
extern HINSTANCE hInst;      // The current instance handle
extern char szAppName[];     // The name of this application
extern char szTitle[];       // The title bar text
```

WINMAIN.C

```
// WINMAIN.C
#include <windows.h>
#include "globals.h"

int APIENTRY WinMain(HINSTANCE hInstance,
                     HINSTANCE hPrevInstance,
                     LPSTR lpCmdLine,
                     int nCmdShow)
{
    MSG msg;

    // register main window class
    if (!hPrevInstance)
```

```
        {
        if (!InitApplication(hInstance))
            {
            return FALSE;
            }
        }

    // create and show main window
    if (!InitInstance(hInstance, nCmdShow))
        {
        return FALSE;
        }

    // process window messages
    while (GetMessage(&msg, NULL, 0, 0))
        {
            TranslateMessage(&msg);
            DispatchMessage(&msg);
        }
    return msg.wParam;
}
```

INIT.C

```
// INIT.C
#include <windows.h>
#include "globals.h"

HINSTANCE hInst;
char szAppName[] = SZAPPNAME;
char szTitle[] = SZDESCRIPTION;

// register main window class
BOOL InitApplication(HINSTANCE hInstance)
{
    WNDCLASS  wc;

    wc.style          = CS_HREDRAW | CS_VREDRAW;
    wc.lpfnWndProc    = (WNDPROC)WndProc;
    wc.cbClsExtra     = 0;
    wc.cbWndExtra     = 0;
    wc.hInstance      = hInstance;
    wc.hIcon          = LoadIcon(hInstance, szAppName);
    wc.hCursor        = LoadCursor(NULL, IDC_ARROW);
    wc.hbrBackground  = (HBRUSH)(COLOR_WINDOW + 1);
    wc.lpszMenuName   = szAppName;
```

```
    wc.lpszClassName = szAppName;

    return(RegisterClass(&wc));
}

// create and show main window
BOOL InitInstance(HINSTANCE hInstance, int nCmdShow)
{
    HWND    hWnd;
    hInst = hInstance;
    hWnd = CreateWindow(szAppName, szTitle,
                        WS_OVERLAPPEDWINDOW,
                        160, 120, 320, 240,
                        NULL, NULL, hInstance, NULL);

    if (!hWnd)
        {
        return FALSE;
        }

    ShowWindow(hWnd, nCmdShow);
    UpdateWindow(hWnd);

    return TRUE;
}
```

CRBMP1.C

```
// CRBMP1.C
#include <windows.h>
#include <windowsx.h>
#include "globals.h"

LRESULT CALLBACK WndProc(HWND hWnd,
                         UINT uMessage,
                         WPARAM wParam,
                         LPARAM lParam)
{
    PAINTSTRUCT ps;
    HBITMAP hBitmap;
    BITMAP bmp;
    HDC hDC, hMemoryDC;
    static int Client_X, Client_Y;
    // store the bits of the bitmap in a BYTE array
    static BYTE Sample[] = {
                    0x00, 0x00, 0x00, 0x00,
```

```
                          0x00, 0x00, 0x00, 0x00,
                          0x00, 0x00, 0x00, 0x00,
                          0x00, 0x00, 0x00, 0x00,
                          0x03, 0xff, 0xff, 0xc0,
                          0x03, 0xff, 0xff, 0xc0,
                          0x03, 0xff, 0xff, 0xc0,
                          0x03, 0xff, 0xff, 0xc0,
                          0x03, 0xc0, 0x03, 0xc0,
                          0x03, 0xc0, 0x03, 0xc0,
                          0x03, 0xc0, 0x03, 0xc0,
                          0x03, 0xc0, 0x03, 0xc0,
                          0x03, 0xc0, 0x03, 0xc0,
                          0x03, 0xc0, 0x03, 0xc0,
                          0x03, 0xc0, 0x03, 0xc0,
                          0x03, 0xc0, 0x03, 0xc0,
                          0x03, 0xc0, 0x03, 0xc0,
                          0x03, 0xc0, 0x03, 0xc0,
                          0x03, 0xc0, 0x03, 0xc0,
                          0x03, 0xc0, 0x03, 0xc0,
                          0x03, 0xc0, 0x03, 0xc0,
                          0x03, 0xc0, 0x03, 0xc0,
                          0x03, 0xc0, 0x03, 0xc0,
                          0x03, 0xc0, 0x03, 0xc0,
                          0x03, 0xff, 0xff, 0xc0,
                          0x03, 0xff, 0xff, 0xc0,
                          0x03, 0xff, 0xff, 0xc0,
                          0x03, 0xff, 0xff, 0xc0,
                          0x00, 0x00, 0x00, 0x00,
                          0x00, 0x00, 0x00, 0x00,
                          0x00, 0x00, 0x00, 0x00,
                          0x00, 0x00, 0x00, 0x00 };
       static BITMAP lpBitmap = { 0, 32, 32, 4, 1, 1,
                                 (LPSTR)Sample } ;

       switch (uMessage)
       {
           case WM_SIZE:
               Client_X = LOWORD(lParam);
               Client_Y = HIWORD(lParam);
               break;

           case WM_PAINT:
               hDC = BeginPaint(hWnd, &ps);

               // set the bit 0 color
               SetTextColor(hDC, RGB(255, 0, 0));
```

```
         // set the bit 1 color
         SetBkColor(hDC, RGB(0, 0, 255));
         hMemoryDC = CreateCompatibleDC(hDC);

         // create a new bitmap
         hBitmap = CreateBitmapIndirect(&lpBitmap);
         GetObject(hBitmap, sizeof(BITMAP),
                             (LPSTR) &bmp);
         SelectObject(hMemoryDC, hBitmap);

         // copy the bitmap from hMemoryDC to hDC
         BitBlt(hDC, Client_X/2 - bmp.bmWidth/2,
                Client_Y/2 - bmp.bmHeight/2,
                bmp.bmWidth, bmp.bmHeight,
                hMemoryDC, 0, 0, SRCCOPY);

         ReleaseDC(hWnd, hDC);
         EndPaint(hWnd, &ps);

         DeleteDC(hMemoryDC);
         DeleteObject(hBitmap);
         break;

   case WM_COMMAND:
         switch (GET_WM_COMMAND_ID(wParam,lParam))
         {
            case IDM_ABOUT:
                    // create an about dialog box
                    DialogBox(hInst, "ABOUTDLG",
                              hWnd, (DLGPROC)About);
                    break;

            default:
                 return DefWindowProc(hWnd, uMessage,
                                      wParam, lParam);

         }
         break;

   case WM_DESTROY:
         PostQuitMessage(0);
         break;

   default:
         return DefWindowProc(hWnd, uMessage,
                              wParam, lParam);
   }
   return 0;
}
```

639

ABOUT.C

```c
// ABOUT.C
#include <windows.h>
#include <windowsx.h>
#include "globals.h"

// procedures for ABOUT dialog box
LRESULT CALLBACK About(HWND hDlg,
                       UINT uMessage,
                       WPARAM wParam,
                       LPARAM lParam)
{
    switch (uMessage)
      {
        case WM_COMMAND:
            switch (GET_WM_COMMAND_ID(wParam,lParam))
            {
                case IDOK:
                case IDCANCEL:
                    {
                    EndDialog(hDlg, TRUE);
                    return(TRUE);
                    }
                    break;
            }
      }
    return FALSE;
}
```

CRBMPI.RC

```
#include "windows.h"
#include "globals.h"
#include <winver.h>

APPNAME ICON ICONFILE

RCINCLUDE ABOUT.DLG

APPNAME MENU
BEGIN
  MENUITEM "&About",     IDM_ABOUT
END
```

ABOUT.DLG

```
ABOUTDLG DIALOG DISCARDABLE  22, 17, 167, 73
STYLE DS_MODALFRAME | WS_CAPTION | WS_SYSMENU
CAPTION SZABOUT
BEGIN
    DEFPUSHBUTTON    "OK", IDOK, 132, 2, 32, 14, WS_GROUP
    ICON             SZAPPNAME,      -1, 3, 2, 18, 20
    LTEXT            SZAPPNAME,      -1, 30, 12,  50, 8
    LTEXT            SZDESCRIPTION, -1, 30, 22, 150, 8
    LTEXT            SZVERSION,     -1, 30, 32, 150, 8
    LTEXT            SZCOMPANYNAME, -1, 30, 42, 150, 8
END
```

CRBMPI.ICO

CASE 9-3: DRAWING ONE BITMAP
ON TOP OF ANOTHER

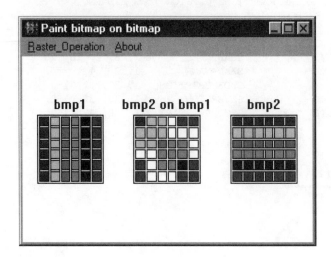

This case shows how to use the BitBlt() function in Windows to paint a bitmap on top of another bitmap. The resulting color is determined by the raster operation code selected by the users. The users choose one of fifteen possible raster operations from the pull-down menu entitled Raster Operation. The main window shows three bitmaps. The one on the left is bmp1; the one on the right is bmp2. The result of combining bmp1 and bmp2 is the bitmap in the center.

The bitmap transfer operation occurs in the function PaintBitmap(), which is a small procedure to encapsulate the steps of creating a memory device context, loading a bitmap into that DC, transferring the bitmap from the memory DC to the screen using BitBlt(), and, finally, doing cleanup with DeleteObject() and DeleteBitmap(). The PaintBitmap() function is called from the WM_PAINT handler, which draws the three bitmaps. To draw the center bitmap, PaintBitmap() is called twice, once to draw bmp1 using the SRCCOPY transfer mode and then again to transfer bmp2 on top of bmp1.

GLOBALS.H

```
// GLOBALS.H - header file for global variables
//               and function prototypes

// Product identifier string definitions
#define APPNAME          BmpOnBmp
#define ICONFILE         BmpOnBmp.ico
#define SZAPPNAME        "BmpOnBmp"
#define SZDESCRIPTION "Paint bitmap on bitmap"
#define SZVERSION        "Version 1.0"
#define SZCOMPANYNAME "\251 M&&T Books, 1994"
#define SZABOUT          "About"

// Global function prototypes.
BOOL InitApplication(HINSTANCE);
BOOL InitInstance(HINSTANCE, int);
void PaintBitmap (HWND, int, int, DWORD, char*);

// Callback functions called by Windows.
LRESULT CALLBACK WndProc(HWND, UINT, WPARAM, LPARAM);
LRESULT CALLBACK About(HWND, UINT, WPARAM, LPARAM);

// Menu item ID
#define IDM_ABOUT        100
#define IDM_BLACKNESS    101
#define IDM_DSTINVERT    102
#define IDM_MERGECOPY    103
#define IDM_MERGEPAINT   104
#define IDM_NOTSRCCOPY   105
#define IDM_NOTSRCERASE 106
#define IDM_PATCOPY      107
#define IDM_PATINVERT    108
#define IDM_PATPAINT     109
#define IDM_SRCAND       110
#define IDM_SRCCOPY      111
#define IDM_SRCERASE     112
#define IDM_SRCINVERT    113
#define IDM_SRCPAINT     114
#define IDM_WHITENESS    115

// Global variable declarations.
extern HINSTANCE hInst;      // The current instance handle
extern char szAppName[];     // The name of this application
extern char szTitle[];       // The title bar text
```

643

WINMAIN.C

```c
// WINMAIN.C
#include <windows.h>
#include "globals.h"

int APIENTRY WinMain(HINSTANCE hInstance,
                     HINSTANCE hPrevInstance,
                     LPSTR lpCmdLine,
                     int nCmdShow)
{
    MSG msg;

    // register main window class
    if (!hPrevInstance)
        {
        if (!InitApplication(hInstance))
            {
            return FALSE;
            }
        }

    // create and show main window
    if (!InitInstance(hInstance, nCmdShow))
        {
        return FALSE;
        }

    // process window messages
    while (GetMessage(&msg, NULL, 0, 0))
        {
            TranslateMessage(&msg);
            DispatchMessage(&msg);
        }
    return msg.wParam;
}
```

INIT.C

```c
// INIT.C
#include <windows.h>
#include "globals.h"

HINSTANCE hInst;
char szAppName[] = SZAPPNAME;
char szTitle[] = SZDESCRIPTION;
```

```
// register main window class
BOOL InitApplication(HINSTANCE hInstance)
{
    WNDCLASS  wc;

    wc.style          = CS_HREDRAW | CS_VREDRAW;
    wc.lpfnWndProc    = (WNDPROC)WndProc;
    wc.cbClsExtra     = 0;
    wc.cbWndExtra     = 0;
    wc.hInstance      = hInstance;
    wc.hIcon          = LoadIcon(hInstance, szAppName);
    wc.hCursor        = LoadCursor(NULL, IDC_ARROW);
    wc.hbrBackground  = (HBRUSH)(COLOR_WINDOW + 1);
    wc.lpszMenuName   = szAppName;
    wc.lpszClassName  = szAppName;

    return(RegisterClass(&wc));
}

// create and show main window
BOOL InitInstance(HINSTANCE hInstance, int nCmdShow)
{
    HWND    hWnd;
    hInst = hInstance;
    hWnd = CreateWindow(szAppName, szTitle,
                    WS_OVERLAPPEDWINDOW,
                    160, 120, 320, 240,
                    NULL, NULL, hInstance, NULL);

    if (!hWnd)
        {
        return FALSE;
        }

    ShowWindow(hWnd, nCmdShow);
    UpdateWindow(hWnd);

    return TRUE;
}
```

BMPONBMP.C

```
// BMPONBMP.C
#include <windows.h>
#include <windowsx.h>
#include "globals.h"
```

```
LRESULT CALLBACK WndProc(HWND hWnd,
                         UINT uMessage,
                         WPARAM wParam,
                         LPARAM lParam)
{
    HDC hDC;
    PAINTSTRUCT ps;
    static DWORD dwRop = SRCCOPY; // raster operation code
    static int Client_X, Client_Y;

    switch (uMessage)
    {
        case WM_SIZE:
            Client_X = LOWORD(lParam);
            Client_Y = HIWORD(lParam);
            break;

        case WM_PAINT:
            hDC = BeginPaint(hWnd, &ps);

            // draw text "bmp1" above left bitmap
            TextOut(hDC, Client_X/6 - 18,
                         Client_Y/2 - 55, "bmp1", 4);

            // paint bitmap 1 on the left side
            // of the client area
            PaintBitmap(hWnd, Client_X/6, Client_Y/2,
                             SRCCOPY, "Sample1Bitmap");

            // draw text "bmp2 on bmp1" above center bitmap
            TextOut(hDC, Client_X/2 - 48,
                         Client_Y/2 - 55,
                         "bmp2 on bmp1", 12);

            // paint bitmap 1 at the center
            // of the client area
            PaintBitmap(hWnd, Client_X/2, Client_Y/2,
                             SRCCOPY, "Sample1Bitmap");

            // paint bitmap 2 at the center
            // of the client area using the raster
            // operation code specified by the user;
            // It is painted right on top of the bitmap 1
            // already painted there
            PaintBitmap(hWnd, Client_X/2, Client_Y/2,
                             dwRop, "Sample2Bitmap");
```

```
            // draw text "bmp2" above right bitmap
        TextOut(hDC, Client_X*5/6 - 18,
                    Client_Y/2 - 55, "bmp2", 4);

        // paint bitmap 2 on the right side
        // of the client area
        PaintBitmap(hWnd, Client_X*5/6, Client_Y/2,
                        SRCCOPY, "Sample2Bitmap");
        EndPaint(hWnd, &ps);
        break;

    case WM_COMMAND:
        switch (GET_WM_COMMAND_ID(wParam,lParam))
        {
            case IDM_ABOUT:
                    // create an about dialog box
                DialogBox(hInst, "ABOUTDLG",
                        hWnd, (DLGPROC)About);
                break;

            // choose the raster operation code
            case IDM_BLACKNESS:
                dwRop = BLACKNESS;
                break;

            case IDM_DSTINVERT:
                dwRop = DSTINVERT;
                break;

            case IDM_MERGECOPY:
                dwRop = MERGECOPY;
                break;

            case IDM_MERGEPAINT:
                dwRop = MERGEPAINT;
                break;

            case IDM_NOTSRCCOPY:
                dwRop = NOTSRCCOPY;
                break;

            case IDM_NOTSRCERASE:
                dwRop = NOTSRCERASE;
                break;

            case IDM_PATCOPY:
```

```
                    dwRop = PATCOPY;
                    break;

            case IDM_PATINVERT:
                    dwRop = PATINVERT;
                    break;

            case IDM_PATPAINT:
                    dwRop = PATPAINT;
                    break;

            case IDM_SRCAND:
                    dwRop = SRCAND;
                    break;

            case IDM_SRCCOPY:
                    dwRop = SRCCOPY;
                    break;

            case IDM_SRCERASE:
                    dwRop = SRCERASE;
                    break;

            case IDM_SRCINVERT:
                    dwRop = SRCINVERT;
                    break;

            case IDM_SRCPAINT:
                    dwRop = SRCPAINT;
                    break;

            case IDM_WHITENESS:
                    dwRop = WHITENESS;
                    break;

            default:
                    return DefWindowProc(hWnd, uMessage,
                                            wParam, lParam);
            }

        // repaint the client area
        InvalidateRect(hWnd, NULL, TRUE);
        break;

    case WM_DESTROY:
        PostQuitMessage(0);
        break;
```

```
        default:
            return DefWindowProc(hWnd, uMessage,
                                    wParam, lParam);
    }
    return 0;
}
```

```
// function for painting the bitmap in window client area
void PaintBitmap(hWnd, Center_X, Center_Y, dwRop, BitmapName)
HWND hWnd;
int Center_X, Center_Y;
DWORD dwRop; // raster operation code
char *BitmapName;
{
  BITMAP bmp;
  HDC hDC, hMemoryDC;
  HBITMAP hBitmap;
    hDC = GetDC(hWnd);
    hMemoryDC = CreateCompatibleDC(hDC);
    hBitmap = LoadBitmap (hInst, BitmapName);
    GetObject(hBitmap, sizeof(BITMAP), (LPSTR) &bmp);
    SelectObject(hMemoryDC, hBitmap);
    BitBlt(hDC, Center_X - bmp.bmWidth/2,
                Center_Y - bmp.bmHeight/2,
                bmp.bmWidth, bmp.bmHeight,
                hMemoryDC, 0, 0, dwRop);
    ReleaseDC(hWnd, hDC);
    DeleteDC(hMemoryDC);
    DeleteObject(hBitmap);
}
```

ABOUT.C

```
// ABOUT.C
#include <windows.h>
#include <windowsx.h>
#include "globals.h"
```

```
// procedures for ABOUT dialog box
LRESULT CALLBACK About(HWND hDlg,
                        UINT uMessage,
                        WPARAM wParam,
                        LPARAM lParam)
{
    switch (uMessage)
```

```
    {
      case WM_COMMAND:
            switch (GET_WM_COMMAND_ID(wParam,lParam))
            {
                case IDOK:
                case IDCANCEL:
                        {
                        EndDialog(hDlg, TRUE);
                        return(TRUE);
                        }
                        break;
            }
    }
    return FALSE;
}
```

BMPONBMP.RC

```
#include "windows.h"
#include "globals.h"
#include <winver.h>

APPNAME ICON ICONFILE

RCINCLUDE ABOUT.DLG

Sample1Bitmap BITMAP sample1.bmp
Sample2Bitmap BITMAP sample2.bmp

APPNAME MENU
BEGIN
    POPUP "&Raster_Operation"
    BEGIN
        MENUITEM "BLACKNESS",    IDM_BLACKNESS
        MENUITEM "DSTINVERT",    IDM_DSTINVERT
        MENUITEM "MERGECOPY",    IDM_MERGECOPY
        MENUITEM "MERGEPAINT",   IDM_MERGEPAINT
        MENUITEM "NOTSRCCOPY",   IDM_NOTSRCCOPY
        MENUITEM "NOTSRCERASE",  IDM_NOTSRCERASE
        MENUITEM "PATCOPY",      IDM_PATCOPY
        MENUITEM "PATINVERT",    IDM_PATINVERT
        MENUITEM "PATPAINT",     IDM_PATPAINT
        MENUITEM "SRCAND",       IDM_SRCAND
        MENUITEM "SRCCOPY",      IDM_SRCCOPY
        MENUITEM "SRCERASE",     IDM_SRCERASE
        MENUITEM "SRCINVERT",    IDM_SRCINVERT
```

```
        MENUITEM "SRCPAINT",      IDM_SRCPAINT
        MENUITEM "WHITENESS",     IDM_WHITENESS
    END
    MENUITEM "&About", IDM_ABOUT
END
```

ABOUT.DLG

```
ABOUTDLG DIALOG DISCARDABLE  22, 17, 167, 73
STYLE DS_MODALFRAME | WS_CAPTION | WS_SYSMENU
CAPTION SZABOUT
BEGIN
    DEFPUSHBUTTON    "OK", IDOK, 132, 2, 32, 14, WS_GROUP
    ICON             SZAPPNAME,      -1, 3, 2, 18, 20
    LTEXT            SZAPPNAME,      -1, 30, 12,  50, 8
    LTEXT            SZDESCRIPTION, -1, 30, 22, 150, 8
    LTEXT            SZVERSION,     -1, 30, 32, 150, 8
    LTEXT            SZCOMPANYNAME, -1, 30, 42, 150, 8
END
```

BMPONBMP.ICO

SAMPLE1.BMP

SAMPLE2.BMP

CASE 9-4: SCREEN BITMAP MAGNIFIER

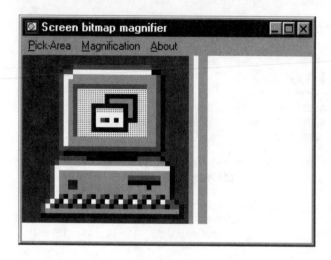

FIGURE 9-4

This program shows how to accomplish a task that is implemented in many drawing or painting applications for Windows. The program allows users to select a portion of the screen display and then paints a magnified version of this image in the main window client area.

Users can set the magnification factor by clicking on the Magnification menu item. To select an area to be magnified, the users first click on the Pick-Area menu item. The program changes the cursor into a "cross" style cursor. Internally, a flag variable bCut is set to reflect the current state. When the bCut flag is ON, the program gets the next two cursor positions when users click the left mouse button (because two points are required to specify a rectangular area). The bitmap of the area defined by these two points is copied to a memory device context. The magnified bitmap is then drawn in the main window client area using the ScretchBlt() function. In   Figure 9-4, a 25x magnification of the "My Computer" icon is painted in the client area.

GLOBALS.H

```
// GLOBALS.H - header file for global variables
//               and function prototypes

// Product identifier string definitions
#define APPNAME        Magnify
#define ICONFILE       Magnify.ico
#define SZAPPNAME      "Magnify"
#define SZDESCRIPTION  "Screen bitmap magnifier"
#define SZVERSION      "Version 1.0"
#define SZCOMPANYNAME  "\251 M&&T Books, 1994"
#define SZABOUT        "About"

// Global function prototypes.
BOOL InitApplication(HINSTANCE);
BOOL InitInstance(HINSTANCE, int);

// Callback functions called by Windows.
LRESULT CALLBACK WndProc(HWND, UINT, WPARAM, LPARAM);
LRESULT CALLBACK About(HWND, UINT, WPARAM, LPARAM);

// Menu item ID
#define IDM_ABOUT      100
#define IDM_PICK_AREA  101
#define IDM_MAG2       102
#define IDM_MAG5       103
#define IDM_MAG10      104

// Global variable declarations.
extern HINSTANCE hInst;     // The current instance handle
extern char szAppName[];    // The name of this application
extern char szTitle[];      // The title bar text
```

WINMAIN.C

```
// WINMAIN.C
#include <windows.h>
#include "globals.h"

int APIENTRY WinMain(HINSTANCE hInstance,
                     HINSTANCE hPrevInstance,
                     LPSTR lpCmdLine,
                     int nCmdShow)
{
```

```
        MSG msg;

        // register main window class
        if (!hPrevInstance)
            {
            if (!InitApplication(hInstance))
                {
                return FALSE;
                }
            }

        // create and show main window
        if (!InitInstance(hInstance, nCmdShow))
            {
            return FALSE;
            }

        // process window messages
        while (GetMessage(&msg, NULL, 0, 0))
            {
                TranslateMessage(&msg);
                DispatchMessage(&msg);
            }
        return msg.wParam;
    }
```

INIT.C

```
    // INIT.C
    #include <windows.h>
    #include "globals.h"

    HINSTANCE hInst;
    char szAppName[] = SZAPPNAME;
    char szTitle[] = SZDESCRIPTION;

    // register main window class
    BOOL InitApplication(HINSTANCE hInstance)
    {
        WNDCLASS  wc;

        wc.style          = CS_HREDRAW | CS_VREDRAW;
        wc.lpfnWndProc    = (WNDPROC)WndProc;
        wc.cbClsExtra     = 0;
        wc.cbWndExtra     = 0;
        wc.hInstance      = hInstance;
```

```
    wc.hIcon         = LoadIcon(hInstance, szAppName);
    wc.hCursor       = LoadCursor(NULL, IDC_ARROW);
    wc.hbrBackground = (HBRUSH)(COLOR_WINDOW + 1);
    wc.lpszMenuName  = szAppName;
    wc.lpszClassName = szAppName;

    return(RegisterClass(&wc));
}

// create and show main window
BOOL InitInstance(HINSTANCE hInstance, int nCmdShow)
{
    HWND    hWnd;
    hInst = hInstance;
    hWnd = CreateWindow(szAppName, szTitle,
                        WS_OVERLAPPEDWINDOW,
                        160, 120, 320, 240,
                        NULL, NULL, hInstance, NULL);

    if (!hWnd)
        {
        return FALSE;
        }

    ShowWindow(hWnd, nCmdShow);
    UpdateWindow(hWnd);

    return TRUE;
}
```

MAGNIFY.C

```
// MAGNIFY.C
#include <windows.h>
#include <windowsx.h>
#include "globals.h"

static HCURSOR hNewCursor;
static UINT iMag;
static BOOL bCopy;
static BOOL bOrder;
static POINT pt1, pt2;
HDC hDC, hScreenDC;
UINT nWidth, nHeight;
RECT rc1;
```

```
LRESULT CALLBACK WndProc(HWND hWnd,
                        UINT uMessage,
                        WPARAM wParam,
                        LPARAM lParam)
{
    switch (uMessage)
    {
        case WM_CREATE:

            hNewCursor = LoadCursor(NULL, IDC_ARROW);
            iMag = 2;
            bCopy = FALSE;
            bOrder = FALSE;
            break;

        case WM_COMMAND:

            switch (GET_WM_COMMAND_ID(wParam,lParam))
            {
                case IDM_ABOUT:
                    // create an about dialog box
                    DialogBox(hInst, "ABOUTDLG",
                            hWnd, (DLGPROC)About);
                    break;

                case IDM_PICK_AREA:

                    // clear the client area
                    InvalidateRect(hWnd, NULL, TRUE);

                    // turn on the bCopy flag
                    bCopy = TRUE;

                    // set the bOrder flag to 0
                    bOrder = FALSE;

                    // set the mouse capture to main
                    // window so all mouse input will be
                    // directed to the main window
                    SetCapture(hWnd);

                    // change cursor to IDC_CROSS
                    hNewCursor = LoadCursor(
                                NULL, IDC_CROSS);
                    SetCursor(hNewCursor);
                    break;
```

```
                // set bitmap magnification factor
        case IDM_MAG2:
            iMag = 2;
            break;

        case IDM_MAG5:
            iMag = 5;
            break;

        case IDM_MAG10:
            iMag = 10;
            break;

        default:
            return DefWindowProc(hWnd, uMessage,
                                    wParam, lParam);
    }
    break;

case WM_LBUTTONDOWN:

    // It required two points to define a rectanglar
    // area. When the bCopy flag is turned on,
    // the program gets the next two cursor
    // positions when user clicks the left mouse
    // button.
    // These two positions are used to define the
    // area on the screen to be magnified

    if(bCopy){
        if(!bOrder){
            // get first cursor position
            GetCursorPos(&pt1); }

        if(bOrder){
            // get second cursor position
            GetCursorPos(&pt2);

            // define a rectangle using
            // these two positions
            rc1.left = min(pt1.x, pt2.x);
            rc1.right = max(pt1.x, pt2.x);
            rc1.top = min(pt1.y, pt2.y);
            rc1.bottom = max(pt1.y, pt2.y);

            // copy the selected screen area bitmap
            // into client area
```

```
    {   nWidth = rc1.right - rc1.left;
        nHeight = rc1.bottom - rc1.top;
         // create a screen DC
        hScreenDC = CreateDC("DISPLAY", NULL,
                                NULL, NULL);

        hDC = GetDC(hWnd);
         // magnify the screen area defined by
         // the rectangle rc1 and copy it to
         // the window client area
        StretchBlt(hDC, 0, 0,
                    iMag*nWidth, iMag*nHeight,
                    hScreenDC,
                    rc1.left, rc1.top,
                    nWidth, nHeight, SRCCOPY);
        DeleteDC(hScreenDC);
        ReleaseDC(hWnd, hDC);
    }

     // turn off the bCopy flag when done
    bCopy = FALSE;

     // release the mouse capture
    ReleaseCapture();

     // change cursor back to IDC_ARROW
    hNewCursor = LoadCursor(NULL, IDC_ARROW);
    SetCursor(hNewCursor);
    }

 // toggle the bOrder flag
    bOrder = !bOrder;
    }
    break;

case WM_SETCURSOR:
    SetCursor(hNewCursor);
    break;

case WM_DESTROY:
    PostQuitMessage(0);
    break;

default:
    return DefWindowProc(hWnd, uMessage,
                        wParam, lParam);
}
```

```
    return 0;
}
```

ABOUT.C

```
// ABOUT.C
#include <windows.h>
#include <windowsx.h>
#include "globals.h"

// procedures for ABOUT dialog box
LRESULT CALLBACK About(HWND hDlg,
                       UINT uMessage,
                       WPARAM wParam,
                       LPARAM lParam)
{
    switch (uMessage)
      {
        case WM_COMMAND:
             switch (GET_WM_COMMAND_ID(wParam,lParam))
               {
                 case IDOK:
                 case IDCANCEL:
                     {
                     EndDialog(hDlg, TRUE);
                     return(TRUE);
                     }
                     break;
               }
      }
    return FALSE;
}
```

MAGNIFY.RC

```
#include "windows.h"
#include "globals.h"
#include <winver.h>

APPNAME ICON ICONFILE

RCINCLUDE ABOUT.DLG

APPNAME MENU
```

```
BEGIN
    MENUITEM "&Pick-Area",      IDM_PICK_AREA
    POPUP     "&Magnification"
      BEGIN
        MENUITEM "&2",          IDM_MAG2
        MENUITEM "&5",          IDM_MAG5
        MENUITEM "&10",         IDM_MAG10
      END
    MENUITEM "&About",          IDM_ABOUT
END
```

ABOUT.DLG

```
ABOUTDLG DIALOG DISCARDABLE  22, 17, 167, 73
STYLE DS_MODALFRAME | WS_CAPTION | WS_SYSMENU
CAPTION SZABOUT
BEGIN
    DEFPUSHBUTTON    "OK", IDOK, 132, 2, 32, 14, WS_GROUP
    ICON             SZAPPNAME,      -1, 3, 2, 18, 20
    LTEXT            SZAPPNAME,      -1, 30, 12,  50, 8
    LTEXT            SZDESCRIPTION, -1, 30, 22, 150, 8
    LTEXT            SZVERSION,      -1, 30, 32, 150, 8
    LTEXT            SZCOMPANYNAME, -1, 30, 42, 150, 8
END
```

MAGNIFY.ICO

CHAPTER TEN

THE
CLIPBOARD

CASE 10-1: CLIPBOARD (TEXT FORMAT)

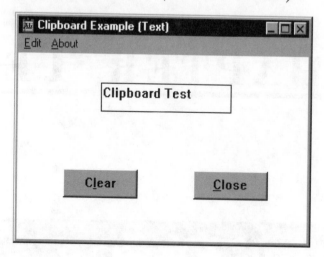

FIGURE 10-1

The Windows Clipboard is a facility that allows users to transfer data from one application to another. Typically, this is done by choosing the cut and paste menu items on the application's Edit menu. Users can cut text, say, from the Notepad text editor, and paste it into a graphics program. Windows provides an API that lets applications transfer data to and from the Clipboard. These data can be in different types and formats—not just text, but also bitmaps and custom application-specific formats.

This case shows how to transfer text data to and from the Clipboard. The main window contains an edit control as well as two push buttons. Copying and pasting text is a two-step process. To copy a string from an edit box onto the Clipboard, the program must first allocate some memory for storing the string. The text string that comprises the edit box's contents is first copied into memory and then copied from memory onto the Clipboard. The paste procedure is the reverse of this sequence.

Looking at the program listing, there is code in the WM_INITMENU handler of the main window procedure to check the state of the Clipboard, seeing if the Clipboard already has some text available. If so, the Paste menu item is enabled; otherwise, it is grayed out. The other important parts of this program are the Copy and Paste menu item handlers in the WM_COMMAND handler. To implement the Copy command, first a string is allocated in global (shared) memory using GlobalAlloc() and lstrcpy(). Then the Clipboard is opened with OpenClipboard(), zeroed out with EmptyClipboard(), and transferred with SetClipboardData(), using the CF_TEXT parameter. Lastly, the Clipboard is closed with CloseClipboard(). The Paste command handler is analogous to the Copy command. The following case shows how to transfer bitmap data.

GLOBALS.H

```
// GLOBALS.H - header file for global variables
//              and function prototypes

// Product identifier string definitions
#define APPNAME        ClipText
#define ICONFILE       ClipText.ico
#define SZAPPNAME      "ClipText"
#define SZDESCRIPTION "Clipboard Example (Text)"
#define SZVERSION      "Version 1.0"
#define SZCOMPANYNAME "\251 M&&T Books, 1994"
#define SZABOUT        "About"

// Global function prototypes.
BOOL InitApplication(HINSTANCE);
BOOL InitInstance(HINSTANCE, int);

// Callback functions called by Windows.
LRESULT CALLBACK WndProc(HWND, UINT, WPARAM, LPARAM);
LRESULT CALLBACK About(HWND, UINT, WPARAM, LPARAM);

// Menu item ID
#define IDM_ABOUT    100
#define IDM_COPY     101
#define IDM_PASTE    102

// Control ID
#define IDC_EDITBOX 103
#define IDC_CLEAR    104
#define IDC_CLOSE    105
```

```
// Global variable declarations.
extern HINSTANCE hInst;      // The current instance handle
extern char szAppName[];     // The name of this application
extern char szTitle[];       // The title bar text
```

WINMAIN.C

```
// WINMAIN.C
#include <windows.h>
#include "globals.h"

int APIENTRY WinMain(HINSTANCE hInstance,
                     HINSTANCE hPrevInstance,
                     LPSTR lpCmdLine,
                     int nCmdShow)
{
    MSG msg;

    // register main window class
    if (!hPrevInstance)
        {
        if (!InitApplication(hInstance))
            {
            return FALSE;
            }
        }

    // create and show main window
    if (!InitInstance(hInstance, nCmdShow))
        {
        return FALSE;
        }

    // process window messages
    while (GetMessage(&msg, NULL, 0, 0))
        {
            TranslateMessage(&msg);
            DispatchMessage(&msg);
        }
    return msg.wParam;
}
```

INIT.C

```
// INIT.C
```

```
#include <windows.h>
#include "globals.h"

HINSTANCE hInst;
char szAppName[] = SZAPPNAME;
char szTitle[] = SZDESCRIPTION;

// register main window class
BOOL InitApplication(HINSTANCE hInstance)
{
    WNDCLASS  wc;

    wc.style          = CS_HREDRAW | CS_VREDRAW;
    wc.lpfnWndProc    = (WNDPROC)WndProc;
    wc.cbClsExtra     = 0;
    wc.cbWndExtra     = 0;
    wc.hInstance      = hInstance;
    wc.hIcon          = LoadIcon(hInstance, szAppName);
    wc.hCursor        = LoadCursor(NULL, IDC_ARROW);
    wc.hbrBackground  = (HBRUSH)(COLOR_WINDOW + 1);
    wc.lpszMenuName   = szAppName;
    wc.lpszClassName  = szAppName;

    return(RegisterClass(&wc));
}


// create and show main window
BOOL InitInstance(HINSTANCE hInstance, int nCmdShow)
{
    HWND    hWnd;
    hInst = hInstance;
    hWnd = CreateWindow(szAppName, szTitle,
                        WS_OVERLAPPEDWINDOW,
                        160, 120, 320, 240,
                        NULL, NULL, hInstance, NULL);

    if (!hWnd)
        {
        return FALSE;
        }

    ShowWindow(hWnd, nCmdShow);
    UpdateWindow(hWnd);

    return TRUE;
}
```

CLIPTEXT.C

```
// CLIPTEXT.C
#include <windows.h>
#include <windowsx.h>
#include "globals.h"

HANDLE hEditText, hClipText, hText = NULL;
LPSTR lpEditText, lpClipText;
HWND hWnd, hEditBox, hClear, hClose;
char EditText[] = "Clipboard Test";

LRESULT CALLBACK WndProc(HWND hWnd,
                         UINT uMessage,
                         WPARAM wParam,
                         LPARAM lParam)
{
    hEditText = GlobalAlloc(GMEM_MOVEABLE,
                        (DWORD)sizeof(EditText));
    lpEditText = GlobalLock(hEditText);
    lstrcpy(lpEditText, EditText);
    GlobalUnlock(hEditText);

    switch (uMessage)
    {
        case WM_CREATE:
            // create an edit control
            hEditBox = CreateWindow("edit", EditText,
                    ES_CENTER | WS_BORDER |
                    WS_CHILD | WS_VISIBLE,
                    90, 30, 140, 30,
                    hWnd, IDC_EDITBOX, hInst, NULL);

            // create a button to clear the text
            // in edit control
            hClear = CreateWindow("button", "C&lear",
                    BS_PUSHBUTTON | WS_CHILD |
                    WS_VISIBLE,
                    50, 120, 80, 30,
                    hWnd, IDC_CLEAR, hInst, NULL);

            // create a close-window button
            hClose = CreateWindow("button", "&Close",
                    BS_PUSHBUTTON | WS_CHILD |
                    WS_VISIBLE,
                    190, 120, 80, 30,
                    hWnd, IDC_CLOSE, hInst, NULL);
```

```
       break;

   case WM_INITMENU:
       // check if the clipboard has text available,
       // if yes, enable the PASTE menu item
       // if not, gray the PASTE menu item
       if (wParam == GetMenu(hWnd)) {
           if (OpenClipboard(hWnd)) {
               if (IsClipboardFormatAvailable(CF_TEXT)
             || IsClipboardFormatAvailable(CF_OEMTEXT))
                   EnableMenuItem(wParam,
                                   IDM_PASTE, MF_ENABLED);
               else
                   EnableMenuItem(wParam,
                                   IDM_PASTE, MF_GRAYED);
               CloseClipboard();
               return (TRUE);
           }
           else return (FALSE);
       }
       return (TRUE);

   case WM_COMMAND:
       switch (GET_WM_COMMAND_ID(wParam,lParam))
       {
       case IDM_ABOUT:
               // create an about dialog box
               DialogBox(hInst, "ABOUTDLG",
                           hWnd, (DLGPROC)About);
               break;

       case IDM_COPY:

               // get the text from the edit control
               GetWindowText(hEditBox,
                               lpEditText, 20);

               // allocate memory and copy the
               // text into it
               hClipText = GlobalAlloc(GMEM_MOVEABLE,
                               GlobalSize(hEditText));
               lpClipText = GlobalLock(hClipText);
               lpEditText = GlobalLock(hEditText);
               lstrcpy(lpClipText, lpEditText);
               GlobalUnlock(hClipText);
               GlobalUnlock(hEditText);
```

```
             // copy the text from memory
             // into the clipboard
         if(OpenClipboard(hWnd) != 0){
           EmptyClipboard();
           SetClipboardData(CF_TEXT,
                         hClipText);
           CloseClipboard(); }

         hClipText = NULL;
         break;

     case IDM_PASTE:

         if(OpenClipboard(hWnd) != 0){
           // copy the text content in clipbaord
           // into allocated memory
          hClipText = GetClipboardData(CF_TEXT);
            if(hEditText != NULL)
                       GlobalFree(hEditText);
             hEditText =
                      GlobalAlloc(GMEM_MOVEABLE,
                        GlobalSize(hClipText));
            lpClipText = GlobalLock(hClipText);
            lpEditText = GlobalLock(hEditText);
            lstrcpy(lpEditText, lpClipText);
            GlobalUnlock(hClipText);
            CloseClipboard();
            GlobalUnlock(hEditText);
            EnableMenuItem(GetMenu(hWnd),
                       IDM_COPY, MF_ENABLED);
              // copy the text from memory into
              // edit control box
            SetWindowText(hEditBox, lpEditText);
         }
         break;

     case IDC_CLEAR:
         SetWindowText(hEditBox, "");
         break;

     case IDC_CLOSE:
         DestroyWindow(hWnd);
         break;

     default:
         return DefWindowProc(hWnd, uMessage,
                         wParam, lParam);
```

```
            }
            break;

        case WM_DESTROY:
            PostQuitMessage(0);
            break;

        default:
            return DefWindowProc(hWnd, uMessage,
                                    wParam, lParam);
    }
    return 0;
}
```

ABOUT.C

```
// ABOUT.C
#include <windows.h>
#include <windowsx.h>
#include "globals.h"

// procedures for ABOUT dialog box
LRESULT CALLBACK About(HWND hDlg,
                       UINT uMessage,
                       WPARAM wParam,
                       LPARAM lParam)
{
    switch (uMessage)
      {
        case WM_COMMAND:
            switch (GET_WM_COMMAND_ID(wParam,lParam))
            {
                case IDOK:
                case IDCANCEL:
                    {
                    EndDialog(hDlg, TRUE);
                    return(TRUE);
                    }
                    break;
            }
      }
    return FALSE;
}
```

CLIPTEXT.RC

```
#include "windows.h"
#include "globals.h"
#include <winver.h>

APPNAME ICON ICONFILE

RCINCLUDE ABOUT.DLG

APPNAME MENU
BEGIN
  POPUP "&Edit"
  BEGIN
      MENUITEM "&Copy",      IDM_COPY
      MENUITEM "&Paste",     IDM_PASTE
  END
  MENUITEM "&About",         IDM_ABOUT
END
```

ABOUT.DLG

```
ABOUTDLG DIALOG DISCARDABLE  22, 17, 167, 73
STYLE DS_MODALFRAME | WS_CAPTION | WS_SYSMENU
CAPTION SZABOUT
BEGIN
    DEFPUSHBUTTON    "OK", IDOK, 132, 2, 32, 14, WS_GROUP
    ICON             SZAPPNAME,      -1, 3, 2, 18, 20
    LTEXT            SZAPPNAME,      -1, 30, 12, 50, 8
    LTEXT            SZDESCRIPTION, -1, 30, 22, 150, 8
    LTEXT            SZVERSION,      -1, 30, 32, 150, 8
    LTEXT            SZCOMPANYNAME, -1, 30, 42, 150, 8
END
```

CLIPTEXT.ICO

CASE 10-2: CLIPBOARD OPERATIONS WITH BITMAP FORMAT DATA

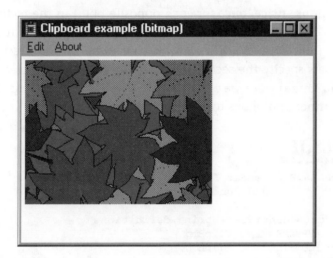

Clipboard example (bitmap)
Edit   About

FIGURE 10-2

This case shows how to transfer bitmap data to and from the Windows Clipboard. Please see Case 10-1 for an introduction to the Windows Clipboard facility and for an example of transferring text data to and from the Clipboard.

To paste a bitmap that is already on the Clipboard into the client area of the application window, the program first uses GetClipboardData() to get the bitmap handle, passing it the CF_BITMAP parameter. Then the program calls our function PaintBitmap() to draw the bitmap in the client area. The PaintBitmap() function encapsulates the work of drawing a bitmap, which consists of creating a memory device context with CreateCompatibleDC(), getting the object and selecting into the device context, and painting it using the BitBlt() function. Lastly, cleanup is done with ReleaseDC(), DeleteDC() and DeleteObject().

Copying a bitmap from the application window to the Clipboard is a bit more elaborate. The code is in the IDM_COPY handler, part of the

671

WM_COMMAND handler of the main window procedure. The code first sets a flag variable bCopy to TRUE, and changes the cursor shape to a cross-hair cursor. The users must specify a rectangular area in the window by clicking on the mouse twice, once for each opposite point in the rectangle. The WM_LBUTTONDOWN handler checks if bCopy is true. If so, it saves the mouse-down coordinates (and also the next time the mouse is clicked). After the users specify the second point, the portion of the screen is transferred using CreateCompatibleDC(), BitBlt(), and the Clipboard API in a manner analogous to the Paste operation.

GLOBALS.H

```
// GLOBALS.H - header file for global variables
//             and function prototypes

// Product identifier string definitions
#define APPNAME       ClipBmp
#define ICONFILE      ClipBmp.ico
#define SZAPPNAME     "ClipBmp"
#define SZDESCRIPTION "Clipboard example (bitmap)"
#define SZVERSION     "Version 1.0"
#define SZCOMPANYNAME "\251 M&&T Books, 1994"
#define SZABOUT       "About"

// Global function prototypes.
BOOL InitApplication(HINSTANCE);
BOOL InitInstance(HINSTANCE, int);
void PaintBitmap (HWND, HANDLE);

// Callback functions called by Windows.
LRESULT CALLBACK WndProc(HWND, UINT, WPARAM, LPARAM);
LRESULT CALLBACK About(HWND, UINT, WPARAM, LPARAM);

// Menu item ID
#define IDM_ABOUT 100
#define IDM_COPY  101
#define IDM_PASTE 102
#define IDM_CLEAR 103

// Global variable declarations.
extern HINSTANCE hInst;      // The current instance handle
extern char szAppName[];     // The name of this application
extern char szTitle[];       // The title bar text
extern HANDLE hClipBitmap;
```

WINMAIN.C

```
// WINMAIN.C
#include <windows.h>
#include "globals.h"

int APIENTRY WinMain(HINSTANCE hInstance,
                     HINSTANCE hPrevInstance,
                     LPSTR lpCmdLine,
                     int nCmdShow)
{
    MSG msg;

    // register main window class
    if (!hPrevInstance)
        {
        if (!InitApplication(hInstance))
            {
            return FALSE;
            }
        }

    // create and show main window
    if (!InitInstance(hInstance, nCmdShow))
        {
        return FALSE;
        }

    // process window messages
    while (GetMessage(&msg, NULL, 0, 0))
        {
            TranslateMessage(&msg);
            DispatchMessage(&msg);
        }
    return msg.wParam;
}
```

INIT.C

```
// INIT.C
#include <windows.h>
#include "globals.h"

HINSTANCE hInst;
char szAppName[] = SZAPPNAME;
char szTitle[] = SZDESCRIPTION;
```

673

```
// register main window class
BOOL InitApplication(HINSTANCE hInstance)
{
    WNDCLASS  wc;

    wc.style         = CS_HREDRAW | CS_VREDRAW;
    wc.lpfnWndProc   = (WNDPROC)WndProc;
    wc.cbClsExtra    = 0;
    wc.cbWndExtra    = 0;
    wc.hInstance     = hInstance;
    wc.hIcon         = LoadIcon(hInstance, szAppName);
    wc.hCursor       = LoadCursor(NULL, IDC_ARROW);
    wc.hbrBackground = (HBRUSH)(COLOR_WINDOW + 1);
    wc.lpszMenuName  = szAppName;
    wc.lpszClassName = szAppName;

    return(RegisterClass(&wc));
}

// create and show main window
BOOL InitInstance(HINSTANCE hInstance, int nCmdShow)
{
    HWND    hWnd;
    hInst = hInstance;
    hWnd = CreateWindow(szAppName, szTitle,
                        WS_OVERLAPPEDWINDOW,
                        160, 120, 320, 240,
                        NULL, NULL, hInstance, NULL);

    if (!hWnd)
        {
        return FALSE;
        }

    ShowWindow(hWnd, nCmdShow);
    UpdateWindow(hWnd);

    return TRUE;
}
```

CLIPBMP.C

```
// CLIPBMP.C
#include <windows.h>
#include <windowsx.h>
#include "globals.h"
```

```
HANDLE hClipBitmap;
LPSTR lpClipBitmap;
HWND hWnd;
LPRECT lpRect;
HCURSOR hNewCursor;
static BOOL bCopy = FALSE;
static BOOL bOrder = FALSE;
static POINT pt1, pt2;

LRESULT CALLBACK WndProc(HWND hWnd,
                         UINT uMessage,
                         WPARAM wParam,
                         LPARAM lParam)
{
    HDC hDC, hMemoryDC;
    PAINTSTRUCT ps;
    UINT nWidth, nHeight;
    RECT rc1;

    switch (uMessage)
    {
        case WM_CREATE:
            hNewCursor = LoadCursor(NULL, IDC_ARROW);
            break;

        case WM_INITMENU:
            // if there is a bitmap available from
            // the clipbaord
            // enable the PASTE menu item
            // otherwise gray the PASTE menu item
            if (wParam == GetMenu(hWnd)) {
              if (OpenClipboard(hWnd)) {
                if (IsClipboardFormatAvailable(CF_BITMAP))
                    EnableMenuItem(wParam,
                            IDM_PASTE, MF_ENABLED);
                else
                    EnableMenuItem(wParam,
                            IDM_PASTE, MF_GRAYED);
                CloseClipboard();
                return (TRUE);
                }
              else
                return (FALSE);
            }
            return (TRUE);

        case WM_PAINT:
```

```
        hDC = BeginPaint(hWnd, &ps);
        PaintBitmap(hWnd, hClipBitmap);
        EndPaint(hWnd, &ps);
        break;

    case WM_COMMAND:
        switch (GET_WM_COMMAND_ID(wParam,lParam))
        {
        case IDM_ABOUT:
                // create an about dialog box
                DialogBox(hInst, "ABOUTDLG",
                          hWnd, (DLGPROC)About);
                break;

        case IDM_COPY:

                // set the cursor to CROSS
                // click mouse button at two different
                // positions in client area to define a
                // rectangle that confine the bitmap to
                // be copied into the clipboard
                // see WM_LBUTTONDOWN case for
                // procedures
                bCopy = TRUE;
                bOrder = FALSE;
                hNewCursor = LoadCursor(NULL,
                                IDC_CROSS);
                SetCursor(hNewCursor);
                break;

        case IDM_PASTE:

                // paste the bitmap from clipboard into
                // main window client area

                if(OpenClipboard(hWnd) != 0){

                    // get bitmap from the clipboard
                    hClipBitmap =
                        GetClipboardData(CF_BITMAP);

                    if(hClipBitmap == NULL) {
                            CloseClipboard(); break; }

                    // paint the bitmap in window
                    // client area
                    PaintBitmap(hWnd, hClipBitmap);
```

```
                CloseClipboard();
                EnableMenuItem(GetMenu(hWnd),
                            IDM_COPY, MF_ENABLED);
                }
            break;

        case IDM_CLEAR:
                // erase the bitmap in client area
            GetWindowRect(hWnd, lpRect);
            InvalidateRect(hWnd, lpRect, TRUE);
            break;

        default:
            return DefWindowProc(hWnd, uMessage,
                                wParam, lParam);
        }
        break;

    case WM_LBUTTONDOWN:

        if(bCopy){
            // copy the bitmap in client area confined
            // by a rectangle rc1 into the clipboard

            if(!bOrder){
                // get the position of first point
            GetCursorPos(&pt1);
            ScreenToClient(hWnd, &pt1); }

            if(bOrder){
                // get the position of second point
            GetCursorPos(&pt2);
            ScreenToClient(hWnd, &pt2);

                // define a rectangle rc1
            rc1.left = min(pt1.x, pt2.x);
            rc1.right = max(pt1.x, pt2.x);
            rc1.top = min(pt1.y, pt2.y);
            rc1.bottom = max(pt1.y, pt2.y);

            {   nWidth = rc1.right - rc1.left;
                nHeight = rc1.bottom - rc1.top;

                    // get main window DC
                hDC = GetDC(hWnd);

                    // create a memory DC and a bitmap
                    // compatible with main window DC
```

```
                         hMemoryDC = CreateCompatibleDC(hDC);
                         hClipBitmap = CreateCompatibleBitmap(
                                       hDC, nWidth, nHeight);

                         // select the bitmap to the memory DC
                         SelectObject(hMemoryDC, hClipBitmap);

                         // copy the bitmap from window DC
                         // into memory DC
                         BitBlt(hMemoryDC, 0, 0,
                                nWidth, nHeight,
                                hDC, rc1.left, rc1.top,
                                SRCCOPY);

                         // copy the bitmap from memory DC
                         // into the clipboard
                         if(OpenClipboard(hWnd) != 0){
                             EmptyClipboard();
                             SetClipboardData(CF_BITMAP,
                                              hClipBitmap);
                             CloseClipboard(); }

                         DeleteDC(hDC);
                         DeleteDC(hMemoryDC);
                       }

                       bCopy = FALSE;
                       hNewCursor = LoadCursor(NULL, IDC_ARROW);
                       SetCursor(hNewCursor);
                       }
                    // toggle the point order flag
                     bOrder = !bOrder;
                 }
               break;

        case WM_SETCURSOR:
            SetCursor(hNewCursor);
            break;

        case WM_DESTROY:
            PostQuitMessage(0);
            break;

        default:
            return DefWindowProc(hWnd, uMessage, wParam, lParam);
    }
    return 0;
}
```

```
// function for painting the bitmap in window client area
void PaintBitmap(hWnd, hBitmap)
HWND hWnd;
HANDLE hBitmap;
{
  HDC hDC, hMemoryDC;
  BITMAP bmp;
    hDC = GetDC(hWnd);
    hMemoryDC = CreateCompatibleDC(hDC);
    GetObject(hBitmap, sizeof(BITMAP), (LPSTR) &bmp);
    SelectObject(hMemoryDC, hBitmap);
    BitBlt(hDC, 4, 4,
            bmp.bmWidth, bmp.bmHeight, hMemoryDC, 0, 0, SRCCOPY);
    ReleaseDC(hWnd, hDC);
    DeleteDC(hMemoryDC);
    DeleteObject(hBitmap);
}
```

ABOUT.C

```
// ABOUT.C
#include <windows.h>
#include <windowsx.h>
#include "globals.h"

// procedures for ABOUT dialog box
LRESULT CALLBACK About(HWND hDlg,
                       UINT uMessage,
                       WPARAM wParam,
                       LPARAM lParam)

{
    switch (uMessage)
      {
        case WM_COMMAND:
            switch (GET_WM_COMMAND_ID(wParam,lParam))
              {
                case IDOK:
                case IDCANCEL:
                    {
                    EndDialog(hDlg, TRUE);
                    return(TRUE);
                    }
                    break;
              }
      }
    return FALSE;
}
```

CLIPBMP.RC

```
#include "windows.h"
#include "globals.h"
#include <winver.h>

APPNAME ICON ICONFILE

RCINCLUDE ABOUT.DLG

APPNAME MENU
BEGIN
  POPUP "&Edit"
  BEGIN
      MENUITEM "&Copy",    IDM_COPY
      MENUITEM "&Paste",   IDM_PASTE
      MENUITEM "&Delete",  IDM_CLEAR
  END
  MENUITEM "&About",       IDM_ABOUT
END
```

ABOUT.DLG

```
ABOUTDLG DIALOG DISCARDABLE  22, 17, 167, 73
STYLE DS_MODALFRAME | WS_CAPTION | WS_SYSMENU
CAPTION SZABOUT
BEGIN
    DEFPUSHBUTTON  "OK", IDOK, 132, 2, 32, 14, WS_GROUP
    ICON           SZAPPNAME,      -1, 3, 2, 18, 20
    LTEXT          SZAPPNAME,      -1, 30, 12, 50, 8
    LTEXT          SZDESCRIPTION, -1, 30, 22, 150, 8
    LTEXT          SZVERSION,      -1, 30, 32, 150, 8
    LTEXT          SZCOMPANYNAME, -1, 30, 42, 150, 8
END
```

CLIPBMP.ICO

CASE 10-3: COPYING THE ENTIRE SCREEN BITMAP TO THE CLIPBOARD

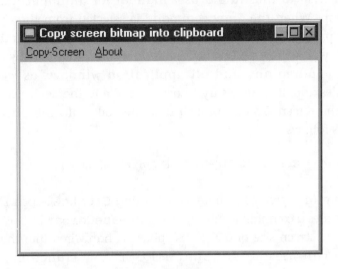

FIGURE 10-3A

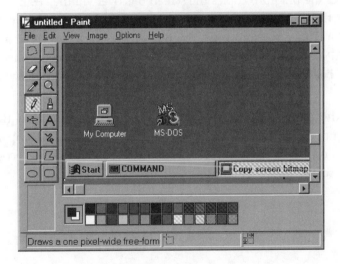

FIGURE 10-3B

This case shows how to make of a copy of the entire screen bitmap and place it on the Windows Clipboard. This procedure is useful if you wish to illustrate a user manual for an application with a screen dump. When the Copy command is selected from the application menu, the program hides itself before doing the screen copy, so that extraneous data won't show up on the screen dump. In order to copy the screen display, including any and all application windows as well as the Windows desktop, it is necessary to get a handle to the device context representing the screen. To accomplish this, the code calls the `CreateDC()` function as follows:

```
hScreenDC = CreateDC("DISPLAY", NULL, NULL, NULL);
```

The program then creates a memory DC using `CreateCompatibleDC()` and also creates a compatible bitmap using `CreateCompatibleBitmap()`. Note that the screen size of 640 x 480 pixels is hardwired into the program code. You can use the `GetSystemMetrics()` function, with the `SM_CXSCREEN` and `SM_CYSCREEN` parameters, to query the system at run time regarding the size of the screen display. After selecting the bitmap into the memory DC, the program copies the screen bits over via the `BitBlt()` function. Then this bitmap is transferred to the Windows Clipboard using the Clipboard API in the usual manner, with `SetClipboardData()` and a `CF_BITMAP` parameter. To make this program work properly, there shall be no overlap between the main window of this program and other windows on the screen.

After the copy is done, the main window shows up on the screen again. Figure 10-3b shows a case in which the screen bitmap has been pasted into a paint program. Please see Case 10-4 for how to copy a portion of the screen to the Clipboard.

GLOBALS.H

```
// GLOBALS.H - header file for global variables
//             and function prototypes

// Product identifier string definitions
#define APPNAME        Screen
#define ICONFILE       Screen.ico
#define SZAPPNAME      "Screen"
#define SZDESCRIPTION  "Copy screen bitmap into clipboard"
#define SZVERSION      "Version 1.0"
#define SZCOMPANYNAME  "\251 M&&T Books, 1994"
#define SZABOUT        "About"

// Global function prototypes.
BOOL InitApplication(HINSTANCE);
BOOL InitInstance(HINSTANCE, int);

// Callback functions called by Windows.
LRESULT CALLBACK WndProc(HWND, UINT, WPARAM, LPARAM);
LRESULT CALLBACK About(HWND, UINT, WPARAM, LPARAM);

// Menu item ID
#define IDM_ABOUT        100
#define IDM_COPY_SCREEN  101

// Global variable declarations.
extern HINSTANCE hInst;       // The current instance handle
extern char szAppName[];      // The name of this application
extern char szTitle[];        // The title bar text
```

WINMAIN.C

```
// WINMAIN.C
#include <windows.h>
#include "globals.h"

int APIENTRY WinMain(HINSTANCE hInstance,
                     HINSTANCE hPrevInstance,
                     LPSTR lpCmdLine,
                     int nCmdShow)
{
    MSG msg;

    // register main window class
```

```
        if (!hPrevInstance)
           {
           if (!InitApplication(hInstance))
              {
              return FALSE;
              }
           }

        // create and show main window
        if (!InitInstance(hInstance, nCmdShow))
           {
           return FALSE;
           }

        // process window messages
        while (GetMessage(&msg, NULL, 0, 0))
           {
              TranslateMessage(&msg);
              DispatchMessage(&msg);
           }
        return msg.wParam;
}
```

INIT.C

```
// INIT.C
#include <windows.h>
#include "globals.h"

HINSTANCE hInst;
char szAppName[] = SZAPPNAME;
char szTitle[] = SZDESCRIPTION;

// register main window class
BOOL InitApplication(HINSTANCE hInstance)
{
    WNDCLASS  wc;

    wc.style          = CS_HREDRAW | CS_VREDRAW;
    wc.lpfnWndProc    = (WNDPROC)WndProc;
    wc.cbClsExtra     = 0;
    wc.cbWndExtra     = 0;
    wc.hInstance      = hInstance;
    wc.hIcon          = LoadIcon(hInstance, szAppName);
    wc.hCursor        = LoadCursor(NULL, IDC_ARROW);
    wc.hbrBackground  = (HBRUSH)(COLOR_WINDOW + 1);
    wc.lpszMenuName   = szAppName;
```

```
    wc.lpszClassName = szAppName;

    return(RegisterClass(&wc));
}

// create and show main window
BOOL InitInstance(HINSTANCE hInstance, int nCmdShow)
{
    HWND    hWnd;
    hInst = hInstance;
    hWnd = CreateWindow(szAppName, szTitle,
                        WS_OVERLAPPEDWINDOW,
                        160, 120, 320, 240,
                        NULL, NULL, hInstance, NULL);

    if (!hWnd)
        {
        return FALSE;
        }

    ShowWindow(hWnd, nCmdShow);
    UpdateWindow(hWnd);

    return TRUE;
}
```

SCREEN.C

```
// SCREEN.C
#include <windows.h>
#include <windowsx.h>
#include "globals.h"

HBITMAP hScreenBitmap;
HWND hWnd;

LRESULT CALLBACK WndProc(HWND hWnd,
                         UINT uMessage,
                         WPARAM wParam,
                         LPARAM lParam)
{
    HDC hScreenDC, hMemoryDC;

    switch (uMessage)
    {
        case WM_COMMAND:
            switch (GET_WM_COMMAND_ID(wParam,lParam))
                {
```

```
case IDM_COPY_SCREEN:
        // hide the main window
        ShowWindow(hWnd, SW_HIDE);

        // copy the screen bitmap
        // into clipboard

        // create a DC for the screen
        hScreenDC = CreateDC("DISPLAY",
                            NULL, NULL, NULL);

        // create a memory DC and bitmap
        // compatible to the screen DC
        hMemoryDC =
                CreateCompatibleDC(hScreenDC);
        hScreenBitmap = CreateCompatibleBitmap(
                        hScreenDC, 640, 480);

        // select the bitmap for the memory DC
        SelectObject(hMemoryDC, hScreenBitmap);

        // copy the screen bitmap into
        // memory DC
        BitBlt(hMemoryDC, 0, 0, 640, 480,
            hScreenDC, 0, 0, SRCCOPY);

        // copy the screen bitmap in memory DC
        // into the clipboard
        if(OpenClipboard(hWnd) != 0){
            EmptyClipboard();
            SetClipboardData(CF_BITMAP,
                        hScreenBitmap);
            CloseClipboard(); }

        DeleteDC(hScreenDC);
        DeleteDC(hMemoryDC);

        // show main window when job is done
        ShowWindow(hWnd, SW_SHOWNORMAL);
        break;

case IDM_ABOUT:
        // create an about dialog box
        DialogBox(hInst, "ABOUTDLG",
                hWnd, (DLGPROC)About);
        break;
```

```
            default:
                return DefWindowProc(hWnd, uMessage,
                                         wParam, lParam);
        }
        break;

    case WM_DESTROY:
        PostQuitMessage(0);
        break;

    default:
        return DefWindowProc(hWnd, uMessage,
                                 wParam, lParam);
    }
    return 0;
}
```

ABOUT.C

```
// ABOUT.C
#include <windows.h>
#include <windowsx.h>
#include "globals.h"

// procedures for ABOUT dialog box
LRESULT CALLBACK About(HWND hDlg,
                       UINT uMessage,
                       WPARAM wParam,
                       LPARAM lParam)
{
    switch (uMessage)
      {
      case WM_COMMAND:
            switch (GET_WM_COMMAND_ID(wParam,lParam))
            {
                case IDOK:
                case IDCANCEL:
                    {
                    EndDialog(hDlg, TRUE);
                    return(TRUE);
                    }
                    break;
            }
      }
    return FALSE;
}
```

SCREEN.RC

```
#include "windows.h"
#include "globals.h"
#include <winver.h>

APPNAME ICON ICONFILE

RCINCLUDE ABOUT.DLG

APPNAME MENU
BEGIN
    MENUITEM "&Copy-Screen",     IDM_COPY_SCREEN
    MENUITEM "&About",           IDM_ABOUT
END
```

ABOUT.DLG

```
ABOUTDLG DIALOG DISCARDABLE  22, 17, 167, 73
STYLE DS_MODALFRAME | WS_CAPTION | WS_SYSMENU
CAPTION SZABOUT
BEGIN
    DEFPUSHBUTTON   "OK", IDOK, 132, 2, 32, 14, WS_GROUP
    ICON            SZAPPNAME,      -1, 3, 2, 18, 20
    LTEXT           SZAPPNAME,      -1, 30, 12,  50, 8
    LTEXT           SZDESCRIPTION, -1, 30, 22, 150, 8
    LTEXT           SZVERSION,      -1, 30, 32, 150, 8
    LTEXT           SZCOMPANYNAME, -1, 30, 42, 150, 8
END
```

SCREEN.ICO

CASE 10-4: COPYING A PART OF THE SCREEN TO THE CLIPBOARD

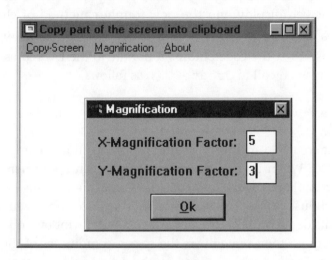

FIGURE 10-4A

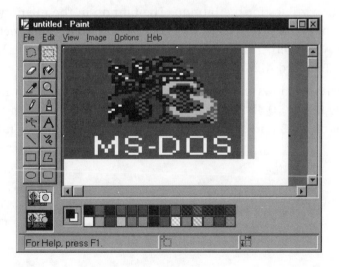

FIGURE 10-4B

This case shows how to copy part of the screen display bitmap to the Windows Clipboard. This example builds upon techniques shown in Case 10-3. This program lets the user specify an arbitrary rectangle on the screen display, via the now-familiar method of clicking the mouse twice, once for each opposite corner of the desired rectangle.

As in Case 10-3, the code obtains a handle to the DC representing the screen display via a call to CreateDC() as follows:

```
hScreenDC = CreateDC("DISPLAY", NULL, NULL, NULL);
```

As before, it creates a memory DC and a bitmap that is compatible with the screen DC. When users click on the Copy-Screen menu item, the code sets the bCopy flag to TRUE and calls SetCapture(). This API function directs all mouse-related messages to this application, even when the mouse is outside its window, traveling across other windows and the desktop. The program then remembers the screen coordinates of the next two mouse clicks. The rectangle defined by these two points is then copied to the memory DC using the StretchBlt() function. StretchBlt() is used instead of BitBlt() because the program allows users to specify magnification values for the bitmap. The bitmap in the memory DC now contains a magnified version of the selected portion of the screen display. This display is then transferred to the clipboard in the usual manner, using the Clipboard API.

Figure 10-4a shows the dialog box that lets users specify a magnification factor. Figure 10-4b shows a screen bitmap that has been magnified by a factor of 5 x 3 and then pasted into a paint program for further processing.

GLOBALS.H

```
// GLOBALS.H - header file for global variables
//              and function prototypes

// Product identifier string definitions
#define APPNAME        CutScn
#define ICONFILE       CutScn.ico
#define SZAPPNAME      "CutScn"
#define SZDESCRIPTION  "Copy part of the screen into clipboard"
#define SZVERSION      "Version 1.0"
#define SZCOMPANYNAME  "\251 M&&T Books, 1994"
#define SZABOUT        "About"


// Global function prototypes.
BOOL InitApplication(HINSTANCE);
BOOL InitInstance(HINSTANCE, int);

// Callback functions called by Windows.
LRESULT CALLBACK WndProc(HWND, UINT, WPARAM, LPARAM);
LRESULT CALLBACK MagProc(HWND, UINT, WPARAM, LPARAM);
LRESULT CALLBACK About(HWND, UINT, WPARAM, LPARAM);

// Menu item ID
#define IDM_ABOUT          100
#define IDM_CUT_SCREEN     101
#define IDM_MAGNIFICATION  102

// Dialog box control ID
#define IDD_MAGNIFICATION 200

// Dialog box control ID
#define IDC_XMAG           103
#define IDC_YMAG           104
#define IDC_OK             105

// Global variable declarations.
extern HINSTANCE hInst;      // The current instance handle
extern char szAppName[];     // The name of this application
extern char szTitle[];       // The title bar text
extern HWND hWnd, hMagDlg;
extern DLGPROC lpProcMag;
```

WINMAIN.C

```
// WINMAIN.C
#include <windows.h>
```

```
#include "globals.h"

HWND hMagDlg;

int APIENTRY WinMain(HINSTANCE hInstance,
                     HINSTANCE hPrevInstance,
                     LPSTR lpCmdLine,
                     int nCmdShow)
{
    MSG msg;

    // register main window class
    if (!hPrevInstance)
        {
        if (!InitApplication(hInstance))
            {
            return FALSE;
            }
        }

    // create and show main window
    if (!InitInstance(hInstance, nCmdShow))
        {
        return FALSE;
        }

    // process window messages
    // if the message is the keyboard input for
    // hMagDlg dialog box,
    // use IsDialogMessage function to process the message
    while (GetMessage(&msg, NULL, 0, 0))
        { if(!IsWindow(hMagDlg) ||
               !IsDialogMessage(hMagDlg, &msg))
            {
             TranslateMessage(&msg);
             DispatchMessage(&msg);
            }
        }
    return msg.wParam;
}
```

INIT.C

```
// INIT.C
#include <windows.h>
#include "globals.h"
```

```
HINSTANCE hInst;
char szAppName[] = SZAPPNAME;
char szTitle[] = SZDESCRIPTION;

// register main window class
BOOL InitApplication(HINSTANCE hInstance)
{
    WNDCLASS  wc;

    wc.style         = CS_HREDRAW | CS_VREDRAW;
    wc.lpfnWndProc   = (WNDPROC)WndProc;
    wc.cbClsExtra    = 0;
    wc.cbWndExtra    = 0;
    wc.hInstance     = hInstance;
    wc.hIcon         = LoadIcon(hInstance, szAppName);
    wc.hCursor       = LoadCursor(NULL, IDC_ARROW);
    wc.hbrBackground = (HBRUSH)(COLOR_WINDOW + 1);
    wc.lpszMenuName  = szAppName;
    wc.lpszClassName = szAppName;

    return(RegisterClass(&wc));
}

// create and show main window
BOOL InitInstance(HINSTANCE hInstance, int nCmdShow)
{
    HWND    hWnd;
    hInst = hInstance;
    hWnd = CreateWindow(szAppName, szTitle,
                        WS_OVERLAPPEDWINDOW,
                        160, 120, 320, 240,
                        NULL, NULL, hInstance, NULL);

    if (!hWnd)
        {
        return FALSE;
        }

    ShowWindow(hWnd, nCmdShow);
    UpdateWindow(hWnd);

    return TRUE;
}
```

CUTSCN.C

```
// CUTSCN.C
#include <windows.h>
#include <windowsx.h>
#include "globals.h"

UINT X_MAG, Y_MAG;
BOOL FAR* bTran;
HBITMAP hScreenBitmap;
HWND hWnd, hMag;
static BOOL bCut = FALSE;
static BOOL bOrder = FALSE;
static POINT pt1, pt2;
DLGPROC lpProcMag;

LRESULT CALLBACK WndProc(HWND hWnd,
                         UINT uMessage,
                         WPARAM wParam,
                         LPARAM lParam)
{
    FARPROC lpProcMag;
    HDC hScreenDC, hMemoryDC;
    UINT nWidth, nHeight;
    RECT rc1;

    switch (uMessage)
    {
        case WM_CREATE:
            // set initial magnification factors
            X_MAG = 1;
            Y_MAG = 1;
            break;

        case WM_COMMAND:
            switch (GET_WM_COMMAND_ID(wParam,lParam))
            {
                case IDM_CUT_SCREEN:
                    // start the copy process
                    // set the bCut flag to TRUE
                    // set the bOrder flag to FALSE,
                    // i.e. next mouse button down will
                    // provide the coordinates of first
                    // point needed for defining a
                    // rectangle on the screen
                    bCut = TRUE;
                    bOrder = FALSE;
```

694

```
                    // direct all cursor input to
                    // this window - hWnd
                SetCapture(hWnd);
                SetCursor(LoadCursor(NULL, IDC_CROSS));
                break;

        case IDM_MAGNIFICATION:
                    // create a magnification factor
                    // dialog box
                lpProcMag = MakeProcInstance(
                            (FARPROC)MagProc, hInst);
                hMagDlg = CreateDialog(hInst,
                    MAKEINTRESOURCE(IDD_MAGNIFICATION),
                                hWnd, lpProcMag);
                break;

        case IDM_ABOUT:
                    // create an about dialog box
                DialogBox(hInst, "ABOUTDLG",
                            hWnd, (DLGPROC)About);
                break;

        default:
            return DefWindowProc(hWnd, uMessage,
                                        wParam, lParam);

    }
    break;

case WM_LBUTTONDOWN:
    if(bCut){
        if(!bOrder){
            GetCursorPos(&pt1); }
        if(bOrder){
            GetCursorPos(&pt2);

            // define a rectangle rc1 using
            // coordinates of pt1 and pt1
            rc1.left = min(pt1.x, pt2.x);
            rc1.right = max(pt1.x, pt2.x);
            rc1.top = min(pt1.y, pt2.y);
            rc1.bottom = max(pt1.y, pt2.y);
            {   nWidth = rc1.right - rc1.left;
                nHeight = rc1.bottom - rc1.top;

                // create a DC for the screen
                hScreenDC = CreateDC("DISPLAY",
```

```
                                 NULL, NULL, NULL);

            // create a memory DC and bitmap
            // compatible to the screen DC
            hMemoryDC =
              CreateCompatibleDC(hScreenDC);
            hScreenBitmap =
                  CreateCompatibleBitmap(
                    hScreenDC, nWidth*X_MAG,
                              nHeight*Y_MAG);

            // select the bitmap for the memory DC
            SelectObject(hMemoryDC,
                            hScreenBitmap);

            // copy a magnified screen bitmap
            // confined by rectangle rc1
            // into memory DC
            StretchBlt(hMemoryDC, 0, 0,
                      nWidth*X_MAG,
                      nHeight*Y_MAG,
                      hScreenDC,
                      rc1.left, rc1.top,
                      nWidth, nHeight, SRCCOPY);

            // copy the bitmap in memory DC
            // into the clipboard
            if(OpenClipboard(hWnd) != 0){
                EmptyClipboard();
                SetClipboardData(CF_BITMAP,
                            hScreenBitmap);
                CloseClipboard(); }

            DeleteDC(hScreenDC);
            DeleteDC(hMemoryDC);
          }

          // when done, set bCut flag to FALSE,
          // release the cursor capture
          bCut = FALSE;
          ReleaseCapture();
          SetCursor(LoadCursor(NULL, IDC_ARROW));
          }

        // toggle the bOrder flag
        bOrder = !bOrder;
        }
```

```
            break;

        case WM_DESTROY:
            PostQuitMessage(0);
            break;

        default:
            return DefWindowProc(hWnd, uMessage,
                                    wParam, lParam);
    }
    return 0;
}
```

MAGNIFY.C

```
// MAGNIFY.C
#include <windows.h>
#include <windowsx.h>
#include "globals.h"

UINT X_MAG, Y_MAG;
DLGPROC lpProcMag;
BOOL FAR* bTran;

LRESULT CALLBACK MagProc(HWND hMagDlg,
                        UINT uMessage,
                        WPARAM wParam,
                        LPARAM lParam)
{
    switch (uMessage)
    {
        case WM_COMMAND:
            switch (GET_WM_COMMAND_ID(wParam,lParam))
            {
                case IDCANCEL:
                case IDC_OK:
                    // get the magnification factor
                    // from the input edit box
                    X_MAG = GetDlgItemInt(hMagDlg,
                                IDC_XMAG, bTran, FALSE);
                    Y_MAG = GetDlgItemInt(hMagDlg,
                                IDC_YMAG, bTran, FALSE);
                    if(X_MAG == 0) X_MAG = 1;
                    if(Y_MAG == 0) Y_MAG = 1;
                    DestroyWindow(hMagDlg);
                    hMagDlg = 0;
```

```
                        break;

                    default:
                        return FALSE;
                }
                break;
        default:
            return DefWindowProc(hMagDlg, uMessage,
                                    wParam, lParam);
        }
        return 0;
}
```

ABOUT.C

```
// ABOUT.C
#include <windows.h>
#include <windowsx.h>
#include "globals.h"

// procedures for ABOUT dialog box
LRESULT CALLBACK About(HWND hDlg,
                        UINT uMessage,
                        WPARAM wParam,
                        LPARAM lParam)
{
    switch (uMessage)
      {
        case WM_COMMAND:
            switch (GET_WM_COMMAND_ID(wParam,lParam))
            {
                case IDOK:
                case IDCANCEL:
                    {
                    EndDialog(hDlg, TRUE);
                    return(TRUE);
                    }
                    break;
            }
      }
    return FALSE;
}
```

CUTSCN.RC

```
#include "windows.h"
#include "globals.h"
#include <winver.h>

APPNAME ICON ICONFILE

RCINCLUDE ABOUT.DLG
RCINCLUDE MAGNIFY.DLG

APPNAME MENU
BEGIN
    MENUITEM "&Copy-Screen",     IDM_CUT_SCREEN
    MENUITEM "&Magnification",   IDM_MAGNIFICATION
    MENUITEM "&About",           IDM_ABOUT
END
```

MAGNIFY.DLG

```
DLGINCLUDE RCDATA DISCARDABLE
BEGIN
    "GLOBALS.H\0"
END

IDD_MAGNIFICATION DIALOG 32, 21, 108, 57
STYLE WS_POPUP | WS_VISIBLE | WS_CAPTION | WS_SYSMENU
CAPTION "Magnification"
BEGIN
    LTEXT           "X-Magnification Factor:",
                    101, 6, 8, 80, 8
    EDITTEXT        IDC_XMAG, 85, 6, 16, 12
    LTEXT           "Y-Magnification Factor:",
                    102, 6, 23, 80, 8
    EDITTEXT        IDC_YMAG, 85, 22, 16, 12
    DEFPUSHBUTTON   "&Ok", IDC_OK, 34, 39, 40, 14
END
```

ABOUT.DLG

```
ABOUTDLG DIALOG DISCARDABLE  22, 17, 167, 73
STYLE DS_MODALFRAME | WS_CAPTION | WS_SYSMENU
CAPTION SZABOUT
BEGIN
```

```
        DEFPUSHBUTTON   "OK", IDOK, 132, 2, 32, 14, WS_GROUP
        ICON            SZAPPNAME,      -1, 3, 2, 18, 20
        LTEXT           SZAPPNAME,      -1, 30, 12,  50, 8
        LTEXT           SZDESCRIPTION, -1, 30, 22, 150, 8
        LTEXT           SZVERSION,      -1, 30, 32, 150, 8
        LTEXT           SZCOMPANYNAME, -1, 30, 42, 150, 8
END
```

CUTSCN.ICO

CHAPTER ELEVEN

THE TIMER

CASE 11-1: USING A TIMER

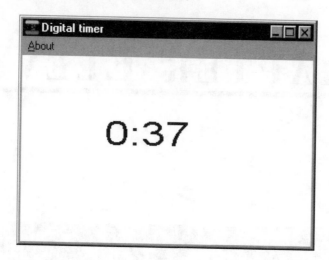

FIGURE 11-1

This case shows how to use a timer in a Windows application. The Windows environment provides an easy way to create and use timers in an application via the SetTimer() function. Using this function is very straightforward. All that you need to do is to create the timer in the WM_CREATE handler, which is invoked when the main application window is created. The parameters to SetTimer() include a handle to the parent window, a numerical identifier for the timer, an interval value in milliseconds, and, lastly, a way for the application to be notified of timer ticks. Applications can receive notification via a WM_TIMER message or, optionally, via callbacks to an application routine. In this case, we opt for the WM_TIMER notification, with a timer interval of one second (1000 milliseconds).

In the WM_TIMER handler in the main window procedure, the code increments a running count of the minutes and seconds, and then outputs a text representation of this elapsed time to the main window client area. Cleanup is done in the WM_DESTROY handler, which disposes of the timer before posting a quit message.

The next case in this chapter shows how to use multiple timers in an application.

GLOBALS.H

```
// GLOBALS.H - header file for global variables
//              and function prototypes

// Product identifier string definitions
#define APPNAME        DTimer
#define ICONFILE       DTimer.ico
#define SZAPPNAME      "DTimer"
#define SZDESCRIPTION  "Digital timer"
#define SZVERSION      "Version 1.0"
#define SZCOMPANYNAME  "\251 M&&T Books, 1994"
#define SZABOUT        "About"

// Global function prototypes.
BOOL InitApplication(HINSTANCE);
BOOL InitInstance(HINSTANCE, int);

// Callback functions called by Windows.
LRESULT CALLBACK WndProc(HWND, UINT, WPARAM, LPARAM);
LRESULT CALLBACK About(HWND, UINT, WPARAM, LPARAM);

// Menu item ID
#define IDM_ABOUT    1000

// Global variable declarations.
extern HINSTANCE hInst;      // The current instance handle
extern char szAppName[];     // The name of this application
extern char szTitle[];       // The title bar text
```

WINMAIN.C

```
// WINMAIN.C
#include <windows.h>
#include "globals.h"

int APIENTRY WinMain(HINSTANCE hInstance,
                     HINSTANCE hPrevInstance,
                     LPSTR lpCmdLine,
                     int nCmdShow)
{
    MSG msg;
```

```
    // register main window class
    if (!hPrevInstance)
        {
        if (!InitApplication(hInstance))
            {
            return FALSE;
            }
        }

    // create and show main window
    if (!InitInstance(hInstance, nCmdShow))
        {
        return FALSE;
        }

    // process window messages
    while (GetMessage(&msg, NULL, 0, 0))
        {
            TranslateMessage(&msg);
            DispatchMessage(&msg);
        }
    return msg.wParam;
}
```

INIT.C

```
// INIT.C
#include <windows.h>
#include "globals.h"

HINSTANCE hInst;
char szAppName[] = SZAPPNAME;
char szTitle[] = SZDESCRIPTION;

// register main window class
BOOL InitApplication(HINSTANCE hInstance)
{
    WNDCLASS  wc;

    wc.style        = CS_HREDRAW | CS_VREDRAW;
    wc.lpfnWndProc  = (WNDPROC)WndProc;
    wc.cbClsExtra   = 0;
    wc.cbWndExtra   = 0;
    wc.hInstance    = hInstance;
    wc.hIcon        = LoadIcon(hInstance, szAppName);
    wc.hCursor      = LoadCursor(NULL, IDC_ARROW);
```

704

```
    wc.hbrBackground = (HBRUSH)(COLOR_WINDOW + 1);
    wc.lpszMenuName  = szAppName;
    wc.lpszClassName = szAppName;

    return(RegisterClass(&wc));
}

// create and show main window
BOOL InitInstance(HINSTANCE hInstance, int nCmdShow)
{
    HWND    hWnd;
    hInst = hInstance;
    hWnd = CreateWindow(szAppName, szTitle,
                        WS_OVERLAPPEDWINDOW,
                        160, 120, 320, 240,
                        NULL, NULL, hInstance, NULL);

    if (!hWnd)
        {
        return FALSE;
        }

    ShowWindow(hWnd, nCmdShow);
    UpdateWindow(hWnd);

    return TRUE;
}
```

DTIMER.C

```
// DTIMER.C
#include <windows.h>
#include <windowsx.h>
#include <stdlib.h>
#include "globals.h"

LRESULT CALLBACK WndProc(HWND hWnd,
                         UINT uMessage,
                         WPARAM wParam,
                         LPARAM lParam)
{
    HDC hDC;
    static HFONT hFont;
    char Timer_Text[9], Second_Text[2];
    char TenSecond_Text[2], Minute_Text[4];
    static int Timer_Second=0, Timer_TenSecond = 0;
    static int Timer_Minute=0;
```

```
switch (uMessage)
{
    case WM_CREATE:
            // create a 1 second period timer
            SetTimer(hWnd, 1, 1000, NULL);

            // create font set for timer digits display
            hFont = CreateFont(40, 20, 0, 0, 400, 0, 0, 0,
                        ANSI_CHARSET, OUT_DEFAULT_PRECIS,
                        CLIP_DEFAULT_PRECIS,
                        PROOF_QUALITY, DEFAULT_PITCH, NULL);
            break;

    case WM_TIMER:
            // increase timer reading by one
            // for every second
            Timer_Second += 1;
            if(Timer_Second == 10){
                Timer_Second = 0; Timer_TenSecond += 1; }
            if(Timer_TenSecond == 6){
                Timer_TenSecond = 0; Timer_Minute += 1; }

            // convert digit number into text
            _itoa(Timer_Second, Second_Text, 10);
            _itoa(Timer_TenSecond, TenSecond_Text, 10);
            _itoa(Timer_Minute, Minute_Text, 10);

            // copy all text into one string
            strcpy(Timer_Text, Minute_Text);
            strcat(Timer_Text, ":");
            strcat(Timer_Text, TenSecond_Text);
            strcat(Timer_Text, Second_Text);

            // display the timer text string
            hDC = GetDC(hWnd);
            SetMapMode(hDC, MM_TEXT);
            SetTextColor(hDC, RGB(128, 0, 0));
            SetBkColor(hDC, RGB(255, 255, 255));
            SelectObject(hDC, hFont);
            TextOut(hDC, 90, 60,
                    Timer_Text, strlen(Timer_Text));
            ReleaseDC(hWnd, hDC);
            break;

    case WM_COMMAND:
            switch (GET_WM_COMMAND_ID(wParam,lParam))
            {
```

```
                    case IDM_ABOUT:
                            // create an about dialog box
                            DialogBox(hInst, "ABOUTDLG",
                                        hWnd, (DLGPROC)About);
                            break;

                    default:
                            return DefWindowProc(hWnd, uMessage,
                                                    wParam, lParam);
                    }
                    break;

            case WM_DESTROY:
                    // kill the timer before closing
                    // the main window
                    KillTimer(hWnd, 1);
                    PostQuitMessage(0);
                    break;

            default:
                    return DefWindowProc(hWnd, uMessage,
                                            wParam, lParam);
        }
        return 0;
}
```

ABOUT.C

```
// ABOUT.C
#include <windows.h>
#include <windowsx.h>
#include "globals.h"

// procedures for ABOUT dialog box
LRESULT CALLBACK About(HWND hDlg,
                        UINT uMessage,
                        WPARAM wParam,
                        LPARAM lParam)

{
    switch (uMessage)
      {
        case WM_COMMAND:
            switch (GET_WM_COMMAND_ID(wParam,lParam))
              {
                case IDOK:
                case IDCANCEL:
                    {
```

```
                        EndDialog(hDlg, TRUE);
                        return(TRUE);
                        }
                        break;
                }
        }
    return FALSE;
}
```

DTIMER.RC

```
#include "windows.h"
#include "globals.h"
#include <winver.h>

APPNAME ICON ICONFILE

RCINCLUDE ABOUT.DLG

APPNAME MENU
BEGIN
  MENUITEM "&About",      IDM_ABOUT
END
```

ABOUT.DLG

```
ABOUTDLG DIALOG DISCARDABLE  22, 17, 167, 73
STYLE DS_MODALFRAME | WS_CAPTION | WS_SYSMENU
CAPTION SZABOUT
BEGIN
    DEFPUSHBUTTON   "OK", IDOK, 132, 2, 32, 14, WS_GROUP
    ICON            SZAPPNAME,      -1, 3, 2, 18, 20
    LTEXT           SZAPPNAME,      -1, 30, 12,  50, 8
    LTEXT           SZDESCRIPTION, -1, 30, 22, 150, 8
    LTEXT           SZVERSION,     -1, 30, 32, 150, 8
    LTEXT           SZCOMPANYNAME, -1, 30, 42, 150, 8
END
```

DTIMER.ICO

CASE 11-2: MULTIPLE TIMER

FIGURE 11-2

This case shows how to use multiple timers in an application. The two timers are defined with a timer period equal to 1 second and 0.2 seconds, respectively. The red ellipse in the main window flashes once every second as triggered by timer 1, while the green ellipse flashes five times per second because it is controlled by timer 2.

As in Case 11-1, the timers are created in the WM_CREATE handler of the main window procedure. Each timer has a different numerical identifier. Both timers are set up to use WM_TIMER notification instead of callbacks to application routines. When the WM_TIMER message is received, the wParam value contains the timer ID. The code merely sets a global variable and calls InvalidateRect(), which precipitates a WM_PAINT message.

The WM_PAINT handler creates various pens and brushes, sets the map mode and viewport-to-window mapping, and then draws the appropriate ellipse depending on the timer ID stored in the static variable Timer.

GLOBALS.H

```
// GLOBALS.H - header file for global variables
//              and function prototypes

// Product identifier string definitions
#define APPNAME        MTimer
#define ICONFILE       MTimer.ico
#define SZAPPNAME      "MTimer"
#define SZDESCRIPTION  "Multiple timer"
#define SZVERSION      "Version 1.0"
#define SZCOMPANYNAME  "\251 M&&T Books, 1994"
#define SZABOUT        "About"

// Global function prototypes.
BOOL InitApplication(HINSTANCE);
BOOL InitInstance(HINSTANCE, int);

// Callback functions called by Windows.
LRESULT CALLBACK WndProc(HWND, UINT, WPARAM, LPARAM);
LRESULT CALLBACK About(HWND, UINT, WPARAM, LPARAM);

// Menu item ID
#define IDM_ABOUT    1000

// Global variable declarations.
extern HINSTANCE hInst;      // The current instance handle
extern char szAppName[];     // The name of this application
extern char szTitle[];       // The title bar text
```

WINMAIN.C

```
// WINMAIN.C
#include <windows.h>
#include "globals.h"

int APIENTRY WinMain(HINSTANCE hInstance,
                     HINSTANCE hPrevInstance,
                     LPSTR lpCmdLine,
                     int nCmdShow)
{
    MSG msg;

    // register main window class
    if (!hPrevInstance)
```

```
        {
        if (!InitApplication(hInstance))
            {
            return FALSE;
            }
        }

    // create and show main window
    if (!InitInstance(hInstance, nCmdShow))
        {
        return FALSE;
        }

    // process window messages
    while (GetMessage(&msg, NULL, 0, 0))
        {
            TranslateMessage(&msg);
            DispatchMessage(&msg);
        }
    return msg.wParam;
}
```

INIT.C

```
// INIT.C
#include <windows.h>
#include "globals.h"

HINSTANCE hInst;
char szAppName[] = SZAPPNAME;
char szTitle[] = SZDESCRIPTION;

// register main window class
BOOL InitApplication(HINSTANCE hInstance)
{
    WNDCLASS  wc;

    wc.style         = CS_HREDRAW | CS_VREDRAW;
    wc.lpfnWndProc   = (WNDPROC)WndProc;
    wc.cbClsExtra    = 0;
    wc.cbWndExtra    = 0;
    wc.hInstance     = hInstance;
    wc.hIcon         = LoadIcon(hInstance, szAppName);
    wc.hCursor       = LoadCursor(NULL, IDC_ARROW);
    wc.hbrBackground = (HBRUSH)(COLOR_WINDOW + 1);
    wc.lpszMenuName  = szAppName;
```

```
    wc.lpszClassName = szAppName;

    return(RegisterClass(&wc));
}

// create and show main window
BOOL InitInstance(HINSTANCE hInstance, int nCmdShow)
{
    HWND    hWnd;
    hInst = hInstance;
    hWnd = CreateWindow(szAppName, szTitle,
                        WS_OVERLAPPEDWINDOW,
                        160, 120, 320, 240,
                        NULL, NULL, hInstance, NULL);

    if (!hWnd)
        {
        return FALSE;
        }

    ShowWindow(hWnd, nCmdShow);
    UpdateWindow(hWnd);

    return TRUE;
}
```

MTIMER.C

```
// MTIMER.C
#include <windows.h>
#include <windowsx.h>
#include "globals.h"

LRESULT CALLBACK WndProc(HWND hWnd,
                         UINT uMessage,
                         WPARAM wParam,
                         LPARAM lParam)
{
    HDC hDC;
    PAINTSTRUCT ps;
    HPEN hPenRed, hPenGreen;
    HBRUSH hBrushRed, hBrushGreen;
    RECT rect;
    static WORD Timer;

    switch (uMessage)
```

```
{
    case WM_CREATE:

        // create first timer with period
        // equal to 1 second
        SetTimer(hWnd, 1, 1000, NULL);

        // create second timer with period
        // equal to 0.2 second
        SetTimer(hWnd, 2, 200, NULL);
        break;

    case WM_TIMER:

        switch(wParam){
           case 1:

                // when receive first timer message,
                // set Timer flag to 1
                Timer = 1;

                // repaint the client area
                InvalidateRect(hWnd, NULL, TRUE);
                break;

           case 2:

                // when receive second timer message,
                // set Timer flag to 2
                Timer = 2;

                // repaint the client area
                InvalidateRect(hWnd, NULL, TRUE);
                break;
           }
        break;

    case WM_PAINT:

        hDC = BeginPaint(hWnd, &ps);
        // create pens and brushes for painting
        hPenRed = CreatePen(0, 1, RGB(255, 0, 0));
        hPenGreen = CreatePen(0, 1, RGB(0, 255, 0));
        hBrushRed = CreateSolidBrush(RGB(255, 0, 0));
        hBrushGreen = CreateSolidBrush(RGB(0, 255, 0));

        SetMapMode(hDC, MM_ISOTROPIC);
```

```
                    GetClientRect(hWnd, &rect);
                    SetViewportExtEx(hDC, rect.right,
                                    rect.bottom, NULL);
                    SetWindowExtEx(hDC, 160, 120, NULL);

                    if(Timer == 1){
                           // if Timer flag is 1,
                           // paint a red ellipse
                           SelectObject(hDC, hPenRed);
                           SelectObject(hDC, hBrushRed);
                           Ellipse(hDC, 20, 20, 40, 40);
                           }

                    if(Timer == 2){
                           // if Timer flag is 2,
                           // paint a green ellipse
                           SelectObject(hDC, hPenGreen);
                           SelectObject(hDC, hBrushGreen);
                           Ellipse(hDC, 120, 20, 140, 40);
                           }

                    EndPaint(hWnd, &ps);
                    DeleteObject(hPenRed);
                    DeleteObject(hPenGreen);
                    DeleteObject(hBrushRed);
                    DeleteObject(hBrushGreen);
                    break;

              case WM_COMMAND:

                    switch (GET_WM_COMMAND_ID(wParam,lParam))
                    {
                       case IDM_ABOUT:
                              // create an about dialog box
                              DialogBox(hInst, "ABOUTDLG",
                                    hWnd, (DLGPROC)About);
                              break;

                       default:
                              return DefWindowProc(hWnd, uMessage,
                                             wParam, lParam);
                    }
                    break;

              case WM_DESTROY:

                    // kill both timers before closing
```

```
        //the main window
        KillTimer(hWnd, 1);
        KillTimer(hWnd, 2);
        PostQuitMessage(0);
        break;

    default:
        return DefWindowProc(hWnd, uMessage,
                             wParam, lParam);
    }
    return 0;
}
```

ABOUT.C

```
// ABOUT.C
#include <windows.h>
#include <windowsx.h>
#include "globals.h"

// procedures for ABOUT dialog box
LRESULT CALLBACK About(HWND hDlg,
                       UINT uMessage,
                       WPARAM wParam,
                       LPARAM lParam)
{
    switch (uMessage)
      {
        case WM_COMMAND:
            switch (GET_WM_COMMAND_ID(wParam,lParam))
            {
                case IDOK:
                case IDCANCEL:
                    {
                    EndDialog(hDlg, TRUE);
                    return(TRUE);
                    }
                    break;
            }
      }
    return FALSE;
}
```

MTIMER.RC

```
#include "windows.h"
#include "globals.h"
#include <winver.h>

APPNAME ICON ICONFILE

RCINCLUDE ABOUT.DLG

APPNAME MENU
BEGIN
  MENUITEM "&About",      IDM_ABOUT
END
```

ABOUT.DLG

```
ABOUTDLG DIALOG DISCARDABLE  22, 17, 167, 73
STYLE DS_MODALFRAME | WS_CAPTION | WS_SYSMENU
CAPTION SZABOUT
BEGIN
    DEFPUSHBUTTON   "OK", IDOK, 132, 2, 32, 14, WS_GROUP
    ICON            SZAPPNAME,      -1, 3, 2, 18, 20
    LTEXT           SZAPPNAME,      -1, 30, 12,  50, 8
    LTEXT           SZDESCRIPTION, -1, 30, 22, 150, 8
    LTEXT           SZVERSION,      -1, 30, 32, 150, 8
    LTEXT           SZCOMPANYNAME, -1, 30, 42, 150, 8
END
```

MTIMER.ICO

CHAPTER TWELVE

MISCELLANEOUS

CASE 12-1: OPEN THE MAIN WINDOW AS A DIALOG BOX

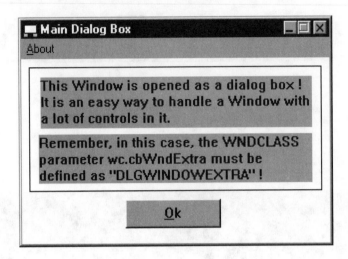

FIGURE 12-1

Sometimes it is more convenient to open the main application window as a dialog box. The advantages of doing this are several. First, you can use the dialog editor to arrange controls in the main window and save it to a resource file (*i.e.*, MAINDLG.DLG). Second, the size and position of the controls in the dialog box are defined in "dialog units," the size of which Windows adjusts automatically, depending on the type of screen display and font size. This function reduces some of the problems with positioning and sizing controls.

However, you must remember several important things. First, the WinClass.cbWndExtra structure element must have the value of DLGWINDOWEXTRA. Second, because the window class name is defined as SZAPPNAME, you must also add the statement "CLASS SZAPPNAME" to the dialog box resource file. Third, instead of using the CreateWindow() function, you must use the CreateDialog() function to create the main window. Fourth, because the window is created as a dialog box, all initialization should occur during or before the WM_INITDIALOG message. As you can see from the listing, the work that, in a regular Windows program, might be found in the WM_CREATE handler is now put in the WM_INITDIALOG handler of WndProc.

GLOBALS.H

```
// GLOBALS.H - header file for global variables
//              and function prototypes

// Product identifier string definitions
#define APPNAME         MainDlg
#define ICONFILE        MainDlg.ico
#define SZAPPNAME       "MainDlg"
#define SZDESCRIPTION   "Open the main window as a dialog box"
#define SZVERSION       "Version 1.0"
#define SZCOMPANYNAME   "\251 M&&T Books, 1994"
#define SZABOUT         "About"

// Global function prototypes.
BOOL InitApplication(HINSTANCE);
BOOL InitInstance(HINSTANCE, int);

// Callback functions called by Windows.
LRESULT CALLBACK WndProc(HWND, UINT, WPARAM, LPARAM);
LRESULT CALLBACK About(HWND, UINT, WPARAM, LPARAM);

// Menu item ID
#define IDM_ABOUT   100

// Control ID
#define IDC_OK      101

// Global variable declarations.
extern HINSTANCE hInst;     // The current instance handle
extern char szAppName[];    // The name of this application
extern char szTitle[];      // The title bar text
```

WINMAIN.C

```
// WINMAIN.C
#include <windows.h>
#include "globals.h"
HWND hWnd;
```

```c
int APIENTRY WinMain(HINSTANCE hInstance,
                     HINSTANCE hPrevInstance,
                     LPSTR lpCmdLine,
                     int nCmdShow)
{
    MSG msg;

    // register main window class
    if (!hPrevInstance)
        {
        if (!InitApplication(hInstance))
            {
            return FALSE;
            }
        }

    // create and show main window
    if (!InitInstance(hInstance, nCmdShow))
        {
        return FALSE;
        }

    // process window messages
    while (GetMessage(&msg, NULL, 0, 0))
        if(!IsDialogMessage(hWnd, &msg)){
        {
            TranslateMessage(&msg);
            DispatchMessage(&msg);
        }
        }
    return msg.wParam;
}
```

INIT.C

```c
// INIT.C
#include <windows.h>
#include "globals.h"

HINSTANCE hInst;
char szAppName[] = SZAPPNAME;
char szTitle[] = SZDESCRIPTION;

// register main window class
BOOL InitApplication(HINSTANCE hInstance)
{
```

```
    WNDCLASS   wc;

    wc.style          = NULL;
    wc.lpfnWndProc    = (WNDPROC)WndProc;
    wc.cbClsExtra     = 0;
    wc.cbWndExtra     = DLGWINDOWEXTRA;
    wc.hInstance      = hInstance;
    wc.hIcon          = LoadIcon(hInstance, szAppName);
    wc.hCursor        = LoadCursor(NULL, IDC_ARROW);
    wc.hbrBackground  = (HBRUSH)(COLOR_WINDOW + 1);
    wc.lpszMenuName   = szAppName;
    wc.lpszClassName  = szAppName;

    return(RegisterClass(&wc));
}

// create and show main window
BOOL InitInstance(HINSTANCE hInstance, int nCmdShow)
{
    HWND    hWnd;
    hInst = hInstance;
    hWnd = CreateDialog(hInstance, "MAINDLG", 0, NULL);

    if (!hWnd)
       {
       return FALSE;
       }

    ShowWindow(hWnd, nCmdShow);
    UpdateWindow(hWnd);

    return TRUE;
}
```

MAINDLG.C

```
// MAINDLG.C
#include <windows.h>
#include <windowsx.h>
#include <stdio.h>
#include "globals.h"

LRESULT CALLBACK WndProc(HWND hWnd,
                         UINT uMessage,
                         WPARAM wParam,
                         LPARAM lParam)
```

```
{
    switch (uMessage)
    {
        case WM_COMMAND:
            switch (GET_WM_COMMAND_ID(wParam,lParam))
            {
                case IDC_OK:
                    PostQuitMessage(0);
                    break;

                case IDM_ABOUT:
                    // create an about dialog box
                    DialogBox(hInst, "ABOUTDLG",
                                hWnd, (DLGPROC)About);
                    break;

                default:
                    return DefWindowProc(hWnd, uMessage,
                                            wParam, lParam);
            }
            break;

        case WM_DESTROY:
            PostQuitMessage(0);
            break;

        default:
            return DefWindowProc(hWnd, uMessage,
                                    wParam, lParam);
    }
    return 0;
}
```

ABOUT.C

```
// ABOUT.C
#include <windows.h>
#include <windowsx.h>
#include "globals.h"

// procedures for ABOUT dialog box
LRESULT CALLBACK About(HWND hDlg,
                        UINT uMessage,
                        WPARAM wParam,
                        LPARAM lParam)
{
```

```
    switch (uMessage)
      {
        case WM_COMMAND:
              switch (GET_WM_COMMAND_ID(wParam,lParam))
              {
                case IDOK:
                  case IDCANCEL:
                      {
                      EndDialog(hDlg, TRUE);
                      return(TRUE);
                      }
                      break;
              }
      }
    return FALSE;
}
```

MAINDLG.RC

```
#include "windows.h"
#include "globals.h"
#include <winver.h>

APPNAME ICON ICONFILE

RCINCLUDE ABOUT.DLG
RCINCLUDE MAINDLG.DLG

APPNAME MENU
BEGIN
  MENUITEM "&About",        IDM_ABOUT
END
```

MAINDLG.DLG

```
MAINDLG DIALOG 76, 38, 156, 100
STYLE WS_MINIMIZEBOX | WS_POPUP | WS_VISIBLE |
     WS_CAPTION | WS_SYSMENU
CAPTION "Main Dialog Box"
CLASS SZAPPNAME
BEGIN
    CONTROL         "", -1, "Static", SS_BLACKFRAME,
                    4, 4, 148, 61
    LTEXT           "This Window is opened as a dialog box !
                    It is an easy way to handle a Window
```

```
                        with a lot of controls in it. ",
                        -1, 10, 9, 137, 25, NOT WS_GROUP
        LTEXT           "Remember, in this case, the WNDCLASS
                        parameter wc.cbWndExtra must be defined
                        as ""DLGWINDOWEXTRA"" !",
                        -1, 9, 37, 138, 24, NOT WS_GROUP
        PUSHBUTTON      "&Ok", IDC_OK, 53, 69, 48, 14
END
```

ABOUT.DLG

```
ABOUTDLG DIALOG DISCARDABLE  22, 17, 167, 73
STYLE DS_MODALFRAME | WS_CAPTION | WS_SYSMENU
CAPTION SZABOUT
BEGIN
        DEFPUSHBUTTON   "OK", IDOK, 132, 2, 32, 14, WS_GROUP
        ICON            SZAPPNAME,       -1, 3, 2, 18, 20
        LTEXT           SZAPPNAME,       -1, 30, 12,  50, 8
        LTEXT           SZDESCRIPTION, -1, 30, 22, 150, 8
        LTEXT           SZVERSION,       -1, 30, 32, 150, 8
        LTEXT           SZCOMPANYNAME, -1, 30, 42, 150, 8
END
```

MAINDLG.ICO

CASE 12-2: START OTHER PROGRAMS USING WINEXEC FUNCTION

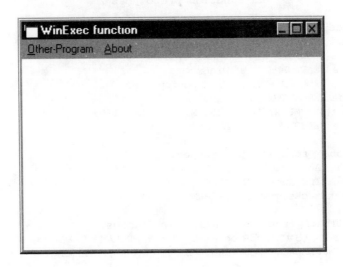

FIGURE 12-2

Windows provides a WinExec() function, that lets you start another program from within your Windows application. This function is especially useful when you need to call a utility program from within the main application. WinExec() can run both regular Windows applications and non-Windows programs (if you supply the PIF file).

In the example here, the menu choice Other Program invokes an executable named OTHER.EXE using WinExec(). The name of the executable is hardwired into the menu handler code. The WinExec() function runs the program whose name is passed as a parameter; when that program returns, WinExec() provides a return value. In this case, there is a custom function, WinExecReturnMessage(), that interprets the error code returned by WinExec() and displays it in a message box. Possible errors include: file not found, path not found, bad format, and out of memory (or out of system resources).

GLOBALS.H

```
// GLOBALS.H - header file for global variables
//              and function prototypes

// Product identifier string definitions
#define APPNAME        WinExec
#define ICONFILE       WinExec.ico
#define SZAPPNAME      "WinExec"
#define SZDESCRIPTION  "WinExec function"
#define SZVERSION      "Version 1.0"
#define SZCOMPANYNAME  "\251 M&&T Books, 1994"
#define SZABOUT        "About"

// Global function prototypes.
BOOL InitApplication(HINSTANCE);
BOOL InitInstance(HINSTANCE, int);
void WinExecReturnMessage(HWND, UINT);

// Callback functions called by Windows.
LRESULT CALLBACK WndProc(HWND, UINT, WPARAM, LPARAM);
LRESULT CALLBACK About(HWND, UINT, WPARAM, LPARAM);

// Menu item ID
#define IDM_ABOUT         100
#define IDM_OTHER_PROGRAM 101

// Global variable declarations.
extern HINSTANCE hInst;     // The current instance handle
extern char szAppName[];    // The name of this application
extern char szTitle[];      // The title bar text
```

WINMAIN.C

```
// WINMAIN.C
#include <windows.h>
#include "globals.h"

int APIENTRY WinMain(HINSTANCE hInstance,
                     HINSTANCE hPrevInstance,
                     LPSTR lpCmdLine,
                     int nCmdShow)
{
    MSG msg;

    // register main window class
```

```
      if (!hPrevInstance)
         {
      if (!InitApplication(hInstance))
         {
         return FALSE;
         }
         }

      // create and show main window
      if (!InitInstance(hInstance, nCmdShow))
         {
         return FALSE;
         }

      // process window messages
      while (GetMessage(&msg, NULL, 0, 0))
         {
            TranslateMessage(&msg);
            DispatchMessage(&msg);
         }
      return msg.wParam;
}
```

INIT.C

```
// INIT.C
#include <windows.h>
#include "globals.h"

HINSTANCE hInst;
char szAppName[] = SZAPPNAME;
char szTitle[] = SZDESCRIPTION;

// register main window class
BOOL InitApplication(HINSTANCE hInstance)
{
    WNDCLASS  wc;

    wc.style          = CS_HREDRAW | CS_VREDRAW;
    wc.lpfnWndProc    = (WNDPROC)WndProc;
    wc.cbClsExtra     = 0;
    wc.cbWndExtra     = 0;
    wc.hInstance      = hInstance;
    wc.hIcon          = LoadIcon(hInstance, szAppName);
    wc.hCursor        = LoadCursor(NULL, IDC_ARROW);
    wc.hbrBackground  = (HBRUSH)(COLOR_WINDOW + 1);
```

```
    wc.lpszMenuName  = szAppName;
    wc.lpszClassName = szAppName;

    return(RegisterClass(&wc));
}

// create and show main window
BOOL InitInstance(HINSTANCE hInstance, int nCmdShow)
{
    HWND     hWnd;
    hInst = hInstance;
    hWnd = CreateWindow(szAppName, szTitle,
                    WS_OVERLAPPEDWINDOW,
                    160, 120, 320, 240,
                    NULL, NULL, hInstance, NULL);

    if (!hWnd)
        {
        return FALSE;
        }

    ShowWindow(hWnd, nCmdShow);
    UpdateWindow(hWnd);

    return TRUE;
}
```

WINEXEC.C

```
// WINEXEC.C
#include <windows.h>
#include <windowsx.h>
#include "globals.h"

LRESULT CALLBACK WndProc(HWND hWnd,
                    UINT uMessage,
                    WPARAM wParam,
                    LPARAM lParam)
{
UINT WinExecReturnValue;

    switch (uMessage)
    {
        case WM_COMMAND:
            switch (GET_WM_COMMAND_ID(wParam,lParam))
            {
```

```
            case IDM_OTHER_PROGRAM:
                    // start a program named "other.exe"
                    WinExecReturnValue =
                       WinExec("other.EXE", SW_SHOWNORMAL);

                    // check the error return code
                    if(WinExecReturnValue < 32)
                       WinExecReturnMessage(hWnd,
                                WinExecReturnValue);
                    break;

            case IDM_ABOUT:
                    DialogBox(hInst, "ABOUTDLG",
                                hWnd, (DLGPROC)About);
                    break;

            default:
                    return DefWindowProc(hWnd, uMessage,
                                            wParam, lParam);
            }
            break;

        case WM_DESTROY:
            PostQuitMessage(0);
            break;

        default:
            return DefWindowProc(hWnd, uMessage,
                                  wParam, lParam);
    }
    return 0;
}

// function for handling the error return code
// from WinExec() function
void WinExecReturnMessage(hWnd, WinExecReturnValue)
HWND hWnd;
UINT WinExecReturnValue;
{
char *xx;
    switch(WinExecReturnValue) {
        case 0:
            strcpy(xx, "Out of memory or system resource");
            break;

        case ERROR_FILE_NOT_FOUND:
            strcpy(xx, "File not found !");
```

```
                break;

        case ERROR_PATH_NOT_FOUND:
                strcpy(xx, "Path not found !");
                break;

        case ERROR_BAD_FORMAT:
                strcpy(xx, "Invalid .EXE file !");
                break;

        default: return;
            }
    MessageBox(hWnd, xx, "WinExec Error",
                        MB_ICONEXCLAMATION | MB_OK);

}
```

ABOUT.C

```
// ABOUT.C
#include <windows.h>
#include <windowsx.h>
#include "globals.h"

// procedures for ABOUT dialog box
LRESULT CALLBACK About(HWND hDlg,
                        UINT uMessage,
                        WPARAM wParam,
                        LPARAM lParam)
{
    switch (uMessage)
      {
        case WM_COMMAND:
                switch (GET_WM_COMMAND_ID(wParam,lParam))
                {
                    case IDOK:
                    case IDCANCEL:
                        {
                        EndDialog(hDlg, TRUE);
                        return(TRUE);
                        }
                        break;
                }
        }
    return FALSE;
}
```

WINEXEC.RC

```
#include "windows.h"
#include "globals.h"
#include <winver.h>

APPNAME ICON ICONFILE

RCINCLUDE ABOUT.DLG

APPNAME MENU
BEGIN
    MENUITEM "&Other-Program", IDM_OTHER_PROGRAM
    MENUITEM "&About", IDM_ABOUT
END
```

ABOUT.DLG

```
ABOUTDLG DIALOG DISCARDABLE  22, 17, 167, 73
STYLE DS_MODALFRAME | WS_CAPTION | WS_SYSMENU
CAPTION SZABOUT
BEGIN
    DEFPUSHBUTTON    "OK", IDOK, 132, 2, 32, 14, WS_GROUP
    ICON            SZAPPNAME,      -1, 3, 2, 18, 20
    LTEXT           SZAPPNAME,      -1, 30, 12,  50, 8
    LTEXT           SZDESCRIPTION, -1, 30, 22, 150, 8
    LTEXT           SZVERSION,      -1, 30, 32, 150, 8
    LTEXT           SZCOMPANYNAME, -1, 30, 42, 150, 8
END
```

WINEXEC.ICO

CASE 12-3: SET SYSTEM COLORS

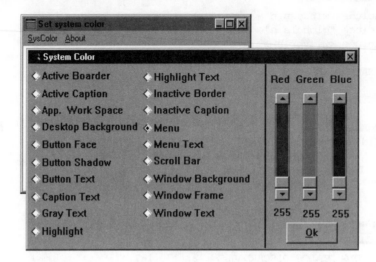

This case shows how to set the colors of various standard elements of the Windows environment, using the SetSysColors() function. This program does all its work within a single large dialog box, which lets the users specify which Windows element needs to be changed and to what color.

The users choose a color via three scroll bars on the right side of the dialog box to set the red, blue, and green components of the color value.

The set of radio buttons on the left side of the dialog box lets the users choose which element will be affected. As you can see from Figure 12-3, elements include the desktop background, button face, button text, window background, window frame, and many more.

This program can be used by users who wish to configure the look of their personal system as well as programmers who are designing the look of an application.

GLOBALS.H

```
// GLOBALS.H - header file for global variables
//              and function prototypes

// Product identifier string definitions
#define APPNAME       SysColor
#define ICONFILE      SysColor.ico
#define SZAPPNAME     "SysColor"
#define SZDESCRIPTION "Set system color"
#define SZVERSION     "Version 1.0"
#define SZCOMPANYNAME "\251 M&&T Books, 1994"
#define SZABOUT       "About"

// Global function prototypes.
BOOL InitApplication(HINSTANCE);
BOOL InitInstance(HINSTANCE, int);

// Callback functions called by Windows.
LRESULT CALLBACK WndProc(HWND, UINT, WPARAM, LPARAM);
LRESULT CALLBACK About(HWND, UINT, WPARAM, LPARAM);
LRESULT CALLBACK SysColorDlgProc(HWND, UINT, WPARAM, LPARAM);

// Menu item ID
#define IDM_ABOUT       98
#define IDM_SYSCOLOR    99

// Dialog box ID
#define IDD_SYSCOLOR 200

// Dialog box control ID
#define IDC_ACTIVEBORDER     100
#define IDC_ACTIVECAPTION    101
#define IDC_APPWORKSPACE     102
#define IDC_BACKGROUND       103
#define IDC_BTNFACE          104
#define IDC_BTNSHADOW        105
#define IDC_BTNTEXT          106
#define IDC_CAPTIONTEXT      107
#define IDC_GRAYTEXT         108
#define IDC_HIGHLIGHT        109
#define IDC_HIGHLIGHTTEXT    110
#define IDC_INACTIVEBORDER   111
#define IDC_INACTIVECAPTION  112
#define IDC_MENU             113
#define IDC_MENUTEXT         114
#define IDC_SCROLLBAR        115
```

```
#define IDC_WINDOW          116
#define IDC_WINDOWFRAME     117
#define IDC_WINDOWTEXT      118

#define IDC_RED_SCROLL      121
#define IDC_GREEN_SCROLL    122
#define IDC_BLUE_SCROLL     123
#define IDC_RED_VALUE       124
#define IDC_GREEN_VALUE     125
#define IDC_BLUE_VALUE      126
#define IDC_OK              127
```

```
// Global variable declarations.
extern HINSTANCE hInst;       // The current instance handle
extern char szAppName[];      // The name of this application
extern char szTitle[];        // The title bar text
extern HWND hWnd, hSysColor;
extern DLGPROC lpProcSysColor;
```

WINMAIN.C

```
// WINMAIN.C
#include <windows.h>
#include "globals.h"

int APIENTRY WinMain(HINSTANCE hInstance,
                     HINSTANCE hPrevInstance,
                     LPSTR lpCmdLine,
                     int nCmdShow)
{
    MSG msg;

    // register main window class
    if (!hPrevInstance)
        {
        if (!InitApplication(hInstance))
            {
            return FALSE;
            }
        }

    // create and show main window
    if (!InitInstance(hInstance, nCmdShow))
        {
        return FALSE;
        }
```

```
    // process window messages
    while (GetMessage(&msg, NULL, 0, 0))
        {
            TranslateMessage(&msg);
            DispatchMessage(&msg);
        }
    return msg.wParam;
}
```

INIT.C

```
// INIT.C
#include <windows.h>
#include "globals.h"

HINSTANCE hInst;
char szAppName[] = SZAPPNAME;
char szTitle[] = SZDESCRIPTION;

// register main window class
BOOL InitApplication(HINSTANCE hInstance)
{
    WNDCLASS  wc;

    wc.style         = CS_HREDRAW | CS_VREDRAW;
    wc.lpfnWndProc   = (WNDPROC)WndProc;
    wc.cbClsExtra    = 0;
    wc.cbWndExtra    = 0;
    wc.hInstance     = hInstance;
    wc.hIcon         = LoadIcon(hInstance, szAppName);
    wc.hCursor       = LoadCursor(NULL, IDC_ARROW);
    wc.hbrBackground = (HBRUSH)(COLOR_WINDOW + 1);
    wc.lpszMenuName  = szAppName;
    wc.lpszClassName = szAppName;

    return(RegisterClass(&wc));
}

// create and show main window
BOOL InitInstance(HINSTANCE hInstance, int nCmdShow)
{
    HWND    hWnd;
    hInst = hInstance;
    hWnd = CreateWindow(szAppName, szTitle,
                    WS_OVERLAPPEDWINDOW,
```

```
                              160, 120, 320, 240,
                              NULL, NULL, hInstance, NULL);

        if (!hWnd)
            {
            return FALSE;
            }

        ShowWindow(hWnd, nCmdShow);
        UpdateWindow(hWnd);

        return TRUE;
    }
```

SYSCOLOR.C

```
// SYSCOLOR.C
#include <windows.h>
#include <windowsx.h>
#include "globals.h"

HWND hSysColor;
DLGPROC lpProcSysColor;

LRESULT CALLBACK WndProc(HWND hWnd,
                         UINT uMessage,
                         WPARAM wParam,
                         LPARAM lParam)
{
    switch (uMessage)
    {
        case WM_COMMAND:
            switch (GET_WM_COMMAND_ID(wParam,lParam))
            {
                case IDM_SYSCOLOR:
                    // create an item selection and
                    // color editing dialog box
                    lpProcSysColor = MakeProcInstance(
                        (FARPROC)SysColorDlgProc, hInst);
                    hSysColor = CreateDialog(hInst,
                            MAKEINTRESOURCE(IDD_SYSCOLOR),
                                    hWnd, lpProcSysColor);
                    break;

                case IDM_ABOUT:
                    // create an about dialog box
```

```
                    DialogBox(hInst, "ABOUTDLG",
                              hWnd, (DLGPROC)About);
                    break;

                default:
                    return DefWindowProc(hWnd, uMessage,
                                         wParam, lParam);
            }
            break;

        case WM_DESTROY:
            FreeProcInstance(lpProcSysColor);
            PostQuitMessage(0);
            break;

        default:
            return DefWindowProc(hWnd, uMessage,
                                 wParam, lParam);
    }
    return 0;
}
```

SCOLOR.C

```
// SCOLOR.C
#include <windows.h>
#include <windowsx.h>
#include <stdio.h>
#include "globals.h"

HWND hSysColor;
HBRUSH hBrushR, hBrushG, hBrushB;

LRESULT CALLBACK SysColorDlgProc(HWND hSysColor,
                                 UINT uMessage,
                                 WPARAM wParam,
                                 LPARAM lParam)
{
    static int DspElements[1];
    static COLORREF RgbValues[1];
    static int RGBV[3];
    HWND hScrollBar;
    DWORD ScrollBarID, RGBindex;

    switch (uMessage)
    {
```

```
case WM_INITDIALOG:

        // create brushes for painting the scroll bar
      hBrushR = CreateSolidBrush(RGB(255, 0, 0));
      hBrushG = CreateSolidBrush(RGB(0, 255, 0));
      hBrushB = CreateSolidBrush(RGB(0, 0, 255));

        // set initial RGB values
      RGBV[0]=255;
      RGBV[1]=255;
      RGBV[2]=255;


        // set scroll bar range and initial position
      for(ScrollBarID = IDC_RED_SCROLL;
          ScrollBarID < IDC_BLUE_SCROLL+1;
          ScrollBarID++)
        { hScrollBar = GetDlgItem(
                            hSysColor, ScrollBarID);
          SetScrollRange(hScrollBar,
                              SB_CTL, 0, 255, FALSE);
          SetScrollPos(hScrollBar, SB_CTL,
                      RGBV[ScrollBarID-121], FALSE);
          SetDlgItemInt(hSysColor, ScrollBarID+3,
                      RGBV[ScrollBarID-121], FALSE);
        };
      break;

case WM_CTLCOLORSCROLLBAR:
      switch(GetWindowLong((HWND)lParam, GWL_ID))
        // set scroll bar color
        {
          case IDC_RED_SCROLL:
              return((WORD)hBrushR);
              break;

          case IDC_GREEN_SCROLL:
              return((WORD)hBrushG);
              break;

          case IDC_BLUE_SCROLL:
              return((WORD)hBrushB);
              break;

          default:
      return DefWindowProc (hSysColor, uMessage,
                              wParam, lParam);
```

```
        }
        break;

    case WM_COMMAND:

        switch (GET_WM_COMMAND_ID(wParam,lParam))
        {
        // choose item which the color is to be changed
            case IDC_ACTIVEBORDER:
                DspElements[0] = COLOR_ACTIVEBORDER;
                break;

            case IDC_ACTIVECAPTION:
                DspElements[0] = COLOR_ACTIVECAPTION;
                break;

            case IDC_APPWORKSPACE:
                DspElements[0] = COLOR_APPWORKSPACE;
                break;

            case IDC_BACKGROUND:
                DspElements[0] = COLOR_BACKGROUND;
                break;

            case IDC_BTNFACE:
                DspElements[0] = COLOR_BTNFACE;
                break;

            case IDC_BTNSHADOW:
                DspElements[0] = COLOR_BTNSHADOW;
                break;

            case IDC_BTNTEXT:
                DspElements[0] = COLOR_BTNTEXT;
                break;

            case IDC_CAPTIONTEXT:
                DspElements[0] = COLOR_CAPTIONTEXT;
                break;

            case IDC_GRAYTEXT:
                DspElements[0] = COLOR_GRAYTEXT;
                break;

            case IDC_HIGHLIGHT:
                DspElements[0] = COLOR_HIGHLIGHT;
                break;
```

739

```
        case IDC_HIGHLIGHTTEXT:
            DspElements[0] = COLOR_HIGHLIGHTTEXT;
            break;

        case IDC_INACTIVEBORDER:
            DspElements[0] = COLOR_INACTIVEBORDER;
            break;

        case IDC_INACTIVECAPTION:
            DspElements[0] = COLOR_INACTIVECAPTION;
            break;

        case IDC_MENU:
            DspElements[0] = COLOR_MENU;
            break;

        case IDC_MENUTEXT:
            DspElements[0] = COLOR_MENUTEXT;
            break;

        case IDC_SCROLLBAR:
            DspElements[0] = COLOR_SCROLLBAR;
            break;

        case IDC_WINDOW:
            DspElements[0] = COLOR_WINDOW;
            break;

        case IDC_WINDOWFRAME:
            DspElements[0] = COLOR_WINDOWFRAME;
            break;

        case IDC_WINDOWTEXT:
            DspElements[0] = COLOR_WINDOWTEXT;
            break;

        case IDC_OK:
        case IDCANCEL:
            DeleteObject(hBrushR);
            DeleteObject(hBrushG);
            DeleteObject(hBrushB);
            DestroyWindow(hSysColor);
            hSysColor = 0;
            break;

        default: return FALSE;
```

```
        }
        break;

case WM_VSCROLL:

    // process messages for scroll bars
    hScrollBar = (HWND)lParam;
    ScrollBarID = GetWindowLong(
                        hScrollBar, GWL_ID);
    RGBindex = ScrollBarID - 121;

    switch(LOWORD(wParam))
      {
      case SB_TOP:
          RGBV[RGBindex] = 0;
          break;

      case SB_BOTTOM:
          RGBV[RGBindex] = 255;
          break;

      case SB_PAGEUP:
          RGBV[RGBindex] =
                    max(0, RGBV[RGBindex] - 16);
          break;

      case SB_LINEUP:
          RGBV[RGBindex] =
                    max(0, RGBV[RGBindex] - 1);
          break;

      case SB_PAGEDOWN:
          RGBV[RGBindex] =
                    min(255, RGBV[RGBindex] + 16);
          break;

      case SB_LINEDOWN:
          RGBV[RGBindex] =
                    min(255, RGBV[RGBindex] + 1);
          break;

      case SB_THUMBPOSITION:
      case SB_THUMBTRACK:
          RGBV[RGBindex] = HIWORD(wParam);
          break;

      default :
```

741

```
                        return FALSE ;
            }

                // set scroll bar new position and
                // display new RGB value
                SetScrollPos(hScrollBar, SB_CTL,
                            RGBV[RGBindex], TRUE);
                SetDlgItemInt(hSysColor, ScrollBarID+3,
                            RGBV[RGBindex], FALSE) ;

                // get new RGB values
                RgbValues[0] =
                        RGB(RGBV[0], RGBV[1], RGBV[2]);

                // change system color
                SetSysColors(1, DspElements, RgbValues);
                break;

        default:
            return FALSE;
        }
    return 0;
    }
```

ABOUT.C

```
// ABOUT.C
#include <windows.h>
#include <windowsx.h>
#include "globals.h"

// procedures for ABOUT dialog box
LRESULT CALLBACK About(HWND hDlg,
                       UINT uMessage,
                       WPARAM wParam,
                       LPARAM lParam)

{
    switch (uMessage)
      {
        case WM_COMMAND:
            switch (GET_WM_COMMAND_ID(wParam,lParam))
              {
                case IDOK:
                case IDCANCEL:
                    {
                    EndDialog(hDlg, TRUE);
```

```
                          return(TRUE);
                      }
                      break;
                  }
              }
        return FALSE;
    }
```

SYSCOLOR.RC

```
    #include "windows.h"
    #include "globals.h"
    #include <winver.h>

    APPNAME ICON ICONFILE

    RCINCLUDE ABOUT.DLG
    RCINCLUDE SCOLOR.DLG

    APPNAME MENU
    BEGIN
        MENUITEM "&SysColor", IDM_SYSCOLOR
        MENUITEM "&About", IDM_ABOUT
    END
```

SCOLOR.DLG

```
    DLGINCLUDE RCDATA DISCARDABLE
    BEGIN
        "GLOBALS.H\0"
    END

    IDD_SYSCOLOR DIALOG 0, 10, 227, 123
    STYLE WS_POPUP | WS_VISIBLE | WS_CAPTION | WS_SYSMENU
    CAPTION "System Color"
    BEGIN
        CONTROL     "Active Boarder", IDC_ACTIVEBORDER,
                    "Button", BS_AUTORADIOBUTTON | WS_TABSTOP,
                    2, 2, 67, 12
        CONTROL     "Active Caption", IDC_ACTIVECAPTION,
                    "Button", BS_AUTORADIOBUTTON | WS_TABSTOP,
                    2, 14, 67, 12
        CONTROL     "App. Work Space", IDC_APPWORKSPACE,
                    "Button", BS_AUTORADIOBUTTON | WS_TABSTOP,
```

```
                          2, 25, 67, 12
          CONTROL         "Desktop Background", IDC_BACKGROUND,
                          "Button", BS_AUTORADIOBUTTON | WS_TABSTOP,
                          2, 36, 77, 12
          CONTROL         "Button Face", IDC_BTNFACE, "Button",
                          BS_AUTORADIOBUTTON | WS_TABSTOP,
                          2, 48, 67, 12
          CONTROL         "Button Shadow", IDC_BTNSHADOW, "Button",
                          BS_AUTORADIOBUTTON | WS_TABSTOP, 2, 60, 67,
                          12
          CONTROL         "Button Text", IDC_BTNTEXT, "Button",
                          BS_AUTORADIOBUTTON | WS_TABSTOP,
                          2, 71, 67, 12
          CONTROL         "Caption Text", IDC_CAPTIONTEXT, "Button",
                          BS_AUTORADIOBUTTON | WS_TABSTOP,
                          2, 83, 67, 12
          CONTROL         "Gray Text", IDC_GRAYTEXT, "Button",
                          BS_AUTORADIOBUTTON | WS_TABSTOP,
                          2, 94, 67, 12
          CONTROL         "Highlight", IDC_HIGHLIGHT, "Button",
                          BS_AUTORADIOBUTTON | WS_TABSTOP,
                          2, 106, 67, 12
          CONTROL         "Highlight Text", IDC_HIGHLIGHTTEXT,
                          "Button", BS_AUTORADIOBUTTON | WS_TABSTOP,
                          80, 3, 67, 12
          CONTROL         "Inactive Border", IDC_INACTIVEBORDER,
                          "Button", BS_AUTORADIOBUTTON | WS_TABSTOP,
                          80, 14, 67, 12
          CONTROL         "Inactive Caption", IDC_INACTIVECAPTION,
                          "Button", BS_AUTORADIOBUTTON | WS_TABSTOP,
                          80, 25, 67, 12
          CONTROL         "Menu", IDC_MENU, "Button",
                          BS_AUTORADIOBUTTON | WS_TABSTOP,
                          80, 37, 67, 12
          CONTROL         "Menu Text", IDC_MENUTEXT, "Button",
                          BS_AUTORADIOBUTTON | WS_TABSTOP,
                          80, 48, 67, 12
          CONTROL         "Scroll Bar", IDC_SCROLLBAR, "Button",
                          BS_AUTORADIOBUTTON | WS_TABSTOP,
                          80, 59, 67, 12
          CONTROL         "Window Background", IDC_WINDOW, "Button",
                          BS_AUTORADIOBUTTON | WS_TABSTOP,
                          80, 71, 78, 12
          CONTROL         "Window Frame", IDC_WINDOWFRAME, "Button",
                          BS_AUTORADIOBUTTON | WS_TABSTOP,
                          80, 82, 67, 12
          CONTROL         "Window Text", IDC_WINDOWTEXT, "Button",
```

```
                        BS_AUTORADIOBUTTON  |   WS_TABSTOP,
                        80, 94, 67, 12
        CONTROL         "", 119, "Static", SS_BLACKFRAME,
                        164, 0, 1, 123
        LTEXT           "Red  Green  Blue", 120, 168, 6, 58, 9,
                        NOT WS_GROUP
        SCROLLBAR       IDC_RED_SCROLL, 171, 19, 10, 72, SBS_VERT
        SCROLLBAR       IDC_GREEN_SCROLL, 190, 19, 10, 72, SBS_VERT
        SCROLLBAR       IDC_BLUE_SCROLL, 210, 19, 10, 72, SBS_VERT
        CTEXT           "", IDC_RED_VALUE, 168, 95, 16, 8,
                        NOT WS_GROUP
        CTEXT           "", IDC_GREEN_VALUE, 188, 96, 16, 8,
                        NOT WS_GROUP
        CTEXT           "", IDC_BLUE_VALUE, 208, 96, 16, 8,
                        NOT WS_GROUP
        PUSHBUTTON      "&Ok", IDC_OK, 179, 106, 35, 14
    END
```

ABOUT.DLG

```
    ABOUTDLG DIALOG DISCARDABLE  22, 17, 167, 73
    STYLE DS_MODALFRAME | WS_CAPTION | WS_SYSMENU
    CAPTION SZABOUT
    BEGIN
        DEFPUSHBUTTON   "OK", IDOK, 132, 2, 32, 14, WS_GROUP
        ICON            SZAPPNAME,      -1, 3, 2, 18, 20
        LTEXT           SZAPPNAME,      -1, 30, 12,  50, 8
        LTEXT           SZDESCRIPTION, -1, 30, 22, 150, 8
        LTEXT           SZVERSION,      -1, 30, 32, 150, 8
        LTEXT           SZCOMPANYNAME, -1, 30, 42, 150, 8
    END
```

SYSCOLOR.ICO

INDEX

ABOUT THE COMPANION CD

All source code files and compiled run time programs are included in the companion compact disc. The files associated with each individual case are stored in the corresponding subdirectory. For example, files for Case 1-1 of Chapter One are stored in subdirectory D:\CHAP1\CH1-1. Assuming that your CD ROM is the D drive. To run the compiled program, simply type the program name with .EXE extension at DOS prompt. You can also use the "My Computer" program in windows session to view the contents of the companion CD. In this case, you can run the compiled program by clicking the icon displayed on the screen. To include the code in your application, simply copy the file from the CD to the hard drive for further editing.